AN INVITATION TO LAW AND SOCIAL SCIENCE

AN INVITATION TO LAW AND SOCIAL SCIENCE

Desert, Disputes, and Distribution

Richard Lempert and Joseph Sanders

upp

University of Pennsylvania Press
Philadelphia

Senior Editor: David Estrin
Developmental Editor: Irving E. Rockwood
Production Editor: Pamela Nelson
Cover Design: Steven August Krastin
Text Art: J & R Services, Inc.
Production Supervisor: Eduardo Castillo
Compositor: Crane Typesetting Service
Printer and Binder: Maple-Vail Book Manufacturing

An Invitation to Law and Social Science: Desert, Disputes, and Distribution

Longman Inc.
95 Church Street
White Plains, N.Y. 10601

Associated companies:
Longman Group Ltd., London
Longman Cheshire Pty., Melbourne
Longman Paul Pty., Auckland
Copp Clark Pitman, Toronto
Pitman Publishing Inc., Boston

The Acknowledgments on page 511 constitute
an extension of the copyright page.

Library of Congress Cataloging in Publication Data

Lempert, Richard O.
  An invitation to law and social science.

  Bibliography: p.
  Includes index.
  1. Law—Philosophy. 2. Social sciences. 3. Socio-
logical jurisprudence. I. Sanders, Joseph. II. Title.
K487.S6L46   1986   340'.115   85-12899
ISBN 0-582-28495-3
ISBN 0-582-28496-1 (pbk.)

        87 88 89 9 8 7 6 5 4 3 2

To Cynthia and Leah Lempert and to Kiyoshi Ikeda:
Each an inspiration
Richard Lempert

To my parents, Robert and Helen Sanders, whose only
demand was that I repay to my children my inestimable debt to them.
Joseph Sanders

Contents

Preface

This book has two goals. The first is to introduce students—advanced undergraduates, graduate students and law students—to law and social science and the many ways in which research in this tradition can enhance our understanding of law and the legal system. The second is to offer something to specialists in this field. We advance a conception of what law and social science is or can be about and we attempt new syntheses of theory and research in various areas.

These goals are not always compatible. Complex analyses that will cause specialists no problems may not be easily understood by students, and the laying out of basic research and theory that is necessary for a student audience will inescapably include much that specialists find familiar. We have often had to choose between the needs and interests of the two audiences for whom we are writing this book. When clashes were apparent, we have tried consistently to favor our student audience. Thus, in proceeding through the book we assume no prior knowledge of law and social science, or even of basic social science, on the part of the reader. We don't avoid complex issues, but in treating them we try to write clearly, to avoid jargon, and to illustrate our points with easy to understand examples. In three chapters we include in appendices material that discusses matters in more depth than might be appropriate in an undergraduate course.

In the course of writing this book we have incurred debts so numerous that we shall, no doubt, fail to recall all those who made significant contributions. To begin where most authors end, we thank our wives, Cynthia Lempert and Mary Sanders, and our children, Leah Lempert, Robert Sanders, Thomas Sanders, and Elizabeth Sanders, who make it all worthwhile and who have been remarkably patient and pleasant despite the stress that writing places authors under. For typing the book we are grateful to Dorothy Blair, Nan Druskin, Noel Harris, Joyce Reese, and Beverly Ward. Kathleen Hayward and Joyce Reese provided general research assistance, and Pat Root's aid was invaluable in reading galleys. Gail Ristow did almost everything: typing, original artwork, research assistance, reading page proof and, no doubt, things we did not ask for and she forgot to mention. We are especially grateful to her. Numerous students were exposed to the manuscript through various metamorphoses. We are grateful to them for their tolerance of less than perfect typescript and incomplete ideas and for the feedback they provided through successive refinements.

Many people read and commented on portions of the manuscript. While we may not have satisfied their every criticism, we addressed many of them and this book is considerably stronger for our having done so. These readers include:

Richard Cohn	Jack Ladinsky
Diane Colasanto	David Nelken
Edward Cooper	Michael Rosenzweig
Alfred Conrad	Theodore St. Antoine
Malcolm Feeley	Terrance Sandalow
Robben Fleming	Kim Scheppelle
Bruce Frier	Steven Seidler
Bryant Garth	Philio Soper
Clayton Gillette	Michael Sosin
Thomas Green	Gunther Teubner
V. Lee Hamilton	Charles Tilly
Keith Hawkins	Joseph Vining
Alan Hyde	Michele White
	Patricia White

Irving Rockwood our publisher's Executive Editor at the time the manuscript was accepted, not only was helpful and understanding in all respects but he gave the manuscript such a close, professional reading that we count him among our valuable critics. Our vision of what we are about owes much to Felice Levine. In her capacity as Program Director for Law and Social Science at the National Science Foundation and through the many roles she has played in the Law and Society Association, she more than anyone has fostered the growth of law and social science as a discipline. She persuaded us that this is the direction in which law and social science has developed, and in doing so she gave our book its name.

Richard Lempert's research was generously supported by the Cook Funds of the University of Michigan Law School. The Centre for Socio-Legal Studies at Wolfson College, Oxford, then codirected by Richard Markovits and Donald Harris, provided a congenial setting for working on the draft manuscript, and Keith Hawkins willingly shared both his office and his stimulating insights. Joseph Sanders was supported in his work on this book by the Center for Research on Social Organization at the University of Michigan and the University of Houston Law Foundation.

Finally we thank each other. This book is coauthored in the full sense that we are both responsible for everything in it. We have found it a pleasure to work with each other, and each of us feels that his thinking about the matters we discuss has been strengthened by the collaboration.

Richard Lempert
Joseph Sanders

AN INVITATION TO
LAW AND SOCIAL SCIENCE

Introduction

LAW AND SOCIAL SCIENCE

This book is intended to introduce the reader to a new discipline: law and social science.[1]

The aim of law and social science is nothing less than an empirically based understanding of all matters pertaining to law and the legal system that can be so understood. It has not achieved its aim, any more than political science has achieved a complete understanding of government, or psychology of the human mind. As with these other disciplines, it probably never will. Nevertheless, a sufficient body of understanding has accumulated to allow numerous generalizations and some theoretical synthesis.

Law and social science is rooted in and grows out of law-related subfields that have long existed in the various social science disciplines. It differs from these subfields because the question it constantly asks is, "What can this (whatever we are looking at) tell us about how law functions in social life?" Other disciplines address their own central questions. For example, studies of the bar (e.g., Smigel, 1964; Carlin, 1962, 1966; Heinz & Laumann, 1982) provide data for both sociology and law and social science, but sociology takes from these studies lessons about the features that characterize the professions while law and

---

1. Some readers who associate disciplines with departments and the titles of advanced degrees or who fully identify with other disciplines even while doing law and social science may bridle at the word *discipline*, preferring to think of law and social science as a field of study, an area of inquiry, or an aspect of sociology—to wit, the sociology of law. Since the value of the chapters that follow does not depend on how law and social science is labeled, we don't wish to enter a terminological debate. For a brief justification of the idea that law and social science is a discipline, see Lempert, 1982.

social science focuses on how the structure of the bar affects the way law penetrates social life.

The method distinctively (although not uniquely) associated with law and social science is to be multidisciplinary. Indeed, if there is one good behavioral measure for identifying work in law and social science, we suspect it can be found in the pattern of citations in articles relating to law and the legal system. Our unsystematic impression is that law and social science articles are far more likely than articles in other disciplinary traditions to refer to work by people whose disciplinary training differs from that of the article's author. One reason for this is that it is only by combining the insights of the various social science disciplines that we can hope to make sense of legal life. A second is that those working in law and social science usually have roots in law or one of the social sciences.[2] The multidisciplinary nature of law and social science is evident in this book. Both of us hold degrees in law and sociology; but in writing this book we have had to draw on work by anthropologists, political scientists, psychologists, economists, historians, criminologists, game theorists, and philosophers as well as on work by lawyers and sociologists.

Another important feature of law and social science is that it treats the law as a variable. Strange as it may seem, many areas of inquiry in which law importantly figures do not focus on the way law and its effects can vary. In academic legal writing, for example, law is often examined only in terms of its doctrinal consistency rather than as a phenomenon that both is shaped by the social structure and in turn shapes it. In criminology, law for years tended to be taken for granted, while scholarly attention was directed at the types of people who violated the law and the circumstances in which violations occurred. In this book, on the other hand, we are concerned with the essential characteristics of different laws, the features that shape law, and the effects that law has on society. We seek to bring the best available empirical evidence to bear on these concerns. Our goal, however, is not simply to catalog what we know, but rather, to construct, wherever possible, new theoretical syntheses. In some areas our ideas are grounded in a body of well-conducted research. In other areas where we know less, we must be conceptual and speculative.

THE HERITAGE OF WEBER

During the last two decades work in law and social science has blossomed and a separate field of inquiry has been defined.[3] The roots of law and social science

---

2. One way in which law and social science does not fit the disciplinary model is that predoctoral specialty training is generally lacking. This nation's colleges and universities provide few undergraduate departments that focus on law and social science (these usually go by the name "legal studies") and almost no Ph.D. granting programs.

3. There is now a professional association, the Law & Society Association, which specializes in this area, and several journals, including most importantly the *Law & Society Review*, which are devoted to work in law and social science.

extend back into the nineteenth century, however, when the social sciences generally were in their cradle. Particularly important was the work of Max Weber, not only because he identified law as an important field of inquiry, but also because his ideas are still very much alive.[4] Although you will find few citations to Weber in this book, our perspective is informed throughout by his work. In particular, we, like Weber, are concerned with the problems of *human action*, and we adopt Weber's favorite methodological device, *the ideal type*, as a mechanism for theoretical generalization (Weber, 1949).

By human action we mean human behavior that has some meaning for the person acting. It is the existence of *subjective* meaning for the actor that distinguishes action from mere behavior or reflexes. The social scientific understanding of human behavior cannot be reduced to some natural science understanding of the physical and biological processes we observe. For example, in viewing a film of someone shooting a gun and killing another person, we may be observing a murder, an act of self-defense, or a patriotic war deed. As behaviors these three possibilities may appear identical, but as actions they are profoundly different. The law is concerned with human action. The degree of concern is a variable that distinguishes both different types of law and different ways of applying it.

In making these and other distinctions, we have found it useful to proceed by the method of ideal types.[5] Weber described the ideal type:

> An ideal type is formed by the one-sided *accentuation* of one or more points of view and by the synthesis of a great many diffuse, discrete more or less present and occasionally absent *concrete individual* phenomena, which are arranged according to those one-sidedly emphasized viewpoints into a unified *analytical* construct. (Weber, 1949, p. 90)

The essence of the ideal type is twofold. First, it is a conceptual abstraction from reality which is sufficiently general that it cannot capture the whole of any actual phenomenon. Second, it is a stylized construct that represents the perfect, and thus unreal, example—it is not the average case; it is the pure one. As a pure case the ideal type is an analytical yardstick against which we might measure actual actions, institutions, or societies. We use such pure types in each section of this book to create generalized statements and to help us understand the

---

4. For an excellent book-length treatment of Weber's sociology of law, see Kronman, 1983. For a fine article-length introduction, see Trubek, 1972.

5. Our reason for employing ideal types reflects another judgment we share with Weber. Weber not only defined human action as the core concern of sociology, he also rejected those social theories which held that social structure was ultimately determined by any one particular factor, such as economic relations, political power, or religious belief. This view of the world poses a problem. The combination of an action orientation and the absence of some fundamental determinant implies an indeterminacy of events and ultimately a science of human behavior that can only explore particular historical phenomena. But to understand law and the legal system, we must move from unique, historical accounts to more general social scientific accounts of causal relationships. The ideal type allows us to maintain this Weberian view of the social world and still generalize about the social order.

intricate workings of the legal order. In the final section our debt to Weber is compounded, for the types we develop are directly influenced by types Weber employed to identify essential differences between possible legal systems.[6]

LAW

For as long as social scientists have been interested in law, they have struggled over how to define it. Their definitions range from Weber's early statement that an "order will be called . . . *law* if it is externally guaranteed by the probability that physical or psychological coercion will be applied by a *staff* of people in order to bring about compliance or avenge violation" (Weber, 1968, p. 34), to Donald Black's recent, simpler proclamation that, "Law is governmental social control" (1976, p. 2). If we had to choose a definition of law, we would be closer to Weber's than to Black's, but like others who have avoided the definitional tangle we find that we do not have to choose. Scholarly definitions are either theories in disguise, or they are designed to establish a set of common meanings between the author and the reader. We do not in this book propose a general theory about what law is or where its boundaries lie, and we believe that the commonsense understanding with which readers will interpret words like "law" and "legal system" is sufficiently accurate that the necessary community of meaning exists.

We do, however, begin with a perspective on law, one that is closely related to common sense. Law, whatever else it is, is a body of rules that relate to (1) how people should behave in society and (2) how the legal system itself should proceed.

Law as a set of rules may be examined at several levels. At one level law divides social behavior into actions that society regards as either obligatory, permissible, or forbidden. It specifies when and how people will be held responsible for shirking obligations or for engaging in forbidden behavior. At a second level law organizes private processes of dispute settlement. At a third level law allocates welfare, by which we mean such things as wealth, status, and power, in society. In large measure, this allocation of welfare is effected by the creation of rights and duties, that is, rules that define behavior as either obligatory, permissible, or forbidden. Thus, we are brought full circle.

The chapters that follow examine the law at each of these levels: as a process of determining *responsibility* for socially consequential behavior, as a process of *dispute settlement*, and as a system for the *distribution* of welfare. Together they form an introduction to some of the most interesting and important issues treated by law and social science.

In the remainder of this introduction we present these core concerns of law and social science and provide a general overview of the chapters that follow.

---

6. For a brief overview of a crucial portion of Weber's analysis see the appendix to this chapter.

DESERT

Allocating responsibility is a central legal task. The business of applying the law is often the business of deciding what people did and did not do, determining what they could and could not have done, and distinguishing the intended from the unintended consequences of behavior. These tasks involve the examination of events and their antecedents as well as that characteristically legal enterprise of considering what might have been had people acted or chosen differently. Ultimately law enforcement is the process of holding people accountable based on an understanding of human action. It requires an appreciation of how actors avoid being held responsible for results apparently attributable to their behavior. Understanding legal judgments of responsibility requires us to consider those decision rules—substantive laws—that specify situations of accountability.

The social scientific study of wrongful behavior has at times floundered on issues of responsibility. The law generally assumes a free will model of behavior. This is sufficiently incompatible with the naturalistic bias of some social scientists that it has led them to disregard responsibility as it is defined and used in the law. Chapter 2 uses the work of analytical and legal philosophers to indicate why the law's free will perspective is important. In it we argue that no objective, behavioralistic language can capture adequately the meaning of key legal statements, such as "He did it," or "She could have done otherwise." We must understand how lawyers use such statements in order to address the question of responsibility.

Responsibility can only be understood within the framework of action language; that is, language that allows for subjective meaning. Given this framework, responsibility can be understood as basically a social process. It exists vis-à-vis other social actors. Responsibility is also a contingent state in that attributions of responsibility are defeasible. One may defeat an attribution of responsibility by providing an adequate excuse. Examining excuses allows us, as we shall see in Chapter 2, to appreciate the differences between responsibility rules and the evidence required to hold someone responsible or not responsible in the first place.

One of the difficulties with discussions of responsibility is that the term *responsibility* has different meanings. We sometimes fail to distinguish these meanings and, consequently, the various ways in which individuals may be held responsible. The second section of Chapter 2 establishes a set of categories with which we can discuss the different meanings of responsibility. One purpose of the chapter, then, is to make responsibility a variable. Some rules allow both intention and ability as excuses; an individual cannot be guilty of first degree murder without the requisite intention to commit murder and the requisite ability to have done otherwise. Other rules allow neither type of excuse. Still others allow one and not the other. We develop the idea of *rule logics* to describe these ideal types of rules.

Chapters 3 and 4 discuss problems of evidence. They look at how we determine the meaning of acts and how we come to understand the circumstances within which action takes place. Although any one adjudication will possess some unique qualities, there are, nevertheless, patterns in the kinds of evidence used to determine responsibility in different types of cases. In Chapter 3 we show how adjudicative processes differ along two important dimensions, the extensiveness of the inquiry and the degree to which the adjudicator tries to determine the mental state of the actor whose behavior is at issue. Chapter 4 builds on Chapter 3 to identify ideal-typical ways in which cases are processed, which we call *case logics*. Then it discusses organizational reasons for the choice of case logics.

Chapter 5 deals with the connections among rules and evidence and the way adjudication is organized. The chapter focuses on the movement from negligence to strict liability in two areas of tort law. The basic argument is that the bureaucratization of adjudication leads to shallow case logics, and these in turn promote movement toward a strict liability rule logic.

DISPUTE SETTLEMENT

Some laws, as we noted earlier, organize legal procedures. A particularly important function of this type of rule is to order processes of dispute settlement. Chapter 6 discusses pretrial settlement with the aid of models drawn from game theory. We shall see that such settlements are often rational for both parties and that rules of evidence and procedure can enhance or minimize prospects for settlement. This chapter also shows how formal modeling can aid in understanding complex social processes, and it discusses some important limitations.

Chapters 7 and 8 adapt and expand on Paul Bohannan's (1965) argument that law is used when primary institutions like peer groups or the family are unable to control conflict. Law "double institutionalizes" the conflict, which means that it provides a distinctively legal framework for the settlement of disputes. What is "distinctively legal" will, of course, vary with the characteristics of societies as will the way disputes are settled within that framework. In the Anglo-American tradition the distinctively legal institution is the court and there is an ideal pattern for proceedings that involve courts: A court should refuse to deal with a dispute unless there is a real conflict among the parties who seek its aid; the party who invokes the jurisdiction of the court should specify the legal norm(s) on which the decision should turn; the court should only consider information that bears on the applicability of the legal norm(s) invoked by the parties; the court should decide its cases on the narrowest grounds possible, and the court should declare a winner and loser in the dispute as well as the consequences that follow.

This Anglo-American vision does not describe a universal ideal. Chapter 7 deals with the question of why different societies and legal systems use different techniques to resolve disputes. The choice of technique appears to be heavily influenced by the typical social relationships of individuals in a society and by the relative autonomy and power of the legal system. Chapter 7 also examines the problems that arise when the settlement techniques employed by a court fail to resolve disputes in ways that are compatible with the expectations and needs of the disputing parties.

Chapter 8 picks up on this last point. Modern societies have come to recognize that their basic model of adjudication is not well suited to all the problems that courts are called on to resolve. Occasionally jurisdictions, like the states of the United States, have tried to design special tribunals to deal with particular problems. Chapter 8 focuses on two such tribunals, small claims court and the juvenile court. In this chapter we assess the relative success of these courts in achieving their objectives. In doing so, we shall learn more about the relationship of legal institutions to patterns of social relations and about the limits of legal reinstitutionalization.

DISTRIBUTION

One of the main functions of law is ordering the distribution of rights and duties in society. Part III examines legal rules that define the relationship of law and the social order.

When we consider law as an instrument of social change, we usually have in mind some attempt to alter the distribution of rights or of economic and social goods. In order to assess attempts to use law as a tool to alter social arrangements, we need to specify the ends of social justice toward which the law should work. Only with these ends in view can we examine how law may be used, with greater or lesser success, to mediate tensions between social ideals and the outcomes of existing social arrangements. But we have no scientific way of validating any particular set of ends, nor do we have special expertise in thinking about the matter.

Chapter 9 attempts to resolve these difficulties by fiat. Drawing on John Rawls's book *A Theory of Justice* (1971), we extract a set of social ideals against which we can measure a society and its legal order. With these ends in view we may evaluate existing social arrangements and the law's ability to alter those arrangements. Rawls's vision of justice, although not necessarily "right," is a respected view, much of which we find congenial. It is useful because it allows us to speak of law as an instrument of justice. But the reader should always be aware that in speaking of justice we refer to a philosophical vision rather than to a scientific concept.

Chapters 10 and 11 examine two specific problems confronting our society: the problem of corporate power and the problem of racial inequality. We shall examine these problems with Rawls's precepts of justice in mind and explore the policy dilemmas that law sometimes confronts in dealing with such problems. When looking at corporate power, we shall pay special attention to the problem of public goods and the difficulties of mobilizing unorganized people to act for their common benefit. We shall contrast their situation with that of organized groups, like corporations and trade unions, that are well situated to advance their special interests. In the case of racial inequality, we shall outline the situations under which the law is most effective in altering the unjust outcomes of social arrangements. In this connection, we shall examine voting rights, employment discrimination, and school desegregation.

The discussions in Chapters 12 and 13 are more abstract. Their topic is the relationship of the legal order to the ultimate aims of social justice, variously defined.

Chapter 12 deals with the possibility of legal autonomy, that is, with the ability of the legal system to act independently of forces emanating from the political, social, and ethical realms of society. We shall see that legal autonomy is an imperfectly realized ideal, but that if legal norms are taken as given, considerable autonomy in the law application process is possible. The key, as we shall see, is whether courts and other agencies charged with the interpretation and enforcement of the law take a formalistic stance toward the law they are applying or, instead, are motivated by the desirability of the results their decisions will produce.

Chapter 13 builds on ideas of legal autonomy and judicial formalism introduced in Chapter 12 as it attempts to explore the relationship between law and the distribution of welfare in society. Different types of legal systems with different implications for the likelihood that law will increase or ameliorate societal inequality are identified. Rawls's theory is used to situate these inequalities against a model of justice. Ultimately we conclude that the two core elements of Rawlsian justice, liberty and equality, are not fully compatible, and a legal system that attempts to maximize one can do so only at some cost to the other.

The concluding chapter briefly ties together some of the different arguments of the book. In it we examine the interrelationships among responsibility rules, dispute settlement rules, and rules concerning distribution.

As this brief description of the chapters that follow indicates, we have chosen to approach the field of law and social science from a problem-oriented or topical perspective. We did not intend to canvass every nook and cranny of this discipline and so have left some aspects unexplored. At the same time, our investigation into each topic ranges far enough to touch on much of the subject matter of law and social science without probing fully the various subfields. For example, had we eschewed a problem-oriented approach to law and social science in favor of a synoptic overview, we might have written lengthy chapters on the bar and the police. We have no such chapters, but we do not ignore these areas. Lawyers and police officers figure importantly in some of the themes developed, and where they do, we draw heavily on what we know of these professions. The same is true of other matters, such as plea bargaining or law and social change, that might merit integrated treatment in a differently organized book. In short, we view this book as an invitation to law and social science. Although it covers a great deal, it is just a first word, not the last. Even when we discuss a topic our citations are necessarily selective. There is much of value in literature that we do not mention—it awaits your discovery.

Appendix: Max Weber and the Rationality of Law

Weber's understanding of how laws are made and cases decided is centered on two basic distinctions. First, law may be made or found by two methods, the rational or irrational. Second, lawmaking and law finding can proceed, rationally or irrationally, with respect to formal or substantive criteria (Rheinstein, 1954, p. xi). These two distinctions create four categories of legal process.

Professor Trubek (1972) provides a helpful analysis of these dimensions. The formal-substantive dimension is primarily concerned with the source of the norms invoked. To the extent a legal system is formal, the norms applied in dispute resolution are *intrinsic* to the legal system. These norms may be of two types: (1) rules that describe the procedures that must be followed if resort is to be had to the law and (2) rules that prescribe appropriate outcomes given the *cognizable* facts of a dispute. The former is often called *procedural* or *adjective* law, while the latter is called *substantive* law. Procedural law affects outcomes in many ways, for procedural rules may systematically advantage one party or another. Indeed, it is procedural law that determines whether certain facts of a dispute or even the dispute itself will be heard in the legal forum.

Substantive law, as the term has come to be used, should not be confused with the substantive dimension of Weber's typology. A legal system is substantive according to Weber to the extent that the source of the norms it applies is *extrinsic* to the legal system. For example, a court would be applying substantive law if it resolved disputes by reference to a religious rather than to a legal code or by reference to a legal code that did no more than enact religious doctrine.

If a legal system is rational it yields outcomes that are predictable from the facts of the case because case outcomes are determined by the reasoned analysis of action in light of a given normative structure. Thus, a legal system is irrational when outcomes are not so predictable. Simplifying only slightly, a legal system is rational to the extent that like cases are decided similarly.

Putting these dimensions together as Trubek (1972, p. 729) did yields the following classificatory scheme:

TABLE 1.1
The Typology of Legal Systems Classified by Formality and Rationality of Decisionmaking Processes

Degree of Differentiation of Legal Norms	Degree of Generality of Legal Norms	
	High	*Low*
High	Logically formal rationality	Formal irrationality
Low	Substantive rationality	Substantive irrationality

Source: Trubek, 1972, p. 729.

A formally irrational procedure exists insofar as a process prescribed by the legal order yields results that do not seek to analyze the meaning of events and are unconstrained by reason. The judgments that are thought by some to follow from the consultation of an oracle or resort to an ordeal are the classic examples.

Substantive irrationality exists when lawmakers and finders do not resort to some dominant set of general norms but, instead, act arbitrarily or decide upon the basis of an emotional evaluation of the particular case. Weber had in mind the type of justice dispensed by the Khadi, a Moslem judge, who, at least as Weber saw him, sat in a marketplace and rendered judgment not by referring to general rules but by making a free and idiosyncratic evaluation of the particular merits of each case.

Substantive rationality exists when lawmakers and finders follow a consistent set of principles derived from some source other than the legal system. These may be religious, economic, or, God forbid, sociological. Weber thought he saw an approximation of this type in Mohammedan law insofar as it tries to implement the thoughts and commands of the Prophet.

Formal rationality could, for Weber, be of two types. The first, *extrinsic rationality*, exists when decisions turn upon perceptible external characteristics that have been made consequential by the legal system. For example, a case might depend on whether certain formal words were uttered or whether a seal was attached to a document. The second, *logically formal rationality*, exists when behavior is evaluated by reference to a theoretically gapless set of legal norms. Logical reasoning allows one, in principle, to determine the implications of the legal norms for any particular behavior. Where logically formal rationality prevails the subjective meanings of actors are important in determining the legal consequences of actions while the importance of extrinsic elements is diminished (Rheinstein, 1954, pp. 63–64). Weber regarded logically formal rationality as the most "advanced" kind of legal ordering and as particularly hospitable to the growth of the capitalist state.

The relationship between formal and substantive law is obviously more complicated than Weber explains it. The ideal types become mixed in important ways. For example, a legal system may be procedurally quite formal, and within the system formal procedures may in large measure determine the outcomes of cases. However, in some fraction of cases the prescribed procedures may lead to situations where the outcome will reflect the influence of some extralegal normative system. This can occur, for instance, where final judgment is left to a group of lay jurors (Green, 1976, 1985; Kalven & Zeisel, 1966). Furthermore, formal law may incorporate—either by statutory enactment or judicial decision— norms that are well rooted in nonlegal institutions. In doing so, the system becomes more substantively rational although it still retains formal character- istics. Thus, as is the case with crimes such as theft and murder, the demands of formal and substantive rationality may to some extent coincide. Even here, however, there is an important difference. In the "hard" case, the formally rational system will decide by logical reasoning from the norm as it has in fact been reinstitutionalized at the legal level. The substantively rational system will look to the implications of the moral system that supports the norm rather than to the logical implications of an enacted norm.

The importance of Weber's categories resides not only in the insight they provide into the decision-making processes of actual legal systems, but also in Weber's effort to link the different types of rationality with different types of societies and legal organizations. According to Weber, a social order based on allegiance to a charismatic leader tends to have an irrational legal order. Formal rationality, on the other hand, appears strongly related to the emergence of the bureaucratic style of organization and the ascendency of secularized, autonomous legal experts. The organization of adjudication, however, is not the only influence producing different types of rationality. The quality of legal rationalization is also affected by the material conditions of collectivities, such as the complexity of exchange arrangements and the balance between contractual and status relations (see Freund, 1969, p. 262).

According to Trubek (1972), Weber considered the calculable legal system represented in formal rationality to offer the optimum combination of coercion and predictability for modern capitalist society. The system as an ideal type promises predictable results when cases are brought to law and the implementation of these results by force if necessary. These factors taken together ensure expectations. Moreover, the formalism of the system allows people to use the law as a shield against those who seek to apply coercion in a manner or for purposes inconsistent with the rules of the law. When the law can be used in this way, it is to some degree autonomous (Trubek, 1972, pp. 742–743). It has a logic and justification that sets it apart from other fundamental social institutions. Law remains the repository of legitimate governmental coercion, but *intrinsic* to the legal system is a set of rules specifying when and how law may be invoked. Although these rules may systematically advantage the more privileged, they also set limits on how the privileged may act and on particular occasions may provide a means for thwarting those with greater social power (Balbus, 1973; Thompson, 1975).

In modern Western societies, the legal order not only tends toward autonomy, it tends toward supremacy as well. The law tends to supersede other forms of normative order. It comes to be perceived as a gapless system within which every type of social conduct can be understood as obedience to, violation of, or application of rules of law. This facilitates economic and political rationality. Rational political and economic arrangements in turn support formal legal rationality.

But there is a darker side to formal rationality. In assuring formal equality and formal rights, the legal order disregards substantive interests. Formal law, as it has developed in Western capitalist societies, gives everyone the equal right to own property but does not inquire into or create rules about the distribution of property in the first place. It tends to disregard ethical and moral considerations of distribution:

> Formal justice guarantees the maximum freedom for the interested parties to represent their formal legal interests. But because of the unequal distribution of economic

power, which the system of formal justice legalizes, this very freedom must time and again produce consequences which are contrary to the substantive postulates of religions, ethics, or political expediency. (Weber, 1968, p. 812)

An important question for Weber and for those who have come after is, How, if at all, can a formally rational legal order be an effective instrument for altering social distributions? To this question we may append the question, What are the costs and benefits of infusing a legal system with substantive concerns and of treating legal actors on the basis of personal and social characteristics rather than as abstract individuals equal before the law? As Weber notes in the preceding quote, formal legalism may yield results contrary to certain ethical positions. But it may also thwart political expediency and the totalitarianism that too frequently accompanies it. This suggests two conditions that must be met if the law is to be used successfully as an instrument to enhance equality. First, the ability of social and economic differences to penetrate the lawmaking and law application processes must be reduced. Second, the ability of law to penetrate social and economic arrangements must be increased. We examine the problems posed by these requisites in Chapters 12 and 13 as we discuss the possibility of legal autonomy and the relationship between law and social justice.

PART I

Desert

SOCRATES: *For surely neither God nor man will ever venture to say that the doer of injustice is not to be punished?*

EUTHYPHRO: *That is true, Socrates, in the main.*

SOCRATES: *But they join issues about the particulars—gods and men alike; and if they dispute at all, they dispute about some act which is called in question, and which by some is affirmed to be just, by others to be unjust. Is not that true?*

EUTHYPHRO: *Quite true.*

The question of responsibility is an intriguing one. It so pervades human relationships that it goes to the heart of the human condition. Responsibility is the glue that binds us together as a species. It is a burdensome privilege that is withheld from those who for reasons of youth, irrationality, and the like are thought unentitled to the complete investiture of a normal personality. Ideas of responsibility shape the moral terrain on which we map social relations and construct social institutions. Part I of this book explores responsibility within the context of law and social science.

Responsibility is the grist the law grinds daily. The business of courts and legislatures is often to establish responsibility. We might go so far as to say that without responsibility we do not have, to use Karl Llewellyn's term, "law-stuff."

In distinguishing among laws and legal systems, we often look to the nature of the responsibility rules embedded in legal proscriptions and to the evidence used to adjudicate disputes. To understand judicial systems, we must also have some understanding of responsibility. Otherwise we can never know what it means for a person "to receive his or her just deserts" or appreciate the role that law plays in this enterprise.[1]

Chapter 2 begins with a discussion of the concept of human action and the proposition that to understand the legal system and the place of responsibility in it we must understand how the law uses statements such as "He did it," or "She could have done otherwise." With the help of modern philosophers we shall see that responsibility can only be understood within the context of language that takes account of human agency and purpose. Building on this base, we then show how legal rules vary depending on their relationship to issues of agency and purpose. To capture this variation, we develop the idea of *rule logics* as ideal types and in concluding the chapter we discuss the ethical dimensions of each rule logic.

Chapter 3 and 4 turn to evidentiary issues. Given that human intentions and abilities often matter when we are ascribing responsibility, how are we to distinguish acts in terms of these criteria, and how are we to understand the circumstances within which action takes place? As we shall see in Chapter 3, different kinds of evidence are used to determine responsibility in different types of cases. In Chapter 4 we identify four ideal-typical ways in which cases are processed, which we call *case logics*. These types or "logics" capture the relationship between different ways that the law holds people responsible and the kinds of proof that these different ways require. We conclude Chapter 4 with a discussion of organizational reasons for the choice of case logics.

With the building blocks of Chapters 2 through 4 in place, we proceed in Chapter 5 to discuss the connections among rules and evidence and the organization of adjudication. We illustrate these connections by examining the movement from negligence to strict liability in two areas of tort law, those involving industrial accidents and automobile accidents.

---

1. In saying that responsibility is inextricably linked with the legal system, we do not mean to stake out a position in any debate concerning the essence of law. It would be misleading to view the law's concern for responsibility as the characteristic that best distinguishes law from other phenomena. Other features that characterize law, such as those that are implicit in Max Weber's definition of law as a normative system guaranteed by the potential for the official use of force, or Bohannan's concept of double institutionalization (see Chapter 7), come closer to suggesting law's unique nature.

2

Human Action and Responsibility Rules

ACTION AND RESPONSIBILITY

The Concepts of Action and Responsibility

"He got his just deserts." When we make this assertion we mean a person got a reward or, more commonly, a punishment appropriate for what he had done. Typically, the person engaged in some action, the action had consequences, and he was held accountable for the consequences because of his relationship to the event. The purpose of this chapter is to explore different types of relationships that people may have to events and how this may affect their legal accountability. We are not concerned here, however, with the character of the consequences that trigger the inquiry into legal accountability, although this feature may have important implications for how the inquiry proceeds and for the eventual outcome. Shooting a gun and killing someone for example, will lead to a different accountability judgment than shooting at someone and missing, even though all other aspects of the action are the same.

Putting aside the consequences of behavior, the key issues in holding a person accountable for what has been done are the issues of *action* and *responsibility*. These are our core concerns in this chapter. Both action and responsibility are everyday ideas that we generally use without thinking. Perhaps for this reason we can and do disagree about what constitutes action or makes for responsibility. Therefore, part of our task is to clarify the different ways in which we use these terms in law and in everyday life. We wish to create a shared understanding of the different meaning of statements like "she did it" and "he is responsible." To do so we must explore issues of action and responsibility at several levels and confront three types of questions: conceptual questions, ethical questions, and evidentiary questions (see Brand, 1970, p. 3).

Conceptual questions ask how we define and describe human action. *Ethical questions* ask by what criteria can we determine that someone is responsible. *Evidentiary questions* ask how do we show that someone has acted so as to be responsible. The first part of this chapter addresses the conceptual question. We establish behavioral meanings for *action* and *responsibility*, and then indicate various ways in which legal rules concern themselves with human action. In so doing, we discuss how the rules address the ethical question of what it is to be responsible. The evidentiary question we postpone until Chapter 3.

Human Action

A mad scientist has implanted an electrode in Fred's brain. She presses a button. He reaches up and scratches his right eyebrow. An observer records, "3:15 P.M., subject reached up and scratched right eyebrow." Sally feels an itch. She knows she is supposed to sit still, but she can't stand it. She reaches up and scratches her right eyebrow. An observer records, "3:15 P.M., subject reached up and scratched right eyebrow." Fred and Sally have behaved in the same way; or have they?

The key conceptual question concerning human action is simply this: Is there something more to human action than mere behavior? The question is at least as old as Aristotle (1951, Bk. III, ch. 1). There are many ways we might approach it. In recent times, analytical philosophers have frequently made this a question about our language. For example, are there essential differences between statements such as "he did it" and statements that fully describe the "it" that was done. Is there a fundamental difference between "I raised my arm" and "My arm rose" such that the first statement may mean something different from the second? (See Melden, 1961, pp. 73ff; Danto, 1965, p. 141.)

Consider the following set of concepts that Richard Taylor (1966, 1969) suggests are fundamental to understanding nature:

1. Existence and nonexistence (being)
2. Motion and rest (change)
3. Cause and effect (causation)
4. Action and passion (agency)
5. Means and ends (purpose)

The question posed by Taylor is whether these are, in fact, basic categories. If they are, none of them can be fully described by concepts that are yet more basic?[1]

The inclusion of agency and purpose on this list, that is, the assertion that they are concepts essential to our understanding of nature, is controversial. In the so-called hard sciences like physics and chemistry the categories of agency and purpose have no recognized, legitimate place and most consider their use to be inappropriate. Not only can the physicist's world be understood without reference to such categories, but the attempt to invoke such concepts may be confusing or worse. What, for example, would one make of the proposition that a ball dropping in a vacuum accelerates because it has decided to go faster or needs to reach the ground quickly. Indeed, at this level of analysis the concepts of agency and purpose have no obvious real-world referents.

Influenced by the natural science model, some social scientists similarly seek to avoid such concepts (see Skinner, 1971). There is, in their eyes, much to be gained by using the same limited set of basic categories to explain the behavior of atoms and the behavior of those collections of atoms called humans. Furthermore, even among those who reject the natural science model, there is a fear that couching explanations in terms of agency and purpose makes it impossible to arrive at a set of law-like statements about human behavior. Yet, the social sciences must be empirical, and it is an empirical fact that legal systems *and* the language of everyday life are permeated with words and phrases that employ concepts of agency and purpose to make sense of human behavior.

Consider, for example, a variation of the earlier statement about arm raising. Suppose a person were to say, "I moved my finger to fire the pistol to shoot the thief." Can we appreciate the full meaning of this statement and the behavior it describes without resort to the idea of purpose?

The statement avows that the declarant moved his finger on purpose. He moved the finger *because* he wished to fire the weapon. Furthermore, the statement implies a still further end—the desire to stop a thief. The *because* in the sentence "I move my finger because I want to fire the pistol" conveys the means-end idea, not simply the idea of causation. The discharge of the firearm is the effect of moving my finger, but it is more. It is the reason for it.

Firing a pistol to stop a thief may also cause other outcomes. For example, the shot may frighten nearby birds or scare a passerby as well as wound the

---

1. Many philosophers have spent much of their life in the attempt to reduce some of these concepts to others, primarily by showing that a concept with a higher number on the list can be reduced to a concept with a lower number. Two of the best-known attempts are those of David Hume and René Descartes. Hume attempted to reduce cause to change, suggesting that what we commonly call causation between events, thereby implying some kind of necessity or "making something happen," is only an invariance or consistency in the joint occurrence of kinds of changes.

Part of the Cartesian enterprise was the attempt to reduce agency to causation. The position argues that whether something is regarded as action or passion (in the sense of being passive) merely depends on how we look at it. Action is a special instance of cause and effect (see Davidson, 1963).

fleeing felon. But the difference between moving my finger to disturb birds and moving it in precisely the same way to prevent an escape is only a difference in the last category. It is neither a difference in what happens (change) nor in how I move my finger (agency) nor in the resultant effects (causation). The difference is one of purpose.[2]

In the language of legal systems, as in the language of everyday life, the relationship of an actor to an event is not only the relationship of cause and effect. When describing what we are doing or what we have done, we usually incorporate the elements of agency and purpose. Consider the following descriptions of an everyday event.

The Description of Action

Gary and Ellen are running around the house while their parents are preparing dinner. Despite being warned that they may hurt themselves, the children continue to play. Soon the inevitable accident occurs, and they come running to their parents full of tears and accusations.

> Gary (age 6): "She pushed me on purpose. She pushed me hard. After I fell down she wouldn't even help me up, she didn't care if I was hurt. I had the ball. She's always trying to take it away from me. Tell her to stop."

> Ellen (age 8): "I didn't push him. I tripped over the board you said you'd fix and bumped into him. I didn't even know he was hurt. I didn't even want the dumb old ball. We were just running around for fun. He thought it was fun until he got hurt."

These two versions of the event illustrate the central questions we ask when searching for a description of an action.[3] To begin with, there are questions of agency. These include questions of act type and mode of action. What did the person do, and how did the person do it? To answer the first question, we typically choose from among the many verbs available to describe actions. To answer the second question, we use those adjectives and adverbs that commonly qualify descriptions of how things happened. Here the choice presented to the distracted parents is between a "hard push" and a "tripping bump."

Disclaiming agency is one way of disclaiming responsibility for an event. The disclaimer may be full as when a person says he was not involved in an event or it may be partial as when a person denies setting a harmful force in motion. In claiming she tripped, Ellen claims that the behavior Gary felt as a push was not her action. It was something that "happened" to her. She was a reactor and not an actor; a victim rather than the agent of the mishap that put

---

2. The preceding discussion is taken from Richard Taylor (1969). The weight of philosophical opinion is in agreement with his position that agency and purpose are irreducible categories. See McIver, 1964; Taylor, 1964; and Chisholm, 1967.

3. The following list is borrowed from Rescher, 1970.

her in contact with her brother. "Yes," says Ellen, "I bumped Gary, but I couldn't help it." In her 8-year-old way she is denying agency.

Next, there is the question of the "setting of the action"—in what context did the person act? The contextual elements define the degree to which a person is constrained in her action and the degree to which she could have foreseen its consequences. By pleading that it was all in fun, Ellen tries to suggest that she could not be expected to have foreseen ill consequences. In pointing to a loose board, Ellen attributes causality to the environment rather than to herself.

Taken together the elements of type, mode, and setting describe whether an individual set some behavior in motion (was an agent), whether she could have *foreseen* the likely consequences of what she did, and whether she had the *ability* to do otherwise. As we shall see, these are key elements in the ascription of responsibility.

Finally, the children address the issue of purpose: Why did Ellen do it? When we ask why she did it, we are, in effect, asking, "What caused her behavior?" Ellen, of course, wishes to answer this question by reference to external conditions and physiological processes not under her conscious control. The cause of the injury was an uncontrollable "bump" caused by an unavoidable, unforeseen "trip." This conclusion is implicit in Ellen's answers to the first three questions. But Ellen's very attempt to provide these answers implies an additional answer to the "why" question, one that deals with her intentions and motives. What she is saying is, "I didn't mean to do it. It wasn't my purpose to hurt him."

Indeed, explanations by reference to external constraints often make sense only because certain intentions or motives are presumed to be salient in particular situations. Thus, the statement "I had the ball" is an intelligible response to the question, "Why did he chase you?" only because we assume children want to play with toys. The statement "I had the ball" would not be an intelligible response to the question "Why did he put on his brown socks?" because we can think of no motive that links the situation and the behavior. Explanations of why people do things are frequently statements of purpose. In this they differ from explanations of why physical objects behave as they do.

Related to the question of why a person did something is the question of why a person failed to do something. Ellen not only describes the contact with Gary as a bump, she describes her failure to assist Gary after the accident as a nonaction, not an intended omission. She and we sense that there is a difference between doing not-X which is an act (i.e., refraining) and not doing X which need not be an action. If Ellen had known Gary was hurt and had not helped him, her behavior of not extending a hand would have a different meaning from what it would have had she thought he did not need a hand. In the first instance the failure to extend a hand is a result of a conscious decision. In the latter, the issue of whether to extend a hand has never reached consciousness. Actions differ from acts in that they are interpretable only by reference to the actor's subjective meanings. Thus, the distinction between nonactions and the action of refraining is primarily one of purpose or intent.

These several elements—act type, modality, setting, and purpose—are all needed for a full description of human action. Only by attending to these features can we understand the stories of Ellen and Gary. People may, like our two children, be responsible in different ways depending on how an action is defined. We shall see examples of this as we explore the issues of responsibility more fully. For the moment, let us simply note that although this is a book about law and not about children, our reliance on Gary and Ellen to illustrate these points is not inappropriate. The rules of the family are protolaw, the mother is a protojudge and, most importantly, the excuses we hear in a family are proto-typical. Add 15 years to the children's ages and we might hear such things as:

> She wanted to steal my watch. She tried to kill me. She ran away and left me there for dead.

or

> I only asked him for the time. He tried to grab the gun and it discharged. I didn't know he had been hit. I thought he'd tripped and I ran.

The courts are full of language like this, replete with references to agency and purpose.

The Concept of Responsibility

Just as human action can be understood at several levels, so too can responsibility. From the mere description of an act it is almost impossible to determine legal responsibility. Attributes of the person, the act-event, and the situation all bear on judgments of responsibility. The following passage by H. L. A. Hart nicely captures some of the different ways in which attributes of individuals or events are employed in assessing responsibility and illustrates the different meanings of the term:

> As captain of the ship, X was responsible for the safety of his passengers and crew. But on his last voyage he got drunk every night and was responsible for the loss of the ship with all aboard. It was rumored that he was insane, but the doctors considered that he was responsible for his actions. Throughout the voyage he behaved quite irresponsibly, and various incidents in his career showed that he was not a responsible person. He always maintained that the exceptional winter storms were responsible for the loss of the ship, but in the legal proceedings brought against him he was found criminally responsible for his negligent conduct, and in separate civil proceedings he was held legally responsible for the loss of life and property. He is still alive and he is morally responsible for the deaths of many women and children. (Hart, 1968, p. 211)

Hart's story uses *responsible* to mean many things. First, there is the preliminary question of whether a person can be responsible at all, whether the person is *accountable*, that is, whether it makes sense to ask for an explanation or account of the questionable behavior (Baier, 1970). Responsibility in this sense might fairly be reproduced by hyphenating the word so that it reads response-able, or able to respond. Some people because of their inability to make sense of the world around them cannot be expected to respond to that world in socially approved ways. If, as rumor had it, the captain were truly insane, we might well conclude that he was not responsible in this sense. An individual must have minimal ability to understand, reason, and control bodily movement to be responsible in the capacity sense (Hart, 1968, p. 218). Young children, like the insane, are often thought to lack the capacity for responsibility.

There are few, if any, rule systems that do not in some way attend to capacity, yet the question of capacity is not decided in a vacuum. Although we might agree that our two fighting children do not have the capacity to be legally responsible for a murder, parents routinely hold their young offspring responsible for fights. Likewise, we might excuse the captain were he truly insane, but his drunkenness is unlikely to be recognized as a capacity defense. This is because the captain had, at least at one time, the ability not to get drunk.

The degree to which we hold people responsible for putting themselves in positions where they are not fully capable of conforming their behavior to what is expected depends on their behavior and the situation, as well as on their position. Some social positions carry with them the responsibility for categories of outcomes, and individuals in such positions are expected to behave always with this responsibility in mind. In the sea captain story this aspect of responsibility is reflected in the statement that, ''as the captain of the ship, X was responsible for the safety of his passengers and crew.'' This second meaning of responsibility Hart calls ''role-responsibility.'' In what follows, we shall focus primarily on this meaning of the term.

To be role-responsible is to be responsible for something by reason of one's social position. The responsibility may be as specific as the responsibility of a meter maid to ticket overtime parkers, or it can be as broad as the responsibility of a police officer to enforce the law. In either case, the exact scope of responsibility is defined by rules of role behavior that are called *norms*. To some extent, one can select the things one will be responsible for by committing or not committing oneself to certain roles or lines of conduct. But, as anyone who has had to wash the family dishes as a child will appreciate, tasks can be assigned and roles can be imposed.

The broadest kind of responsibility is that which the state attaches to the unavoidable condition of personhood. Persons within the jurisdiction of the state must obey the law. However, in ordering behavior, the law, as we shall see, takes roles into account. Many legal rules apply to persons in some positions but not to those in others or make different demands of people occupying different positions. The captain is responsible for the ship. The galley hand need only assure that the potatoes are properly peeled.

Responsibility, as we see from these examples, is not an attribute of an individual like height or hair color. *Responsibility exists only in relation to an event or a status.* It is contingent on relationships before, during, and after events and may vary accordingly. Whether a role has been voluntarily assumed or imposed, questions of responsibility arise when the task assigned to the role is not performed according to expectations.[4]

A third meaning of responsibility is *answerability*. If an individual has the capacity to be accountable and has apparently failed to satisfy a norm (i.e., a rule of role behavior), that person may be required to answer the question of why he failed to conform to the norm. Usually it takes the occurrence of an untoward event to motivate an inquiry into whether an individual has breached a norm. Such events, like the sinking of the captain's ship, suggest that some person or persons have not performed as they should and call for a response to the charge. The captain attempted an answer when he blamed winter storms for the ship's sinking. Sometimes an untoward event may not be necessary to trigger the inquiry. A mere failure to perform up to expectations may be enough. The captain's drunkenness would have required an explanation whether or not the ship was lost.

In either case, responsibility in the sense of answerability emphasizes the important point that *responsibility is a relationship between or among individuals*. The proverbial man alone on a desert island is responsible for nothing in this sense because no one will or can question his behavior.

In conceptualizing responsibility as a relationship between people, we do not mean to imply that a person's sense of responsibility is a meaningless concept, or that the law is uninterested in this psychological state. Clearly, people can feel responsible and be motivated by these (guilt) feelings. Furthermore, legal actors may take genuine feelings of responsibility (remorse) or the behavior they engender into account when deciding cases. However, in the legal sphere the determination of responsibility usually entails the *evaluation of a person's answer to the charge that he failed to perform as required and so caused an untoward action or event*. Responsibility, as we are interested in it, is an attribution process.

Types of Answers

The availability of answers indicates another important aspect of attributions of responsibility. They are *defeasible* (Hart, 1949). The accused has some opportunity to indicate how it is that the ascription of responsibility for an untoward event or impermissible behavior is mistaken. Many types of answers are available. An answer may admit fully the charged failure and the actor's responsibility for it, or an answer may seek, in whole or in part, to defeat the suggestion of responsibility.

One type of answer, which attempts to wholly defeat responsibility, is the *demurrer*. A demurrer is an answer that says "so what?" It admits the alleged connection between the act and the event but denies the existence of a rule

---

4. One may also wish to determine responsibility in order to accord praise or give a reward. The law, however, is almost always concerned with determining responsibility for untoward events.

making the actor accountable for the event. For example, one thief argued that he had committed no federal crime in transporting a stolen airplane across state lines because an airplane was not a vehicle and only the interstate transportation of stolen vehicles was prohibited by the relevant act. A unanimous Supreme Court agreed [*McBoyle* v. *United States*, 283 U.S. 25 (1931)[5]]. Of course Congress quickly corrected this oversight.

What is unique to the demurrer as an answer is that it rests the denial of responsibility entirely on rule interpretation. The facts that are alleged to constitute irresponsible behavior are acknowledged to be both accurate and complete. The party responding with a demurrer is saying, in effect, "I have nothing to add to the accuser's story of how and why the event occurred, but so what!"

The availability of the demurrer makes it clear that *responsibility exists in relation to rules*. In ordinary life the rules are social norms that define a person's roles. In legal life the rules, at least in most modern societies, are explicit enactments or judicial precedents that impose obligations on individuals in certain circumstances. Thus, the demurrer as a legal response admits the particular act or event for which a person is asked to account but denies the existence of any law that makes the act or event an occasion for the ascription of legal responsibility.

When successful, the demurrer works by asserting that the act as described meets the standards of all applicable substantive rules. Another type of answer attempts to avoid the attribution of responsibility without confronting the merits of the complaint. This kind of answer does not deny the alleged irresponsibility; instead, it questions the right of the accuser to call an individual to account. If the defense succeeds, the accused, however irresponsible her behavior, has no one to whom she must answer. Thus, a child told by a friend not to chew gum in class might respond, "What's it to you?" or "Who are you to complain?"

At law, defenses that avoid the merits in this way are called *collateral defenses*. They are "collateral" in the sense that they raise collateral or side issues, usually of a procedural nature. The legal analog to the question "Who are you to complain" is the objection to "standing." A taxpayer, for example, who wants a court to halt covert aid to rebels in a Latin American country on the theory that it is an unauthorized expenditure of tax payments may be told

---

5. As this is the first case we have mentioned, it is a good place to explain legal citations. Law cases are published chronologically in series of books called reporters. Reporters come in two varieties: official reporters, published by states or by the federal government; and unofficial reporters, published by private corporations. They contain the same case texts, and, indeed, some states and some federal courts rely entirely on "unofficial" reporters. "U.S." in the citation indicates that the case is taken from the U.S. Reports, the official reporter of United States Supreme Court cases. The numbers before the (U.S.) indicate in which volume the case is to be found. The numbers after the (U.S.) indicate the page number in the volume where the case starts.

When the number of volumes in a reporter reaches some high number, the publishers may decide to start all over with volume 1. They then note this by indicating that this is part of the second series. This has not, however, happened with the U.S. Reports. The date at the end is the year the case was decided.

that since the injuries he alleges are not personal to him his suit will be dismissed for lack of standing. The court will not even examine the accusation that tax money is being illegally spent, although this may well be the case.

Other collateral defenses are answers that challenge factors such as the jurisdiction of the courts, the constitutionality of procedures used by the police to "build" a criminal case, and the timeliness of the complaint. For example, complaints that are brought while threatened harm is inchoate may be dismissed as "unripe," while those brought too long after the allegedly wrongful act may be dismissed for "latches" or because a "statute of limitations" has run. Most of these answers, however, have a commonsense basis. Thus, one reason courts refuse to adjudicate unripe claims is because to do so would waste judicial resources whenever the unfolding of events would have meant that the parties never actually came into conflict. For instance, an auto industry challenge to a proposed air bag regulation might be dismissed as unripe because the fact that a regulation is proposed does not mean that it will be enacted. Statutes of limitations, on the other hand, are designed to protect people from having to answer for actions that occurred long ago. The protection is justified because much of the evidence bearing on the action complained of is likely to have vanished over time, and viable, long-standing accommodations to the situation are likely to have occurred that will be costly to disturb.

Collateral defenses appeal to norms that condition the applicability of more substantive legal norms. The norms that are appealed to are peculiarly "legal." They are often rooted not in the popular culture but in the training of lawyers, and so are not readily perceived, understood, or accepted by those without legal training. Norms of this sort are the hallmark of and flourish in formally rational legal systems such as those found in modern Western democracies. They are the constitutive law of such systems in the sense that they specify the arenas in which and the occasions on which substantive legal norms will be enforced.

This implies for a legal system such as ours that substantive rules and policies may be overriden by formal requirements. Thus, evidence may be thrown out and a burglar freed because a police officer stopped the burglar and searched him illegally. "How can it be illegal," a layperson may ask, "to stop a burglar and seize the fruits of his crime?" "It is illegal," the lawyer answers, "because rules of proceeding, in this case constitutional rules, preclude the state's agents from stopping a person and seizing evidence from him without 'probable cause' to believe he has been involved in a crime."

When formal procedural rules and substantive norms clash, accommodations must be reached. There is no necessary hierarchy that guides the choice of which norms are to prevail. A rule limiting searches and seizures to situations of probable cause, need not, for example, exclude illegally seized evidence from trials. Until 1961 and the Supreme Court case of *Mapp* v. *Ohio*, 367 U.S. 643 (1961), this was the situation in many states. Similarly, statutes of limitations may be thought generally desirable but may be made specifically inapplicable to murder or to certain types of land transactions, personal injuries, or tax frauds. Indeed, when procedural rules are closely scrutinized, the distinction between procedure and substance often breaks down, for procedural rules frequently have consistent substantive implications. Nevertheless, except at the border there is a perceptible difference between the spirit or concerns of procedural law and the spirit of substantive enactments. One focuses on what is grist for the legal mill and on how legal action is to be accomplished. The other focuses on substantive ends to be achieved and regulates with an eye toward their attainment.

Modern legal systems can be characterized by the degree to which formal or substantive concerns prevail when the two clash. Ordinarily it is only when formal norms generally prevail or are thought to prevail that we honor a governmental system with the approbation "rule of law." We shall see in Chapter 13 that a regime of law in this sense is a mixed blessing, but on balance, in our view, a blessing nonetheless.

Defenses other than demurrers or collateral attacks raise what we call "justiciable events." The presence of a justiciable event means that there is considerable work to be done before an ascription of failed role responsibility can be made. It is between the allegation of such responsibility and the decision on the allegation that justice (and injustice) resides. It is here where rules take on meaning and where the fate of individuals is finally determined.

The predominant answers at this stage are the *denial* and the *excuse*. The denial, as the name implies, denies the connection between actor and event that is the basis for the attribution of responsibility in the first instance. "I didn't do it" is a defense that 3-year-olds scolded for taking chocolate chip cookies and adults charged with multiple murders have had in common.

When an allegation of responsibility is answered with a denial, a factual question is raised. If the connection between actor and event cannot be shown with the degree of certainty the law requires, exoneration is, in theory, complete. In fact, doubts may linger and an acquitted accused may continue to suffer from having been under suspicion. He may face private sanctions as when an individual charged with a crime and acquitted cannot by reason of the charge find employment (cf. Schwartz & Skolnick, 1962), or when after a publicized civil suit consumers avoid a product that the plaintiff could not show to be a cause of his disease or injury. The effects of suspicion may also have a public dimension as when the police, implicitly rejecting the judgment of a court, treat an acquitted defendant as a "usual suspect" when investigating a crime similar to the one of which he was acquitted.

In some instances, there is good reason to believe that the legal system's decision to accept a denial is *as a factual matter* mistaken. In criminal cases, for example, the state's burden of proof may be "beyond a reasonable doubt," which means that the law's fact finder should accept some denials that are more likely than not to be unworthy of belief. Even more important are the implications of a legal system with formal rules regulating the way matters may be proved. In the Anglo-American system the most prominent among these are the "rules of evidence." It is conceivable that over the range of cases these rules minimize error, but it is clear that in particular cases the rules, by preventing the admission of probative evidence, may interfere with accurate fact finding.

Finally, when an individual's factual relationship to an untoward event cannot be denied and when demurrers and collateral defenses are unavailing, excuses come into play. If the accused is able to convince others that her behavior is in some sense excusable, she will not be held responsible, or her responsibility will at least be mitigated. Excuses are a type of what Erving Goffman calls "remedial work." Goffman defines such work as action designed "to change the meaning that otherwise might be given to an act, transforming what could be seen as offensive into what can be seen as acceptable" (Goffman, 1971, p. 109). A sufficient excuse turns an apparent rule violation into an acceptable (if not admirable) piece of behavior. It offers an explanation and definition of a situation that absolves or mitigates the offerer's responsibility for an untoward event (see Austin, 1956–1957; Scott & Lyman, 1968; Blum & McHugh, 1971).

Most excuses go to the two distinguishing elements of human action, agency and purpose. Excuses are the answers we provide when we wish to describe our behavioral relation to an event as something other than a fully intended act of a conscious agent. In one sense excuses are the last line of defense; but in another sense excuses are the fundamental answer, for they define the law's relationship to what it is to be a human actor. As we shall see in the next section, rules may be understood in terms of the excuses they admit.[6]

SUMMARY

When an individual is accountable, and role responsible, and when excuses along with all other answers have failed, he is responsible in a final sense. He may face sanctions. This last sense might, therefore, be called *sanction-responsibility* (cf. Baier, 1970, p. 107). Putting the various meanings of the word *responsible* together, we can conclude that the attribution of responsibility for an untoward event: (*1*) *is to be understood in terms of the roles and tasks of different actors*; (*2*) *is a relationship between individuals*; (*3*) *is defeasible*; (*4*) *involves the relationship of some act to some rule*, and (*5*) *exposes the accused to possible sanctions.*

The two final elements, the relationship of acts to rules and the sanctions that attach to particular actions are central concerns of law. The determination

---

6. We may distinguish analytically an additional way of defeasing claims of responsibility. This is the "justification," which ordinarily goes more to the intended consequences of the behavior in question than to issues of responsibility. Justifications occur when actors admit their involvement in an event and their responsibility, but deny that they have done anything wrong or, indeed, claim they acted virtuously. Those who offer justifications may be challenging the law itself, at least as it applies in a particular context. What is to be judged is not the actor or his relation to the event, but the event itself. For example, those who refuse to register for the draft do not deny their failure to register nor do they deny that they are responsible for this failure. Instead, they argue that their action is justified because the disruption it entails or its symbolic import serves the cause of peace. On other occasions the law itself recognizes justifications. We shall treat justifications that the law recognizes as a kind of excuse.

of responsibility is not resolved solely by looking to statutes or rules. But the rules do help define the various ways in which actors are held accountable for their connection to untoward events. In the next section we present a set of rule categories that we call *rule logics*, which vary in terms of the excuses they allow. In discussing these rule logics, we shall raise a number of questions both about the ethical bases of responsibility rules and about our legal system.

RULE LOGICS

Defining the Logics

In this section we discuss a set of responsibility rules that taken together classify and define most types of legal responsibility. Our classification has two objectives. First, it should enable us to capture most of the ways in which we think about the relationship of human action to moral responsibility. It must, therefore, incorporate the concepts of agency and purpose. Second, the scheme should allow us to categorize actual laws in a relatively efficient and unambiguous fashion.

With respect to the first objective Francis Raab has suggested that there are two criteria for full moral responsibility. They are that the "agent did what he did intentionally and that he could have helped doing what he did" (1968, p. 702). The first element clearly refers to the element of purpose. The second, ability to do otherwise, is a way of raising the agency question that deserves some elaboration.

The essence of the "could have done otherwise" element is captured by the maxim "ought implies can." We should not require people to do things that cannot be done. There are, however, many different senses in which something may be said to be impossible (see Austin, 1956–57; Brand, 1970).[7] If an individual is able to show impossibility in certain of these senses his behavior will be excused, for from an ethical point of view he will not have been fully responsible for his action (see Rawls, 1971, p. 236). To plead that one could not have done otherwise is to argue that one was not the free author of the event.

Most of us would agree with Raab that both intention and ability to do otherwise are necessary for full moral responsibility. But the two elements are

---

7. Consider a man locked in a prison cell. We may ask, "Can he play the piano?" One answer is yes, he has played many times before. Another answer is no he cannot, there is no piano in the cell. The first answer is in the *ability* sense of can. The second is in the *opportunity* sense. If a person has both ability and opportunity then he "can" in an *all-in* sense. To these three meanings we might add a *capacity* sense—not having the ability to play the piano but having the ability to learn. And in still another usage we may speak of a *capability* sense—having the capacity to learn to play but having no opportunity to learn, for example, being unable to afford lessons. Finally, there is a sense, important in law, of *ill-consequence*—a person can play but she avoids doing so because she has severe arthritis in her hands. No doubt, there are other nuances that can be suggested.

not always required for the ascription of legal responsibility. A particular responsibility rule may require both of these elements, either one, or neither. Thus, a particular statute may make intention either relevant or irrelevant to a finding of responsibility. The situation is the same with the ability to do otherwise. Crossing these possibilities gives rise to four ideal types, as shown in Table 2.1.

The first cell defines a rule logic where both criteria are relevant. We must have both an intention to do the untoward act and the ability to have done otherwise. The label "criminal liability" is used because the criminal law, at least in the Anglo-American tradition, is interested in both aspects of human action. It is important to note at the outset, however, that what we call the criminal rule logic, like all our labels, describes an ideal. Actual criminal statutes vary greatly with respect to the excuses they allow. Strictly speaking, only a crime that is *malum in se* (or, evil in itself) fits the criminal law rule logic ideal. *Malum in se* crimes are those that reinforce norms of popular morality by directing the power of the state's enforcement apparatus against actions, like burglary or murder, that are self-evidently evil.

It is not surprising that capacity and intent, characteristics that are essential to popular judgments of immorality, are elements of *malum in se* offenses. Crimes that are *malum prohibita*, that is, crimes defined by acts that are not self-evidently evil, like driving over the speed limit or radio broadcasting without a license, may or may not require both the intent to violate the law and the ability to do otherwise. We will return to this point when we discuss the range of excuses available under each logic.

The second cell defines negligence liability. Intention is not relevant, but being able to do otherwise is. The tort of negligence involves this type of responsibility as do certain crimes such as negligent homicide. This rule logic applies in situations where a harmful event has occurred and some actor, other than the victim, is linked causally to the event. The issue is whether the actor who "caused" the harm should make amends by compensating the victim or paying a penalty exacted by the state. Since the excuse "I couldn't do otherwise" is acceptable, a person who suffers harm may find that she has no claim against the party who injured her. Thus, if the brakes on a new car fail suddenly, injuring a pedestrian, the driver will not be liable in negligence so long as she had no

TABLE 2.1
Rule Logics

	Intention Is Relevant	*Intention Is Irrelevant*
Ability to do otherwise is relevant	Criminal liability (*malum in se*) (1)	Negligence liability (2)
Ability to do otherwise is irrelevant	Witchcraft, contractual liability (in a sense) (3)	Strict liability (4)

reason to believe the brakes were bad and she could not have taken reasonable steps to avoid the accident.

On the other hand, the excuse, "I didn't intend the harm" will not defeat an attempt to impose responsibility. Thus, had the driver in the preceding example known her brakes were bad, her honest claim that she did not intend to injure anyone would not have defeated the victim's demand for compensation.

Cell 3, where intention is relevant, but being able to do otherwise is not, defines a situation that is in a sense approximated by contractual liability. In certain situations impossibility will be no defense for a failure to perform an obligation; that is, for a failure to perform a contract. This is most likely to be true where the impossibility is personal to the nonperformer and not the result of unexpected conditions that affect everyone (Simpson, 1965, p. 360).[8]

Grant Gilmore (1974, p. 45) quotes the following opinion by Judge Morton speaking to this point:

> [W]here the law imposes a duty upon anyone, inevitable accident may excuse the non-performance; for the law will not require of a party what, without any fault of his, he becomes unable to perform. But where the party by his agreement voluntarily assumes or creates a duty or charge upon himself, he shall be bound by his contract, and the nonperformance of it will not be excused by accident or inevitable necessity; for if he desired any such exception, he should have provided for it in his contract. [*Adams* v. *Nichols*, 19 Pick (Mass. 1837) pp. 275, 276]

As this passage indicates, the role of intent in such situations is somewhat unusual. The intention that is relevant is not the party's intention at the time of the breach. If it were, an individual could always defend by claiming he had no intention to breach but found it impossible to do otherwise. What is crucial is the party's intention at the time the contract was made. If the contract contemplated that the parties be bound despite their personal circumstances, each party will be held to have accepted the risk that performance would turn out to be impossible. Judge Morton is simply announcing the rule that if the parties did not speak to this issue in their agreement, the law will assume that they each meant to be so bound.

We should not be surprised that this type of liability is largely limited to situations where a person has explicitly or implicitly promised to perform before the occurrence of the impossibility. Liability like that defined by our third cell implies a type of existential responsibility that makes an individual accountable for all actions done as a conscious agent even though he could not help doing (or not doing) the act (cf. Sartre, 1977). Hence, such responsibility is rarely imposed in a modern society unless its risk is willingly assumed. However, the logic is not inherently limited to situations where such responsibility is inten-

---

8. When a party for personal reasons is unable to fulfill obligations under a contract, this is generally not an excuse. This situation is often called "subjective impossibility," and is distinguished from "objective impossibility," where the thing or duty under question cannot be performed by anyone; for example, an agreement to sell a house that is destroyed by a tornado before the closing date.

tionally assumed. We see this in certain societies that believe in witchcraft. Everyone in the society may admit that a witch cannot help being possessed by demons, but the witch may nevertheless be held responsible for acts of witchcraft (Seidman, 1965). The "fact" on which all agree, that the acts are properly attributed to a demon that "possesses" the witch, is not an acceptable excuse. The witch is like the person who through nonperformance breaches a contract in that the circumstance leading to the violation may not be her fault, but she is nonetheless held accountable for what has happened.[9] At the same time, it is ordinarily assumed that the harm the witch does the victim is intended, and the process of identifying a witch often involves an attempt to identify a person likely to have intended harm to the victim. Once such a person is identified she may be tried—usually by ordeal—to determine if she is in fact possessed. Presumably those with no apparent intent to harm the victim are unlikely to be suspected of witchcraft in the first instance.

The fourth cell requires neither intention nor the ability to do otherwise for findings of responsibility. It is the logic of strict liability. Within a strict liability rule logic behaviors are generally inexcusable. Restaurant owners, for example, are held strictly responsible for selling contaminated food even though they did not intend to do so and may have had no way of knowing that the food was contaminated.

Strict liability does not, however, mean that there is no defense. Demonstrating that there is no causal connection between the accused agent and the event will defeat the accuser's claim. A person may not be able to plead "I didn't mean the harm," but he can still plead "I didn't cause the harm." Moreover, pleas by way of demurrer and collateral defenses may also be entered. That is, a person may always argue that the strict liability rule logic does not apply, or if it does, he may plead technical defenses, like the statute of limitations.

Excuses

As the preceding discussion suggests, each rule logic can be described in terms of the types of excuses it allows. Table 2.2 presents the rule logics in terms of the types of excuses they typically allow.

The legal types we used to label the rule logics in Table 2.1 are as we previously noted ideal types. They are one-sided and simplistic as compared to the often mixed logics of the actual laws that are subsumed under these labels. By examining the variety of excuses that are in fact used in different situations, we can better understand the complex stances that laws take to excusing circumstances.

---

9. Different cultures have different conceptions of witchcraft. In some, as in Renaissance Europe and the colonial United States, possession is not considered involuntary; it is the perceived result of a "pact with the devil" or other voluntary action (Erikson, 1966; Currie, 1968).

TABLE 2.2
Typical Excuses In Rule Logics

	Intention Is Relevant	*Intention Is Irrelevant*
Ability to do other-wise is relevant	Fully excusable	Situationally excusable
Ability to do other-wise is irrelevant	Motivationally excusable	Largely inexcusable

Most intention and ability excuses are unavailable when liability is strict, but there are usually limits to the law's disregard of these matters. Strict liability is rarely absolute liability. By way of example, the old common law action for trespass made a person strictly liable for invading another's land, even if he had not intended an invasion or realized that one had occurred. Yet, if a person were bodily seized and carried on another's land, an action for trespass would not lie. When intention and the ability to do otherwise were not only missing but any desire not to invade was overborne, the trespass was excused.

Within the logic of contractual liability and criminal liability "I didn't mean it" statements are typical pleas. But the pleas have different meanings in the two contexts. To say, "I didn't mean it" in response to a criminal complaint is to deny one of the elements that constitutes the crime. It is to assert that what one "did" is qualitatively different from the act that one is accused of having engaged in. The defense is possible whenever a crime is defined so as to take account of the actor's subjective meaning. Assault with intent to kill is qualitatively different from simple assault. We see this in the penalties provided. A legal actor can defeat the former charge by showing an intention to kill was lacking. Even simple assault requires the intent to place another in fear of injury. Where no such meaning applies to an act, such as where an actor is accidentally pushed into another, no criminal assault has occurred. As Justice Holmes once said, "Even a dog distinguishes between being stumbled over and being kicked" (Holmes, 1881, p. 3). Much of the criminal law turns on this distinction.[10]

The "I didn't mean it" statement in response to a claimed breach of contract does not dispute the quality of the act that is immediately antecedent to the litigation, for whether or not the breaching act was done intentionally is usually irrelevant. "I didn't mean it" in a contract suit means "I didn't mean to be

---

10. Often in the criminal law actions done in reckless disregard of the life or person of another are treated as if they were done with criminal intent. One justification for this compromise position between the criminal and negligence rule logics is the belief that a person who recklessly disregards the life or person of another is so depraved that he deserves to be punished criminally. Another more pragmatic justification is that because it is difficult to prove subjective intent when the actor denies it, if the objective circumstances suggest that an act was either intentional or done in reckless disregard of another's physical well-being, it makes sense to proceed as if the act was intentional. Although we cannot prove intent, we are confident that if we could know the actor's mind we would find in most such cases that the action was intentional.

obligated in the way you claim.'' This excuse denies that the act that the complainant points to was a breach, whether intended or unintended, for it denies the existence of a contract imposing obligations with respect to the act in question. The denial may question the existence of any contract, or it may simply dispute the claim that the contract was intended to regulate behavior in the way the complainant alleges. In either case, it refers to a purpose that existed before the alleged breach when promises about future behavior were exchanged.

Motivational excuses are particularly complex within the criminal law. Statements about intention, motivation, purpose, reason, aim, objective, to name but a few of the words in the teleological vocabulary, are all in order when responding to a criminal charge. A person might, for example, argue that he had no intention at all as when claiming that a bullet accidentally discharged when he dropped a gun. The danger with such a plea is that it may open the person up to negligence liability since it admits responsibility for an injurious event without justifying its occurrence.

Another kind of excuse is that of ''alternative purpose.'' Some alternative purpose excuses are those that the criminal law traditionally calls *justifications*.[11] A person who advances such an excuse is arguing that his act should be seen as proper or even praiseworthy. The most common example is the plea of self-defense. A person who makes this plea is claiming that he was not trying to harm another but was merely trying to protect himself. If so, he may be justified in intentionally doing something (e.g., shooting another) which is ordinarily punishable as a crime. Other alternative purpose pleas attempt to place known facts in a perspective which suggests that one or more elements of a crime are lacking. For example, a person charged with acting as a get-away driver in a bank robbery might defend by testifying that she thought she was doing a friend a favor by taking him to and from the bank and had no idea that the friend had intended to rob the bank.

An accused may also admit that an act was intended but plead a good motive.[12] The distinction between intention and motive is a distinction between the desire to bring about an act and the reason for that desire. Thus, murder requires an intention to kill someone. A person may intend to kill for a variety of reasons—because he has been paid to do so or because he cannot stand to see a dear relative suffer from a terminal illness.[13] In American criminal law,

---

11. See footnote 6. As we point out there, justifications may be seen as something analytically different from excuses rather than as a variety of them. When, however, justifications are recognized by law we think they can be profitably seen as a kind of excuse.

12. The plea of good motive may also be a form of justification.

13. The law uses the term *motive* to refer to a person's reason for desiring the event that is the occasion for a determination of responsibility. There is nothing in the abstract that defines some of our purposes as intentions and others as motives. The distinction only emerges when we have settled on some event as the untoward event. If the event that gives rise to assessing responsibility is the reduction of suffering, a court would ask whether an individual's intention was or was not the reduction of suffering. If the event is a death, the intention at issue is causing death, and the purpose of reducing suffering is a motive. The distinction between motive and intention is often crucial. In American criminal law, for example, a person may show a lack of intention to kill and be excused. Generally, however, if intention is present, ''good'' motives will not excuse homicides.

demonstrations of good motive will only rarely fully excuse behavior that is otherwise criminal. But a good motive may reduce the level of the offense, from first degree to second degree murder, for example, or present a reason for leniency in sentencing. Thus, a "mercy" killer can expect a lighter sentence than a contract killer, although as a matter of law both may have been found guilty of the same crime.

Occasionally motive will be an element of a crime, in which case the negation of the motive will be a defense to the crime. The situation is confusing, however, because where motive is an element of a crime, the statute will usually speak of intent. For example, a statute may make it a crime to reveal the names of intelligence agents with the intent of interfering with the activities of the CIA. Here intent is relevant in two senses of the term. The first, which is implicit, is that the accused has intended to reveal the names of intelligence agents. If, for example, the accused published a list of CIA agents thinking it was a list of State Department civil servants, intent in this sense is lacking and a cell 1 type of crime has not been committed. Yet, even if the person knew she was publishing the names of CIA members, criminal liability under our hypothetical statute would still be problematic. There remains the question of whether the act was done with the intent (for the purpose) of interfering with CIA activities. Here intent is synonymous with motive and the showing of a good motive, or more precisely, the government's failure to prove the existence of the proscribed motive, would mean that an accused could not be held responsible under the statute.

Within the logics of negligence liability and criminal liability, excuses that suggest an individual could not be expected to have done otherwise are typical. Constraint, compulsion, duress, mistake, unforeseeability, irresistible impulse, and many other words and phrases suggest this inability. Various more specific claims are subsumed under these categories. Some based on foresight, knowledge, and ability deal with what Austin calls the "machinery of action" (1956–1957). An individual cannot be expected to have done otherwise where the untoward results of an action and thus the need to act differently cannot be foreseen. Other excuses seek to avoid responsibility by reference to cultural circumstances or biological drives that are allegedly so compelling as to have made actions other than the one taken impossible. Some such excuses seek to treat as compelling circumstances cultural values that allegedly serve to "dictate conduct" (J. Stone, 1966, p. 556; see also Seidman, 1965, for belief in witchcraft as such an excuse). Religious beliefs, may, for example, require a person to take certain actions such as refusing to work on the Sabbath or not registering for the draft. In a modern pluralistic state like the United States, cultural excuses are only occasionally recognized by law. Not only are cultural constraints thought, rightly or wrongly, to be less binding than more immediate situational constraints and threats, but to allow such excuses generally would permit too many people to establish reasons for ignoring too many laws. Consider, for example, the attractions of a religion that proclaims the payment of taxes a sin.

Not only is the variety of excusing conditions quite complex, but similar excuses meet with different acceptance even in areas of law that are formally alike. Herbert Packer makes this point nicely in a passage that illustrates the differential openness of the criminal law to the excuse of mistake:

> Arthur is charged with homicide and claims that he thought the man he shot at was really a deer. Barry is charged with stealing a raincoat that he claims he thought was really abandoned property. Charlie is charged with possessing heroin; he says he thought the white powder in the packet was talcum powder. . . . Evan is charged with statutory rape; he claims the girl told him she was over the age of consent. Frank is charged with selling adulterated drugs; he says that so far as he knew the drugs conformed to requirements. George is charged with failing to file his income tax return; he says that he didn't know about the income tax. Harry is charged with carrying a concealed weapon; he claims he didn't know it was against the law to do so.
>
> Under existing law Arthur, Barry, and probably Charlie will be listened to. That is, the trier of fact will decide whether each of them really did make the mistake he claims to have made. If it is believed that he did and (ordinarily) if the mistake is thought to be "reasonable," no crime has been committed. . . . Evan is probably out of luck, although there is a developing trend in his favor. Frank, George, and Harry might just as well save their breath; their exculpatory claim of mistake will not be listened to.
>
> If all this seems confusing and arbitrary, that is only because it is confusing and arbitrary. Traditional criminal law has fallen into the deliberate, and on occasion inadvertent . . . refusal to pay attention to a claim of mistake. (Packer, 1968, pp. 122–123)

Packer notes that the occasions where mistake will not be considered as an excuse are of several general types. First, there are certain basic offenses that dispense in whole or in part with mental state requirements. Statutory rape is an example in point. Any act of sexual intercourse with a girl under the age of consent, however old she looks and whatever her prior sexual experience, is, in some jurisdictions, rape. An individual cannot plead an honest and reasonable misapprehension of the girl's age because knowledge of the girl's youth is not an element of the crime. Other crimes that make similar inroads on the criminal liability rule logic are bigamy and felony-murder.

Second, resort to the excuse of mistake is limited by the barrier of *ignorantia legis*, ignorance of the law is no excuse. On this ground the pleas of George and Harry will fail. In the case of *malum in se* crimes, such as murder, this limitation is unproblematic. The law reflects community standards of minimal behavior, and it is unlikely that any normally participating member of the society will be unaware of these standards. There are other laws, however, that are neither so well publicized nor so rooted in ordinary morality that an individual cannot reasonably claim to be unaware of the illegality of the acts they proscribe. When the courts will not listen to credible excuses of ignorance, they have moved from the criminal law rule logic toward one of strict liability.

Third, there are crimes that are judged by a negligence logic. Manslaughter and negligent homicide are the clearest examples. Each involves the killing of another human being without the intention to kill. The distinction between manslaughter, negligent homicide, and an excusable accidental killing depends largely on the degree to which the accused should have foreseen the possibility that his actions would cause life-threatening harm. Pleas that one did not mean to kill are to no avail. In Packer's story, Arthur's plea that he thought he was shooting a deer would, if believed, save him from a conviction for first degree murder, but depending on the reasonableness of his decision to shoot, it might not save him from a manslaughter or negligent homicide conviction.

Finally, there are a group of offenses, commonly called *public welfare offenses*, that do not allow either motivational or situational excuses. As Packer notes, these offenses openly flout their rejection of such excuses (1968, p. 130). Violations of food and drug regulations, violations of liquor regulations, and some traffic offenses are frequently encountered strict liability crimes. These kinds of crimes are what we alluded to earlier as *malum prohibita*.

As the actions we have discussed suggest, in the world of real statutes and rules there are no clear, sharp lines between rule logics. They shade into one another. Our examples also raise a number of questions. Why do we have rules that disregard those considerations that make for full moral responsibility? Is there something "wrong" with strict liability crimes? What ends justify strict liability in civil actions? How do different rules relate to the ethics of responsibility? We address these and other questions in what follows.

The Ethics of Responsibility

Accepting Raab's point that full moral responsibility requires a consideration of both agency and purpose, we may begin by asking, "Why do different rules and statutes allow different excuses?" In the criminal law, full criminal responsibility is generally the rule for crimes that are *malum in se*. Why is this so? One answer is that capacity and intent are relevant because of the relationship of this part of the criminal law to popular morality. The classic *malum in se* crimes restate norms of popular morality in terms that the law will enforce. In these circumstances it is not surprising that those characteristics essential to popular judgments of immorality—capacity and intent—are incorporated into the criminal law. However, some crimes that require capacity and intention are not simply the legal restatement of folk morality. Income tax evasion and espionage, for example, presuppose the existence of the state. If these are "popular crimes," it is because an official morality has become accepted at the folk level. Yet, in the case of income tax evasion, at least, the degree of popular acceptance is questionable. "Why then," we might ask, "are these and other novel crimes often defined so as to require a full moral responsibility?" We can only venture an answer.

First, there is the matter of habit. Legislators are accustomed to defining crimes in terms of capacity and intent. Thus, some new crimes allow the full set of excusing conditions because it never occurred to the drafters who defined the crime to state otherwise. Second, there is a relationship between the responsibility we require and the punishment we mete out. It is generally felt that severe punishment is appropriate only when action has been generally immoral, and in some circumstances, as when death is the punishment, this might be constitutionally required (cf. *Lockett* v. *Ohio*, 438 U.S. 568, 1978). In order to discourage some undesirable behavior, legislators may make the behavior a crime, and provide a severe punishment. To justify the severe punishment they may feel that they must define the crime so as to require capacity and intent.

Finally, there is the issue of stigmatization. Stigmatization refers to the degradation of a person's moral character that typically accompanies the conviction of a crime. Some people believe that much of the force of the criminal law lies in the stigmatizing consequences of a criminal conviction. If crimes were routinely defined so that capacity and/or intent were irrelevant, the criminal conviction would lose much of its stigmatizing consequences because the judgment of guilt could not be taken as a judgment of moral character. Where crimes do not require capacity, a conviction usually carries with it little or no stigmatization.

Moving beyond criminal liability, we might ask, "How are rules requiring less than full responsibility justified? Is there an ethical dimension to negligence, contractual or strict liability?"

In the case of negligent conduct where the actor did not intend the untoward act but could have in some way avoided it, most of us feel that the actor nonetheless has some moral responsibility. Although "intention" may be a requisite for the ascription of *full* moral responsibility, it is not essential to the ascription of *some* moral responsibility. Agency alone is sometimes sufficient for moral judgments. An agency-linked morality appears particularly attractive in situations where a loss has occurred and the question is whether (or how) to apportion that loss between a negligent actor and an innocent victim. This is the classic problem in tort law.

People expect others to be alert to their surroundings and to take special care when they engage in potentially dangerous activities. These expectations have a moral quality, and sanctions are applied when they are not met. One of us remembers very well the occasion during his childhood when he spun a Lazy Susan so fast that one of the dishes flew off and broke. The plea "I didn't mean to do it" neither forestalled punishment nor assuaged guilt. If the law can be taken as a mirror of the social norm rather than vice versa (cf. Lempert, 1972), the general obligation is to avoid any action that might injure the person or property of another unless the benefits of that action outweigh the likely harm.

Unlike a lack of intention, many types of impossibility appear to preclude stigmatization. No moral opprobrium applies to a person who breaches a contract in a situation where performance is impossible. Agency is in some ways a more fundamental element of moral responsibility than purpose.

Perhaps more interesting is the fact that even the intentional breach of a fulfillable contract may escape condemnation as immoral so long as the breacher is willing to pay for the damages he or she has caused. This is because the standard measure of contract damages requires the breacher to place his contracting partner in as good a position as he would have been in had the contract been performed; and the other party to a contract is often indifferent, or so it is assumed, between performance and money. Some have argued that breaching contracts promotes efficiency because the resources that would have gone to fulfilling the contract are presumably used for a more valuable purpose (Posner, 1977). From this perspective, it would be socially harmful if the breach of contract by those willing to pay damages were discouraged by being treated as immoral. Others, however (e.g., Finnis, 1980), focusing on the general obligation to keep promises and the value of trust, reject this view.

The ethical justification of strict liability, like the justification of contractual breaches where the breacher is willing to pay damages, is distributive rather than personal. Strict liability frequently exists in situations where injuries attributable to the behavior of some actor are regarded as unpredictable, and in a certain sense, inevitable. The issue is whether the agent of the harm or the victim, neither of whom is thought to have acted carelessly or intentionally, should pay for injuries that would not have occurred but for the harm doer's activity. Thus, for example, a drug company may be held responsible without any showing of wrongful behavior for damages attributable to an impurity present in a drug it sold. The decision to hold the harm doer responsible is like the decision to hold a contracting party responsible for a breach he could not help, except that ordinarily one cannot argue, without resort to legal fiction, that the harm doer intended to assume the risk of damage caused by his permissible, or even socially beneficial, activity.

A frequently used rationale for strict liability in cases such as those involving impure drugs is to recognize that if drug companies must pay for such harms, the costs will, over the long run, be borne by all drug purchasers. Compensating those hurt by impure drugs is, in other words, a cost of doing business. Making harm attributable to defective products a cost of doing business is considered a better way of allocating the costs due to the distribution of a product than the essentially random assignment of very large costs to the injured subset of the product's users (Calabresi, 1970). Thus, to impose strict product liability is not to ignore morality; it is instead to opt for a morality of distributive rather than personal justice.

There is another dimension that is also important to the ethical justification of strict liability rules. Recall our statement that the injuries that give rise to strict liability are regarded "in a certain sense" as inevitable. The inevitability of injuries in most cases is only relative to the general level of effort made to preclude them. Thus, if a drug company inspected a product for purity 200 times during the manufacturing process rather than just 10 times, injuries due to impure drugs would, no doubt, decrease. Yet, at some point further inspections would be counterproductive, for the costs of such efforts would far exceed the costs attributable to the impurities that would be found by additional inspections.

The moral implications of this situation might be best appreciated by considering the Ford Pinto cases, which arose out of the fact that the Pinto's gas tank was allegedly positioned in a location that increased the probability that it would explode in the event of a collision from the rear. Ford's engineers apparently conducted a cost-benefit analysis, as shown in Table 2.3, prior to placing the gas tank where they did. Benefits of $49.5 million consisting of the deaths, injuries and vehicle damage avoided are contrasted with the $137 million cost of moving or shielding the gas tanks in 12.5 million vehicles. Ford's engineers did what the law's "reasonable" person would do in the circumstances. They concluded that since the cost of future harm would be less than the cost of placing the tank elsewhere, they would not move it. If Ford's analysis were accepted, most courts would not hold the company responsible under a negligence logic, for Ford was acting neither carelessly nor unwisely. With a strict liability rule logic the case is closer, although even here there are limits to liability for such "design defects." If there were no limits, automobile manufacturers would be liable for injuries suffered in all automobiles not built like Sherman tanks. Yet, even such a strict rule might not induce Ford to invest further in safety. If the cost of the remaining "inevitable" injuries was less than the cost of the changes in the manufacturing process needed to eliminate the injuries, the lowest cost alternative for Ford would be to increase the cost of each car by enough so that Ford could pay for all compensable injuries that might occur.

The choice between a negligence rule logic that places the burden of cost-justified design defect injuries on the victims and a strict liability rule logic that more frequently places the cost on the manufacturer is basically a choice about the distribution of costs and the efficiency of different systems of accident law. The morality that argues for placing the costs on Ford is, as with the drug company, one of distributive justice. There is, in addition, the pragmatic justification that strict liability gives those who weigh costs and benefits an incentive to value human life and injuries as highly as popular opinion—speaking through the jury—does. What is most offensive about Ford's alleged cost-benefit analysis, in our opinion, lies not in the fact that it was done, but in the low values that were placed on human life and suffering and in the equation of the marginal cost of the first $11 required to locate the gas tanks more safely with the last $11 that victims would expend on grief and suffering.[14]

Each of the rule logics we have discussed reflects an underlying morality, even those logics that do not label as immoral actors who are held responsible. However, it is only in cell 1 (in Table 2.1) that to be responsible is to be held

---

14. This last point, that Ford apparently ignored the fact that an $11 charge which most people would find a meaningless increment to the price of the Pinto was aggregated to overbalance extreme pain and suffering that would be felt by a small number of individuals, would not be discouraged by a regime of strict liability since the company would only attend to the aggregate cost of compensation as compared to the aggregate cost of avoidance. However, if such cold-blooded assessment of the worth of human injuries was thought morally offensive despite its bottom line rationality, punitive damages—a penalty that tort law allows for particularly willful or reckless behavior—might be appropriate. In *Grimshaw* v. *Ford Motor Co.*, No. 19-77-61 (Super. Ct., Orange Cty., Calif., Order Dated March 30, 1978) an original jury award of $125 million in punitive damages was reduced by the trial judge to $3.8 million. Although a $125 million judgment may seem hugely excessive, note how it would affect Ford the next time they evaluated the costs and benefits of different gas tank locations.

TABLE 2.3
Benefits And Costs Relating To Fuel Leakage Associated With The Static Rollover Test Portion of FMVSS 208

Benefits	
Savings	180 burn deaths, 180 serious burn injuries, 2100 burned vehicles
Unit Cost	$200,000 per death, $67,000 per injury, $700 per vehicle*
Total Benefit	180 × ($200,000) + 180 × ($67,000) + 2100 × ($700) = $49.5 million
Costs	
Sales	11 million cars, 1.5 million light trucks
Unit Cost	$11 per car, $11 per truck
Total Cost	11,000,000 × ($11) + 1,500,000 × ($11) = $137 million

Source: Owen, 1982, p. 56.
* The dollar estimates for fatalities and injuries were based on National Highway Traffic Safety Administration calculations.

accountable for one's actions in the full moral sense. This explains the special nature of the sanctions that may be applied to those who violate the criminal law as well as the stigma that attaches to convicted criminals. The corollary to this is, as we have noted, that a person found criminally responsible is generally perceived to be more morally culpable than a person who is found to be negligent; and a negligent person in turn is perceived as more culpable than a person who promises more than she can eventually perform or one held strictly liable.[15] The criminally liable person has chosen wrongly in a situation where choice is allowed. Thus, each of the rule logics is associated with its own ethic of responsibility.

In the preceding discussion we have been addressing the question of the moral justifications of the various rule logics. In the case of both contract liability and strict tort liability there is a justification we have mentioned but not emphasized: *efficiency*. Efficiency relates to morality in that it minimizes costs for a given return and so maximizes the resources available for human well-being. Contract liability and strict liability may both promote efficiency in the sense that actors facing potential liability can in theory choose the course of action that fully compensates any victims while maximizing their own gains.[16]

---

15. This analysis is confirmed by a laboratory study by Weiner and Kukla (1970), where hypothetical students were punished most severely when they had the ability but didn't try (criminal liability), and least severely when they tried but had no ability (strict liability).

16. This is not to say that regimes of contract law and strict liability are in the economist's technical sense necessarily efficient ways of organizing social behavior. Although contract law tends to be efficient in that it facilitates exchanges that are in the interests of both parties, third parties may sometimes be adversely affected, and the specific performance remedy that contract law sometimes allows may thwart an "efficient" breacher. Although strict liability laws may encourage those responsible to act as efficiently as they can, the strict liability system as a whole may not be efficient because, as contrasted with a scheme of negligence, it may discourage accident prevention measures by the party who is the cheapest cost avoider.

Strict liability is also efficient in a different sense. Because it is unconcerned with issues of agency and purpose, a regime of strict liability is relatively cheap to administer. Were the law concerned solely with administrative efficiency, there would be much to be said for strict liability. Since the problem of human action does not emerge under such a rule logic, the decision about responsibility is, therefore, simplified. But being human and having a sense of the moral, we choose laws that make human action a central concern. Herbert Packer puts the issue well in the following passage:

> The reasons for recognizing excuses do not, then, have much to do with the prevention of antisocial conduct. They have to do with other values that, to put it bluntly, interfere with absolute efficiency in the prevention of antisocial conduct. They have to do with preserving human autonomy and with maximizing the opportunity to exercise choice. (Packer, 1968, p. 112)

The conflict between the virtues of a rule that recognizes human autonomy and abilities and a rule that efficiently disposes of cases forces hard choices. In Chapter 5 we shall discuss the conflict between these objectives in tort law. Let us simply presage this discussion by noting that the choice is not solely a matter of moral reflection. It is not enough to point out an underlying morality and identify a logic that corresponds to that morality. The moral quality of a situation is not always self-evident; and even if it were, we could always ask what makes it so. The adoption of a particular rule logic to deal with a particular problem is a political as well as a moral decision.

The adoption of a rule logic is political in two senses: (1) It is a response to values, (2) It is a response to power. For example, the choice between a strict liability and a negligence logic for compensating injured workers will, as a sociological matter, reflect the relative interests and power of labor and management as well as the values that surround the question of how injured workers should be treated. Similarly, in the movement toward "no-fault" automobile accident compensation, Keeton and O'Connell (1965) and others have acted as "moral entrepreneurs," arguing that no-fault compensation is more efficient and distributionally fairer than a negligence system because it eliminates middlemen (i.e., lawyers), and because it allocates funds more equitably to those injured in accidents. Trial lawyers and others have argued against no-fault and its accompanying strict liability logic. They too raise arguments of efficiency and morality. The efficiency argument is one from deterrence (we can expect fewer accidents under the tort regime), while the morality argument focuses on issues of both desert—people should pay for the harm they (negligently) cause—and distribution—the severely injured are undercompensated under schemes that exclude full compensation for their special pain and suffering.[17] Which side prevails in a particular jurisdiction depends not only on the persuasiveness of the competing arguments from efficiency and morality—which is the language in which

---

17. One frequent finding in studies of accident compensation is that the severely injured are undercompensated while the slightly injured are overcompensated. This is true in negligence systems as well as in strict liability schemes (see, for example, Conard, 1964, p. 291).

the debate is conducted—but also on the pressures and rewards that each side can bring to bear on the legislators who will resolve the issue.

There is, within law and social science, relatively little systematic empirical study of how and why different rule logics are enacted or maintained. In Chapter 5 we shall discuss one area about which something is known as an example of what the enterprise might look like.

In concluding, we return briefly to some matters noted earlier. There are those who would argue that focusing on issues like human agency and purpose in an effort to explain human action is misguided and irrelevant (Skinner, 1971). The arguments of those who take this position are based on a particular conception of determinism. It is not profitable for us to engage in the deterministic debate. We are content to show that concepts of agency and purpose are needed to understand responsibility, and we believe that understanding the meanings of responsibility is essential in order to understand law. Whether, when we have a purpose, that purpose is itself determined (caused), is a separate question (see Nagel, 1961; Ofstad, 1961; Schleffler, 1963; McIver, 1964).

As to whether one could construct a legal system that did not attend to agency and purpose, Isaiah Berlin responds:

> What can and what cannot be done by particular agents in specific circumstances is an empirical question, properly settled, like all such questions by an appeal to experience. If all acts were causally determined by antecedent conditions which were themselves similarly determined, and so on *ad infinitum*, such investigations would rest on illusion. As rational beings we should, in that case, make an effort to disillusion ourselves—to cast off the spell of appearances; but we should surely fail. . . . To try to place ourselves outside the categories which govern our empirical ("real") experience is . . . regarded as an unintelligible plan of action. (Berlin, 1959, p. 681)

Berlin, of course, may be mistaken. Perhaps we could create a legal system that always disregarded agency and purpose. To the degree that the law could do so it would, in turn, make this plan of action intelligible. By acting as if agency and purpose were irrelevant concepts, we would help make them so. A legal system that takes cognizance of agency and purpose in defining the human condition helps make those elements part of the human condition. Whether or not our freedom to choose is metaphysically real, the legal system helps make it empirically real. The maintenance of this empirical reality is one of the functions of the concept of responsibility (Hart, 1968).

3

The Answering Process

Rule logics and their attendant excuses provide a skeletal structure for understanding the answering process. They allow us to categorize rule systems and to recognize gross shifts in the underlying logic of such systems. They do not, however, tell us how cases get processed. Where rule logics are abstract, cases are concrete. Litigants argue over the rules that pertain to their behavior and often give conflicting accounts of what transpired. A third party, whom we shall conventionally call the *judge*, is present to resolve matters in conflict. It is the judge in the various forms this figure may take (including in some societies large groups of people and in others nominal partisans of the parties) who gives the attribution of responsibility its public character.

It is in the context of being judged that excuses are advanced and liability is assessed. As we have already indicated, excuses are of many types that inescapably shade into one another. Further complexities can arise because although no excuse fits a behavior, the behavior may be described so as to fit an excuse. As J. L. Austin notes:

> Many disputes as to what excuse we should properly use arise because we will not trouble to state explicitly *what* is being excused. . . . To do so is all the more vital because it is in principle always open to us, along various lines, to describe or refer to ''what I did'' in so many different ways. . . . It is very evident that the problems of excuses and those of the different descriptions of actions are throughout bound up with each other. (Austin, 1956–1957, p. 17)

The problem of describing events and actions that Austin raises is at its base epistemological. That is, it concerns a theory of knowledge with special reference to the limits and validity of information. The practical discipline of law turns many epistemological questions into problems of evidence. The problem is not how *can* we know when some individual in a given circumstance has acted so as to be responsible? It is, "How *do* we know?" What counts as evidence?

In this chapter we discuss the problem of evidence in its most general sense. We explore the ways in which events are described and human actions are understood. We are concerned not with particular items of information or the legal rules of evidence, but with the ways in which circumstances and actions are *typified* in the answering process.

TYPIFICATION

Typification is the process by which we organize and categorize experience (Schutz, 1970). It is intimately related to knowledge. For example, our ability to distinguish dogs and cats is based on typifications about the nature of the two species. We can lump all dogs into one category and all cats into another. Yet, strictly speaking, each dog or cat is unique. Thus, we need not stop with two categories. If we choose, we can distinguish *between* dogs (or cats) rather than lumping them into a single typification. We may, if we wish, distinguish setters from bulldogs, or, with closer inspection, Irish setters from English setters. Sometimes, of course, a detailed examination may not lead to a clear identification of a subgroup. Perhaps our dog is a crossbreed of indistinguishable origins. In such a case, in order to know more, we shall have to investigate its ancestry, perhaps concluding that the dog is half cocker spaniel and half beagle, or we may simply forego the investigation and call the dog a mutt. However we describe the animal, we have made a choice between relying on a more general typification (dog, hound) and delving more deeply into the particular nature of the animal before us.

Similar processes are used in calling individuals to account. We decide how closely to scrutinize actions and events. Where highly typified accounts are acceptable only a superficial analysis of a situation is necessary. In such circumstances we usually consider fewer excuses, and those we do accept are themselves likely to be typified. When making a more detailed analysis, we delve into the circumstances and meaning of action and listen to a wider range of excuses.

For example, statutory rape categorizes as criminal any act of sexual intercourse with a person below a certain age, while ordinary rape makes criminal only those acts of intercourse that are knowingly done without the sexual partner's consent. The former is more highly typified than the latter because, starting with the sex act, it focuses on only one dimension of what has occurred: Was the woman below the age of consent? A searching inquiry is not needed to answer this question, and once it is answered we know the type of person before us, a criminal rapist or an innocent fornicator. However, when ordinary rape is charged, a court must probe more deeply. Beginning at the same point, it must explore both the woman's state of mind and that of the man. Men may not be typified as people who have had intercourse; they must be broken down further by considering what was on their minds at the time. Classifying women into easily defined age categories is of little aid here in deciding guilt or innocence.

The legally relevant distinctions depend on less certain processes of attitude reconstruction. Moreover, with more matters demanding more complicated proof, the accused has greater scope for his defense. As the example illustrates, one consequence of increased typification is to restrict the range of relevant excuses.

In calling people to account, we use typifications primarily to *understand circumstances* and *determine meaning* (Schutz, 1970, pp. 120–121). When we categorize an event or action as a certain kind of circumstance, we are saying that for our purposes it is essentially similar to other actions and events that have been similarly classified. Thus, a police officer who finds a man unconscious in the road may at first be puzzled, but putting together various clues, he may typify the event as "another hit and run" and radio his fellow officers to look for freshly dented cars speeding from the area. Had he decided the event was "another mugging," he would have acted differently.

Typifications are used to determine meaning because we can never be certain of what others intend. Rather than confront another's action in its uniqueness, we simplify by assuming that people who act in typical ways for their situations proceed from similar motives and have a common end in view. Thus, we assume that a driver speeding away from an accident is trying to escape and not attempting to secure help for an unconscious victim.

Typification occurs at both the rule and case levels. Rules may specify that apparently different circumstances deserve identical treatment or that recognizably different actions are, for legal purposes, the same. Thus, under the law of statutory rape, the circumstance of having sexual intercourse with a girl who is 12-years-old and looks and claims to be 12 is the same as the circumstance of having sexual intercourse with a girl who is 12 but looks and claims to be 18. The only meaning that is relevant in this case is the intent to have intercourse. On the other hand, the meaning of killing a person during the course of a felony such as an armed robbery is assimilated to—that is, deemed to be of the same type as—deliberately killing a person. The different circumstances are recognized in the required proofs, but both are presumed to be done with malice aforethought and to justify the state's highest penalty.

Where rules do not impose typifications, social processes may nonetheless lead to typical ways of interpreting cases. For instance, larceny, which includes stealing from a building by day, is a less serious crime than burglary, which involves breaking into a building by night, yet burglars who have done little damage and stolen only a small amount may be treated as if they had committed larceny. The circumstantial difference between burglary and larceny as recognized in the law is, in this example, obliterated in practice. What actually happens is that the lawmaker's attempt to typify crimes by the time and manner of their occurrence is replaced by a typification that is more congenial to those who process cases. "Two bit" thefts are differentiated from more consequential offenses whenever they occur.

The case examples that follow show how adjudication processes differ in the degree to which they use typifications to define circumstances and determine meaning. With these examples in mind, we develop a more general theory of when disputes are likely to be more or less typified. Throughout we are concerned with the connections between the process of understanding circumstances and the process of determining mental states.

Understanding the Circumstances

To begin, let us consider the relative particularity with which we describe the circumstances surrounding an untoward event. It is costly to search out information, so we must at the outset of any investigation reach some decision about the depth of our inquiry. Questions of depth arise with any description, but they are especially troublesome in the process of bringing someone to account. This is particularly true when we seek to apply negligence or criminal rule logics since how we see surrounding circumstances affects our understanding of past behavior. Although mental states are conceptualized as internal to actors, the inferences we make about mental states accompanying acts are likely to be situationally dependent. For example, a man who throws a live grenade into a crowd of people at Times Square on New Year's Eve is either crazy or evil. The same act done on a battlefield might earn the adjective "heroic," which is one way of saying that the action is not the same.

Two elements determine the depth at which an adjudication is conducted. The first is the "fine grainedness" of our investigation, that is, the degree to which we attend to the special characteristics of a situation in order to identify its unique aspects. The second is our willingness to search out evidence extended in time and space from the immediate event. We call these two elements *uniqueness* and *extensiveness*. We discuss them in turn.

Uniqueness. Events may be seen as more or less typical and actions may appear as relatively unique or not unique depending upon the particularity with which the situation is described. In characterizing a situation, we might use highly typified descriptions—for example, "This animal is a dog"—or we might be much more specific—"This animal is a reddish-brown cocker spaniel that has a scar on its ear, walks with a slight limp, etc." The more detail we attend to, the more we are able to distinguish one object, action, or event from others that are similar.

The level of description is crucial in common law systems where the rules decided in prior court cases are used to determine the correct outcome of an existing case. The central doctrine in this process is *stare decisis*, "adhere to the decision." This means that if the instant case resembles a previous case in relevant detail, it should be decided in the same way as the earlier one. The most important recurring question in a common law system is whether the facts of some earlier case (a precedent) are sufficiently like the facts of the present case so as to govern the present decision. This system encourages relatively unique analyses, both in arguing to the trial judge and on appeal.

An earlier case that is similar in every relevant respect to the adjudicated case is said to stand "on all fours." Finding a favorable case on all fours is the goal of the legal researcher. But, as one would expect, there can be considerable disagreement about whether some previous case stands in that posture. In discussing whether the case is sufficiently identical so as to constitute controlling precedent, opposing counsels argue about the unique elements of the cases.

An example of this process is found in Summers and Howard's (1972, pp. 43–94) detailed discussion of the otherwise unassuming case of *White* v. *Island Amusement Co.*, 378 P. 2d 953 (Ore. 1963). *White* arose out of a suit brought by a 15-year-old girl who was injured when she dove into the defendant's public swimming pool and struck her head on the bottom. The girl apparently knew that the pool had no very deep section, but the pool was somewhat misleading in the way its floor sloped. The issue was whether the amusement company could be considered negligent for its failure to alert users to this fact and its failure to specify the pool's depth at various locations. The trial judge had overturned a jury verdict for the girl on the ground that the evidence did not show the defendant company to be negligent, and the appellate court, with one judge dissenting, affirmed.[1]

Much of the argument on appeal concerned the proper interpretation of a 48-year-old case, *Johnson* v. *Hot Springs Land & Improvement Co.*, 76 Ore. 333, 148 P. 1137 (1915). In the *Johnson* case a 19-year-old was killed in a similar accident. He struck his head on the bottom of a public swimming pool by diving into it. In *Johnson* the court ruled that the pool owners were not the insurers of the safety of the pool's patrons. The question of whether the decision in *Johnson* "controlled" *White* was hotly disputed.

The defendant in its brief argued that the holding in *Johnson* governed:

> This case is basically the same as *Johnson*, . . . excepting in *Johnson* defendant provided a diving board at the place where plaintiff dove and such diving board was an invitation to use it for diving. In *Johnson* plaintiff was told upon entering the pool that the water was shallow, and was 3 to 3½ feet deep, but was coming in fast, and it would not be long until the tank was full. . . . Plaintiff thereupon waited "about twenty minutes" and then apparently made his own assumptions as to the depth of the water at that time. . . . Apparently, without having any precise information as to how much deeper the water had gotten, he dove off the diving board and sustained injury, for which he sued, making a similar allegation as that upon which plaintiff relies in this case, that defendant failed to warn (him) that on account of the shallowness it was dangerous to dive into the water. . . . He claimed that he was unfamiliar with the premises and did not know the risk of diving, and that he

---

1. Judges in civil cases or on behalf of defendants in criminal cases may reverse jury verdicts when they believe that the verdict is unreasonable given the facts presented at trial and the legal standard to be applied.

had a right to rely upon the assurances of the defendant arising from the fact that defendant had rented him a bathing suit and charged him an admission.

The defendant, Island Amusement, then quoted a passage from *Johnson* arguing that if the plaintiff knew of the danger incident to diving from a springboard, whether or not the defendant had told him of the danger, diving into the pool was an act of contributory negligence. The defense counsel concluded with:

> We submit that this holding in *Johnson* is apropos to our case because in our case plaintiff knew that the water was shallow, although there is evidence that she did not know the precise depth. She appreciated the consequences of diving into a shallow pool and she dove anyway.

Not unexpectedly, the plaintiff's counsel found distinctions between Johnson's situation and White's:

> In *Johnson*, . . . the decedent knew exactly how deep the water was or at least reasonable men would all agree he should have known. He and his friends had been swimming and diving into a half-filled pool for fifteen minutes. . . . The plaintiff was entitled to rely upon what she observed to indicate the depth of the water. Unlike the *Johnson* case, supra, this was the plaintiff's first visit to defendant's pool. Unlike the *Johnson* case, supra, there was no warning given regarding the depth of the water, nor was there any warning she should not dive into the defendant's shallow pool, or that she did so at her own risk. . . . The plaintiff did not have any knowledge of the actual depth as the decedent must have had in the *Johnson* case, supra, since she had not been in the water.

Each side is attempting to characterize the "facts" of *White* to make it appear more or less similar to *Johnson*. The defendant tried to make this another case of "heedless patron dives into shallow water." The plaintiff, on the other hand, attempted to distinguish this case from *Johnson* by emphasizing facts that were unique to *White*, namely, what the plaintiff knew and could have known about the pool into which she dove. These positions are responses to the outcome of the prior case. If *Johnson* had been decided for the plaintiff, *White*'s attorney would be arguing for the typical similarity of the two cases and the defendant's counsel would be pointing to what made the later case unique.

The preceding dispute, which illustrates the importance of the uniqueness-typicality dimension, concerns a matter that is itself a type. It involves the meaning of *precedent*. Precedential cases are especially significant in determining the legal implications of facts in a common law system. They are one way in which the uniqueness-typicality dimension may be important when responsibility is in issue. In judging individuals, we often compare their actions in certain circumstances with their past actions in other situations; with others' actions in other situations; and with others' actual or presumed actions in the same situation (see Kelley, 1967).

These kinds of comparisons are made both in and out of courts. They not only can bear on the legal implications of facts, but they can also affect our view as to what the facts are in the first instance. To borrow an example from

Kelley (1967), if Harold trips over Maude's feet while waltzing, if no one else has ever tripped over Maude's feet while waltzing, and if Harold often trips over people's feet, Harold is, *in fact*, clumsy. If, on the other hand, everyone trips over Maude's feet while waltzing and Harold never trips over the feet of any of his other dance partners, it is Maude who is the source of the problem. The exact same sense data—a boy tripping over a girl's feet to the strains of Chopin— has very different implications depending on the uniqueness of the behavior.

In law as in most things, sense data are translated into facts by humans who give them meaning. What is special about the legal context is that the translation of data into facts is routinely and openly contested. Moreover, even when the facts are established, their legal implications may remain open to dispute. Thus, a lawyer after losing the battle to establish that her client was in fact careful when she dove into a shallow pool, may still argue that the factual situation, including her client's carelessness, is essentially identical to one in which a higher court allowed recovery.

Whether or not an adjudicator will see two situations as being essentially the same type depends on the scope of the inquiry. An adjudicator who skims the surface is less likely to see differences than the one who probes deeply. But the importance of deeper probing varies with the matter in issue, and whatever the legal question, inquiry must stop somewhere. Since every case is to some degree unique, a system of precedent requires that there be rules or understandings about what facts are important. Such rules and understandings exist. The law may explicitly make certain facts relevant or irrelevant to the resolution of particular disputes. In addition, general familiarity with the legal system and the ability to ascribe purpose to particular laws leads to shared understandings of what facts make for "admissible" distinctions. Thus, *White*'s lawyer did not try to distinguish *Johnson* on the ground that the plaintiff in *Johnson* was a boy and his client was a girl or on the ground that the diver in *Johnson* died and his client lived. At another time or in another culture, these differences might have supported the conclusion that *Johnson* was not controlling.

We know relatively little about how legal systems come to regard certain facts as relevant and others as irrelevant, yet the importance of the issue can hardly be overemphasized. Indeed, *lawmaking* may be conceptualized as the process by which a society changes the facts its courts are willing to hear. For example, in the 1950s and 1960s most states by either statute or judicial decision abrogated their doctrines of charitable immunity. That is, they changed a rule which said that charitable institutions could not be compelled to compensate the victims of their negligence. Now, in most states when a charity, say, a hospital, is sued, it can no longer defend itself by pointing to its charitable status. Courts in these states are no longer concerned with how a hospital is funded or whether it aims to make a profit. The transfer of hundreds of millions of dollars has been affected by making evidence that goes to these issues irrelevant. Profit-making and charitable hospitals as a legal matter are more of a type than they once were, because one possible way to distinguish them no longer counts in court.

Extensiveness of the Inquiry. The second element involved in characterizing circumstances is extensiveness. Here we are concerned with neither the details of the event before us nor the detailed comparison of two events to determine whether they match. Rather, the question is how far back in time and how far afield should we look in deciding whether a person is responsible? Just as the relevance of details may be spelled out in rule logics, so may be the relevance of time and situation. Extensiveness, like uniqueness, shapes decisions as to meaning.

The philosopher Roderick Chisholm provides an example of how an inquiry into an individual's actions may be more or less extensive:

> Suppose we say to a man, "This morning you could have arranged things so that you would be in Boston now but you didn't," meaning thereby that he had it within his power this morning to arrange things and that he did not exercise this power. How is one to understand this sense of "could" and of "in his power"? (1967, p. 409)

Chisholm notes that in making such a statement we mean to emphasize its temporal dimension. We mean that *this morning* the man could, if he so chose, have arranged things so as to be in Boston now.

The statement implies that there are no known laws of nature, either in general (people cannot travel more than 6 miles in a day) or in this particular case (the pilots union went on strike this morning) that would have made it physically impossible for the man, had he acted this morning, to be in Boston now. But conditions change, with time. Although this morning the man might have arranged the journey, at some point during the day the possibility disappeared. How does this relate to excuses?

Assume that the person to whom the statement is addressed is due in Boston now. His absence is an untoward event. We cool our heels waiting for him, and then we angrily phone his Seattle apartment. When he answers we say, "You should have been in Boston at 5 P.M." His response is that he did not get to the airport in time and so missed his flight. "But," we say, "you could have gotten to the airport sooner." We are proceeding back in time.

He says, "I overslept." We respond, "You should have set your alarm clock." He says, "I did but I didn't hear it because I was out late the night before." We answer, "You should have gone to bed earlier." He rebuts, "I was attending an important meeting and could not leave."

In the abstract, the regress is infinitely open. Yet at some point the judgment process must come to a close, either out of sheer exhaustion, leaving the conflict unresolved, or because we find him guilty ("no more excuses") or innocent ("Yes, the meeting was important"). At some point we must draw the line. We might, for example, forgive a woman who stole a loaf of bread if she could prove she was starving at the time. However, we are less likely to forgive her if she could only show she had gone hungry as a child. We would probably not even listen if her only excuse was that her mother never had enough to eat.

Extensiveness is not confined to explorations in time. The law may confine what is important within narrow parameters, or it may permit a broad ranging inquiry. In a conspiracy case, for example, action that took place in South America may be relevant to a charge of *conspiring* to distribute cocaine in Los Angeles. If only the distribution itself is charged, action removed from the point of sale is less likely to matter.

In this instance it is the substance of the charge that determines the permitted scope of the inquiry. A more interesting and peculiarly legal example is *Ermolieff* v. *R.K.O. Pictures Incorporated*, 122 P. 2d 3 (1942). Here the core dispute was over what the scope of the inquiry would be. The parties knew that whoever won this dispute would win the case. *Ermolieff* v. *R.K.O. Pictures* arose out of a contract in which Ermolieff in 1936 granted R.K.O. the exclusive right to distribute an English version of a motion picture, entitled *Michael Strogoff* to "those countries or territories of the world" listed in the contract. "The United Kingdom" was among the places listed. Ermolieff retained exclusive distribution right in all unlisted areas.

After the production of the English version, entitled *A Soldier and a Lady*, a dispute arose as to whether the United Kingdom included the Irish Free State (then Eire, now the Republic of Ireland). Politically and legally Southern Ireland was no longer part of the United Kingdom. According to the defendant, however, the normal practice in the motion picture industry was to treat Eire as part of the United Kingdom.

In American contract law there is a legal rule called the *parol evidence rule*. According to this rule, evidence of oral agreements made prior to or contemporaneous with a written contract that conflict with the written contract or would modify it is not admissible. The court, in other words, will not look beyond the language of the contract to determine its meaning. The intention of the parties, which is what is presumably controlling in a contract action, must be determined by reference to the written instrument. The parol evidence rule operates to narrow the scope of inquiry by confining the parties' proofs to the written language of the contract in its generally understood meaning. Applying the rule in this form to *Ermolieff* would have prevented R.K.O. from introducing testimony that they and the plaintiff were using the term United Kingdom in a special, uncommon sense.

There are, however, several well-entrenched exceptions to the parol evidence rule. One of these is that parol evidence is admissible to establish trade usage. Under this exception, R.K.O. was entitled to prove trade usage by either oral testimony or writings other than the contract. In doing so, they could thereby alter the commonly accepted geographical meaning of the term United Kingdom and the otherwise apparent intent of the parties.

The court in *Ermolieff* gave the following justification for the trade use exception:

> The basis of this [exception] is that to accomplish a purpose of paramount importance in interpretation of documents, namely, to ascertain the *true* intent of the parties, it may well be said that the usage evidence does not alter the contract of the parties, but on the contrary gives the effect to the words there used as intended by the parties.

The usage becomes a part of the contract in aid of its correct interpretation. [122 P.2d 3, 6 (1942)]

So much for a German film in a California court in 1942! The important point, however, is not the justice of the outcome, but the expansiveness of the inquiry. The parol evidence rule requires that contractual intention be determined only by reference to the language of the written instrument. The trade usage exception permits a more extended analysis.

Note that the issue is *not* at any point what the parties *really* meant by "United Kingdom." They may have always disagreed on this point. But knowledge of the special meaning is presumed when a general trade-specific understanding is established. Indeed, the presumption of knowledge may be applied even though one party can show that she was unaware of the usage.

Despite what the court in *Ermolieff* says, evidence of trade usage does not necessarily aid in ascertaining the true intent of the parties in a given case. However, because it is likely to help in determining intent over the run of cases, trade usage is an allowable aid to interpretation. The legally correct interpretation of a contract is not what the parties meant—judges cannot read minds—but what they probably meant. In ordinary contracts, this explains the parol evidence rule. In businesses that commonly draft contracts against a background of trade usage, an analysis that extends beyond the written document—that is, an expanded analysis of meaning—is essential to a legally correct interpretation.

We may, in short, have a more immediate or a more extensive analysis of an event under examination. The extensiveness of an inquiry like our willingness to perceive detail helps to determine the "facts" of the case, and thus may alter our belief as to what a person could have done or meant to do in particular circumstances. We shall see how this happens as we look at how the law attributes meanings to actions.

The Meaning of Action

The second dimension along which action is typified relates to the determination of its meaning. The central problem is the degree to which we try to ascertain an actor's actual mental state.

An act may mean one thing to an actor and something quite different to those who observe him or learn about what he has done (cf. Kaplan, 1964, pp. 32–33). Thus, a man traveling down a highway at 85 miles per hour may see his behavior as an effort to get his wife to the hospital before she gives birth. To the cop looking at a radar screen, however, he is only a speeder. We shall call the meaning an actor gives to his own behavior its *actor meaning* and the meaning the behavior has in the eyes of others its *social meaning*.

The social meaning is in a sense the normal or "typical" meaning of a particular behavior (Schutz, 1970). Individuals may and often do ascribe normal meanings to their own actions. For example, a shoplifter, caught red-handed, may admit he was trying to steal a watch. Thus, a person's account of an action may correspond to an observer's version. However, it is also possible for the two versions to differ because, like our speeding driver and traffic cop, actors and observers occupy different positions. The observer's account is literally objective, since it treats the actor's behavior as an object explainable from without. The actor's account is literally subjective, since it is the view of the subject. As such, the actor's version reflects not only a natural tendency to see oneself in the best light but also the fact that the actor is particularly well situated to perceive the variety of historical and contextual forces that impinge on his behavior and compel him to action. We see this when an actor takes into account unique features of a situation in explaining behavior that an observer readily typifies. For example, an observer may characterize as "stealing" the act of pocketing a watch and then leaving the store. But an actor may argue that he had placed the watch in his pocket for safekeeping and then forgot about it, or that it was an act of self-help, compensating for a defective watch that the store had sold him and unreasonably refused to replace.

Differences between actor and observer interpretations also emerge because typifications are not standardized, and more than one normal meaning for an action often exists (Schutz, 1970). Consider, for example, a ghetto youth who runs away when hailed by the police. There are at least two normal meanings of such an action. One reflects the belief that people do not run from the police unless they have something to hide. Flight so interpreted is evidence of guilt. The other recognizes that a person may fear or dislike the police so much that he will flee whenever they approach. Flight from this perspective reflects an attitude toward the police. The propensity to accept one or the other interpretation as the normal meaning of flight is not randomly distributed throughout society. The second meaning is, no doubt, more common among ghetto youths and the first more characteristic of the police and, one suspects, of juries.

One reason that the actor/social meaning issue is so troublesome is that different actions may be behaviorally identical. For example, an eye closing because of a nervous twitch and an eye closing because of a purposeful wink are different actions, but the movements they entail may appear the same to a movie camera. Moreover, a given behavior may have more than one normal action meaning. A wink that one observer might characterize as a friendly gesture might be characterized by another as a leer. When we accuse a person of a leering wink and he pleads that it was really a friendly wink, what are we to do? Stephan Toulmin is perhaps right in saying:

> Our everyday modes of explanation being what they are, the reasons explaining why a man acted as he did are commonly "for him to say." Normally, at any rate, the relevant language games are ones in which the agent speaks with special authority. What he says, goes. (1969, pp. 97–98)

Normally, maybe, but not always. The more abnormal the explanation is, the less likely it is to be accepted. Indeed, people, knowing this, may choose to "make up" normal accounts of their behavior rather than to give subjectively true but abnormal accounts. Thus, a student who would rather read great literature than dance and drink may explain his decision to skip a fraternity party to finish reading Homer's *Iliad* by citing an upcoming test instead of the preference that motivates him. Language may also encourage normal accounts. "Unspeakable" is more than a metaphor to describe horrible behavior. How can one give a reasonable account of the forces that compelled him to beat a young child?

In short, the very qualities that give an actor's account its special authority mean that an observer can never be sure that an explanation is not "made up" or the result of self-deception. Consequently, we are reluctant to accept fully the meaning an actor gives his behavior. In settings like a courtroom where accounts are closely tied to probabilities of reward or punishment, we are particularly suspicious of the stories we hear. In every case the problem of the lie is present. At the same time, legal rules often make subjective states—states known in principle only to the actor—crucial. Thus, a homicide may be punishable by death if done with "malice aforethought," but it may not even be criminal if committed in the honest belief that the killing was necessary in self-defense.

The tension between the belief that justice requires us to explore the boundaries of private worlds and our inability to trust those best able to describe these worlds is obvious. Not so obvious is the tension that might exist if we, nevertheless, tried to grasp subjective states precisely. Identical behavior with identical consequences would meet with very different social responses depending on the subjective state that was thought most likely to have accompanied the act. Such differences based on states that are, in principle, unobservable and could never be certainly known, might also strike people as unjust (Fuller, 1964).

Unable to avoid these tensions, the legal system must strike a balance between the distinctly human claim that subjective states matter and the need of any enforcement system for objectivity. At both the law-making and fact-finding levels the legal system continually confronts the question of what weight to accord subjective claims in ascribing responsibility for specific behavior. What, for example, should we do when someone argues that his mental state is legally sufficient to excuse his otherwise actionable behavior? When will we listen to an actor's argument about what he meant? H. L. A. Hart notes that problems of proof become especially difficult when we move away from questions such as whether a person lacked volitional muscular control or whether he knew a certain fact (e.g., the gun was loaded) toward questions of self-control (e.g., was he mentally unbalanced) and questions of will. In the latter two situations the law is more likely to insist on social meanings:

> The law is accordingly much more cautious in admitting "defects of the will" than "defects in knowledge" as qualifying or excluding criminal responsibility. Further difficulties of proof may cause a legal system to limit its inquiry into the agent's "subjective condition" by asking what a "reasonable man" would in the circumstances have known or foreseen, or by asking whether "a reasonable man" in the circumstances would have been deprived (say, by provocation) of self-control; and the system may then impute to the agent such knowledge or foresight or control. (Hart, 1968, p. 33)

Problems of meaning arise in both civil and criminal cases. As an illustration consider a pair of cases relating to the gerrymandering of political jurisdictions.

In 1960, after many years of refusing to involve itself in the "political thicket" of reapportionment and gerrymandering issues, the Supreme Court accepted the case of *Gomillion* v. *Lightfoot*, 364 U.S. 339 (1960). *Gomillion* grew out of a statute passed by the Alabama State Legislature in 1957 which redefined the boundaries of the City of Tuskegee. Under Act No. 140, the political shape of Tuskegee was altered from a square to a 28-sided figure. A group of black citizens of Alabama, who were residents of Tuskegee at the time of the act brought an action in the federal district court charging that Act No. 140 violated their rights under the Fourteenth and Fifteenth Amendments to the Constitution. The complainants alleged that the effect of the redefinition of Tuskegee's boundaries was to remove from the city all but 4 or 5 of its 400 black voters, while not removing a single white voter.

The federal district court dismissed the plaintiff's complaint and so upheld the gerrymandered boundaries on the ground that the legislature had absolute power to establish municipal boundaries regardless of motive. In doing so, the federal district court refused to treat the objective situation created by Act No. 140 as unconstitutionally discriminatory even though it effectively removed the black vote as a force to be reckoned with in Tuskegee city government. It also avoided the question of whether the observable outcome of Act No. 140—the 28-sided figure—was dispositive evidence of the actor meaning that underlay the act. Speaking through Mr. Justice Frankfurter, the Supreme Court reversed:

> These allegations [that the boundaries of the city of Tuskegee had been switched from a square to a 28-sided figure that removed all but 4 or 5 Negro voters from the city without removing a single white], if proven, would abundantly establish that Act 140 was not an ordinary geographic redistricting measure even within familiar abuses of gerrymandering. If these allegations upon a trial remained uncontradicted or unqualified, the conclusion would be irresistible, tantamount for all practical purposes to a mathematical demonstration, that the legislation is solely concerned with segregating white and colored voters by fencing Negro citizens out of town so as to deprive them of their pre-existing municipal vote. [364 U.S. 339, 341 (1960)]

Justice Frankfurter took the consequences of Act No. 140 as a "mathematical demonstration" of the legislative purpose, which was the segregation of voters due to race and the exclusion of black voters from the municipal voting lists. Apparently, the plaintiffs needed to prove only the fact that a change from a square to a 28-sided figure disenfranchised almost every black in town. Those arguing for Alabama, the Court pointed out, never suggested that there was any municipal purpose behind the redistricting. Yet even had they done so, the Court's language suggests that the evidence was so probative of actual discriminatory intent that the legislature could not prevail on a claim that its actor meaning was different from the social one. The Court made clear its willingness to invalidate "statutes that, *however speciously defined*, obviously discriminate against colored citizens" (364 U.S. 339, 341, 1960; emphasis added).

A similar case arose 4 years later in *Wright* v. *Rockefeller*, 376 U.S. 52

(1964). In this case the plaintiffs were citizens and registered voters in the 17th, 18th, 19th, and 20th congressional districts of New York (all in Manhattan). They challenged Chapter 980 of New York's reapportionment statute which redefined these four districts in response to the 1960 census. The plaintiffs alleged that Chapter 980 created discriminatory congressional districts and segregated eligible voters by race and place of origin. Specifically, they complained that the statute had created one district, the 17th, which was largely limited to white citizens. Nonwhites and Puerto Ricans were crowded into the other three districts, especially the 18th.

The plaintiffs offered maps, statistics, and testimony in their effort to prove that the district boundaries could not have been drawn as they were unless "they were drawn with regard to race." The statistics were: 18th District, 86.3 percent Negro and Puerto Rican; 19th District, 28.5 percent; 20th District, 27.5 percent; and 17th District, 5.1 percent. The plaintiffs also showed irregularities in the boundaries of the districts that tended to segregate the districts further. In response, the named defendants, including the governor and several other state officials, presented historical maps, a table from the Bureau of the Census, and a message from the president to the Congress on the subject of reapportionment.

The case was tried before a three-judge panel in the district court, and a majority found that the plaintiffs had not made out their case on one central issue. Judge Moore found that, "no proof was offered by any party that the specific boundaries created by Chapter 980 were drawn on racial lines or that the Legislature was motivated by considerations of race, creed or country of origin in creating the districts." Judge Murphy, in dissent, echoed Justice Frankfurter's language in writing that the evidence presented was, "tantamount for all practical purposes, to a mathematical demonstration" that the legislation was "solely concerned with segregating" white voters from colored and Puerto Rican voters, "by fencing colored and Puerto Rican citizens out of the 17th District and into a district of their own (the 18th)."

When the case reached the Supreme Court, Justice Douglas noted that the 17th District was altered in three respects: (1) The legislature had added an area on the upper East Side whose Negro and Puerto Rican population was 2.7 percent. (2) It had added an area on the lower East Side called Stuyvesant Town which had almost no Negro and Puerto Rican residents. (3) It had dropped from the 17th District, and added to the 18th District, a two-block area from 98th Street to 100th Street between Fifth and Madison Avenues. This area was 44.5 percent Negro and Puerto Rican:

> The record strongly suggests that these twists and turns producing an 11-sided, step-shaped boundary between the Seventeenth and the Eighteenth Districts were made to keep out of the Seventeenth as many Negroes and Puerto Ricans as possible. [376 U.S. 52, 60–61 (1964)]

But Justice Douglas was writing in dissent. The Supreme Court, per Mr. Justice Black, affirmed the district court's finding and said that the plaintiffs "failed to prove that the New York Legislature was either motivated by racial considerations or in fact drew the districts on racial lines. Compare *Gomillion* v. *Lightfoot*, 364 U.S. 339."

What Justice Black must do, however, is contrast *Gomillion*, not compare it. In two cases, not altogether different on the facts, one set of facts was "tantamount to a mathematical demonstration" of segregative intent, while the other set left the plaintiffs still having to "prove" racial motives.

Of course, there are distinctions to be made, beginning with the simple differences between a 28-sided figure and an 11-sided boundary. Mr. Justice Black refers to geographical factors that would have made it difficult to create Manhattan districts with an equal percentage of minorities. However, what we suspect was more important was the fact that some blacks, including Adam Clayton Powell who represented the 18th District, intervened on the side of the defendants and argued in support of the constitutionality of the apportionment act. The intervenors' actions tended to undermine the claim that discrimination was the only plausible normal meaning of the legislative action. In addition, we might note that in the Alabama case Negroes were more nearly disenfranchised, whereas in New York they were only shuffled between districts. Indeed, the shuffling guaranteed that Manhattan would have at least one nonwhite Congressional representative. All of these factors distinguish *Wright* from *Gomillion*. Each case is unique.

Still, we might add at least one more "fact" for consideration. *Wright* arose in New York State, while *Gomillion* arose in Alabama. Although nothing in the Constitution suggests that location is an important distinction in assessing claims of discriminatory reapportionment, many cases apparently turned on it. Plaintiffs in the South often prevailed, while those in the North invariably lost. The reason apparently lay in the differential receptivity of the courts, from the Supreme Court on down, to evidence bearing on the legislature's purpose in redrawing political lines.[2] In cases arising in northern states the courts not only attended

---

2. In a number of cases involving northern states the defendants provided alternative motives for actions that were apparently discriminatory, and the plaintiffs stumbled over the requirement that they "prove" discriminatory motive. *Ince* v. *Rockefeller*, 290 F. Supp. 878 (S.D.N.Y. 1968); *Jones* v. *Falcey*, 48 N.J. 25, 222 A. 2d. 101 (1966); *Cousins* v. *City Council of the City of Chicago*, 466 F. 2d 830 (7th Cir. 1972); *Whitcomb* v. *Chavis*, 403 U.S. 124 (1971) (an Indiana case). In similar cases arising in southern states, the courts either inferred improper intent from the legislation itself, *United States* v. *Democratic Committee of Barbour County*, 288 F. Supp. 943 (M.D. Ala. 1968); *Fortson* v. *Dorsey*, 379 U.S. 433 (1965; Georgia), or were easily persuaded that the legislature had a racist intent. In one case, *Smith* v. *Paris*, 257 F. Supp. 901 (M.D. Ala. 1966), the trial judge cited "the long history of racial discrimination in Alabama" as part of his "firm . . . conviction that (the statute) was racially motivated" 257 F. Supp. at 905, and in another the distinction between the North and South was used to distinguish an Indiana case, *Whitcomb* v. *Chavis*, from the case at hand: "*Whitcomb* arose in Indiana, a state without the long history of racial discrimination evident in Alabama" *Sims* v. *Amos*, 336 F. Supp. 924; 936 (M.D. Ala. 1972).

In some cases, partly due to the impact of the 1965 Voting Rights Act, which applied only to southern states, district courts went so far as to say that even though an election change was made for legitimate purposes and "was not enacted because of a racially discriminating motive," that fact

to such evidence, but in some cases seem to have gone so far as to require the plaintiffs to prove that the legislature had a racially discriminatory purpose when a statute was passed. In cases involving southern states the courts have been less receptive to defense attempts to show proper motive. Statements suggesting racially neutral purposes have been met with great skepticism and at times the courts simply refused to consider the possibility.

What we see are courts that are differentially receptive to claims of a non-discriminatory subjective meaning. In the northern cases the courts treat actor meanings as problematic and place the burden of proving improper motives on the plaintiff. It has not been enough to show that a plausible social meaning for the action is discrimination. In the southern cases of the same period the courts were so confident of their social meanings that they in effect presumed that the actor meanings were identical.

Thus, actor meanings and social meanings became assimilated in very different ways—at least for purposes of the law—in the two regions. In the North, discriminatory intent could not be shown so actions that gave rise to racial imbalance were not, in the eyes of the law, perceived as "discrimination." In the South, actions that gave rise to racial imbalance were seen as discrimination, so a discriminatory intent was imputed to the legislation mandating the action.

We should not be surprised at this. In the North there are, or at least in the 1960s there were, competing normal meanings that could explain reapportionment decisions that had segregative effects. Northern defendants were allowed to argue which meaning was appropriate to explain their behavior. In the South there was one, overriding, normal meaning—racial discrimination. Accounts providing a different meaning were seen as "abnormal" and given little credence.

Also, there is no mystery about where these differences came from. The courts were engaging in an extensive analysis. Each region had its history, and their histories made them different. The Supreme Court by the 1960s had spent 35 years dealing with the attempts of southern legislatures to thwart black voting through discriminatory legislation. Many of these attempts, such as grandfather clauses, poll taxes, and literacy tests had been on their face neutral. In dealing with such legislation, the courts learned to ignore the neutral actor meanings that southern lawyers advanced. Both the context and effects of such legislation compelled imputations of discriminatory intent. Thus, by the time of *Gomillion*, the Alabama Legislature was a "known offender" whose description of purpose could not be trusted and whose cumulative deeds spoke for themselves. The New York Legislature did not bear such a stigma. It was at least reasonable to assume that the New York act at issue in *Wright* was a "normal" political

---

did "not dispose of these cases in view of the apparent discriminatory effect" *Sellers* v. *Trusell*, 253 F. Supp. 915 (M.D. Ala. 1966). We shall examine the 1965 Voting Rights Act in Chapter 11. It had the consequence of turning some activities of legislators and registrars into strict liability offenses. We should note, however, that the *Sellers* position was never adopted by the Supreme Court, even though Justice Douglas argued for such a position in his dissents in the *Wright* and *Whitcomb* cases.

bargain which, if attentive to race, was at least not motived by a desire to discriminate invidiously against or disenfranchise black people.

WORKING A CASE: THE OPENNESS OF ADJUDICATION

We have now shown that adjudications may differ in ways that affect how data are processed. There remains the more practical question: When will an excuse work? Here we have less to say. Rule logics and typifications can only tell us what types of excuses will be entertained, not whether once considered, they will be accepted.

We can, of course, suggest some commonsense considerations in judging excuses. First, there is the issue of *truthfulness*. Sometimes stories are simply not to be believed, as in the case of the woman who, when apprehended with a $1,350 diamond and emerald pin (with price tag) in her bra and a $1,300 diamond ring, two men's wrist watches, and other assorted jewelry in her panties, claimed she had no idea how the merchandise got there (Goffman, 1974, p. 330). But, of course, truthfulness is to some extent determined by descriptions of events. If it were shown that the bejeweled lady had been hypnotized by a known jewel thief who had accompanied her in the store, our judgment of her story might be different.

There is also the issue of sincerity. An implausible story well told may "carry the day." Witness the following daring escape:

> A young lady in Los Angeles invited a director of a private Hollywood school to her apartment, after she had secreted a recording machine under her couch. She recorded his amorous intentions and later began to blackmail him. The school director, however, went to the police department and the district attorney's office, and the young lady was arrested. However, she was acquitted when she demurely testified that the recording had been a joke and that she had actually expected the school director to marry her. (Goffman, 1974, p. 334)

"Demure" hardly seems the word for what must have been an Oscar-winning performance.

Finally, there is the basic issue of adequacy, or as J. L. Austin would call it, the standard of acceptability:

> We may plead that we trod on the snail inadvertently: but not on a baby—you ought to look where you are putting your great feet. Of course it *was* (*really*), if you like, inadvertence: but that word constitutes a plea, which is not going to be allowed, because of standards. (1956–1957, p. 14)

What occurs at the case level is an attempt to reconstruct reality, for the consequences that the law prescribes assume that a particular version of "what happened" has been established. In court the process usually involves the presentation of conflicting stories to a fact finder, in some cases a judge and in others a jury, who is asked to choose between them (Bennett & Feldman, 1981).

The fact finder's choice will reflect the appearance of truth and sincerity and, above all, the judgmental standard applied. This standard will in large measure reflect an understanding of the law, but it may also reflect the way the fact finder's own values apply to the person or action in question (Kalven & Ziesel, 1966). We address the question of how understandings of the law affect case decisions in the next chapter. We look at how a fact finder's values can systematically affect adjudicative outcomes in Chapters 12 and 13.

Particular cases are always in some way open. There are many modes of describing what happened and what we were thinking. However, here too there are general patterns in how cases are processed. In the next chapter we examine evidence from social psychology that suggests two basic patterns of judging behavior, and we seek to explain why one pattern or the other is used in different circumstances.

CONCLUSION

In this chapter we have been concerned at the most general level with how the law responds when it must analyze human action in allocating responsibility. The law, we have seen, tends to typify or categorize actions, and legal rights and responsibilities turn on how these typifications are made. We have identified two dimensions that are especially important to understanding the circumstances of a legally problematic action: (1) the perceived uniqueness of the action and (2) the extensiveness of the inquiry into what has occurred. Uniqueness refers to the degree to which we attend to the special characteristics of a situation in identifying its legal implications. Extensiveness of the inquiry refers to the degree to which we search out and accept evidence that is temporally or spatially removed from the event in question. The two dimensions are obviously related. In seeking to establish uniqueness, we are more likely to engage in an extensive inquiry. In engaging in an extensive inquiry, we are likely to uncover evidence that makes the event in question appear relatively unique. However the result of an inquiry into legally problematic action is not predetermined.

4

Case Logics: Some Determinants and Consequences

As noted in the conclusion to Chapter 3, adjudications are open in the sense that responsibility is determined only as the answering process proceeds, but the answering process is itself patterned. The difficulties of predicting the outcomes of particular cases do not mean that one cannot explain how cases typically are processed or give the reasons that they are processed in certain ways. In the first section of this chapter we argue that typified analyses of circumstances and normalized meanings tend to be associated so as to form what we call *shallow and deep case logics*. In the second and third sections we examine factors such as the adjudicator's knowledge and objectives and the structure of the adjudicative setting that lead adjudicators to adopt deep or shallow case logics. In the last section we note how different case logics produce different meanings of justice.

CASE LOGICS

Jones and Nisbett (1972, p. 79) writing about the divergent perceptions of actors and observers begin by reflecting on a typical interaction between a teacher and a student.

> When a student who is doing poorly in school discusses his problem with a faculty adviser, there is often a fundamental difference of opinion between the two. The student, in attempting to understand and explain his inadequate performance, is

usually able to point to environmental obstacles such as a particularly onerous course load, to temporary emotional stress . . . or to a transitory confusion about life goals that is now resolved. The faculty advisor may nod and may wish to believe, but in his heart of hearts he usually disagrees. The advisor is convinced that the poor performance is due neither to the student's environment nor to transient emotional states. He believes instead that the failure is due to enduring qualities of the student—to lack of ability, to irremediable laziness, to neurotic ineptitude. (1972, p. 79)

How are we to explain these different explanations for failure? Jones and Nisbett believe that an important source of such differences is the information available to actors and observers. They discuss two general types of information: effect data and cause data. Effect data include information about the act itself, about environmental outcomes, and about the actor's reaction (e.g., embarrassment, anger, etc.). The observer and actor have a similar opportunity to view the behavior and its environmental consequences, but they are situated quite differently with respect to the actor's personal reactions. Often the observer does not witness any expressive behavior at the time of the act, or available cues such as a flushed face or an angry voice may be ambiguous or even misleading.

With respect to causal data, actor–observer differences are even greater. Actors presumably know their intentions, but observers must either rely on an actor's explanations or infer intentions from the actor's behavior and the "logic" of the situation.[1]

Actors and observers are most similar in their access to information about the environment immediately surrounding the act. Both may know, for example, that A in insulting B was responding to a taunt by B. In the broader temporal context, however, the information available to actors and observers will vary. Jones and Nisbett argue:

[There is] the likelihood that the actor is responding to events more extended in time than those available to the observer. The particular taunt that triggered the actor's outburst may have been the straw that broke the camel's back—the latest in a series

---

1. The Anglo-American legal system eschews "trying intentions" that are unaccompanied by actions. Without behavioral clues, the attribution of intentions is regarded as too uncertain to justify legal action. In the words of the old English epigram, "The thought of man shall not [be] tried, for the devil himself knoweth not the thought of man" (C. J. Brian in Y.B. 7 Edw. IV f. 2). Not all legal systems have taken this stance. The following passage is from *The Gulag Archipelago*. The comments are attributed to Andrei Y. Vyshinsky in 1934. Vyshinsky became the chief prosecutor in the show trials of 1936–1938:

One important additional broadening of the section on treason was its application "via Article 19 of the Criminal Code"—"via intent." In other words, no treason had taken place; but the interrogator envisioned an *intention* to betray—and that was enough to justify a full term, the same as for actual treason. True, Article 19 proposes that there be no penalty for intent, but only for *preparation*, but given a dialectical reading one can understand intention as preparation. And "preparation is punished in the same way [i.e., with the same penalty] as the crime itself" (Criminal Code). In general [and the following is Vyshinsky speaking], "we draw no distinction between *intention* and the *crime* itself, and this is an instance of the *superiority* of Soviet legislation to bourgeois legislation." (Solzhenitsyn, 1973, pp. 61–62)

of frustrations. The observer is more likely to work instead with the data from one slice of time. (1972, p. 84)

This quote speaks to both the uniqueness and the extensiveness of the attribution. Jones and Nisbett continue:

> Because the actor knows his past, he is often diverted from making a dispositional attribution. If the actor insults someone, an observer, who may assume that this is a typical sample of behavior, may infer that the actor is hostile. The actor, on the other hand, may believe that the sample is anything but typical. He may recall very few other instances when he insulted anyone and may believe that in most of these instances he was sharply provoked. . . . We suspect that because of the differences in the availability of personal history data, actors and observers evaluate each act along a different scale of comparison. The observer is characteristically normative and nomothetic: He compares the actor with other actors and judges his attributes accordingly. The actor, on the other hand, is more inclined to use an ipsative or idiographic reference scale: This action is judged with reference to his other previous actions rather than the acts of other actors.
>
> Much of the discrepancy between the perspectives of observer and actor arises from the difference between the observer's inferred history of everyman and the concrete individualized history of the actor himself. (1972, pp. 84–85)[2]

To state this in terms of our evidence dimensions, observers are more likely to attribute cause and ascribe responsibility on the basis of *typical and immediate analyses*, and actors are more likely to employ *unique and extended analyses*.

During the past two decades numerous social psychological studies have explored the question of how people explain the behavior of others. Evidence from this body of research, much of which goes by the name "attribution theory," suggests that when individuals employ immediate, typical analyses they are likely to produce normalized accounts of the general mental state of the actor (see Thibaut & Riecken, 1955; Kelley, 1967; Kelley, 1971; Ross, 1977). This means they ascribe to the actor whatever intent is thought ordinarily to accompany the given behavior in the observable circumstances. Thus, a man who shoots his wife's lover will be thought to have been crazed by jealousy, a man who

---

2. Actor–observer differences are likely to be great, especially with respect to information on motive and intent. Alfred Schutz, whose writings influenced much of our discussion of actor and social meanings, feels that an actor's understanding of what he did is always different from an observer's understanding:

> Subjectively it [motive] refers to the experience of the actor who lives in his ongoing process of activity. To him, motive means what he has actually in view as bestowing meaning upon his ongoing action, and this is always the in-order-to motive, the intention to bring about a projected state of affairs, to attain a preconceived goal. As long as the actor lives in his ongoing action, he does not have in view its because motives. . . . Only insofar as the actor turns to his past and, thus, becomes an observer of his own acts, can he succeed in grasping the genuine because motives of his own acts. (Schutz, 1970, pp. 127–129)

Support for Schutz's position may be found in a study by Storms (1973, p. 165). When actors are specifically directed to retrospectively "observe" their own conduct through videotapes, their attribution processes become more like those of observers.

TABLE 4.1
Correlates Of Case Logics In Adjudication

Aspects of Adjudication	Deep Case Logic	Shallow Case Logic
Precondition		
Desired level of understanding	Actor meaning	Social meaning
Quality of Adjudication		
Perspective toward act		
Probable distinctiveness	Unique	Typical
Relevant environment	Extended	Immediate
Output		
Account produced	Unique actor account	Shared social account

shoots an acquaintance after quarreling in a bar will be thought to have been crazed by drink, and a man who shoots ten people apparently at random will be thought to be simply crazy.

Typical and immediate analyses bias attributers toward gross typifications and "social meanings." When circumstances and behavior fit a convenient stereotype, an attributer is less likely to consider the possibility that a particular actor meaning accounts for behavior. The ideal types of Table 4.1 summarize our analysis.

The table specifies those adjudicatory characteristics that when taken together characterize what we call deep and shallow case logics.[3] These characteristics do not have to be associated in the ways we indicate, but they often are. Deep case logics are likely when the adjudicatory search is for an actor meaning, that is, an understanding of the action from the actor's point of view. Shallow case logics occur when social meanings satisfy whatever situational demands the adjudication imposes.

The desired or satisfactory level of meaning is contingent on normative, organizational, and situationally specific characteristics, factors that are not necessarily congruent. Legal norms, for example, may purport to require decisions based on actor meanings, but pressures for organizational efficiency may mean that in the settings in which the norms are enforced social meanings are tolerably precise; or, more specifically, the imprecision of social meanings is tolerable. We see this in busy misdemeanor courts that devote no more than a few minutes to each case, making it virtually impossible for a defendant to show that his action was not as it appeared (Mileski, 1971). At the same time, situationally specific characteristics, such as the presence of a particularly effective defense

---

3. The terms *shallow* and *deep* are borrowed from Jack Katz, who suggested the distinction to Joe Sanders while they were fellow graduate students. Much of the discussion in the first part of this chapter is indebted to Katz's insights.

counsel, may mean that even in a setting geared to the production of social meanings, an actor meaning will occasionally be sought. Thus, even a busy court that rushes cases and sanctions those who would delay the legal process may appreciate the difference between ordinary breaches of the peace and the raucous welcome of two brothers for a third brother who has just been discharged from military service (Mileski, 1971, p. 523).

Where an actor meaning is sought and a deep case logic applied, the act will be approached with the assumption that it is unique, and the adjudicator's task will be to specify the legal implications of the unique features that constitute the action. Consider, for example, the trial of a simple assault: Smith, let us assume, stabbed Jones in a bar. If an actor meaning is sought, the assault will not be immediately characterized as just another drunken brawl. The judge will be concerned with such facts as the amount of drinking that preceded the quarrel; whether Smith drew the knife intending to wound, kill, or merely frighten; the danger Smith was in; and Smith's perception of that danger. Furthermore, the judge's attention will not be confined to the immediate setting in which the assault occurred. Past quarrels between Smith and Jones will be relevant, as well as the presence of spectators who might have taken sides and the combatants' past histories of violence.

If, on the other hand, an understanding of social meaning is sufficient, the inquiry will be limited. The judge's primary concern will be whether the action fits readily into some preestablished type. If so, well-defined consequences follow. In the case of the barroom knifing, the question is whether Smith stabbed Jones in a typical barroom brawl. The shallower the case logic is, the less likely the judge is to distinguish the fight from others that are superficially similar, and the more likely is an outcome of stereotyped labeling. If Smith tried to point out that Jones had drawn a gun on him a week before, he would be told that the tribunal is only concerned with what happened in the bar, and if Smith said he feared for his life, he might be scornfully asked, ''The bar door wasn't locked was it?''

The product of inquiries that follow deep case logics are unique accounts:

> The assailant, Smith, ordinarily a mild-mannered man had been drinking heavily because his wife had left him for another man. Jones, who was equally drunk started to taunt Smith about his wife's unfaithfulness. Smith cursed Jones and when Jones reached into his pocket Smith was afraid he was reaching for a gun because he had seen Jones pull a gun on a man a week before. Smith pulled a knife, stabbed Jones in his gun arm and fled out the door. It took seven stitches to close Jones's wound.

Shallow case logics on the other hand are associated with typified accounts. They are, as a rule, much less revealing. In our example the judge's final assessment might be:

> Typical barroom brawl. The assailant and the victim were both drunk and quarreling and one pulled a knife on the other. The assailant claims the victim was going for a gun, but nothing other than the fact the victim had put his hand in his pocket suggests this. The victim was not seriously cut.

The difference in case logics does not necessarily mean that the accounts one logic generates are more serviceable than those provided by the other. This depends on how judgments are to be used. Indeed, for some purposes the accounts might have similar implications. It is conceivable that Smith would receive the same guilty verdict and sentence from a judge who had adjudicated the matter using a deep logic as he would from a judge who accepted the shallow analysis.

The step we have labeled a precondition—the desired level of understanding—seems causally primary and likely to determine whether an adjudicator will approach an act as one that is presumptively unique and deserving of extensive inquiry or as one that may be safely typified on the basis of its most salient characteristics and immediate surroundings. This is often the case. When cultural or policy norms require judges to approach acts as unique, judges are more likely to do so than when no such norms exist. However, the process may be reversed. If a judge learns facts that suggest an act is unique or that an extensive analysis is needed to understand the true quality of an event, the inquiry may change from one in which a social meaning would have been sufficient to one in which an actor meaning is sought. Thus, the level of meaning sought may affect the depth of the case logic, but the depth of the case logic may also affect judgments about the desired level of meaning. The informational basis that allows a deep understanding of circumstances establishes empathetic pressures in order to understand meaning from the perspective of the actor. When this informational basis is not present, it is difficult to engage in an actor meaning account except insofar as the adjudicator is willing to rely on the unsubstantiated, introspective account of the actor.

From the point of view of the actor whose behavior is being judged neither case logic is necessarily more advantageous. Some actions appear less culpable when subjected to closer scrutiny, while others may appear more culpable. In the barroom brawl as previously described, Smith would probably benefit if the court approached the matter with a deeper logic. However, if Smith had really been quite sober and intended to kill Jones under the guise of a drunken quarrel in order to marry Jones's wife, Smith would be better off if the court were content with a shallower approach that characterized the matter as just another drunken brawl. Good lawyers seek to influence the depth at which cases are processed because this may substantially affect the outcomes their clients receive. One way to do this is to muster information that impels adjudicators toward deeper case logics. Another way is to push for standard settlements in cases that may grow weaker if all the facts come out.

Our characterizations of case logics as deep or shallow are, like many of the other concepts we introduce in this book, ideal types. Thus, an adjudicator may approach a judgmental task at a greater or lesser depth. However, this is not the only type of variation that occurs. In a single case, certain aspects may be treated as unique and subject to in-depth analysis while other aspects are subjected to shallow typifications. Indeed, legal rules may conduce to this. In our barroom brawl, for example, the court might closely examine the relationship between Smith and Jones, but, except in special circumstances, the rules of evidence would prevent the court from exploring Smith's past violent behavior. Furthermore, an adjudicator may change logics in the middle of the adjudicatory process. Thus, a police officer, prosecutor, or judge may be interested in the details of Smith's relations to Jones up to a point, but after that point may decide that the assault was in fact a typical barroom brawl and no longer attend to Smith's arguments about the ways his action was unique.

TOWARD DEEPER CASE LOGICS: OBSERVER KNOWLEDGE AND ADJUDICATION STRUCTURE

Observer Knowledge

One implication of the earlier Jones and Nisbett discussion is that the closer an observer is to sharing an actor's world, the more attentive he will be to the special circumstances of the event. This, in turn, makes it more likely that the adjudicator will come to appreciate the meaning the actor gives to his acts. Cornelius Moynihan (1962) provides an interesting legal example of how shared experiences can increase an attributer's awareness of the unique aspects of a situation. The example concerns the *rule against perpetuities*, a rule of property law designed to encourage free trade in land by preventing landholders from conveying interests in real property that unduly restrict future conveyances. *Undue restrictions* are those that restrict the sale of property for what is deemed to be too many years. An example would be that of a gift of a life estate[4] to one's eldest child and to all succeeding eldest children of eldest children. Under the terms of this gift no lineal decedent taking possession could sell the property, for the right to use the property would always have to be maintained for the next child in line.

A lawyer might state the rule against perpetuities as follows: "a future interest that, by any possibility, may not vest within 21 years after the end of a life or lives in being at the time of its creation is void from its inception." Translated from the lawyerese into English: When land is conveyed by will, gift, or sale, it must be the case that within 21 years after the death of some person alive at the time of the conveyance someone will have acquired a title that allows him to dispose of the land fully; if not, the attempted conveyance is void.[5] Thus, a farmer who seeks to keep his farm intact and in his family by bequeathing a life estate to his eldest child and to the eldest child of each eldest child after that is at least possibly preventing a sale of the full interest in the land (called a fee simple) for more than 21 years after the death of anyone living

---

4. A life estate gives the holder the right to use land for life but not the right to sell the land or fully deplete its resources.

5. The difficulty of stating this rule clearly and concisely in ordinary English is one reason the legal profession like other professions has developed a specialized jargon.

at the time of the bequest. As a result, the attempted bequest will be void, and the land will be distributed as if the farmer had died without a will. If the farmer was survived by three children, the intestacy laws would distribute a third of the land to each, and the farm would be broken up immediately. If the farmer were survived by just one child, that child would receive a fee simple title under the laws of intestacy rather than the life estate the farmer sought to convey, and the child might, if he wished, sell the land to a developer the next day.

As we discovered in writing the preceding paragraph, explaining the rule against perpetuities in plain English is difficult. The rule is equally difficult for law students to learn, and in practice is fraught with technicalities. Thus, it is not surprising that lawyers, from time to time, run afoul of the rule in drafting wills and disinherit intended beneficiaries. Such a lawyer is like the surgeon who leaves a sponge in a patient. He has made a grievous error. In an action for legal malpractice, we would expect a jury to award damages to the disappointed beneficiary. After all, legal problems are legal problems, and what are lawyers for if they cannot draft a valid will? Yet the California Supreme Court, in a decision that was path breaking because it held that lawyers are *in principle* liable for damages attributable to their malpractice, did not see matters in this way. Moynihan writes:

> The Supreme Court of California has held that an attorney who drafted a will . . . that violated the Rule against Perpetuities was not liable for negligence to the intended beneficiaries . . . *Lucas* v. *Hamm*, 364, P. 2d 685 (Cal. 1961), reversing *Lucas* v. *Hamm*, 11 Cal. Rptr. 727 (1961). After quoting Professor Leach's description of the Rule as "a technicality-ridden legal nightmare" and "a dangerous instrumentality in the hands of most members of the bar" (67 *Harvard L. Review* 1349) the court concluded that "it would not be proper to hold that defendant failed to use such skill, prudence, and diligence as lawyers of ordinary skill and capacity commonly exercise." (1962, p. 205)

The Supreme Court of California was made up of attorneys who at some point, even if only as law students, had had to wrestle with the rule against perpetuities. They could view the rule as a distinctive circumstance whose arcane features meant that even a competent lawyer might not get things right. It was, in other words, the rule and not the lawyer that was primarily responsible for the failure of what was in *Hamm* a seven-figure bequest. The fact that the court's view was particularly well informed, no doubt, was small solace to the disinherited beneficiaries. The lawyer's plea that his erroneous application of the rule was not so unskillful as to constitute negligence would probably have fallen on deaf ears before an audience without special information about the difficulty of the rule.

Not all defendants are lucky enough to find a knowledgeable and sympathetic adjudicator. Consider the plight of the juvenile delinquent. Sykes and Matza (1957) and Matza (1964) have developed a theory of delinquency that argues "that much delinquency is based on what is essentially an unrecognized extension of defenses to crimes, in the form of justifications for deviance that are seen as valid by the delinquent but not by the legal system or society at large" (Sykes & Matza, 1957, p. 668). A fine article by Werthman and Piliavin (1967, p. 56) presents a powerful example of such a situation. Juveniles in some neighborhoods consider parts of what is legally public land to be private property that they have a right to defend.

> Sherri Cavan has suggested that a house is a place where "activities which would be unlawful in public places such as poker games and nudity, and activities which would be a source of embarrassment in public places such as family arguments and love making can be freely engaged in." On the basis of this criterion, the plots of public land used as "hangouts" by gang members must also be considered a sort of "home" or "private place." (Werthman & Piliavin, 1967, p. 58)

Around this "private place" boys may establish certain "rules of trespass." The rules neither exclude nor are threatened by the ordinary passersby since the gang members recognize that what is private to them is in fact a public way, and those who pass through neither assert a special interest in the "turf" nor challenge the gang's special claim of entitlement. The situation is different when it is a rival gang that invades or the police that intrude. The former recognize the gang's special claim and seek to destroy or usurp it. The latter act as if there is no validity to the claim. The property is only and entirely public. If necessary, it will be reclaimed for the public by force.

Police who challenge a gang's ownership of the corner may well understand the ecology of the street.[6] They simply choose not to recognize it or, implicitly recognizing it, openly feign misrecognition in order to emphasize their dominance. Werthman and Piliavin note that the Chicago police have a phrase that constitutes both an assertion of dominance and an implicit recognition of the relationship of the boys, the corner, and the society. When bothered by a gang's use of a hangout they may say "Gi'me that corner!" (1967, p. 62). With no officially cognizable claim to the land, gangs have little choice but to at least passively recognize the police officer as the "public's official landlord." They are like a group of squatters who may disperse when the landlord says so, but reappear when he goes away. Other gangs, however, do not have the police

---

6. The relation of street corner boys and the law ranges from the sharing of a set of experiences to the sharing of a whole world view. People may be closer or further apart in this respect as well. Substantial differences occur between cultures and within cultures over time. C. Wright Mills gives a good example of the latter situation:

> A medieval monk writes that he gave food to a poor but pretty woman because it was "for the glory of God and the eternal salvation of his soul." Why do we tend to question him and impute sexual motives? Because sex is an influential and widespread motive in our society and time. Religious vocabularies of explanation and of motives are now on the wane. In a society in which religious motives have been debunked on rather wide scale, certain thinkers are skeptical of those who ubiquitously proclaim them. . . . But from the monasteries of medieval Europe we have no evidence that religious vocabularies were not operative in many situations. (1940, p. 910)

officer's overwhelming force, and physical conflict may ensue if a rival gang encroaches.

When a rival gang attacks a streetcorner hangout, they have chased the gang that resides there to their last stronghold; in other words, they have pushed them "to the wall." Being pushed to the wall is important in the law. If an individual has been pursued by an aggressor to the point where his back is to a wall, violent behavior that would otherwise be considered criminal, up to and including the use of deadly force, will be permissible in self-defense. Nor need a "wall" exist as a concrete object. The term is a symbol for places from which a threatened person cannot or should not be expected to escape without resort to counterviolence. Thus, a person attacked in his home generally need not attempt to escape before resorting to violent self-defense. If one cannot stand and fight in his home—so the law reasons—to where can one escape?

With this in mind, consider the situation of a gang attacked at its street corner hangout. To the gang members their street corner is a home, a place where even in the eyes of the law counterviolence is an appropriate response to aggression. However, for a judge who does not understand the ecology of the corner, the jump from "a man's home is his castle" to "a boy's corner is his castle" is unlikely. Not sharing the boy's background, a judge will see the excuse of self-defense as unreasonable and as out of place as a layperson will see a lawyer's plea that the complexities of the rule against perpetuities excuse a $1 million mistake.

Alternatively, the knowledgeable judge may be aware of the ecology of certain neighborhoods and yet either not allow the delinquent to tell his story or be unmoved by it. In such cases the rejection of the "defense case" does not reflect a failure to appreciate the youth's view of the situation. Instead, for policy reasons, perhaps in an attempt to get youth gangs to change their definitions of territory and "property rights," the law refuses to act on the basis of a deep case logic analysis of behavior. The preference for action reflecting a shallower logic exists because the judge is less concerned with the meaning of the act to the child than with future understandings of what constitutes private and public places. We shall return to the more general issue that this concern raises later in this chapter.

The Structure of Adjudication

Generally speaking, the evidence in a legal case is the dominant factor in determining outcomes. If the evidence strongly favors one party, that party is likely to prevail. There are, however, other factors that affect the attribution of responsibility. They are likely to be especially important when cases are, on the facts, close. In particular, the way the legal system structures cases for adjudicative decision making may be important. As an example, we shall discuss two aspects of how cases are structured for decision making. These concern the way evidence is presented to the fact finder and the rules of decision that the fact finder is told to follow.

The Method of Presentation. Attributers may have biases that lead them to process particular evidence in certain ways. Some lawyers have argued that a consequence of bias is a tendency to typify cases prematurely. In a laboratory setting Thibaut, Walker, and Lind (1972) explored the question of whether the way evidence was presented had an effect on the attribution process.

They took their working hypotheses from Professor Lon Fuller, a distinguished jurisprudent, who wrote:

> What generally occurs in practice [as evidence is heard] is that at some early point a familiar pattern will seem to emerge from the evidence; an accustomed label is waiting for the case and without awaiting further proofs, this label is promptly assigned to it. It is a mistake to suppose that this premature cataloging must necessarily result from impatience, prejudice or mental sloth. Often it proceeds from a very understandable desire to bring the hearing into some order and coherence, for without some tentative theory of the case there is no standard of relevance by which testimony may be measured. But what starts as a preliminary diagnosis designed to direct the inquiry tends, quickly and imperceptibly, to become a fixed conclusion, as all that confirms the diagnosis makes a strong imprint on the mind, while all that runs counter to it is received with diverted attention.
>
> *An adversary presentation seems the only effective means for combating this natural human tendency to judge too swiftly in terms of the familiar that which is not yet fully known.* (Fuller, 1971, pp. 43–44)

The hypothesis is, in other words, that an adversary process, with opposing sides alternatively presenting evidence, helps forestall the premature imposition of labels. In our terms it increases the likelihood that the unique aspects of a case will be appreciated and that the case will be processed in depth.

In the experiment by Thibaut and his colleagues (1972), student subjects were presented with a hypothetical case arising out of a barroom fight that had broken out during a card game. The defendant who had been knocked to the ground had responded by stabbing the victim in the stomach with a piece of glass. The plea was self-defense. The legal issue was whether the defendant had used more force in repelling the attack than was reasonably necessary.

The evidence in the experiment consisted of 50 brief factual statements, half of which suggested that the defendant's response was lawful (i.e., reasonable self-defense), and half of which tended to indicate that it was unlawful. An example of a *lawful* fact was "[the victim] had been lightweight boxing champion of the First Marine Division." An example of an *unlawful* fact was "the defendant holds the black belt, awarded for high proficiency in karate." These facts, as the examples indicate, frequently provided general information about the defendant and the victim.

The experiment contained three manipulations. First, there was an "adversarial" and an "inquisitorial" method of presentation. In the adversarial method two persons read the facts. One wore the label "Defense" and read all 25 lawful facts. The other was labeled "Prosecution" and read the 25 unlawful facts. In the inquisitorial presentation the same person read all 50 facts.

The second manipulation involved the order in which the evidence was presented. Half the subjects first heard all the lawful facts, then the unlawful facts. For the other half the order of the evidence was reversed. This was true for both the adversarial and inquisitorial manipulations. Thus, for the adversarial subjects, half heard the defense first, and half the prosecution first. All subjects heard all 50 facts.

The third manipulation involved subject bias. Bias was created in half the subjects by giving them summaries of six assault cases that were generally similar to the test case. Five of the six cases were made up primarily of unlawful elements and one case primarily of lawful elements. Biased subjects were informed that in five of the six cases the defendant was found guilty. This was designed to make the subjects expect that cases of the type used in the experiment involved unlawful behavior. Pretests indicated that this manipulation produced the desired expectation in the "biased" subjects.

The dependent variable, that is, the factor that was supposed to be affected by these manipulations, was a rating of the lawfulness of the defendant's act on a 1 to 9 scale (1 = unlawful; 9 = lawful) that the subjects were asked to give. The results of the experiment are presented in Table 4.2

The data indicate that all three manipulations had statistically significant effects on the final judgments of the subjects. The last received evidence had a stronger influence on judgments than the first received evidence; biased subjects were signficantly more likely than unbiased subjects to find the defendant's act unlawful, and subjects exposed to the adversarial method of presentation were less likely to find the act unlawful than those who heard only one presenter. The last finding is, however, subject to an important qualification. The method of presentation strongly affected the biased subjects but did not significantly affect the judgments of the unbiased subjects. Table 4.2 also suggests that the overall order of evidence had less impact on subjects who heard the "adversary" evidence than on those who heard the "inquisitorial" evidence (compare differences within columns). This is true for both biased and unbiased subjects.

Overall, "adversary" subjects generally reached more moderate conclusions about the case. One of the most interesting findings in the experiment is that

TABLE 4.2
The Effect Of Procedure On Decision Making:
Mean Final Opinions*

Order	Biased Subjects		Unbiased Subjects	
	Inquisitorial	Adversary	Inquisitorial	Adversary
Unlawful-lawful	3.00(13)	4.20(10)	5.53(15)	5.00(13)
Lawful-unlawful	1.33(15)	3.13(15)	2.00(16)	3.47(19)

* Number of subjects in parentheses.
Source: Thibaut, Walker & Lind, 1972, p. 395.

when biased subjects were given *unlawful* evidence first in the adversarial mode they tended to react against their biases and were more likely to find the defendant's act *lawful*. They refused to immediately typify the case as "another unlawful assault." This effect does not appear in the inquisitorial mode (Thibaut et al., 1972, pp. 397–401). The adversary mode seemed to cause subjects to keep an open mind, await more particularistic facts about the case and engage in a unique, rather than a typifying, analysis before arriving at a final verdict.

Some people might question our reliance on this study. Professor Damaska (1975) and others have pointed to serious flaws in the experiment. In particular, it cannot be taken as evidence that an adversary system is superior to an inquisitorial system when there are preexisting biases. In an inquisitorial system a judge does not read the facts found to a third-party adjudicator but reaches a decision himself, and an inquisitorial system may have safeguards against bias that an adversary system lacks (cf. Sheppard & Vidmar, 1980; Vidmar & Laird, 1983). Furthermore, differences between the experimental setting and legal trials are such that any generalization must be cautious. The experimenter's order manipulation, for example, was much purer than that found in courts because in courts parties alternate throughout the case with opening statements direct questioning and cross-examination, and closing statements exposing the fact finder first to the position of one party; next, to that of the other; then, to that of the first party; and so on. Finally, the subjects in this experiment were students who in important respects are different from actual jurors, and the case consisted of only 50 facts read from cards.

Nevertheless, the very weakness of the most interesting manipulation—the difference between facts read by one person and facts read by two persons, one labeled prosecution and the other defense—makes the resulting judgmental differences an impressive finding. Although the experimental trial has little in common with real trials, the study may nonetheless speak indirectly to those interested in understanding legal processes by suggesting that as a matter of basic psychology a person's orientation to information will depend on whether it is perceived as coming from one consistent or two conflicting sources. One experiment cannot prove that different modes of presenting evidence lead to different methods of case processing, but in our view this study is good reason to take seriously the hypothesis that styles of decision making are affected by how information is presented to adjudicators.

The following experiment deals with another aspect of adjudicative decision making: How—or by what standard—adjudicators are told they should decide a case. The results suggest that this too may affect the attribution process.

The Rules of Decision. In this experiment Colasanto and Sanders (1976) asked jurors to pass judgment on a defendant who was charged with theft. The accused according to their scenario had used a large quantity of bricks, taken from the land upon which an old house had burned down, to build a backyard barbecue pit. The bricks, part of the remains of the house, had been set in a pile in the yard and had rested there, uncleaned, for 9 months. The crucial manipulation in this experiment involved what the judge told the jurors about how they were to decide the case. In one version, called *general intent*, the judge instructed the jury:

> In determining the defendant's intention, the law assumes that every person intends the natural consequences of his voluntary acts. Therefore, the defendant's intention is inferred from his voluntary commission of the act forbidden by law, and it is *not* necessary to establish that the defendant knew that his act was a violation of law.

In another version, called "specific intent," the judge instructed the jury:

> The crime charged in this case requires proof of specific intent before the defendant can be convicted. Specific intent means more than the general intent to commit the act. To establish specific intent the government must prove that the defendant knowingly did an act which the law forbids, purposely intending to violate the law. Such intent may be determined from all the facts and circumstances surrounding the case. The word "knowingly" means that the act was done voluntarily and purposely, and not because of mistake or accident. Knowledge may be proven by the defendant's conduct and by all the facts and circumstances surrounding the case. No person can intentionally avoid knowledge by closing his eyes to facts which should prompt him to investigate.

These instructions contain different rules of law. The first or general intent version tells the jurors that they are expected to presume meaning from the conduct of the defendant. So long as the defendant intended to take the bricks, they can assume that he intended to take property belonging to another person and can characterize the taking as theft. Under the second or specific intent version the act of taking is not sufficient to give a legal meaning to the defendant's intent. Deeper analysis is necessary.

The defendant in this case responded to the charges by claiming that he believed the bricks to be abandoned and so thought he could take them. The judge's instructions in the specific intent condition told the jury to consider this issue. The instructions did not tell the jurors that they had to believe the defendant, that is, accept the meaning the defendant attached to his behavior, nor were the jurors instructed that if they believed the defendant, they had to find him not guilty. "No person can intentionally avoid knowledge by closing his eyes to facts which should prompt him to investigate." All that was required of the jurors was that they seriously consider the issue of meaning in light of the unique facts of the case.

The case was constructed so as to be ambiguous on the facts. There was conflicting evidence bearing on the defendant's likely beliefs. Supporting his claim that he reasonably believed the bricks had been abandoned were the facts that the bricks had sat in a pile for the better part of a year and that the property generally appeared unkempt and unused. Also, the defendant took the bricks in broad daylight and never denied taking them. On the other hand, the property was posted with a sign designating ownership, and there was a rundown fence around the property. Moreover, the defendant had never asked anyone about the status of the land or the bricks. In addition, although there was no evidence on

TABLE 4.3
Legal Instructions And Jury Decision Making*

| | Specific Intent | | | General Intent | | |
Jury Verdict	Jury Law (%)	Judge Law (%)	Total (%)	Jury Law (%)	Judge Law (%)	Total (%)
Guilty	25 (3)	50 (6)	38 (9)	54 (7)	83 (10)	68 (17)
Not guilty or hung	75 (9)	50 (6)	63 (15)	46 (6)	17 (2)	32 (8)
Total	100 (12)	100 (12)		100 (13)	100 (12)	

* Number of juries in parentheses.
Source: Colasanto & Sanders, 1976.

this, the jurors must have known that a pile of bricks is worth money and that the defendant would have been aware of this.

The jurors were also subjected to a second manipulation. Half the juries were told by the judge that his instructions were binding and that they must follow the law as he presented it. This is called the *judge law* instruction. The others were told that the instructions were meant to be helpful but were not binding. It was their job, they were informed, to determine both the law and the facts in the case. This is called the *jury law* instruction. Table 4.3 presents the verdicts returned under these different conditions.

Both manipulations had a significant effect on the verdicts returned by the juries. In the extreme case where the jury was told that intent was presumed from the act (general intent) and that it must follow the judge's instructions (judge law), 10 out of 12 juries found the defendant guilty.[7] At the other extreme, where the jurors heard the jury law (specific intent instruction) 9 out of 12 juries did not find the defendant guilty. The specific intent instruction must have led the jurors to attend to the defendant's assertion of meaning, and, because not all juries in this condition found the defendant not guilty, to the circumstances surrounding the case.

When jurors heard the general intent instruction but were told they could decide the law as well as the facts, nearly half the juries did not find the defendant guilty. This suggests that the judge law, general intent jurors may have been dissatisfied with the standard they were given but deferred, by and large, to what they believed was the law.

Perhaps the most interesting results, given our current concerns, are those from judge law juries that received the specific intent instruction. Although this standard tends to favor the defendant, half the juries hearing it found the defendant guilty. The meaning of this result is clarified by the responses of the jurors to two questions in a postexperiment interview. The jurors were asked to rate, on

---

7. If we look at the verdicts of individual jurors rather than the verdicts of juries, the results are even more extreme. Of 69 jurors in this treatment, 64 found the defendant guilty.

a scale of 1 to 7, the degree to which they felt that (1) the defendant really believed the bricks were abandoned and (2) a reasonable person would have believed the bricks were abandoned. Many of the jurors tended to believe the defendant's claim that he thought the bricks had been abandoned, yet they also felt that a reasonable person would not have thought so. The jurors in the judge law cell apparently took seriously the judge's statement in the specific intent instruction that a person could not avoid knowledge by closing his eyes to facts that should prompt him to investigate, and judged the defendant by a "reasonable man" standard. They interpreted the defendant's behavior with a less subjective, more *normal* standard of meaning. The jurors in the jury law cell, on the other hand, apparently felt less bound by this standard and tended to judge the defendant on a more *introspective* standard that increased the probability of acquittal. The jury verdicts reflect these juror understandings.

Thus, rules of decision as well as methods of presentation apparently make a difference in the way evidence is used. The trade usage exception to the parol evidence rule had a similar effect on expansiveness in *Ermolieff* v. *R.K.O.* Nor should the above results surprise us. The legal system has long affirmed that the rules of evidence and procedure make a difference. At times such ideas are debunked by lawyers and nonlawyers alike on the theory that lay people will decide cases as they see fit and that nothing will alter this. This "perfidy" theory of human behavior finds little support in the previous data. Decision rules structure the problem the fact finder must resolve, and so alter the ways in which cases are decided.[8]

TOWARD SHALLOWER ADJUDICATION: REPETITIVE DECISIONS AND FUTURE ORIENTATIONS

Repetitive Decisions

In the preceding sections we considered organizational arrangements that tend to increase the likelihood of extended and unique understandings of evidence. Of course, adjudications can be structured to produce the opposite effect. Perhaps the most important factor leading to shallow decision making is experience in judging similar issues. Experience supplies a stock of stereotypes that may be

---

8. Again, one cannot rest too much on the results of a single study. This is true even though the Colasanto and Sanders (1976) study was considerably closer to the actual jury experience than the study conducted by Thibaut, Walker, and Lind (1972). The stimulus was a videotape, people eligible for jury duty were used as subjects, and the mock jurors had a chance to deliberate. Moreover, the predeliberation judgments of individual jurors were completely consistent with the jury results presented and the difference between conditions attained higher levels of statistical significance because of the larger numbers involved when juror rather than jury verdicts were analyzed. Although there are data in other studies suggesting that jurors do not always comply with what they are told to do, Colasanto and Sanders's findings that legal instructions affect jury deliberations have been substantiated by a number of other researchers (see Severance & Loftus, 1982), and is consistent with the seminal work of Kalven and Zeisel (1966).

applied with some accuracy on minimal cues. Where an adjudicative setting is structured so that there are pressures for the quick and inexpensive resolution of masses of similar claims, shallow case logics are almost inevitable.

The two studies we have just discussed looked at jurors. Jurors are "one-shot" adjudicators. They are called on to decide a single case. Although a juror will occasionally have heard of or even decided a similar case in the past, judgment in one case need not—indeed, should not—take account of what occurred in the other case. Moreover, if potential disputants not before the court are likely to be influenced by the outcome in the case at hand, this should not concern the juror.[9]

Most cases, as is now well known, are not decided by a jury. In fact, most cases are not decided by a trial. They are "settled" in advance of trial if they are civil cases, or in the criminal law jargon, they are "plea bargained." Of the nonbargained cases, many are tried before a judge.

A study by David Sudnow (1965) shows how repetitive decision making leads attributers to typify or "normalize" the cases with which they deal. Sudnow studied the behavior of prosecutors and public defenders in cases involving indigent defendants. Prosecutors try cases on behalf of the state, and public defenders are one way of meeting the state's constitutional obligation to supply counsel to indigents charged with criminal behavior. The public defender like the prosecutor and judge, is a regular employee of the judicial system. In urban areas the amount of criminal activity coupled with the large proportion of criminal defendants who cannot afford private counsel (estimated to be about 65 percent) renders the job of public defender a full-time occupation, and multilawyer public defender offices are common.

In some jurisdictions public defenders are assigned to defendants and like private attorneys handle all aspects of their clients' cases. But in the jurisdiction Sudnow studied, as in many others, the public defender occupies a station. His "beat" is typically a given courtroom, where his job is to defend all comers. A new defender soon finds that he has special privileges such as access to the court's telephone to contact his office or the perquisite of leaving his material at the defense counsel's table when a private attorney "interrupts" to argue a motion. Unlike private attorneys, who come and go from the court, the public defender works there. He and the prosecutor handle case after case together. The courtroom setting rather than the client is the most salient feature of the public defender's work.

Defendants in the jurisdiction Sudnow studied move from courtroom to courtroom as their cases proceed. A typical defendant might be represented by

---

9. Judges, however, as Emerson (1983) documents, may decide cases with an eye toward past cases or to the implications that a decision will have for future cases. For example, a traffic court judge may hesitate to acquit a person who disputes the validity of a traffic ticket if that person's case is called early in the day, for fear that an acquittal will induce other persons to dispute their tickets. Although it is proper for a judge to consider past cases or implications for future cases when considering issues of legal precedent, it is not proper to let such considerations affect judgments on the facts. With respect to the facts, each litigant is entitled to his or her own day in court.

one defender at arraignment, another at the preliminary hearing, a third at the trial, and a fourth when sentenced (1965, p. 257). Most of the communication between the public defender staff and the defendants they represent comes at the first interview. Whoever handles the initial interview talks to the client. For those defenders who occupy later stations, the "client" is often a stranger. A file prepared at the first interview and added to as the case proceeds furnishes those who occupy the different outposts with information about the particular person they are called on to defend. At times, a file is first reviewed by the trial defender an hour or so before the trial begins.

Given the importance of the first interview for all subsequent proceedings, it is important to understand what goes on there. Sudnow's central observation is that during this interview the public defender, "attends to establishing the typical character of the case before him and thereby instituting routinely employed reduction arrangements" (1965, p. 259). In other words, the public defender tries to pigeonhole cases for later plea bargains. Sudnow reports typical comments of public defenders on first interviews:

> [H]e had me fooled for a while. With that accent of his and those Parliaments he was smoking I thought something was strange. It turned out to be just another burglary.

> I could tell as soon as he told me he had four prior drunk charges that he was just another of these skid row bums. You could look at him and tell.

> When you see a whole string of forgery counts in the past you pretty much know what kind of case you're dealing with.

> From the looks of him and the way he said "I wasn't doing anything, just playing with her," you know, it's the usual kind of thing, just a little diddling or something. We can try to get it out on a simple assault. (Sudnow, 1965, pp. 259–260)

The last comment indicates the step that will follow the interview. After categorizing the cases into typical crimes, public defenders assign them typical penalties. "Diddling" with a little girl is a simple assault. This is a typical plea in a typical child molestation where the defendant is not the type who would actually engage in sex with the girl. Another possible charge is loitering around a school yard. Sudnow notes that this latter charge may be used even in a case where there is no school anywhere near the site of the alleged offense. The charge captures what this defendant "is like." He is the type who loiters around school yards. He is an average, *normal* molester, to be handled routinely with an offense that typifies his behavior. It is just bad luck that he was apprehended in the park and not near a school.

To the extent that Sudnow's observations generalize, few if any of the questions public defenders ask of their clients are designed to elicit information concerning the particulars of the alleged offense, nor, indeed, to match the facts to the specific requirements of a possible charge. The client is usually assumed to be guilty, and the issue is how to typify the case. The public defender is not planning to go to trial; he is determining the going price for the crime in question, that is, the plea-sentence bargain that is routinely struck in cases of that type. Moreover, if we could listen in on plea bargaining discussions, as Douglas Maynard (1984) did, we would find that much of the discussion between the prosecutor and defense counsel concerns the proper way to characterize the case.

If the client is unwilling to cop a plea and unable, as he usually is, to convince the defender that his case does not fit an established type, the public defender's response is usually to tell the client that he can do little for him. This is not play acting, for the public defender is usually right. In most cases, the police and prosecutor do not make serious mistakes, and a jury acquittal is the exception rather than the rule. To suggest that the defendant plead guilty to some charge is only to suggest that the defendant act reasonably in his own interest. A defendant claiming innocence despite solid incriminatory evidence is making an "innocence pitch," "being wise," and "not knowing what's good for him."

Trials in the run of the mill case are not much different. Even if there is a trial it is a matter of routine. Sudnow writes:

> With little variation the same questions are put to all defendants charged with the same crimes. The P.D. [public defender] learns with experience what to expect as the "facts of the case." These facts, in their general structure, portray social circumstances that he can anticipate by virtue of his knowledge of the normal features of offense categories and types of offenders. (1965, p. 274)

The tendency to typify cases that Sudnow reports is not unique to the public defenders he studied. Skolnick (1967) reports similar behavior by the private defense counsel and prosecutors in the same jurisdiction that Sudnow studied. Maynard's (1984) conversations include privately retained as well as appointed counsel. Ross (1970) finds that automobile accident insurance claims adjusters typify cases in a similar fashion. In any rear end collision, for example, the second driver is, for settlement purposes, always at fault. Emerson (1969) reports that juvenile court judges react the same way to the burdens of getting the job done and the weight of a wealth of experience. They have "seen it all before."

However, not every case is just another case. Even in a bureaucracy geared to typification, an unusual case can be recognized. Cases that do not fit in any pigeonhole, which includes both celebrated crimes and those where the possibility of innocence seems real, are handled more in accord with the law's normative model. In the office Sudnow studied, the prosecutor and defendant would on occasion, in notorious homicide cases, for example, stop shadowboxing and actually slug it out. But the vast majority of cases in that office as in legal and judicial offices generally are handled routinely. *Routinely* means an immediate typical understanding of the circumstances and an attribution of some normal meaning. *Routine adjudication* means shallow adjudication—a way to get through the job. In Chapter 5 we return to this topic and look more closely at the effects of bureaucratization on decision making.

Future Orientation

The objectives of the adjudicator may also influence the depth of an adjudication. A common objective is to shape the future behavior of people other than the accused. When this is the objective, the adjudicator may be concerned primarily with the message that will be conveyed to third parties. Actor meanings may be understood but ignored for fear that a decision that recognizes such meanings will be misconceived. Thus, the military in wartime may punish all collaboration with the enemy even that which is unknowing or a result of irresistible torture. To do otherwise might lead those who know only that collaborators are not always punished to regard the offense as less serious than it actually is. Thus, as some social psychological research has shown, moral norms may be invoked even against those known to have good external excuses (Schmitt, 1964; Kelley 1971, p. 23). In other words, an adjudication may proceed with a deep case logic, but the adjudicator, for policy reasons, may ignore much of what has been learned and render a verdict that could as easily have followed a shallow analysis.

A good example of how a concern to structure behavior may affect legal decision making is found in the situation of English colonial judges confronted with the cases of accused slayers of alleged witches (Seidman, 1965). The defendant, or group of defendants (sometimes whole villages) who killed a "witch" was, in the British colonies, tried by British courts. Although it was generally agreed that the defendant, as a normal member of his society, believed in witchcraft and the power of his victim to destroy him and his family, these cases almost invariably led to a death sentence in the British courts. Just as invariably the defendants received a royal pardon or clemency (Seidman, 1965, p. 204; cited in Chambliss & Seidman, 1971).

Chambliss and Seidman compare one such case with a case arising in England that they see as similar. In both cases the accused sought to excuse his homicide with the plea that it was done to protect the well-being of another person. In *Konkomba* (Gold Coast) 14 W.A.C.A. 236 (1952) the defendant dutifully consulted a "juju" man after his first brother died. The juju man pointed to the eventual victim of the homicide as a witch who had caused the defendant's brother's death. A second brother became ill and the juju man again pointed to the eventual victim. The defendant killed the victim, and when he was tried for homicide he argued that his action was necessary to save the life of another. Verdict: Guilty. In the case of *Rex* v. *Bourne* 1 K.B. 687 (1939) a prominent English doctor was charged with committing an unlawful abortion on a 14-year-old rape victim. The case turned on whether the operation was done "in good faith for the purpose of preserving the life of the girl" [1 K.B. 687, 695 (1939)]. Dr. Bourne's defense was that he had thought continuation of the prègnancy would cause serious, perhaps life-endangering, injury to the victim. He was supported in this defense by a psychiatrist who testified that if the girl gave birth to the child, she would most likely become a mental wreck, and disastrous consequences would ensue. The jury was instructed that this evidence together with Dr. Bourne's views might properly cause them to doubt the prosecution's claim that the operation, however well motivated, was not done to save the girl's life, and a "not guilty" verdict was duly returned.

Chambliss and Seidman (1971, p. 205) argue that the only apparent difference between the cases they describe is that British judges believed in psychiatry but not in witchcraft. This is one way to explain them. British doctors can rely on speculative psychiatric linkages between a patient's mental health and her life, but the reasonable reliance of an African native does not serve as a standard of judgment. For example, the Chief Justice for the appellate court in *The Attorney General for Nyasaland* v. *Jackson (Federation)* R. & N. 443 (1957), held that the standard for such a case:

> is what would appear reasonable to the ordinary man in the street in England. . . . On this basis, and bearing in mind that the law of England is still the law of England even when it is extended to Nyasaland, I do not see how any court, applying the proper test, could hold that a belief in witchcraft was reasonable so as to form the foundation of a defense that the law could recognize.

In other cases in which witches were killed by defendants who honestly believed their victims were dangerous, other standard legal defenses to homicide have also failed to excuse the killing. Among the defenses that have proved unavailing are: mistake, *Gadam* (Nigeria) 14 W.A.C.A. 442 (1954); self-defense, *Erika Galikuwa* (Uganda) 18 E.A.C.A. 175 (1951); insanity, *Philip Muswi s/o Musola* (Kenya) 23 E.A.C.A. 622 (1956), and partial delusion, *Skekanja* (Tanganyika) 15 E.A.C.A. 158 (1948). Between the world view of the English judiciary and the African defendant there lay a chasm that could not be bridged.

Before passing too harsh a judgment on the British colonial judiciary, however, we should reflect on the width of that chasm and the self-appointed mission of the judges. There is more to these cases than the fact that the English judges do not believe in witchcraft, and therefore refuse to accept witchcraft as an excuse. After all, English judges may not believe that a man has property rights in yams grown by his mother's brother but would consider a tribe's shared understanding in such a matter in adjudicating a claimed theft. The ethnocentrism in the case of witchcraft runs deeper, and the issue of control is critical. To understand why the English judges acted as they did, we must consider the nature of witchcraft.

In Chapter 2 we suggested that liability for witchcraft can approximate an ideal type of legal liability in which intention at some level matters but the ability to do otherwise is irrelevant. This means that ability excuses are generally unavailable. Chambliss and Seidman (1971) give the following summary of one tribal group's theory of witchcraft:

> The Akan (one of the largest West African tribal groupings), for example, postulate man as tripartite. His physical body, a mere shell, encloses two indwelling souls, the *kra*, or life-soul, and the *sunsum*, or personality-soul. A wicked entity, the *obayi*, on occasion seizes dominion of the *sunsum* of a witch. Without her volition, her *sunsum*, makes excursions from her earthly body. Free of physical restraint, it attacks

the *kra* or *sunsum* of its victims by sucking it forth secretly from its material shell. As the *kra* is devoured, sometimes by degrees, sometimes in a rush, so the physical body of the victim withers. (1971, pp. 203–204)

Given that the witch, at least in some societies, is regarded as unable to avoid being possessed and cannot, by the very nature of the crime, plead any situational inability excuses, the trial of witches is a trial of mental states. Moreover, there may be no objective evidence that a person is a witch except the harm that is attributed to his witchcraft. It is not surprising that trials for witchcraft often take the form of trial by ordeal. Since there is no visible act, the proof must come from either magical revelation or confession (see, e.g., Parrinder, 1965, pp. 177–178). In extreme cases, not only witchcraft itself, but the very accusation of witchcraft approaches a strict liability crime; yet it may be punishable by death.[10]

Both the substantive plea of witchcraft and the logic by which a person was found responsible as a witch clashed with English notions of responsibility. In attempting to stamp out this evil, the English were trying to eradicate one meaning of what it is to be responsible and a whole method of deciding cases. Where world views are as different as those of the English judge and African native, even a full, extended historical understanding of the meaning of an action (here, killing a witch) is unlikely to sway an adjudicator completely.

Harold Kelley, in his seminal article on attribution theory, notes:

> There is a strong intuitive appeal, however, in the notion advanced by Stevenson that "ethical judgments look mainly to the future. Even when they are made of past or imaginary acts, they still serve a dynamic purpose—that of discouraging (or encouraging) similar acts later on." (1971, p. 17)

Judgments, in other words, may be guided by estimates of future responsibility rather than, or in addition to, evaluations of past responsibility.

The English judiciary saw the prospective teaching of new rules as a central task. This task was regarded as more important than the retrospective adjudication of past behavior. As one judge proclaimed in a case of death caused while attempting to exorcise a demon:

> It . . . seems to me that even where moral guilt is absent a court may, in a proper case, where a very large section of the community, especially an unenlightened one, requires to be protected against dangerous practices, disregard the existence of that form of mitigation. (*Zanhibe*, 1954 (3) S.A. 597, cited in Chambliss & Seidman, 1971, p. 216 n.86)

---

10. Adamson Hoebel (1969) reports such a process among people of the Keresan Pueblo of New Mexico.

> The culprit was made to stand within a three-foot cornmeal circle while being unceasingly interrogated. If he fainted or stepped outside the circle, he is said (by my informants) to have been forthwith shot by one of the War Captains, who stood by with drawn bow and arrow throughout the entire trial. When he confessed, he was subsequently executed. To be charged with witchcraft was to be sentenced to death. (1969, p. 110)

The world of witches was so alien to the British that virtually all "witch killings" were treated the same.[11] They were typified and normalized in a way that ignored differences between them and justified a verdict of murder. Because the judges believed they should eliminate the "evil" of witchcraft, they were not swayed by their recognition that the killing of witches was rooted in basic cultural beliefs. Knowing that cultural beliefs change slowly, they convicted witch killers and sentenced them to death in order to deter and instruct others. Such motives might similarly be imputed to the U.S. federal judiciary in the southern racial districting cases we discussed in Chapter 3.

At the same time, there was a complexity to the typifications used in witchcraft trials that is not normally found in shallow adjudications, for part of the stereotype was a rather sensitive attribution of subjective meaning. The British understood that the typical witch killer had not, from his perspective, done anything wrong. Thus, the death sentences of convicted witch killers were routinely commuted. This despite the fact that deterrence might have been greater had the sentences been actually carried out. The British could appreciate what it meant to be morally culpable in a tribal society. In the routine administration of colonial justice, witch killers may have been sentenced to death but the actual penalty was reserved for those whose moral culpability was greater.

This suggests that there was more at stake in the witchcraft trials than the simple desire to eliminate unacceptable beliefs. This something more had to do with the integrity of the British legal system. The system's claim to be a civilized and civilizing institution would have been undercut had its rules excused the

---

11. There is one exceptional case reported by Chambliss and Seidman, but it is in the nature of the exception that "proves the rule." In *Fabiano* (Uganda) 8 E.A.C.A. 96 (1941), the victim had been found crawling naked in the defendant's compound at night and the defendant had killed him. The court's opinion read in part as follows:

> We think that if the facts proved establish that the victim was performing in the actual presence of the accused some act which an ordinary person of the community did generally believe to be an act of witchcraft against him or another person under his immediate care [which act would be a criminal offense under the Criminal Law (Witchcraft) Ordinance of Uganda . . .] he might be angered to such an extent as to be deprived of the power of self-control and induced to assault the person doing the act of witchcraft. And if this is to be the case a defense of grave and sudden provocation is open to him (quoted in Chambliss & Seidman, 1971, p. 207).

Can it reasonably be said that the defendant in this case suffered any more provocation than the defendant who had one brother die and another dying? The difference between the cases is not in the amount of provocation, but in the behavior of the victim. The victim, who presumably knew what he was doing, acted in a way that in his community was regarded as threatening. Moreover, the English courts appreciated neither the African procedures for identifying witches nor the reason why once a witch was identified a self-help remedy rather than a public trial was appropriate. In this case the victim's involvement was not problematic and the court could appreciate the need for quick action in defense of self and family. Since the victim was not selected mystically or killed solely for a status crime, the court listened to the defense of provocation. It is, no doubt, more than a coincidence that an Englishman who killed an intruder in similar circumstances would be excused if he reasonably thought the victim was committing a felony.

slaying of witches who the British jurisprudents knew (rightly or wrongly) could have done no harm. This systemic claim was not threatened when sentences were commuted for moral rather than legal reasons. Again, there may be a parallel with the behavior of federal judges in the southern racial districting cases. The southern states attempted to use legal "technicalities" and delays built into the litigation process in order to avoid or forestall the impact of *Brown v. Board of Education* and its progeny. Some of the tactics the states used threatened to make a mockery of the legal system. Eventually the judges would have none of it.

TWO CONSEQUENCES OF CASE LOGICS: FAIRNESS AND EFFICIENCY

What difference does it make whether an adjudicator employs a shallow or a deep case logic? The question can be answered at several levels. The choice of case logic may make a difference to the accused, both in terms of her likelihood of "getting off," and in her punishment if she is found responsible. The choice may also make a difference to the adjudicator in terms of the effort required to resolve a case. Finally, the choice of case logics has implications for the different rule logics that are or may be made available to assess responsibility in different types of situations. In this section we discuss the impact of the choice of case logic on the accused and the adjudicator. In the next chapter we shall deal with the complex relationship among case logics, rule logics, and changing standards of responsibility.

Consequences for the Actor: The Success of Excuses and the Meaning of Fairness

For the actor whose behavior is being tried, the use of a shallow case logic usually means a reduced opportunity to advance successfully excuses that might exculpate or mitigate his act. Typification restricts the range of possible excuses that one may advance. In so doing, it hampers the accused who seeks to redefine a situation so as to suggest that the original accusation is mistaken. Adjudicators using shallow case logics tend not to consider the extended situations of different actors, the precise circumstances of untoward acts, or special actor meanings in deciding how responsible actors are. Other things being equal, shallow adjudications are more likely to produce findings of unmitigated responsibility. But, by the same token, shallow adjudications are less likely to arrive at findings of special responsibility. Thus, a person caught with a relatively large supply of heroin that he has stockpiled for personal use may find that he is convicted of possessing a narcotic drug with intent to sell, while someone who has bought a small amount of heroin for resale may only be convicted of possession.

The choice of case logic has important implications for the meaning of one of the basic precepts of justice: the meaning of fairness (see Rawls, 1971, p. 235). Fairness implies, if nothing else, that similar cases should be treated similarly. But what constitutes similarity is not an easy issue. It is, we argue, contingent on case logic.

Consider the example of two men, let us call them Fred and Tom, who have been sentenced to prison for armed robbery. Fred has received a sentence of 5 years and Tom a sentence of 10 years. Is this fair? Well—it all depends. If the normal term is 10 years, but Fred managed to get 5 years by bribing the judge, it is unfair. But what if the normal term is 5 years, and Tom is a repeat offender? Or perhaps Fred was armed with a penknife, while Tom used a sawed-off shotgun. Should such a detail matter?

Consider now the discrepancy from the perspective of the two felons. Tom may feel he has been treated unfairly. He might argue that since he and Fred are both armed robbers, it is unreasonable to make him serve twice as long. Fred, however, may find the distinction easily justified. As Plato long ago observed, there is no greater injustice than to treat unlike cases the same. Circumstances, or past record, or any number of other factors should be worth something. To Fred it would be unfair if he and Tom received the same sentence.

Fairness in sentencing criminals is but one aspect of the issue. In any adjudicatory process the choice of what arguments and evidence to allow or disallow will affect the degree to which cases can be distinguished. From one perspective, fairness consists of the more or less equal treatment of people in basically similar situations, and judgments of dissimilarity should attend to only relatively gross distinctions. From another perspective, no two cases are entirely alike, and fairness requires attention to all the relevant ways in which cases might be distinguished.

Shallow case logics, which use only normal meanings, recognize only typical situations, and care only about immediate circumstances, yield results that appear relatively equal and hence fair to those who cannot or do not wish to perceive any but the grossest differences between cases. Deep case logics, on the other hand, come closer to fair results insofar as fairness requires attention to details that distinguish facially similar behavior.

Just as a preference for case processing by shallow logic may reflect a concern for future behavior that overrides intuitions about justice in a particular case, so the preference for such a logic may be affected by the likely reactions of an audience to the *apparent* morality of a decision. Thus, a judge sentencing two teenagers for a mugging may feel constrained to give each the same sentence although he feels one is a hardened criminal while the other is not committed to a life of crime. The judge does not attend to those aspects of character that distinguish the defendants because he believes that people not in a good position to appreciate the distinction will perceive it as grossly unfair if one of two muggers receives a jail sentence while the other gets probation. Perceptions of unfairness are particularly likely if there are irrelevant but visible distinctions between the muggers that under some popular theory might explain their different treatment. Consider the criticism that a judge using a deeper logic might be open to if the hardened criminal whom he chooses to jail is black and the less committed criminal who receives probation is white. Of course, the decision to treat the muggers similarly in such a situation does not specify what the equal treatment will be. Both may get probation or both may get jail or some intermediate level of punishment may be found. In any event, each will be sentenced, in part, for the company he keeps.[12]

Which case logic provides the better approach to criminal or civil cases? There is no universal answer. There is one criterion, however, that we may use to judge the appropriateness of a case logic. This is its *reliability*. Case logics may be considered unreliable when they mistakenly hold the innocent blame-worthy and/or find the culpable blameless. But what constitutes innocence and culpability depends on the rule logic being used.

A shallow case logic is likely to be unreliable if it uses typifications that take no account of purpose in situations where the legal standard makes purpose important. The unreliability of judgments based on shallow case logics is usually attributable to the fact that evidence on important parts of the responsibility question is "glossed over" in the typification process. Unreliability will be mitigated to the extent that those aspects of the event on which the shallow logic focuses are good proxies for the intent that the legal standard makes relevant.

Deep case logics may be unreliable in a different sense. They may require the adjudicator to make decisions about aspects of the situation or mental state of the actor that are very difficult to get right. If the adjudicator cannot or will not make reliable distinctions, a deep case logic will fail to distinguish fairly the culpable from the innocent. In the next chapter we discuss a situation where deep case logics are unreliable in this sense.

The suitability of a case logic also depends on the purpose of the adjudication. To the extent that the purpose of adjudication in criminal cases is to classify people as guilty or not guilty in order to generate deterrence or create the popular impression that justice is being done, shallow logics may work tolerably well. For purposes of deterrence at least, errors may cancel out in the aggregate. If some guilty people are acquitted and some innocent people convicted, the apparent severity and certainty of punishment will remain about the same. Shallow case logics may also be adequate for those kinds of civil cases where it is more

---

12. The issue of which criteria to consider in making such decisions has been confronted directly in the area of parole decisions. A 1972 study of these decisions funded by the Law Enforcement Assistance Administration generated a set of guidelines that consisted of a scale of offense severity and "salient factor" scores designed to predict parole success. Using base-rate actuarial expectancies, the Guidelines give a range of months to be served for each combination of offenses and offender characteristics. Included in offender characteristics are the offender's age at first commitment and whether the offender was employed or in school for at least 6 months in the preceding 2 years (Gottsfredson et al., 1978). The Guidelines were formally adopted for use in federal parole decision making (Coffee, 1978). Many additional individual characteristics might have been included, and, indeed, several indicators such as age, education, and family ties are better predictors of parole success. These, however, were not in the "control" of the individual and it was felt that their use would be unfair.

important that matters be settled so that commercial life can proceed than that each matter be settled correctly. Thus, the question of whether Sue, who stopped short, was more responsible for an accident than Karen, who plowed into her, may be less important than informing Sue what, if anything, she will receive for her injuries and telling Karen's insurer what, if anything, it will have to pay.

The situation is different if an adjudication seeks to reconcile people by resolving tensions that underlie a dispute or if society seeks through its adjudicatory processes to inform itself about what is really going on in certain areas of conflict. A marriage counselor, for example, would soon be out of business if he responded to the news that a husband had hit his wife by saying that the wife must have done something to deserve it or by remarking that the husband should be sent to jail. But marriage counselors in Western societies are not generally adjudicators. Part of their training is in learning how not to pass judgments.

The pressure toward shallow logics in formal adjudication is such that when truly deep analysis is required, adjudication as we know it in the West must be either avoided or substantially transformed. Transformation in routine styles of adjudication can occur as when judgments of sanity in criminal cases are, in effect, entrusted to psychiatrists. Substantially different processes that allow deeper analysis but are nonetheless recognizable as adjudications are found in some non-Western societies. Here we simply state these propositions as conclusions. In Chapters 7 and 8 we discuss in detail examples that support them.

Consequences for the Adjudicator: Speed and Efficiency

In Chapter 2 we quoted Herbert Packer (1968) who states that allowing excuses is likely to make a legal system less efficient. Packer was talking about efficiency in preventing antisocial conduct. This is often spoken of as the general deterrence function of the law. *General deterrence*—as distinguished from what is called specific or individual deterrence—is the tendency of legal sanctions to lead people other than the one being punished to refrain from doing proscribed acts. The punished are, for purposes of general deterrence, examples whose unpleasant fate leads others to avoid emulating their criminal behavior. If law is to deter in this sense, it must not only tell others what to expect if they breach the rule; it must also provide a relatively clear message about what constitutes a breach.

Thus, it appears that shallow adjudications in criminal cases should be more likely to deter than deeper adjudications and in this sense they should be more efficient. This is because when fewer excuses are allowed, justifications and exceptions to rules do not cloud the message conveyed by punishing others. The message is not "Thou shalt not do X, unless . . . except . . . or in the circumstances. . . ." It is simply, "Thou shalt not do X."

Since exceptions are built into legal rules for good reason, if the deterrent message conveyed by criminal convictions were fully heeded, shallow adjudications would overdeter. However, the message we convey by convicting accused criminals is not fully effective in ordering the behavior of others, or even close to it. Thus, shallow adjudications may bring us closer to the desired level of general deterrence than adjudications that are consistently deep. This analysis is, however, entirely speculative, for evidence relating the level of adjudication to general deterrence is lacking.

There is another sense in which shallow adjudications may be more efficient than deep adjudications when general deterrence is at issue. By limiting relevant excuses, shallow case logics make convictions more likely. This is important because studies of different crimes suggest that the certainty of apprehension and punishment is positively related to the level of general deterrence (Lempert, 1981–1982, pp. 513, 516). Deeper adjudications may be expected not only to lower conviction rates by enhancing the prospects for acquittal of those actually lacking criminal intent, but also to give those who are in fact guilty the opportunity to secure acquittals by dissembling and creating doubt in the minds of their adjudicators. Widespread belief in the ability to "beat raps" might have a devastating effect on general deterrence.

However, the relationship of case logics to deterrence is not all one way. Although certainty of punishment is, within the range of natural variation, apparently more strongly related to deterrence than severity of punishment, the evidence suggests that for most crimes more severe punishments have a somewhat greater deterrent effect than less severe ones. Under the Anglo-American system of justice, the criminal can exercise some degree of control over the depth of the case logic employed by his ability to choose among bench trials, jury trials, and guilty pleas. The shallowest adjudications—those attendant on a willingness to plead guilty—are associated with less severe sentences than those that follow jury trials. Consideration at sentencing appears to be the price that the state pays in order to elicit guilty pleas or, from a different perspective, the risk of a severe sentence is the price a defendant pays for a jury trial (Church, 1976). In either case, leniency associated with more routinized forms of adjudication may undercut deterrent effects attributable to higher conviction rates. Furthermore, the deeper adjudications that occur in celebrated trials may draw so much more attention than routine proceedings that, despite their greater ambiguity, they effectively communicate the messages of the criminal law.

There is also the matter of *specific deterrence*, the tendency of punishment to decrease the likelihood that a punished offender will offend again. It is at least plausible to suppose that a person whose behavior has been closely examined on its own terms and found wanting will be less cynical and less likely to offend again than a person whose case has been processed by some shallower form of adjudication.

Finally, there is another, less problematic sense in which shallower case logics are likely to be more efficient. Making distinctions costs time and money. Deep case logics are organizationally inefficient. Trials take longer than pleas or settlements, and the deeper the adjudication at trial, the longer the trial is likely to take. Furthermore, trials are just the tip of an iceberg. When deep adjudications are contemplated, substantial amounts of time and money may have to be invested to understand the unique circumstances surrounding an event. Thus, deep case logics are also socially inefficient so long as the returns, by whatever standard of value, are not substantially greater than the returns to shallower adjudication. Someone must pay the cost of running the system.

The lower cost of shallow adjudications is purchased in part at the expense of people's claims to be considered as full human actors. But where problems are viewed as societal rather than individual, a state may well be willing to pay this price for an adjudication process that requires less time to dispose of cases and takes fewer tax dollars to run. Furthermore, when adjudicators face substantial docket pressure, cheap, efficient processing becomes a desirable goal for personal as well as organizational reasons.

We shall return to some of these themes and illustrate systems that process cases in different depths in Part II of this book when we focus more directly on dispute processing. The concern for efficiency, as we shall see, figures in the following chapter. It was one of the elements causing a change in the case logics, and ultimately in the rule logics, used in the legal response to two types of civil harm.

5

Case Logics, Rule Logics, and Legal Change: The End of Negligence

In Chapter 2 we developed the idea of rule logics and indicated how they relate to our understanding of responsibility. In Chapter 4 we developed the idea of case logics and discussed several social and organizational factors that influence what case logic will be used. We also explored some of the consequences of using different logics. In this chapter we discuss case logics and rule logics together as we examine changes in the rule logics of two aspects of tort law. The first part of the chapter describes these changes. In the second and third sections, we analyze them, noting how social changes and changes in adjudication structures affect case logics and how these in turn affect rule logics. In the final section we briefly discuss the ethics of responsibility.

FROM NEGLIGENCE TO STRICT LIABILITY: LORD ABINGER'S LEGACY

In the last half-century the American legal system has witnessed a slow but clear shift away from a negligence rule logic toward a strict liability rule logic in several substantive areas. Most prominent among these are: workers' compensation,[1] automobile accidents, and products liability. In this section we treat only the first two, reviewing briefly the legal changes in these areas over the last 100 years or so. The next section discusses certain underlying patterns that were present in both. First, consider the workers' compensation revolution.

---

1. The system of no fault liability for workplace injuries has been known throughout most of its history, including all of the period we shall be discussing, as workmen's compensation. Recently, another kind of revolution has occurred as society has come to realize that many of the "workmen" covered by compensation plans are women. Thus, such plans are today often described by the sex neutral title "workers' compensation." We shall use the sex neutral term.

Workers' Compensation

Before workers' compensation statutes, an employee who sought to recover for an injury sustained during the course of his employment had to make out a case under the tort law of negligence.[2] Under this system an injured employee had to prove that his employer was negligent, that is, unreasonably careless, and that this negligence caused his injury. Complicating this system was the doctrine of *respondeat superior*: let the master, or employer as we would say today, answer. This doctrine relates to situations in which employees can financially obligate their employers. Originally, if a servant incurred a debt on behalf of an employer, the employer was liable. By early in the nineteenth century the employer's liability to persons injured by the negligence of his servants, so long as they were acting in the normal scope of their employment, had also been established. This was important because employers could usually afford to pay damage judgments while their employees were typically "judgment proof."[3]

In 1837 the famous English case of *Priestly* v. *Fowler*, 3 Mees. & Wels. 1 (Exchequer, 1837), raised the question of whether a master's "vicarious liability" for his employee's negligence extended to the situation where the victim was at the time of his injury also employed by the master. The court could easily have held that this question was answered in the affirmative by existing law, but the judges chose to perceive it as a novel issue.

The defendant in *Fowler* was a butcher, who had ordered two employees to haul some goods in a van. The facts are somewhat obscure, but the van had apparently been overloaded by one employee. The plaintiff and the one who did the loading set out, the van broke down en route, and the plaintiff's leg was broken. He sued the master, claiming that under the doctine of *respondeat superior* the master was responsible for the loader's negligence. Had the plaintiff and the master been "strangers," the plaintiff's right to recover would have been clear. Was the situation any different when he worked for the master and his injury was due to the carelessness of a co-worker? Lord Abinger thought that it was. Writing for the Court of the Exchequer, he held that a master was not liable to his servant for injuries caused by the negligence of a fellow servant. This doctrine soon took on the name of the *fellow servant rule*.

In 1841 and 1842 the rule was adopted in South Carolina and Massachusetts, respectively [*Murray* v. *South Carolina Railroad Co.* 1 McM. 385 (S.C., 1841); *Farwell* v. *The Boston and Worcester Railroad Corp.* 4 Metc. 49 (Mass., 1842)]. It quickly spread to most American jurisdictions. The two leading cases, as is clear from their names, involved the emerging railroad business. *Priestly* v.

---

2. Negligence is not, however, an ancient tort. Negligence as a separate cause of action did not fully emerge until the nineteenth century in England.

3. A person is "judgment proof" when he is so lacking in funds or other assets that there is no way to collect any monetary judgment rendered against him. Suing a judgment proof defendant is usually a waste of time and money.

Fowler arrived on this side of the Atlantic just in time for the Industrial Revolution.

A rule allowing an employee to sue his employer for a job-related injury only if the employer had been personally negligent would have had relatively little impact in a society where most employers had only a few employees who worked alongside their employers and under their supervision. But in a growing industrial society, it effectively insulated those who owned the new businesses from liability for the injuries that inescapably accompany industrial enterprise (Licht, 1983). Almost as effectively, it denied injured employees compensation for their injuries because the right that remained, the right to sue a fellow employee, was likely to be a barren remedy.[4] The cost of industrial injuries was to be borne by the injured workers, by their families, and by society in the form of almhouses and other local charities rather than by the growing industrial sector.

At least, this is one way to view the situation. Some courts saw it differently. Lemuel Shaw, the great Chief Justice of the Masachusetts Supreme Court, wrote in *Farwell* v. *The Boston and Worcester Railroad Corp.*:

> The general rule, resulting from considerations as well of justice as of policy, is that he who engages in the employment of another for the performance of specified duties and services, for compensation, takes upon himself the natural and ordinary risks and perils incident to the performance of such services, and *in legal presumption*, the compensation is adjusted accordingly. (4 Metc. 49, 57, emphasis added)

This analysis puts a different distributional face on the consequences of the rule. The transfer involved is not seen as one between classes, that is, between capital and labor; rather, it is one within a class, that is, within the ranks of labor. Industry pays all the costs of its injuries in the form of wage premiums needed to lure workers to the more dangerous occupations. It is within the ranks of labor that unfairness, at least when viewed after the fact, occurs. Most workers— those who remain uninjured—are overcompensated because they receive payment for an event that never occurs. The seriously injured minority are, however, substantially undercompensated, for the increment to their wages attributable to the relative danger of their occupation does not nearly compensate them for the harm they suffer.

Shaw's statement does not, however, say that the employees as a class are *in fact* compensated for the danger inherent in their occupations or that individual employees are compensated for the risk of danger. These conclusions are reached as matters of legal presumption, not matters of evidence. Indeed, the conclusions are better seen as something other than legal presumptions. They are conclusions that follow from an economic theory, one that assumes a free labor market, perfect information, and risk neutral parties. For our purposes, however, the

---

4. Many employees were judgment proof, and few had the "deep pockets" that would have permitted them to pay the costs of a truly serious injury.

importance of Shaw's statement does not depend on whether labor markets were free or on the empirical inadequacies of information. What is most interesting is that even in 1842 a judge was suggesting a market solution to the problem of accidents and formulating a legal rule enacting that solution. As we shall see, in the last 144 years we have in some ways come full circle.

As might be expected, labor interests immediately began to work for the overturn of the fellow servant rule, but little changed in the period before the Civil War. With the end of the war and the maturing of American industry, however, courts and legislatures started to have second thoughts. In various ways they began to limit the scope of the fellow servant rule.

New statutory and case law exceptions soon made employee injuries one of the most complex and confusing branches of law. The fellow servant rule came to be "shot through" with exceptions, such as the "vice principal" doctrine, which said that the rule did not apply where the negligence was attributable to some person having authority over the defendant. Then there was the "departmental" rule, which held that the employer was not relieved of liability if the two employees were not in the same department of the business (and in this sense not fellow servants). Perhaps most important was the idea that certain duties of the master were not "delegable." He must do them or have them done in his name, and any failure to do them correctly could open the master to liability. Among these nondelegable duties was the duty to provide a safe workplace and safe tools.

As Friedman and Ladinsky (1967) observed, the courts, had they so desired, might have *sub silentio* abolished the fellow servant rules by adding further exceptions. They did not, and the rule hung on. Indeed, there were exceptions to the exceptions, which reimposed the rule. Thus, the "simple tool" rule said that in the case of simple tools, such as hammers, the "safe tool" exception to the fellow servant rule exception to the doctrine of *respondeat superior* did not apply!

While this process was going on, the legislatures of several states abolished or limited the fellow servant rule. This movement started as early as the 1860s in cases involving railroad employees. Over the next half-century the legislatures abolished the fellow servant rule in some instances and passed laws defining and specifying the "safe place" duty of employers in other instances. Moreover, some courts abolished or limited other defenses that employers routinely raised, such as the "assumption of the risk" defense, under which the defendant-employer would prevail if he could show that the injured employee had, perhaps by the very act of taking a dangerous job, assumed the risk of any injury he might suffer.

What was crucial in litigation arising out of workplace injuries was whether a plaintiff-employee's case could get to the jury. The fellow servant rule meant that if an employee sued an employer for injuries allegedly due to the negligence of a fellow servant, as in *Priestley* v. *Fowler*, the judge would dismiss the action, for under the law there was nothing for a jury to decide. The plaintiff's allegations of an injury at the hand of a fellow employee did not describe an injury that was remediable at law. Suppose, however, the plaintiff in *Fowler* had alleged that it was his *master* who had negligently overloaded the wagon, and the master had responded with the claim that it was the plaintiff's fellow servant who was responsible. The situation would have been different. Unless the defendant's evidence was so persuasive and the plaintiff's evidence so weak that a reasonable juror could not have concluded that the chances were better than 50–50 that the master had loaded the wagon, the judge would not have taken the case from the jury. And once the case reached the jury, no one could be sure what would happen.

A jury deciding for the plaintiff in our variant of *Fowler* might have done so because the jurors believed, on the basis of all the evidence, that it was more likely than not that the master had loaded the wagon himself. Or the jurors, persuaded that the plaintiff's fellow servant probably loaded the wagon, might have disregarded the court's instructions and found for the plaintiff because they thought the fellow servant rule was unfair or because they believed the master could easily afford to pay for the plaintiff's injury or because they did not want the plaintiff to burden their community as a ward of charity, or because of some other reason. Furthermore, the jurors might have genuinely disagreed about who probably loaded the wagon. Those who thought that it was most likely the fellow servant might have agreed to waive their objections and allow a verdict to be returned provided the other jurors agreed to give the plaintiff less than what they thought was appropriate. This kind of compromise contravenes the jurors' instructions, but like a verdict that goes against what the jurors know to be the weight of the evidence, the illegality is invisible to a reviewing court, and the verdict will stand so long as it is within the realm of reason. What the proliferation of exceptions to the fellow servant rule did was to give plaintiffs' attorneys ways of formulating their cases that made it more likely they would reach the jury. Once a case reached the jury, juror sentiments or a sense of popular justice might, and were often thought to, tip the balance.

Friedman and Ladinsky (1967) tell us that these common law and statutory changes, together with the perceived unwillingness of juries to follow the law,[5] made the field ripe for litigation. The legal rules were not settled, and the fellow servant rule was not so ironclad that injured employees would not risk a suit. This was especially true because many attorneys accepted these cases, as they later accepted products liability and automobile accident cases, on a contingent

---

5. Friedman and Ladinsky (1967, pp. 50–82) report that by 1907 a total of 307 workers' personal injury cases had appeared before the Wisconsin Supreme Court. Although nearly two-thirds of these cases had resulted in victories for the employee at trial, only two-fifths of the employees emerged victorious from the state Supreme Court. What this suggests in part is that trial judges differed substantially from the Supreme Court judges in their reading of law and their sense of when a case was sufficiently two-sided to get to the jury. It also suggests that the Supreme Court was willing to focus on technical evidentiary errors, which are present in almost every trial, to reverse cases that could not be reversed as a matter of law. Although such reversals typically left open the possibility of a retrial, the expense of again litigating the matter must have been a substantial barrier to retrial in many cases.

fee basis—that is, plaintiffs who lost were charged no fees, while plaintiffs who won paid a percentage of the settlement rather than an hourly rate.

The vagaries of the law of employee injuries, the existence of the contingent fee, and the mounting number of job-related injuries in an industrializing society turned the stream of worker injury cases into a flood. In time these cases came to dominate the civil dockets of most courts. Significant delays arose, and litigation costs could be great, although the sum reaching the typical litigant was often meager. The New York Employers' Liability Commission of 1910 reported delays of from 6 months to 6 years in resolving cases arising out of work injuries. The commission found that only 8 of 48 families of employees suffering fatal injuries recovered as much as three times the deceased breadwinner's annual wage and that 18 of the families recovered nothing. They also noted that the costs of running the system were remarkably high. In 1907, of $193,000 paid out by employers as a result of lawsuits or to avoid suit, only $81,000 went to the beneficiaries. This is about 42 percent. Close to one-third of the amount paid went to plaintiffs' counsels.

States, looking for an alternative to this unsatisfactory situation, learned of a plan adopted in 1884 in Germany which set up a fund for the compensation of injured employees. Employees could collect from the fund without proving that their injuries were due to an employer's fault. In 1910, New York, which in those days was often a model for legal reform, passed a compensation statute along similar lines that, among its other features, made coverage compulsory for certain "hazardous employments." But the statute was held unconstitutional the next year by the New York Court of Appeals on the ground that it imposed liability without fault upon the employer. This, according to the court, was taking property without due process of law and so forbidden by both the state and federal constitutions (Larson, 1952, pp. 33–39). This opinion occasioned a state constitutional amendment permitting a compulsory law, and thus a new law was passed although the federal constitutional question was still unresolved.

Other states responding to the questionable constitutionality of compulsory compensation statutes made their systems voluntary, but to encourage participation these states also abrogated the traditional common law defenses of fellow servant, assumption of the risk, and contributory negligence[6] for employers who chose to remain outside the system. In 1917 the U.S. Supreme Court held several types of plans, including New York's new compulsory plan, constitutional. The system quickly spread. By 1920 all but eight states had adopted workers' compensation acts. In 1949 the last holdout, Mississippi, adopted the system.

Before the process had run its course, Jeremiah Smith, writing in 1914 in the *Harvard Law Review* foresaw with trepidation the extension of strict liability

---

6. We have not mentioned the defense of contributory negligence before, because it was a common defense in all types of negligence actions and was not peculiarly associated with worker injury suits. Nevertheless, it was an important common defense. For now, this is all you need to know. We discuss the defense in more detail later when we examine the movement toward "no fault" automobile accident insurance.

to other areas. He feared the ultimate result would be the end of a fault-based system of tort liability (Smith, 1914, p. 235). Although the breadth of Smith's fears has not as yet been realized in America, his foresight was at least partly correct. The triumph of workers' compensation has been followed by the spread of strict liability rules to injuries attributable to defective products[7] and most recently by the adoption of "no fault" schemes for the compensation of automobile accident victims.

No Fault Automobile Insurance

Almost from the time workers' compensation became the law of most American jurisdictions, there have been people who have argued for some type of strict liability for automobile accidents. As the twentieth century progressed, the automobile accident victim took the place of the injured worker as the single most frequent plaintiff on the civil docket. The courts became swamped with cases, and delays as long as or longer than those that had plagued workers' suits became common (see Zeisel, Kalven & Bucholtz, 1959). Moreover, the law of negligence as it applied to automobile accidents became, in its own way, as complex and confusing as the older workers' compensation law.

One source of complexity was the rule of contributory negligence. *Contributory negligence*, as the phrase implies, is negligent behavior on the part of the plaintiff that contributes in some causal sense to his injury. Its legal consequences were determined by precedents such as *Butterfield* v. *Forrester*, 11 East 60 (K.B. 1809). In this English case the defendant, while making some repairs to his roadside home, put a pole across one side of the road, leaving

---

7. The liability of manufacturers for injuries due to defective products, like liability for industrial and automobile accidents, was traditionally governed by a negligence rule logic. The last 20 years, however, have seen the triumph of a strict liability rule logic. Strict liability was originally based on the theory that manufacturers and other sellers implicitly warranted their products against defects. (*Hennington* v. *Bloomfield Motors, Inc.*, 32 N.J. 358, 161 A. 2d 59, 1960). Later the courts abandoned the warranty theory in favor of the direct statement that manufacturers are strictly liable in tort for the harms caused by their dangerous or defective products (*Greenman* v. *Yuba Power Products, Inc.*, 59 Cal. 2d 57, Cal. Rptr. 697, 377 P. 2d 897, 1963). The liability may extend beyond buyers and consumers to others like pedestrians and bystanders, who could foreseeably be injured by a defect in the product in question (*Piercefield* v. *Remington Arms Co.*, 375 Mich. 85, 133 N.W. 2d 169, 1965).

To recover under a strict products liability theory, one must prove that an injury was incurred because the manufacturer's product was unreasonably dangerous or defective. There is no unreasonable danger in a hammer simply because it might smash a thumb in the hands of an unskillful user. But once a danger or defect, such as the fact that a hammer head flew off, is shown, the plaintiff does not have to prove negligence on the part of the manufacturer or the seller.

Much of the argument we shall make concerning the process of change in industrial and automobile accidents could also be applied to products liability, especially insofar as the courts have come to see these injuries as a collective, structural problem rather than as problems of individual carelessness.

passage on the other side. The plaintiff left a "public house" around 8 P.M. one August evening, mounted his horse and, according to a witness, rode violently down the road into the pole. He said he did not see the pole in the twilight, although a witness testified that enough daylight remained to see the obstruction at 100 yards. The plaintiff sued the defendant for negligence in leaving a pole across the road, but a verdict was directed against him. In an opinion affirming the lower court's ruling, Lord Ellenborough wrote:

> A party is not to cast himself upon an obstruction which has been made by the fault of another, and avail himself of it, if he do [sic] not himself use common and ordinary caution to be in the right. . . . One person being in fault will not dispense with another's using ordinary care for himself. Two things must concur to support this action, an obstruction in the road by the fault of the defendant, and no want of ordinary care to avoid it on the part of the plaintiff. (11 East 60, 61)

The contributory negligence rule is a harsh one. In its classic formulation, contributory negligence is a complete bar to recovery, no matter how slight the plaintiff's negligence, and no matter how careless the defendant.

Given the harshness of the rule, it is not surprising to find that exceptions developed. For example, a plaintiff's ordinary negligence will not bar recovery when the defendant has been grossly negligent. Nor will contributory negligence bar recovery when the defendant had the "last clear chance" to avoid the accident. This important exception may be traced back to 1842. A man who owned a donkey had placed it at the side of the road to graze and, to keep it from running away, he had fettered its front feet. The defendant's servant, driving a wagon and horses down the road at a "smartish pace," ran into and over the donkey. The owner sued for the death of his donkey and received the verdict at trial. The defendant moved for a new trial, arguing that the trial judge should have told the jury that the case was governed by the contributory negligence doctrine: The defendant's servant may have been negligent, but so was the plaintiff for leaving his donkey fettered in the road where it might be struck.

It was in this posture that the case, *Davies* v. *Mann*, 10 M. & W. 545 (Exchequer, 1842) came to Westminster. Again, Lord Abinger was there. Here are his comments:

> I am of the opinion that there ought to be no rule in this case [i.e., the verdict should stand]. The defendant has not denied that the ass was lawfully in the highway, and therefore we must assume it to have been lawfully there; but even were it otherwise, it would have made no difference, for as the defendant might, by proper care, have avoided injuring the animal, and did not, he is liable for the consequences of his negligence, though the animal may have been improperly there. (10 M. & W. 545, 548)

Note first that there is an issue in the case as to whether the plaintiff was negligent. If he was not, and this is how Lord Abinger appears to have read the evidence, the case has nothing to do with contributory negligence.[8] If this were

---

8. Note that Abinger's statement does not imply a belief that the plaintiff was not careless. The legality of the donkey's presence is apparently to be presumed by the failure to plead otherwise.

established, everything after the semicolon in Lord Abinger's opinion would be *dictum*, a gratuitous statement of a legal rule that is unnecessary for the decision of the case. This is important because at common law, dicta, unlike the holdings of cases, are not considered to be precedents and so are not treated as *prima facie* binding in future cases.

A second opinion by Baron Parke in *Davies* v. *Mann* is also unclear on the issue of the plaintiff's contributory negligence, but it is even more forceful in arguing that whether or not the plaintiff was negligent he should still recover. Parke wrote, "the negligence which is to preclude a plaintiff from recovering in an action of this nature, must be such as that he could, by ordinary care, have avoided the consequences of the defendant's negligence" (pp. 548–549). Thus, there was born the *last clear chance rule*: Even if the plaintiff is contributorily negligent, if the defendant had the "last clear chance" to avoid the accident, the plaintiff may recover.

Whether the last clear chance doctrine was actually necessary to the holding of *Davies* v. *Mann* soon became irrelevant. In both England and the United States the rule was applied often enough that its legal status was clear. Last clear chance clearly favors negligent plaintiffs, but its boundaries have never been clear. Some of its less avid admirers have given the rule the name "jackass doctrine." The appellation has less to do with its origins than with the inconsistencies and complexities that have come to be associated with it. Dean Prosser comments:

> The last clear chance cases present one of the worst tangles known to the law. In some jurisdictions the application of the rule has been limited to cases where the plaintiff is helpless and the defendant has in fact discovered the situation; in others it is extended to cases where the defendant might have discovered it by the exercise of reasonable care. In still others it is applied to situations where the plaintiff is not helpless at all and continues to be negligent, but is unaware of his danger, while the defendant has discovered it. In still others it is applied to cases where the defendant's antecedent negligence, as in driving a car with defective brakes, has rendered him unable to take advantage of the "last clear chance" he would otherwise have had. . . . (1953, p. 465)

The application of the contributory negligence rule as well as exceptions to it like the last clear chance doctrine requires the unique examination of the events surrounding an accident in order to figure out the causal sequences of who could have done what when. As with workers' compensation, a complex rule encourages litigation. Litigation is further encouraged because the willingness of lawyers to take personal injury cases on a contingent fee basis means that securing counsel is not problematic. Indeed, some personal injury specialists, in violation of the bar's code of ethics, maintain networks of "runners" to steer injury victims to them.

The administrative costs of this system for compensating injured accident victims are substantial. Conard and his colleagues (1965, pp. 60–61), looking at the situation in Michigan in the late 1950s, estimated that less than half of every tort liability dollar paid out reached the pocket of the accident victim. Furthermore, some automobile accident victims receive nothing, for plaintiffs to establish their right to recover must show that defendants are negligent. Not only is this often difficult to do, but some accidents are just that—unavoidable mishaps in which no one is in any meaningful sense at fault. Finally, even when fault can be shown, defendants may be judgment proof. The plaintiff who has the misfortune to be injured by an uninsured, impoverished defendant is often without a remedy.

To cope with the financial consequences of automobile accidents, states have passed "financial responsibility" laws, created "uninsured motorists" funds, or even made insurance compulsory. These laws all increase the likelihood that injured parties will find defendants who are able to pay judgments, but they do not help those involved in accidents where no one is at fault or where they themselves have been negligent. Only those victims who have purchased their own health or accident insurance policies can recover in these situations, and payments under first party insurance are often limited in ways that tort judgments are not.

Strict liability solutions to the problems posed by automobile accident victims were suggested as early as the 1930s when the Columbia Report (Columbia University, 1932) proposed a system modeled on workers' compensation that made the owner of each vehicle strictly liable for harms caused by the vehicle. In order to pay for these injuries, owners, under the proposed plan, were required to carry insurance. Although the Columbia plan was never adopted in any jurisdiction, a somewhat similar scheme was enacted in the Canadian province of Saskatchewan. This plan provides a provincial insurance fund, which is used to compensate all auto accident victims regardless of fault. It is funded by fees all drivers pay at the time they register for their license plates. Rates of payment to injured parties are established, as in workers' compensation plans, by a statutory compensation schedule. In some circumstances, injured parties can sue for additional compensation on the basis of fault if they can prove it.

During the past decade several American states, including Massachusetts, Colorado, Florida, and Michigan, have passed some type of "no fault" insurance law. Most of the American plans have followed, in general outline, the proposal of Professors Robert Keeton and Jeffrey O'Connell (1965) that each motorist insure himself. When an accident occurs, drivers in no fault states are compensated in the first instance by their own insurance companies. As with most other first-party insurance, payment is made regardless of fault. Others, not compelled to have insurance, such as passengers and pedestrians, claim against the insurer of the car they were in or of the one that hit them. In addition, most of the enacted no fault plans allow injured parties to sue for negligence if their injuries exceed some threshold of severity as measured by monetary loss or physical disability. These no fault plans are strict liability with a twist: One is strictly liable to oneself.

As with workers' compensation schemes in their early days, the no fault plans have met with legal challenges. In some states (e.g., Illinois), plans have been found to be unconstitutional. In others (e.g., Massachusetts and Michigan), however, their essential elements have been found constitutional by state supreme courts. Indeed, at one point, it appeared that Congress would pass a federal no fault law, and bills are still being introduced that would make no fault the law of the land. Although in recent years the impetus toward no fault appears to have slowed down, it is still possible that federal action or the action of the several states will, over time, make no fault rather than negligence the dominant rule logic in automobile accident cases.

THE PROCESS OF CHANGE: ORGANIZATION OF ADJUSTMENT

What happened in these areas? Why has our system for compensating job-related injuries changed, and why is our system for compensating those injured in automobile accidents changing? As we shall see, there are substantial similarities in the processes tending toward change in these two areas. Before discussing the similarities, however, we should note one key difference. Under the schemes of workers' compensation someone (the employer) is responsible for injuries to someone else. Under the newer no fault automobile plans, except in the most serious cases, drivers are liable for their own injuries. This difference reflects the reciprocal nature of the risk of automobile accidents and, perhaps, the efficiency of having drivers insure themselves rather than unknown others (Fletcher, 1972). It also, no doubt, reflects the models available at the time problems in these areas were seen as particularly acute.

Our effort to understand these movements from a negligence rule logic to one of strict liability has three aspects. We are concerned with: (1) the changes in the way adjudication was organized as the problem of accidents became widespread; (2) the effects these changes had on the way cases were processed, that is, on the case logics employed; and (3) the impact of these changes on important social actors and their resultant efforts to have legislatures alter the rule logics employed.

The Adjudication of Widespread Trouble

A tort[9] action for negligence requires a fairly detailed analysis of circumstances. In areas like industrial and automobile accidents, a tort action also requires, in theory, a rather difficult decision as to the mental state of the defendant. Leon

---

9. *Tort*, the French word for "wrong," is a legal term that encompasses a wide range of harms that people may inflict on one another through their wrongful behavior. Common torts include harms engendered by negligence, assault, battery, fraud, defamation, and invasion of privacy. An important feature of torts is that they are privately remediable; that is, a victim may sue the tort-feasor (tort doer) for the damages attributable to the tortious behavior.

Green once commented as follows on the physical and resultant legal complexities of driving a car:

> The duties placed by statute and common law upon the operator during any moment of his operation of a motor vehicle can scarcely be catalogued in a dozen pages. Summarized only in part and in the briefest fashion they are the following: The operator must observe the operation of other vehicles, front and rear and to the sides—those he is meeting, those that pass, and those that may cross his path. He must observe road signs, stop signs, cautions, traffic lines, light signals and those of traffic officers. He must observe his speed and he must watch for signals of other motorists and give proper signals himself. He must know the operating mechanisms of his machine, check their operations as he travels, and maintain his rapidly moving and complex machine under control at all times. These and other duties may be required of him every moment of his travel, made specific for the particular situation, and all overtopped by the common law duty to use reasonable care under all circumstances.
>
> Multiply the same duties and hazards by any number of other operators in the immediate vicinity; add the duties and hazards of highway maintenance, passengers, pedestrians, and adjacent landowners, the conduct of any one or more of whom may impose upon all operators in close proximity duties and hazards requiring instant and perhaps unerring judgment and action. Add further the hazards of climatic conditions; the imperfections of the human being in sight, judgment, muscular reaction, health, strength and experience. Bring any combination of these duties and hazards into focus on a collision at high speed at a particular point of time and place. Who can name all the factors involved in causing the collision? Who can know or discover or describe the conduct of the parties involved? Who in retrospect from the tangled fragments of evidence given by the participants or bystanders and those who arrived on the scene at a later time; from marks and measurements, calculations of time and speed, is expert enough to reconstruct the fleeting scene with any assurance of its accuracy. If the picture by some miracle could be truly presented, who could pass a rational judgment in the allocation of responsibility as between the parties on any basis of fault? (1958, pp. 66–68)

Add the basic requirements of care, such refinements as the contributory negligence rule and the assumption of the risk doctrine along with the exceptions these rules engendered and one has a body of law that might well be expected to make all cases somewhat ambiguous. Complex legal rules, in other words, make the outcomes of legal claims uncertain, and outcome uncertainty can encourage litigation.

This is so for several reasons. First, outcome uncertainty means that litigating may be profitable. If the parties, which means, in practice, their lawyers, know exactly how a court will respond to a case, there is little point in spending the money needed to formalize that response. Thus, a pedestrian who was hit by a car while crossing against a red light would be throwing good money after bad if she sued the car's driver for her injuries in a jurisdiction that had held crossing against a light to be contributory negligence as a matter of law. But if the jurisdiction followed the rule of last clear chance, and if it had never been decided whether the doctrine applied when the plaintiff had violated a safety statute, there would be a point to the plaintiff's suit—perhaps hundreds of thousands of dollars. Furthermore, as legal rules grow more complex, the number of factual issues whose resolution is relevant to legal rights tends to increase. Thus, if the last clear chance doctrine applied even when the plaintiff had crossed against a light, there might be a close factual question as to whether the defendant in fact had a clear chance to stop. Without the last clear chance exception, or if the exception did not apply in "red light" cases, the factual question—here one open to jury resolution—would never arise.

Second, ambiguous statutes may give people conflicting senses of entitlement, and this rights consciousness may fuel litigation. In a jurisdiction where crossing against a red light abrogates a defendant's last clear chance obligations, a pedestrian who learns of this from a lawyer might feel that his own stupidity in crossing against the light extinguished any right he had to claim compensation from the driver and so would not feel impelled to press the matter. In a jurisdiction where last clear chance applied despite a plaintiff's statutory negligence, a defendant told of this fact by his lawyer and knowing that attentive driving would have avoided the accident might blame himself for what had happened and not resist the plaintiff's demands, and, if he was insured, the insurance company would certainly want to settle early if it were sure it would lose at trial. But if the law were ambiguous, natural tendencies to blame the environment (in this case another person) for one's failings might lead each party and their attorneys to place the bulk of the blame on the other, and so dispute the matter with the special intensity displayed by those who are convinced they are in the right.

Finally, uncertainty means there is no such thing as a worthless claim. Every legal claim has a chance of prevailing however slight, and in the personal injury area if a claim does prevail, however poor its initial prospects, damages may be substantial. This means that claims have both a risk value and a nuisance value. The risk value is the amount likely to be recovered discounted by the probability of recovery. Thus, the risk value of a $100,000 claim with a 10 percent chance of prevailing is $10,000. The nuisance value is the cost to the defendant of establishing that the plaintiff's claim has no legal basis. Thus, a $100,000 claim with no chance of prevailing may have a nuisance value of $5,000 if that is what it will cost the defendant to prove the claim is groundless. When legal claims have value, they are likely to be made even if the prospects of victory in litigation are low because, as we shall show in Chapter 6, defendants have substantial incentives to settle. Legal uncertainty can increase the risk value of tenuous claims and increase the investment that must be made in their defense, thus increasing their settlement value. So long as the costs of making a claim are sufficiently modest, as they are when lawyers take cases on a contingent fee, people have substantial incentives to sue for possibly compensable injuries.

But not all or even the bulk of the increase in work injury or auto accident litigation can be attributed to increased legal complexity. In both these areas the primary force making for increasing resort to the judicial process was the increasing number of injuries. More and faster cars and more exposure to industrial machinery produced more injuries. Thus, legal complexity encouraged a higher percentage of claims on an ever-expanding base. As the number of accidents increased and as the incidence of plausible claims rose, the way cases were handled began to change.

A person with an unsatisfied claim of legal entitlement will, if what is at stake is substantial, seek the assistance of a lawyer. The lawyer may convince her that her claim is baseless, arrange a settlement without filing suit, or take the case to litigation. When a type of dispute is not widespread, lawyers are more likely to see cases as unique, each requiring an examination of its merits and a decision about whether to proceed toward a settlement or trial. However, when types of disputes become common, specialities arise and disputes of that type gravitate toward those who routinely handle such claims. This is what happened as first industrial accidents and then motor vehicle accidents became more common. The routine processing of cases which is often a concomitant feature of specialization has, as we have seen, important implications for case logics. Ultimately, as we shall see, rule logics may also be affected.

The Plaintiff's Counsel. Over the years personal injury litigation has been a substantial source of income for a significant portion of the bar. Indeed, personal injury litigation along with divorce, criminal defense, and probate-related work has been the mainstay for those lawyers whose clients are primarily individuals rather than organizations. Lawyers who specialize in plaintiff's personal injury litigation are, within the organized bar, something of a "status group." They coordinate their activities through the American Trial Lawyer's Association, the nation's second largest (after the American Bar Association) private bar association, and lobby effectively for matters they believe to be in their interest and in the interests of their clients. Typically, these plaintiffs' lawyers work on a contingent fee basis, which means that they get nothing unless the plaintiff recovers something. If there is a recovery they usually get between 25 and 50 percent of the recovery, depending on state law and at what stage the case is resolved, plus any litigation expenses they may have paid on the client's behalf.

The contingent fee as a method of payment has much to recommend it. It allows middle- and lower-class clients to have the benefit of counsel in situations where they otherwise might not be able to afford to pursue their claims in court. This can be especially important for people who are injured in accidents since they may incur substantial medical expenses at a time they are unable to work. Furthermore, lawyers working on a contingent fee basis often advance litigation expenses to their clients. These can be substantial, running into the thousands of dollars. Although the client remains, in principle, liable to the lawyer for these expenses, lawyers often require no more than a nominal contribution where there is no recovery. The lawyers know their clients are unlikely to be able to bear the burden of litigation costs on top of their medical expenses, and it is unseemly as well as, should the word get around, bad business to sue a client over such matters.

The contingent fee also has its unfortunate effects. As Douglas Rosenthal (1974) has shown, it is the source of an inescapable conflict of interest between lawyer and client. Since the lawyer gets paid only when he wins, there can be considerable pressure to take a settlement rather than risk a trial. This is particularly true of those less serious cases that are not going to result in large verdicts in any event. In dealing with such cases, the profit-maximizing lawyer benefits from quick turnover. Even so, clients rarely lose by taking smaller cases to lawyers since, as Ross (1970) discovered, once a case gets to a lawyer, insurance adjusters will usually up the last offer they made when the client was unrepresented by at least enough to pay the lawyer's fee. This is because when a lawyer enters a case, both the nuisance value and the risk value of the case are raised, and insurance companies know that it is almost impossible for a lawyer to persuade a client to settle for less than the client would have received without representation.

The potential for a conflict of interest between the lawyer and client is most serious when a quick settlement is available in a case that might yield a more substantial sum if fully litigated. Although the client's recovery may be considerably more if the case goes to trial, counsel's return, at least on an hourly basis, is likely to be substantially greater if there is a quick settlement. For example, assume a lawyer can settle a case for $10,000 after 10 hours of research and negotiations. If the lawyer charges a relatively modest 25 percent contingent fee, he will have received $2,500 or $250 per hour while the client will get $7,500. If, on the other hand, the lawyer puts in 100 hours and settles on the eve of the trial for $25,000, the lawyer's return, assuming he takes a hefty 50 percent of the recovery, will be $12,500. Yet this is only $125 per hour or half his hourly return to a quick settlement. The client will also receive $12,500 which is $5,000 more than he would have received following 10 hours of negotiation. If, as might well be the case, the lawyer's fee was 33⅓ percent in both instances, these discrepancies would be substantially greater.

Many lawyers who handle personal injury cases as part of a general private practice barely eke out a living, but others who specialize in this area are among their profession's highest paid practitioners, some earning substantially more than most senior partners at major Wall Street law firms. Indeed, there is so much money involved in personal injury practice that the search for potential plaintiffs has given rise to various kinds of professional deviance. Some rules of professional conduct that are routinely circumvented, such as proscriptions on referral fees, may not be in the public interest. At the other extreme, deviations such as "ambulance chasing" may degenerate into criminally creating cases out of "whole cloth," that is, out of the perjured testimony of scheming plaintiffs and the uncritical prognoses of dishonest physicians. Given our concern in this chapter with changing rule logics, this is not the place to discuss issues relating to the structure and ethics of the legal profession. But when we examine personal injury compensation as a social problem, the reader should be aware that for a portion of the bar, particularly those with a more elite corporate practice, part of the problem is the effect that fault-based compensation schemes and the associated system of contingent fees have on the structure of their profession and the repute in which it is held.

The Defense. Specialization in personal injury work is not limited to plaintiffs' attorneys. There are lawyers and firms that handle only defense litigation as well as nonlawyer agents who deal with unrepresented claimants and plaintiffs' attorneys in cases that are not yet clearly headed to trial. These agents, whose practices are described in this subsection, are insurance adjusters.

Insurance as a widespread phenomenon is a central social invention of the past century. In fact, it is difficult to imagine a more important social invention unless it is the modern corporation. Death, disease, theft, accident, fire, natural disaster; all these events are in the aggregate sufficiently predictable as to allow reliable actuarial calculations.

Automobile insurance policies are sold by insurance companies to individuals or to groups of individuals on a pooled risk basis. They may protect against theft, the risk of collision, and the risk that a person will be injured in an accident. Their primary protection, however, and the reason insurance coverage is frequently mandated by law, is against the risk that one person will be liable to another for injuries due to negligence. Such coverage is widespread. According to Ross (1970), between 70 and 90 percent of all drivers have some form of liability insurance.

When an insured motorist is involved in an accident, his insurance company investigates the accident, and if the driver has potential liability, the company handles his defense. Both the task of determining what happened and the responsibility for settling claims that others might bring against the motorist are initially delegated to an insurance adjuster.

Adjusters when faced with a plausible claim are, like plaintiffs' lawyers, not averse to settlement. Indeed, for several reasons they are under considerable pressure to settle. First, if a case can be settled before the plaintiff retains a lawyer, the final settlement is likely to be lower by at least the amount of the attorney's fees and typically by more than that. Second, the more a file is handled, the more expense the insurance company incurs. Third, when claims are made, the companies set up "reserves" to pay for potential settlements or judgments. If a case is settled quickly, the money held in reserve can be invested in riskier but more lucrative enterprises than the reserve procedure allows. In the area of automobile insurance the profit margin for insurance companies comes largely from the interest earned from the investment of premiums rather than from the premiums themselves. Fourth, the fear exists that if a case continues, the unscrupulous claimant will "pad" the damages. Fifth, a settlement can be conditioned on an agreement not to pursue other legal remedies. This at once forecloses the nuisance value and risk value of the claim. Finally, and most importantly, the case loads that adjusters must cope with pressure them toward early settlements. This is not only because of the need to maintain a manageable load, but also because within the insurance company's bureaucracy moving cases is desirable for the preceding reasons, and the ability to move cases is a convenient way of measuring adjuster performance.

Adjuster work, therefore, is judged on the basis of closing files. As one automobile adjuster put it, "Closing files, two words, describes our job in the ultimate—closing files'' (Ross, 1970, p. 61). Making some payment is often, perhaps usually, preferable to denying a claim, particularly from the viewpoint of an adjuster who may have to account for cases that remain open for an exceptionally long time but will not raise any supervisory eyebrows with a string of small settlements. All this suggests that a high percentage of claimants will be paid something. The data on settlement patterns in automobile accident cases indicate that this in fact occurs.

The earliest study in this area, the Columbia Report (Columbia University, 1932), found that some payment was made in 87 percent of the serious cases when there was tort liability insurance. Roughly similar figures have been produced by James and Law (1952, 95 percent in the case of substantial injuries) and Rosenberg and Sovern (1959, 84 percent). H. Laurence Ross, in *Settled Out of Court*, the most thorough study of the settlement process to date, found recovery rates of 81 percent in the more serious cases. These recovery rates exist although liability rules require negligence on the part of the insured driver and freedom from negligence on the part of the claimant.

Ross also presents figures for less serious injuries. He reports that even when injuries are minor or unknown, the claimant is paid 63 percent of the time. Indeed, people who might never have made a claim are sometimes compensated, for as Ross tells us, it is usually the claims adjuster who gets in touch with the potential claimant, not the other way round:

> The claim is rather initiated by the insured, who is required by the conditions of his insurance policy to notify the company if he has an accident. The company could perhaps merely note the incident in its records and wait for the claimant to bring his demands, on the theory that sleeping dogs may lie. In the companies studied, however, all people reported as involved in the accident were treated as potential claimants, and were approached by an adjuster as quickly as possible. Among the reasons for this procedure are: (1) the assumption on the part of the insurance company that most victims do in fact make claims, that delay in approaching the victims increases the likelihood that the claimants will have retained attorneys, and that represented claims are more expensive to settle; and (2) the need for investigation of the claim while physical evidence is fresh and the memories of witnesses are relatively clear. (Ross, 1970, p. 67)

Once an insurance company becomes aware of a case, the probability that a potential claimant will recover something is a good deal higher than what one knowing only the formal tort rules of recovery would expect. Recall that Ross found recovery rates of between 63 and 81 percent depending on the seriousness of the injury.

> For comparison, consider that if the insureds were negligent, strictly speaking, in as many as three quarters of all reported accidents, and if the claimants were free of significant [contributory] negligence in half of these, one would expect liability payments to be justified in only about 38 percent of all claims. (Ross, 1970, p. 200)

Although Ross's estimate of contributory negligence rates is probably high because passengers in vehicles are unlikely to be at fault, his basic point is sound.

Recovery rates generated by the institutional arrangements that insurance companies have made for dealing with potential claimants are substantially higher than what one would expect from a strictly accurate application of the legal liability rules. But this is only part of the picture. Many of those who are seriously injured in auto accidents recover nothing. In part this is because some people have no claim under the tort law—as, for example, the drunk who goes off the road into a tree—and in part it is because those at fault in accidents may not be identified or, if they are, they may have no insurance or other resources to pay for the damage they caused. More importantly, as Conard and his coauthors (1964) report, when liability claims are settled, the settlements tend to overcompensate the slightly injured but undercompensate, often substantially, the more seriously hurt.

Compromise processes tend to favor those whose claims are small or have only nuisance values because in less serious accidents the value of closing files leads to settlement offers that are small but generous given the likely legal liability. When injuries are severe and claims are large, insurance policy limits may be exceeded, and even where they are not, cases are no longer routine. An insurance company will often find it cheaper to close a file than to bargain a $300 claim down to $200. The situation is different when the opposing offers are at $300,000 and $200,000. Moreover, seriously injured accident victims may be willing to accept considerably less than the full value of their claims. Not only may the seriously injured be in desperate need of cash to pay medical expenses and make up for lost wages, but their refusing to settle can result in substantial litigation costs, and the liability situation may be such that litigation results in no recovery whatever. In addition, there is evidence in the work of Rosenthal (1974) that the conflict of interest that the contingent fee engenders will lead some lawyers to press their clients to settle for less than the full value of their claims.[10]

As a consequence of the incentives that both plaintiffs and defendants have to settle, very few cases ever go to trial. The best estimates are that between 2 and 4 percent of all cases end with judicial judgments (Conard et al., 1964; Department of Transportation, 1971). In the Conard study the authors looked at 86,000 persons injured in automobile accidents in Michigan in 1958. Of the 12,100 claims handled by lawyers, in only about 4,000 was a suit ever filed (1964, p. 154). Of these, fewer than 15 percent went to trial, and only 2 percent reached an appellate court (1964, p. 241). The authors comment:

> The law of torts as it is written in books, debated in law review articles, and taught in law schools, is based on those cases which are ''appealed.'' These represent only 2 percent of all the cases on which suit is filed, and about one-tenth of one percent

---

10. However, recent research by Kritzer et al. (1985) suggests that when large sums of money (more than $6,000) are at stake contingent fee lawyers put in at least as much time as their hourly-fee counterparts would in similar litigation. This calls Rosenthal's conflict of interest hypothesis into question insofar as it applies to serious personal injury litigation.

of the total number of persons suffering economic loss in personal injury automobile accidents. What a small view of what a large universe! (1964, p. 242)

To summarize, as the injuries attributable to auto accidents increased, organized ways of handling them developed. Two actors emerged, the plaintiff's lawyer and the claims adjuster, who both found themselves in a position where settlement was preferable to litigation and speedy processing was a virtue. The result was that as automobile accident cases proliferated, the case logic for handling them was transformed.

The Case Logic of Settlement

Judging from the law as it appears in that small percentage of cases subjected to appellate review, one might think that negligence claims require decision makers to apply a deep case logic. *Fact finders must determine whether conduct was unreasonably risky given those adverse consequences that the actor might reasonably have foreseen.* Judges must decide whether in certain situations behavior is so obviously reasonable or unreasonable that as a matter of law it cannot or must constitute negligence.

Since almost all human activities carry with them some small risk of harm, to adjudicate negligence we must look closely at each situation. How is one to decide that a certain line of conduct is sufficiently risky so as to constitute negligence? It is partly a matter of the likelihood that some harm will stem from the behavior, but only partly. The probable seriousness of the injuries that might occur is also relevant. The chance of being hit by a train at a crossing is small, but the seriousness of potential injury is so great that a railroad may be negligent in maintaining an unguarded crossing.

In addition, the utility of the line of conduct in question and the costs of reducing the probability of injury must be balanced. A man may be justified in dashing before an advancing train to save his child, but he would be a negligent fool if he did so to save his hat. On the other hand, the Supreme Court's attempt to impose on drivers the duty to stop their cars and get out and look when they came to railroad crossings did not establish an enduring precedent. Even assuming that this would have reduced the accident rate, the likely savings of life and limb would not have justified the inconvenience the rule would have caused.[11]

Professor Prosser summarizes:

---

11. Of course, the rule would not in fact have inconvenienced anyone, for drivers were not likely to stop their cars and get out to look at each railroad crossing simply because a court said that this behavior was a condition precedent to their or their estate's recovering damages should they happen to be hit by a train. The analysis of the costs and probability of complying with the rule is, nevertheless, the type of analysis a court should go through in determining whether the failure to stop and look at each crossing is so unreasonable as to constitute negligence or, in this example, contributory negligence.

It is fundamental that the standard of conduct which is the basis of the law of negligence is determined by balancing the risk, in the light of the social value of the interest threatened, and the probability and extent of the harm, against the value of the interest which the actor is seeking to protect, and the expedience of the course pursued. For this reason, it is seldom possible to reduce negligence to any definite rules; it is "relative to the need and the occasion," and conduct which would be proper under some circumstances becomes negligence under others. (1971, p. 149)

Thus, not only does negligence as it appears in the case law require a detailed examination of circumstances, it also requires a deep examination of the actor's understanding of those circumstances and an assessment of the reasonableness of this understanding.

The relativeness of negligence does not mean there are no standards. The fact that a person did not stop and think or that he is clumsy will be of no avail when haste or clumsiness cause another person harm. Nor are such standards unreasonable. Even if it were not nearly impossible to prove basic clumsiness, the rest of us would have a right to expect more of a man who is congenitally careless than the assurance that he did the best he knew how.[12] As Justice Holmes noted:

If, for instance, a man is born hasty and awkward, is always having accidents and hurting himself or his neighbors, no doubt his congenital defects will be allowed for in the courts of Heaven, but his slips are no less troublesome to his neighbors than if they sprang from guilty neglect. His neighbors accordingly require him, at his proper peril, to come up to their standard, and the courts which they establish decline to take his personal equation into account. (Holmes, 1881, p. 108)

But even if the standard to which the law of negligence holds people is not completely subjective, there remains the question of what a reasonable person could have foreseen or known about a situation. This depends less on general considerations than on the particular circumstance in which the actor found himself. An objective and normalized standard is rarely adequate.

The difficulty of the judgmental task is obvious. Thus, it should not be surprising that even as a matter of law, rules developed to simplify decision making by allowing a less penetrating inquiry than the full, formal, deep case logic of negligence seems to require. These are evidentiary rules of correspondence. They specify that certain more easily ascertainable behavior is sufficient to prove, or even constitutes, actionable negligence. Foremost among these rules are *per se* negligence and *res ipsa loquitur*.

Per Se Rules. Most American jurisdictions hold that a violation of a statute that exists in part to promote safety is negligence *per se*; that is, for the plaintiff to

---

12. However, when there are more objectively ascertainable causes of bad judgment or clumsy behavior such as extreme youth or age or physical disability and the like the law may sometimes take them into account in judging the reasonableness of the actor's actions. Perhaps this is because the claimed disability may be reliably established and is not potentially open to any tort-feasor. In addition, such conditions are usually visible to those who interact with the individual and may be taken into account by them.

recover he needs to show no carelessness on the part of the defendant other than the violation of the statute. For example, if a defendant did not contest the plaintiff's allegation that he lost control of his car because he was speeding, the trial judge would ordinarily instruct the jury that the driver was, as a matter of law, negligent. If the defendant claimed he was traveling within the speed limit, the jury would be instructed to determine whether the defendant was in fact speeding, and if they so determined to find him negligent. Violating a speed limit is ordinarily conclusive on the issue of negligence.[13]

Per se rules by focusing on one aspect of an event assimilate dissimilar circumstances to one type. They reduce complexity by making only one thing matter, and in the process eliminate unique circumstantial excuses that might otherwise allow the defendant to escape liability. For example, the excuse that the defendant could not know of the danger he was creating is unavailing, because, regardless of the facts, he is charged with knowing that excessive speed may create danger (see, e.g., *Frazier* v. *Pokorny*, 359 P. 2d 324 Wyo., 1960). Courts have similarly rejected any excuses based on the unforeseeability of potential injury.

Res Ipsa Loquitur. A second presumption used to simplify cases goes by the name *res ipsa loquitur*, a Latin phrase roughly meaning: the thing speaks for itself. It helps circumvent difficulties that might arise in showing that negligence caused an injury.

By and large negligence is not presumed. The fact that there is a dead man on a highway or even the fact that the defendant admits that his car struck the man does not mean that the death was due to negligence. If all the plaintiff's estate could show was that the victim died after being struck by the defendant's car, the estate's negligence claim would be dismissed. They must show that the striking was not only tragic but that it was in some sense wrongful. This might be done by showing that the defendant was drunk, or was speeding or kissing his girlfriend or engaging in some other careless behavior at the time of the accident. Thus, the conjunction of an accident and the defendant's involvement is insufficient to prove negligence because this conjunction is equally consistent with a defendant's faultless behavior. For example, the victim in our case may have rushed out from between two parked cars or a manufacturing defect may have led to a sudden brake failure that in turn caused the accident.

This does not, however, mean that negligence can only be proved by direct

---

13. It should be noted, however, that to dispose of the issue of negligence is not to decide that the plaintiff should prevail. Still open are questions of contributory negligence, assumption of risk, and proof of some legally sufficient causal relationship between the statutory violation and the injury. Thus, the interesting argument that the speeding of a bus brought it to a certain point on the road just in time to have a tree fall on it, would not support a plaintiff's judgment even if the analysis is accurate. Here the accident was not of a type that laws against speeding were designed to prevent [see Hart & Honore, 1959, pp. 111–112, *Horton* v. *Greyhound Corp.*, 128 S.E. 2d 776, 241 S.C. 430 (1962)]. In addition, the fact that a defendant is found to have not violated a safety standard does not mean that he was not negligent.

evidence, that is, by testimony from someone who saw the defendant acting carelessly. Negligence is inferable from circumstances. In the case we posit, testimony that the defendant 20 minutes before the accident staggered out of a tavern into his car or the fact that the skid marks he laid down indicated that when he began to brake he was going 15 miles over the speed limit would probably be enough to bridge the gap between tragic involvement and negligent responsibility.

Res ipsa loquitur is a phrase used to describe those situations in which the circumstances of an accident are sufficient to establish both negligence and the defendant's responsibility. A plaintiff who can argue *res ipsa loquitur* will not necessarily win the case, but he will be able to get to the jury. This means that the circumstances of the accident are sufficiently suggestive of the defendant's negligence that it would not be unreasonable for the jury to return a plaintiff's verdict even if the plaintiff's only evidence is a description of the untoward event.

In the case from which *res ipsa loquitur* originated, a barrel fell from a window of the defendant's second story business establishment and injured the plaintiff. The plaintiff could only show how the injury occurred. He had no other information tending to show that the barrel was carelessly stacked or why it had fallen. The English high court held that the description of the accident alone was sufficient to support a verdict. The justices reasoned that barrels will almost never fall from upstairs windows unless they have been carelessly stacked or handled. They further noted that the defendant had control of the premises from which the barrel fell and so, if he had not himself been negligent, he was almost certainly vicariously liable for whoever had engaged in the careless behavior. Typical situations where the principle of *res ipsa loquitur* has been applied over the years are falling elevators, explosions of boilers, defective equipment, tainted food, and the more obvious forms of medical malpractice such as leaving surgical sponges in patients.

Case Logic Before Trial. These simplifying procedures often help the plaintiff's cause, but they do not relieve him of his basic obligation to show the defendant's negligence. Both appellate opinions and jury trials are normally replete with details about the circumstances of accidents. This might suggest that accident victims must muster detailed proof in order to recover. We must remember, however, that jury trials and cases that go to appeal represent a very small proportion of all accident cases. What about those settled before trial? How do plaintiffs' attorneys and adjusters assess these cases?

We should not fall into the overstatement that insurance companies pay all comers. They do not. Nor should we conclude that they pay randomly. The law casts a shadow (Lempert, 1978, p. 99; Mnookin & Kornhauser, 1979). Ross (1970) in his study of automobile accident cases compared the settlement percentage in cases where the claims adjuster's initial judgment was that the insured was responsible for the accident with the settlement percentage in cases where the adjuster concluded that the insured was not responsible. When the insured was deemed responsible, payment was made in 91 percent of the cases. When the adjuster thought the insured was not responsible, only 34 percent of the cases were paid. The question is "How do insurance adjusters (and plaintiff's counsel) decide who is responsible?"

Ross concludes that adjusters decide cases in a mechanical way. In terms of our evidence dimensions, they typify immediate circumstances and normalize meaning:

> The formal law of negligence liability, as stated in casebooks from the opinions of appellate courts . . . deals with violation of a duty of care owed by the insured to the claimant and is based on a very complex and perplexing model of the "reasonable man," in this case the reasonable driver. . . . It is not with this intellectual model, however, that claims men must deal. In their day-to-day work, the concern with liability is reduced to the question of whether either or both parties violated the rules of the road as expressed in common traffic laws. Taking the doctrine of negligence *per se* to an extreme doubtless unforeseen by the makers of the formal law, adjusters tend to define a claim as one of liability or of no liability depending only on whether a rule was violated, regardless of intention, knowledge, necessity, and other such qualifications that might receive sympathetic attention even from a traffic court judge. (Ross, 1970, p. 98)

It appears that the adjusters have also developed their own version of *res ipsa loquitur* which they use in a similar way. For example, if the insured were emerging from a street governed by a stop sign, this alone would justify payment to the claimant. It would do so regardless of whether the sign was seen, whether there was good reason for not seeing the sign, or whether the insured had in fact stopped at the sign before proceeding. "In short, in the ordinary case the physical facts of the accident are normally sufficient to allocate liability between the drivers" (Ross, 1970, p. 99).

Ross quotes an adjuster discussing the importance of the accident configuration:

> You can almost tell when you get the report of the accident whether or not your insured is responsible, simply on how the accident happened. Right off the bat you know which way you're going to go. . . . And if your insured admits making a left turn in front of somebody, or admits hitting somebody in the rear end, you know right away that he was negligent. (1970, p. 99)

Rear-enders, the most common form of minor accidents, are good examples of the presumptions made by adjusters. In one case Ross reports a discussion between an adjuster and his supervisor about a case where the claimant's demands seemed excessive. The adjuster asks, "Want me to tell the [attorney] to go to Hell?" meaning sue to recover. The supervisor replied, "No, it's for settlement. We rear-ended him" (1970, p. 174). The technique is clearly one of shallow adjudication. This type of typification of circumstance does a fairly poor job of determining what the insured driver could have done, but adjusters are unable or unwilling to invest effort in deeper adjudications.

The use of a shallow case logic is not surprising when we consider the situation of the adjuster. He is confronted by high case loads and the task of deciding numerous cases of a similar nature. His situation is like that of the public defender discussed in the last chapter. It is also similar to the way workers' compensation cases are handled by some agencies. Consider Philippe Nonet's description of case processing by the California Industrial Accident Commission:

> Routines are needed to organize the processing and disposition of the masses of cases that pass through the IAC. The agency has little time for analyzing issues, debating procedural strategy, or condoning a subtle casuistry.[14] Cases must be fitted into readily identifiable categories, the path to be followed must be quickly pointed, alternative outcomes must be easily specified and promptly weighed. . . . In a couple of minutes before the hearing, a referee can, by a glance at the case file, get an idea of the story, of the issues that will be raised, and of what he is going to hear in the next hour. . . . Routine has similarly affected the quality of the justifications the IAC offers in its decisions. The "findings of facts and conclusions of law" the agency is required to produce in support of its awards have often become standardized formulas, devoid of any reference to the concrete issues of the case. (Nonet, 1969, pp. 224–227)

Max Weber believed that the structure of Western law was moving toward a type of formal rationality characterized by "the logical analysis of meaning." This calls for deep adjudication to determine how legal rules apply to actions in the specific circumstances of a case. Weber contrasted this "logically formal rationality" with another type of formal rationality, "extrinsic rationality," or the rationality of "tags and forms." Procedures that are rational in this sense rely on typified and routinized "facts" to decide the meaning of acts. Weber thought that this type of rationality was less suited to modern society than were logically formal procedures. But Weber, also a preeminent student of bureaucracy, did not reckon with the consequences of adjudicative bureaucratization.

As Lawrence Friedman argues, extrinsic rationality has come to predominate:

> But if we look at the legal system as a whole, we get a quite different picture. We see that the area of regulation is growing as government grows. Government regulation, however, quite typically adopts as one method of controlling conduct the use of external signs which permit legalism (mechanistic logic) in making decisions. The answer, then, to our question of the decline of legalism is that it has not declined at all; it has merely moved from courts to other agencies. Mechanistic decision making is efficient decision making. (1966, p. 20)

---

14. "Casuistry" is an interesting word. It has two meanings in the dictionary. The first meaning is "a method or doctrine dealing with the cases of conscience and the resolution of questions of right or wrong in conduct." The agency has no time to deal with subtle casuistry. The second meaning, however, is more pejorative; it is "the false application of principles especially with regard to morals or law." Max Weber used the word in this sense in describing the formalism used by agencies, "In so far as the absolute formalism of classification according to 'sense data characteristics' prevails, it exhausts itself in casuistry" (Weber, 1967, p. 64).

In general, officials in bureaucratic organizations find it convenient to fall back on rules of thumb and mechanistic precedent that embody shallow logics. This allows them to process their dockets quickly and diminishes the uncertainty surrounding decisions (March & Simon, 1958; Cyert & March, 1963). Official needs of this sort stand against the formal ideal of an extended legal and logical analysis of the content of action, and for a type of bureaucratic law that weighs costs against benefits in the interests of an efficient administrative policy (Balbus, 1973, pp. 15–25; Unger, 1976, p. 24). Where cases must be closed, and where the adjudicator, whether she be a public defender, a referee, or a claims adjuster, hears case after case of a similar nature the pressure is clearly toward a "mechanistic logic," a logic of forms and tags.

Abetting this tendency in the case of the adjusters is the relative powerlessness of their "clients." We have already described the relative powerlessness of the criminal defendant vis-à-vis the public defender. The insured is in much the same position vis-à-vis the adjuster. Most insurance policies provide that the insurance company will defend actions against the insured and require the insured to promise that he will cooperate with the company's efforts to "defend" him. Cooperation includes not refusing offers of settlement. A full refusal of cooperation is grounds for cancellation of the insurance, although this is apparently rare. But then, the insured rarely fails to cooperate. After the accident, he is relatively indifferent as to what is done so long as any settlement is within the policy limits, for it is not his money that is at stake.

In summary, it appears that when cases of a particular type become common (which occurs when an underlying social problem becomes widespread) the adjudication and settlement of such disputes is likely to involve a group of people who are or become specialists in dealing with such matters. So long as the cases are numerous and their commonalities obvious,[15] those responsible for resolving them are likely to organize their work in some bureaucratic fashion, and, in doing so, they are very likely to move to a method of processing cases that relies on a shallow case logic.

Much of the evidence needed to make a full negligence analysis in settling accident claims is either not collected or not used. When we look at the pattern of aggregate outcomes in claims arising out of accidents involving insured drivers or the way that lawyers and adjusters use evidence to resolve individual cases,

---

15. One feature of expertise and the experience that comes with specializaion is the ability to perceive regularity in what a naïve observer might see as a disparate body of information. Thus, there may be a "chicken and egg" problem and a feedback effect with respect to the development of organizational patterns to deal with the kinds of cases we are discussing. Routinized processing may seem feasible in the first instance because cases seem similar, but similarities may become more obvious to those involved as they process more cases in a routinized fashion. It appears to us that in the kinds of cases we are discussing it does not take great training to spot relevant similarities. The kinds of categories that public defenders and insurance adjusters use seem to be commonsense typifications of moral norms and the norms of the legal system. It is always possible, however, that this appearance is an artifact of the categories available to the sociological observers who have reported on these matters.

we see the effects of a case logic that resembles strict liability. The formal rule logic, however, remains one of negligence liability and in a minority of cases it is applied. But the dominant pattern means that the ultimate move to some type of strict liability rule logic to resolve auto accident cases is not as extreme as one would surmise from reviewing the decisions that are published by appellate courts and made the basis of law school instruction.

The examples indicate an important relationship between rule logics and case logics. Through differential attention to particular kinds of evidence, rule logics can be made to shade into one another. Much legal change occurs not in the sudden announcement of a new rule, but in the growth of typifications and slow changes in the ways in which actual cases are decided.

It might be possible to continue indefinitely a state of affairs in which adjusters and lawyers generally use a shallow logic while maintaining the façade of a negligence system.[16] Indeed, there may, especially in the area of criminal justice, be good reason to preserve the possibility that cases will be adjudicated by some deeper logic where facts are truly special or where the litigants insist on it. Inconsistencies between the way most cases are in fact decided and the legal norms that in theory apply does not guarantee that rule logics over time will come to mimic case logics by calling for shallower analyses. Fundamental change in our methods for compensating job-related injuries and automobile accident victims has depended on legislative action. Thus, to understand the change in rule logics, at least as it has occurred in the United States, we must look not only at how individual cases were decided but also at actors in the legislative arena.

FROM NEGLIGENCE TO STRICT LIABILITY: THE POLITICS OF LEGISLATIVE CHANGE

Laws are ideal in two senses of the term. First, they are ideas, or at least begin as ideas, about how to organize particular aspects of social life. Second, they are goals. They specify and are designed to bring about desired states of affairs. One can ask of any law where did the underlying idea originate and why was the state of affairs the law aimed at thought desirable? One can also ask how the law came to be enacted.

This last question takes us out of the realm of ideas into the world of politics. One person's ideal is another's nightmare. Laws often change prior distributions of resources and entitlements. When this is likely, those who believe they will

---

16. Indeed, the courts themselves have done something like this under a statute called the Federal Employers Liability Act (FELA). The act was passed to protect railroad workers in the early days of industrial injury reform, but it did not establish a strict liability standard. Rather, it maintained a negligence standard with many common law defenses stripped from the defendant. The courts, however, have taken a very liberal view of the statute, and most observers would agree that concepts of negligence have had very little to do with the litigation of cases under the FELA.

benefit from the change are likely supporters of the law, and those who fear they will be disadvantaged are likely opponents. The effectiveness of these groups depends on their members' social positions, their access to legislators, and the resources they can bring to bear on the issue. When each side has substantial resources compromise is likely. We have a good clue to the likelihood that some bill will pass and the form it will take if we can identify which special interests are bringing what messages to which legislative offices.

Although the "rough and tumble" of politics often has much more to do with interests than ideas, the two cannot be clearly separated. Ideas may be generated by particular interest groups that then work to establish the ideas as goals. This is most evident in instances where there is the least conflict, that is, in what we might call "private legislation."

If we examined those bills that are enacted, we would find that many of them deal with the relatively narrow interests of one or a small number of persons or organizations. The best examples are probably corporate charters that at one time had to be issued by legislatures, and during some periods, as Willard Hurst (1956) tells us, constituted a large proportion of enacted legislation. No one seeking a charter in the nineteenth century could claim to have invented the idea of the corporation, but it was the charter seekers' idea that the organizations they represented should be chartered and that to grant such charters was in the public interest. The legislatures went along with whichever member had been persuaded to introduce the bill because the matter—the idea that the organization in question should be incorporated and the goals therein implicit—was regarded as noncontroversial and routine. When, however, an organization tried to secure an unusual privilege in its charter, the matter might prove controversial in the legislature, and if the applicant achieved his goals there, the bill might be vetoed by the governor (Hurst, 1956, p. 16).

In the United States today private bills continue to be enacted. At the federal level they are common with regard to matters of immigration and citizenship. Private legislation may also take the form of narrowly drawn provisions in bills of general relevance. Thus, a tax bill may contain a provision that an arcane method of accounting shall be allowed companies who are depreciating certain kinds of equipment in certain industries. Upon investigation it might turn out that only one company is affected by that provision, a company that has its home office in a district represented by a powerful member of the House Ways and Means Committee, the body that initiates tax legislation.

It is impossible to draw a line between bills that are essentially private and what we might call public legislation. The sociological characteristic of a bill is a function not only of the number of actors affected by the legislation but also of the kind of attention it receives. A bill introduced at the instance of and directly affecting only one actor will, if it attracts general attention because it is seen to raise an issue of principle, lose those qualities that distinguish the enactment of private legislation from the enactment of statutes of more general application and interest.

For present purposes we need not be concerned with boundaries, for we are discussing legislation that was, in the case of workers' compensation, and is, in the case of no fault auto insurance, clearly controversial and affects a multitude of private interests. In the areas with which we are concerned, the wealthiest and best organized interests—industry and the business community in the case of workers' compensation and insurance companies in the case of no fault auto insurance—tended initially to favor the status quo. Since the legislative process tends to favor defenders of the status quo because of the many ways in which bills can be sidetracked, the central event to be explained is why the business community and insurance industry switched sides and supported some type of reform. But we are getting ahead of ourselves. Before the positions of potential defenders of the status quo can be relevant, there must be pressure for reform and an idea as to what shape that reform might take. We shall see that the features leading to workers' compensation and the no fault movement are in many respects similar.

The first step for those seeking legislative change is to redefine what might be considered a personal, occupational, or class problem so that it is seen as a social problem—affecting the well-being of society. In the compensation area, it appears that labor succeeded in convincing many people that the question of compensating injured workers involved not just the issue of fairness to individual workers but the whole problem of poverty in industrialized society. Philippe Nonet (1969, pp. 18–19) quotes the chairman of The California Industrial Accident Commission (IAC), writing in 1914 and 1915:

> Workmen's compensation is only one of the numerous problems causing our present social unrest . . . approximately 40 percent of the poverty is chargeable to work accidents; and when we have poverty, we have crime, insanity, and all other forms of social evils. . . . It is apparent on the face of it that if these injured people, instead of being unable to bear their burden directly, had been compensated at the time of their injury by industrial compensation . . . so that they could have rehabilitated their earning power and thus kept [themselves] from dropping over into the poverty line, that society would have been richer, private property safer, and our taxes much less.

> * * *

> Whenever any considerable portion of the population of any country falls definitely below the poverty line life becomes unsafe, property insecure, and the preservation of social order a matter of pure brute force. There comes to be, first, what we call "unrest," then disturbances, "direct action." . . . As a consequence of unrelieved distress . . . there frequently follows the turning of children loose upon the streets while the mother is earning their keep, or the breaking up of family ties, the putting of children into orphanages or giving them away like surplus puppies or kittens to whoever will take them, all of which experiences are absolutely destructive of the bonds which hold society together. . . .

[C]ompensation "as a system of dealing with the third greatest cause of poverty" was founded on the:

> incontrovertible principle that society has the right to protect itself from those influences which tend to force large numbers of persons below the poverty line, thereby

making them a menace to social order and social safety. This is why society has said to its industries that they must take care of their own killed and wounded. It is in obedience to the first law of nature, the right of self-defense. . . .

When it becomes reasonable to even discuss a problem in the terms used by the chairman of the IAC, tremendous pressures for change are generated. The direction of change is not foreordained, but the described situation is intolerable and legislators are expected to do something.

In the case of auto accidents the problem was defined in somewhat different terms. Undercompensation of the seriously injured and the maldistribution of the insurance premium dollar were seen as serious problems without any pretense that they led to some more fundamental problem such as poverty. The argument is one of efficiency and distributive justice. Perhaps the distributive justice claim, which is implicit in arguments concerning undercompensation, was better able to stand on its own in the auto accident area than in the workers' compensation area because those injured in auto accidents come from all walks of life. Thus, to argue that the injured should be fully compensated regardless of fault is not to argue for the apparent interests of one class—labor—vis-à-vis another class— business. Justice arguments may be more readily accepted when everyone is a potential beneficiary from a more just distribution.

In both the compensation and auto accident areas there was a subsidiary problem that was salient to some people and may have had more influence than popular concerns suggest. Worker injury cases were perceived as dominating the civil docket in the late nineteenth century just as auto accident cases came to be perceived three generations later. The result was delays in processing not only personal injury cases but other civil matters as well. Lawyers are particularly sensitive to crowded dockets; the disproportionate representation of lawyers in legislatures and among lobbyists probably meant that this aspect played more of a role in shaping legislative perceptions of the crisis than it has in the popular mind. Of course, lawyers differed dramatically on the issue of whether a no fault approach to injury compensation was a desirable way of coping with court congestion, and in recent years there has been no more effective lobby against the extension of no fault auto insurance than those lawyers who specialize in plaintiffs' personal injuries.

This brief overview necessarily slights many of the social problems that reformers in the two areas attributed to the existing systems, and it does not describe the dynamics by which people came to view the status quo as problematic and a no fault compensation system as an answer to its deficiencies. Some interesting differences between the two movements may help explain the ultimate triumph of workers' compensation schemes and the current slowdown in the spread of no fault auto insurance.

The movement toward workers' compensation in the United States predates that social invention. Organized labor throughout the nineteenth century fought for more adequate compensation for injured workers. Throughout much of this period the fight was not for a no fault system of compensation but for the legislative or judicial overruling of the harsh common law defenses we have mentioned. Then, in 1887, a system of no fault compensation was instituted in

Germany. The idea soon reached the United States, and organized labor became the prime pressure group lobbying for its implementation. Having succeeded, labor has maintained a special interest in compensation programs and over the years has lobbied for liberalized benefit schedules and similar "improvements." The labor movement has also been instrumental in judicializing the adjudication of claims, trusting the cases that workers' attorneys can make under claims of right more than the paternalistic orientation of those who administered compensation programs during the early years of their existence (Nonet, 1969).

In the area of no fault auto insurance there has been no such monolithic lobby, although in some states some insurance companies have been important proponents of change. Instead, the movement has its roots in legal scholarship and in social science research. Surveys of accident victims played a role in establishing the inadequacies of fault-based compensation. Particularly important was a massive survey of accident victims conducted by Professor Alfred Conard and his colleagues (1964) at the University of Michigan. Professor Conard's basic finding, consistent with prior research, was that 45 percent of those seriously injured in automobile accidents received nothing from automobile liability insurance, and, of those who recovered something, the ones who were least seriously injured tended to be adequately and even overcompensated, while those who were most severely injured received substantially less than the amount needed to make them whole. Conard's findings, based on Michigan victims was confirmed in a nationwide investigation conducted by the Department of Transportation (DOT) and published as a report to Congress and the president in March 1971. The DOT investigators found, for example, that none of those who suffered less than $1,000 in measurable economic loss and received any compensation under the tort system, received less than one-half of their loss, while 87 percent were fully or more than fully compensated. On the other hand, 85 percent of those who suffered over $10,000 in measurable economic loss and recovered something received less than half of their loss.

Thus, survey researchers were instrumental in defining what has come to be viewed as the central problem with fault-based accident insurance. Academics, this time law professors rather than social scientists, have also been instrumental in suggesting a solution. A particularly important book, *Basic Protection for the Traffic Victim* (1965), by Professors Robert Keeton and Jeffrey O'Connell provided the blueprint for the system of no fault insurance adopted by the Massachusetts legislature and helped shape the systems of no fault insurance adopted in other jurisdictions. Moreover, Keeton and O'Connell did not treat their scheme as an academic exercise to be left for further research. Instead, they tried in many ways to encourage legislatures to adopt their proposals. O'Connell has been particularly active over the years, acting as what Howard Becker (1963, pp. 147–163) once called a "moral entrepreneur," that is, an individual who feels strongly about the morality of a particular legal reform and takes the lead in defining the new morality and organizing support for its implementation. Of course, Keeton and O'Connell (1965) could not have played such a significant role if their program had not secured the support of certain powerful interest groups and struck many people, legislators included, as being in the public interest. The fact that their plan did capture the support needed to become law in a number of states is, in part, a testimony to the power of both ideas and social science to shape our view of reality.

But the story of these changes in rule logics cannot be told entirely at the level of ideas and their role in legal change. The final chapter, still being played out with respect to no fault auto insurance, requires us to look at the political arena. The question remains why powerful groups like the transportation and manufacturing interests that dominated business at the turn of the century and large segments of the insurance industry today came to favor no fault approaches to accident compensation. Ideas are seldom, if ever, powerful enough to persuade such groups that their interests should be sacrificed to the greater good. What is more likely to persuade such groups is the belief that their own interests might benefit from reform.

One important factor that contributed to reform in both areas is that structural variables peculiar to the tort system mean that the total payout under a no fault scheme can be substantially less than what would be expected if the average cost of fully compensating plaintiffs under the tort scheme applied to all injury victims. In the first place, securing compensation in a tort scheme entails high transaction costs, the most important of which are attorney's fees and court costs. These take between one-third and one-half of the typical plaintiff's recovery under a contingent fee agreement and may be substantial for defendants even when plaintiffs recover nothing. No fault schemes typically contemplate the virtual elimination of litigation, thus allowing the transaction costs of the fault system to be reallocated to plaintiffs without adding to defendants' expenses. Although the expectation that litigation would be virtually eliminated in compensation schemes has not been met in the case of workers' compensation and is also not fully realized in no fault auto states, what is important at the time statutes are enacted is the expectations of relevant interest groups and not the systems that actually emerge. (It is, no doubt, also the case that transaction costs under no fault compensation programs are less than under the fault-based systems they replace, so expectations are not entirely disappointed.)

A second way in which victims may be compensated without forcing defendants to dig deeper is to reallocate awards among victims. Recall that where tort law applies research has found that many victims are overcompensated. This means that some victims receive more than their measurable economic loss; that is, more than the total of their medical expenses, property damage, and lost wages. Two important reasons for this are that the claims of victims with no measurable loss have both nuisance and risk values and victims with measurable losses may be compensated for their immeasurable pain and suffering as well. No fault compensation schemes typically set limits on recovery geared to discernible physical and economic losses. This reduces both the nuisance and risk value of the claims of the less seriously injured by rendering the threat of litigation to secure more than what is obviously deserved less credible. It also means that money that would have been used to compensate successful tort plaintiffs for their pain and suffering is available to compensate those who under the tort system would not have recovered their real economic loss.

Finally, there is the collateral source rule. This rule means that tort plaintiffs can recover their full losses from negligent defendants even if the losses have been paid from other sources. Thus, an individual injured in an auto accident who has her $10,000 hospital bill paid under a Blue Cross policy may nonetheless recover that $10,000 from a negligent defendant. The theory behind the rule is that a wrongdoer does not deserve to benefit from the fact that he injured someone prudent enough to have provided for her own health care in the event of an accident. There is also an economic justification for ignoring collateral source payments. Tort compensation, at least in theory, helps ensure that activities bear the costs of the risks they create. This provides actors with an incentive to prefer safer ways of proceeding except where the costs of safety measures exceed the costs of the injuries they will forestall. If the costs of accidents borne by collateral sources were not also charged to the tort-feasors, the social costs of accidents would be higher because potential tort-feasors would be insufficiently motivated to choose safer methods of operation, or so runs the argument from economic theory.

However one evaluates these arguments, one result of the collateral source rule is that an accident may prove to be a windfall for the victim who has first party insurance that pays his medical expenses and lost wages. No fault plans, by focusing on what the victim has in fact lost, compensate actual expenses only to the extent that they have not been paid by other sources. This has been particularly important in keeping down the costs of no fault auto insurance because many people today have first party insurance that covers the cost of medical treatment.

These features, particularly the first two, were important in the genesis of workers' compensation because they meant that the costs of expanded accident protection were not borne entirely by industry. All three have been important to no fault auto insurance because they have allowed insurance premiums to be kept at a level the public will tolerate. Indeed, a strong selling point of no fault auto insurance is that it promises to lower the cost of insurance while expanding recovery. Although this promise has remained largely inchoate, at least costs have not substantially escalated.

But money is not free. If industry did not bear all the new costs of workers' compensation and the insurance buying public has not paid the full costs of the expanded coverage under no fault, who has lost so that others may receive? One set of losers are those who for a fee facilitate the transfer of money from negligent defendants to injured plaintiffs. Lawyers predominate in this group but they are by no means the only actors whose compensation is, from an economic per-spective, a "transaction cost." To the extent that no fault succeeds in reducing the overall transaction costs of the tort system, less money will be paid to those actors who share in the tort recoveries of plaintiffs or assist defendants in settling or resisting claims. There has also been a substantial transfer within the ranks of injury victims. The losers come from the ranks of those who would have recovered under the tort system, especially those who would have recovered substantial sums for pain and sufferings, those whose claims had only nuisance value, and those whose economic losses were substantially covered by first party insurance. Gainers include those who, for the various reasons we have outlined, could not have recovered in a tort suit or would have recovered only a fraction of their measurable economic loss.

There are also transfers among those who remain uninjured. Under no fault auto insurance relatively safe drivers with high incomes do less well—vis-à-vis the fault system—than relatively unsafe drivers with low incomes, and the demise of the collateral source rule means that some of the costs of auto accidents are transferred from purchasers of automobile insurance to purchasers of health insurance generally.

Now we are ready for the last part of the story. A social problem has been identified, a solution proposed, popular support exists for reform and conditions are such that the full cost of reform need not be borne by the party whose liability will be expanded. It is still necessary that those powerful institutional actors who might block reform come to realize that reform is not obviously against their self-interest and may, in fact, advance it.

Friedman and Ladinsky (1967) in their fine article on the triumph of the workers' compensation movement outline the remaining crucial factors. Chief among these were the fact that the costs to business of processing cases in the tort system, that is, the transaction costs of settling cases or mounting a defense, grew substantially and the payout that the tort system required became, both in individual cases and over the long run, increasingly uncertain. Uncertainty in individual cases stemmed from the increasing complexity of the law and the discretion accorded judges and juries. One could rarely be sure that a case would not reach the jury, and if it did the award might be extravagant. Uncertainty about the long run resulted from the fact that the rules that provided employers with most of their protection were becoming increasingly eroded, and there was a possibility that if the system were not thoroughly reformed the balance of advantage in tort litigation might at some future point swing to the workers. In sum, although many injured workers were inadequately compensated under the tort system, the total payout by business was high and the returns from main-taining the common law were—particularly as the assumption of the risk and fellow servant rules became riddled with exceptions—questionable.

Friedman and Ladinsky remark:

> Assuming that employers, as rational men, were anxious to pay as little compensation as was necessary to preserve industrial peace and maintain a healthy workforce, the better course might be to pay a higher *net* amount direct to employees. Employers had little or nothing to gain from their big payments to insurance companies, lawyers, and court officials. Perhaps at some unmeasurable point of time, the existing tort system crossed an invisible line and thereafter, purely in economic terms, represented on balance a net loss to the industrial establishment. (1967, pp. 66–67)

Employers who reached this conclusion were likely to change sides, moving from opposition to workers' compensation to support for the idea, insofar as it served their interest.

In 1910 the National Association of Manufacturers appointed a committee to study new ways of dealing with industrial accidents. By 1911 the association apparently was convinced that a new plan was called for. Not only was the old system economically undesirable, it also led to acrimonious relations between labor and business. With the support of business as well as of labor, a new system was assured. But with business support also came business interests, and these interests helped shape the new law.

The most important items on the business agenda were that the new plans be actuarially predictable and as inexpensive as possible. A plan that compensated all injured workers in the amounts that juries awarded workers who could prove tort liability would have been intolerable. In return for certainty of recovery for the workers, the employers wanted a reasonable and predictable loss. In this case the demand translated to limitations on recovery; statutory amounts were established as fair and maximum compensation for various injuries. Labor, of course, wanted certainty coupled with high compensation. The resulting statutes were the end product of a bargain balancing the interests of labor and management. In the bargain, the role of the judiciary was greatly limited, and the uncertainty of the jury trial disappeared.

Perhaps because we are in the middle of the move toward no fault insurance, we lack a good account of the forces that have led many automobile insurance companies to support the change. Nevertheless, we can point to some features of the proposed change that help explain the automobile insurance companies' position. First, the insurance companies have less reason to be hostile to the change than industry did with respect to workers' compensation. The dollars that industry had to pay to injured workers would otherwise have been profit to the company. Insurance companies, on the other hand, are regulated industries, and the dollars that insurance companies pay to accident victims redistribute premiums that are set largely on the basis of accident experience and the reasonable costs to the company of administering the system. This does not mean that insurance companies are indifferent to premium levels. As insurance premiums increase, there is increasing political pressure to restrain the rising costs, and this may lead insurance regulators to delay justifiable increases or set rates at levels likely to eat into the companies' traditional profit margins. Furthermore, where insurance is not compulsory, and even to some degree where it is, higher premium levels mean that less insurance will be sold. Thus, it is not surprising that Massachusetts, the first state to opt for no fault auto insurance, had what were by far the nation's highest insurance costs at the time it changed rule logics. One would also expect insurance company support for no fault auto insurance to be higher in those states where transaction costs are greatest and where awards for pain and suffering are high because such jurisdictions promise the greatest savings or the least extra costs from the switch to no fault.

Organizationally, the greatest difference that the switch to no fault makes to insurance companies is that they are no longer negotiating solely with "opponents" but, instead, are often trying to strike deals with their own customers. A company that is strict or hostile when dealing with its own insureds may find that word gets around and business falls off. Thus "good will" value may come to replace nuisance value in negotiating the claims of the less visibly injured. On the other hand, those only slightly injured may tend not to claim against their own companies for fear that their premiums will be raised.

Not all the organizational consequences of no fault are likely to be such a mixed blessing for the insurance companies. Since states that adopt no fault typically require all drivers to purchase insurance, there will be additional customers to be shared by the companies doing business in the state. Furthermore, to the extent that no fault eliminates jury judgments as well as awards for pain and suffering, the uncertainty of the current system and the concomitant costs of uncertainty in a rational organization will be minimized. However, in practice, this potential advantage of no fault for insurance companies has not been fully realized. The passage of these statutes has inevitably involved compromises with legislators who are influenced by their own belief in the tort system and by groups of plaintiffs' personal injury lawyers and other defenders of the status quo. A common compromise has been to retain the negligence suit and the right to recover for pain and suffering for certain kinds of injuries or for cases in which damages exceed a specified amount. Ironically, although the undercompensation of severely injured accident victims was a principal source of dissatisfaction with the tort liability system and a spur in the movement to no fault, the fear that the seriously injured would be undercompensated under no fault has led legislatures adopting no fault to allow them to opt back into the negligence system.

In summary, the movements toward no fault and the workers' compensation statutes were rooted in dissatisfaction with the tort compensation system and the perception that it was a source of social trouble. In each case an idea for resolving the trouble was suggested, an idea that, taking advantage of certain costly features of tort compensation, placed the costs of broadened coverage on several groups. The possibility of reform became a reality when powerful interest groups that had traditionally supported the status quo changed sides. The reason they changed was that the old systems became or promised to become more expensive to operate than the new ones. Indeed, in the case of no fault auto compensation, by the time the change comes to most jurisdictions, it will not be much of a change at all. The change in rule logics is the final, small step in a long change process rather than a radical new direction in the law.

RULE LOGICS, CASE LOGICS, AND THE MORALITY OF THE LAW

The reformulation of the tort law in favor of no fault systems of injury compensation marks a retreat from a full consideration of human action in assessing liability. To put it bluntly, the law has come to ignore part of what it is to be human in deciding these personal injury cases. Strict liability makes both the careless and the careful responsible. In this sense, the change is a retreat from morality.[17] Indeed, it might be argued, as Jean Piaget does, that movement in the other direction is the essence of moral development, at least in Western societies.

The Process of Moral Development

In his seminal book, *The Moral Judgment of the Child*, Piaget (1965) argues that as children develop moral judgment, they move from a logic of strict liability to a morality concerned with intentions and abilities. Piaget reached this conclusion from his observations of children at play and from the assessments of responsibility made by children of different ages when confronted with stories about children who had misbehaved.

For example, one story involved broken cups. As with most of the stories, there were two versions. The first version read:

> A little boy who is called John is in his room. He is called to dinner. He goes into the dining room. But behind the door there was a chair, and on the chair there was a tray with fifteen cups on it. John couldn't have known that there was all this behind the door. He goes in, the door knocks against the tray, bang go the fifteen cups and they all get broken. (p. 122)

The second version was:

> Once there was a little boy whose name was Henry. One day when his mother was out he tried to get some jam out of the cupboard. He climbed up on to a chair and stretched out his arm. But the jam was too high up and he couldn't reach it and have any. But while he was trying to get it he knocked over a cup. The cup fell down and broke. (p. 122)

Piaget asked his young respondents two questions about paired stories of this type. They were: (1) Are the children equally guilty? (2) Which is the naughtiest? Geo represents a typical response of a 6-year-old child:

> Q: Is one of the boys naughtier than the other? A: The first is because he knocked over twelve cups. [In some replications of the story, only twelve cups broke.] Q: If you were the daddy, which one would you punish most? A: The one who broke twelve cups. Q: Why did he break them? A: The door shut too hard and knocked them. He didn't do it on purpose. Q: And why did the other boy break a cup? A: He wanted to get the jam. He moved too far. The cup got broken. Q: Why did he want to get the jam? A: Because he was all alone. Because his mother wasn't there. Q: Have you got a brother? A: No, a little sister. Q: Well, if it was you who had broken the twelve cups when you went into the room and your little sister who had broken one cup while she was trying to get the jam, which of you would be punished most severely? A: Me, because I broke more than one cup. (p. 125)

---

17. As we noted in Chapter 2, strict liability systems have their own underlying moralities, but these are concerned with questions of deterrence and distribution and not with what it means for a human being to be responsible for his actions.

Mol (age 7) and Corm (age 9) give answers that are typical of older children. First Mol:

> Q: Which is naughtiest? A: The second, the one who wanted to take the jam-pot, because he wanted to take something without asking. Q: Did he catch it? A: No. Q: Was he the naughtiest all the same? A: Yes. Q: And the first? A: It wasn't his fault. He didn't do it on purpose. (p. 129)

And Corm:

> A: Well, the one who broke them as he was coming isn't naughty, 'cos he didn't know there was any cups. The other one wanted to take the jam and caught his arm on a cup. Q: Which one is the naughtiest? A: The one who wanted to take the jam. Q: How many cups did he break? A: One. Q: And the other boy? A: Fifteen. Q: Which one would you punish most? A: The boy who wanted to take the jam. He knew, he did it on purpose. (p. 129)

It is obvious that to the younger children evidence of intention is irrelevant. The meaning of the event, even as a matter of morality, is determined entirely by objective criteria. Piaget summarizes his results as follows:

> Thus these answers present us with two distinct moral attitudes—one that judges actions according to their material consequences, and one that only take [sic] intentions into account. These two attitudes may co-exist at the same age and even in the same child, but broadly speaking, they do not synchronize. Objective responsibility diminishes on the average as the child grows older, and subjective responsibility gains correlatively in importance. (Piaget, 1965, p. 133)

Not only does the issue of intention take on greater importance as children become older, but age also brings with it a tendency to develop rules that take into account the unique features of a situation. Piaget spent considerable time asking young boys about the rules of the game of marbles. Younger children reflected a moral realism that helps explain their response patterns to marbles and to broken cups alike. The rules come from God or Daddy. They never vary, and there always has been and always will be only one correct way to play marbles. The rules must not be changed, and they allow no exceptions in their application. For older boys, the rules become remarkably complex and are contingent on circumstances. These circumstances depend not only on the immediate position of the marbles in the circle, but also on how the game has gone; that is, on a more extended analysis of circumstances. The older boys "take pleasure in juridical discussions, whether of principle or merely of procedure" (1965, pp. 42–43). Thus:

> Our three legal experts [three boys ages twelve and thirteen] also point to the measures of clemency in use for the protection of the weak. According to Vua "if you knock out three at one shot and there's only one left [one marble in the square], the other chap [the opponent] has the right to play from half-way [half-way between the coche and the square] because the first boy has made more than his 'pose'". Also, "the boy who has been beaten is allowed to begin." According to Gros, "If there is one marble left at the end, the boy who has won, instead of taking it, can give it to the

other chap." And again, "When there's one boy who has won too much, the others say 'coujac,'[18] and he is bound to play another game" (1965, p. 49).

Piaget's work with young children is intriguing in several respects. It again indicates the connections between rule logics and admissible evidence. For the younger children adjudicating the broken cups case, the standard of judgment is one of strict liability. Evidence of the offender's intention is basically irrelevant. Older children care about intentions. Responsibility is, for them, no longer a unitary concept, and they are more open to unique extended analyses in determining justice. For them, the rules of marbles change with the ever-changing circumstances of the game.

The thrust of Piaget's argument, and of research in this tradition, is that children undergo a process of moral development (see Kohlberg, 1969). Older children are morally more sophisticated. Does that mean that the movement to strict liability is a move backward? From the perspective of individual morality, yes. Indeed, arguments about responsibility have been persuasively employed by those fighting the spread of no fault auto insurance. But individual morality is not the only consideration in choosing a responsibility rule logic. Other considerations may argue for strict liability in certain cases.

Accidents and the Social Morality of Strict Liability

C. Wright Mills (1959) described the sociological imagination as the ability to grasp history and biography and the relations between the two (p. 6). Perhaps this is the essence of the sociological imagination, but it is also at the heart of the legal imagination. Mills suggests that the most fruitful distinction to be made in this regard is "between the personal troubles of milieu and the public issues of social structure" (p. 8). Troubles are personal problems that beset individuals and are to be understood and dealt with in terms of unique individual situations. Issues go beyond the realm of the person. An issue is a public concern.

Yet personal problems and issues cannot always be distinguished. Presumably if only one person is in some way afflicted, the affliction is a problem, or trouble in Mills's sense, and not an issue. At the other extreme some public issues involve no personal problems. The analysis becomes difficult, however, when a particular kind of personal problem is widespread. At some point we tend to perceive not just individual problems but a social problem, an issue requiring political attention. If a man is unemployed, that is his problem, and if we are moved to help him we do so by looking for a suitable job. If two people are unemployed, we find jobs for both. But if millions of people are out of work the situation no longer seems to be an aggregation of personal problems that might be alleviated by finding jobs for specific individuals. Systemic change

---

18. The word "coujac" is only appropriate under the circumstances of a lopsided win; in other circumstances it has no "legal" significance.

seems necessary, for the problem lies in the system and not with specific individuals.

People frequently disagree about whether a social problem is essentially a reflection of troubled individuals to be dealt with at that level or rooted in the social system and so inescapably raising the issues of whether and how to change the system. Often this debate is structured along the lines of placing the blame. Unemployment may be blamed on the laziness of the idle or on the government's fiscal policies, school failure on the ignorance of the uneducated or on poor student–teacher ratios, and poverty on the race of the poor (see Ryan, 1971) or capitalist exploitation.

Every set of misfortunes has both public and individual causes. We must decide on which to focus. In the areas that we have been examining in this chapter there was a slow movement from viewing uncompensated injuries as personal troubles to viewing them as a public issue. We have already noted the importance of this change to what followed. Here we discuss this aspect of the matter in more detail.

The change in public perception was in part a consequence of the increase of accidents in these areas. Both in our factories and on our highways, the accident and death rate has grown from modest beginnings to enormous proportions. By the end of the nineteenth century it was estimated that two million injuries and 35,000 deaths were occurring annually in industrial accidents (Friedman & Ladinsky, 1967, p. 60). By 1970 the toll on the highways had surpassed these figures. Nearly 15 million accidents, about 2 million injuries, and 55,000 deaths were reported in 1968 (National Safety Council, 1969, p. 40).

The increased frequency of accidental injuries coupled with complicated and changing technology have led numbers of people to conclude that many, if not most, accidents are, for all practical purposes, unavoidable. Even careless behavior, the kind that qualifies as negligence, is in a statistical sense inevitable. The law's reasonable man sets a standard of behavior that humans cannot always achieve. Whether harm results when we do fall short is in large measure a matter of luck, that is, of random processes. On most occasions when a driver's head is turned in conversation there will be no child on the street. But when a child is present there will be an accident, unless for any one of dozens of reasons, either the driver or child are lucky enough to avoid it.

Most inattentive or ill-considered action has no consequences, for actors are usually not in a position where they can easily injure themselves or others. However, as people increasingly find themselves in charge of heavy, complicated, or fast-moving machinery, the consequences of human slipups become greater. The machine-dominated environment has less tolerance for error; hence, the skyrocketing rate of industrial and highway accidents. And in more and more of these accidents, even if a tort-feasor can be identified, the deviation from the behavior that society has a right to expect will be small, and the ill that befalls those who are injured due to their own carelessness or that of others will be quite disproportionate to the sin.

As accidents come to be seen as more or less random events, the blame for which lies largely with the environment, it becomes increasingly difficult to justify the allocation of accident costs on the basis of who might have avoided the harm in some individual and immediate sense. Although the examination of individual accidents may often suggest they were avoidable, when we look at the mass of accidents, we realize that the microscope in some ways misleads. This view is confirmed when we see the effects that social policies can have on accidents, such as the dramatic dip in highway deaths that occurred when speed limits were lowered from 70 to 55 miles per hour for reasons that had nothing to do with safety. Although investigation might reveal human failings that contributed to the thousands of "excess" deaths that occurred at the higher speed limit, the deaths are also attributable to a social policy, the policy of setting speed limits so high. And going 70 miles per hour when that was the speed limit was not negligence, however more deadly it made the consequences of other careless behavior.

What we have just described may not be the dominant view even today. It is perhaps more accurate to say that over the years the environmental component of accident rates has come to dominate the personal component and there is an increasing tendency to see accidents in the aggregate as events for which no one is really responsible. None of this happens quickly, and the changing nature of a type of accident and the way we perceive it does not immediately lead to legal change. In the case of automobile accidents, for instance, these are not horse and buggy times; 1983 is not 1903 when the "horseless carriage" was just beginning to make its appearance. On the other hand, one might hazard a guess that the situation of highway driving is no worse in the 1980s than it was in the 1950s. Driving 55 (or even 70) miles per hour on a present-day interstate seems a more rational venture than doing 55 on the poorly graded two-lane highways of 30 years ago. Clearly, the change in perspective is as much a social creation as a recognition of changing conditions.

Recognizing the change in these cases appears to involve not only the perception of social causes of misfortune, but also the perception of a social solution. This solution itself helps to reorient our view. In the accident area our perception of both the problem and its solutions has been fundamentally colored by the institution of insurance.

The impact of insurance on the choice of compensatory rule logics is twofold. First, it seriously undermines any unique deterrent effect the tort law might otherwise have. The employer with industrial accident insurance, the manufacturer with products liability insurance, and the driver with liability insurance may try to act carefully because they fear an increase in premiums, but this is an effect that exists whether the responsibility rule is negligence or strict liability.

Secondly, insurance allows those who have it to alter radically the impact of a finding of negligence. Negligence understandings in these areas are by definition individual understandings. But one who is insured avoids the consequences—the payment of damages—that society seeks to attach to such understandings. Insurance aggregates and depersonalizes the social judgment, and it imposes a new understanding about accidents. Never mind how careful or careless

Johnny is; note only that he is 19 years old, unmarried, and male. As our understanding gravitates more toward allocation and less toward individual action, the tort remedy of negligence seems less and less adequate. A social problem needs a social solution, and strict liability is a social solution *par excellence*.[19] It is, as we showed in Chapter 2, moral at an aggregate level.

There is, however, another side to these movements. The movement toward strict liability is caused not only by the changing nature of accidents but also by the changing nature of how claims of negligence are resolved. Specifically, the growth of bureaucratic decision making tends to produce shallow case logics, and rule logics other than strict liability are poorly served by shallow adjudication. We have presented examples of this not only in the area of negligence but also in the criminal law as well.

Although some may regret the movement to strict liability in cases of industrial and automobile accidents, what is more disturbing to many is the apparent ease with which lawyers and judges adopt a shallow case logic in the case of accused criminals. Shallow case logics restrict the law's commitment to the full humanity of individual actions. It is true that shallow case logics tend to reduce transaction costs in the criminal area as they do with torts, but the savings do not have the same implications, for the criminal law is not primarily concerned with the allocation of costs. Bureaucratic adjudication, as Weber feared, undermines the ethical dimension of law embodied in the concept of desert. In situations where individual desert is the central concern, we risk important values when we allow adjudications to be transformed into a mode of bureaucratic decision making. One solution is to refocus our concerns and forego moral judgments. With the spread of insurance and the extension of strict liability, this has been happening to a large extent in the tort law.[20] If, on the other hand, we remain interested in judging the morality of behavior, and this is what the criminal law purports to do, we are, if we take the task seriously, committed to a deep case logic.

---

19. In the legal literature, there has been a great debate as to whether, in fact, strict liability is more likely than negligence liability to reduce accidents, or, more precisely, accident costs. The result of the debate is presently a standoff. Both systems should reduce accident costs, but the overhead costs of a strict liability system seem to give it a slight advantage (Calabresi, 1970; Shavell, 1980). Also, to the extent that one party, such as a large employer, creates an environment that can be more or less conducive to accidents, strict liability might be expected to lead to changes that will reduce accident costs if the maintenance of an environment more conducive to accidents than some other economically feasible arrangement would not be held to constitute negligence. Strict liability arrangements may also be more efficient in generating information about a total accident picture, and thus may make it easier to discern trouble spots and effective accident reduction procedures.

20. At the same time, although the matter has not to our knowledge been systematically studied, it appears there has been an upsurge in tort cases demanding punitive damages. Punitive damages are sanctions against a tort-feasor for particularly gross negligence or other immoral behavior. They bear no relation to the injury done to the victim. Thus, it may be that the tort law is developing in a direction that tends to separate the compensation judgment from judgments about the morality of behavior (Rabin, 1983).

SUMMARY: THE DILEMMA OF RESPONSIBILITY

In the first section of this book we have examined issues of responsibility. We began by arguing that the concept of responsibility cannot be understood unless we are willing to view human action as something more than mere behavior. From both a sociological and a legal perspective human action has the qualities of agency and purpose. It is the presence or absence of these qualities that define different types of human action and different types of responsibility. Legal rule may be distinguished by the degree to which they treat agency and purpose as essential factors in determining responsibility. The rule logics developed in Chapter 2 formalized these distinctions.

Beyond the question of rules, there is the question of evidence, that is, the application of rules to particular cases. As the quote from Plato that introduces this section suggests, many arguments are not about the general rule, but, rather, are about the particular case. In Chapter 4, we developed two ideal typical ways in which cases may be decided—by a shallow or a deep case logic. Sometimes the choice of a case logic may be quite purposive. As we shall see in Chapter 8, a court may adopt a shallow case logic to increase the legal impact of certain laws. But the adoption of a case logic is not always the result of a deliberate policy choice. In Chapter 4 we discussed some of the organizational factors that influence the type of case logic that will be employed in particular kinds of cases. Of greatest importance is the tendency of bureaucratic organizations to adopt shallow case logics. Whenever adjudicative tasks are vested in bureaucracies, shallow logics tend to emerge. This chapter has examined two areas of tort law, industrial and automobile accidents, where this process has occurred.

A shallow case logic has the advantages of speed and efficiency. But as used by attorneys and adjusters in cases arising out of automobile accidents, the logic is unreliable in the sense that it fails to distinguish adequately between occasions when drivers are negligent and occasions when they are not. As such, it undermines the negligence rule logic that has traditionally governed this civil harm. Indeed, the widespread use of a shallow case logic has caused automobile accident law as it affects most accident victims to drift away from the formal rule logic of appellate court opinions. The widening gulf between the formal rule logic of negligence and the shallow case logics of settlement helped create a situation ripe for change.

The point applies more generally. Rule logics and case logics are closely connected. They must be consistent with one another if we are to have a stable system of adjudicating responsibility. When rule logics mandate the consideration of factors that case logics ignore, tensions develop because either the legal system is expected to live up to ideals it does not meet or the law appears increasingly irrelevant to those who work with it, and the occasional consideration of factors that are not routinely accorded attention appears unfair or inefficient.

In the case of no fault auto insurance and perhaps in the case of workers' compensation as well, the shift to a strict liability rule logic is a much smaller movement than it would appear to be if one looked only at appellate decisions.

In part, the movement reflects the fact that under the influence of routinized decision styles, many such cases were being decided on the basis of evidence that had little to do with the responsibility analysis prescribed by the formal law of negligence. Thus, the movement toward strict first party liability for auto accidents may be understood in part as a process whereby the old rule logic is succumbing to an entrenched case logic.

Of course, many have argued that rule logics should not succumb to case logics in this way. The law, they argue, should not always follow the path suggested by the exigencies of the situation. We have already noted the protests of the plaintiffs' personal injury bar against no fault auto insurance. But this group, however effective they have been in forestalling the movement, stands largely alone, and even if their motives are public spirited, their self-interest is also obvious. In other areas, most notably in the area of criminal justice, the concern for shallow case processing is more widespread. This concern exists because when criminal sanctions are at issue the adoption of a shallow case logic, which fails to give full consideration to questions of agency and purpose, threatens the moral foundations on which the law must rest if it is to respect each sane adult citizen as a full human actor.

The sociological implications of this retreat from morality are not, however, clear. Whether the modern social order depends in some way on the degree to which its criminal justice system in fact attends to issues of agency and purpose is a question we do not address. We do, however, know that the criminal law has witnessed a considerable routinization of case processing both in the way cases are handled by lawyers, be they prosecutors, public defenders, or private attorneys, and in the way cases are disposed of by plea bargaining or in abbreviated trials. As in the negligence area, these processes of bureaucratic decision making tend to undermine the existing logic.

We do not, however, wish either to leave the impression that the bureaucratization of decision making is the only factor that influences the movement from rule logics that appear to call for deep case logics to those that seem consistent with shallower ones, or to suggest that selecting a rule logic that eschews a deep understanding of human behavior necessarily slights moral concerns. The movement toward strict liability, for example, has been influenced by a growing belief that personal injuries constitute a collective, structural problem, best settled by a collective, structural remedy. Some see this movement, as it is embodied in workers' compensation and no fault auto insurance (as well as products liability), as a retreat from morality because it ignores issues of fault. Others, ourselves among them, see the use of strict liability in these circumstances as reflecting moral judgments about how best to deal with collective problems.

Indeed, the refusal to adopt a strict liability rule logic in the face of a structural problem may be a failure to pursue the general interest that is attributable to the special interests of those who are causally responsible for or otherwise benefit from the trouble of others. But, however compelling the justification for strict liability, it is also true that the adoption of a strict liability rule ignores much of what it is to be human. Speaking, for the moment only, more as lawyers than as social scientists, we believe that regimes of strict liability should not be too hastily embraced. A legal system that routinely fails to consider the questions of agency and purpose not only abandons commonly shared understandings of morality and justice, but it also destroys part of our liberty by failing to provide us with a system that respects personal choice. In establishing responsibility rules, we must constantly balance the right of the collectivity to expect that law will work toward the amelioration of structural problems with the right of the individual to expect that the law will give considered attention to personal autonomy and the ability to exercise choice.

PART II

Disputes

Only twice in my life have I felt utterly ruined: once when I lost a lawsuit, and once when I won.

Voltaire

In Part I we examined the law as a process of determining responsibility. In this part we treat law as a device for conflict resolution. Part I was concerned largely with substantive rules. Part II focuses on the logic and rules of processing disputes.

When we focus on the role that judgments of responsibility play in the legal process, we tend to see the law as a moralistic enterprise. When we shift our attention to law's role in conflict resolution or dispute settlement, the legal process appears to be more like a game where the important issues are whether and what one wins or loses. Rules from this perspective provide ammunition for the parties involved.

Neither image of the law, as a moral process or as a game, is wholly accurate. Each viewpoint must be leavened by the other, and, as we shall see in Part III, even then the picture is not complete. As we discuss the bargaining part of the legal process, we should not forget that the law's substantive and procedural rules establish the parameters within which bargaining occurs.

In labeling the issues of Part I moral and likening the issues of this part to a game, we do not wish to imply that Part I dealt with the honest and good side of the legal process while this part addresses the dark underside. One virtue of the rule of law is that it provides institutionalized and usually nonviolent ways of resolving disputes. The compromises that occur in the dispute settlement process and the rules of thumb applied are as integral to the rule of law as the rules themselves.

A dispute is often resolved at law by deciding that one side or the other side is "responsible." Thus, judgments of responsibility not only carry moral connotations, as we have noted, but are also ways of describing outcomes or settlements. From one perspective, what is important is not that one side is judged responsible, but that a dispute has been settled. This is most evident in situations where the law's role in allocating responsibility bows before the demands of dispute settlement. Less formal tribunals, for example, often refrain from judgments of responsibility or spread responsibility more or less equally among all disputants in order to facilitate the reconciliation of the parties. And court-endorsed settlements that reallocate millions of dollars often state as part of the settlement agreement that the defendant in compensating the plaintiff does not admit responsibility for the matter at issue.

When parties turn to law to settle their disputes, they relinquish part of their control over the course of the dispute. The legal system imposes a definition of what is in dispute and establishes the parameters of possible resolution. In modern societies the legal system goes further and reworks disputes between parties into conflicts concerning a specific set of legal issues. The legal process then focuses on what the law has established as important and ignores other matters. George Simmel captured this sense of the ideal Western procedure nearly one hundred years ago when he noted:

> For legal conflict has *an object,* and the struggle can be satisfactorily terminated through the voluntary concession of that object. . . . In respect to the *form* of conflict, however, legal quarrel is indeed absolute. That is, on both sides the claims are put through with pure objectivity and with all means that are permitted; the conflict is not deflected or attenuated by any personal or in any other sense extraneous circumstances. Legal conflict is pure conflict in as much as nothing enters its whole action which does not belong to the conflict *as such* and serves its purpose. (1955, p. 36)

This ideal, however, does not always prevail in our society, and in some societies such an ideal would appear as a perversion rather than as a goal.

In this part we examine methods of dispute settlement and the way disputes are processed in various circumstances. In the present-day United States what is most striking about legal disputes is that they are usually settled out of court. Only a small proportion of the cases that are officially commenced ever proceed to a trial. In Chapter 6 we indicate, in a general sense, why this is so, by using game theory models to describe the nature of lawsuits and their potential for settlement. Game theory, like so many of the less formal models on which we have relied, specifies an ideal, in this case one that allows us to better understand the bargaining situation in which people who turn to law to settle their disputes find themselves. The basic idea is that lawsuits are non-zero sum games; that is, one party's gains do not necessarily have to come at the other party's expense, and often both parties by settling can exceed what they expect to gain from going to trial.

Given that cases are usually settled out of court, we can also ask whether such settlements are fair. The second section of Chapter 6 discusses this issue, again within the framework of a game theory analysis.

In some circumstances the role of law is not so much to establish clear rules of responsibility, as it is to arrange the bargaining space in which parties negotiate and to control the relative power they can bring to bear. In the appendix to Chapter 6 we examine an attempt to establish through law the ground rules for labor–management negotiations.

Parties going to law commonly find that the legal system is concerned with only part of what they think of as the dispute. Thus a person who hits another as the culmination of a year-long quarrel may find that the law is only concerned with those aspects of the quarrel that occurred within a few minutes of the blow. Chapter 7 confronts the issue of how the legal system selects certain aspects of disputes to be the subject of official attention. We shall see that, while in some societies tribunals attend to more than what the parties thought was in issue, in other societies tribunals are concerned with less. In Chapter 7 we present four ideal-typical ways that legal systems have defined the nature of the bargaining space created when the parties go to law, and we explore their implications for the treatment of disputes.

Chapter 8 seeks to explain the primary reasons why legal systems vary in their dispute settlement strategies. We discuss two courts: the small claims court and the juvenile court, each of which was designed to alter the normal way in which disputes are processed in the American legal system. We attempt to assess the relative success of these innovative courts and to indicate some of the limits of law as an instrument of dispute resolution.

6

Conflicts and Settlements: The Logic and Fairness of Bargains in a Game Theory Perspective

Legal disputes involve conflicting interests. Usually one person has something the other wants and both parties make claims of entitlement. Since the claims cannot be simultaneously satisfied, there is a true conflict.[1]

In this chapter we examine legal disputes as occasions of conflict. Parties turn to law when they are unable to settle their conflicts privately. Law provides third-party adjudicators—in our society we call them judges and jurors—to de-

---

1. Indeed, the jurisdiction of the so-called Article III courts, that is, the courts provided for in Article III of the Constitution is limited to "cases and controversies." This means that there must be a real dispute between two parties before the federal judiciary will hear the case. If Sam and Sally wished to settle a rule of law in the abstract, or if Sam were upset at what Sally was doing to someone else, but her conduct did not hurt him, the federal courts would not hear a suit between them. There are two basic arguments for this requirement. First, the rule reduces the pressure on the courts and saves their time and resources for actual cases of conflict in the society. Second, requiring a real controversy more nearly ensures that the parties will care about the outcome. In a system such as ours, where the adversarial process is used as an "engine for truth," it is essential that the opposing parties be true adversaries, each interested in presenting the strongest possible case for his or her side, and the concrete facts of real cases may provide the most reliable bases for intelligent decisions. In addition, to the rule that there must be a case or controversy, there is the old legal axiom *de minimis non curat lex,* the law will not concern itself with trifles. Trivial matters may not be litigated. A court may refuse to hear a suit to recover a 1 cent overcharge even if the cause appears just.

termine which party should prevail as well as the coercive resources to guarantee that the legal determination will be honored. Since lawsuits are typically instituted only after the parties have failed to reach an agreement, the fact that most legal cases are eventually settled by agreement is striking. It appears as if after the power of the court has been officially invoked, the parties discover that going to law was not necessary. However, appearances are deceiving. An out-of-court settlement does not mean that the ultimate resolution of the controversy is unaffected by the initial invocation of the law. It is affected in crucial ways. Norms that structure the legal settlement may differ substantially from the norms the parties invoked in their prefiling settlement attempts. Guarantees that attach to court-ordered resolutions, such as the ability to call on the sheriff to enforce a judgment may also attach to settlements that courts merely ratify. And, as we shall see, there is good reason to believe that most settlements would not have been reached but for the possibility of a court-ordered resolution (cf. Lempert, 1978, pp. 90, 99).

This chapter addresses two questions about this process. The first section treats the question: Why are most but not all cases "settled out of court"? The second section addresses the question: Are most settlements "fair"? It also deals with the preliminary question of what it means to say that a settlement is fair or unfair.

Although legal norms may suggest a solution when the parties cannot agree upon a settlement, the primary role of law is often to structure the situation in which parties may bargain (Teubner, 1983). Here the law may be used to give the parties more or less bargaining strength. It may also be used to encourage settlement. The National Labor Relations (Wagner) Act (NLRA) is a law that does both. Its purpose is to set the bounds on the arena of collective bargaining between labor and management. In an appendix to this chapter we look at the effects of two provisions of the Wagner Act in controlling bargaining power and encouraging settlement.

THE NATURE OF LEGAL CONFLICT

How can one examine the nature of conflict in a lawsuit? Fortunately, we do not have to start from scratch in addressing this issue. Since World War II there has developed a set of conceptual and mathematical models that go by the name of *game theory*. This chapter borrows from this body of theory to explain the settlement of and the failure to settle lawsuits (see generally, Luce & Raffia, 1957; Raffia, 1982; Shubik, 1982).

Fundamental to this analysis is the fact that in certain respects a lawsuit is like a lottery. Rarely are suits sure things. Rather, they promise only some probability of a return. The plaintiff, that is the party bringing the suit, may win or lose. At best he can give a good estimate of his chances.

Consider a suit in which if the plaintiff wins he receives $5,000. Since the suit is not a sure thing, the plaintiff may estimate a probability of victory. He may decide, for instance, that the appropriate probability is .50. That is, he has a 50 percent chance of getting $5,000 and a 50 percent chance of getting nothing. If the plaintiff could try suits of similar strength over and over again, he would expect to receive an average return of $2,500 from each suit filed. We may call this sum, which is the amount he wins discounted by the probability that he will not win, the *expected value* of the lawsuit.

Of course, the situation may be more complex. The plaintiff may not be certain of what he will get if he does win. He may think he has a 50 percent chance of winning a judgment that will range between $1,000 and $9,000, and he may place a different probability on each amount within this range. This is the situation in most negligence suits, where the jury, if it decides that the defendant has been negligent, must also establish the amount of damages. For our purposes, however, we can focus on the simpler case where the only probability to be estimated is the probability of winning. So long as one can estimate the average sum that the plaintiff will receive if he wins, the simple and complex cases can be analyzed in basically the same fashion.

Going to trial and receiving the verdict of a judge or jury is only one of the possible outcomes of a lawsuit. Some lawsuits are unilaterally dropped by plaintiffs who realize they have no chance of winning or who decide to forget the whole thing because of the psychological or financial costs of litigation. Other lawsuits are settled in advance of trial. When suits are settled, many different kinds of outcomes are possible.

Each of the possible outcomes of a lawsuit has a different value for each party. Each party may set a value on the likely outcome of going to trial, which will be an *expected value* since the parties can never be certain of what the judgment will be, and a value on each of the alternative settlements that might be reached. The latter will not be expectations because the parties can specify these alternatives precisely in advance. In the language of game theory we may call these values, whether actual or expected, *utilities*. Going all the way to trial and judgment has an expected *utility* for both the plaintiff and the defendant. Since defendants ordinarily lose when plaintiffs gain,[2] these expected utilities are almost certain to be different.

The possibility of settlement from a game theory perspective depends on whether there are outcomes that will make both the plaintiff and defendant better off than they expect to be if the case goes to final judgment. If there are such outcomes and if the parties can agree upon any one of them, a settlement is to

---

2. It is possible for both parties to gain from pursuing a case to a verdict. In a prisoners' rights suit, for example, the prisoner plaintiffs may gain because the court orders improvements in a state's detention facilities, but the prison board that is defending the suit may also gain because the court orders the state to allocate more money to it. Arguably the state will also gain if the benefits from the improvements exceed their cost. Possibilities for simultaneous gains of this sort do not apply in situations like the tort suit that will be our paradigm for discussion.

be expected because it is in the parties' mutual self-interest. Usually there is some set of such outcomes.[3]

One reason, and probably the most important reason for this is that litigation takes time and money.[4] In order to illustrate this point and others, we shall diagram various bargaining situations using Cartesian graphs, in which the vertical axis represents the defendant's utility and the horizontal axis, the plaintiff's utility (see Figure 6.1).

---

3. In game theory terms this means as we have noted in our text that lawsuits are non-zero sum games, for they are not strictly competitive. Formally, non-zero sum games may be defined as follows: There is at least one pair of outcomes (or lotteries) X and X^1 such that one player prefers X to X^1 and the other player does not prefer X^1 to X. For such games it is impossible to choose payoff values (i.e., a positively valued gain for one party and a negatively valued loss for the other) that sum to zero (Luce & Raffia, 1957, p. 88). Such games are sometimes called "mixed motive" games because the players have incentives both to disagree and to cooperate. Non-zero sum games may be divided further into cooperative and noncooperative games. In cooperative games the parties may communicate with each other before "playing" and, in addition, may make binding agreements before play. In noncooperative games there is no preplay communications. Of course, there may be types of games that share elements of these extremes. For instance, the parties might be able to communicate but not to enter into binding agreements. By and large lawsuits are types of cooperative games. Parties to a suit may bargain to a settlement, which, if agreed upon, is binding on both. In the appendix to this chapter we discuss a type of noncooperative game commonly known as the prisoner's dilemma.

4. There are other reasons why certain suits are not zero sum games. In a particularly thoughtful article, Carrie Menkel-Meadow (1984) reviews various considerations that may be the subject of bargaining in a lawsuit, all of which tend to make the suit less of a zero sum game. Furthermore, even where money is the only thing of value at issue in a lawsuit, for some parties utility is not linear with money and nonlinearities may be different for different parties. The following figure graphs this possibility:

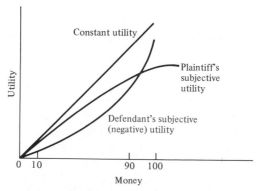

In the figure, if utility were linear with money each dollar increase in money would represent a unit increase in personal "subjective" utility. For most individuals, however, as one acquires more and more money, each additional dollar has less utility. This is indicated by the curved line which shows that the dollars between 90 and 100 do not increase utility (satisfaction) by as much as the first $10 did. When one has to pay judgments the situation is often the reverse. Small sums can be easily managed, but each additional dollar is the source of increasing anguish. In the graphed situation, the plaintiff does not gain much satisfaction by holding out for 100 rather than 90 units of money, but the defendant stands to lose a lot should his final payout be at 100 rather than at 90 units. Thus

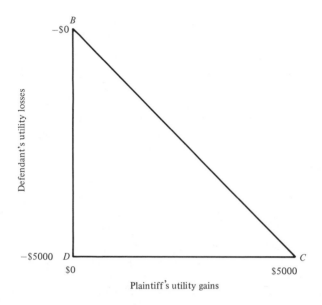

Figure 6.1

The graph in Figure 6.1 and many of those that follow portray, by way of example, the situation of a simple suit. The suit arose after Peter Plaintiff was struck by Diane Defendant's car as he crossed Main Street.[5] He seeks $5,000 to compensate him for his medical expenses. We assume that the only uncertainty is whether Peter will in fact win. If he does, he is guaranteed $5,000. In this situation the best outcome from Peter's point of view is represented by point *C*. Here he gets $5,000 and Diane pays $5,000. We see this by reading across the horizontal axis to determine the plaintiff's recovery and down the vertical axis to determine the defendant's payout. Similarly, the best outcome from Diane's point of view is point *B*. Point *B* is the outcome where she pays Peter nothing. Now we are at the top of the vertical axis where the defendant pays nothing and at the extreme left of the horizontal axis where the plaintiff collects nothing. Any point on the graph can be specified by the joint outcomes that exist at that point. Thus, noting the defendant's "payoff" first, point *B* might also be written (−0, 0), while point *C* is specified by (−5,000, 5,000).

In our case the defendant, Diane, who was arguably negligent, has through her actions cost Peter $5,000, which he has had to pay in medical expenses. Before Peter attempts to recover for Diane's alleged negligence, the parties are

the plaintiff has less incentive to hold out for a 100-unit award than the dollar difference between that and a 90-unit settlement would suggest, and the defendant has more incentive to avoid the possibility of a 100-unit judgment than the dollar difference between that and a 90-unit settlement would suggest.

5. We give our parties names because some readers may find that personifying the parties makes the subsequent discussion easier to follow. As the names we have chosen indicate, Peter's position may be generalized to that of all plaintiffs and Diane's to that of all defendants.

at position *B*. Diane has paid nothing and Peter has received nothing. Since Peter prefers outcome *C,* he asks Diane to pay the full $5,000 or some part of it. If they cannot agree on some settlement, the outcome remains at point *B*. In this sense, point *B* is the original *no agreement outcome*. By *no agreement outcome*, we simply mean it is the outcome that occurs if the parties cannot agree on some settlement. If Peter is not satisfied with this outcome he may sue.

Once a suit is filed, the utility of the suit is the no agreement outcome. This is because if Peter and Diane fail to agree, their outcome will be the one the judge imposes at the end of a trial. The suit guarantees to each party a no agreement outcome, by which we mean an outcome that either party may force on the other by refusing to settle and instead proceeding with the suit.[6] Peter and Diane, of course, do not know exactly what that outcome will be, but they have expectations. These expectations determine the utility of the suit to them at every point in time and guide their decisions. Their expectations need not be symmetrical, because if they view the case differently, Peter may expect a gain that is different from what Diane expects to lose. These expectations may also change over time.

Where in our *BCD* triangle should we locate the no agreement point that is represented by our lawsuit? This depends on a number of factors. The two most important ones are: (1) the merits of the case and (2) the cost of litigation.[7] If a suit is totally worthless; that is, if in our example it is obvious that Peter was contributorily negligent, the no agreement point would not move very far from point *B*. Even if the case goes to trial, it is very unlikely that Peter will win. If, on the other hand, the suit is ironclad, filing the suit would move the no agreement outcome to a point near point *C*.

In these extreme cases, lawsuits are unlikely. If a suit is worthless, a plaintiff will not file, unless the threat of a suit promises to extort some ''nuisance value'' from the defendant and a lawyer can be found who will ignore his ethical responsibility not to file baseless litigation. If, on the other hand, both the defendant's liability and the plaintiff's damages are clear, the defendant has a substantial incentive to settle before a suit is filed in order to save litigation costs. Typically, however, suits are not sure things. The no agreement point, therefore, will move somewhere in between the extremes which are represented by the damages the plaintiff seeks to recover and the guarantee that the suit will fail.

Peter, as a typical plaintiff, presumably has some idea as to how likely he is to win if the case goes to trial. He can place an expected value on his suit. This value may be represented as some point in the *BCD* bargaining space.

Figure 6.2 assumes that Peter believes he has a 50–50 chance of winning

---

6. Strictly speaking, the defendant is not quite in this position, for the plaintiff usually has the option of forgetting the whole thing and dropping the suit. In our discussion we are assuming that the plaintiff has decided the suit is worth more than the original no agreement outcome (-0, 0).

7. In an actual lawsuit, the timing of payment may matter since investment opportunities mean that a defendant would rather pay a certain sum 2 years hence than now, while the plaintiff would rather receive that sum now than 2 years from now. By dealing with utilities measured in dollars instead of actual dollars, we are implicitly incorporating such preferences in our model. But this is not particularly important, for the model has its heuristic value regardless.

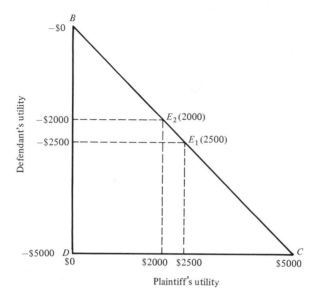

Figure 6.2

his $5,000 suit, and so places an expected value of $2,500 on going to judgment. If there were no expenses involved in bringing a lawsuit, the utility of the suit for Peter would be its expected value, which in our example is represented by point E_1 in Figure 6.2. Diane Defendant, on the other hand, might believe that Peter Plaintiff has only a 40 percent chance of winning. Again, if suits cost nothing, the utility of the suit would be its expected value, in this instance— $2,000 which is represented by point E_2 in Figure 6.2. Peter and Diane are unlikely to settle, because Diane does not expect to pay as much as Peter expects to receive.

Lawsuits, however, impose various costs. Some are largely psychological, such as the stress of having one's integrity questioned in court. Others are obviously financial, such as the costs of hiring lawyers and paying filing fees.[8]

---

8. Trubek and his coauthors (1983) in a large-scale study of civil litigation tried to measure the extent of the measurable costs (attorney's fees and litigation expenses). One of their measures, which they call "plaintiff success," (p. 114) employs the following formula:

$$\text{Plaintiff success} = \frac{\text{recovery} - \text{fees}}{\text{plaintiff's highest stakes estimate}}$$

where recovery is the amount the plaintiff receives in settlement or judgment, fees are attorney fees in the case, and plaintiff's highest stakes estimate is the plaintiff's attorney's estimate of what the case should settle for. By this measure plaintiffs on the average recovered between 50 and 60 percent of the highest stakes estimate, and the average attorney fee was between one-third and one-fifth of the total recovery (Trubek et al., 1983, pp. 111–115). The study also found that the longer the time is between filing and settlement or adjudication, the lower is the plaintiff success rate, and that cases that go to trial have on the average lower plaintiff success than cases that are settled in advance of trial. In the following discussion we focus on costs (and benefits) like attorney's fees that are readily translatable into dollars. One should keep in mind, however, that the argument applies more generally.

Assume now that for both Peter and Diane the expected value of the judgment is $2,500, which is represented by point *E* in Figure 6.3, and that pursuing the litigation will require the expenditure of $500 in court costs, attorney's fees, and the like. In this case the suit at the time it is filed has a utility of $2,000 ($2,500 − $500) for Peter and a utility of −$3,000 (−$2,500 − $500) for Diane. This joint payoff (−$3,000, 2,000) is represented by point *A* in Figure 6.3.

Given Peter and Diane's utilities, there are outcomes that both should see as preferable to the no agreement outcome of going to trial and receiving the court's judgment. They are the outcomes that fall in the shaded area, *AFG*. This area may be called the *negotiation set*. All agreements should fall in this area.

Consider why this is the case. Since Diane expects to pay $3,000 if an agreement is not reached, she would never agree to an outcome like point *C*. A settlement here would cost her $5,000, which is $2,000 more than pursuing the suit to judgment. Similarly, Peter would not agree to take less than $2,000 which is the utility of the suit to him.

The most Diane might agree to pay Peter is $3,000. This is point *G*. Diane by definition is indifferent between point *A*, that is, the expected outcome of the trial, and point *G*. Both represent a $3,000 cost to her. At the other extreme, Peter might settle for $2,000. This is point *F*. He is indifferent between points *A* and *F*. Both represent a utility of $2,000 to him.

Of course, a settlement at either point *F* or point *G* is not likely. It is more probable that Peter and Diane will settle for some amount between these points. The line connecting points *F* and *G* constitute what is called a *Pareto optimal*

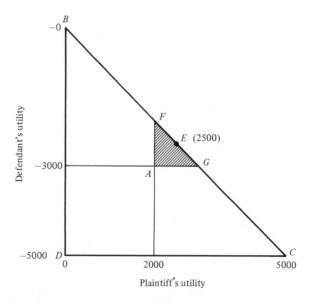

Figure 6.3

set. All points along this line are optimal in the sense that once one point on this line is chosen, there is no other outcome that is better for *both* parties. Furthermore, points off this line but in the negotiation set may leave both parties worse off than they would be if they settled at some point on this line. At a minimum, one party will be worse off than he would have been had the settlement occurred at some point on the line, and the other party will be no better off than she would have been had the settlement occurred at the line point.

If Peter and Diane cooperate, they will end up agreeing to settle at some point between *F* and *G* because these points constitute a set of cooperative solutions that have, for both of them, a higher utility than the suit. Thus point *E* has a value of $2,500 for Peter and a value of −$2,500 for Diane. Both can "save," or at least will believe at the time they are negotiating that they can save, $500 by settling here rather than going to trial. Under such circumstances it is not surprising if a case is settled. Given that this is the situation in most lawsuits, one might ask why cases ever go to trial?

Why Cases Go to Trial

There appear to be two central reasons why some cases go to trial: disagreement about the utility of the suit and gamesmanship. In the pages that follow we discuss these reasons.

Failure to Agree About the Utility of the Suit. Failure to agree about the utility of a suit is one important way in which settlement may be thwarted. Figure 6.4 portrays a situation where Diane believes that there is a 40 percent (E_2) chance that Peter will prevail while Peter believes he has a 60 percent (E_1) chance of winning, and each estimates litigation costs of $400. Thus Diane will be willing to settle for any sum less than $2,400 (.40 × 5,000 = $2,000 + 400 = $2,400), while Peter will be satisfied with anything more than $2,600 (.60 × 5,000 = $3,000 − $400 = $2,600). The negotiation sets, *P* and *D*, do not overlap. There will be no settlement because both Peter and Diane believe that they will be better off if they let the jury decide than if they take what the other is willing to offer. Of course, the estimates of one or both of them must be mistaken; but so long as each is convinced that it is the other who has erred, they will remain at loggerheads.[9]

9. Raffia (1982, p. 75) reports that in experiments where subjects are given identical information about an actual case and their assigned roles, those assigned the plaintiff's role assessed their probability of victory at 75 percent, while those assigned the defendant's role assessed the probability of a plaintiff victory at 55 percent. If people playing roles make this type of self-serving assessment, we should expect that actual litigants would do likewise. One task of lawyers is to help parties take a more realistic view of their chances in court.

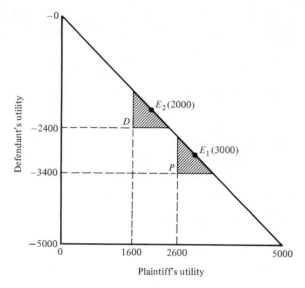

Figure 6.4

Interestingly, from this perspective, the more costly litigation becomes, the more likely the parties will find some middle ground that both prefer to pursuing the litigation. Figure 6.5 is identical to Figure 6.4 except that both sides perceive the costs of litigation to be $800 rather than $400.

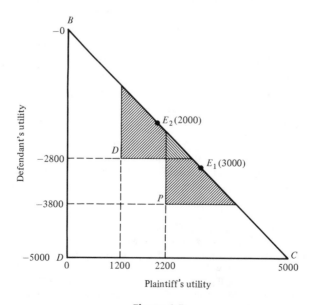

Figure 6.5

Diane, adding litigation costs of $800 to her expected value of $2,000, should be willing to consider settlements of up to $2,800, while Peter, subtracting $800 in litigation costs from his expected value of $3,000, will consider settling for as little as $2,200. Their negotiation sets now overlap since for each of them the utility of a settlement of between $2,200 and $2,800 exceeds the utility of taking the case to judgment. Thus there are settlement points that both find preferable to the prospect of a trial even though they retain their disparate views about the expected value of the suit.

For small suits such as our $5,000 case, costly litigation may, therefore, increase settlement potential.[10] For very large suits this is less likely. If our hypothetical case involves a potential liability of $5,000,000 rather than $5,000, the costs of litigation are likely to comprise a smaller proportion of the total expected value. If Peter believes that the expected value of the judgment is $3,000,000 and Diane believes that the expected value is $2,000,000, expected litigation costs of even $400,000 will not cause their respective negotiation sets to overlap.

In recent years, however, litigation over large amounts has become a very expensive proposition, and the costs of litigation are compounded by the costs that uncertainty respecting large contingent liabilities has for companies that must regularly enter the financial markets. Thus settlements are common even when hundreds of millions of dollars are potentially at stake. Other factors making for the settlement of such cases include the relative risk averseness of the parties, the different utilities that each party places on the marginal dollar or other matters at stake in the controversy, and the ability that parties may have to structure settlements so that their tax or other consequences differ from the consequences of judgments by shunting some costs to third parties.

One may also expect suits for large sums to be settled when the plaintiff has a small chance of prevailing so long as litigation costs promise to be substantial. Thus if a plaintiff estimates his chances at prevailing in a $5 million patent infringement suit at 5 percent and anticipates litigation costs of $200,000, he should be willing to settle for anything in excess of $50,000 (.05 × $5,000,000 = $250,000 − $200,000 = $50,000), while a defendant who anticipates similar litigation costs should be willing to settle for anything under $200,000, even if she believes the plaintiff's chance of prevailing approaches zero. In these circumstances an unscrupulous plaintiff might be willing to bring suit even if he shares the defendant's judgment that the suit has no merit, for an economically rational defendant might prefer to pay the plaintiff a substantial sum rather than allow the matter to proceed.[11] Thus even cases demanding large sums can have

---

10. Trubek et al. report that the smaller the civil suit is, the less likely it is to "pay." Looking at hourly-fee lawyers (lawyers paid by the hour), they note that plaintiffs' attorneys' fees equaled almost 20 percent of the amount recovered in state court cases under $10,000 and 40 percent in federal cases. On the other hand, in both state and federal cases over $50,000 plaintiffs' attorneys' fees amounted on the average to but 5 percent of the recovery (1983, pp. 120–121).

11. If economic rationality were the only criterion, the defendant should be willing to pay up to $200,000 so long as payment in the instant case will have no adverse long-run effects such as encouraging others to bring frivolous litigation.

a nuisance value. The implications of this will vary depending on each party's ability to inflict costs on the other, the symmetry of litigation costs, and the way in which costs are accumulated. We shall return to this matter at the conclusion of this section when we discuss the limitations of the model we are using.

Although more costly litigation does in general increase the probability that the negotiation sets of the parties will overlap, the potential for settlement is not necessarily great. In cases where the overlap is small, for the parties to settle they must agree on a point that is only slightly better than what they expect to receive by going to judgment. Moreover, the dynamics of the process by which each party tries to convince the other party that the other's estimate of the expected value of the suit is mistaken may effectively preclude agreement (see Ross, 1970, p. 164).

Modern trial procedures, particularly in civil cases, allow a lawyer to acquire substantial familiarity with his adversary's case before the trial itself commences. "Discovery" devices allow one side to question the other party's witnesses and examine documents and other evidence in the adversary's possession. One study (Glaser, 1968) finds little evidence that these devices increase the potential for settlement, but there is reason to believe that they should do so. In the first place, extensive discovery is expensive, so the availability of discovery will usually raise each party's anticipated costs of litigation. Second, discovery should allow each party to better anticipate the other's case (it is this point that Glaser questions); and so, as discovery proceeds, the parties' estimates of the likely value of the verdict should converge, which, other things being equal, means that negotiation sets are more likely to overlap.

Other things, however, do not remain equal. As the trial draws closer, the costs of litigation that serve to discount the expected value of the case for each party are progressively being incurred. By the time of the trial the costs of discovery, medical examinations, pretrial motions, and the like have already been borne. Thus although the negotiation sets may come to overlap, they also become smaller and the potential savings from negotiating a settlement diminish (see Figure 6.6).

In Figure 6.6 the large negotiation sets for the plaintiff and defendant illustrate the situation when suit is filed. P_1 is our plaintiff Peter's estimate of the utility of the suit and D_1 is the defendant Diane's. Assume that Peter's expected utility of \$3,000 reflects an estimated verdict of \$3,800 discounted by \$800 in expected litigation costs, while Diane's utility of \$2,000 reflects her belief that Peter will receive \$1,200 and that she will have to pay \$800 on top of this for litigation costs. In these circumstances, Peter and Diane's views of the likely verdict are so disparate that there is no room for settlement even though litigation costs are substantial. As the case progresses, Peter and Diane will learn more about each others legal theories and supporting evidence, and so they are likely to come to closer agreement on the value of the suit. In Figure 6.6 this is portrayed by a shift in Peter's estimated utility from P_1 to P_2 and a shift in Diane's estimate from D_1 to D_2. At the same time, however, the utility of going to trial (no agreement) moves closer to the expected value of the suit since some costs have

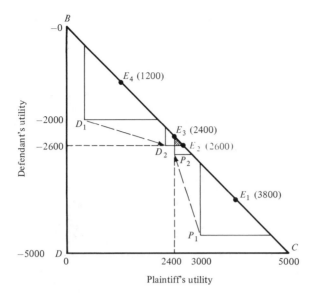

Figure 6.6

already been borne. Thus, by the eve of trial after three quarters of the litigation expenses have been incurred, Peter may expect a verdict of $2,600 ($E_2$), while Diane may anticipate paying $2,400 ($E_3$) if the case goes to judgment. Since in this example both Peter and Diane anticipate remaining costs of $200, there is a negotiation set, but it is confined to a relatively small space—between $2,400 and $2,600. Had the two litigants known at the outset of the case what they knew at the eve of trial, the negotiation set would have ranged between $1,800 and $3,200. Although Peter and Diane would probably have found it more difficult to settle on a specific figure within this range than they would have if the range were the narrower one that existed on the eve of trial, the considerably greater savings available through early settlement would have provided substantially more of an inducement to settle. Thus pretrial negotiations may be seen as a race between contracting negotiation sets and mutual agreement about the value of going to judgment.

To generalize, when parties to a lawsuit originally disagree about the value of going to judgment and cannot persuade each other to change their estimates, the fact that money is spent as the case progresses means that the prospects for settlement should diminish as the trial draws closer. It appears, however, that the parties are usually able to establish overlapping negotiation sets as the trial approaches. This is particularly likely in cases that do not require or justify extensive discovery, for trials of such cases are typically quite costly relative to pretrial proceedings. Indeed, in such cases the mutually acceptable negotiating set may have been obvious from the beginning, but one or both parties may have delayed settling either on the chance that helpful information would turn up during inexpensive pretrial proceedings or in order to give the other side the impression that more than obvious concessions were necessary to induce a settlement.[12]

Gamesmanship. In any lawsuit the range of possible settlements is, as we have seen, limited by what the parties expect to achieve should the case go to trial. We cannot expect a party to consider any settlement that will leave him worse off than he would be if he went to trial. The range of outcomes that leave a party no worse off than he would expect to be by going to trial is, as we have said, that party's negotiation set. The area of possible agreement is the area in which the parties' negotiation sets overlap or the mutually beneficial negotiation set. As this area of mutually beneficial outcomes[13] grows smaller, it may become more difficult to spot; but if it is perceived, the potential for settlement should increase since the *absolute* amount of conflict will be less. Put another way, in settling on a specific figure within the range of mutually acceptable outcomes, the smaller the area of overlap the less the parties have to fight about.

Figure 6.7 illustrates this in the context of the lawsuit we have been considering. We assume that at the time the litigation is begun Peter and Diane agree that the suit has an expected value of $2,500 and each expects costs of $500. Thus the area of overlap between the parties' negotiation sets is defined by triangle *AFG*. By the day of the trial $300 has been spent by each. The mutually beneficial negotiation set is now defined by triangle *XYZ*. Its range has been reduced from $1,000 (the space between $2,000 to $3,000) to $400 (the space between $2,300 to $2,700), for each party now has only $200 left to save by settling rather than by going to trial. From one perspective, it may appear that the parties will be more intransigent, because Diane who once would have paid up to $3,000 to settle will now pay no more than $2,700, and Peter who once would have accepted a settlement of $2,000 now insists on at least $2,300. Yet in a real sense the absolute amount of conflict has been more than cut in half. With the larger set, Peter and Diane had to fight over how to split the $1,000 savings that a settlement made possible. Now they only have to argue over $400. In both settings the precise division of the savings, and indeed the question of whether there will be a settlement and hence any savings at all depends on their skill at bargaining.[14]

---

12. It may also be that one or both parties is behaving irrationally or that one or both parties thinks that the threat of trial is needed to get the other to behave rationally. In our discussions of the game theory model, we are assuming that each party is acting rationally to maximize his or her expected utility.

13. The bounds of this area consist of points at which one or both parties are indifferent between the prospects of a trial and an offered settlement. At all points within the bounds both parties are better off than they would expect to be by going to trial.

14. We are assuming a two-party negotiation. Third parties help disputants reach settlements by pointing to mutually beneficial negotiation sets that the parties do not perceive and by suggesting points within that set on which it would be appropriate to settle.

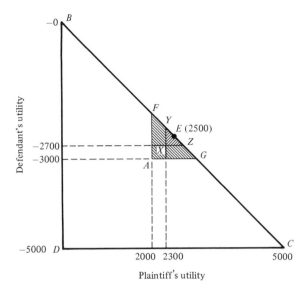

Figure 6.7

This is because the perception of a mutually beneficial negotiation set does not guarantee that a mutually beneficial solution will be reached. Agreement about the range of possible settlements is not sufficient. To settle, the parties must agree upon a sum certain. Negotiations within the context of a mutually beneficial set is a game of pure bargaining. Both parties would like to reach a settlement that comes as close as possible to their maximum. The farther apart these "best" positions are, the greater will be the amount of absolute conflict. Speaking of the situation where negotiation sets overlap substantially, Ross notes:

> This situation presents a large range of potential agreement, but paradoxically, it may result in no agreement whatsoever. Each side will try to insist that the bargain be set at its own target, knowing that the other side would prefer settlement at that point to trial, and one possible outcome of the situation is the trial that no one prefers. To reach a bargain, the parties require a point from which they cannot reasonably be expected to depart and from which they cannot reasonably expect the other to depart. (Ross, 1970, p. 159)

The various techniques that a party uses to get the other party to settle at a favorable point may be thought of as techniques of negotiation or gamesmanship. Three strategies are common: The first is to try to manipulate the opponent's negotiating set by changing his assessment of the expected value of the judgment or of its utility. Consider Figures 6.8, 6.9, and 6.10. Figure 6.8 is our standard situation, but we shall leave Peter and Diane and talk more generally. The plaintiff and defendant believe that the expected value of the judgment is $2,500 and − $2,500, respectively, and each anticipates litigation costs of $500. One strategy each party can follow is to attempt to change the other's expectation about the

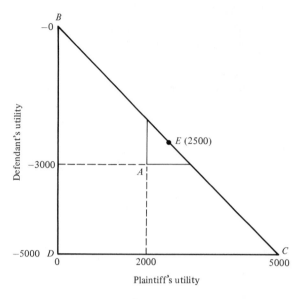

Figure 6.8

judgment. This can be done in a variety of ways. For example, at a crucial point in the negotiations one attorney may disclose evidence of which the other party was unaware. "You act as if it's your client's word against mine, but there were three eyewitnesses on the corner who saw the whole thing, and they say that your client was speeding."

Or the argument instead of being over what actually happened may focus on how jurors will react to the evidence of what happened. "You forget that my client was pregnant at the time and even though your doctors will testify that she lost her baby for other reasons, some of the jurors will think the accident had something to do with it."

Both procedural and substantive rules of law figure in such negotiations. "You know the judge will tell the jury they can't award damages for the loss of her child," or "The loss of the child is irrelevant. You won't be able to get it into evidence."

At times the negotiation process will lead counsel to seek a legal ruling on a particular issue that will affect the structure in the case. This is so common that there is a name for it—*motion practice*. In the example we are pursuing the defense counsel might make a motion before trial (called a *motion in limine*) asking the judge to rule that the loss of the child is irrelevant and that no evidence relating to it can be mentioned at trial. The expected value of a judgment and the prospects for settlement are dramatically affected by the way judges rule on such motions.

Figure 6.9 illustrates the situation where the plaintiff has persuaded the defendant to expect a judgment, E_2, of $3,000. The plaintiff's secret expectation

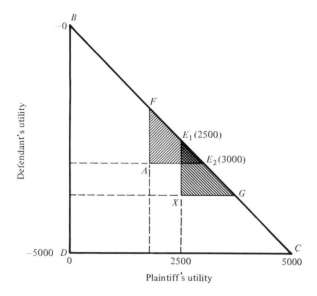

Figure 6.9

of $2,500 ($E_1$) remains unchanged, but the defendant who does not realize this will think that the negotiation space is the area XE_1G. E_1, the midpoint of settlements acceptable to the plaintiff, is likely to become the lower bound on any solution. Thus interpreted Figure 6.9 portrays the situation of the cynical or deceptive plaintiff who does not believe his own claims about the likely judgment.

Although such "puffing" is common in negotiations of all sorts, it is also common for the plaintiff and defendant to disagree honestly about the likely value of a judgment. Negotiation over the reality behind the lawsuit is especially important in such instances because unless the parties can be persuaded to a similar view of the case, settlement becomes unlikely. Thus Figure 6.9 also illustrates the situation where a defendant who initially believes that the expected value of a lawsuit is E_1 is persuaded by a plaintiff, who honestly believes that the expected value of the suit is E_2, to increase her estimate of the plaintiff's likely verdict.

Figure 6.10 depicts another strategy open to counsel, namely, to raise the other party's estimate of his litigation costs and thus diminish the utility of a judgment. In the example the plaintiff has succeeded in making the defendant anticipate litigation costs of $1,000, thus moving the no agreement point (going to trial) from A_1 to A_2 and diminishing the defendant's utility of going to judgment on a case valued at $-2,500$ (E_1) from $-$3,000 to $-$3,500. This should make the defendant more anxious to settle the matter and willing to consider offers that she would, with lower anticipated costs, have summarily rejected. Furthermore, if the increased costs are asymmetric in either dollar amount or in the

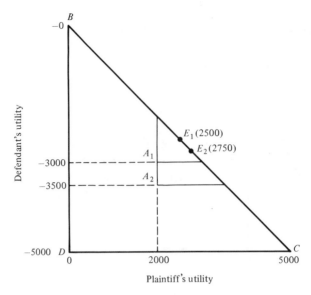

Figure 6.10

capacity of the parties to bear them, this asymmetry is likely to be reflected in the settlement even though the parties may share a common assessment of the expected value of the judgment. In the example the plaintiff's anticipated litigation costs remain at $500 and his lower bound (which we shall henceforth call his *resistance point*) remains at $2,000. If the final settlement were to split the difference between the parties' resistance points, and in a crude way this often happens, the plaintiff would recover $2,750 [(2,000 + 3,500) divided by 2]. This is $250 more than the $2,500 [(3,000 + 2,000) divided by 2] the plaintiff would recover if the parties' anticipated costs were equal.

The strategy of raising the opponent's anticipated litigation costs is most effective at the level of threat, since once the opposing side has incurred the threatened costs, they can no longer be avoided by settlement. However, on some occasions it is necessary to impose some costs on the opposition before threats are accepted as credible. Thus one party may notice (tell the other party that he must make his witnesses available for) a series of depositions in the belief that this will induce a settlement, and, when it does not, make the first depositions especially time-consuming in order to emphasize how much the litigation will cost (cf. Schrag, 1968; Stern, 1976). Again, motion practice will yield preliminary legal judgments that may have important implications for the negotiations. A party might, for example, seek a ruling that certain matters are privileged in order to avoid being obligated to answer sensitive questions or to make particular witnesses available. The threat to raise costs, like other threats in negotiations, may be declaratory in the sense that the party is simply stating what good practice requires him to do if the matter is not settled, or it may be tactical in that it would not be made but for its likely effect on the negotiations. In the latter instance the threat may or may not be carried out.

Thus the exigencies of gamesmanship mean that negotiations often involve threats and counterthreats as well as assessments of the threats that have been made. The following fictitious dialogue between a plaintiff's attorney (P.A.) and an insurance adjuster (Adj.) illustrates some of the options:

ADJ.: Six thousand dollars is our last offer.

P.A.: I'm afraid my client won't let me come off $10,000.

ADJ.: Maybe you'd better go back to your client and tell him that if he doesn't settle now, I'm going to put this on the back burner. You know the case won't come to trial for 2 years. We're earning a lot more than the legal interest (i.e., the interest the court would assess on a judgment—typically at a level set by law) on our reserves, so I don't care if the case is postponed forever, but your client needs his money now.

P.A.: I wouldn't delay if I were you. Who knows what the medical bills will be by the time of trial?

ADJ.: He's been fully treated by now. I don't see where you're going to get any more doctor's bills.

P.A.: I wouldn't be too sure about that. He's been complaining that his back is still sore, and I was thinking of bringing in a few specialists.

ADJ.: You'll have to eat those costs. Even your own doctor pronounced him 100 percent. Look, if $10,000 is your last word I'm leaving. I imagine you'll hear from our counsel in about 18 months when they set a trial date.

P.A.: Come off it—you know that your company doesn't let cases of this size lie fallow for more than 3 months. I'll split the difference. Make it $8,000 and it's a deal.

ADJ.: I can't go above $7,500.

P.A.: $7,750.

ADJ.: Look, do you want to see my instructions—$7,500 is my max.

P.A.: I think I can sell my client on that.

In the preceding dialogue each side begins with its purported final offer. The insurance adjuster then makes a threat. He points out that delay is far more costly to the defendant than to the insurance company and threatens substantial delay if the case is not settled on his terms. The plaintiff's attorney responds with a counterthreat, the plaintiff's medical costs will rise in the interim. The adjuster dismisses the threat, but the attorney rather than giving in tries to make it more explicit. The adjuster responds with an ambiguous observation, "You'll have to eat the costs," whose double meaning is clear to both parties. Not only will the costs be deemed unnecessary and so not be compensable, but it may turn out that the attorney, who has been advancing litigation costs, will end up paying for the examinations himself. The attorney will find it difficult to charge the costs of an examination to the client if the court holds that it was unnecessary. The adjuster repeats his threat to let the matter lie fallow, but the attorney drawing on his knowledge of the insurance company makes it clear that he knows the threat to be empty and then offers to "split the difference," a common way of settling on a specific point when there is a range of Pareto optimal points from which to choose. The adjuster responds that he cannot go that high, and, when the attorney again tries to split the difference, he offers to prove that he is firmly committed to a top figure. Rather than insult the adjuster by accepting the invitation to verify what he has said, the attorney accepts; but since he began by saying that his client would not settle for less than $10,000, he must make the settlement contingent on his ability to persuade his client. Obviously, he thinks he can do this. Indeed, he may already have the authority to settle for $7,500, but given the dynamics of the negotiation process and the prospect of future negotiations he cannot admit it.

The last portion of this dialogue illustrates a third important tactic of negotiation, namely (to take the plaintiff's point of view), to convey the impression that one's negotiation set has its lower bound near the defendant's upper bound. Consider for example Figure 6.11.

If a defendant who would prefer any settlement under $3,000 to a trial accurately estimates that the plaintiff would prefer any settlement above $2,000 to a trial, the negotiation set is defined by triangle AFG, and there is $1,000 to be contested. A defendant in these circumstances would be reluctant to settle for as much as $2,800 because, even though he would prefer such a settlement to a trial, he knows he can do a lot better. If, however, the defendant believes that the plaintiff is truly unwilling to settle for less than $2,800, the negotiation set is defined by the shaded area A_1F_1G, and the defendant is likely to settle for $2,800 or even $2,900 because he prefers such a settlement to trial and knows he cannot get a better deal. Thus negotiators try to convey the impression that unless they can get a settlement toward the top (bottom) of the other party's settlement range, they would prefer going to trial and there will be no deal.

One way for a plaintiff to convey this impresssion is to convince the defendant that he believes that the expected value of the judgment is higher than the defendant thinks. Thus even if the plaintiff's attempt to convince the defendant to change her resistance point fails, the plaintiff may have gained from the effort because he may have laid the groundwork for a settlement near the boundary of the defendant's settlement range.[15]

Similar results can be obtained if the plaintiff can convince the defendant that he honestly believes that his costs of litigation will be low. If, for example, the plaintiff and defendant both agree that E_1 is the expected value of the judgment, but the plaintiff persuades the defendant that he expects the litigation

---

15. The plaintiff, however, is not indifferent between persuading the defendant that the expected judgment is higher than the defendant initially believed and persuading him that the plaintiff sincerely believes that it is. If, for example, the defendant actually believed the cost of going to judgment was $3,300 plus $500 in litigation costs, the negotiation set would be defined by A_2,F,G, meaning that negotiations seeking up to $3,800 might succeed. But if the defendant did not think the case would cost him more than $2,500 plus $500 in litigation costs, he would not settle for more than $3,000 regardless of what he thought the plaintiff believed.

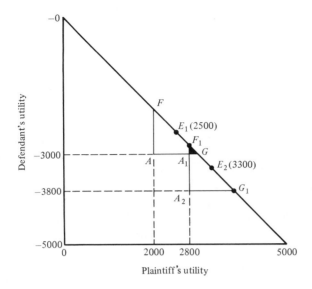

Figure 6.11

to cost no more than $200, the plaintiff's resistance point will be at $2,300 rather than at $2,000 and the Pareto optimal line will run from $2,300 to $3,000. The plaintiff is likely to fare better in such a negotiation than in one in which the line stretches downward to $2,000.

It is not, however, necessary to change the other party's views about how one values the case or about what one expects his costs to be in order to negotiate a settlement that is relatively favorable given the range of Pareto optimal points. One need only convince the other party that he will not budge from a point that is within the other's settlement range. In the preceding dialogue, both parties use a common ploy—they attribute a figure to a third party who may not appreciate the range of rational settlements and who is not present to change his mind. Thus the lawyer originally says that his client will not move off $10,000. The adjuster refused to accept this ploy, however, and suggested that the lawyer go back and talk to his client. Had the lawyer thought that $10,000 was within the insurance company's settlement range, he might have adjourned the meeting and then come back and explained to the adjuster that despite his entreaties to be flexible, the client had a fixation on the figure of $10,000. ("I honestly believe that if you offered him $11,000 he would turn it down and say he wanted ten grand.") Had the adjuster thought the lawyer could not influence his client on this issue and if $10,000 was within his settlement range, even at the upper end, the adjuster probably would have settled. It would have been uneconomic to refuse.

This technique is like the other techniques we have discussed in that the allegation of a fixed resistance point may be honestly conveying information to the other party or it may be assumed for the purposes of the negotiation. Good negotiators can bluff, which means making reality appear otherwise than it really is.

One problem with conveying the partial or misleading information that is essential to a bluff is that the parties may so successfully mislead each other that they may decide that a settlement is impossible even when there are settlements that both would prefer to going to trial. Bluffing, in other words, can compound the problems that are posed by the fact that even when the parties realize that a range of mutually beneficial settlements is possible, it may be difficult to settle on a figure within that range. With the possibility that negotiation sets might not, or might not be perceived to, overlap and with the difficulties of fixing on a settlement point even when sets do overlap, one might wonder how it is that settlements are common. The primary reason is, of course, the financial advantages to settlement. Although it may be difficult to find a point of agreement, the incentives to search for one are great. Moreover, the parties are aided in their search by aspects of the negotiation process that help them to perceive what is in their mutual interest and aid in overcoming problems of pure bargaining.

Some aspects make it likely that a party will perceive that he shares a negotiation set with his adversary and that his adversary realizes this. The most important of these is the legal culture that is shared by the attorneys on both sides. Ordinarily attorneys are likely to assess the law similarly, which means they are apt to reach similar judgments about the expected value of the judgment. If they do not because the attorneys interpret the law differently or have a different view of the facts, prospects for the eventual reconciliation of views are enhanced by the availability of discovery devices, the possibility of securing rulings on preliminary questions of law, and the factual disclosures and legal arguments that each side can make in the course of the negotiation process. In tort litigation a particularly important bit of information, usually available through discovery although not generally admissible at trial, is the liability limits of any insurance carried by the defendant.

We saw in our discussion of responsibility rules that when cases are routine and repetitive, deep case logics tend to be replaced by shallow ones. Shallow logics enhance the prospects for negotiated settlements because they allow for less ambiguity, hence there is less to be disputed. When the typical auto accident of low to moderate severity is negotiated, liability, as we have noted, may be determined by a rule of thumb such as ''the driver emerging from the controlled intersection is responsible for the accident.'' Similar ''rules'' develop on the issue of damages. Plaintiff's attorneys and insurance adjusters will apparently begin and often end their discussion about what the plaintiff should receive for his injuries at a figure that is three times the ''specials,'' that is, three times the medical expenses in the case.

In addition, there are norms for conducting negotiations that help the parties perceive the existence of a shared negotiation set when this is in fact the case. Negotiators are expected to make initial offers in turn (sometimes there is considerable jockeying about who begins), and an offer by one party is expected to be met by a counteroffer from the other. The level of the opening offers and the rate at which offers converge will give experienced negotiators a good idea of whether they share a negotiation set.

When there is a negotiation set, the choice of which Pareto optimal figure to settle on is, as we have seen, one of pure bargaining.[16] In principle, either party should be willing to settle on any figure within the range. Domain specific rules like the "three times specials" formula in minor auto accident cases help establish specific points of agreement. A more general rule is that at some point it is appropriate to split the difference. Round numbers also facilitate agreement. To drop a claim that deviates slightly from a round number is a sign of magnanimity; a similar concession to a point lacking in cultural meaning may suggest that one is weak, or a fool (Goffman, 1970). Thus in a negotiation that has reached the stage where the defendant offers $850 and the plaintiff demands $1,100, if the defendant's next move is to offer $950, it is a fair bet that the parties will settle on $1,000.

When parties share a negotiation set but are unable to reach an agreement, it is often because each party has placed himself in a position from which he cannot retreat without "losing face." Thus if each party has used the ploy of firmly committing himself to a figure that is toward the favorable end of his settlement range, each may find that he is unable to compromise further without appearing dishonest in the context of the instant negotiation and losing credibility for future ones. An interesting form of cooperation in negotiation occurs when one party tries to provide the other with a face-saving excuse to move from a point of commitment (Raffia, 1982, p. 129). When the plaintiff's attorney says that his client will not settle for less than $1,000 and the defendant's counsel responds with a detailed analysis showing that the injuries cannot be worth more than $700, the plaintiff's attorney may respond by emphasizing how attractive the client is and how likely he is to attract jury sympathy. This gives the defendant a way to raise her offer without retreating from her analysis of what the injuries are objectively worth.

Of course, not all cases are settled. When they are not, the parties will have to settle for the no agreement point, the trial outcome. Settlement attempts may fail because there was never a range for possible agreement or because the parties misestimated each other and failed to reach a firm point within a mutually beneficial negotiation set. Parties may also lose the opportunity to settle because information may not be transferred with sufficient speed and clarity or because neither party knows crucial information until it is too late. Thus on the eve of trial the parties may realize that it would have made sense for them to have settled the case when suit was first filed. However, by the time this realization

---

16. As we mentioned earlier, lawsuits are best understood as non-zero sum games. However, on the Pareto optimal line within the negotiating set, bargaining is on a zero sum basis. Within this restricted range of mutually advantageous solutions to the original contest, one party's gains come entirely at the expense of the other. One way of attempting to reach a settlement in such a situation is to add an item to the negotiating agenda so that this no longer need be the case (Menkel-Meadow, 1984).

occurs so much of the litigation costs may be ''sunk'' that a settlement no longer makes sense. Generally speaking, as the trial draws nearer, the range of possible settlements lessens; but if there is some overlap in the parties' negotiation sets, the potential for finding a point to settle on increases. Settlements right before trial are common, and on occasion settlements are reached while the jury is deliberating its verdict or, indeed, after a jury verdict has been returned, pending appeal.[17]

Relative Amount of Conflict of Interest

Thus far we have been discussing legal disputes in which the outcome is some monetary transfer from the defendant to the plaintiff. In the figures we have used, as in Figure 6.12, the line between B and C has been drawn as a straight line at a 45° angle to the axis. This diagonal portrays the situation where any agreement represents a certain dollar loss to the defendant and a corresponding dollar gain to the plaintiff. Not all lawsuits, however, are over some fixed dollar amount. We must consider the criminal trial.

Most criminal cases are settled before trial. Either the case is dismissed, in which case the charges are dropped, or the defendant pleads guilty to the charged offense or to some lesser charge. Pleas of guilty are usually seen as being a *quid pro quo* for concessions regarding sentencing. Hence the process that generates guilty pleas usually goes by the name ''plea bargaining.''

In the criminal courts of the United States trials are relatively rare events. In some big cities 90 percent and more of the verdicts in criminal cases that reach judgment are agreed to by the parties (see Heumann, 1975, p. 515). Why are settlements so remarkably frequent? No doubt many forces are at work. Yet considerations of financial cost, which were central to our analysis of civil cases, do not explain these agreements. Criminal litigation often has nothing to do with the allocation of dollars between parties, and the state commonly pays the litigation costs of each side. We must search further to explain bargain justice in criminal cases.

In his work on plea bargaining, Milton Heumann (1975, 1977) notes that the perception of the actors in the criminal courts he studied is that most defendants are guilty of the crime charged. (Estimates range between 80 and 90 percent.) They are legally as well as factually guilty. Furthermore, there is a general belief that if defendants plead guilty they are likely to be rewarded with a reduced charge or sentence (Heumann, 1975, p. 525). Although the accuracy of this belief has been disputed (Eisenstein & Jacob, 1977; Rhodes, 1978), it appears that defendants convicted by trial rather than by plea do pay a penalty, particularly if their case was not close and they chose a jury trial (Uhlman & Walker, 1979; Brereton & Casper, 1981–82).

---

17. Since appeals are always possible, the threat of an appeal and the costs that go with it may be used to increase the bargaining range before and after trial. In this sense even formal trial court judgments have only an expected value. They too are not sure things.

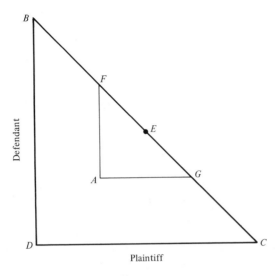

Figure 6.12

Given these perceptions, it is not hard to understand why many defendants plead guilty. Most have little chance of being acquitted at trial or at least they or their lawyers think so. (But see Finkelstein, 1975.) Thus the expected value of the judgment is low and any prosecutorial commitment to reduce the charge or sentence comes close to being the best outcome a criminal defendant can hope for. Indeed, guilty pleas would not disappear if prosecutors ceased bargaining. In some cases the system is overdetermined, meaning that there are a number of factors, any one of which would lead a defendant to plead guilty. Thus, abolishing all prosecutorial concessions for guilty pleas, as has apparently been done in some jurisdictions for some types of crimes, would not reduce the guilty plea rate to zero or anywhere near it (Rubenstein & White, 1979). Genuine remorse and the desire to avoid the hassles of a trial also leads defendants to plead guilty. Furthermore, even without a promised concession, a defendant may feel that he will do better at sentencing if he does not protest his guilt. Finally, defendants often take their counsel's advice in deciding whether to plead, and defense counsel may have substantial interests, both financial and organizational, in encouraging their clients to plead (Sudnow, 1965; Blumberg, 1967; Altschuler, 1975). In the analysis that follows, we focus on the formal logic of the system and ignore factors other than the defendant's opportunity to get a good deal. We discuss the limitations of this focus later.

Prosecutors also perceive benefits from plea bargains (see, generally, Heumann, 1977, pp. 92–126). First, guilty pleas guarantee convictions. Prosecutors, especially those who must run for reelection, may feel that they will be judged in part by their conviction rates. Second, guilty pleas are organizationally efficient. They make the prosecutor's job easier and allow him to concentrate his office's resources on "big" cases heading for trial. Pleas also conserve court time and money. This too can be important to prosecutors, who together with judges form the core of the state's criminal justice establishment. Third, the plea bargain enables the prosecutor to retain more control over the ultimate disposition of the case than he would have if the matter proceeded to trial and conviction. After conviction the prosecutor's sentencing recommendations are just recommendations, but plea bargains typically limit and may in practice foreclose a judge's sentencing discretion.

Fourth, prosecutors by virtue of their control over the charging process and greater knowledge of the system may feel that they give up nothing in the bargain. Thus a prosecutor may overcharge initially (i.e., charge more crimes or more serious crimes than his evidence supports) and agree in exchange for a guilty plea to some charges to dismiss or downgrade those charges on which he did not expect to secure a conviction. Even when a prosecutor has not overcharged he may be willing to drop a number of counts of a multicount indictment, because when defendants are convicted on multiple counts, they often receive the same sentence on each to run concurrently. A prosecutor may similarly ''con'' a defendant by offering one who faces a 10-year sentence, a 2-year sentence contingent on a guilty plea, knowing that 2 years is the usual sentence for those in the defendant's circumstances who are convicted at trial.

Fifth, even where plea bargains yield lighter sentences than those that would follow convictions at trial, if the case is of low visibility, there is usually little reason for the prosecutor to be concerned with small differences in sentence length or in the seriousness of the charge on which the defendant is convicted. Finally, some defendants can offer real value in return for generous plea concessions: They can turn state's evidence; they can clear those who are falsely suspected; they can inform on fellow criminals; or they can make the police look good by admitting to more crimes than could ever be proved against them, thus enhancing the police clearance record. The last appears to be a particular perverse trade-off, but apparently it happens (Skolnick, 1966).

Focusing on the interests of the prosecutor in maximizing his conviction rate while keeping costs to a minimum and the interests of accused criminals in minimizing their expected sentences, we can best represent the situation of the criminal trial by using a diagram such as the one in Figure 6.13.

The *BC* line is no longer straight. Rather, it has one (or more) kinks in it so that it bends out from the axis. If the parties can reach an agreement at a point like *H*, they can both come closer to achieving their best outcome than they could if the situation were characterized by a *BC* line that was straight.

Since there is no common unit like dollars with which we can measure either the prosecutor's or the defendant's utilities, we will in order to illustrate this point more clearly *normalize* the two situations. This requires us to assign arbitrary values to the extreme outcomes. Point *A* (the no agreement point, that is, the utility of going to trial) is the worst either party can do since they always have this option. We give this worst point a value of zero for both parties (0, 0). The best the defendant can hope for is point *F*, because the prosecutor would never agree to a better deal than what he would gain from a trial after all the costs of a trial (including such matters as court congestion and the possibility

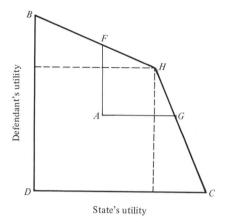

Figure 6.13

of an acquittal) have been accounted for. We give it a value of 1 for the defendant. For the prosecutor *F* is equal to *A* and is the minimum "payment" that he can expect, for if *F* were less than *A* the prosecutor would by definition rather try the case than bargain it out. In the language of game theory, the prosecutor is indifferent between *A* and *F*; both have the value of zero. Thus the overall value of *F* is 1 for the defendant and zero for the plaintiff (1, 0). The same argument in reverse applies to point *G*. Point *G* represents the best the prosecutor can do, and so has a value of 1 from his perspective. This, however, represents the worst the defendant can do—being as bad as the trial—and so is worth zero to the defendant. Thus this point is specified by the joint value (0, 1).

Figures 6.14 and 6.15 represent the normalized versions of Figures 6.12 and 6.13. Compare point *E* in Figure 6.14 to point *H* in Figure 6.15. Point *E* in Figure 6.14 represents one point on the Pareto optimal line connecting *F* and *G*. We may give it a numerical value. Since for the defendants point *E* is halfway between points *F* and *A*, it has a value of .5 for the defendant. Since it is also halfway between points *A* and *G*, it has a value of .5 for the prosecutor as well. The combined payoff at point *E* is (.5, .5). In Figure 6.15 point *H* is, for the defendant, closer to point *F* than to point *A*. Since point *F* is the best outcome for which the defendant could hope, point *H* comes closer to realizing the defendant's best outcome. In the figure it represents an outcome that is 70 percent of the most that the defendant could hope for. It is, therefore, given a value of .7. The situation is similar for the prosecutor since point *H* comes closer to point *G* than to point *A*. As we have drawn the figure an outcome at point *H* gives the prosecutor 70 percent of what he would get from his preferred outcome.

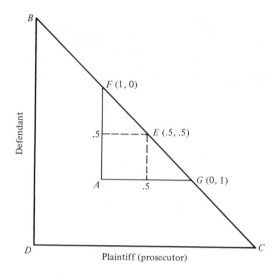

Figure 6.14

Again, the point has a value of .7. Thus the combined payoff at point H is (.7, .7).

By comparing the two figures, we see that in the trial represented by Figure 6.15 there is less conflict, for the parties can simultaneously come closer to achieving their best outcome than they can in the trial represented by Figure 6.14. Our argument is that criminal trials typically resemble Figure 6.15 more

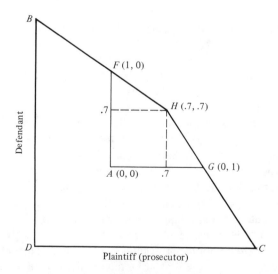

Figure 6.15

than Figure 6.14.[18] The reason for the difference between our models of criminal and civil trials is that in the ordinary civil damage action both parties are concerned with maximizing their monetary well-being, so concessions that enrich the plaintiff tend to be at the defendant's expense and vice versa.[19] In a criminal case, however, the parties have, as we have noted, more disparate stakes. The defendant will be concerned primarily with avoiding or minimizing the stigma of being labeled a criminal and with minimizing the time or monetary cost of any penalty he will face. The prosecutor will be concerned with factors such as maintaining an efficient office, avoiding court congestion, keeping up his conviction rate, avoiding bad publicity, and ensuring that the defendant is properly but not excessively punished. When parties have stakes that vary in these ways, satisfying the concerns of one party does not necessarily require a more or less equivalent diminution in the satisfactions of the other party. Indeed, one can conceive of a situation where a prosecutor feels he must secure a conviction but has no further desire to punish an accused while the accused does not care if he has a criminal record but is terrified by the prospect of spending time in jail. In these circumstances a guilty plea followed by a suspended sentence might leave each party feeling that he had achieved virtually everything he wanted from the litigation. In short, criminal cases may lend themselves to bargained settlements because, as indicated by the bulge in our normalized diagram, there often is a comparatively low level of relative conflict of interest.

Thus it is neither surprising that plea bargaining rates in some cities reach 90 percent or more nor that rates and styles of plea bargaining are sensitive to changes in legal and political systems. Mandatory sentencing for certain crimes may, for example, lead the parties to bargain over the charge to be preferred rather than over the specific sentence (Newman, 1966). Prosecutors desiring to show toughness toward some or all criminals may, by strictly controlling their subordinates, largely eliminate overt bargaining, although this may be taken into account when charges are initially preferred or by judges in sentencing those

---

18. Some civil cases fit the model we apply to the criminal trial more closely than they do the pure dollar bargaining model that applies best to tort and some breach of contract cases. For example, in divorce cases issues of child custody, alimony, and property settlement make for a situation with many kinks of the kind we see in Figure 6.15. Indeed, one skill of a good negotiator or mediator may be to introduce issues that create kinks and so reduce the relative conflict of interest (Raffia, 1982; Menkel-Meadow, 1984.)

19. As the preceding footnote indicates, we do not mean to suggest that the stakes in a civil suit must be limited to money. Even when money damages are sought, other "goods" are often also at stake, and sometimes they will be the predominant concerns. A corporate defendant in a products liability case, for example, may be more concerned with bad publicity or the precedent a case will establish than with the money that it might have to pay the plaintiff. In civil rights actions both parties may be concerned primarily with the symbolic implications of the court's verdict and the way in which future behavior may be changed. When the parties have qualitatively different stakes in a civil action, the potential for settlement may increase because, as we show for criminal cases, the relative conflict of the parties diminishes. Thus a personal injury plaintiff's promise not to share information acquired in a products liability action may be crucial to an out-of-court settlement in an amount the plaintiff will accept.

who have pled guilty without an overt bargain (Loftin, Heumann, & McDowall, 1982). Also, procedures may develop that minimize overt bargaining because they give at least one party and perhaps both a relatively desirable mix of rewards without the need to reach an explicit agreement. When such procedures are available, they can replace the full trial as the no agreement point and so diminish one or both parties' incentive to bargain. Thus for many years in Los Angeles defendants had the option of being tried on the basis of the transcripts of the testimony given at their preliminary hearings,[20] and they received sentencing concessions for agreeing to this procedure. The process required little court time and the verdict was generally preordained; hence it has been called a ''slow plea of guilty'' (Mather, 1974, 1979). Schulhofer (1984) describes a similarly abbreviated trial that substitutes for guilty pleas in Philadelphia, but suggests that the verdict is sufficiently in doubt that the process cannot be dismissed as a ''slow plea.''

THE FAIRNESS OF SETTLEMENTS

Thus far we have presented models indicating why most cases are settled. The basic point of the argument is that in most cases the costs of going to trial are such that there exists a range of outcomes that both parties prefer to the situation they expect to be in should they pursue the matter to a judicial judgment. It may be against a party's self-interest to be embroiled in litigation, but once a case is commenced, neither party is likely to agree to a settlement unless it is in his perceived self-interest. The fact that a settlement is agreed upon does not, however, mean that the settlement is fair. But, what is a ''fair settlement?'' It is to this question we now turn.

In the case of sophisticated businesspeople fighting over a contract claim, we might feel that any agreement they both assent to is fair. In the case of a criminal defendant, however, people argue both that the plea bargaining process is unfair to the accused and that it allows some criminals to get off too easy. Similarly, some people feel that severely injured accident victims are often forced to settle for less than they deserve, while others believe that insurance companies pay too much. Are these views correct in any sense, or are they simply romantic siding with the underdog on the one hand and conservative hardheadedness on the other? The answer to this question as to so many others depends on one's point of view and on the factors one is willing to consider in deciding issues of fairness.

---

20. A preliminary hearing is a hearing closely following an arrest at which the state presents a limited amount of testimony to show that there is probable cause for holding the defendant for trial. The defendant may or may not testify.

Fairness Given a Negotiation Set

One approach to the issue of fairness is to accept the legitimacy of any mutually beneficial negotiation set and to ask what constitutes fairness given that set. Clearly, a fair agreement will not lie outside the negotiation set, for that would impose on at least one of the parties a worse outcome than the party would achieve by refusing to settle and pursuing a judicial judgment. Yet a litigant might be forced to accept such a settlement if he could not afford to litigate the matter fully even though the expected payoff from litigation was far greater than the anticipated costs. Personal injury victims might find themselves in this situation if the contingent fee were outlawed, and it may describe the situation of classes of victims whose aggregate damages are great but who, for reasons we shall describe in Chapter 10, cannot raise sufficient funds to invest adequately in litigation.

A second constraint, although perhaps not essential to fairness, is that an agreement should be chosen from among those outcomes that constitute the Pareto optimal set. The outcome should be on the *FG* line in Figure 6.16. Any outcome off the line is inferior because there will always be an outcome on the line that can make at least one party better off without hurting the other. The difficult question is whether there is some particular point on the *FG* line that, more than any other, constitutes a fair agreement? A possible candidate is the "split the difference" solution. This implies an outcome at point *E* (.5, .5) in the normalized Figure 6.16.

Such an outcome is sometimes called the Nash solution, for John Nash (1950), who was the first to present the argument and mathematics for this result.

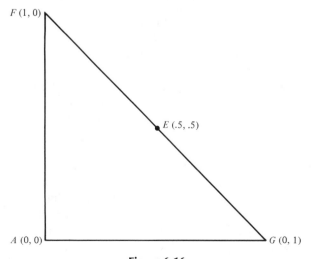

Figure 6.16

It is also known as the *product maximization* solution because the product of the two points (their value when multiplied) is the largest possible (i.e., .25, the product of .5 × .5, is larger than the product of any other two numbers that define a point in the *AFG* triangle). If a case were before an arbitrator who was told only the parties' resistance points and who had to choose some figure at which to settle, he might choose the Nash solution as basically fair. Indeed, if he chose otherwise, we might consider him a bad arbitrator. In cases of pure bargaining, however, the Nash solution appears to be but one of many "fair" bargains. A voluntary non-Nash settlement within the negotiation set can only be called unfair if one has an ethical theory that requires people, who can by acting jointly maximize their wealth, to split equally the dollar amount by which they expect to increase their well-being. We are not aware of any such theory.

The argument that the Nash solution, or, indeed, that any point on the Pareto optimal line is fair, is, of course, premised on accepting the mutually beneficial negotiation set as itself fair. However, the negotiation set is mutually beneficial only in the sense that it allows solutions that both parties prefer to a final judgment. When we look beyond the negotiation set to the utility of the suit, the question of fairness becomes truly problematic because factors that influence the parties' preferences may themselves be regarded as unfair.

Fairness Beyond the Negotiation Set

Earlier we noted that the utility of a lawsuit is primarily a function of two factors: the merits of the legal claim and the cost of litigation. The utility of the suit represents the expected value of the judgment minus the costs of going to judgment. Insofar as these are the only factors involved in determining utility, the negotiation set that emerges seems fair. Of course, one side may be put in a poor bargaining position because from his perspective the expected value of the judgment is low. But this does not constitute unfairness unless we believe the rule of law that governs the case is itself unfair. If, however, we believe a party should do as well as the law entitles him to, or better if mutual savings can be achieved by a settlement, unfairness emerges when the utility of the suit is influenced by factors other than its cost and expected value. Such factors include delay and extra-legal threats. We have already alluded to them. Here we discuss them in more detail.

Delay. Lawsuits take varying lengths of time to reach trial. When they take a long time the cost of not reaching an agreement, for at least one party, tends to increase. Delay is one of many possible ways in which litigation expenses grow. Sometimes, however, delay should not be treated as just another factor influencing the cost of a legal judgment. There is some truth in the old saying that "justice delayed is justice denied." This is so because delay often works to the advantage of defendants. When a plaintiff seeks money damages, the defendant's calculation of the suit's utility will reflect her estimate about *when* any judgment will have to be paid. If the likely trial date is 5 years away, the expected loss from the suit may be discounted by the fact that no payment will be necessary during the intervening time. The money that might be paid to the plaintiff can earn interest over that period.

For the plaintiff the opposite is true. Delayed payment means that any final award must be discounted to its present value. Moreover, some plaintiffs may find themselves extremely hard pressed to make ends meet in the intervening time. They need money now. Money that, if it is to be paid at all, will not be paid for 5 years may be worth very little. Thus the expected length of the time to trial may alter the negotiation set. For this reason defendants in some cases actively seek delay. Here legal rules are important. Rules like discovery rules may be used not for their intended purpose, but for the time the procedures they prescribe take. Certain rights—such as the right when certain matters are at issue to take interlocutory appeals (i.e., appeals that interrupt the litigation before a verdict has been returned) can add years to the time it takes to reach a final judgment. Other rules can encourage settlements or speed up the litigation process.

In criminal cases the effects of delay on the negotiation set depend on whether the defendant is in jail or on bail. Delay usually aids bailed defendants, because the prosecution, which bears the burden of proof, may find that its witnesses disappear or that their testimony becomes less convincing as memories fade. For those who do not make bail, the situation is quite different since by being confined to jail they are paying a penalty in advance of conviction.

The most obvious solution to this problem is, of course, speedy trials. In the criminal law there is a right to a speedy trial written into the Constitution. Moreover, many states and the federal government now have statutes requiring that indicted defendants be brought to trial within a specified period (usually 3 to 6 months) following the indictment. Even though these statutes have enough exceptions that they are sometimes honored in the breach, delays of a year or two in trying criminal cases are no longer common. In civil cases there is no right to a speedy trial and cases can sometimes take 5 or 6 years or even longer to reach final judgment. On the civil side one way to redress the balance is to require that the defendant pay interest on any final judgment either from the time of the wrong or from the time when the suit was first filed. However, statutes that provide for "legal interest" have historically not been indexed to market interest rates or inflation and so may remove only a portion of the defendant's incentives for delay. Moreover, the prospect of a fair award in the future does not restore fairness to the negotiation set for the penniless defendant who cannot afford a long wait.

Extra-legal Threats and Deception. The second way in which negotiation sets may be unfair is when one party is able by threat or deception to convince the other that he faces especially harsh consequences if he goes to trial and loses. Fear of such consequences will reduce the opponent's utility judgment. If such threats and deceptions are empty, the resulting negotiation is unfair because the opponent does not appreciate the quality of the "game" in which he is involved.

If the threats are honest, the situation is unfair because the defendant faces worse consequences than he would have received had negotiation been impossible. The possibility of these kinds of unfairness may explain the uneasiness that some people feel about plea bargaining in criminal cases. Tactics apparently used to make pleas more attractive to criminal defendants include: setting high bail, overcharging in the initial indictment, and threatening harsh sentences for those who demand a trial.

Setting High Bail. Bail allows criminal defendants to remain free between the time of arrest and the time of trial. If a defendant cannot meet the bail set for him, he will remain in jail until his trial date. Pretrial incarceration has a number of adverse consequences for the defendant. First, it limits his ability to aid in the preparation of his defense. He will be unable to find or talk to witnesses, and he may be restricted in his discussions with his lawyer. Inability to prepare for trial reduces the expected value of the judgment for the defendant by reducing the likelihood that he will be acquitted (Ares, Rankin & Sturz, 1963; Hagan, Nagel & Albonetti, 1980).

The inability to make bail also reduces the utility of the judgment because it reduces the utility of an acquittal. This is because some of what a person might gain from an acquittal will be lost if he must await the trial in jail. For example, family or employment relationships that are unlikely to be ruptured by a short trial ending in an acquittal might be irreparably broken by an extended pretrial confinement regardless of the verdict. Thus one of the costs of conviction that might have led a defendant to hold out for trial will not be avoided even if he wins. Indeed, jailed defendants who are offered fines, probation, or suspended sentences in exchange for their guilty pleas may find that the costs of admitting full guilt immediately are less than the costs associated with a delayed acquittal. The utility of going to trial is further reduced because pretrial jail time is commonly but not always offset against the final sentence a defendant receives. If a defendant who receives a one-year sentence has already served 6 months awaiting trial, this time will usually be deducted from the sentence. The utility of the trial, with its possibility of acquittal, is thereby reduced because the defendant has already served half the time he faced. In the extreme case, a prosecutor will offer to accept a plea in return for time served. It is the principled defendant, indeed, who will prefer further time in jail awaiting trial to immediate freedom with a criminal record.

For these reasons if a judge sets bail at a level the defendant cannot meet, the prosecutor is likely to be bargaining within a negotiation set that makes a guilty plea quite likely. Within that set, the prosecutor is not necessarily going to strike a deal that is more favorable to him than to the defendant, but the set itself is quite different from what it would have been if time had the same meaning for each.

Overcharging and Multiple Charging. A second way in which prosecutors can threaten or deceive the defendant about the utility of the no agreement point is by overcharging. The prosecutor may charge a defendant with a crime that is greater than the evidence can sustain or the act warrants in order to convince him that going to trial may be more risky than originally contemplated. Similarly, the prosecutor may charge the defendant with several crimes stemming out of the same incident. This may not only lead the defendant to lower his expectations that he will be acquitted at trial and to see the prospects of a severe sentence as greater, but it may also be used to get the judge to set high bail (Balbus, 1973, p. 167).

Threatening Penalties for Those Going to Trial. Finally, prosecutors may benefit from the defendant's fear that if he goes to trial the judge will be particularly harsh on him for wasting the court's time. Newman reports a general fear among some defendants "that the judge would be especially severe in sentencing if they did decide to fight and then lost" (Newman, 1956, p. 784). Newman's defendants also felt that going to trial might offend the prosecutor who would "get even" when the time came to recommend a sentence. According to one defendant:

> "When the day comes to go and the D.A. stands up and says you're a dirty rat and a menace to society and should be locked up and have the key thrown away—then look out! You're going away for a few years." (1956, p. 784)

Empirical research has not consistently shown the existence of such a trial "premium," but our reading of the evidence is that such premiums often exist, although this varies by court and by judge (Klein, 1976, Baldwin & McConville, 1977; Miller, McDonald & Cramer, 1978; Feeley, 1979a,b). Also, in some jurisdictions there is apparently no penalty if trial is to a judge rather than to a jury or if a case is sufficiently close that the judge believes that it was reasonable for the defendant to use court time. One does not, however, have to sort out this picture fully to note that whether judges or prosecutors in fact attach a special penalty for the exercise of the right to trial, they do little to disabuse defendants of such beliefs. To this extent, they deceive defendants about the utility of the lawsuit.

As we noted in our discussion of gamesmanship, threats and deception are also commonly employed in civil litigation. We shall not elaborate on our discussion of the techniques that may be used. What is of interest is that techniques involving threats and deceptions seem intuitively to be less unfair when used in a civil context. We believe there are at least two reasons for this. The first is that the institutional resources of the parties seem more equal. If a personal injury plaintiff has a more immediate need for cash, a defendant insurer has a special bureaucratic interest in closing files. Where imbalance in the parties' capacities to use threats and deception is greater, the resulting negotiation set is likely to appear less fair.

The second reason is that the devices the prosecutor uses are governed by norms that have nothing to do with the inducement of plea bargains. Bail, for example, is supposed to reflect the likelihood that a defendant will show up for trial, or, if popular morality is accepted, the danger inherent in allowing a defendant to remain at large. It should have nothing to do with a defendant's decision to stand trial, and failure to make bail should certainly not work to induce innocent defendants to plead guilty.[21] The prosecutor who uses the fact that a defendant is jailed pending trial, especially if high bail was sought with a view toward its impact on the plea bargaining process, appears to be cynically misusing his office. Even pretending that the state's case is stronger than it is may be regarded as an unfair manipulation of the negotiation set, for the norms that govern the prosecutor's office demand that his primary allegiance be toward securing justice rather than accumulating convictions.

On the civil side, the threats and deceptions that are part of the negotiation process are often the subject of no norms external to that process other than general norms of honesty and fair dealing, which, it is understood, are somewhat relaxed in the context of negotiations. Thus it does not seem unfair when a civil attorney pretends to have more confidence in his case than he in fact has or threatens to litigate the matter to the hilt if the opponent rejects his "final" offer. There is, however, a sense of impropriety when civil litigants seek to gain an edge in the negotiation process by using litigation devices in ways that are not part of their *raison d'être*. Whether this leads to a negotiating set that seems unfair depends in large measure on whether the parties are equally capable of misusing the devices.[22] Thus it is wasteful and improper but does not necessarily seem unfair for one major oil company to commence discovery proceedings that threaten to cost millions of dollars in order to induce another major oil company to settle an antitrust suit. The same abuse of discovery might seem unfair if the opponent were a small company that could neither afford such costs nor threaten to escalate them.

Using legal machinery for the purpose of harassing or coercing an opponent violates the bar's code of professional responsibility, but the rule is almost never enforced because so long as the lawyer can point to a permitted purpose for his behavior whatever his actual motive, the offense cannot be proved. The primary legal protection against such abuses lies in the discretion that judges have to limit the use of legal tactics that might unfairly burden a party, to provide for cost sharing when certain demands are made, and to impose all costs relating to some action on the moving party when it appears that the action was taken for improper purposes.

---

21. This may be one reason why speedy trial laws in some states allow less delay for jailed than for bailed defendants. Other more obvious reasons are the costs of maintaining defendants in jail, jail overcrowding, and the desire to minimize the pain suffered by those who will be eventually found "not guilty."

22. However, a party equally capable in most senses may not be equally willing, and the negotiating set may be changed somewhat if that party values settlement because it will enable him to avoid responding in kind to an opponent who is misusing the legal process.

THE LIMITS OF MODELING

Models are inevitably simplifications. Indeed, one of their prime virtues is that they simplify and organize reality so that we can grasp the essence of what is involved in a pattern of behavior. Models can distort reality if they leave out crucial variables. When working with models of the kind used in this chapter, there is the particular danger that a variable will be omitted not because it is unimportant but because it is difficult to incorporate in the chosen model. The reader who has followed our argument as we developed it by reference to a series of Cartesian graphs might have found him or herself saying on more than one occasion, ''Surely there is more to negotiated settlements than that.'' Surely, there is. But before we discuss some of the complexities our model does not capture, we should note our view that, as models go, the one we have presented does pretty well in explaining the fundamental dynamic that underlies negotiated settlements, particularly when what is at stake is money damages in civil cases.[23] In such suits the parties are basically trying to maximize their dollar returns. Information that leads to converging views about the value of going to judgment and high anticipated costs are almost certainly crucial factors in motivating parties to settle.

The most important factor that is left out of our model is any reference to the interests of third parties, especially plaintiff's attorneys in civil litigation (Johnson, 1980–81) and defense counsel in criminal matters (Blumberg, 1967). Counsel may have motives other than maximizing their client's interests that lead them to urge settlements on their clients. Both plaintiff's attorneys on contingent fees and criminal defense counsel are, so long as they face no shortage of clients, likely to earn substantially higher hourly returns from cases that are settled quickly than from cases that go to trial. This possibility of divergent interests poses no fundamental problem for the application of the model in civil cases. It simply means that to the extent that the lawyer's judgment is motivated by self-interest rather than the client's interest and to the extent that it is the lawyer and not the client who decides at what point it pays to settle, one must

---

23. Gerald Williams, in a recent primer on negotiation (1983, p. 116) cites Robert L. Simmons's (1974) formula for determining the fair settlement value of a personal injury case:

> Simmons, invites the attorney to subdivide the case into six categories and estimate a value for each. They include: PAV—The probable average verdict. PPV—The probability of a plaintiff's verdict. UV—The uncollectible portion of the verdict. PC—The plaintiff's cost in obtaining verdict. DC—The defendant's estimated cost of defense. I—The value of the intangible factors. FSV—The fair settlement value. Expressed algebraically, the formula looks like this: $(PAV \times PPV) - UV - PC + DC \pm I = FSV$. (Williams, 1983, p. 116)

This formula is in a handbook written to aid lawyers in negotiating cases. Its consistency with the approach of this chapter is obvious.

consider the lawyer's expected returns from various possible settlements rather than the client's.[24]

In criminal cases the matter is more complex, because what the lawyer is presumably trying to maximize (his income) bears little relation to the "commodities" that are the subject of the bargain. Here if the lawyer is entirely self-interested, fears no adverse reputational effects from securing a lousy deal, and is in control of the client, the model will not apply, for such a lawyer cares only about the speed with which the case can be resolved and is indifferent to the outcome the client receives. However, it is unclear how often these conditions are met, particularly since the lawyer with only a little effort can usually secure a decent deal. Furthermore, the lawyer must secure the client's consent to a plea. Even if the model does not apply to the lawyer–prosecutor bargaining because the lawyer is purely self-interested and will accept the prosecutor's first offer, it is likely to portray accurately the client's analysis of the situation when the lawyer tries to persuade him to accept the arranged deal.[25]

Some may find the model deficient because it omits considerations of justice. Certainly there are some litigants who believe their cause just and will refuse to settle unless their claims are fully satisfied even though such recalcitrance is not

---

24. Even if a plaintiff's attorney is self-interested rather than client-oriented, there is a considerable congruence of interest between attorney and client since higher rewards for one are correlated with higher awards for the other. The model of self-interested lawyer behavior which the contingent fee might be expected to engender, draws heavily on the work of Rosenthal (1974). Rosenthal's suggestions have recently been challenged by Kritzer et al. (1985) who find that contingent fee lawyers appear to put in less time than their hourly fee counterparts only when $6,000 or less is at stake. Where more than $6,000 is involved, the data suggest that if there is any difference in the time put in by the two groups the advantage lies with the contingent fee lawyer. One conclusion we draw from this is that in civil cases self-interested behavior attributable to the contingent fee does not greatly confound our client-focused model.

25. Other third parties may also influence the settlement process. A crucial witness who is unwilling to testify may substantially diminish the value of a suit. Pressure from the police to protect an informer or to throw the book at someone who resisted arrest may lead a prosecutor to deviate from his normal plea bargaining practices as may the desire to avoid further traumatizing a rape victim at a public trial. These factors influence the value of the suit because they are consciously taken into account by the litigant and may affect the likely outcome of the case or the values that the litigant places on settling versus going to trial. Thus such interests are, in principle, incorporated in our utility-based model. Lawyers are special because they actually participate in the negotiation process and can influence it directly. The ability to impose costs on third parties also facilitates settlements. Thus the different tax consequences of child support payments (income to the paying spouse) and alimony (a deduction to the paying spouse and income to the recipient) allows parties to transfer some costs to the government in the form of lower tax receipts and so can encourage settlement. If, for example, the paying spouse has a higher income than the receiving spouse, a settlement of $200 a month in child support and $400 a month in alimony may bring the custodial parent more money after taxes and cost the paying spouse less than a settlement of $500 a month in child support with no alimony. Thus the parties have an incentive to settle on the first formula so that a court will not impose the second one. This is true only because a third party, the government as tax collector, has a stake in the payment arrangements. As a general rule, whenever possible settlements differ from the no agreement point in that costs that would otherwise be borne by the negotiators can be inflicted on third parties, the likelihood of a negotiated settlement increases.

likely to maximize their economic well-being. But such litigants are rare, at least among civil litigants who seek money damages. Leon Mayhew (1975) in a survey of Detroit area households reports that when respondents were asked how they wanted their most serious problems to be resolved, few listed justice as a goal they sought to achieve. Only when problems involved discrimination did more than 10 percent (31 percent in fact) speak in these terms. In none of the 92 problems arising out of the landlord–tenant relationship was justice listed as a reason for pursuing the matter. Erich Steele (1975) reports similar results in a study of consumer disputes. Civil litigants in our society are by and large economic actors. Even when what they seek is not money damages but specific relief, such as the recision of an eviction order, they are usually in court to secure the relief they seek and not to contend for a general principle.

There are, however, some organizations such as the NAACP (National Association for the Advancement of Colored People) and ACLU (American Civil Liberties Union) that specialize in bringing actions to establish principles, and the model of negotiations that we have used will generally not apply to them. Indeed, such organizations sometimes face problems when their adversaries offer to satisfy the personal demands of the individual(s) in whose name suit has been brought. The lawyer's allegiance to his client means that a favorable settlement should be accepted, but the purpose of the lawsuit and of the organization that has invested its funds in it is to secure a legal pronouncement by a court that will change the law in some area. To avoid conflicts between the client's particular interests and the litigation's goals broadly defined, "public interest" law firms try, if they cannot sue in their own names, to consolidate the cases of numbers of plaintiffs or bring actions on behalf of classes of individuals. This increases lawyer control over the litigation because there is no one client to answer to, and it makes the strategy of buying off the plaintiff unduly expensive or even self-defeating. A welfare agency, for example, might be willing to pay Mrs. Smith an allotment withdrawn from her without a hearing rather than risk the pronouncement of a principle that will entitle all welfare recipients to hearings before their aid is cut. But if the suit is brought on behalf of most or all of those who claim the right to a hearing, the agency must either concede the principle or battle for its views in court.

Organizations that have an essentially economic interest in the outcomes of court cases may on occasion also play the litigation game for principles, *i.e.*, to secure favorable precedents (Macaulay, 1966; Galanter, 1974). The reason is that they perceive that their long-run financial interest may conflict with their short-run interest in a particular case. Our model would have to be modified to accommodate this temporal dimension, and so, even when the motivation is economic, it does not portray litigation for precedent very well.

Consider, for example, a major auto company that regularly terminates the licenses of its franchisees. Initially, there was little to keep it from being arbitrary, but eventually the National Automobile Dealers Association succeeded in lobbying through Congress a Dealers Day in Court Act designed to ensure that franchise terminations are in "good faith." Parts of the act are inescapably ambiguous, and the company is very concerned with how these ambiguities will be resolved. Assume that the first case requiring an interpretation of a key provision involves a family-owned, rural franchise that is terminated because sales fell to an unacceptable level during the wife's extended illness. The plaintiffs sue for $100,000 and appear serious about holding out for that amount. The auto company's lawyer estimates that the plaintiffs have a 50 percent chance of winning and that the litigation expense will be about $10,000, yielding a resistance point of $60,000. Nevertheless, the company settles for the sum demanded. In the next case a franchise is terminated for insufficient sales attributable to the fact that the owner-manager was often drunk on the showroom floor. The franchisee sues for $200,000 but makes it clear he would settle for $10,000. The company's lawyer estimates that the franchisee has about a 10 percent chance of winning and that litigation costs will be about $10,000. Although the defendant's demand is well within the company's settlement range, the company does not settle, but instead, spends an additional $50,000 to pursue the matter to the Supreme Court.

What is going on? The answer is simple. The company, knowing that it will often be accused of wrongfully terminating franchises, wishes to establish crucial precedents in the context of a case where their justification for the alleged breach of the franchise agreement was the plaintiff's drunkenness rather than an illness in the plaintiff's family (cf. Macaulay, 1966). Put another way, the company is willing to pay a substantial sum to have a 90 percent chance of establishing a favorable precedent rather than a 50 percent chance. Marc Galanter (1974) has argued that this ability to play for precedents is a major advantage that wealthy "repeat players" of the litigation game have over less wealthy litigants who are likely to be involved in a particular kind of litigation on only one occasion. Over the long run Galanter is right; particularly when what is at issue is how the law allocates wealth in society. Yet if you are a rural franchise owner whose sales dropped below contractual levels when your spouse was ill, you might negotiate a better result than you had a right to expect on the one occasion that matters to you.

Our model is also descriptively less adequate when the government is a party. We have already noted the modifications needed to apply the model to plea bargaining and the difficulties that exist even then, but the point applies to civil litigation as well. In some cases the government will be litigating over principles, and when this is the case it is likely to be even less constrained by costs than the ordinary institutional litigant. But even when the government is seeking damages, its behavior may be different from that of most litigants. It may act as if costs are less important in setting the boundaries of the negotiation set than they are to private plaintiffs or defendants, and it may be more willing to litigate on principle, even when precedents are not at issue, than are most litigants. The reason is that there is often no person or entity whose role is like that of the bill-paying client. Indeed, the litigation expenses may be charged to a budget other than that of the agency on whose behalf the suit is brought or defended. When any good is free or priced below cost, it will tend to be "over-consumed,'' which in this case will translate into an economically irrational preference for litigation as opposed to settlement. Whether this will be offset by bureaucratic pressures to fit cases into a routine, another factor our model does not take into account, is an empirical question about which we have no information.

The suggestion that governments will value money differently from most clients applies more generally as a reason why our model, even if it captures the essence of negotiations, may not precisely fit any actual negotiations. The model assumes that both parties value money in the same linear fashion[26] and that both are risk neutral.[27] In fact, the marginal utility of the last dollar at stake in a lawsuit is likely to be less than the marginal utility of the first one, and these utilities may be quite different for different parties as may be their taste for risk. For example, a risk avoider who estimates that litigation will cost $10,000 might prefer a settlement of $38,000 in a suit for $100,000 to a 50 percent chance of winning at trial. In this case a settlement will be possible for an amount that according to our model should be below the plaintiff's resistance point. Tastes such as these may, however, be captured by models of the same general form as ours if they are only known. Thus our model retains its heuristic value although actual litigants may have nonlinear tastes. The insight it offers into the dynamics of negotiation is unaffected by the fact that it might err if one tried to use it to predict which of a group of lawsuits would be settled.

Finally, there are aspects of the negotiation process that our model does not purport to address. It does not tell us what the parties discuss when they are attempting to persuade each other of the appropriate settlement point. There is some evidence that the parties negotiate about the reality of the case (Ross, 1970; Utz, 1978; Maynard, 1984). This may be done in an attempt to convince the other party of the likely outcome if the case reaches judgment, in which case it is completely consistent with our model of settlement behavior. But it may also be done to convince the other party where justice lies. To the extent that this is important to the final settlement, our model, which has no place for justice except insofar as the concepts of Pareto optimality and the negotiation set are useful in thinking about fairness, is in a fundamental sense incomplete.

Our model also does not extend to a second ''negotiation'' that may take place if the lawyer must convince a reluctant client to accept the settlement that he has achieved. The problem of selling a settlement to a client is also important in understanding the lawyer's negotiation behavior. One task of the negotiator may be to convince the opposing counsel that he can ''sell'' a proposed settlement to his client, and information may be disclosed largely for this purpose. Thus,

---

26. By this, we mean that all dollars are worth the same to both parties. This implies that one party does not need money more than the other party and that the last dollar a party gains or pays is as desirable to get or as painful to part with as is the first dollar.

27. A risk neutral person is indifferent between receiving, for example, $1,000 or receiving a ticket in a lottery that gives her one chance in a hundred to receive $100,000. A risk averse person would rather receive the $1,000, while a risk preferrer would choose the ticket.

in a criminal case where the routine bargain is clearly appropriate, the prosecutor may show the police report to the defense counsel so that the latter will be able to convince an unreasonably stubborn client to accept the deal that is offered.

SUMMARY

It is common to indict the legal system because so many disputes are settled out of court. Some people believe that this reflects a failure of the legal system. The critiques come in several varieties. Sometimes the objection is that by settling out of court one side or the other avoids "justice." Rules do not mean anything if you can simply bargain them away. From this point of view the law is a moralistic enterprise and "justice should be done though the heavens may tremble." As we said in the introduction, however, the purpose of law is not only to do justice, but it is also to settle disputes. Settlements do this. Moreover, the fact that there is a settlement does not mean that there has been an injustice. Settlements, if entered into fairly, take account of those substantive rules that define justice. The value of a suit or the probability that someone can be proven to have committed a crime helps establish the negotiation set within which any bargain will be reached. Although the all or nothing character of a trial may be more satisfying than a compromise, every verdict carries with it some probability of error. Settlement and justice are not incompatible ideas (but cf. Fiss, 1984).

Sometimes the objection to settlement is of a different nature. It is that the settlement is somehow unfair. This is a more substantial criticism. The unfairness, however, is not in being forced to play the game of settlement. Rather, it is in being forced to play the game when the deck is stacked. If the negotiation set is fair, then in a certain sense the settlement itself, whatever it may be, is fair as well. It is when the negotiation set is rigged by delay or by extra-legal threats that bargain justice is no justice at all.[28]

In this chapter we have attempted to model the negotiation processes that resolve most lawsuits. We have examined the amount of conflict in disputes and the nature of a "fair" solution to conflict. In general, we treated the lawsuit only as a no agreement point. In the next two chapters we take a more dynamic perspective on the trial as we examine ways in which different types of courts process and resolve disputes.

The behavior of courts is a central concern of law and social science for a number of reasons. First, styles of judicial dispute settlement affect the value of suits and the nature of the bargains that the parties reach. Both the likelihood of settlement and the "fairness" of possible settlements reflect estimates about what will happen at trial. Second, the ways in which courts process disputes

---

28. A further objection that we mention only in passing, is that the bargain may be unfair to parties other than those involved in the suit. Thus one might object that a plea bargain that is fair to the prosecutor and the defendant fails to take into account the interests of the general public which has a stake in the outcome of the trial. Insofar as the prosecutor fails to concern himself with the needs and interests of the public he is employed to serve, this criticism is reasonable.

affect and are affected by the law's relationship to other institutions and groups in society. The following chapters present a typology of dispute settlement techniques and relate these techniques to both the likelihood of settlement and the relationship of the law to other institutions. Finally, as we shall see, dispute settlement techniques are interesting in their own right. The study of dispute settlement is often the best way to grasp the relationship between a society's legal life and the larger culture of which the law is a part.

Appendix: Conflict of Interest and the NLRA

In our discussion to this point we have examined dispute settlement within the context of a lawsuit. Here the law's primary function is to establish the consequence of failing to agree which helps define the range of possible settlement outcomes. Although we shall discuss such situations further in the following chapters, it is worth noting that this is not the only way in which law may be used to promote bargains.

In some situations the role of law is to encourage and produce fair settlements. Indeed, laws may be enacted specifically to achieve this end (Teubner, 1983). In this appendix we discuss one such statute, the National Labor Relations Act. This statute, usually called the Wagner Act for Senator Robert Wagner, its chief architect, was passed in 1935.

Examining the Wagner Act allows us to expand on our game theoretic approach to dispute settlement. We shall discuss how law may facilitate "fair" settlements within the context of collective bargaining and how it may promote fair bargaining between labor and management.

The National Labor Relations Act (NLRA) as amended is wide-ranging in its regulation of labor–management relations. We focus on only two of its sections: 8(a)(3) and 8(a)(5). Section 8(a)(3) says that it is in an unfair labor practice for an employer "by discrimination in . . . employment to encourage or discourage membership in any labor organization." Section 8(a)(5) makes it an unfair labor practice for an employer "to refuse to bargain collectively with the representatives of his employees." First, we discuss 8(a)(3) and then 8(a)(5).

8(a)(3): "FAIR" BARGAINING AND THREATS

In our earlier discussion of game theory we suggested "solutions" to non-zero sum bargaining games and also a method of measuring the conflict of interest in such games. To do this, we *normalized* the games, setting each player's utility on a scale from zero which represented the worst he could do to 1 which represented his best. One of the benefits of this scheme is that it makes the game symmetrical. For purposes of abstraction and the comparison of different games, this is a reasonable procedure. The cautious reader may wonder whether this is an acceptable abstraction.

The answer is "yes" and "no." It is certainly not unreasonable to put utilities on a scale ranging from a person's most preferred outcome to his least preferred. Moreover, if we are indifferent between two parties, other approaches might not be fair. Normalizing the game attends to each player's "threat capabilities," that is, to the fact that either party may force the other to go to trial. The normalized game takes this threat as a given and assigns to it a value of zero.

If we stipulated that threats could play no role, we would change the game altogether. It would no longer be a bargaining game. If I have an apple and you have an orange and we try to strike a deal, it seems only fair that you should not do any worse than retain your orange. We might say that you should be able to "threaten" me with this possibility. That is, you should be able to say, "I will agree to no outcome worse than my keeping the orange." Setting at 1 the best a player can do, given his opponent's threat, also seems fair in the apple–orange trading game. Who is to say whether I prefer your orange more than you prefer my apple? Normalization creates a formal equality between players *given their initial position and threat capabilities*. Is this always intuitively fair as it appears to be in the fruit trading game? Many would say no, because initial positions and threat capabilities may not be fairly distributed.

Consider a situation where the players are an employer and an employee, and assume that the issue is how to divide the fruits of increased earnings in a company. In this situation the employer offers a settlement that gives him four-fifths of the increase, and the employee counters with a demand that gives him four-fifths. If they fail to agree, the employee will stop working, at some cost to each party. A possible payoff matrix is represented in Figure 6.17.

The game as presented has some interesting properties. First, it is meant to be understood in monetary terms, not in utilities. We could imagine the numbers to represent hundreds of dollars, for instance, so that position B represents an outcome where the employer gets $400 of the increased profits, while the employee's earnings go up $100.

Second, the game is such that one party's best is not the other party's worst. It is important to recognize why this is so. The employer realizes that an attempt to take all of the increased productivity will, in fact, seriously reduce his employees' incentive to increase productivity in the future. Likewise, the employee recognizes that to demand all the increase is to put the employer in a position of being unable to make the capital investments needed for future wage gains.

Third, the game is not symmetrical. The cost of no agreement (the employee refuses to work) in the bargaining process we have modeled is greater for the employee. A normalized version of the situation in Figure 6.17 is presented in Figure 6.18.

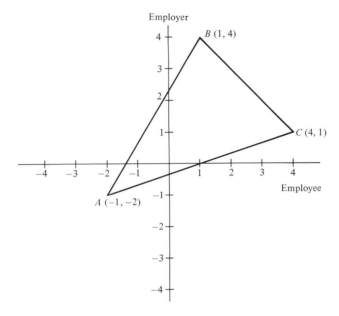

Figure 6.17

Point *A*, the no agreement point, is set at (0, 0). Since point *B* is the best the employer can do, it is given a value of 1 for him. Point *B* is given a value of .5 for the employee because as we can see in Figure 6.17 an outcome of 1 is halfway between his best (+4) and his worst (−2).[1] Point *C* is the employee's best and so is given a value of 1 for him. Point *C* is given a value of .4 for the employer because the outcome (+1) is two-fifths of the way between his worst (−1) and his best (+4).

Thus far the case seems well on its way to settlement. It has a rather low level of relative conflict of interest. The parties only need to find some position between payoffs *B* and *C*. But the employee may believe he can improve his position if he and his fellow employees bargain collectively. Assume that if they form a union and threaten a strike as the no agreement outcome the collective nature of their threat will shift the no agreement point in Figure 6.17 from (−1, −2) to (−2, −2). This makes the game symmetrical in both dollars and the parties' utilities.

But what if the employer finds out that employee *X* is talking union and in fact has begun discussions with the International Brotherhood of Workers? At that point the employer may well follow the employee's lead and enter the threat business himself. He fires employee *X*, and he and his fellow employers blackball

---

1. Under both the common law and the Wagner Act an employer may impose any result. We assume, however, that in the short run the employer cannot impose his best result because the employee will not immediately accept it and cannot be easily replaced.

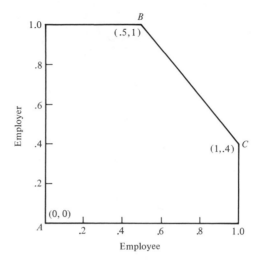

Figure 6.18

X from any employment in the industry. He then tells the remaining employees that they will also be fired and blackballed unless they each sign "yellow dog" contracts, that is, contracts in which they agree to work for the employer and to refrain from joining a union so long as they are working for him. This contract also specifies a wage level that gives the workers $100 and the company $400 of the new profits. Yet the contract appears hardly binding, for it is "terminable at will," meaning that the workers under contract can quit their jobs at a moment's notice should they find more satisfactory employment and that the company can fire them almost instantly should their work be unsatisfactory, or, perhaps more importantly, should they show any further interest in joining a union.

What is the point of such a contract? We see it when the remaining employees, intimidated by the employer's threats or simply in need of a job, sign the contracts offered. To make sure there is no future union nonsense, the employer enlists the help of the law by getting a court to say that no union can try to organize the people he has under contract. This means that the court will enter an injunction against any union that tries to organize the employees, forbidding it from trying to induce the employees to break their contracts with the employer. Violation of such an injunction is punishable as a contempt of court, which can mean a substantial fine or up to a year in jail [see *Hitchman Coal & Coke* v. *Mitchell*, 245 U.S. 229 (1917)].[2]

This virtuoso performance by the employer can be admired in the abstract.

2. Statutes that attempted to prevent discharging an employee because he joined a union were at one time struck down by the Supreme Court as an invasion of the employer's freedom of contract [*Adair* v. *U.S.*, 208 U.S. 161, 277 (1908); *Coppage* v. *Kansas*, 236 U.S. 1 (1915)]. We are talking here in the present tense to provide an example that lays the ground for the discussion that follows. Our discussion of the law of injunctions describes the situation at the time of our example—before the Wagner Act and other labor law reforms. Today there are substantial constraints on the use of injunctions in labor disputes.

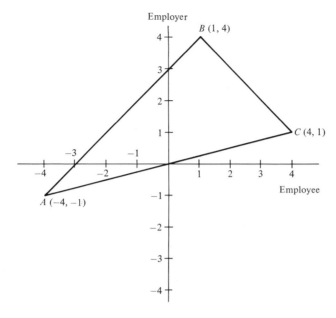

Figure 6.19

In one fell swoop he has managed to greatly increase his threat capabilities by the use of the blackball, and through the use of yellow dog contracts and legal injunctions has prevented any unfriendly union from organizing the employees. After these moves, the payoff matrix might resemble Figure 6.19. Figure 6.20 presents a normalized version of Figure 6.19 with the earlier version of the employee–employer relationship (Figure 6.18) in dotted lines.

After these maneuvers, a \$450–\$50 split would be a relatively more attractive deal than the \$400–\$100 split was in the earlier situation. Indeed, the employer, to show his generosity, might settle for the Nash solution to the game in Figure 6.20 (point *E*). Given the new game, it would be a fair solution. Yet many would feel that the employer has gone too far. Why do we feel this way? Perhaps we believe that it is unfair for a big company to gang up on poor employee X. It isn't "nice" to threaten someone that way. But we must be cautious about our feelings in these cases, for most of labor relations in this country involves threats and counterthreats and the "ganging up" of one side on the other.[3] Also,

3. The United Auto Workers (UAW) typically gangs up on one of the Big Three automobile manufacturers by threatening to strike that company while continuing to work for the other two. This tactic has the double advantage of letting that company know it is losing production and sales to the other two companies while a strike goes on, and preserving the union treasury, since strike benefits need to be paid to only part of the membership while dues are collected from those still working. The UAW typically rotates its "strike target" from contract to contract so that the average member will experience a strike once every 9 years, but in recent years the relative economic conditions of the Big Three companies have been an important consideration in the choice of a target.

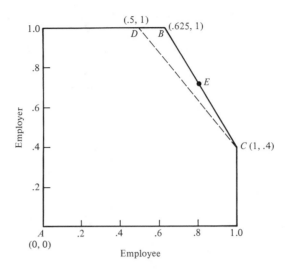

Figure 6.20

before we become too exercised by the employer's behavior, we should recall that in our example the employees induced the employer's maneuvers by their threat to form a union and perhaps to strike. In a sense, the employees wanted to gang up on the employer.

Still, our sense that the new game is unfair can find some neutral grounds to stand on. Two elements in the employer's actions changed the conflict from one involving just one company and its workers. First, the employer was backed up by his fellow employers who joined in the blackball. Second, he used the legal system to make certain counterthreats illegal. We might wish to argue that a fair bargaining game requires at a minimum that employers, whose resources are substantially greater than those of their employees, be limited to their own capacities for reward and punishment. The blackball violates this requirement. Moreover, we might say that if it is to be a free-for-all, it should be one for both sides. The law should not limit the employees' ability to counter with the threat of organizing a union.

These considerations suggest that a fairer game would prohibit both blackballs and judicial injunctions against attempts to organize employees working under yellow dog contracts. Both devices were, in fact, restricted by the labor law legislation of the New Deal: the Norris–LaGuardia and the Wagner acts.

On the other hand, what about the employer who agrees to these restrictions? He does not blackball, and he does not resort to injunctions, but he still argues that he should be allowed to fire any employee who tries to organize or join a union. Such a move does not bring a third party into the fray, nor does it absolutely restrict unions. It simply provides a counterthreat. If all the employees hang together, the employer's threat probably fails, for he would have to fire his entire work force. The costs of doing this are likely to be greater than those of acceding to the union's demands.[4]

If all the workers hang together, they probably will not hang separately. If they do not hang together, why should the law make it impossible for an employer to hang them separately by firing those who join unions? One answer is that for good policy reasons (e.g., the promotion of industrial peace) our society wishes to encourage organized collective bargaining, and this requires viable unions. Another reason is that society does not want relationships among workers to fall into certain competitive patterns. A third reason is that society finds it inherently unfair that a powerful company can fire workers, who as individuals are relatively powerless, when they seek to redress the power imbalance by joining a union. These reasons are by no means mutually exclusive. Although some or all of these reasons may seem intuitively obvious, there is an interesting logic behind the intuition that firing workers for joining labor unions hampers collective bargaining unfairly. It stems from an inescapable inequality in the bargaining game and what this implies.

The fundamental inequality is that the employer is one unit, with one set of interests bargaining with a single voice. The employees are separate individuals with different interests. The unionization issue is to a large extent a dispute over whether they should be allowed to bargain with one voice. One might say that if they have genuinely common interests, fairness requires that they be allowed to articulate them, subject to whatever pressure the company can legally place on the workers as a group to forego their interest (e.g., the honest argument that extravagant salary demands will cause the company to shut down). When workers are fired for joining unions, it inhibits the articulation of genuinely shared interests. The battle between labor and management may be over before it is fairly joined. This is because when an employer fires workers as they join unions he is *preventing his employees from bargaining with one another*. He is, in effect, forcing them into a game in which they cannot effectively communicate with each other and reach binding agreements. Game theory clarifies what this implies.

Non-zero Sum Noncooperative Games

In Footnote 3 of Chapter 6 we divided non-zero sum games into those that are and those that are not cooperative. In cooperative games the parties may communicate with each other before playing and, in addition, may make binding agreements. The employees would like to discuss among themselves whether they want a union, and, if they do, they would like to be able to enter into a binding agreement whereby those who join do so for better or worse. The

---

4. This is not to say that firing most or all of a striking work force is an option that is never taken. The best known recent example was the federal government's decision to fire most air traffic controllers following the PATCO strike. In this instance, of course, the government had a special justification for their actions since the strike was in violation of federal law.

employer, by firing anyone striving for unionization, makes communication costly and binding agreements difficult to reach. He forces, indeed, wishes to force, the players (workers) into a game where communication is limited. As an ideal, he would like to force the players into a type of noncooperative game commonly called a *prisoner's dilemma*. Figure 6.21 represents such a game.

This game is between two employees rather than between an employer and his employee. It is named the prisoner's dilemma because its dynamics are most easily understood by considering the situation of two prisoners, A and B, arrested for the same crime, who are separately interrogated and promised rewards for confessing. Each is told that if he alone confesses he will be allowed to turn state's evidence and go free, while the other serves a 20-year sentence. He is also told that if both he and his partner confess, there will be no need for one to turn state's evidence so they will both be sent to jail for 5 years. In addition, being old hands at crime both prisoners know that if neither confesses, the state will only have enough evidence to convict them of a lesser charge, and they will each get only a year in jail.

This game is interesting because the prisoners' joint return (i.e., the best they can do together) is greatest if neither confesses. Yet each is made better off by confessing no matter what the other does. If A confesses and B does not, A will avoid 1 year in jail since he will be set free, and if B confesses and A does also, A will save 15 years which is the difference between 5 years and 20. Thus if each does what is best for him, A and B will each serve 5 years in prison. They would have served only 1 year each had neither tried to maximize his self-interest.

The situation of two employees confronting a hostile employer is, at least in the short run, not dissimilar. If one joins the union and the other does not, the union member will be fired, while his fellow employee will not only have a job, but may be rewarded for not joining the union or for informing on the joiner. If neither joins the union, they will have to settle for a bargaining space

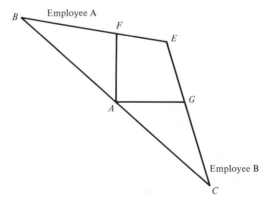

Figure 6.21

dominated by the employer's threat capability. If both join, collective bargaining is likely to allow them to improve their positions.

In Figure 6.21, *A* represents the situation if neither joins; *B* and *C*, the position if one joins but the other does not, and *E*, the position if both join. The important point to note about the game is that positions *B* and *C* are possible outcomes precisely because the parties cannot communicate and enter into binding agreements. If communication and binding agreements were possible, then presumably the worst either could do would be within the area *AEFG*. Neither would agree to anything worse than the payoff for no agreement. Here, however, if one man says "I'll join" and the other does not follow, the joiner is left with *B* or *C*, commonly called "the sucker's payoff."

The employer would like to make the sucker's payoff as high as possible (firing and blackballing). He would also like selectively to reward nonjoiners, thus increasing the temptation to defect[5]; to make joining an independent union more difficult for those who might desire joint representation (the yellow dog contract); and to diminish the rewards of unionization (by, e.g., refusing to bargain with a union). The employer's overall strategy (although none would have phrased it this way) is to make the contest between the company and its employees a prisoner's dilemma in which the employees do not realize that their joint interest lies in cooperation or, if they do realize this, are unable to trust their fellow employees to act so as to maximize their joint interest.

The NLRA in Section 8(a)(3) tries to ensure that employees who have an opportunity to form a union will not be placed in a prisoner's dilemma situation. Thus it prohibits any employment discrimination that is designed to encourage or discourage trade union membership.[6]

SECTION 8(a)(5): ENCOURAGING A BARGAIN

Section 8(a)(3) appears aimed at making a fairer bargaining arena. It is designed to control the parameters of the bargaining game. Section 8(a)(5) which makes it an unfair labor practice for an employer to refuse to bargain with official union representatives was probably included in the statute for much the same purpose. Although not all scholars agree about what this section of the statute was orig-

---

5. See, *Budd Mfg. Co.* v. *NLRB*, 138 F. 2d 86 (1943) and the extraordinary case of Walter Weigand, a company man of whom the Court of Appeals said, "If ever a workman deserved summary discharge it was he." In point of fact, he was given an easy job while he was a company man but immediately fired when he expressed an interest in a union.

6. Some courts have tried to narrow this rule, fearing that it might infringe upon traditional management prerogatives in hiring and firing. What management cannot do is fire a person because he or she joins or attempts to join a union. As the Fifth Circuit says, "Management can discharge for good cause, or bad cause, or no cause at all. It has, as the master of its own business affairs, complete freedom with but one specific, definite qualification: it may not discharge when the real motivating purpose is to do that which Section 8(a)(3) forbids" [*NLRB* v. *McGahey*, 233 F. 2d 406, 413 (5th cir. 1956); *NLRB* v. *Transportation Mgt. Corp.*, 462 U.S. 393 (1983)].

inally intended to do, the dominant view is that it was meant only to lead the parties "to the office door"[7] (see Smith, 1941; Cox, 1958; Duvin, 1964; but see Miller, 1965; Klare, 1978).

The courts, however, gave provision 8(a)(5) a liberal interpretation which compelled more than simply meeting with employee representatives. When the statute was amended in 1947 this interpretation was formalized in section 158(d) which reads:

> To bargain collectively is the performance of the mutual obligation of the employer and the representative of the employees to meet at reasonable times and confer in good faith with respect to wages, hours, and other terms and conditions of employment, or the negotiation of an agreement, or any question arising thereunder, and the execution of a written contract incorporating any agreement reached if requested by either party, but such obligation does not compel either party to agree to a proposal or require the making of a concession. [29 U.S.C. Sec. 158(d)]

Reread section 158(d). What does it say? The last clause seems to contradict the first part of the section. The section might be paraphrased "We want you to really try, but we don't want you to do anything you don't want to do." Moreover, a problem that was only implicit in section 158(a)(3)—determining the intention of the parties—becomes painfully obvious in this provision. Although it may be difficult to determine why a given individual was fired, the surrounding information is often sufficient to allow courts to decide whether it was for union activities. But who is to determine what constitutes "good faith" bargaining? How can a court decide this? This section taxes to the utmost the attribution skills of an adjudicator. What exactly does section 158(d) require an employer to do? Most importantly, how much can it require him (and the union) to do without the court, in effect, imposing an agreement upon the parties?

Deciding how to interpret the statement is difficult in the best of circumstances, but what if the employer really wants to let the union strike and be damned? Is a "take-it-or-leave-it" attitude illegal? If it is (there is some authority to suggest this), can the employer not achieve the same result by beating around the bush with different proposals and then presenting "a last and best offer"?

The answer to the preceding question is probably "yes." Is there, then, any virtue to sections 8(a)(5) and 8(d)? Can they encourage settlements? Again, the answer is probably "yes." One final excursion into game theory indicates how this is so.

8(a)(5), 8(b)(3), and deceit

Most of our discussions of bargaining and game theory thus far have included an assumption that is in actuality rarely tenable. In our figures and matrices the

---

7. A comment by Senator Walsh in Senate hearings on the bill was it "does not go beyond the office door." Once a union is formed the employer must recognize it.

utility schedules of the parties have been available for all to see. We know what each party prefers and how much each prefers it. More importantly, when discussing what each party should do if he is rational, we have assumed not only that he knows his own utility schedule (in itself often questionable), but also that he knows the utility schedule of his adversary. Not only do adversaries rarely go around announcing their utility schedules, but they are likely, as we have already noted, to go out of their way to disguise their preferences. Figure 6.22 illustrates how deception may work in labor management negotiations.

In this figure we might imagine that point A represents the utility of the no agreement point for each party. This might be a strike, for example. Point B represents the outcome that the employer first suggests, and point C_1 the outcome the union first suggests in the negotiation. If it is a bargaining game, these two suggested solutions are presumably outside the negotiation set since one typically begins negotiations with extreme demands. If points B and C_1 represent the true utility of these points to the parties, they would reject any agreement that is not bounded by AFG. The employer, however, would like to have the union believe that point C_1 is truly a terrible solution. Indeed, he might well say that the wage increase that is part of the union's solution C_1 is not economically feasible. "Such a demand," he might tell the union, "would place the company in an intolerable competitive position vis-à-vis other manufacturers, lead to the layoff of many employees, and ultimately bankrupt the company, harming everyone."

The employer's argument is designed to make it appear that the union's suggestion is not at point C_1 but at point C_2. In pleading his case, the employer seeks not only to make the union believe that the offer has less utility for him

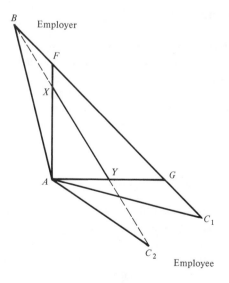

Figure 6.22

but also to make it believe that it has less utility for the union itself. The employer wants the union to believe that the game is really ABC_2 and that the negotiation set is AXY.

This is a game, however, that both parties can play. The union negotiators may portray the management's offer as being somewhere below and to the left of point B. Should such deception be allowed? If not, how should one draw the line between hard bargaining and impermissible deception? Under section 8(a)(5) the courts have generally held that in cases such as the preceding example where the employer pleads financial impossibility, he will commit an unfair labor practice if he refuses to back up the plea with the economic data about the firm that the union needs in order to assess his claim [see *NLRB* v. *Truitt Mfg. Co.*, 351 U.S. 149 (1956)]. In the *Truitt* case the Court said:

> Good-faith bargaining necessarily requires that claims made by either bargainer should be honest claims. This is true about an asserted inability to pay an increase in wages. If such an argument is important enough to present in the give-and-take of bargaining, it is important enough to require some sort of proof of its accuracy. (351 U.S. 149, pp. 152–153)

Indeed, it has been held that the employer has an obligation to furnish the union a wide range of information relevant to bargaining. Such information has long included wage-related data on job rates and classifications, piece rates, incentive earnings, merit increases, overtime payments, group insurance costs, and individual employee earnings. More recently, requirements for disclosure have been extended to job quality information such as lists of chemicals used in the workplace or discrimination complaints. Unions in turn are obligated under section 8(b)(3) of the act to share with employers certain job-related information, like information about the internal operations of a union-run hiring hall (see Note 1957; Bartosic & Hartley, 1972; Shedlin, 1980).

This use of sections 8(a)(5), 8(b)(3), and 8(d) by the NLRB and the courts increases the likelihood of agreement. The danger in attempting to mislead an opponent in negotiations is that joint misrepresentation may lead to the no agreement solution (strike), because the parties fail to perceive their mutual interest. Forced disclosure of information makes this less likely. The public interest in industrial peace and a healthy collective bargaining system can justify such rules regardless of whether they are essential to fairness between the parties.

8(a)(5) and bargaining style

The forced disclosure of information removes some gamesmanship from bargaining. But oddly, section 8(a)(5) has been used at times for the opposite purpose, to force some gamesmanship. One of the most controversial, and often condemned, uses of 8(a)(5) has been to regulate "bargaining style." Recall that section 8(d) concluded with language stating that nothing in the section compels either party to agree to a proposal or to make a concession. Consider an employer who comes to the bargaining table with a "fair and firm" proposal which he has determined is "right" for both the company and its employees. He is not unwilling to talk, but he makes it clear that he will not budge from his proposal unless new information on economic conditions makes it clear that his position is in some way "wrong." The union is told in advance that the threat of a strike will be futile, because the employer will "take" a strike of any length to resist doing what it considers to be "wrong." This "fair and firm offer" approach, or as some call it, a "take-it-or-leave-it" approach, is a bargaining style that achieved notoriety in a case involving the General Electric Company. It may, of course, be used in nonlabor negotiations as well (Ellsberg, 1975).

People who adopt this style may extol its virtues. It is a straightforward, direct style that lets the other party know exactly where one stands. The "ask-and-bid" or "auction" strategy in which different offers are exchanged, may be disparaged as "a flea-bitten eastern type of cunning and dishonest but pointless haggling" [150 N.L.R.B. 192, 208 (1964)].

To this the labor board has responded:

[A] party who enters into bargaining negotiations with a "take-it-or-leave-it" attitude violates its duty to bargain although it goes through the forms of bargaining, does not insist on any illegal or nonmandatory bargaining proposals, and wants to sign an agreement. . . . This "bargaining" approach undoubtedly eliminates the "ask-and-bid" or "auction" form of bargaining, but in the process devitalizes negotiations and collective bargaining and robs them of their commonly accepted meaning. . . . In practical effect, Respondent's "bargaining" position is akin to that of a party who enters into negotiations "with a predetermined resolve not to budge from an initial position," an attitude inconsistent with good-faith bargaining. In fact Respondent here went even further. It consciously placed itself in a position where it could not give unfettered consideration to the merits of any proposals the Union might offer. Thus, Respondent pointed out to the Union, after Respondent's communications to the employees and its "fair and firm offer" to the Union, that "everything we think we should do is in the proposal and we told our employees that, and we would look ridiculous if we changed now." General Electric, 150 N.L.R.B. 192, 194–196; enforced 418 F. 2d 736 (2d cir. 1969)

It is clear that with this opinion the board is involving itself in the "style" of bargaining. Such involvement has been criticized as a futile attempt to legislate "good faith." The union, it is argued, seeks to use rules regulating style as tactical weapons to get through legal means what it could not get through economic means alone. (It is perhaps worth noting that the General Electric case which is celebrated for having raised this issue was pursued by the union after an unsuccessful 3-week strike.) Finally, it is argued that the board should not involve itself in the "nuances" of bargaining. Bargaining styles it is argued are mainly a matter of taste, and the board should keep hands-off. (See Cooper, 1966.)

From the perspective of game theory, however, we may detect some virtue in the regulation of style. In the General Electric case the board is really making two related arguments: (1) the parties should use a stepwise approach to bargaining in which they alternatively present and respond to a variety of positions; (2) the parties should not at an early stage in the negotiations make offers from which they will not move. They should not issue ultimatums or otherwise "burn their bridges." We shall deal briefly with each of these points.

If both parties select a "fair-and-final offer" before bargaining, they may well select a pair of positions that lie outside the negotiation set. If, as in Figure 6.23, the union has a "final" position at C and the management has one at B, they will presumably not agree even though there are many possible agreements that both would prefer to a strike. The results will be the same if only one party makes a firm offer so long as it is outside the negotiation set and the other party believes it is firm. Thus if management makes a firm and final offer at point B, a union whose resistance point is at F will see no sense in further discussion.

Of course, requiring an "ask-and-bid" system almost guarantees that initial positions will lie outside the negotiation set, but it also compels the parties to keep talking. Presumably, they are more likely to find a position within the negotiation set, for the give-and-take of the negotiation will allow each party to better judge what the other can be reasonably expected to accede to.

Moreover, the stepwise approach should help the parties find positions that are most mutually advantageous and, therefore, increase the likelihood of settlement. Labor contracts are rarely only over money wages. They involve pensions, vacations, overtime, working conditions, and other matters. Thus there is seldom maximum relative conflict of interest in the labor negotiation game. It will have numerous "kinks" like point E in Figure 6.23, because the parties

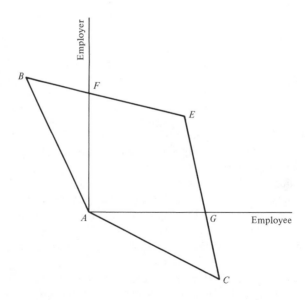

Figure 6.23

will differ in their preferences for different mixes. For instance, the union may be willing to give up 6 cents an hour in increased wages for an attractive vacation plan. The company may prefer the plan to a 5 cents an hour wage increase. Or, management's plan may offer night workers a 20 percent shift differential over day workers, while the union, which knows more about its worker's preferences, may believe that the workers will be more content if the same amount of money is used to establish a higher base rate and a 10 percent shift differential. Joint utility would be increased if the negotiators could find such compromises (Walton & McKersie, 1965; Raffia, 1982, ch. 10).

If, as Axelrod (1970) has hypothesized, agreement is more likely when relative conflict of interest is lower, barring "take-it-or-leave-it" offers should make settlements more likely. This is because the stepwise strategy increases the chances that the parties will find mutually beneficial solutions on the Pareto optimal line. In some cases this might make the difference between a settlement and a strike.

It is, however, difficult to test empirically this implication of game theory. Ross (1965) in an examination of meritorious cases (not, however, involving initial take-it-or-leave-it offers) in which a return to the table was ordered under section 8(a)(5) found that in 54 of 67 cases (80 percent) the return produced a contract (1965, p. 185). Although this does not prove the effectiveness of section 8(a)(5), or, especially, of any given decisions under it, Ross's findings do suggest that the section has not been a serious impediment to agreement and that many cases of apparent impasse do not involve intransigent unions and management bent upon economic warfare. The requirement of stepwise negotiations may well lead parties willing to cooperate toward a mutually satisfactory agreement.

The power to regulate bargaining style without the authority to order the parties to adopt reasonable substantive positions means that the requirement of good faith can be subverted by a clever and careful party. Although not bargaining in good faith is economically unwise in the context of a given negotiation, it might make economic sense as part of a long-run strategy to bust a union or it might reflect principles that are not wholly economic at their core. Except when a party does not desire a mutually advantageous short-run settlement, proceeding by stepwise negotiations may improve the chances of settlement, and, indeed, improve the settlement itself.

The second issue raised by the take-it-or-leave-it offer relates to the practice of "burning one's bridges." In game theory terms, this requires two maneuvers: moving first and restricting one's alternatives. It might seem that neither move is a wise one. After all, if one moves first, the other party knows what he has done and thus has additional information on which to base his move. Likewise, restricting one's options reduces "bargaining room." Yet both moves can work to a player's advantage. In Figure 6.24 the employer moves first by saying that point H is his position. Moreover, he says that this is his final offer. He has told the press, employees, and the company's stockholders that this is the best he can do, and therefore, he cannot make a better offer without substantially harming his credibility and leadership capacity. If the asserted harms are credible, the union is forced into a bargaining situation where the area *AFHI* comprises the negotiation set. Indeed, point *H* is the best bargain for which it can hope.

If the union were to accept the employer's ploy and treat the area *AFHI* as the arena in which the game must be played, there would be a very low level of relative conflict of interest, indicating that an agreement should be easy to reach. However, since all possible Pareto optimal agreements are quite favorable to management, it is likely that the union will resist the employer's effort to redefine the bargaining space. The union would like to see the game defined by the area *AFSG*, in which case the conflict of interest would be very high.

To secure this, the union might try to burn its bridges first or it might respond to management's action by showing that its hands are similarly tied and that point *J* is its best position. Such a joint strategy makes the area *AKLI* the negotiation set and dramatically increases the relative conflict of interest.[8]

In sum, allowing the parties to state final, unmovable positions is likely to decrease agreement which in this case means an increase in strikes. The ask-and-bid requirement at least as a matter of theory should reduce the frequency with which the parties fail to agree.

But suppose all this is true in fact as well as in theory. Why should the parties not be allowed to adopt negotiating styles that are likely to leave them obstinately at loggerheads? This questions brings us back to the rationale for the NLRA. Federal intervention in an area that had hitherto been governed largely

---

8. For a technical discussion of what is meant by relative conflict of interest see Axelrod (1970). Axelrod argues that we can compare the conflict of interest presented by different situations by comparing the area within the negotiation set to the area formed by the square that is created when we extend perpendicular lines from the "1" points for each party on the normalized graph to the point where the perpendiculars intersect. In Figure 6.24, if management and labor agree that because management's hands are tied the optimal result for management is at point *F* and for labor it is at point *I*, extending perpendiculars yields the square *AFRI*. Since the area of this square is only slightly greater than the area of the negotiation set *AFHI*, relative conflict of interest is low. If the union refuses to accept the employer's commitment, but sets its best return at point *G*, the point that represents the most that the company can give the union without faring worse than they would if no agreement were reached, extending perpendiculars leads to an area of conflict defined by *AFSG* and a negotiation set bounded by *AFEG*. The proportion of the total area encompassed by the negotiation set is smaller than in the *AFRI–AFHI* comparison, so the relative conflict is greater. When the negotiation set is limited by firm mutual commitment to *AKLI* the total area of conflict remains *AFSG* and relative conflict is immense with the chance of reaching agreement accordingly small.

To see why relative conflict is defined in this way, suppose that *FSG* were the Pareto optimal line. If this were the case, the agreement would always fix on point *S* where each party got everything he wanted. There would be no sense in stopping at a point like *U* or *V* since one party could give the other party more by moving to *S* without losing anything of value. Thus where the Pareto optimal line and hence the bounds of the negotiation set runs along the top and right-hand sides of the unit square (a "unit square" because in the normalized space the length of each boundary line is "1"), there is no conflict of interest. To the extent that the Pareto optimal line is within the bounds of the unit square, it is impossible to give more to one party without taking something away from the other party. Thus the conflict of interest increases. Settlement chances diminish despite the existence of a negotiation set because even though mutually beneficial solutions are available, the parties have more to fight about.

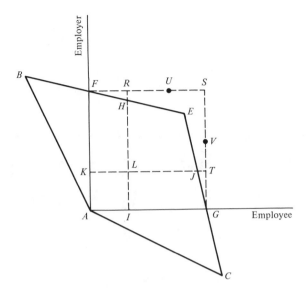

Figure 6.24

by state law as limited by the constitutional protections accorded freedom of contract was regarded as appropriate not just because some people believed that power was unfairly distributed between labor and management, but because in the midst of the Great Depression the public was regarded as having a substantial interest in industrial peace. The portions of the NLRA that we have been discussing may be seen as an attempt to balance this public interest, which might best be served by compulsory arbitration, against the private economic interests of labor and management, which only the parties can meaningfully define. The solution is an ingenious compromise. Private interests must ultimately prevail. Hence no solutions will be imposed on the parties. But the public has a right to demand that the parties diligently search out accommodations that are in their mutual interest. Therefore, the law requires the parties to bargain within an arena structured so as to maximize the probability that mutually beneficial solutions will be discovered.

7

Alternative Styles of Dispute Processing

Paul Bohannan (1965), in a article entitled "The Differing Realms of the Law," engages in that most dangerous of quests, the search for the meaning of "law." More than one reputation has been scuttled in the attempt. If Bohannan did not come back with the "Golden Fleece," the fact that he did come back at all, and with his reputation enhanced, is sufficient reason to treat his observations seriously.

THE DOUBLE INSTITUTIONALIZATION OF LAW

Bohannan begins by making a point we have emphasized: There is "law-stuff" everywhere. Many institutions in society are in the business of creating and enforcing norms (rules if you prefer). These bodies of norms shape, and so in a real sense are the customs of, the institution. Different types of institutions have different norms to deal with their unique circumstances, but similar norms may appear in several institutions. Both schools and factories, for example, have norms concerning tardiness and absenteeism. (But schools usually do not have norms concerning collective bargaining, at least among the "workers.")

Even similar institutions, however, do not have the same customs. Not all schools enforce the same rules; not all families raise children in the same way. We recognize this fact when we say such things as "They are stern disciplinarians," or "It is a very progressive school."

By and large, social institutions, like schools, businesses, churches, and families, do quite well without outside help. They create and enforce rules that bind their members and enable the institution to function adequately. Occasionally, however, institutions find that they are unable to maintain important rules. Or they find themselves involved in conflicts with other institutions that they are unable to resolve. Furthermore, individual interests can clash in settings that provide no convenient, agreed-upon body of norms with which to settle differences. This may be because the clash occurs outside any institutional context, or it may be that jurisdiction can be plausibly lodged in two or more institutions, and the disputants cannot agree on which set of institutional norms is to apply. In these circumstances informal institutional "law-stuff" is not sufficient, and one must turn to some other authority. The body of organizations and rules designed to deal with the trouble cases that other institutions cannot handle Bohannan calls the distinctively legal. Law is:

> "a body of binding obligations regarded as right by one party and acknowledged as the duty by the other" *which has been reinstitutionalized within the legal institution so that society can continue to function in an orderly manner on the basis of rules so maintained.* In short, reciprocity is the basis of custom; but the law rests on the basis of this double institutionalization. Central in it is that some of the customs of some of the institutions of society are restated in such a way that they can be applied by an institution designed (or, at very least, utilized) specifically for that purpose. (1965, p. 36)

Bohannan's conception of law has both strengths and weaknesses. It is as much a theory as a definition, but it is a partial theory stated in universalistic language. As a definition, the statement is clearly inadequate. It slights procedural rules like the rules regulating pretrial discovery or the rules of evidence in court. It also fails to take account of the fact that in modern societies many of the laws enacted by legislatures are designed to deal with newly perceived social problems, the disposal of toxic wastes for example, and have no deeper institutional roots. However, Bohannan's statement does capture an important characteristic of much of what we call law, including many of those norms that we believe are essential to the social order. Furthermore, Bohannan derives from his definition a useful theory about the crucial tasks that must be accomplished if disputes are to be settled by law.

When Bohannan speaks of a rule being "reinstitutionalized" within the legal institution, he means that a customary rule guaranteed (i.e., enforced) by the resources of the institution in which it is lodged becomes accepted as a law and so is guaranteed by the resources of the legal institution as well. Because the norm is a rule of two institutions and is guaranteed by each, there is double institutionalization. Consider the situation of a church whose doctrine commands monogamy. The norm, "thou shalt not have more than one spouse at a time" is rooted in a single institution—the church. The church has ways of guaranteeing, that is, enforcing, the norm. It can refuse to marry those with living spouses, it may bar bigamists from its sacraments, it may excommunicate bigamists, and, if it is sufficiently dominant, it may effectively isolate bigamists from the day-to-day life of the community. If the church is strong and its authority generally accepted, bigamy should be rare. Most people will have been taught directly by the church or indirectly through their schools or families that bigamy is wrong and will not consider marrying a second spouse before divorcing the first. Such people have been socialized (taught the social rule) so that they internalize (accept as in the nature of things) the norm. The remainder, those who are tempted by bigamy and so consider it, will be deterred by the threat of the sanctions that the church can impose. However, some nonbelievers who do not value their association with the orthodox, will, if sufficiently tempted, contract bigamous marriages. The church cannot effectively sanction them.

The situation changes if the norm institutionalized in the church is made into law, or, in Bohannan's terms, "reinstitutionalized in the legal institution." Now the norm will be guaranteed by the resources of the legal institution as well as by those of the church. In plain English, bigamists will not only be excommunicated from the church, but they will also be thrown into jail. Presumably, there will be a further decline in the rate of bigamy. This is not only because the threat of going to jail may scare those who laugh at excommunication, but also because the law may directly or indirectly encourage socialization. The family of nonbelievers who would not raise their son or daughter to accept unthinkably a rule of the church may do so when the rule is one of law.

In our example the law has a residual role, for we posited a strong church. Had the church been weak, the law might have been the only effective defense against temptations to bigamous marriage. Where legal norms are not firmly rooted in other institutions, as is the case with tax laws, the importance of legal guarantees to normative conformity are obvious.

As with bigamy, community norms are often reinstitutionalized as crimes, but double institutionalization may be important on the civil side as well. Consider the normative obligation to fulfill contracts within the business community and the underlying obligation to keep promises that is institutionalized in the church, the family, and other settings. One might think that nonlegal norms regarding promising would mean that the business community has no need for a law of contracts, that is, a law that comes into play when obligations are arguably unfulfilled. Often this is true. Most contracts are carried out, and when they are not fulfilled the failure is often for what are, within the business community, normatively permissible reasons. This is not surprising. Norms of honesty and fair dealing within the business community have powerful guarantees. A businessperson can incur substantial costs if he develops a reputation as one whose word cannot be trusted. This is especially true if he depends for products or sales on a small set of others with whom he has ongoing relationships. However, some people do not have to worry about their business reputations, or the gains from breaching a contract may so far outweigh the costs of compliance that expected reputational losses count for little. Since these circumstances can occur, contract law plays an important backup role, although contract actions are, even relative to the number of breaches, rare events. Contract law gives A, who must invest substantial amounts in reliance on B's promised performance, some guarantee that B will either perform his end of the bargain or provide A with compensation for any failure to perform.

Bohannan lists three tasks that legal institutions must perform if the reinstitutionalization of norms at the legal level is to be effective:

> (1) There must be specific ways in which difficulties can be disengaged from the institutions in which they arose and which they now threaten and then be engaged within the processes of the legal institution. (2) There must be ways in which the trouble can now be handled within the framework of the legal institution, and (3) There must be ways in which the new solutions which thus emerge can be re-engaged within the processes of the non-legal institutions from which they emerged. (1965, p. 35)

What Bohannan means is that legal institutions must have regularized ways of "interfering" with nonlegal institutions, both in taking "trouble" cases from those institutions and in generating legal solutions that can be fitted into the ongoing life of the nonlegal institutions.

If this seems uncomfortably abstract, narrowing the focus slightly may help. Henceforth, rather than speaking of legal institutions, we will talk of courts and court-like bodies. These are the legal institutions that have been of most interest to Bohannan and his fellow anthropologists. What Bohannan is telling us is that there must be both procedures by which cases can be brought to court and ways of ensuring that court decisions have, to some meaningful degree, their intended impact within the institutional arena in which the disputes that they process arose. These can be difficult and delicate tasks. Although they might be accomplished by brute force, the consequence might be to destroy an institution under the guise of saving it. Closed circuit television monitors in bedrooms and kitchens, for example, might bring many more cases of family violence to judicial attention, but the institution of the family as we know it might disappear. The NLRB (National Labor Relations Board) might by fiat "settle" industrial disputes, but if it regularly did so, the institution of collective bargaining would dissolve.

Courts not only must develop ways of acquiring cases, they must also develop rules for handling cases once they are brought to law. Part of the task is to devise substantive rules (law) that can be used to decide cases. In Part I of this book we discussed some of the reasons for and consequences of the rules chosen. The other part of the task is to devise rules on how cases should be handled. These rules are as a body just as important as the substantive law and, in fact, often determine case outcomes. Rules about the handling of cases include rules of procedure, evidence rules, and rules concerning the consequences of legal judgments.[1] We shall call these rules *secondary rules* to distinguish them from the *primary rules* of substantive law (Hart, 1961).

The task of disengaging trouble cases from and reengaging them in other institutions and the task of providing primary and secondary rules for their

---

1. Social scientists often overlook the fact that rules concerning the consequences of a judgment are at least as important as other rules. Law schools teach whole courses on parts of this topic. They have titles such as Equity, Restitution, and Damages. The question in these courses, crudely stated, is: If you win, what do you get and how do you get it?

settlement are closely connected. Intervention in ordinary (by which we mean nonlegal) life may be more or less disruptive depending on the way in which the legal institution defines the problem and the type of solution it imposes.

Although no brief statement can describe all the ways in which American legal institutions intervene and settle disputes, a fair generalization might be that intervention is guided by three principles. First, it should be limited to situations where there is a clear showing of a genuine, unresolved conflict. Second, courts should decide cases on the narrowest grounds possible. Third, courts should clearly declare winners and losers.

The first principle is reflected by the common requirement that there must be a "case or controversy" before the courts will intervene.[2] We might add that except with respect to certain crimes and regulatory violations, our legal system is primarily *reactive*; that is, it is one of unofficial *party initiation*. Courts and other legal actors will intervene only at the request of one of the disputants. Someone must sue, and that someone must have a stake in the dispute. These seem to be characteristics of most legal systems, but they do not always pertain in any society. Unilaterally intervening in some matter when no one is especially aggrieved takes concentrated power. It is only when police or police-like organizations develop in response to social threats that *proactive* enforcement of the law is both common and, in some measure, effective.

The second principle, that the law should decide on narrow grounds, we call the *narrow res gestae rule*. The *res gestae* of a case is not the complete transaction under consideration in all its richness. Rather, it is the actual thing or issue being litigated and is to be distinguished from other events and circumstances that have no necessary implications for the core legal issue.[3] Modern Western courts are supposed to narrow the controversies presented to them to the core of what they have been told is in dispute. They should accept as proven all matters on which the parties agree and exclude evidence pertaining to disputes not intimately connected with the one cited when their jurisdiction was invoked.[4]

---

2. For a discussion of what the "case or controversy" requirement means and justifications for it, see note 1 in Chapter 6. Some states do not impose a case or controversy requirement on their courts. This means that their courts can give "advisory opinions," i.e., statements about what the law means although an occasion to apply the law has not arisen and may not occur. Such opinions, however, do not usually require courts to be actively involved in the resolution of problems rooted in other institutional spheres.

3. *Res gestae* has a slightly narrower meaning in law. It distinguishes the circumstances immediately surrounding a legally relevant act from those separated by time and/or space. As a phrase it has been used by courts to characterize statements closely related to an act for purposes of defining an exception to the rule excluding hearsay evidence. This use is disappearing since the label *res gestae* is avoided in modern codes of evidence. Here we are using the term with a wider meaning to distinguish the actual issue(s) to be decided from surrounding issues and circumstances.

4. Anglo-American common law also has a preference, often, however, honored in the breach, that cases should be decided on the narrowest grounds possible. If two rules could be used to decide a case, one of which speaks only to the specific issues of the present case and the other that speaks to these issues as well as related issues that might arise in the future, the first rule should guide the decision. This is not what we mean by a narrow *res gestae*. As we use the concept, it is concerned with the information a court will consider and not with the breadth of the rule or principle the court uses to decide the case.

The third principle is that if the parties cannot settle their differences, the law should declare a winner and a loser rather than impose some kind of compromise (Eisenberg, 1976). We call this the *binary decision* rule. We saw a good example of this in our discussion of contributory negligence in Chapter 5. Under the classic doctrine even slight negligence on the part of a personal injury plaintiff destroys his legal right to recover. Although most states have now modified this rule, in most areas of law it is still generally true that trials to judgment do not eventuate in some "splitting of the difference" depending on the relative guilt or responsibility of the parties. The primary rules usually require the fact finder to determine which party is legally right and which is legally wrong. The winner takes all.

Not all legal systems operate under these principles. Indeed, no system does all the time. In the next section we draw on studies by anthropologists to discuss different modes of dispute settlement and their different consequences. The anthropological literature, by examining legal systems and cultures different from our own, provides a valuable perspective from which to view American legal institutions.

SETTLEMENT TECHNIQUES IN OTHER CULTURES

The Barotse of Northern Rhodesia (Zambia)

In one of the classics of the anthropology of law, Max Gluckman (1967) used a case method to explicate the legal system of the Lozi tribesmen in what was then Northern Rhodesia (now Zambia). Before Gluckman's work, most reports [a notable exception being Llewelyn & Hoebel's *The Cheyenne Way* (1941)] on the legal systems of tribal groups were written as if the tribes had European-style civil codes that clearly delineated the rules that governed the society. Not only was this misleading—most of the societies had no written law whatsoever—but it also led to the conceptual separation of legal norms from the process by which they were applied. By using a method that discussed and grouped *cases*, Gluckman was able to present the rules as they were actually applied, as well as to show how cases came to be decided.

The Lozi (the tribe Gluckman studied, and at the time the ruling people of Barotseland) have councils of men who both decide cases and perform other administrative acts. When sitting as a court, the councillors are called a *kuta*. After a case has been argued, each member of the court announces his opinion in ascending order of rank until the senior *induna* ("judge") speaks. He is the last to speak and his statement is the judgment of the kuta.

"The Case of the Biased Father" illustrates the general nature of the *secondary* rules used by the Lozi in deciding cases. A, B, and C sued their "father" (i.e., their father's elder brother) who was the headman in their village. This "father," Y (see Figure 7.1), was not only their "classificatory father;" he had in fact raised A, B, and C since their biological father had died when they were

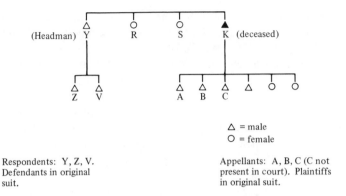

Respondents: Y, Z, V.
Defendants in original
suit.

Appellants: A, B, C (C not
present in court). Plaintiffs
in original suit.

Figure 7.1   The Case of the Biased Father

children. The suit concerned some gardens in the village. In a modern Western court it would have been called a property case.

What a Westerner might consider the legally relevant facts were undisputed. For reasons we will get to, A, B, and C had left the village and another "brother," Z (Y's biological child) had taken over their garden. Moreover, the Lozi legal rule was equally straightforward: "If you leave the village, you lose your gardens in it."[5] But, as we shall see, the case is not so simple.

The evidence given by A (the eldest of the nephews) was that Z had committed adultery with C's wife. This began a quarrel that, according to A, eventually led Y to tell C to leave the village. When A intervened, Y also told him to leave. Shortly thereafter, B returned from White country where he was working and joined A and C. When they found that Z was working their gardens they brought the case to court. A testified:

> I protested to our "father" Y who said it was done without his agreement—he would put it right. He did nothing, so I saw that he was supporting his own son, Z, against the children of his younger brother. We complained to the induna SIKWA who said we could not live together, we must separate. [Sikwa, who in our terms was a lower court judge, had feared that more serious harm might develop as accusations of sorcery had been made.] The induna said we had lost our land. I cannot see how a person without a fault can lose his land, and his mangoes and other crops, so we have appealed. (Gluckman, 1967, pp. 37–38)

As one might expect, this version of what had happened was not the same as that told by the defense. Z testified and admitted the adultery. He denied, however, that he or his father had driven the plaintiffs away. He then went into a long series of allegations of ways in which the nephews had insulted him and his father.

---

5. The rule itself tells us much about Barotse life. Rights of ownership of land come from membership in a village and kin group. A different rule might seriously threaten the basic social unit and the unity of the village. Western property laws can cause havoc in such situations. Rights in real property severed from social position promote absentee landlordism and various ensuing problems (Paige, 1975).

B then testified that when he returned from the White country he went to Y to call the parties together to settle the quarrel, but Y said it was no longer possible. He accused Y of partiality for siding with his biological son.

Y took the stand and "began with a diatribe on how wicked and irresponsible the modern youth are" (1967, p. 38). He repeated and added to Z's statement about all the ways in which his "children" had not respected him.

There was additional testimony by the aunts R and S and by V (Z's sibling), all of whom tried to make no statement against either party. Then the judges began cross-examining the witnesses. The parties stuck to their stories. Y denied that B had ever asked him to call the parties together. B reaffirmed that he had. The judges asked A and B whether they had generally given Y food, and whether they had given him clothes when they returned from working in White country. They recited a long list of gifts. Y and Z denied receiving such gifts. The councillors asked about C, who was not present. What gifts had he given?

Then one judge asked Y, "Do you want your sons back?"

Y replied, "Yes, I do, emphatically."

He asked A and B, "Do you want to return?"

B answered, "Yes, it is to our father; if the gardens . . ."

Several councillors interrupted: "Leave the gardens, that is easy. Do you want to go home?" (1967, p. 40)

The councillors then began to render their judgments. Some of the less senior councillors stated the legal rule. Thus the Induna Mbasiwana: "You children return home. As for the gardens, no one lives elsewhere and cultivates in the home. It is good that you return, and if you refuse to return home, you cannot return to your gardens" (1967, p. 41). The more senior councillors, however, rarely even referred to the point that brought about the suit. They spoke instead about the duties and obligations of the parties to one another. Consider this statement by a councillor named Awami.

> Y, in my opinion you have not handled the village well. You must see that your children like one another. A man loves all his children and they strengthen him. The country is well-built when a man and his children love one another. If they refuse to live with you, I would see that they refuse to eat the land of their father. Now I've heard from them that they will return. If they do return and you withhold their gardens, I shall see that you agreed only in the kuta. A child has no soil but from his parent, and a parent is only worked for by his child. Thus if you refuse them the gardens, we shall see that it was you who drove them away. If you give them the gardens, I shall see that you still love them. I shall thank you greatly.
>
> Now for you, Z. Y is their father, you must give them their gardens. They have only him as their father. You are only one of the children. The man who is oldest in the family, it is just that he is born first.[6] You are not their lord, but merely the first by birth. Hold your brothers well, and they will care well for you. It is

---

6. Although Z as Y's oldest son may assume that he will succeed Y as headman of the village upon Y's death, the councillor is reminding him that this is not necessarily the case. When the headman dies an heir is selected by all the cognates from among themselves. No one succeeds as a matter of law. Y may think Z will succeed him and Z may also believe this, but the family may choose V or A or B or C.

good to love one another. Also, you are the one with power. I heard your father say that he may live only another year, and may not see much more. You will be in difficulties. If they rejoin the village, it is to strengthen you. Now you, A and B—do not take this affair by another path. Do not think that the kuta has returned your gardens. They are the gift of your father. Also, for the poles you took back— bring your small gifts and work for your parents. I was born as you were and know. Every day your father fed you, morning and evening, and now he is old the position is reversed: you are the parent. He cannot go to the bush to fell hard trees. Do not take your poles from him.[7] He is a parent. We thank you because you said in the kuta you wish to return to your father. (Gluckman, 1967, pp. 42–43)

Justice in a Mexican Zapotec Court

Laura Nader (1969), in an article entitled "Styles of Court Procedure: To Make the Balance" reports on court proceedings in the Mexican village of Ralu'a, a town of 2,000 deep in the Sierra Madre. The town has three officials who act as judges: the *presidente*, the *alcalde*, and the *sindico*. The latter deals primarily with crimes. The other two handle civil matters, usually with the more "serious" cases reserved for the *alcalde* when the *presidente* is unable to "work a solution."

The judges are chosen because they are deemed to be men who are capable of *erj goonz*, "making the balance" between the plaintiff and the defendant. The case discussed here is before the *presidente*.

"The Case of the Bossy Wife" began with a complaint by Sr. Jaime Ruiz against his wife, Carmen Ibarra. The complaint was that the wife had cut his coffee without his consent.[8] The wife was called and the husband made a fuller plea.

"Mr. President, I am here to complain with the help of your authority that this woman, who is my wife, had my coffee cut from a piece of land that belongs to me. I know that the helper of my wife did the cutting on her order, but without consent or permission, and this is why I am here to claim that this coffee should be delivered to me."

To this the wife responds:

"Mr. President, this man really does not think at all. Why shouldn't I cut the coffee as it belongs to both of us, and besides we have children to support and feed. I am a woman. I do everything to look after our children, and he has left us, left the house. . . . Now he is complaining about the coffee—it is true, I ordered the coffee to be cut. What do I do—me, I have to [take] care of his children, so I think I have my rights, after all we are legally married, and nobody hindered him in carrying out his own wish to get out. . . . Look Mr. President, my little girl is at this moment

---

7. One of the accusations against A and B was that Y had taken some poles from them to build a partition in his house. During the quarrel they had come and taken them back. They claimed this was before any partition had been built.
8. Coffee was the main cash crop in the area, and thus the case had real economic significance.

in Mexico [City] for a treatment because she is sick and he does not even think that his daughter needs some money for treatment. [The plaintiff interrupts to claim he did not even know the daughter had gone, she did not ask or tell him.]''

The defendant continues:

"Now he says that I didn't say anything about her going—If she were dying, would you want me first to ask you permission so that she could die? When there is urgency for a treatment, one has to look for a way." (1969, pp. 76–77)

The husband responds to all of this by saying the wife never tells him any of her affairs. Apparently she has a liquor store, the profits from which she keeps to herself. Then he says, "and there are more things she has been doing, but now I don't want this case to drag on longer—I only want her to return the coffee to me."

But Carmen will not isolate the coffee issue.

"Yes, I will deliver the coffee, which you said I took, but you have to pay in front of the President the bills of the treatment that our daughter had to have—poor little girl—who wants so much to be cured as she says in her postcard, 'Mama, do sell some interests of my part for the treatment.' And I am doing everything to get hold of some money so that she can take the treatment—and this man, for a little bit of coffee which I went and cut off, he is making such a terrible fuss."

The plaintiff made one final attempt to narrow the case.

"I planted the coffee seeds for my wife and she has sufficient, and now she tries to take mine and wants to have more, but the only thing I want is for her not to cut [my coffee] without my permission." (1969, p. 77)

The *presidente* gave his opinion. It would be well received in the Lozi kuta. He tells both parties to forget their troubles of the past and worry about their sick daughter. He tells the husband he should return home and the wife that the husband should give the orders and it is her duty to follow them as long as the orders are for the good of the household. Also, it is the wife's duty to inform the husband about what she is doing.

After this the parties become more reasonable. The husband will go home when the daughter returns from Mexico City. The wife agrees. The *presidente* leaves the case open until the daughter's return from her mysterious "treatment." Nothing was said about the coffee.

Who won this case? Who won the Lozi case? The results of the cases are not so ambiguous that the questions cannot be answered. From a Western perspective, the wife won the Mexican case (she did not have to pay damages), and A, B, and C won the Lozi case (their land was restored), although in the latter instance the Lozi declared Y the winner on the theory that his "sons" were allowed to retain gardens they had forfeited only because Y welcomed them back. But the important point of the cases is not that we can translate the results into winners and losers; rather, it is that a wide set of activities were examined in each case and the parties each "gave" something.

This fact is noted by both Gluckman and Nader. Indeed, one of their most important findings is that the courts employ these types of secondary rules. Gluckman notes:

> In order to fulfill their task the judges constantly have to broaden the field of their enquiries, and consider the total history of relations between the litigants, not only the narrow legal issue raised by one of them. . . . The result is that in cases of this sort the court's conception of "relevance" is very wide, for many facts affect the settlement of the dispute. . . . There is no refinement of pleadings in Lozi procedure to whittle a suit down to certain narrow legal claims so as to present the judges with a mere skeleton of the facts relevant to those claims. The judges are immediately made aware of the moral perspective of the suit, and they themselves can take judicial notice of anything that falls in their own knowledge which they consider relevant. (1967, pp. 21, 51)

Nader's comments are not dissimilar:

> The judge is a warden of order and fair play among peers. He resolves conflict by minimizing the sense of injustice and outrage felt by the parties to a case. His investigation of the truth is nondirective and flexible much of the time. His patient stance functions to encourage litigants to decide what relevant issues should be discussed, to present both real and abstract evidence to support their claims. In family cases he is more directive and paternalistic and seeks to remind kinsmen of their responsibilities. He is expected to make use of what he knows of town affairs and is selected for just such knowledge. He is expected to render a verbal and written agreement for each case—an agreement that consensus would label equitable.
>
> The judgment that the *presidente* gives on a matter is always a compromise in that the decision is the "result or embodiment of concession or adjustment." . . . In the case of the bossy wife, the *presidente* thought that neither damages nor punitive fines would aid restoration of peace—but that conflict over the division of property would be eliminated if both returned to a normal marital state.
>
> . . . The contenders talk about anything they consider relevant, without the *presidente's* attempting to confine the discussion to the original charge(s). Points of fact are not definitely settled; matters of fault are not ultimately pursued. . . . There is no fiction of judicial ignorance. (1969, pp. 84–86)

The style of decision making in the Mexican and Zambian cases is obviously different from the style that is thought ideal in American courts. In the Mexican and Zambian courts the *res gestae* is expected to be wide rather than narrow, and *flexible, integrative outcomes* are sought rather than *binary* ones. The procedural and evidentiary rules followed by these courts reflect these norms of decision making. Nothing is totally irrelevant, and the determination of particular facts seems at times hopelessly vague. What was wrong with the daughter in Mexico City? What is "the treatment"? How much does it cost? Holding someone at fault for a particular action, which is essential for a binary decision, is often not done. Or if it is, the complaining party is frequently found to have also been at fault in some respect. The tribunal's job is to resolve the conflict fairly between the parties, or in Nader's felicitous phrase, "to make the balance." The idea of making the balance implies an effort to restore the relationship between disputing individuals or groups of individuals by specifying a course of action that each disputant can accept as a basis for peaceful interaction. Declaring one side a winner on all counts and the other a loser and distributing praise and sanctions accordingly seldom facilitates such reconciliation. Also it is often the case that harmonious relations cannot be restored simply by resolving the quarrel that the disputants have brought to court. The judicial net must be widened to determine what is really dividing the parties. The litigants in such systems know what to expect. Indeed, some plaintiffs admit to bringing their legal claims so that the court will help settle more fundamental differences between them and those they accuse.

TYPES OF LEGAL DECISION MAKING

The fact that a court seeks to resolve social conflict flexibly and is open to compromise solutions does not, however, mean that the differences between the parties before the court will inevitably be split down the middle. One party may be more in the right than the other, and courts such as the Lozi kuta recognize this.[9] Binary outcomes are not necessarily inconsistent with resolving conflicts and reconciling disputing parties. The outcome, as well as the procedures employed, may encourage reconciliation. In addition, law itself, as Bohannan's perspective makes clear, can be an important integrative device. A tribunal may hew closely to a legal rule that demands a binary decision because of the importance of maintaining the rule, even when it would prefer a compromise outcome. In such circumstances, however, the all or none nature of the official decision may be tempered by other action flowing from the litigation.

Three cases that Gluckman describes are instructive. In the first, the "Case of the Vain Garden-Holder" (p. 309), W left his uncle's village, W's home village, expecting to be appointed heir in his mother's village. When his expectations were not realized he was ashamed and wanted to build in a nearby village with his mother's relatives but to work his old gardens. His uncle said he could not do this, and W complained to the kuta. The kuta affirmed the uncle's judgment, and W returned home. Although Gluckman's description of the case is sparse, here an all or nothing decision apparently reconciled the youth

---

9. June Starr and Barbara Yngvesson (1975) in a thoughtful commentary on the work of Gluckman, Nader, and others argue that the overwhelming majority of the cases that Gluckman describes ended in zero sum (binary) outcomes rather than in compromises reconciling the parties. Although one might reasonably classify many of Gluckman's cases differently than these authors do, their cautionary message is sound and important. Decision styles that allow flexibility and aim at integration do not necessarily result in compromise decisions or successful reintegration. There is an association with intermediate outcomes when systems that allow flexible, integrative approaches are contrasted with those that aim from the start at binary solutions, but the association is statistical rather than necessary. We see this in Chapter 8 as well when we look at mediation programs attached to small claims courts. Mediation is more likely to yield compromise solutions than adjudication, but a surprising number of mediated cases end with one party or the other getting everything in dispute.

to returning home. Knowing how the kuta works, the virtues of remaining in the home village must have been expounded in the kuta, and the judges probably extracted a commitment from W to return home before they rendered their decision.

The second case, the "Case of the Immigrant Land Borrower" (pp. 62–64), involved S, an immigrant to B's village, who had been loaned a garden by B. For 7 years B and S lived as close neighbors, with S doing many valuable favors for B. Then King I, who was related to B through B's mother told B that he must tell S to leave, for the land was needed for their own kin. S was outraged. He complained bitterly of B's ingratitude, and B replied with a list of S's faults. Eventually, a kuta was called. S admitted the land was loaned to him but claimed his brother-like ties to B, his dependency on B, and the many things he had done for B meant that B had no right to expel him. B responded angrily denying S's favors. The kuta followed the law and ruled for B. Although M, B's brother tried to soothe S by pointing out that he had always been a good neighbor and was not being expelled for any fault of his own, S was not mollified. He grumbled and threatened to sue B for repayment of his favors. The kuta said he would get nothing, for it was right to help a neighbor, and the judges pointedly asked who would give S a place to stay should he demand repayment.

So far we have in this case two binary decisions and a disgruntled loser. This seems to be a poor example of flexible, integrative justice. But the night of the decisions S was visited by N, the head of the kuta, who lectured him on what it meant to be a good neighbor and on the advantages of not bearing grudges. N suggested that S yield his land with good grace to B and ask the king for a gift of land. S took N's advice and was placed on royal land in the neighborhood. Thus the formal kuta did not end the dispute resolution process. N's visit to S was crucial, and Gluckman suggests that N helped S obtain the new land with a more secure title.

Finally, we have "The Case of the Prince's Gardens" (pp. 56–61). A local prince, P, was seeking to evict M from some gardens. P claimed that his father had loaned M the gardens and M defended by claiming he had been given the gardens and by questioning the validity of P's claim of title. It appears that all the witnesses called, including M's son, testified on behalf of P, and the evidence was largely confined to the issue of title. Ultimately, P won a clear victory. At the same time, however, judge after judge was careful to emphasize the overwhelming weight of the evidence on behalf of P and that the court was not being swayed by the fact that P was a "big person" and M was a "small person."

Two facts stand out about this case. First, the ties between P and M were less multiplex than the ties between any of the other litigants whose cases we have discussed. So it is not surprising that the kuta narrowed the *res gestae* in this case and issued a clearly binary decision that did not blame the winner and offered little material consolation to the loser.[10] At the same time, the kuta was

---

10. Several judges did mention that M's children worked P's land, and they suggested that P might be angered by M's suit and might take back the children's land but that he should not do so.

careful to emphasize the weight of the evidence and the way the testimony in the case compelled them to decide as they did. In a dispute between neighbors who had relatively little to do with each other, this may be all that is necessary to make the balance, at least when the stronger party prevails.

As these cases suggest, what differentiates courts like the Lozi kuta from modern Western courts is not that the latter generally render binary decisions, while the former never do. The difference is more subtle. The modern Western court is oriented to binary decisions that resolve opposing claims of right. They are its ideal. We might say that such courts are *rights based* and *binary decision driven*. Courts like the Lozi kuta, on the other hand, are flexible in their outcome orientation. They will render a binary decision if the situation calls for one, but they will render graduated, compromise decisions as well. What drives them are more integrative concerns. The purpose of a court decision is apparently not to vindicate rights (even if this at times occurs). Rather, it seems to be to restore the relations between disputing parties to the extent feasible and to maintain collective understandings insofar as they are essential to a stable society.

In Table 7.1 we have taken the two factors, outcome orientation (binary or flexible) and *res gestae* (narrow or wide), and constructed a table specifying four ideal types of settlement processes.

We have given names to the decision process of each cell. Each is an ideal type of *secondary* rule structure that is used to resolve controversies. The upper left-hand corner, which we call "issue decision," represents the idealized process in American courts. The courts are supposed to decide in favor of one party or the other the issue(s) formally presented to the court in the case. The lower right-hand cell, "relationship settlement," is an idealization of the style of settling relationships that we see in the courts studied by Gluckman and Nader.

We have not as yet discussed decision processes that approximate the other two types in this table; "issue settlement" or "relationship decision." Issue settlement does not ordinarily occur in courts, but it takes place constantly in negotiated settlements of the type we discussed in Chapter 6. Courts may facilitate such settlements, as they do when judges in pretrial proceedings urge intermediate solutions on the parties, and issue settlements are common in court-annexed mediation programs where third parties without the power to impose solutions suggest possible outcomes. We examine issue settlements in the context of small claims court mediation programs in Chapter 8. Issue settlements are usually spurred by the implicit threat of a worse result should the more resistant party

TABLE 7.1
Types of Settlement Processes

Res Gestae	Outcome Orientation	
	Binary	*Flexible*
Narrow	Issue decision	Issue settlement
Wide	Relationship decision	Relationship settlement

pursue a binary decision. Also, there is often normative pressure brought to bear on both parties, suggesting either that one is in the right and further litigation by the other is wrong or fruitless or that a compromise outcome is more appropriate than the extreme claims the parties make (Eisenberg, 1976).

Compromise, however, is not easy to come by when only one issue is at stake, except insofar as there are mutual savings to be had through the compromised outcome. The major source of such mutual savings is, as we have seen in Chapter 6, litigation costs. However, by the time a case has reached the pretrial conference stage or when a case has been channeled to pretrial mediation, a large proportion of the litigation costs may have been expended. For this reason, in such settings there is often a push toward expansion of the *res gestae*, not to the point of relationship settlement, but at least to the point where several issues rather than one issue are open to discussion. When several issues are involved, even if each is approached somewhat narrowly, the potential for settlement increases, because expanding the issues provides one way of graduating results in a binary decision system. Instead of giving a party that is expecting a binary decision more or less on an issue, the mediator can suggest solutions that give one party everything on one issue and the other party everything on some other issue. Thus both parties will feel they are partially in the right, and if the parties value victory on the various issues differently, the relative conflict of interest will be reduced. For this reason, it has been suggested that expansion of the issues is a promising tactic for negotiators who are interested in achieving settlements (Raffia, 1982; Menkel-Meadow, 1984).

The fourth cell, the relationship decision, involves decision-making processes that focus not on particular behavior with an eye toward characterizing it as legal or illegal, but rather, on the basic character or situation of the person before the tribunal. The goal is to characterize what that person is in essence. The juvenile court as it existed throughout much of this century is an example of a tribunal geared largely toward rendering relationship decisions. We discuss the juvenile court in some detail in the next chapter. For the remainder of this chapter we return to the outcomes that most interest us here: issue decisions and relationship settlements.

WHY DIFFERENT TECHNIQUES?

To avoid leaving the impression that all "primitive" societies use a relationship settlement technique and all "civilized" societies use an issue decision technique, let us consider an example that cuts the other way. This example is taken from a study by Lloyd Fallers (1969) of the Basoga in Uganda and is reported in Fallers's book *Law Without Precedent*. As with "The Case of the Biased Father," one needs a scorecard to keep track of the players.[11]

---

11. Gluckman (1967) only gave letters for the names of the parties in "The Case of the Biased Father." Fallers provides party names, but with names like Gwampiya Kire, it seems preferable to maintain the convention of using letters.

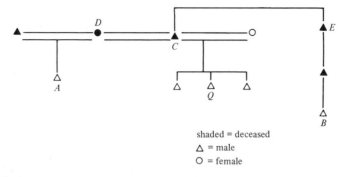

shaded = deceased
△ = male
○ = female

Figure 7.2   The Case of the Headman's Stepson (Fallers, 1969, p. 287)

"The Case of the Headman's Stepson" like the Lozi case concerns property rights. B is the subvillage headman in the village where the property is located. A accuses B of removing him without reason "from my garden, in which I have lived for twenty-four years and which was given to me by C in 1927." All agree that A has occupied the garden since the 1920s when his mother, D married C. At the time E was the subvillage headman. E gave C the garden to provide for his new wife and her son (A), then a young boy.

Later E died and C succeeded to the subvillage headmanship. Within the 3 years preceding the suit both C and D had died. B, the grandson of E, succeeded to the subvillage headmanship, and, he claimed the garden being used by A. (As with the Lozi, the headmanship of Soga villages may move from one line to another in a lineage. The headmen do not strictly inherit, but are chosen by the clan. In this case Q was the main inheritor of C's land, but joined with other villagers in giving B the headmanship.)

When B told A to leave the garden, A refused. B took the issue to the village headman, who decided in his favor. A then brought the case to court.

B's claim is that when C died he inherited the garden with the headmanship, and that the clan intended this to be the case when they gave him the headmanship seems fairly clear. Also, it is clear that A cannot inherit the land from C. In Soga law, widows and stepchildren have no rights in a husband's estate. A's claim is not based on inheritance, however. Instead, he alleges that the garden was a gift from C to him. When C was the headman the land was his to allot, and he could legally have given A the garden as a tenant. A argues that since C gave it, B could not inherit it. Furthermore, A points out that the garden was allotted many years ago, and the arrangement has been acquiesced in ever since.

B responds that A "went to the land with his mother." The claim is that the land was never the property of either A or his mother, but was only given to them to use because A's mother had married C.

The Soga judges concentrate on the legal issue. They first want to know how A holds the land: as a tenant or as his mother's son? The evidence is unclear.

A calls several witnesses to testify that C gave him the land as a tenant, but under the judge's questioning no one testifies directly that he witnessed the transaction. In a society without written deeds the fact that there is no *mukwenda* (agent) who was present at the alleged transaction is a telling point against A. Moreover, the village headman reports no knowledge of such a transaction. This is even more damning, for usually a new tenant is introduced to the headman. But A has a further argument: acquiescence. This long acquiescence is the central flaw in B's case. The following question (Q) and answer (A) dialogue occurs between a judge and B:

> Q: [A] says that he has spent twenty-four years in the garden, but you say he just went to visit his mother. Which is correct? [Fallers: the two statements are not, of course, literally contradictory, but the first tends to affirm A's rights, the second to deny them.] A: My statement is right. Q: Do you agree that the accuser [A] grew up there and first paid taxes there? A: I am sure of it. Q: Did the accuser have another place, which he left? A: He has nothing else. . . . Q: Are there any witnesses to testify that the accuser has not used that holding for twenty-four years? A: Mpango and Waibi; I appeal to them because they know that the accuser was never given that garden, but that it is mine. (Fallers, 1969, p. 289)

The two are called, but like A's witnesses, they refused to say flatly whether A was given the land by C. Without any direct testimony as to whether C gave the land to A, the long unchallenged use of the land, A's record of paying poll taxes there, and the fact that A has no other place to which he belongs proves decisive. By collecting the taxes, the headmen have been implicitly treating A as a landholder. A man pays no taxes in a community in which he holds no land.

The court's opinion reads as follows:

> The accuser has won the case. It is true that he owns the garden, which was given him by Balugambire, who had married his mother Mudola. During the twenty-four years which the accuser has spent in the garden, the accused should have initiated the case. . . ." (1969, p. 290)

This case is not so different from "The Lozi Case of the Biased Father" in its legal outlines. Both involve rights in a garden that are disputed by collateral kin. Moreover, it is clear that the general rules governing the law of real property are not radically different in the two societies.

But compare the opinion of this court with that of the judges in the Lozi case. The latter opinion is one of compromise, legal generality, and moral upbraiding. The Soga opinion by comparison is a firm decision, characterized by legal specificity and moral neutrality.[12]

> A "case" for [the Basoga], is a proceeding to decide whether or not a particular set of "facts" falls within the reach of one particular concept of wrong. All sorts of other issues may be raised in argument, but only those relevant to the reach of

---

12. This characterization should not be read as suggesting that the decision is in any way immoral or unjust. Indeed, it is just the opposite. Acquiescence and reliance play a central part in the decision. The judges clearly feel it would be a great injustice to turn A out at this point. But this view is pronounced as a legal rule, not in an effort to persuade the parties of some fair compromise.

the particular concept of wrong enter into the decision; and the latter is delivered quite unilaterally, with little attempt to elicit consent. (1969, p. 327)

Why are the Soga courts more legalistic than the Barotse courts?[13]

Both Gluckman and Nader argue that the dispute settlement techniques of the groups they studied were strongly influenced by the nature of the relationships of the people in the society. Gluckman calls Lozi relationships *multiplex*:

> Most Lozi relationships are multiplex, enduring through the lives of individuals and even generations. Each of these relationships is part of an intricate network of similar relationships. Inevitably, therefore, many of the disputes which are investigated by Lozi kutas arise not in ephemeral relationships involving single interests, but in relationships which embrace many interests, which depend on similar related relationships, and which may endure into the future. This, at least, is usually the desire of the parties and the hope and desire of the judges and unbiased onlookers. The Lozi disapprove of any irremediable breaking of relationships. (1967, p. 20)

Nader makes similar points. Among her observations about the Zapotec are the following:

> The decisions of the court emanate from the characteristics of a multiplex society. Regardless of who the litigants are, it is the wider network of relations that influence a decision. The greater social relevance is considered in solving a particular dispute. Utilitarian thinking is valued. . . . Reasoning is prospectively oriented. (1969, p. 88)

But in this respect Soga society resembles Lozi society. Many relationships are multiplex and enduring. Why then is there a difference in the way cases are resolved? Fallers suggests that one reason is that Soga courts are purely judicial bodies, whereas Lozi kutas engage in administrative, executive, and judicial functions. In fact, Fallers compares four ethnographies of African tribal legal systems, the Soga and Barotse as well as the Tiv of Nigeria (Bohannan, 1957) and the Arusha of Tanzania (Gulliver, 1963). Styles of judging are consistent with Fallers's hypothesis. The more purely judicial the courts are, and the more the judicial role is divorced from other political and administrative tasks, the more legalistic the system is (Fallers, 1969, pp. 326–332). Thus the Barotse seem to stand between the Arusha and Busoga in both the purity of the judicial function and the legalism of the judicial process.

It follows from Fallers's research that a society built around enduring multiplex relationships is at most a necessary condition for the emergence of a conciliatory style of dispute settlement. It is not, however, sufficient. One reason for this may be that when officials are charged only with the resolution of legal disputes, they increasingly become specialists in the application of legal norms

---

13. Fallers (1969, p. 321) notes that although Soga courts are more legalistic, they are less prone to explicit legal arguments. The legalistic style of the Soga is concrete and factual. This observation suggests that the Soga system is able to function with narrow statements connected to the immediate, particularistic facts of the given controversy.

and so tend to resolve conflicts by reference to the normative framework that is at once their special province and the source of their special status. Interestingly enough, there is at least tangential support for this position in U.S. data. Stewart Macaulay (1963) in a study of contractual relationships among businesses found that when businesses had long-term (enduring) relationships, arguable breaches of contracts rarely gave rise to lawsuits; instead, compromise solutions were reached (see also Palay, 1984). Compromise was most likely when the negotiations concerning the breach were conducted by the management staff. There was a general feeling among managers that if the disputants' lawyers were allowed to become involved the resolution would be less sensitive to the situation of the two parties. It would be more legalistic and litigation would be more likely.

To this argument we add a further point, which Bohannan makes. In the article we discussed at the beginning of this chapter, Bohannan distinguishes among several types of "law." The key variables are whether the social system in which the legal system is embedded contains one or more than one culture and whether there is a unicentric political power structure or a bicentric (or multicentric) one. Crossing the two dimensions produces Table 7.2.

Of relevance here is what Bohannan calls "law in stateless societies." Power in such societies tends to reside in lineage groups:

> In such a situation, all trouble cases are settled by some form of compromise, more or less in accordance with a set of overt "rules." Instead of "decisions" there are "compromises." In a unicentric system, it is possible to have judicial decision and a recognized mechanism of enforcement which presents problems merely of efficiency, not of substance. In a bicentric situation, nobody can be in a position to make decisions—it is organized so that there cannot be. . . . Instead of implementing decisions, the parties are made to accept the principles and provisions of a compromise. (Bohannan, 1965, p. 39)

Although Fallers's (1969) society is far from being a modern state, it appears that to some extent the existence of a separate judiciary creates or is a creature of more concentrated power than that which the Barotse enjoy. If we weave together the comments of Fallers and Bohannan with those of Gluckman and Nader, an important point emerges. The way disputes are settled is affected both by the nature of the formal legal order and by the social relationships of people

TABLE 7.2
Power, Culture, and Types of Law

	Unicentric Power	*Bicentric (or multi-centric) Power*
One culture	Municipal systems of law	Law in stateless societies
Two (or more) cultures	Colonial law	International law

Source: Bohannan, 1965, p. 38

in the society. The relative importance of these factors has been disputed by numerous legal scholars.

FORMALISM AND LEGAL REALISM

Some scholars such as John Austin (1955) and Hans Kelsen (1967) have treated the law as a closed system. Focusing on formal legal reasoning and the formalistic study of legal functionaries, they looked to the law to explain how legal institutions functioned and to the decisions of legal institutions to determine what the law was. Ultimately for such scholars, law was a command backed by force and for this reason one could expect it to be obeyed. Other groups of scholars reacted to this "positivist" position. Collectively, they were relatively less concerned with pure deductive theories of the law and more interested in how the law in fact operated. The most prominent American group was called the "Legal Realists."[14] Included in this illustrious group were men such as Roscoe Pound (1922), Karl Llewellyn (1930, 1960), Jerome Frank (1949), and Justice Oliver Wendall Holmes (1897).

If the desire of positivists such as Austin and Kelsen was to produce a consistent closed system of legal reasoning, the desire of the realists was to study law not as doctrine but as the imperfect product of human decision making. Although the positivists and their opponents differed on several points, we are concerned here only with their different perspectives on the relative importance of the formal organization of legal rules and decision making, on the one hand, and the effects of the social situation in which legal institutions operate and legal rules are applied, on the other. Pound expressed this as a concern for the relative importance of the "law on the books" and the "law in action." Holmes and Frank were interested in comparing the social determinants of judicial decisions with their legal determinants.

A discussion of the ideas of these men is relevant here because their conflicting perspectives are still important in the study of law. Reacting to the positivist view that the law is a coherent closed system in which results are rather clearly ordained by rules, some theorists have treated the law on the books as if it had little or no impact on the law in action. Social prejudices, bureaucratic policies, and the like are seen as controlling legal outcomes. In our view relegating substantive legal rules and the secondary rules that govern legal processes to a residual explanatory role is as misguided as the blind faith that when the law demands that something be done, that thing will follow. What is needed is a balanced perspective. Legal anthropology suggests that both social relationships and legal institutions are important in understanding dispute settlements. The work of Macaulay (1963), McBarnet (1981), and others shows this to be true

---

14. A related reaction to the positivists, more in the European tradition, goes under the heading "Sociological Jurisprudence." Eugene Erlich (1936) was the most prominent figure in this movement.

of modern societies as well. Given that both the system of legal rules and the social arrangements of people and institutions are important in understanding the operation of the legal process, the question is how do they go together?

The law has a life of its own. So do people and other institutions. At times social relationships and legal settlement techniques may be compatible. Most Lozi disputes are easily handled in a relationship settlement forum. At other times incompatibilities exist. In such circumstances the interface between the law and other institutions is disrupted. The legal machinery may have difficulty disengaging, working on, or reengaging disputes and disputants. This creates tensions in the settlement process that must be dealt with in some way lest the settlement process breaks down.

The fact that there are tensions is obvious. In "The Case of the Bossy Wife," the husband felt that the court's dispute settlement technique did not give him justice. He wanted a judicial decision that would have determined straightforwardly the legal rights that he and his wife had to the coffee and, on the basis of that determination, given the coffee or its monetary equivalent to the legal owner. In other words, he wanted an issue decision. The village legal system was unable or unwilling to provide him with such a decision.

Nevertheless, we might feel that the logic of the system both fitted and befitted the relationship of the litigants. The relationship settlement style is, as Nader and Gluckman note, useful if the goal is to maintain multiplex relationships. But if relationships are not multiplex, this style is unlikely to work. Indeed, it hardly makes sense.

Gluckman (1967, p. 21) and Nader (1969, p. 58) both note that the courts they observed tend to narrow the range of relevant facts when confronted with disputes between strangers. Here issue decisions are more likely. Gluckman reports an interesting case involving the Watchtower Pacifists, a group of Jehovah's Witnesses (1967, p. 158). The defendants were charged with refusing to pay a war tax imposed by the Barotse government. Their response was "Whoso sheddeth man's blood, by man shall his blood be shed, for in the image of God made He man" (Genesis, IX.6). The judges began to search for a common ground, to persuade the parties of their unreasonableness. Gluckman reports:

> As the judges failed to establish consensus with the accused, they became heated, and men at the sides of the kuta joined in to an extent I had not seen in any other case. Quotations from the Bible were bandied about by pagans as well as Christians. The irate judges began to attack the Watchtower people with commonly held taunts on their general immorality: they had no church buildings but worshipped in the bush like animals, they held their women in common, they did not respect authority. The accused calmly denied the first two accusations, and said that God had ordered them in the Third Commandment not to bow down to anyone but Him, and therefore they would not kneel to king or induna or District Commissioner; and moreover in Hosea viii.4, He had said, "They have set up kings, but not by me; they have made princes, and I knew it not." After some hours debate the irritated judges, seemingly helpless, fined the accused and sent them to the Provincial Commissioner. (p. 158)

This is perhaps the only case reported by Gluckman where the trial was a complete failure. The Jehovah's Witnesses refused both every compromise and all attempts to widen the relevant issues in the case. In the process they confounded and dismayed the Lozi judges. The Lozi system of dispute settlement is inadequate unless the parties and judges hold basic cultural understandings in common. [15]

TENSIONS IN ISSUE DECISION SYSTEMS

Modern Western courts are, as we have noted, unlike the Lozi kuta or the Zapotec courts because the ideal outcomes of their processes are issue decisions. In the criminal process the ideal manifests itself in the focus on whether the accused did in fact violate a particular statutory provision. In contract cases the issue to be decided is whether a particular provision of an agreement has been breached, and in tax cases the question is whether a citizen owes the government a particular sum of money. In each area the goal is to pose a narrow question on which legal rights depend and to answer it decisively. Disputants are viewed as judicial entities whose legal conflict may be abstracted from other aspects of their relationship. Thus if a woman sues her brother-in-law for repayment of a loan, they appear in court not as relatives by marriage but in the abstract roles of plaintiff and defendant. Indeed, it is possible that testimony about their family relationship would not be admissible in evidence. When the court answers the narrow question it addresses, the answer reorders the relation of the parties not because they have been convinced that the new order is better or fairer, but because the courts are by and large invested with sufficient power to enforce their decrees against losers.

Not infrequently, however, situations arise that make this binary decision system difficult to operate. The needs of the legal system or the relationships of the parties may in some measure be inconsistent with the ideal. In this section we discuss some of these inconsistencies, the tensions they create, and the solutions (if any) that are attempted.

---

15. The case has an interesting parallel in a dispute settlement attempt reported by Paul Wahrhaftig (1982). The Community Boards Program in San Francisco is a community-based mediation system grounded in the community, which uses community pressure to obtain individual appearances and compliance. Wahrhaftig reports complete failure in a case where an elderly man fed pigeons from his back porch, creating a significant health problem for his neighbors. The man felt the feeding was a religious obligation. The CBP staff pulled out all the stops to obtain participation, including two personal visits to his home by CBP staff, obtaining an appeal from his pastor to attend a hearing, and getting the leadership of his local Kiwanis lodge to bring pressure on him to participate in the hearings. All efforts failed. In San Francisco, as among the Barotse, a shared value system is essential for mediation-based systems.

Organizational Constraints: Tensions Between the Settlement Ideal and the Task of the Legal Agent

Keeping the Peace. Police officers, like other legal agents in our society, are officially expected to perform in an issue-oriented manner. Their job is law enforcement. They are supposed to arrest individuals who have violated the law and leave alone those who have not (Goldstein, 1960). Law enforcement, however, is only one of the tasks that we assign to police in our society. If Fallers (1969) is correct, their responsibility for other tasks means they are likely to find an issue-oriented approach constraining at times, and they will perceive a conflict between the "legalism" of the system and what the performance of their tasks requires. Studies of policing in America indicate that this, in fact, occurs. A device that could infallibly determine whether there was sufficient evidence of any illegal action to justify an arrest would not solve all or even most of the problems faced by the cop on the beat. One reason for this is that the police are "peace officers" as well as "law officers." Their task is not only to enforce the law, but also to keep the peace. Although enforcing the law is often part of keeping the peace, in some circumstances the two may not be fully complementary. Indeed, they may conflict. Egon Bittner (1969) in a study of "Police on Skid Row" makes the point well.

On skid row peacekeeping is very important. The skid row police officer must keep things under control in a setting where inhabitants cannot or will not be held totally responsible for their actions. The alcoholics who are the officer's primary concern do not lead "normal" lives; they live in an environment where the everyday certainty of ordered relationships cannot be taken for granted.

> Good faith, even where it is valued, is seen merely as a personal matter. Its violations are the victim's own hard luck, rather than demonstrable violations of property. . . . The overall air is not so much one of active distrust as it is one of irrelevance of trust; as patrolmen often emphasize, the situation does not necessarily cause all relations to be predatory, but the possibility of exploitation is not checked by the expectation that it will not happen. (Bittner, 1969, p. 143)

The police officer on skid row sees his basic task as ensuring peace on his beat. Order maintenance takes precedence over law enforcement. "They tend to proceed against persons mainly on the basis of perceived risk, rather than on the basis of culpability. And they are more interested in reducing the aggregate total of troubles in the area than in evaluating individual cases according to merit" (1969, p. 154). According to skid row officers, most of what they do is directed toward protecting persons and preventing trouble. To this end they use the criminal law primarily as a *resource* to solve problems in keeping the peace.

Usually the general criteria of some legal rule are met, for example, those arrested for drunkenness are usually drunk, but even this is not always the case. Bittner reports one incident where a police officer arrested a man who, if not completely sober, had not achieved his usual high. The arrest was one of convenience more than anything else, for the arrestee was seen stumbling across the street just as the police van the officer had summoned for another person he had arrested was about to depart. When the second man complained that he "wasn't even half drunk yet," the officer responded, "OK, I'll owe you half a drunk" (1969, p. 152).

Even when a law violation is clear, "compliance with the law is merely the outward appearance of an intervention that is actually based on altogether different considerations" (1969, p. 149). The decision to arrest may turn on whether someone "needs" to be arrested rather than on the strict legal rules of probable cause. If a person "needs" to be arrested to keep the peace, the police officer selects a general catchall offense such as begging or drunkenness or disturbing the peace that will justify taking the man in. Sometimes these arrests are called "preventive arrests," and on occasion what they prevent is trouble the arrestee would face if he remained on the street.

Throughout, there is what Bittner calls "the restricted relevance of culpability." The following case is reminiscent of "The Case of the Bossy Wife."

> For example, an officer was called to help in settling a violent dispute in a hotel room. The object of the quarrel was a supposedly stolen pair of trousers. As the story unfolded in the conflicting versions of the participants, it was not possible to decide who was the complainant and who was alleged to be the thief, nor did it come to light who occupied the room in which the fracas took place, or whether the trousers were taken from the room or to the room. Though the officer did ask some questions, it seemed, and was confirmed in later conversation, that he was not there to solve the puzzle of the missing trousers but to keep the situation from getting out of hand. In the end, the exhausted participants dispersed, and this was the conclusion of the case. The patrolman maintained that no one could unravel mysteries of this sort because "these people take things from each other so often that no one could tell what 'belongs' to whom." In fact, he suggested, the terms owning, stealing, and swindling, in their strict sense, do not really belong on skid row, and all efforts to distribute guilt and innocence according to some rational formula of justice are doomed to failure. (1969, p. 150)

The main difference between the patrol officer and the Zapotec judge appears to be that the officer feels a need to justify his inability to decide in an issue decision fashion. But like the Zapotec judge, the police officer wants to put disputes into context. According to one officer:

> If I want to be in control of my work and keep the street relatively peaceful, I have to know the people. To know them I must gain their trust, which means that I have to be involved in their lives. (1969, p. 148)

These police officers *use* the criminal law more than they uphold it. It is a valuable resource for maintaining the peace. To use the criminal law in this way is to depart from the ideal of issue-oriented adjudication.

Police face other problems as well. Issue decision techniques are almost always accompanied by some opportunity and incentive to bargain. We saw the reason for this in Chapter 6. Although the police may not appear to fit nicely into the models we presented there, often for organizational purposes there are outcomes they prefer to the arrest or even the conviction of particular suspects. And suspects frequently would rather contribute to such outcomes than be arrested or convicted.

Society's model of the police, however, presumes that they should not bargain. Police officers should arrest or leave alone. Consistent with this model is the fact that they are given little with which to bargain. When crimes such as rape and murder are involved, this presents little difficulty. If there is to be bargaining, it can take place in the prosecutor's office. In other situations, however, the lack of bargaining chips is a severe handicap. Often the only thing the police can offer is the underenforcement of the law.

The Good Pinch. Jerome Skolnick's (1966) fine book *Justice Without Trial* is to a significant extent a book about what police do when they want to bargain rather than simply to arrest. Police officers are generally on the lookout for a "good pinch," that is, for an arrest that will lead to a felony conviction. Some pinches, such as those of major narcotics distributors, are especially good. Other arrests, although part of the job, do little to enhance the public's view of the police department or the career of the individual officer. Beyond this the police want to clear (to close the police book on) serious crimes by arrest. The unresolved crime is to the police department much like the adjuster's open file is to the insurance company. Not only does it require intermittent attention, but crime clearance rates are a mark of departmental success. The police consider a crime cleared when they are able to "charge" an arrestee with the crime. This does not require that the charge be formally lodged, and where a formal charge is lodged, it need not result in conviction. We shall see shortly that this allows some arrestees to strike bargains that would not otherwise be available.

In some police work the good pinch comes from information supplied by the victim of the crime or by other witnesses. However, for many crimes there is no victim or at least none who is able to assist the police. Police work here must almost always be proactive rather than reactive (Reiss, 1971; Black, 1980). In other words, the police must set out looking for crime rather than wait to respond to complaints, since when there are no victims to complain, complaints are unlikely. "Victimless" crimes that are generally policed proactively include prostitution, narcotics violations, gambling, and the like.[16] To arrest for such crimes, police must engage in undercover work and/or they need the aid of informants. Securing the aid of informants presents difficulties since those with access to information the police seek usually have no natural inclination to help the police and may have good reasons for not wanting to cooperate.[17] Thus the police must bargain for information. To bargain one needs something to give.

---

16. Because of the difficulty of apprehension, and because some in our society view many of these crimes as "legislated morality," the argument is frequently advanced that these offenses should be decriminalized. Recently, marijuana offenses have been substantially decriminalized. Also gay liberation groups have repeatedly called for the decriminalization of homosexuality and have to some extent succeeded.

17. We should note, however, that the special problems of arrest presented by the lack of a willing victim is not restricted to what are typically called victimless crimes. As Skolnick (1966) notes, burglary presents much the same problems as narcotics violations. There is a victim who would be willing to cooperate, but he usually has no information. He did not see the thief. Thus the apprehension of burglars requires many of the same techniques as the apprehension of narcotics sellers.

At times the police give money, the most general of bargaining chips. When money is available, it often suffices, but police departments are not given large supplies for their informants. A more important resource available to the police is their power of arrest and their concomitant control over the charging process. Ideally, arrest has a binary quality and the charge should be the most serious that is factually justified. One is either arrested and tried on a charge or he is not arrested. But police routinely turn arrest and the power to charge into negotiable commodities.

One interesting and imaginative example of how the police turn a legal absolute into a bargaining chip is given by Skolnick in his discussion of the way police deal with prostitutes. Prostitutes are generally considered to be small fry in the law enforcement world. This does not mean that the police do not pursue them. Those on vice squad duty actively attempt to arrest prostitutes using informants, plainclothesmen and others as would-be "tricks." Nevertheless, the police view prostitution as a less serious offense than drug or theft crimes.[18] What is most salient about prostitutes to the police is not that they are criminals but that they are denizens of the criminal world who are possible sources of information that will lead to the arrest of more serious offenders. The problem is to extract information from these women. To do this the police must be able to give them something in return.

In the city that Skolnick (1966) studied there was a general police order and a stated policy by the district attorney that every woman arrested for prostitution should be held for a venereal disease check by the local health department. The order was straighforward and clear. Every woman arrested for prostitution was to be quarantined. The quarantine (in the city jail) could last for up to eight days. In fact, only 38 percent of arrested prostitutes were held. Skolnick notes:

> Holding a prostitute for quarantine is not considered a "credit" to the policeman's record. Neither the policeman nor the prosecutor is primarily interested in anything but the central "product" of law enforcement: felony convictions. To achieve these . . . may require resources that the prostitute can provide. For her, "cooperation" with the police may mean more than a simple absence of aggression. It also may include her agreement, if "requested," to act as an informant or a special employee [undercover decoy], especially in the enforcement of narcotics laws. The threat of quarantine hold doubtless exerts some anticipatory pressure on the prostitute to "cooperate" with police.[19] The quarantine hold, however, can serve as a threat only if it is not uniformly administered. Conformity to the rule of uniform administration would, therefore, result in the loss of a valuable item of exchange. (1966, pp. 108–109)

---

18. The police view is, of course, similar to that of most people. The police generally view as serious those crimes that are defined as serious by the criminal law and that the public regards as serious and presses them to do something about. Should the public come to regard prostitution as a more serious crime than drug dealing and should the law be changed to reflect this, the scenario we describe below might be reversed.

19. We might add that the prostitute is often willing to cooperate because of the potential for future dealings. She is likely to be arrested again and can ill afford to make an enemy by standing on her rights (see Skolnick, 1966, p. 148).

In this case police officers find it impossible to work with a secondary rule structure that imposes a binary decision rule on them. They therefore create a currency with which to bargain.

The third major resource of the police lies in their cooperative arrangements with the prosecutor's office. Police and prosecutors are in the same business and have many similar goals. Often police can persuade the prosecutor to drop charges or can help the accused negotiate an especially "sweet" sentence. Skolnick (1966, pp. 174–179) describes two cases in which burglars confessed, apparently as part of plea bargains, to substantially more burglaries (over 400 in one instance) than the police could prove. In exchange for their help in improving the department's clearance record, the burglars received *lighter* sentences than they might have received had they confessed only to the crime charged. Whether the burglars committed all the crimes they confessed to we will never know. What we do know is that the police could tell a number of indignant home owners that they had arrested and jailed the man who robbed them, and the burglary squad's clearance record that year looked better than it otherwise would have looked. Here the police with the help of the prosecutor and, implicitly at least, the judge created a currency with which to bargain—time to be served.[20]

In the first two situations we have described, the police find themselves in circumstances that constrain the use of an issue decision secondary rule system. In each of these cases their relative power is diminished. Prostitutes and bums have little to fear from the normal sanctions of the law. A compromise (sometimes self-created) must be made to settle cases. Police officers in effect modify the system to fit their needs, much as Lozi judges change the scope of relevance to fit their needs. In the third situation a burglar with a lot to lose also has much to give. Here the police are not so much constrained by the law as they are buffeted by political and organizational pressures. Because police can manipulate the legal system, the law offers them release from these pressures.

Law as a Resource. At several points in our discussion of police work we referred to the law as a "resource." The idea of a *resource* is in many ways an excellent metaphor for thinking about the law. As with most resources, people draw on the law when it is the "cheapest" way of meeting their needs. When

---

20. From this perspective it is interesting to note the general disdain with which many people view plea bargaining. Plea bargaining in criminal cases as we saw in Chapter 6 is similar to bargaining in other legal contexts. Nevertheless, there is a general feeling that plea bargaining is not "justice." From a purely dispute settlement perspective this position is difficult to justify. By definition, unless one of the parties is irrational, the bargain serves both parties better than the no agreement outcome of a criminal trial. From other perspectives presented in this book, however, the practice of plea bargaining may be attacked. From the perspective of "just desert" one may feel that there simply should be no bargain with criminals. They should not be allowed to bargain away their responsibility. From the distributive justice perspective that we discuss in the next part of this book, one might argue that although the bargain between the prosecutor and the defendant may serve their needs, it is at some cost to the rest of us who are not present to participate in the bargain. Of course, the prosecutor and police are legally our representatives. But they have their own axes to grind and their own livings to make. Their objectives may differ from ours.

cheaper alternatives are available, resort to law is unlikely.[21] Since law is a subsidized resource, even on the civil side, it is also true that people "consume" more law than they would if they had to pay all the cost of enforcement. Thus if the police, like plumbers (at one time we would have written "doctors"), charged for their house calls, earplugs or fights would probably be the predominant remedy for noisy parties, and more battered spouses might leave their homes. Finally, resources must be exploited. Just as people and organizations are differently situated to exploit natural resources, so they are differently situated to exploit the law. Some have advantages of expertise and position that others lack. Marc Galanter (1974) in an important theoretical statement that we have mentioned before argues that the situational advantages that the "haves" have in litigation is an important reason why they come out ahead. As both wealthy parties and repeat players in the litigation game, haves have a special ability to exploit the system. Among the advantages are their special familiarity with courts, their access to the best legal talent, and their ability to litigate with an eye toward precedent.

Some people and organizations are yet more favorably situated to exploit the law. The police are the best example. They do not have to go to the law; they carry it with them. If Skolnick's example of the plea bargaining burglar is more shocking than the case of the informant-prostitute or peacebreaking drunk, it is because the police appear to be exploiting the law for narrow personal or organizational ends rather than for the ends that have led society to vest them with legal authority. And yet more shocking examples of police who exploit the law for personal gains may be given. The cop who trades traffic tickets for bribe money is a well-known figure, and Paul Chevigny (1969) has documented a number of cases in which resisting arrest charges were apparently lodged to cover instances of police brutality.

From one perspective the cop who rips up a ticket for $10 is no different from the office worker who xeroxes his tax return on the company machine. It is just that the resource that the cop has special access to is the law, while the bureaucrat is fortuitously situated with respect to copying machines. From another perspective the cop's exploitation of his position not only violates legal norms, it perverts them.

---

21. Several of the propositions in Black's (1976) general theory of law accord well with the implications of the resource metaphor. Thus Black notes that the law is less likely to be invoked within social groups than between them. An important reason why this is so is that people often have other, cheaper ways of controlling the behavior of those within their own class. Within classes, reputation may be particularly important, but people in one social stratum may be unconcerned with what those in another are saying about them. Thus gossip, a relatively cheap form of social control, may play a role within classes that the law must play between them. The same analysis may apply to more violent activity. If one lower class man bloodies the nose of another because he objects to his behavior, that is likely to be the end of the matter unless there is retaliation in kind. If the bloody nose were attached to the face of someone of a higher class, it is more likely that the police would be called. The higher-status person expects to be believed if there is a conflict in stories, and it is "cheaper" for one of his status to call the police than to risk further injury by striking back.

Ordinarily, disputants unlike legal officials find it difficult to alter the law's secondary rules even when they find the decision-making style inadequate. They can, however, avoid them. In the next section we discuss two studies that describe situations where this occurs. In both cases the parties are too intimate to feel comfortable in a style of decision making that seems to operate best for people with no connection except for their lawsuit. In one case, avoidance is legal and even favored. In the other case, the means of avoidance may themselves contravene the law, but the force that leads to avoidance is so great that the law has given way.

Social Constraints: Tension Between the Settlement Ideal and the Relationship of the Parties

Business Contracts. Stewart Macaulay (1963), as we noted earlier, became interested in how businesspeople settle conflicts that may emerge when someone breaches a contract. If there is any part of American law that ideally formulates the issue decision mode, it is contract law, especially as it pertains to business transactions. In fact, many writers saw the development of modern contract law as one of the prime indicia of the movement from feudalism to capitalism. In Maine's (1963—original edition, 1861) famous phrase, the great movement in society was "from status to contract." The idea underlying this observation is that for many centuries the trend in social relationships has been away from interpersonal linkages based on positions in a complex status hierarchy (the relationship of a serf to his lord, for example) toward linkages based on more specific but more limited agreement-based obligations. In a status relationship an individual has no choice about what duty entails. One is what one is and that status carries a set of inescapable obligations with it. In a contract relationship a person has the obligations he assumes. The trend Maine described both reflects and contributes to a decline in the importance of multiplex relationships and a movement toward a multiplicity of more or less independent relationships.

The development of contract law, like no other body of law, is associated with this trend. Not too many centuries ago an Englishman's ability to enter into binding, court enforceable agreements was quite limited. The most important aspect of the civil law was the law of property and the related law that regulated what a person could do with property. The emergence of modern contract theory accompanied the movement from feudalism. Indeed, it was in the developing law of contract that the ideal of the narrow, binary decision rule partly emerged, for the issues in contract litigation lend themselves to yes–no answers. A promise was either made or was not made. A signature was forged or was not forged. The contract was sealed or was not sealed. Such issues admit of neither degree nor compromise.

However, binary decision rules, even when they are operable, do not mean that hard questions cannot arise. For instance, who loses when I write a check and give it to Mr. X, who then adds a zero behind the last number and signs it over to you in payment for some merchandise. Mr. X, of course—if we catch him, but such men tend to be hard to find after the fact. As between you and me, who must pay whom? Or, suppose I send you an offer by telegram to sell 10,000 pounds of butter at 62 cents a pound, but the telegraph company makes an error and the telegram offers 10,000 pounds of butter at 60 cents a pound. You, in good faith, snap up the offer. Am I bound? Perhaps the issues seem tedious, but then again we are not really talking about your money. Contract law must deal with specific issues like these, and it must be precise enough to allow the courts to say that either I win or you win. The courts will not hold, whatever else they might conclude, that the price for the butter was 61 cents.[22]

Contract law as it applies to business transactions is now generally codified at the state level in a statute called the Uniform Commercial Code (UCC). Although not all versions of the UCC are identical, they are close enough so that on most matters the legal implications of agreements are the same across jurisdictions. The uniformity and relative precision of the UCC combine to form a body of law that is well suited to the needs of businesspeople who want to know exactly where they stand in their buying and selling relationships. Yet Macaulay found that the businesspeople he studied rarely took their contract disputes to court.

Most large companies, according to Macaulay, plan carefully before entering into agreements. When a business deal is important and has special characteristics, detailed contracts are written, often with the assistance of numerous attorneys. More routine transactions are handled by "standardized planning." The items sold and their price are specified, usually on an order or confirmation form. The remainder of the contract is standardized (lawyers call it "boiler plate") and is often printed in small type on the back of the form. The standardized provisions may have been drafted originally by house counsel or by a trade association, or they may even have been borrowed from a competitor. As one might expect, the boiler plate may fail to consider some important point that is peculiar to the contract. For example, the specifications of the product to be bought and sold are often so general that they give little guidance should a dispute later develop. Moreover, the standardized planning may break down altogether,

---

22. See UCC Section 2-305. However, even within the confines of the UCC there lurks the idea of compromises. For example, Section 2-615 on "Excuse by Failure of Presupposed Conditions" contains the following comment by the reporter:

> In situations in which neither sense nor justice is served by either answer when the issue is posed in flat terms of "excuse" or "no excuse," adjustment under the various provisions of this Article is necessary, especially the sections on good faith, on insecurity and assurance and on the reading of all provisions in the light of their purposes, and the general policy of this Act to use equitable principles in furtherance of commercial standards and good faith (UCC Section 2-615, comment 6). See also *Aluminum Company of America* v. *Essex Group, Inc.*, 499 F. Supp. 53 (W.D.Pa, 1980), but note that the case was settled on rather generous terms by Alcoa while on appeal (Macaulay, 1984).

as when the seller makes an offer on his form and the buyer accepts it on his form. The seller's boiler plate favors him, of course, while the buyer's has the opposite slant. This is so common that lawyers have a name for it: the battle of forms, and a portion of the UCC specifies circumstances in which, in the event of a legal dispute, one party's form will prevail.

A battle of forms can develop because when a routine business transaction is consummated, no one bothers to read and compare the forms. Macaulay tells us of one manufacturer of packaging materials who audited its records to see how often it had failed to agree with its contracting partners on terms and so had failed to create legally binding contracts. An examination of five days of orders in four different years showed that in 60 to 75 percent of the transactions there was insufficient agreement to form a contract. Macaulay concluded that in many exchanges there is little or no effective planning with respect to the consequences of defective performance. The fact that business exchanges flourish in these circumstances suggests that the parties to most routine business deals perform to each other's satisfaction.

Even where businesspeople have not ignored the niceties of contract law in arranging deals, they often relegate the norms of contract law to what is at most a secondary role when it comes to settling disputes and adjusting relationships. In law, if a buyer and seller agree on the sale of 10,000 widgets (the widget is the contract law student's universal commodity) at one dollar per widget and the buyer finds after a period of time that he needs only 5,000 widgets, the seller could sue to recover his expenses up to the time of the breach plus the profits he will lose because of it. Yet businesspeople often treat cancellations, even when the seller's rights are clear, in a different manner. Buyers expect to be allowed to cancel orders so long as they pay the seller for such major expenses as scrapped materials. According to Macaulay, the buyer who does not live up to his agreement speaks of "cancelling our order" rather than "breaching our contract."

> Disputes are frequently settled without reference to the contract or potential or actual legal sanctions. There is a hesitancy to speak of legal rights or to threaten to sue in these negotiations. Even where the parties have a detailed and carefully planned agreement which indicates what is to happen if, say, the seller fails to deliver on time, often they will never refer to the agreement but will negotiate a solution when the problem arises apparently as if there had never been any original contract. (1963, p. 61)

When we consider the special characteristics of the business world, this reluctance to define differences in legal terms is not surprising. First, there are personal relationships that grow up between members of the two organizations. Salespeople entertain purchasing agents. The engineering staffs of two companies may work together to solve problems. Top executives often know each other in a variety of contexts, ranging from serving together on trade commissions to the fellowship of country clubs. Second, there are business norms that define reasonable behavior in ways that may be quite inconsistent with what the legal norms provide:[23]

> [I]f something comes up, you get the other man on the telephone and deal with the problem. You don't read legalistic contract clauses at each other if you ever want to do business again. One doesn't run to lawyers if he wants to stay in business because one must behave decently.
>
> Or as one businessman put it, "You can settle any dispute if you keep the lawyers and accountants out of it. They just do not understand the give-and-take needed in business. (1963, p. 61)

Third, and most important, businesses have considerable capacity to reward and punish each other apart from any legal remedies. A seller who unreasonably refuses to accept a cancellation may be unable to sell to that buyer again. A buyer who insists on his rights vis-à-vis a seller may find that if a shortage develops he has no stable source of supply, and even during times of plenty he may find that he has to pay a premium for a "bad reputation." Moreover, in the modern business world, corporations often deal with each other as both buyers and sellers. Thus the buyer who accepts a seller's default may more than make up his losses with the profits from a large sale to the former seller. Macaulay summarizes:

> Not only do the particular business units in a given exchange want to deal with each other again, they also want to deal with other business units in the future. And the way one behaves in a particular transaction, or a series of transactions, will color his general business reputation. (1963, p. 64)

A lawsuit for breach of contract may settle a particular dispute, but it may foreclose future business relations, since a contract action is likely to carry charges with at least overtones of bad faith, and the action is itself a signal that the parties have been unable to work well together.

Thus, businesspeople seem to have little desire to determine precisely what the law demands. Yet legal rights are not irrelevant: "it makes a difference if one is demanding what both concede to be a right or begging for a favor" (1963,

---

23. The norms of contract law do not, however, require anything. They simply specify the procedures the parties must follow if they wish to enter into a binding agreement. These procedural norms are "open" norms (Lempert, 1972). By following these procedures the parties may create specific rules that have normative force between them. But nothing about contract law requires the parties to comply with the rules they have created. That requirement is contingent on the demands of the party whose rights under the contract are being infringed. If that party voluntarily consents to the infringement, there is no violation of the contract. Rather, the contract is, in effect, "reformed." Even when a party has not consented in advance to a deviation from required behavior, no norm requires the aggrieved party to bring the infringer to court. In these ways contract law differs from criminal law. The norms of the criminal law are, as a formal matter, not generally open to respecification through dyadic agreement. Conformity with these norms is expected, and where there is nonconformity, violators *should* be taken to court.

p. 62). So long as it is only the law's shadow that affects the negotiation, the business of reformulating a contract in the light of events is a "cooperative venture" rather than a "horse trade." To demand precision and conformity is to invite a dispute as to what that entails.

To file a suit or even to threaten to do so is to imply that the situation of the parties has changed from one in which their interests are congruent—hence the original agreement—to one that is fraught with conflict. Personal relationships are likely to be destroyed because the negotiation process will be changed from one that seeks a reasonable mutual accommodation to one in which threats of the kind we describe in Chapter 6 will come to predominate (cf. Galanter, 1983, p. 25). Control over decisions will pass from the hands of management to those of lawyers. Transaction costs, which help neither party, will grow. Finally, regardless of which party prevails the legal solution, usually the awarding or denial of damages, will not, unless the parties' goals are to maximize one time profits, achieve most of what was sought from the original agreement. Buyers will not have acquired a product that meets their needs, and sellers will not have established a dependable outlet for their products.

Thus when we look at situations in which contractual relations develop between businesses, it is the decision to sue rather than the failure to assert legal rights that appears most problematic. Here again we can generalize from Gluckman. Businesses often have substantial ties of mutual self-interest that bind them to each other in much the same way that multiplex relationships bind the Lozi.

To the extent such ties exist, businesses in conflict may be expected to seek a relationship settlement rather than an issue decision. Since the law only provides the latter, litigation will be avoided. Indeed, the more binding the ties between businesses the less likely it is that even the "shadow of the law" will be relevant to the way contracting parties resolve unanticipated difficulties.

This point is nicely illustrated in a recent study of the railway shipping industry by Tom Palay (1984). Palay looked, on the one hand, at shippers who use railway equipment, like ordinary boxcars or flattops, that is highly fungible. If the shipper does not secure such equipment from one railroad, he can secure it from another one, and if the railroad does not assign such equipment to one shipper, another shipper can always make use of it. On the other hand, Palay looked at the situation where railway equipment is shipper-specific as is the case with railway cars built to hold a specific model of a specific auto manufacturer's fleet. Here the shipper is locked into a particular railroad because only its cars can carry the shipper's product. At the same time, the railroad is dependent on the shipper because if the shipper does not use its cars, they have only their scrap value. Palay found that when problems arose between shippers and the railways, if the parties were using fungible equipment that was widely available and generally in demand, they tended in negotiations to hold out for their legal contract rights, since if the relationship broke down a new one could be easily substituted. However, where the parties were highly dependent on each other and expected to remain so, they were cooperative and accommodating to the extent that one shipper paid a railway more than a million dollars without any legal obligation to do so because the shipper had not used specially constructed equipment to the extent that was originally contemplated.[24] Interestingly, when specialized equipment was required, the shippers and railroads planned their relationships in detail, but they typically did so in documents that were not legally binding contracts.[25]

Of course, even those shippers and railways that used fungible equipment had an interest in maintaining each other's business and in their own reputations for fair dealing. Perhaps, for these reasons Palay does not report any instances where the parties actually took each other to court. When the ties of prospective business relationships do not exist, a lawsuit becomes more likely. Macaulay comments:

> [P]erhaps the most common type of business contracts case fought all the way through to the appellate courts today is an action for an alleged wrongful termination of a dealer's franchise by a manufacturer. Since the franchise has been terminated, factors such as personal relationships and the desire for future business will have little effect; the cancellation of the franchise indicates they have already failed to maintain the relationship. (1963, pp. 65–66)[26]

Again, the metaphor of law as a resource helps make sense of the data. Terminated franchise holders unlike businesspeople in ongoing contractual relationships have few if any bargaining chips that can be used to get some measure of satisfaction from the franchising company. In these circumstances they resort

---

24. One might expect that where two businesses were truly locked into a relationship the likelihood of taking contract disputes to law would increase since even if the suit tended to alienate the parties, the relationship would continue. This can happen (Galanter, 1983, p. 25, note 118), and the dangers of such fallings out are one reason why businesses may choose to absorb suppliers on whom they are highly dependent (Williamson, 1975). However, it appears that accommodations like those described in the text are the more ordinary outcome where parties have a long history of interdependent interaction.

25. Palay also reports on the intermediate case of equipment that is available in only limited supply and has only a limited range of uses. Patterns of relating in this case were intermediate between the two extremes. Palay also tells us that in some cases involving very specialized equipment that requires special treatment, like cars for shipping dangerous chemicals, shippers often preferred to purchase their own equipment. Finally, Palay emphasizes the importance of the fungibility dimension by noting that where shippers have different departments, some dealing with readily accommodated material like iron ore and others with hard-to-accommodate items like finished automobiles, the style of railway–shipper relations depends on the kind of materials shipped and not on the companies involved.

26. In a retrospective look at his 1963 study Macaulay (1984) notes that in recent years other kinds of contract disputes are being regularly brought to court. These include cases involving companies threatened with bankruptcy, cases involving expensive technical failures that cannot be adjusted by cooperative tinkering by the engineers of the two companies, and cases in which huge sums of money are at stake, typically because economic cataclysms like the energy crisis were not anticipated. In these cases legalistic negotiation and even litigation are consistent with the model we have presented either because future relations are not anticipated as when a near bankrupt is a party or because so much is at stake that one party's well-being is threatened by a relationship on anything close to the prior terms and the other party has so much to gain from enforcing the apparent agreement that the value of a continued relationship on reformed terms pales by comparison.

to law. They also draw on law because they typically occupy a relatively weak position vis à vis the company. Since law is backed by the power of the state, when it can be successfully invoked it is a great equalizer between the strong and the weak. Finally, the costs of exploiting the law are relatively low because the defendant has already withdrawn the rewards that a lawsuit between ongoing contractual parties might have jeopardized.

In this last respect the situation of the terminated franchise holder differs from the situation of the small company that supplies nonspecialized goods to a large manufacturer. Such a company might find that its contract has been arbitrarily breached and that it is expected to bear the entire burden. Although the company might have legal redress, the manufacturer's ability to terminate all its business with the company is likely to make the costs of even threatening to use the law prohibitive. This possibility should caution us against the romantic view that the noncontractual resolution of business disputes necessarily represents a fair accommodation of conflicting interests based on what businesspeople think is right.

The police officers in Bittner's and Skolnick's studies altered the secondary rule structure when it failed to meet the constraints posed by their working environment. Macaulay's businesspeople take a different course of action. They avoid the system by refusing to sue and often do not bother to create legally binding norms in the first instance.[27] However, not all litigants or participants are able to avoid or alter the secondary rule structure. Some people must take the legal system for dispute settlement as they find it or relinquish the law's imprimatur on their action. They may still, however, be able to avoid the full impact of primary legal norms. For an illustrative example, we draw on O'Gorman's (1963) interesting book on the role lawyers played in matrimonial cases at a time when divorces were not easily acquired.

The Law and Divorce. O'Gorman's work was done in New York in the early 1960s. At that time the grounds for divorce in New York were severely limited, with adultery being the most important. The resulting system for securing divorces was fraught with perjury, which the courts, in their uncritical reception of certain evidence, apparently acquiesced in. For example, some courts apparently indulged in the presumption that an unrelated man and woman could not spend a night together in a hotel without having sexual intercourse. Thus, or so rumor has it, a woman would be hired to enter a hotel room with a man in the evening under the watchful eye of a private detective and leave in the morning, again observed. Even though the woman may have spent the entire night reading a good book or may have left when the private detective retired and returned before he awoke, such evidence was held to furnish grounds for divorce. Of course, obtaining grounds in this way was only possible when the husband and

---

27. Businesspeople also have access to an intermediate position in resolving contract disputes. They may hire a private judge (arbitrator) who attends closely to the details of the contract but is also sensitive to industry custom. If the parties agree, the arbitrator need not be tightly bound to the binary decision rule.

TABLE 7.3
LAWYERS' IMAGES OF MATRIMONIAL CASES

Images	Percent
Emotionally upset clients	74
Clients ignorant of the law	37
Strain on lawyer	28
Female clients	27
Personal problems	23
Involvement of lawyer	17
Nonlegal problems	16

Source: O'Gorman, 1963, p. 82).

wife cooperated in the effort to separate. Cooperation to circumvent the law was necessary because the New York divorce law did not respect private agreements to dissolve a marriage.[28] One party was granted a divorce because of the fault of the other. However mutual the desire to part, formally, the husband and wife were adversaries.

At other times, of course, the parties were adversaries in fact and wished to go at it "tooth and nail." O'Gorman asked 82 New York divorce lawyers to list what they thought were the most salient characteristics of their matrimonial cases. Table 7.3 summarizes the images presented by 82 informants. Since each lawyer mentioned several attributes, percentages total to more than one hundred (O'Gorman, 1963, p. 82).

The preceding table is revealing in terms of the special problems that divorces present to matrimonial lawyers. The lawyers report that their clients are often "subjective," "tense," "excited," "unobjective," and "emotional." When emotions are aroused, clients are likely to think they are entirely in the right and will resist bargaining to secure a divorce and settlement. "They think that something's wrong with a lawyer who compromises" (O'Gorman, 1963, p. 85). The fact that clients in the end usually do bargain says something about both the influence of lawyers and the costs of "no holds barred" litigation.

The lawyers report that "getting even" and "getting revenge" is often important to their clients and that these clients frequently expect their attorneys to feel the same as they do. The legal dissolution of the marriage is often not enough:

> The one thing they all want is for the lawyer to shoot the other side. They'd like it if we went after the other side with a knife, a blade. Then they'd be happy. (p. 86)

> They don't look at it logically or rationally. They demand instead of thinking. They're emotional and so unrealistic. (p. 89)

---

28. Indeed, in many states if one spouse willingly had sexual intercourse with the other spouse after knowing that grounds for divorce existed, the courts would not allow divorce solely on the preexisting grounds. One spouse's willingness to welcome the other back to the marital bed despite grounds for divorce was held to be "condonation."

Lawyers who characterize their clients in these terms do not necessarily lack understanding or compassion for them. They know better than most the strains that are involved in the breakup of a marriage. Thus the lawyer can say; "They are very disturbed emotionally and *for good reason*" (p. 84). But perceiving this does little to make the lawyer's task easier. However good a client's reasons, it is also the case that, "They are so emotional and excited that they can't see things in the right perspective" (p. 89).

The question is what is the "right perspective?" What makes this type of case difficult? Why does it create a strain for the attorneys?

An important source of strain is that some clients who feel they have been personally wronged are not content with just their legal remedies. The compensation of being unmarried even when coupled with alimony or child support payments does not make up for the hurt the other spouse has inflicted. These wronged clients would like to subject their spouses to what Harold Garfinkel (1956) has called a status degradation ceremony; that is, a process designed to alter the identity of a person to show how bad he truly is. Status degradation is most likely when the *res gestae* is wide, since to show the essential badness of a person requires that a judgment be passed on his essential character. At a minimum, the tribunal must be able to apply a label that suggests the person is evil at the core.

For matrimonial lawyers the "wronged spouse" perspective on divorce litigation, even in an attenuated form, is misplaced. Divorce courts like all American courts are ill equipped to pass judgments on whole persons—although something like this may occur in certain child custody disputes—and their product is an order regarding the marriage rather than a label implying that one party is essentially evil. Lawyers see their own role as acquiring specific goods for a client (e.g., the dissolution of the marriage, custody of a child, high alimony) rather than as satisfying the client's emotional needs. Thus it is not surprising that lawyers often find working with divorce clients more stressful than working with clients who share the lawyer's view of what is at stake.

> The claimant in a negligence action may be angry, and the man who is closing a real estate deal may be apprehensive, but these marital ones are usually *deeper emotional problems*. . . . In a negligence case, the client has a grievance against a stranger and is out to get some money. In a matrimonial case, the client is not merely interested in making money, *he has a grievance against a family* member. (O'Gorman, 1963, pp. 91–92)

The difference in perspective leads to conflicts over how the case should be presented. Clients seek an extensive analysis of the marriage. They constantly confront their lawyers on evidentiary and procedural questions.

> Matrimonial clients don't understand that the quibbles and quarrels of the marriage do not constitute evidence. What they call cruelty is not necessarily the legal definition of cruelty. (p. 93) They don't understand that it is not enough that they know something happened. They must have proof, be able to prove it in court. They want

to know why can't the lawyer do something. (p. 94) I explain the law, the requirements of the law, the procedures of the courts, but they still don't truly comprehend. . . . They don't understand why we, the lawyers, can't *do something about the whole business.* (O'Gorman, 1963, p. 95, emphasis added)

What the lawyer must do is attempt to fit the client's case to the legal framework within which the lawyer must operate (see Galanter, 1983, p. 19). Both lawyers and clients are frustrated by the conflict between the secondary rule system of the courts and the way the client would like the case to be decided. The clients want to litigate the marriage, but the law is designed to litigate the divorce.

It would be a mistake to draw too close a comparison between people seeking a divorce and businesspeople resolving a contract dispute. As we have noted, the businessperson is primarily concerned with prospective dealing and with compromise. The subset of bitter divorce clients we have been discussing wants to specify the implications of past dealings and is apparently unconcerned with compromise. Thus the businessperson's problems with the law's dispute settlement technique stems primarily from the binary decision rule. The bitter spouse's concern is primarily with the narrow *res gestae*. Put another way, the spouse sees the law as a resource that can be used to gain revenge on an ex-mate. The law's formal rules do not allow private appropriation for this purpose, and its secondary rules will frustrate, although they will not always defeat, divorce clients who attempt to use law for such ends.

The emotional, revenge-seeking divorce clients about whom O'Gorman's interviewees complained are, and probably were, in the minority among those seeking divorce. Although emotion is commonly associated with the dissolution of a marriage, most divorcing spouses are more concerned with getting out of the marriage quickly, simply, and cheaply than they are with the possibility of inflicting pain on each other. For these people the major difficulty with the law's dispute settlement process lies in its primary rules. If one must demonstrate wrongful action by one's partner to secure a divorce, difficult problems of evidence arise, and the partner can frustrate one's desire to be legally free of the marriage by convincing the court that he or she did not engage in the alleged acts. The difficulties of securing a divorce are exacerbated if the grounds for divorce are limited to a small subset of reasons why a person might wish to leave a marriage, as they were in New York at the time of O'Gorman's study. Furthermore, the primary rules can promote conflict and stress that would not otherwise have existed. Although divorce proceedings may be insufficiently condemnatory to satisfy those who seek to totally degrade their spouses, the allegations that have to be made in a fault system carry with them some measure of moral opprobrium. A spouse publicly accused of "mental cruelty" or being an adulterer may be indignant and tempted to return the charges in kind, particularly if a monetary award (alimony) will turn in some measure on the court's assessment of his or her moral character. Thus the primary rules cannot only make it difficult to establish the grounds needed to terminate a marriage, they can also heighten the adversarial nature of the parties' relationship with a concomitant increase in emotional stress and monetary costs.

However, the divorce client, unlike the business contractor, cannot opt out completely when the law's mode of dispute settlement is unsatisfactory. Legally terminating a marriage requires a judicial imprimatur. Without this imprimatur it is a crime to marry again. This does not, however, mean that the rigidities of the fault-based system of divorce cannot be circumvented. In New York in the early sixties there were a number of ways of coping when legal grounds for divorce did not exist. Perhaps the most common one, particularly among those who before the spread of legal aid could not afford lawyers, was to give up on the idea. This was not so much opting out of the law's dispute settlement process as it was not being allowed in. Being undivorced does not mean being together. Many spouses went their separate ways without stopping at the courthouse on route. But, each could face substantial costs from being legally married while living apart.

A second way of coping was to establish residence in a state that allowed more grounds for divorce than New York. This was expensive because one marital partner had to move to and reside in the chosen jurisdiction for the period needed to establish residence, and that person might also have to lie under oath about his or her intentions to remain in the state. Nevada, because of its liberal grounds for divorce and short residency period, became notorious as a "divorce haven."

A third way to get around the primary rules was to falsely create the appearance that they had been satisfied. Perjury was common and staged incidents, such as the woman in the hotel sequence that we mentioned earlier, also occurred. These techniques were largely dependent on the cooperation of both parties. Thus they gave bargaining leverage to the party who was less desirous of securing the divorce. A man, for example, might agree not to contest his wife's allegation of adultery so long as she did not demand alimony. The woman, who might have had no legal grounds for divorce but who would have been entitled to alimony if she had had such grounds, would have to sacrifice the one to secure the other. Deals might also be made regarding the level of child support payments, although it was the child's independent rights that were technically at stake.

O'Gorman's study indicates again that legal systems have a life of their own. The Lozi judges had difficulty with the Watchtower Pacifists. New York courts had similar trouble with divorces. In both cases, the traditional rules for deciding cases could not easily be adapted to those cases in which the dispute processing style was inappropriate given what the parties wished to accomplish. The law in the books is not unchangeable, however. Since O'Gorman wrote his book, the law of divorce has radically changed in this country. "No fault" divorce has been adopted in most jurisdictions. Under no fault plans a spouse does not have to prove any wrongdoing to obtain a divorce. He or she need only claim irreconcilable differences to have the marriage dissolved. There is nothing the other spouse can do to prevent this. The legislatures have by this act relieved the courts of much of the controversy that once surrounded divorce cases.[29]

It is interesting, however, to note the nature of the legal reform. Legislatures did not alter secondary rule structures; they altered the primary rules governing divorce. They moved from a type of criminal or negligence logic to one that makes responsibility—even in its causal sense—irrelevant. This means that divorcing parties need no longer litigate the quality of their marriage, and the courts can dismiss most attempts to do so as irrelevant. In most cases the courts act as administrative agencies affixing a legal stamp to the decision of the parties. This reflects the fact that many divorcing couples wish this, but it also suggests something that is at first a bit surprising: It is often easier for a legal system to alter its substantive rules than to alter the way it does business. No doubt the Lozi judges felt the same way. It was easier to allow the provincial commissioner to alter the rules governing war taxes than to reason with the Jehovah's Witnesses.

INSTITUTIONAL INTEGRATION: A SUMMARY

In recent years a number of scholars have addressed the issues discussed in this chapter. Indeed, dispute settlement has been one of the "high growth" areas in law and social science. Perhaps the most significant finding is that there is a general correspondence between secondary rule systems and the social relationships of the parties using the system. This insight reflects the integration of research into modern societies and the studies of legal anthropologists who have examined non-Western societies. Writers such as Marc Galanter (1974, p. 96) and Lawrence Friedman (1975, p. 260) have done much to summarize recent thought.

From this body of writing, including that which we have just discussed, it appears that two elements of the relationship between parties to a dispute have a particularly strong influence on the type of settlement technique they prefer. These are: (1) whether they have multiplex relationships (the density of the relationship) and (2) whether they will have prospective dealings (whether the relationship will endure into the future).

Table 7.4 defines four types of party relationships and specifies the form of dispute settlement that is most appropriate to each. The forms of dispute settlement were derived earlier by crossing the scope of the hearing (wide or narrow *res gestae*) with the court's outcome orientation (binary or flexible). Table 7.4 reports both a tendency and an hypothesized fit. The forms of dispute settlement tend to be associated with different patterns of party relationship and appear to work better—in Bohannan's sense of developing solutions that are easily inte-

---

29. Problems still emerge, however, especially in the case of children where custody fights occur. Interestingly, some judges are trying to cope with this problem by a retreat from official judgment of the parties as parents like the retreat embodied in the no fault laws themselves. They allow even fairly young children to "vote with their feet" and choose the parent with whom they wish to live.

TABLE 7.4
Preferred Mode of Dispute Settlement

Density of relationship	Future dealings	
	Enduring	Episodic
Multiplex	Relationship settlement	Relationship decision
One-dimensional	Issue settlement	Issue decision

grated into the institutional context in which the dispute arose—when relationships are of the specified types. Where a particular type of party relationship predominates in a society, one can expect that that society's predominant dispute settlement institution will be oriented to produce outcomes of the form specified. It is also likely that parties who are not in the law's typical relationship will find alternative ways of dealing with their disputes.

Thus Lozi courts operate most effectively and with the least trouble when dealing with parties who share enduring, multiplex relationships. Our courts operate most effectively and are most widely used by people in one-dimensional, episodic relationships. When people in modern society are, like Macaulay's businesspeople, in enduring relationships, they avoid going to court, seeking instead to achieve issue settlements through private negotiations. This is one way of dealing with the tensions that develop when the relationship of the parties does not correspond to the dispute settlement techniques specified by the legal system's secondary rules. Other methods include the development of alternative tribunals, and, as with no-fault divorce, changing for a subset of cases the legal system's primary rules.

If these observations are, as we believe, correct, there remains the question of why certain patterns of relating tend to be associated with certain modes of dispute processing. It is not likely that the Lozi and the Zapotec developed accidentally a relationship settlement mode of dealing with disputes, and it would be surprising if our issue decision techniques were not in some way related to the changing nature of an advanced industrial society.

We do not know enough to specify fully the causal relationships between the nature of a society and the characteristics of its dispute settlement institutions. We can, however, make a start. The most obvious explanations are of the type that is called "functional." The linkage exists because the characteristic forms of dispute settlement promote the well-being of the societies in which they are embedded. If they did not benefit society, they would have long since disappeared and been replaced by those that did. No doubt there is some truth to this explanation. In a close-knit community, where leaving is difficult for individuals and costly to those left behind, it may be especially important to have ways of dispute settlement that resolve bundles of tensions so that quarrels are not continually being rekindled. On the other hand, in a society where capital can flow to its "highest" uses only if property is unencumbered by traditional role expectations, a legal system that abstracts disputants from their multiple role relationships by focusing only on issues between parties may contribute to the growth of the market economy that developments in industry and commerce make possible.

At the same time, it is unlikely that the causal arrows go in only one direction. It may be that unless a community is as close-knit as the Lozi its legal system will lack the information or the influence needed to expand disputes so that entire relationships are considered and reconstructed. It may also be the case that in modern societies most disputes that are worth taking to law arise out of limited relationships such as contracts, accidents, and crimes. Thus there is no sense in maintaining a legal system geared to searching out hidden tensions between persons tied together in diffuse ways. Most disputants who go to law have no such ties.

Functional arguments, however, are unlikely to explain all we would like to know. No matter how skilled we are in matching the characteristics of legal systems with those of the societies in which they are embedded, the characteristics of legal systems are not so uniquely associated with the characteristics of societies as to suggest that only one type of legal system can flourish with a particular type of social organization or that only one type of society can endure with a particular mode of resolving disputes.

The Busoga alert us to the fact that not all African societies have traditional relationship settlement techniques. The Japanese and Chinese warn us against the inevitability of convergence at the other end of development (see Kamashima, 1963; von Mehren, 1964). Functionalist interpretations place substantial emphasis on social structure but little on legal tradition and culture. It is well to remember that English law, from which our legal system was derived, has been quite "legalistic" for some time, beginning long before the Industrial Revolution. First causes may be lost in history, but their effects can linger long after the moving cause has disappeared. The status quo at any one moment in time is causally related to what has preceded and to what follows.

There is also an economic dimension to all this. We said that in the industrialized West most disputants who take their cases to law are not tied together in diffuse, multiplex ways. This does not, however, mean that most people have most of their disputes with relative strangers. It only means that the subset of disputes taken to law tend to be of this type. One might argue that if our dispute settlement institutions were different, disputes between diffusely tied individuals would be taken to law. This is no doubt, to some extent true, and there has been considerable effort in some Western societies to develop informal, localized tribunals to resolve disputes between neighbors and intimates. However, informal tribunals geared toward relationship settlement or issue settlement tend to have a great deal of trouble in acquiring cases. This suggests that the issue decision style that predominates in modern Western courts is not itself the prime reason why most of the cases brought to them involve one-dimensional, episodic relations that are well suited to issue decisions.

Another important reason has to do with the value and cost of going to law. There are psychological and economic costs of involving third parties in disputes even when efforts have been made to provide inexpensive, easily accessible tribunals. At the same time, going to court is likely to be least necessary when parties have enduring multiplex relations. People in such relations can get their opposites to listen to their complaints (itself an important reason to invoke the law), and they usually have the capacity, independent of the law, to reward and punish each other. This means that the law is a less valuable resource to them than it is to those in socially less dense or episodic relationships.

One might say that the same argument should apply to the Lozi, and to an extent it probably does. It is likely that most disputes arising among the Lozi are resolved privately. One would expect the psychological and economic costs of litigation together with the parties' capacities to reward and punish each other to be generally sufficient to ensure that the law need not be invoked. However, there is a residue of cases where ruptures are more serious and informal social control less workable, so the parties turn to law. Given the structural characteristics of Lozi society,[30] these disputes, like those that are resolved privately, generally involve people in enduring, multiplex relationships. The tribunal that developed in Barotseland reflects the social structure and the typical relations of litigants before it. This fit of tribunal to dispute type as well as the relative accessibility of the Lozi kuta probably encourage people to bring disputes to it. Were the fit less close, we would expect court utilization to be less and private dispute resolution efforts to be greater. We have, however, no data that bear on these two last propositions.

In our society, too, there is a residue of disputes involving people in enduring and multiplex relations that the parties have difficulty resolving on their own. However, this residue is dwarfed by disputes involving people in one-dimensional, episodic relationships, so the court system that has developed is primarily geared toward the latter type of dispute. This gives disputants, who if they were Lozi would go to a kuta, further incentives to resolve disputes privately. It leads to mediation and counseling programs that aim at relationship settlement, and, perhaps most frequently, it results in "lumping it," William Felstiner's (1974) term for doing nothing about a grievance because no possible remedy is worth its apparent cost.

These last actions may all be seen as responses to the tensions created when the parties find that the dominant mode of legal dispute settlement is ill-suited to the resolution of their dispute. Other reactions have been portrayed in our examples. At one extreme we have business contractors who in most cases avoid the formal system because of their special incentives to settle. Interestingly, the businessperson's behavior is in some way the best advertisement for an issue decision system. It works almost like the textbooks say it should. If one assumes that litigation is not desirable for its own sake and that settlements should be

---

30. The most important characteristics include the relatively small scale of Lozi village life; the ties that develop through marriage and other reciprocal relationships; and the difficulty, in part due to the preceding factors, of exiting from the situation in which the dispute is rooted. In our society it is relatively easy to exit from most relations, and even multiplex relations may often be broken with relative ease (Felstiner 1974; cf. Hirschman, 1971).

preferred, one should have little quarrel with the body of contract law. It informs the businessperson in detail about legal rights and obligations; it provides rules for situations where the important thing is the existence of a clear standard, and it provides a way of imposing solutions in those rare cases where businesspeople fail to resolve their own conflicts. The system permits businesspeople and their lawyers to have the degree of precision they deem appropriate for their endeavors. In doing so, it allows them to make fairly precise estimates of the utility of lawsuits in different situations, and thus, as seen in Chapter 6, it facilitates bargaining when that is sensible and spurs litigation when it is not.

Studies of the police, by contrast, present a less attractive picture of the results of our system for resolving disputes and the differential access that people have to the law. It is easy to dismiss prostitutes and drunks as people who should not be able to place moral demands on society, yet, given our legal ideology, it does not seem right that drunks are likely to be arrested more because of who and where they are than because of what they have done. Still, the solutions of the police in the face of complex problems of law enforcement and order maintenance are those of people who are trying to do a job we gave them and not the work of people who aim to subvert the system. Considering what we ask of police, their basic solution is not unreasonable. Faced with a situation where the secondary legal rules make it difficult to resolve certain types of disputes, the police have altered the system.

The last case we considered, that of divorcing spouses, is the most difficult. These people cannot avoid the legal system, nor can they establish legally effective alternatives. For those who simply want out and who are coping well emotionally, no fault divorce seems to be a workable solution. But for O'Gorman's emotionally involved clients who seek to litigate the marriage, there is no obvious way to alter the law's process for resolving disputes. One might conclude that what is needed is an alternative that fits the parties' needs. But what are these needs? The desire of one spouse to enlist the law's aid in degrading the other is a need of one party, not both. We might imagine a legal tribunal that sought by passing judgments on relationships to recognize the special circumstances of parties terminating multiplex relationships. However, the decisions of such a tribunal would be more likely to exacerbate social conflict than to reinstitutionalize a set of rules that could maintain peace when familial and social pressures failed. This suggests that there are limits to the degree to which the legal system can accommodate itself to the relationship of parties in primary institutions. But this does not mean that accommodation is impossible. Nonlegal institutions, such as therapy or support groups, for example, might be able to help aggrieved spouses with their problems. Indeed, the law in its primary rules can recognize its own limits. Thus, in ordering a divorce, a court might order one party to pay for care that is essential to the other's mental well-being.

Party relationships are not, however, the only limitation on the choice of decision rules. Max Weber saw as a defining element of law, as he generally used the term, the existence of a staff of people who could be called upon when needed to coerce compliance with the legal order and punish violations of it

TABLE 7.5
Predominant Mode of Legal Dispute Resolution

| | Adequate coercive power | |
	No	Yes
	Special legal staff	
No	Relationship settlement	Relationship decision
Yes	Issue settlement	Issue decision

(Weber, 1968a, pp. 311–15). The idea that a coercive staff is necessary for a legal order best fits the situation of the modern nation-state where there is a monopoly of force that is sufficient to ensure obedience to most legal rules and a group of people (police, lawyers, and judges) whose special task is to enforce legal norms.[31] These two elements—monopoly of force and special staff—do not characterize all societies. As they vary, so does the dominant mode of dispute settlement.

Table 7.5 embodies the hypothesis that the type of dispute settlement in society will reflect the available coercive apparatus as well as the relations between the parties. We would also argue that, as an empirical matter, societies that tend toward the configurations of coercive power and special staff that figure in this table tend also to be characterized by the relationship patterns specified by the similarly labeled cells in Table 7.4. However, this overlap is by no means perfect and both help explain the kinds of legal decision making that figure in different societies. By and large, Table 7.5 specifies the kind of dispute processing procedure it is possible for a society to maintain, while Table 7.4 indicates the kind of procedure that is best suited—taking Bohannan's perspective—to the relationships that parties typically find themselves in.

The relationships in Tables 7.4 and 7.5 are, of course, ideal types, and we should be cautious not to overstate the strength of the relationships they portray. Nevertheless, in societies like the Lozi it would be difficult to operate an issue decision system even if the parties had one-dimensional, episodic relationships. More importantly, in societies such as ours the tendency toward an issue decision system is considerable. Legal specialists tend to define disputes in terms of legal issues, and the coercive power available to the courts facilitates binary outcomes by allowing the imposition of decisions that give nothing to one side. At the same time, however, the system can tolerate considerable opting out by parties whose relations are not conducive to an issue decision. The Lozi, on the other hand, could not force the Jehovah's Witnesses to opt into their system. They

---

31. Weber did not, however, require that the coercive staff be full time law enforcement specialists. Thus his definition allows for the possibility of law in primitive societies since a subset of the community may, along with their other roles, act as a law enforcement staff. Moreover, Weber recognized that the coercion supporting a legal order might be psychological as well as physical and that it might work indirectly.

had to refer them to a court that had legal specialists and adequate coercive power.

In the next chapter we shall examine two modern court systems that were intended to counter the dominant trend of legalistic dispute processing. Those who designed these courts—the small claims court and the juvenile court—have tried to reduce tensions between formal legal rules and informal relations by altering secondary rule structures. The small claims court has met with some success. The juvenile court has been branded a failure by many and has changed substantially in response to legal challenges and criticism. In examining the problems confronted by these courts, we shall learn more about the relationship of legal institutions and social relations and about the limits of legal reinstitutionalization.

8

Creating New Systems: The Limits of Double Institutionalization

INTRODUCTION

When we think of important legal changes we typically think of Supreme Court pronouncements that state new constitutional principles or of new rules that alter what it means to be responsible in some situation or of new statutes that reallocate social goods. The adoption of a no fault auto insurance statute, for example, would be recognized by everyone as a legal change, as would the Supreme Court's decision in *Roe* v. *Wade,* 410 U.S. 113 (1973), which held that a state cannot regulate first trimester abortions. These kinds of changes are significant, but often changes in the legal institutions themselves are more fundamental. In this chapter, which concludes our discussion of dispute processing, we examine two courts, the small claims court and the juvenile court, which were specially created to ameliorate perceived problems with our legal order.

Changing institutional structures is a continuing process in legal systems. Not so long ago most American and English civil law was governed by what were called the "forms of action." These forms, the great invention of medieval English jurisprudence, imposed narrow, formal limits on the availability of legal remedies. The "forms" specified types of situations that, if they could be shown in fact to exist, were remediable in the royal law courts. If the facts of a case could not be stated in a way that was actionable under one of the forms, suit could not be brought.

In a sense each form stated a "legal theory" justifying recovery for a particular type of harm. Over the years the forms and the system of secondary rules that grew up around them became ossified. Since new forms were rarely introduced, the old forms were expanded in complex ways to subsume situations that were not contemplated when they were originally created. Legal fictions were patent. Moreover, technical aspects of pleading might prove more important than the substantive merits of a case. If a plaintiff who had a right to recover under a well-established legal doctrine failed to characterize his case correctly and so invoked the wrong form, he would not be allowed to correct his error but would instead lose the case, although if a statute of limitations had not lapsed he would ordinarily be able to bring a new action using a different form. Thus, the right to a remedy was only partly a matter of substantive law. The niceties of procedure were at least as important.

To give but one example of the problems that came to surround the forms, consider the writ of *trespass*, one of the oldest forms, and its companion writ *trespass on the case* (usually shortened to *Case*). The writ of trespass had several varieties. One of these was *trespass vi et armis*, that is, trespass with force and arms. *Trespass vi et armis* (hereafter called Trespass) was originally the appropriate allegation for injuries committed by a defendant with direct and immediate force or violence against a plaintiff or his property.[1] Under this writ a plaintiff could, for example, recover from a defendant who had wrongfully struck him or had thrown a stone that struck him or his horse. Trespass was, however, unavailable where the defendant's wrongful conduct was less immediately responsible for the plaintiff's harm, as when the defendant created a hazard to which the plaintiff fell victim. The action for trespass on the case developed to fill this gap.

Thus if a man hit you with a stick, you could recover in Trespass. If, however, he placed a pole across the road and you ran into it, the action, if any, would lie in Case. If you brought an action for Trespass when the proper action lay in Case, or vice versa, your case was dismissed. The distinction, esoteric to begin with,[2] appears almost absurd in cases such as *Pearcy* v. *Walter*, 6 Cur, & p. 232, 172 Eng. Rep. 120 (1834). The case arose following a collision of a horse with a wagon, and turned on the question of whether the shaft of the

---

1. Today we usually associate the word *trespass* with the unwanted invasion of another's land. This too fell under the general trespass writ, and was called *trespass quare clausum fregit* or "trespass wherefore he broke the close"; the "close" being the real or imaginary boundary enclosing the land. Other writs of trespass were *trespass de bonis asportatis*, a writ for injury caused by unlawfully taking away another's personal property; and *trespass for mesne profits*, a form of action to recover profits wrongfully received by one during his occupation of land.

2. The strangeness of the distinction is partly a product of our present views of the nature of responsibility. Given the English law of the time, the distinction had merit. Both writs specified forms of strict liability as the term is used in Part I of this book. If you hit someone, you paid. In the case of indirect harms, however, there are many ways this might occur. Some of these are the hard to foresee consequences of simply going about one's business. The courts were presumably reluctant to make all of these injuries matters of strict liability. Thus the writ of trespass on the case at first was narrowly limited to a few circumstances where the defendant had a strong duty to protect the plaintiff or his goods, for example, common carriers or innkeepers. Only later did the concept of negligence come along to distinguish indirect injuries which were actionable from indirect injuries which were simply accidents.

wagon was driven into the horse or the horse driven against the shaft. For cases to turn on such issues seemed as quixotic in 1834 as it does now (Malone, 1970, p. 26).

In 1873 and 1875 the Judicature Act in England abolished the forms of action for a more liberal pleading system in which the individual simply had to state the appropriate facts. This move also occurred in the United States. Yet long after formal abolition it was possible for Maitland, a leading legal writer, to say, "The forms of action we have buried, but they still rule us from their graves" (Maitland, 1936, p. 2).

It was not until a generation of lawyers and judges had passed away that the changes really took hold, because lawyers trained in the language of the forms saw legal problems with the forms in mind. The new ways of pleading required a different conceptual universe, and the old one was not easily abandoned. The new liberalized procedures were designed to ensure that formal mistakes did not affect access to justice. The early changes and the more substantial liberalizations that followed have gone a long way toward achieving this end. Yet the tension between the formal requirements of a legal system and the substantive rights that law guarantees is still with us, for it is inescapable. The law must prescribe not only what the rules are, but also the conditions under which they may be invoked. If the conditions are not met, there is by definition no legal remedy. But the conditioning rules themselves may be conditioned to allow for waiver or for a second chance to come into compliance. Indeed, the ability to correct procedural defects after they have been pointed out is one of the least visible but most important legal changes of the last century. Yet not all defects are correctable, and the process must end somewhere. People still can and do lose cases for reasons that have nothing to do with the merits of their complaints or defenses.

The otherwise ordinary case of *Logan* v. *Zimmerman Brush Co.*, 455 U.S. 422 (1982) nicely illustrates the tension between form and substance, for the courts that heard it were divided about which claim was stronger. Under Illinois law a person who claims he has been discriminated against in employment must, if he wants a remedy under the Illinois Fair Employment Practices Act, complain to the Illinois Fair Employment Practices Commission which must then schedule a fact-finding hearing within 120 days after receiving the complaint. Five days after being dismissed from his probationary position as a shipping clerk with the Zimmerman Brush Company, Laverne L. Logan filed a complaint with the commission. He claimed that he had been discriminated against because of a handicap, a short left leg that according to the company made it impossible for him to perform adequately. Due to a clerical error, the required fact-finding hearing was not scheduled until 125 days after the filing of Logan's complaint. At the hearing, counsel for the Zimmerman Brush Company did not address the merits of the complaint, but instead argued that the complaint should be dismissed because the hearing had not been held within the required 120-day period. This argument would have done a common lawyer proud. It elevates form over substance in much the same way as do demurrers to technically deficient pleas.

Yet it might have been malpractice had Zimmerman's lawyer not advised the company that this defense was possible. It took the Supreme Court of the United States to rule that when the procedural failure was clearly not the responsibility of the complainant, form could not constitutionally be elevated over substance in this way.

The Supreme Court's decision was—even in 1982—by no means preordained. The Supreme Court of Illinois, which is not known as a conservative court, had decided the other way. Moreover, had Logan, even inadvertently been responsible for the untimely hearing, the Supreme Court would probably not have agreed to hear the appeal in the first instance. An argument that Logan's substantive right to be heard on his discrimination claim should outweigh the state's interest in timely proceedings would probably have been dismissed by the Supreme Court for ''want'' of a substantial federal question.

Two themes that clashed in the demise of the forms of action—the sense that liberalized litigation procedures would better serve the values of a changing society and the conservative influence of the bar and accepted legal thought on legal innovation—provide the point and counterpoint in many stories of legal change. On the one hand, there may be pressure on the legal system to change the way it reinstitutionalizes rules in order to better serve the perceived needs of litigants or the larger society. On the other hand, the possibilities for legal change are typically restricted by the existing legal framework (cf. Teubner, 1983) and may be resisted by lawyers accustomed to or interested in traditional ways of doing things. The histories of the small claims court and the juvenile court which we discuss in this chapter are histories of the conflict between perceived needs for change and imaginations and interests rooted in the status quo.

THE SMALL CLAIMS COURT

One of the major practical projects of the early legal realists was to establish a court specifically designed to handle the disputes of the average citizen. Led by Roscoe Pound (1906), the original proponents of the small claims court saw procedural technicality as a major problem with American law. Procedural reform it was thought could make the legal system available to every person.

An influential early article entitled ''Small Causes and Poor Litigants'' (Scott, 1923) identified two types of cases that could not be handled effectively by then existing institutions. First, there were cases involving small amounts of money. Second, there were cases where the plaintiff was so poor that he could not afford to sue (Scott, 1923, p. 457). The proposed solution was to simplify court procedures, eliminate lawyers and in other ways streamline the judicial process. The modest idea has much to recommend it. Not only does it allow more disputes to be brought to law, but it also gives some bargaining power to aggrieved plaintiffs who would otherwise have no credible threat to back up their complaints.

By and large the early small claims courts did not go far beyond procedural simplification and cost reduction. However, some reformers argued for changes designed to transform the basic settlement technique. The thrust of these suggestions was to maintain the substantive rules while relaxing substantially the strictures of the secondary rules. For example, formal rules of evidence were to be discarded and judges were empowered to alter the timing and payment of judgments in light of the financial situation of the defendant (Yngvesson & Hennessey, 1975, pp. 223–224). A few small claim courts, in Cleveland, Minneapolis, and New York, among other places, went further and sought to achieve less formal, more conciliatory modes of dispute processing, but these were exceptional. Most small claims courts were simplified versions of traditional dispute decision courts using adversary processes to reach binary decisions.

In recent decades this traditional small claims court model has generated considerable criticism:

> Most small claims hearings follow the adversary model. Although the process is speedy and inexpensive, it remains too complex for many litigants to handle on their own. In spite of the goal that lawyers should not be necessary, they are present in most courts, a factor which seems to increase rather than reduce complexity. In spite of the goal of a radical change in the role of the judge, he remains a judge in the traditional sense in most courts, although this role is unsuited to proceedings in which one or both parties may be unrepresented and may need judicial assistance. (Yngvesson & Hennessey, 1975, p. 257)

Criticisms like those of Yngvesson and Hennessey are criticisms of a model of dispute processing. Judges who follow this model remain aloof and refrain from actively questioning and participating in proceedings. Cases are rushed through without time to give a "full" airing of grievances. Lawyers only make things worse because they behave like—well—like lawyers. They concern themselves with legal rights and rules of evidence. The thrust of the recent criticism like that of the early radical reformers is that the dispute decision model is ill-suited for small claims courts given the types of claims that are appropriately brought and the kinds of people who litigate there. Those who take this position often also argue that certain kinds of small claims, such as the bad debt cases routinely brought by businesses, should not be heard in small claims courts.

Several writers have discussed the problems of small claims courts in terms of the cross-cutting roles of lawyers and judges. Thus Galanter (1974, p. 118) argues that although lawyers may be ideologically committed to certain types of legal reform, they "have a cross-cutting interest in preserving complexity and mystique so that client contact with . . . law is rendered problematic." Lawyers should not be expected to be proponents of reforms that are optimum from the point of view of clients. Likewise judges trained in regular courts have a difficult time behaving in a nonjudicial fashion. In America the prevailing "judicial fashion" is to play a passive, umpire-like role and to render a binary decision.

Small claims courts that allow attorneys and follow the dispute decision model produce what is to some an anomalous situation. Although they were designed to be legal weapons that poor claimants could invoke against those who abused them, it has turned out that the poor are more often a target of their processes. In many, although by no means all, of these courts the bulk of litigation is brought by businesses against customers, tenants, and other debtors. It appears that small claims courts that combine inexpensive, relaxed procedures with a fairly formal system of decision making are ideally designed for bill-collecting plaintiffs.[3]

But this decision-making style is not well tailored to the everyday disputes of ordinary people, which some believe should be the bulk of the small claims court's business. Several writers have suggested that to deal effectively with such disputes small claims courts must move toward a "conciliation model" (see, e.g., McFadgen, 1972). Yngvesson and Hennessey summarize this position:

> The main feature distinguishing conciliation from adjudication is that the "judge" is not a judge, but an active agent in eliciting the true nature of the dispute and in bringing the parties toward a mutually acceptable resolution. The process is meant to be therapeutic rather than judgmental, and with this in mind, the parties to the dispute are encouraged to express their feelings as well as telling the facts of the matter in dispute, with a view to increasing mutual understanding. (1975, p. 260)

The judge, in other words, should be part therapist and part mediator if the proceeding is aimed at conciliation. The proposal sounds like a recipe for justice in an African village or a Mexican town. This is no coincidence. Such proposals have been inspired by the work of anthropologists, including that which we have previously discussed. The question is whether a model that is well suited to a tribal village will work in an urban American neighborhood. Research in Moscow suggests that an urban setting does not foredoom the approach to failure.

---

3. A small claims court judgment like the judgment of any court may, if it is not paid, allow a victorious plaintiff to seize assets of the defendant or to garnish the defendant's wages. Furthermore, a plaintiff may get a judgment by default if the defendant, however sound the merits of his defense, does not show up in court to rebut the plaintiff's claim. An unsophisticated defendant, not appreciating the need to show up in court, may not realize the importance of defending a case until the plaintiff shows up with an order attaching his car or garnishing (docking and transferring to the plaintiff) his weekly wages. Some think the ability of businesses and loan companies to use courts that were ostensibly set up to benefit the "little guy" is a scandal. But this pales besides a true scandal that has occurred in some jurisdictions. This is the institution of "sewer service." Where this occurs the process server, whose task it is to deliver a subpoena to the defendant notifying him of the time and place of the hearing, signs an affidavit swearing the defendant received the subpoena, when it has actually or in effect been thrown down a sewer. In these cases the defendant does not know there has been a suit until the plaintiff, armed with a default judgment, tries to take his property. At that point it is likely to be difficult to have the judgment overturned and will almost certainly require a lawyer's help.

On the other hand, many defendants, especially those involved in default judgments may be unlocatable or may have no assets that can be taken to satisfy a judgment. Thus in many cases a small claims court judgment is not worth the paper it is printed on. Interestingly, it appears that judgment against businesses are more likely to be paid than judgments against individuals (McEwen & Maiman, 1984).

Justice in Moscow

The idea of conciliation is not new in industrialized societies. Part of the ideology of the Soviet revolution in Russia was that the law should be returned to the people and that eventually formal courts, indeed, formal law, would no longer be necessary (Pashukanis, 1980, original edition 1924). George Feiffer (1964) in his book *Justice in Moscow* discusses a type of "court" that, ideologically at least, is a prototype of this type of justice. It is called the comradely court, and its jurisdiction, like that of the small claims court, is limited. It concerns itself with such minor issues as violation of labor discipline, truancy, tardiness and sloppy work, drunkenness, damage to public property, and violations of apartment rules. Feiffer summarizes:

> Nothing major, in a word, I suppose for this reason the Comradely Court should be thought of as lower than the People's Court (to which it may turn for advice), although in another sense it is higher than the Supreme Court of the U.S.S.R. For, we are told, it is a prototype of the court of the future: under Communism something like the Comradely Court will settle—simply in an *obshchestvennoye*[4] way—any minor social disputes that still exist. (1964, pp. 114–115)

Feiffer sat in on four cases heard by the comradely courts. He learned of the sessions from public notices in different areas of Moscow. Although one must be cautious about generalizing from only four sessions, these were not "show" trials, and they were basically alike. The first case Feiffer reports, that of Citizeness Kliuchkova, provides a sense of the comradely court in action.

The case was heard on April 10, 1962, in a common room in an apartment building. The table was covered with a flaming red cloth and the walls were strewn with banners proclaiming, "Glory to the Communist Party," "Brotherly Greetings to All Peoples Fighting for the Complete Eradication of Colonialism," "The People and the Party are Indivisible," "Glory to Our Cosmonauts," and "Glory to Communism, Shining Future of All Mankind."

Benches were squeezed into the small room and there were about 75 spectators, mostly older women. Three "judges" and a secretary made up the court staff. The chairwoman, an elderly person who was a retired people's court judge, began by asking the parties whether they would make it up? This was met with calls from the audience to get on with it and begin the case. Apparently the audience knew, even if the judges did not, that conciliation would be no easy matter.

The "complaint," a letter from the complainant, was read. The complainant, named Sobeleva, was complaining about the demand of a woman named Fe-

---

4. *Obshchestvennost* is a difficult term to translate. It pertains to situations or individuals that are "public but nongovernmental" or pertaining "directly to the people" (Feiffer, 1964, p. 103). In the present context the idea is that the comradely courts are expressions of the public interest and concern, but are not strictly part of the Soviet government. The People's Courts mentioned in the passage are, contrary to their name, not popular courts. They are ordinary courts of law.

derovna Kliuchkova, that Sobeleva pay her share of an electricity and gas bill. (Sobeleva, Federovna, her husband and son, and at least one other lady, shared the same apartment. Housing in Moscow at the time, and still to some extent today, was extremely crowded. There is a whole body of law in the Soviet Union that deals with the allocation—down to the square centimeter—of floor space in apartments. The parties to this suit shared the apartment, and thus the utility bills.)

Sobeleva's argument was that she was in the hospital almost the entire month of February, yet Federovna wanted her to pay her share of the utility bill. Sobeleva's portrayal of Kliuchkova makes the Bossy Wife seem retiring.

> When I said, "No, I was in the hospital that month," she started insulting me in the filthiest language. It was frightful. This is not the first time she behaved like an animal; you can expect only all sorts of unpleasantness from her mouth. Once she was about to beat me with her fists. Her son stopped her just in time. She constantly swears and insults me vilely, as well as all the others in our apartment. To live with her is to live in filth. I ask that the Comradely Court stop her from making my life miserable. (Feiffer, pp. 116–117)

The judge asked when the payment problem occurred and Sobeleva answered sometime in March. She remembered that it was her *dezhurstvo* or duty day, that is, her day to clean the common bathroom, kitchen, and halls. At the word *dezhurstvo* Sobeleva's worthy opponent weighed in.

FEDEROVNA: *Dezhurstvo*! Why don't you say anything about your refusing to clean up, you obscenity? How many times did you skip *dezhurstvo*? How many times did I have to clean up for you? You slanderer! . . .

SOBELEVA: I never skipped my *dezhurstvo*. Once, just after I left the hospital. What are you trying to invent, you liar and hussy?

FEDEROVNA: *You're* the liar. What about before? What about this winter? You worm, you sneaked out of your turn. (Feiffer, p. 117)

Things degenerated from this point. Despite attempts of the judge to return to the issue of the utility bill, the parties complained about cooking smells, use of the kitchen, taking down each other's wash when it was still wet, noise in the apartment, and other matters. Every accusation was accompanied by insults and obscenities. The audience joined in with catcalls, cackles, and shouts of encouragement to one side or the other.

After the restoration of a semblance of order other witnesses were called: first, other members of the apartment, then the apartment house chairman, then other neighbors. Some supported Sobeleva, some Federovna. The level of the testimony did not improve. "Sobeleva keeps a dirty room." "Federovna pushes her son too hard." "Sobeleva swears." "Federovna spits." The testimony went on for over an hour. The chairwoman admitted she did not know whom to believe. Finally, she and the other two judges went behind a curtain to deliberate. Nearly two hours after the whole thing began a verdict was rendered.

The court concluded both women were at fault and that their arguments could be easily, amicably resolved! Yet hear the rest:

> It [the court] encouraged them to face their problems gracefully, in a socialist, comradely spirit, and warned that further scandals would be punished strictly. There was no punishment and no censure; the twenty-eight kopek debt [for utilities] was divided in half. A cackle of comments followed the decision—"Correct!" "Very Good!" "Sensible!"— and Sobeleva and Federovna looked at each other with shy, tentative smiles. (Feiffer, pp. 119–120)

What a trial! And yet if it ended as Feiffer describes, what a settlement! Of course, the two women probably went on fighting, and maybe they even came back to the comradely court. But they did get a lot out of their system, as did the rest of the apartment building, and they did smile at the end.

However, Feiffer's commentary on this and other cases gives the impression that he was disappointed by the comradely courts. From one perspective they are disappointing. They do not live up to the high ideal of a court to replace all others. Yet in an apartment building in Moscow something like a conciliation model seems to have worked as well as anything might have to ameliorate a dispute in a situation where the parties were bound by the housing market to a future life together. Is there a place for such courts in the United States?

The U.S. Situation

William Felstiner (1974, 1975) cautions against the romantic appeal of informal conciliatory modes of decision making, such as the comradely courts. He argues that in societies like ours *avoidance* is often an acceptable or even a preferable alternative to conciliatory tribunals. People react to serious disputes by ceasing to associate with their individual and organizational adversaries. We shop at a different store, or get a different job, or move to a different apartment.

Felstiner argues that avoidance is a viable way of responding to disputes where relationships are unidimensional. In such situations few costs are attached to avoidance. Where, however, relationships are multiplex, avoidance is a more expensive alternative. A store and its customer can cease associating with fewer costs than a child and his parents (1974, p. 76). Moreover, the Moscow example teaches us that in some relationships, simple or multiplex, avoidance is impossible. Given a choice, Sobeleva and Federovna would, no doubt, have preferred separate apartments. In Moscow at that time this was impossible, so they turned to a forum to settle their dispute.

In some settings, however, even the impossibility of avoidance does not mean that some forum is required. As Felstiner points out, people need not press their grievances to the point where they ripen into disputes. This kind of passivity, which Felstiner calls "lumping it," is most likely when an actor has a dispute with a more powerful party who will not give satisfaction but cannot be easily avoided. Thus if a man purchases sour milk in the neighborhood's one supermarket and the market will not refund his money, the man may "lump it" and continue shopping there if other supermarkets are sufficiently distant. The only effect of the experience will be that the man's attitude toward the supermarket may take on the flavor of the milk, and even this may change over time.

Lumping it can also occur when a tribunal is available, for the rewards of even large recoveries may not be worth the costs of litigation. Thus the supplier of rearview mirrors to a large auto company may lump it when slackened demand leads the manufacturer to cancel its order for 10,000 mirrors that the supplier has already produced. A lawsuit is out of the question, not because of the financial cost, but for fear that the manufacturer will not renew other contracts. The supplier of mirrors, like the man in the one supermarket town, has nowhere else to take his business.

Danzig (1973) and Danzig and Lowy (1975) differ from Felstiner in that they believe there are in the contemporary United States many neighborhoods in which people—including those in business—tend to share common values and be closely tied. They see the fact that disputants in these situations usually have no "remedies" other than avoidance as a serious problem. Avoidance, Danzig and Lowy point out, is not without its costs, both psychological and economic. Furthermore, its costs are not necessarily confined to the avoider and the person avoided. Society in general may be weakened because of a breach in social relationships. Lumping it is seldom a preferred remedy, but it exists because there is no alternative in American law. Danzig's suggested solution is, in part, to create informal neighborhood tribunals that will mediate local disputes.

Is Danzig correct? Are avoidance, lumping it, self-help, and our current judicial system sufficient, or do we need this new type of forum? In our society relationships between nonfamily members and between people and organizations are usually unidimensional. Where this is the situation, self-help or avoidance often suffices. When they do not, lumping it is likely to occur. This clearly has costs, but no dispute settlement forum is frictionless. Mediation also has its cost, and success is not guaranteed. There are not many relationships that could survive a mediation like that between Sobeleva and Federovna. It seems easier to move out where possible. Problems in other relationships are better resolved by lumping it or through self-help. One of us has a son who at age 4 would announce almost daily that because of what daddy had done, he didn't like him any more. And, if the truth be told, the feeling, if not the statement, was often reciprocal. Yet, depending on the circumstances, lumping it or self-help sufficed and love abides.

Have we convinced you that our current options are sufficient? We have not really convinced ourselves. Soaring divorce rates and quarrels between neighbors are troublesome, and their costs often extend beyond the quarreling parties. Self-help often fails to resolve such disputes, and as Danzig and Lowy argue, avoidance may be an overused alternative in our society. In recent years community-based alternative dispute resolution forums have proliferated. If these programs take roots and grow, they will add to our repertoire of dispute settlement techniques (see Abel, 1982a; Dubois, 1982).

Those who argue for a conciliatory model of small claims litigation recognize that the value of this reform is contingent on the kinds of cases parties bring and their willingness to accept conciliatory procedures. The ideal is a court that could use different procedures depending on the nature of the case. The conciliation model is thought to be most appropriate in cases involving parties who share enduring multiplex relationships (McFadgen, 1972, pp.73–75).

Conciliatory courts can work if they are removed from the formal legal process. Litigation that is controlled by lawyers or under the authority of regular judges is almost certain to be dominated by dispute decision tendencies. Indeed, the very solemnity of the traditional courtroom is deemed by many to subvert conciliation. The body of American law is designed to answer narrow questions in the light of clear binary rules. To transform litigation without transforming courts is to ask lawyers and judges to ignore their training and expertise and to ask the state to disregard its monopoly of power. In short, if the desired outcome of litigation is a relationship settlement, the tribunal should, like the comradely court, be *obshchestvennost*: operated in the public interest but not directly part of the judicial machinery.[5]

If the decision is made to foster mediative tribunals, one must decide whether they should replace or only supplement traditional small claims courts, and whether they should be able to compel unwilling parties to participate. Both questions raise the issue of whether we wish to force individuals to use the new tribunal, which we may attempt to do either by direct compulsion or by failing to provide alternatives.[6]

Beyond this, there is a question of whether mediative tribunals can be successful when both parties are not willing participants. To some extent they can be. The Bossy Wife probably did not relish the idea of being hauled into court by her husband, and it is likely that many Lozi defendants would avoid the kuta if possible. But these are people in multiplex relationships. When relationships are unidimensional the prospects for a conciliatory process that begins by threatening to punish one party should he not show up is bleaker. One cannot turn down a traditional judicial verdict; it is effective whether or not one likes it. But a person need not accept a mediator's suggestions and can refuse to be reconciled. This does not mean, however, that coercion to conciliation is doomed to failure when relationships are unidimensional. A skilled mediator

5. The separation must extend to the procedures that link cases the conciliatory tribunal does not resolve satisfactorily with the ordinary courts. If appeals are regularly allowed from the former to the latter the conciliatory tribunal would almost certainly be drawn into the formal legal process. (see Yngvesson & Hennessey, 1975, pp. 264–265). An ability to seek an entirely new trial in the traditional courts would not pose as severe problems.

6. This point has been made recently about the many alternative dispute settlement forums such as neighborhood justice centers that have sprung up to resolve disputes outside traditional court structures. In an acerbic essay denouncing most of the alternative dispute settlement apparatuses as informal extensions of the state legal system, Jerold Auerbach quotes federal judge Leon Higgenbotham as saying that the diversion of disputes to alternative forums risks transforming powerless people "into victims who can secure relief neither in the courts nor anywhere else" (1983, p. 125; see also Abel, 1982b; but see Henry, 1985).

can lead parties to see commonalities of interest of which they were not aware. If the alternative to mediation is costly litigation, the horse that has been forced to water may want to drink.

Without coerced participation, however, it appears that tribunals designed to mediate interpersonal and small claims type disputes are underused. The party complained about, unless threatened with other legal action, seldom consents to mediation or consents verbally and then does not show up at the hearing. This may be because that party prefers the status quo to any alteration that might result from the hearing—he, after all, is not complaining. Also, one or both parties to possible mediation may find the prospect unappealing.

Wariness about mediation is not without reason. The broadening of issues that occurs in conciliatory adjudication and the pressures for compromise can lead participants to feel that their autonomy is threatened. In addition, the normative and other pressures that can be brought to bear in mediation may make the process stressful to endure and may lead litigants to "agree" to solutions that they did not really want to reach.

However, the primary reason most people in Western societies apparently prefer the traditional small claims court to mediation has to do with the nature of the disputes brought to third parties for solutions. In most cases when the third party is a court, what is sought is a vindication of rights. Thus business creditors and debt collection agencies would, no doubt, prefer the current small claims court to a revamped procedure that offered only mediated solutions. Not only do they prevail by "default judgment" if those they sue do not show up, but they are likely to win a complete victory when, as is apparently the usual case, they are legally in the right (Vidmar, 1984).[7] Moreover, businesspeople are not the only ones who might prefer a traditional court. When a ghetto dweller sues Jack's Appliance Store for the money he paid for a "guaranteed new" 5-year-old refrigerator, he wants all his money back. Generally speaking, people with clear legal rights seek binary decisions, for apart from litigation expenses, they will rarely see a good reason to compromise what is by law theirs. Forcing mediation, either by compulsory process or by not providing adequate alternatives, is asking citizens to give up something: the implicit promise that they can use legal rules as guarantors of rights. Yet, even from the party's standpoint, this is not necessarily undesirable.

We see this in two excellent studies (McEwen & Maiman, 1981, 1984; Vidmar, 1984) of small claims courts that encourage mediation. The "encouragement" by these courts is so intense that most (Vidmar, 1984) or many (McEwen & Maiman, 1981, 1984) parties feel they have no choice but to attempt mediation before proceeding to trial. Because these mediation programs are

---

7. A default judgment is a judgment entered on the assumption that a defendant who refrains from contesting the case does so because he knows the plaintiff is in the right. For this reason, when we refer to a "complete" victory in small claims court, we mean only legally complete. However, as we point out in footnote 3, some defendants may not realize the importance of defending the case or may not care if they lose because they have no assets to satisfy a judgment.

closely tied to traditional small claims courts, the disputes they hear are the kinds of disputes that would otherwise appear in small claims courts. The parties to these disputes usually differ over who owes how much money to whom, and their relations are rarely multiplex. Yet the mediation process seems reasonably effective. A substantial proportion of the mediated cases are settled either at the hearing or sometime after the hearing but before the case goes to trial. And it seems that agreed-upon settlements are more likely to be complied with, at least in part, than imposed judgments.

The mediation does not, however, follow the model of the Barotse. Only occasionally is there an effort to expand the *res gestae* and then in only a limited way to allow for the consideration of counterclaims that may be brought by the defendant against the plaintiff. Instead, the mediator takes a legalistic attitude toward the dispute. For example, in the jurisdiction Vidmar studied, the mediators are neither judges nor lawyers, but they often do not correct litigants who refer to them as ''Your Honor'' or otherwise identify them as judges, perhaps because the misapprehension facilitates settlement. And the mediators may side wholly with one party or the other on legal or factual grounds.

What we have here, in terms of our ideal types, appears to be an *issue settlement* system. The *res gestae* is narrow as it is in most lawsuits, but the third party does not—indeed cannot—impose a binary outcome. Rather, solutions may fall anywhere in the range that both parties are willing to consider. To some degree what drives the parties toward agreement are the same kinds of self-interested forces that, as we saw in Chapter 6, lead parties to settlements on their own. But a skilled mediator makes a difference. By expressing a judgment on the facts or law, he may lead one or both parties to change the expected values that they have assigned to the judicial decision. He may also suggest solutions that the parties would never have considered, especially solutions that impose burdens on both parties and apparently for this reason are particularly likely to be complied with (McEwen & Maiman, 1984). In addition, a mediator may impose substantial normative pressure on the parties to come to an agreement (Merry, 1982). In particular, it appears that parties to small claims disputes are often simply claiming their legal rights and that if they can be persuaded that the law is entirely on one side or the other they will act accordingly. Thus Vidmar (1984) found that agreements of plaintiffs to drop their cases or of defendants to pay everything in dispute were not uncommon outcomes of the mediation process.

The research of McEwen and Maiman and Vidmar suggests that the issue settlement logic is well suited to dispute settlement in modern society when the parties lack substantial ties and seek to resolve quarrels that center on a single incident.[8] Not only do the parties have an incentive to resolve their disputes at

---

8. Mediation has long been used successfully as a way of helping parties—particularly labor unions and management—agree to contracts. More recently, there is some evidence that mediation is being used successfully on a purely voluntary basis to help parties resolve the various distributional issues that arise in the course of a divorce. In both cases the *res gestae* is wider than it is in small claims

mediation and so avoid the greater expense and potentially greater risk of a trial, but there also appears to be a complex legitimation structure that makes compliance with mediated settlements especially likely. The following factors apparently contribute to this structure: (1) Consensual (mediated) outcomes are more likely than imposed (adjudicated) outcomes to be seen as fair. (2) People feel a special obligation to comply with outcomes they have agreed to (cf. Lempert, 1972). (3) Mediated settlements are more likely than adjudicated outcomes to include features such as reciprocal obligations, time payment provisions, or partial awards that, whether agreed to or imposed, increase the likelihood of compliance. (4) Parties learn more about their legal rights and responsibilities in mediation than in adjudication and grant legitimacy to the law once they understand what it demands.

Where small claims disputes are not successfully mediated or where there are no mediation programs, the case will be taken to the small claims court. Here an issue decision logic prevails. However, the contrast between issue settlement that we associate with small claims mediation and issue decisions that we associate with the small claims court does not mean that legal rights are always perfectly preserved in existing small claims courts or that compromises do not occur. The world, as we have often noted, is not divided neatly into the "pure" types of our tables. It has been estimated that about one-fourth of all small claims cases are settled before trial and that a significant number may be compromised in some way at trial (Gould, 1972). As is so often the case, differences that appear stark when we look at legal rules in the abstract are often attenuated in practice. Indeed, it is likely that the relative informality of the small claims court, coupled with the limited amounts at stake, encourages judges to compromise differences and attend to equities in ways they would avoid if the litigation involved more "significant" matters and judicial behavior was open to close scrutiny on appeal.[9]

The range of legal formality that one finds in small claims courts is nicely illustrated by the following two cases that Douglas Matthews (1973) describes in his delightful little how-to-do-it book on the small claims court called *SUE THE B*ST*RDS*. The first case, heard in Los Angeles, involved car repairs. The mechanic, an owner of a small gas station, had sold a Mexican-American a car and later performed needed repairs on the vehicle. He was suing for the balance due on the repair work. The mechanic had numerous work orders signed by the

---

mediation, but it is not so unconfined as it is with a relationship settlement logic. We may think of this "impure" type as "multi-issue settlement." With total stakes of equal moment, multi-issue settlement despite its potentially greater complexity is sometimes easier to achieve than pure issue settlement, because if the parties place different values on the different issues to be resolved, the absolute conflict of interest may be reduced. Thus one technique that may be used by mediators or negotiators to encourage settlements is to add issues to the agenda so that a party who loses on one matter may gain on another. (Menkel-Meadow, 1984)

9. Appeals from the judgments of small claims courts are limited and transcriptions of small claims court litigation are almost never made. Thus the actions of a judge in small claims court are largely invisible to his legal superiors.

defendant, who had little to say except that he could not afford all of this money for a car.

The plaintiff as Matthews notes had a strong case. The sale was an ordinary business transaction, and the car had been sold "as is." In these circumstances the general principle *caveat emptor* (let the buyer beware) supposedly applies. The repairs were authorized and performed as promised and the defendant had acknowledged the debt by making partial payments on his account. As a matter of law the "good guy" looked to be the loser. But in this court at least, good guys did not always finish last.

The judge looked down to the plaintiff and asked him for the blue book price (standard used car list value) of the car. Then he asked how much the defendant had already paid the plaintiff. The latter figure, which included some money paid for repairs was several hundred dollars more than the blue book price. Matthews continues:

> Then, fixing the mechanic with a look that George C. Patton might have reserved for a private caught trying to go over the hill, he gave him approximately the following lecture: "You mean to stand here and tell me that you've gotten $1100 out of this man for a five-year-old car and have the nerve to come here and ask for more? Well, you and your sort have another think coming. You're not to go around cheating people and expecting this court to back you up. You're not going to get another penny out of this man as long as I'm sitting here. Judgment for the next [sic] defendant." Plaintiff's protests were cut short by a curt, "Next case." (Matthews, 1973, p. 93)

The judge's actions in this case violated several legal rules. Yet, as in most small claims courts the plaintiff was stuck, for he had no right to appeal. Matthews asked the judge about this case later. The judge responded:

> "Look, we both know what happened. This guy saw a defenseless sucker coming, sold him a piece of junk, and charged him through the nose to fix it up. He got plenty of money out of that car, and I'll be damned if I'm going to make the buyer pay him more." . . . Here was a man who felt that ignoring the letter of the law was perfectly just in order to fulfill its basic purpose and wasn't afraid to take a reasonable guess about what happened (about which he was almost certainly correct). (p. 94)

The second case involved an employment broker suing for a fee. The broker and the defendant presented conflicting stories. According to Matthews, it seemed that the defendant was a liar and that the broker deserved his fee, but the broker's only evidence was his self-serving testimony. The judge could "guess" who was telling the truth, or he could refrain from making a factual judgment. To refrain from deciding between the two stories was to deny the plaintiff, who in law has the burden of proof, any recovery. This is what happened: The judgment was for the defendant. Again, Matthew interviewed the judge. The judge agreed with Matthew's judgment about who was telling the truth, and explained his decision as follows:

"You know," he said, shaking his head and pursing his lips in disgust, "I just knew that bastard (the defendant) was lying. But there was nothing I could do about it. There was just not enough evidence." Here was an honest judge obviously upset by what he had "had to do," but scrupulously adhering to the standard of regular court. (p. 94)

Matthews calls the first kind of judge a *fundamentalist*. He gets to the heart of the matter and sweeps away any "legalisms" that get in his way. The second judge Matthews calls a *formalist*. He sticks more rigidly to the formal legal decision-making rules in reaching a judgment (p. 95).

The fundamentalist in the used car case not only ignored any procedural niceties in reaching his judgment, he also ignored a considerable body of substantive law. One suspects that this is not an unusual situation. Attending to equities, like the movement toward relationship settlement, implies a movement away from clear legal rules. We may applaud this fundamentalist's decision, for the result seems just. Yet, what seems proper in one case could have substantial costs if it were the dominant mode of deciding cases. Whatever one thinks of legal formality, clear legal rules have their place, especially in market situations. Max Weber, for one, saw formal law as a key component in modern exchange (capitalist) economies:

> Though it is not necessarily true of every economic system, certainly the modern economic order under modern conditions could not continue if its control of resources were not upheld by the legal compulsion of the state; that is, if its formally "legal" rights were not upheld by the threat of force. (Weber, 1967, p. 65)

From this perspective, whatever else the fundamentalist's opinion was, it was not a good judicial performance.

But this image of good judicial performance is precisely what the critics of the traditional small claims court are complaining about—power resides in a judge who is concerned with being judicious. Eckoff (1966, p. 165) explains the tension:

> It is difficult to combine the role of the judge and the role of the mediator in a satisfactory way. . . . By mediating one may weaken the normative basis for a later judgment and perhaps also undermine confidence in one's impartiality as a judge; and by judging first one will easily reduce the willingness to compromise of the party who was supported in the judgment, and will be met with suspicion of partiality by the other.

How should we conclude? The small claims court has not lived up to the ideal some have set for it. It remains primarily an adjudicatory forum. Not surprisingly, most of the disputes it deals with are brought by parties who are not adverse to issue decisions. If it were designed differently, different kinds of disputes might be brought there, and the problem might be to design a tribunal to handle the kinds of cases that the current small claims courts consider. Furthermore, we should remember that, although the logic of the tribunal is geared to issue decisions, resort to small claims court does not lead inevitably to pure, binary outcomes. A large proportion of cases instituted there are settled, and the availability of the court may result in some grievances being satisfied to forestall legal claims. In these two ways the court gives bargaining strength to parties who because of the size of their claim or their poverty would otherwise not be able to enlist the aid of the law. The fact that businesspeople have used small claims courts to increase their leverage over the poor upsets many. But this result is not inevitable. Some small claims courts do not greatly aid businesses in the debt collection process because they either will not hear cases arising out of business debts or they limit the number of cases any one plaintiff can bring to court. Even where small claims courts do process business debts, it is not clear—so long as the debt was honestly incurred and fair procedures followed—where the harm lies. If there is an evil here, it lies either in abuses, such as sewer service,[10] which the informality of small claims court may facilitate, or in the substantive law that in the eyes of some is distinctly tilted in favor of creditors. Such evils can be corrected without eliminating the small claims court.

The small claims court cannot, and perhaps should not, change exclusively to a conciliatory style. It is not set up to reinstitutionalize rules in this fashion. The issue facing society now is whether we should spend the money needed to experiment with mediative forums outside the formal system. Conciliatory courts may fill a gap in our ability to keep the peace, especially for those who cannot afford to hire experts to perform this service. It would be surprising, however, if they became a major forum for processing disputes in a country like the United States.[11]

THE JUVENILE COURT

In the preceding section we discussed a court that has met with at least partial success. Recent criticisms notwithstanding, the small claims court has made legal remedies available to some who otherwise would be cut off from the resources of the law. Yet we have seen tension in the system. The dispute settlement technique does not always conform to the relationship of the parties, and, given the nature of our legal system, it is difficult for an official court in the United States to do so. People in multiplex and ongoing relationships are by and large left to work out their problems outside the formal legal order. Indeed, except when one or both parties want to terminate the relationship, this is typically their preference.

---

10. See the discussion in Note 3, *supra*.

11. We should point out that mediation on a private basis and in some cases with government sponsorship is important in settling labor disputes as well as disputes between businesses and disputes between businesses and government agencies. Also private conciliation services, such as marriage and family counseling, are a booming business. The latter may benefit from being less formal than any official state tribunal can hope to be.

If the absence of conciliatory courts is a fault, it is a fault of omission; something our system fails to provide. In the present section which focuses on the juvenile court we discuss what is arguably a more serious fault, a fault of commission. Unlike ordinary criminal courts whose jurisdiction is based primarily on the quality of the alleged crime (felony or misdemeanor), the jurisdiction of the juvenile court turns on the age of the alleged offender. To understand the problem, we must go back nearly 90 years to when the juvenile court was created.

In 1899 the first juvenile court in this nation was founded in Cook County (Chicago), Illinois.[12] It was the product of a group of concerned citizens who had the best of motives. They wanted to "save" our children. That numbers of children needed saving was obvious to these people. The movement to establish such courts became an important part of the agenda of the organized charities movement of the time (Sutton, 1985) and a special project of a number of "moral entrepreneurs," including several of the early juvenile court judges.

The children who motivated the reformer's concern were either abandoned or neglected or involved in criminal activity. The latter especially needed help. Too often they were treated like adults, tried for their crimes and put in jails and prisons.

The reformers attributed the criminal activity of children largely to their environment. Consider the lament of Louise Bowen, an important leader in the Chicago movement:

> Here we are, Chicago, a great city sprawling over vast territory, people with many nationalities, calling ourselves the commerce center of the world. . . . It is said that we are going to be the largest and most beautiful city in the world, but what is it going to profit us if our children lose their souls! (Quoted in Platt, 1969, p. 91)

To upper-class women who, like Mrs. Bowen, were raised in rural areas and moved to large metropolises, the city was full of sin and woe. Brothels, alcohol, comic books, and amusement parks were all threats to the moral development of children. What was the solution? Enforcement of law and the development of "character." Character could be built by parental authority, discipline, and moral education. As Platt notes, these "child savers" had much in common with other social reformers of their time. They shared a boundless faith in the virtues of the rural Protestant life-style. They shared the temperance movement's model of correcting problems by regulating and bringing them under governmental control. Social progress they thought depended on strict supervision of a child's life, especially his leisure time. They also shared the nativism

---

12. In our discussion of the juvenile court we shall occasionally refer to other achievements of the juvenile justice reform movement which the court came to represent and embody. These include such things as the juvenile reformatory, incarceration for status offenses, the idea of the neglected child, and separate pretrial detention facilities for juveniles. These other achievements did not always arrive with the institution of the juvenile court. They could follow the institution of a juvenile court or precede it (Sutton, 1983, 1985).

of the temperance movement and other crusades of the time. In the eyes of the reformers, one of the main problems with city children was that they (and their parents) were not like "us." They did not share the nativist's well-regulated Protestant roots. If a child went wrong it was probably due to his heritage, which at the individual level means "upbringing." The solution was obvious—to raise the child in an appropriate manner, even if this meant taking him from his parents and home.

The development of the juvenile court was a natural by-product of such views. The reformers were confident that the existing system, which could involve incarcerating adults and children together, bred crime. Frederick Wines, Chairman of Chicago's Board of Public Charities, noted:

> We make criminals out of children who are not criminals by treating them as if they were criminals. That ought to be stopped. What we should have, in our system of criminal jurisprudence, is an entirely separate system of courts for children. . . . We ought to have a "children's court" in Chicago, and we ought to have a "children's judge," who should attend to no other business. (Frederick Wines in a speech in 1899; quoted in Platt, 1969, p. 132)

The juvenile court was not supposed to treat children as criminals, even when they had committed criminal acts. At the same time, it was not to sit passively by and wait for the worst. By then, as the Board of Public Charities noted, it would be too late:

> If the prevention of crime is more important than its punishment, and if such prevention can only be secured by rescuing children from criminal surroundings before the criminal character and habits become firmly established, then it is evident that the state reform school cannot accomplish all that we desire, since it does not receive children at a sufficiently early age, nor does it receive children who still occupy the debatable ground between criminality and innocence, who have not yet committed any criminal act, but who are in imminent danger at every moment of becoming criminals. (Sixth Biennial Report of the Board of State Commissioner of Public Charities of the State of Illinois; quoted in Platt, 1969, p. 107)

Past conduct, in other words, should not be the only grist for the juvenile court's mill. It must also consider the prospective relationships of children to society. To do this well required the court to examine the whole of a child's behavior. The examination was not to search out criminal conduct; rather, it was necessary to guide the court in determining what was needed to make the child a good citizen. What this often meant in practice was that once a child was in court, even conduct that was not criminal might impel the court to severe action. As one of the early judges in Boston's juvenile court said:

> The court does not confine its attention to just the particular offense which brought the child to its notice. For example, a boy who comes to court for such a trifle as failing to wear his badge when selling papers may be held on probation for months because of difficulties at school; and a boy who comes in for playing ball on the street may . . . be committed to a reform school because he is found to have habits

of loafing, stealing or gambling which cannot be corrected outside. (Baker, 1910, p. 649; quoted in Platt, 1969, p. 142)

Indeed, a youth did not have to engage in criminal activity for the court to take jurisdiction. Truancy, incorrigibility, using indecent or profane language, sexual profligacy, growing up in idleness, and other "status offenses" were grounds for judicial involvement. Deviations like these in the young were seen as predicting to at best bad citizenship and at worst a life of crime: Thus in most states they justified labeling children delinquent. It would have been tragic not to correct such tendencies at a time when correction was still possible.

The juvenile court movement, as Judge Baker's comment makes clear, was aimed at creating a new backup institution to step in where primary institutions such as the family and the school had failed. The theoretical objective of the juvenile court was *relationship settlement*. In some cases the relationship that needed repairing involved a youth and his family or a youth and his school, but more often it involved the relationship between a youth and all of civil society as represented by the judge and the juvenile court staff. As would be expected in an institution geared to relationship settlement, the formal law was considerably relaxed. Notice of the charged offenses was often vague and minimal, for there was no need to commence cases by information or indictment nor was there a preliminary hearing. Jury trial was not an option. Counsel was rarely appointed, and in some courts the right to retain counsel was not clear. Everything about the child and his situation was potentially relevant. Thus juveniles were confronted by judges whose attitudes and, on occasion, commands suggested they were obligated to talk rather than given the adult's right to remain silent. Furthermore, there were neither binary decisions nor set penalties for children found delinquent. As Judge Baker's comment suggests, the juvenile could be found not to have been involved in the act that brought him to court, but still in need of "help." Since the court's purposes were corrective, youth involved in serious offenses might escape with a lecture, but at the other extreme, trivial offenses or disfavored behavior could lead to incarceration until the age of majority. At one time more girls were in juvenile corrections institutions for sexual promiscuity than for any criminal offense.

The juvenile court as it flourished for decades, came as close as any American court has ever come to the jurisprudence of totalitarianism. Compare Judge Baker's statement of the purposes of the juvenile court with Alexander Solzhenitsyn's description of the work of Soviet Troikas.

(Please forgive us, reader. We have once more gone astray with this rightist opportunism—this concept of "guilt," and of the guilty or innocent. It has, after all, been explained to us that *the heart of the matter is not personal guilt, but social danger.* One can imprison an innocent person if he is socially hostile. And one can release a guilty man if he is socially friendly. But lacking legal training, we can be forgiven, for the 1926 Code, according to which, my good fellow, we lived for twenty-five years and more, was itself criticized for an "impermissible bourgeois approach," for an "insufficiently class-conscious [by Vyshinsky] approach," and for some kind of ''bourgeois weighting of punishments in relation to the gravity of what had been committed.'') (Solzhenitsyn, 1973, pp. 282–283)

We do not mean to imply that Judge Baker and Comrade Vyshinsky, the chief prosecutor in the Moscow show trials, are cut from the same cloth. If nothing else, there is considerable difference between one year in reform school and 25 years in Siberia. It is also clear that Judge Baker was an idealist. Whether Comrade Vyshinsky was an idealist or a cynic we cannot say. But the logic of the two approaches is uncomfortably similar regardless of the different motivations and consequences.

The juvenile court movement spread widely throughout the United States in the years following 1899, and eventually every jurisdiction had some special court to handle juveniles. The court did not escape criticism (see, e.g., Allen, 1964, pp. 43–61), but it was not until 1967 that anyone mounted a successful assault on the system. In that year the U.S. Supreme Court handed down its opinion in the case of *In Re Gault*, 387 U.S. 1 (1967). The Gault opinion required juvenile courts to: (1) give timely notice of *specific* charges, (2) notify accused youths of the right to be represented by counsel in any proceedings that might lead to commitment to an institution, (3) honor the right to confront and cross-examine witnesses, and (4) alert accused youths to the privilege against self-incrimination and their right to remain silent. These changes did not necessarily make the juvenile court a dispute decision forum, but they moved it in that direction. Mr. Justice Fortas did not mince words.

[H]owever euphemistic the title, a ''receiving home'' or an ''industrial school'' for juveniles is an institution of confinement in which the child is incarcerated. . . . Under our Constitution, the condition of being a boy does not justify a kangaroo court. (*In Re Gault*, 387 U.S. 1 (1967), pp. 27–28)

What was wrong with the juvenile court as it once flourished? Consider the case of Gerald Gault. At the age of 15 he was accused of making an obscene phone call to a woman. Neither he nor his parents were notified before his hearing of the specific charges he was to answer. They were also not told that Gerald might be represented by counsel, and when the judge questioned the youth they were not informed of the constitutional privilege against self-incrimination. The complaining witness was not present at the hearing and could not be cross-examined. Her accusations were presented by a probation officer reporting a conversation he had with her. In an adult court the officer's testimony would have been excluded both as hearsay and as a violation of the defendant's Sixth Amendment right to confront witnesses against him. Ultimately, Gerald Gault was found delinquent and was sentenced to the state industrial ''school'' until he reached the age of 21, unless released sooner. Had he been an adult convicted of the same offense, the maximum penalty would have been a fine of up to $50 and a jail sentence of up to 2 months.

This description of apparent injustice or, at least, excessive punishment is just one way to answer the question of what is wrong with the juvenile court. In a fundamental sense the question goes beyond the court itself. An examination of the problems of the juvenile court requires us to consider the limits of rein-

stitutionalizing norms through the legal system. For present purposes there are
at least four areas of tension when juvenile courts are structured along relationship
settlement lines. These are:

1. The juvenile is forced to use the court. He cannot reject the jurisdiction.
2. The court brings together two disputants of greatly unequal power—the state
   and a child.
3. The court's rhetoric of solicitous concern for the child's welfare disguises
   the actual relationship of the child and the state.
4. As a result of (2) and (3), the court's secondary rule logic is often subverted
   so that what occurs is not a relationship settlement but, rather, a relationship
   decision.

We shall briefly discuss each of these points.

Forced Use

The youth brought to juvenile court has no choice in the matter. He can neither
escape his legal involvement nor opt for a tribunal that proceeds formally to an
issue decision. The general issue is one that we touched on in the preceding
section. It is one thing to set up community mediation boards that the citizenry
can or cannot turn to as they desire. It is another thing to compel participation.
Intrusive systems that compel participation give rise to the danger of abuse. This
is all the more likely when the parties are of unequal power, and it is almost
inevitable when one party can impose a solution on the other.

Unequal Power

In most of the systems that ordinarily use the relationship settlement model, the
parties are of roughly equal power or can align themselves with allies to redress
serious imbalances. In the cases of the Bossy Wife, the Biased Father and
Citizeness Kliuchiova, power relationships were fairly equal. Insults and slan-
ders, accusations and counteraccusations could be traded back and forth in the
process of jockeying for position. Indeed, the trading of such charges is an
integral part of this dispute settlement technique. One cannot allow the opponent
to have a monopoly on virtue.

Robert Emerson (1969), in a thoughtful investigation of the operation of
one juvenile court, discusses the ability of juveniles to counter accusations against
them. He lists four possible defensive strategies that the child might use: innocence, justification, excuse, and counterdenunciation (1969, pp. 142–143).

Innocence. The defense of innocence appears straightforward and conclusive.
It is not in juvenile court, for the usual rules involving the state's burden of

proof do not always pertain.[13] Consider the case of a boy who was accused in connection with an auto theft (Emerson, 1969, p. 147). The police had captured the boy after a long foot chase, but could not say they saw him in the car or jumping out when it stopped. The boy said he was only walking by when three boys stopped, jumped out of a car and began to run. When the police began shouting at them to stop, he ran too. The boy had a long arrest record of serious offenses, and the judge found him delinquent in connection with the car theft. When there are competing versions of what happened, a youth with a police record, which means most youths who reach the stage of a "formal" hearing, has an almost unsurmountable credibility problem.

Justification. Justifications are often powerful defenses. The Bossy Wife did not try to deny that she took the coffee; she justified her act in the name of her sick daughter. Emerson distinguishes two types of justification: *principled justification* and *situational justification*.

Principled justifications argue for some moral or social value that takes precedence over or perhaps denies the value threatened by one's act. Such justifications are rare in any circumstance. The only example that we have encountered in this book is the statement of the members of the Watchtower Pacifists. Emerson found no examples of such a justification in his study of the court. It would have been foolish to make them in a setting in which one could be incarcerated for being "incorrigible," since denying that one's act is in principle wrong not only questions the official morality of the juvenile court, but it also is perhaps the best evidence of likely repetition that one can provide.

Situational justifications are less extreme. Such justifications argue that an apparently questionable act was proper, or at least permissible, given the circumstances of the situation. The Bossy Wife's argument is of this variety. Cutting one's spouse's coffee is wrong unless it is to meet his unfulfilled obligations to his child. Situational justifications may help mitigate wrongness in the juvenile court, but they rarely exculpate. Attempts at complete justification are routinely met with judicial counterassertions reestablishing the child's culpability (Emerson, 1969, p. 151).[14]

Excuse. The excuses most commonly employed by juveniles are duress, accident, and ignorance. Although excuses that diminish *mens rea* can be helpful, when

---

13. In 1970 in *In Re Winship*, 397 U.S. 358 (1970) the Supreme Court held that "proof beyond a reasonable doubt" is an essential element of due process and that this standard must be met when a juvenile is tried for an act that would be a crime if committed by an adult. Thus in this respect the "law on the books" is the same in juvenile court as it is in adult court. However, differences may persist in practice (see generally, Stapleton and Teitlebaum, 1972).

14. Note we are talking only about cases that reach the juvenile court hearing stage. Principled or situational justification may work for some juveniles, but when they are viable excuses, they are likely to lead the police not to arrest or youth authorities to drop charges. The excuses offered by youth before the juvenile court are likely to have been offered at earlier stages in the juvenile justice process to no avail.

a child's story conflicts with that of an adult the child is unlikely to be believed. Emerson reports a case of three young boys accused of purse snatching in a subway. They claimed it was an accident, that they merely bumped the woman and her shopping bag when running by. The woman claimed the boys grabbed the purse when they ran by. When the oldest boy attempted to argue again that it was an accident, the judge responded angrily, "What do you think, the lady's lying? Is that what you want me to believe?" (1969, p. 154).

Counterdenunciation. In a Lozi court or Mexican village the questions the judge asked of the boy would not have been treated as rhetorical, but would probably have been answered "yes." A long counterdenunciation, reciting a number of occasions where the woman was a known liar, would have probably followed. In the case Emerson reports, the boy merely stood with his head bowed before the judge's glare. He was smarter than some. He sensed that a counterdenunciation was an unwise strategy.

> Use of this strategy, however, is extremely risky in the court setting. While counterdenunciation may appear to the delinquent as a "natural" defense as he perceives the circumstances of his case, it tends to challenge fundamental court commitments and hence, even when handled with extreme care, often only confirms the denunciation. (1969, p. 156)

Occasionally, when other youth are the target, a counterdenunciation will help spread responsibility around. The strategy is also sometimes effective when family members are denounced. Emerson reports a case where a girl successfully blamed her mother, who had brought her to court, for part of her misbehavior, and another where a runaway girl explained her behavior by showing that her father beat her for inviting a boy friend into her house while her parents were out (1969, pp. 161–162). It is worth quoting Emerson on the circumstances of a successful counterdenunciation.

> The relatively high probability of successful counter-denunciation in cases arising from family situations points up the most critical contingency in the use of this protective strategy, the choice of an appropriate object. Denouncers with close and permanent relations with the denounced are particularly vulnerable to counter-denunciation, as the accusation is apt to rest solely on their word and illegitimate motives for the denunciation may be readily apparent. But again, where relations between the two parties are more distant, counter-denunciation has more chance of success where the denouncer is of more or less equivalent status with the denounced. Thus, the judge can be easily convinced that a schoolmate might unjustly accuse one from jealousy, but will reject any contention that an adult woman would lie about an attempted purse-snatching incident. (1969, pp. 162–163)

Most dangerous of all are counterdenunciations against those frequent accusers of children—the police. The judge will often openly reject such attacks, and they may be read as evidence of the juvenile's bad character which justifies an unusually stringent sanction.

The power inequalities in juvenile court reflect inequalities that exist in the social standing of the various actors. The court does nothing to mute them. In this respect the juvenile court differs from an issue decision court in which weaker parties, although disadvantaged, often prevail against stronger ones. The failure to ameliorate preexisting power differences is not a necessary feature of dispute settlement tribunals. The village headmen in both Fallers's and Gluckman's work are important men. Relatively speaking, they are much more important than a police officer in our society. Their power, however, is muted when their disagreements with others spill over into the legal arena. The judges attend to everyone. Moreover, the litigants, whether or not they are headmen, are in complicated relationships with each other. Each party often ''has something'' on the other side that can be used in the conflict.

The power of the police in the juvenile court is not the power of money or politics. It is the power of distance and relative position. The police officer is credible because he or she does not have an obvious reason to ''get'' the youth. The social distance between them would make counterdenunciation difficult, even if counterdenunciations were not necessarily suspect because of the denouncer's self-interest. Furthermore, the relative positions of child and police officer are extreme. Many social relations are upset when one believes a youth rather than an officer of the law. For this reason, too, the power of the police is the power of being believed. In a court of law one can ask for no greater weapon. The result is that in a factual dispute between a police officer and a delinquent, the outcome is effectively preordained.

The Relationship of Child and Court

The rhetoric of the juvenile court has from its beginnings been dominated by expressions of a solicitous concern with the whole child. What was supposedly paramount was the child's welfare and his place in society. ''We must reach into the soul-life of the child,'' and ''get the whole truth about a child'' said one early judge (Platt, 1969). Such remarks were not cynical justifications for the institution that was being built. They expressed the ideals of a group that was supremely confident that it knew where morality lay and that it could instill in the young strict Protestant virtue. If this led to the creation of status offenses, it also meant that some children who committed serious crimes were treated with what would have been for adults remarkable leniency.

The societal institution that most obviously combines punishment, forgiveness, and coercion toward virtue is the family. This was the institution that was thought to have failed society when children were delinquent. Thus it is not surprising that in speeches about the new court the imagery frequently employed was that of a family. In the dedication of the Chicago juvenile court building in 1907 the program affirmed that:

> the hearings will be held in a room fitted up as a parlor rather than a court, around a table instead of a bench. . . . The hearing will be in the nature of a family

conference in which the endeavor will be to impress the child with the fact that his own good is sought alone. (Quoted in Platt, 1969, p. 143)

Judge Tuthill of the Chicago court affirmed that:

I have always felt, and endeavored to act in each case, as I would were it my own son who was before me in the library at home, charged with some misconduct. (Quoted in Platt, 1969, p. 144)

Such rhetoric was more than idealistic chitchat. It was part of the formal argument for the court's power. Its legal foundation rested on the concept of *parens partriae*, the right of the state as a sovereign to act as guardian over those under a disability—in this case the disability of youth. Indeed, it was the image projected by this concept, that the court was not punishing crime but was looking after the welfare of children who could not be adequately cared for by other institutions, which allowed the juvenile court to escape the procedural and evidentiary restrictions that have traditionally accompanied criminal proceedings in the United States.[15]

The approach of acting as if each child were one's own son or daughter is in the abstract admirable. John Griffiths (1970) makes this point in an article that contrasts what he calls the "family model" with Herbert Packer's (1964) "crime control" and "due process" models of criminal justice. Griffiths argues persuasively that the latter two "models" are end points of a perspective that sees the criminal process as a battle. Whether the advantage is heavily tilted toward the state as in the crime control model or arguably tilted the other way as in the due process model, the criminal trial is an arena in which there is a maximum of conflict of interest. The accused will either be labeled a criminal or will go scot-free. Griffiths suggested the family model, which is designed not to declare winners and losers but to reconcile the individual to society.

In the context of the family the ideal of reconciliation is reasonable. If my child tears up my first draft of this chapter I am likely to punish her, and I may, if I have a legal turn of mind, even consider what she did to be a crime; but she is my child, not my *criminal* child. We might analyze my reaction by observing the multiplex and prospective nature of the parent–child relationship, but Griffiths is in some ways closer to the mark when he submits that what moves the family model is love.

The juvenile court attempts after a fashion to follow something like the

---

15. The rhetoric, however, could not completely hide the reality, even in the statements of the functionaries. Judge Julian Mack, an important and influential early juvenile court judge, wished to dispense with "ordinary trappings of the court room" but also wished to impress on the child the fact that he was confronting the "power of the state" (Platt, 1969, p. 44). And in the Boston court, although the judge did not sit on a high bench, the child and his parents were required to stand throughout the hearing so that "the fact of the court being a department of public authority and having power to compel compliance should be indicated distinctly" (Platt, 1969, p. 145). Over the years attempts at informal physical arrangements seem to have diminished, and in most courts the judge has gone back to a more traditional courtroom appearance.

family model in passing judgment on children. Griffiths notes this attempt and laments its failure. He attributes the failure to the lack of institutional resources and the inadequate training of those associated with the courts. Here we believe he is wrong. The obstacles are more fundamental. We doubt if there is one person in a thousand who can love delinquent after delinquent in the way she would love her own child. Both the long-standing emotional attachment and the very real self-interest that parents have in their own children are lacking.

Moreover, there are pressures leading the judge away from the ideal of reconciliation. Chief among these is the idea that incarceration will incapacitate dangerous people and deter others, who are potentially dangerous, from pursuing lives of crime. The pressure on courts to sentence so as to achieve these goals is, in many communities, immense. Where juvenile crime is rife, the pressure to sentence severely may be particularly strong with respect to delinquents. Countervailing pressures that might exist if judges or the police who are often complainants had close supportive ties to the youths are largely absent. And when parents are complainants, also a common occurrence, the very fact that the court has been invoked means that the usual expectations of familial support are likely to be lacking.[16] In these circumstances the conflict between the youth and society—as represented by the court—is clear. It is a lie to speak of the juvenile court's relationship to an accused as if it were essentially like a family head's relationship to a wayward child.

Nor is this the only "lie" of the juvenile court. The other fundamental deceit is the court's claim that its dispositions are chosen in order to aid the child. Although this may be true of some sentencing decisions, it is certainly not always true of the decision to incarcerate, even if the pretense is maintained by calling walled prisons "training schools." The deceit is perhaps defensible so long as the bulk of those interned are serious offenders who by the standards of the criminal law deserve to be in prison. But for many years juvenile court judges, some no doubt honestly fooled by the family image, were exiling, under conditions of greater or lesser security, youth whose most serious offenses were avoiding school, having sex, and not getting along with their parents. These "delinquents" were told that removal to a more restrictive community was for their own good, but one could hardly blame them if they did not believe it.

The problems of what to do with such difficult youth as the unmanageable child or habitual truant, on the one hand, and the 14-year-old who is an alleged armed robber or rapist, on the other, are genuinely difficult ones. In neither case, however, are they solved by labeling the easiest solutions for the adult community as being "in the interest of the child" and then lowering the procedural protec-

---

16. One study (Dannefer, 1984) indicates that holding the offense constant, youth are treated more severely after arrest and receive more severe dispositions when family members are the complainants than when the police are. This is not surprising, for the family is an important resource for the youth ensnared in the juvenile justice system. If a child's family will not plead for him, find counsel, and propose nonincarcerative rehabilitative programs, the child, despite provisions for appointed counsel, is in serious trouble. Consider the likely reaction of a judge when a child's own parents admit he is beyond their control.

tions we offer accused children because we have so labeled the outcomes. Yet the image of the child-centered *parens patria* court was powerful, perhaps because the ideal of the family model juvenile court was honestly hoped for by many if not honestly held. It is no coincidence that *Gault* was handed down at a time when many people had come to realize that juvenile offenses were often serious criminal business. They did not involve the kinds of youthful excesses that the well-regulated, middle class handled within the family.

The Emerging Logic—Relationship Decision

The birth of the juvenile court was accompanied by the invention of the *delinquent*. Children would no longer be criminal. They would simply be delinquent youth in need of help. The term *delinquent* was not meant to carry with it the stigma that comes with the label "criminal," for delinquency covered not only serious crimes but also sins like truancy which only children could commit. Moreover, there was a feeling, despite the relatively serious crimes of some delinquents, that youth signified a malleability of character, which meant that with proper treatment even apparently hardened delinquents would change their ways. Today these ideas seem quaint.[17] When we think of the serious delinquent, we think of a person who but for age would be standing in the docket in a criminal court. Even though many children are still being labeled delinquent for behavior that would not be criminal if committed by an adult, the word conjures up the image of a little felon, or at best, a prospective felon. Indeed, the term delinquent is in some ways even more condemning than the label criminal, for a delinquent not only did something wrong, but there is something wrong with him. This perception of what it is to be adjudicated a juvenile delinquent reflects the secondary rule structure of the traditional juvenile court.

The dispute logic that emerged in the juvenile court took the "whole child," as the proper focus of attention. Everything about the child was relevant. Performance at school, attitude at home, and behavior at play were scrutinized for signs that something was wrong. The stigma of being a juvenile delinquent, not to mention the possibility of probation or reform school, were not conducive to the caring model originally envisioned. If there was to be a compromise, the power relationships did much to ensure that it would be the child who did the compromising. The result was a decision-making process that produced outcomes that were more binary than the court's rhetoric would have had us believe.

---

17. It is true that many delinquents do not grow up to lives of adult crime, but it is not clear that involvement in the juvenile justice system has much to do with it. Some have suggested that such involvement actually increases prospects for future crime (Gold, 1970). Others find an individual deterrent effect to serious penalties visited on youth (Murray & Cox, 1979), but it is not clear that the effects are greater than with first time adult offenders, many of whom, following an experience with prison, are never subsequently arrested. If delinquents are less prone to recidivate than older criminals, we think it is more likely to be due to the dramatic change in social situation and job opportunities that come with age than to any interventions of the juvenile justice system.

But the choice the juvenile justice system made was seldom the familiar one of guilty or not guilty. Instead, the system seemed more concerned with determining whether the child was essentially a good kid or basically a delinquent. The former might purposely be given a taste of jail by slow case processing following arrest and could expect a severe scolding by the judge which might include a threat of incarceration or even a sentence of incarceration reluctantly withdrawn at the last moment. Ultimately, however, the "good child" was released on probation, or for minor offenses, in the care of his parents. The court's bluster was justified as the "kick in the pants" needed to get the youth back on the right path. On the other hand, even if his offense seemed minor the youth judged *essentially* delinquent might be sent away, with less ceremony than the good kid received, for an indefinite period of time (Wheeler, 1968).[18] As more and more juveniles have become involved in more serious crimes, however, the incarceration of essential delinquents for relatively minor offenses has become a luxury that many jurisdictions cannot afford. Indeed, as youth crime has grown more serious, those whose offenses are minor are likely to appear to judges as less essentially delinquent (Emerson, 1983).

The dispute settlement style that emerged in the juvenile court is one we call *relationship decision*. Recall our table of dispute settlement logics (see Table 8.1). By and large we have until now discussed cases that fall in either the issue decision or the relationship settlement cells, although we mentioned issue settlement in connection with mediation programs appended to some small claims courts. The tensions we have discussed have been between the use of these techniques, the underlying relationship of the parties, and the nature of the legal order. When the problems brought to court are appropriate, these techniques are reasonable and coherent. Issues, if made specific enough, can be decided. Relationships can be settled.

The juvenile court could not let go of the idea that it must examine the whole child to determine what should be done, nor could it disregard the pressures and the power to make decisions about the type of children before it. The former implies a low level of conflict between the child and the state, and the latter implies a potentially high level. Only in the juvenile court could Gerald Gault be sent to an institution that might incarcerate him for several years for an offense (an obscene call) that could lead to no more than 3 months in jail for an adult. The tension is not between the social reality of relationships and the way norms governing these relationships are institutionalized; rather, the tension is internal.

---

18. Although the matter has not been thoroughly researched, it appears that the quality of a child's family influenced the court's assessment of the child's essential character as well as the decision regarding the disposition. A child who had no familial support or whose family was clearly part of the problem might well end up—even if adjudged a good kid—in foster care or in an institution. Similarly, a family that promised to supervise a true delinquent carefully might buy the child a few more arrests before he was finally sent away. Also, it appears that incarcerative decisions have changed over the years. Early on it appears that even good kids were sent away in the belief that institutionalization would do them some good.

TABLE 8.1

Res Gestae	*Binary*	*Flexible*
Narrow	Issue decision	Issue settlement
Wide	Relationship decision	Relationship settlement

The court is pulled by two conflicting objectives. The resulting case logic, which is one of relationship decisions, reflects these inconsistencies.[19]

The court is in this position for two reasons. First, the pattern of the emerging rule structure follows the social relationship of children to the society. If the secondary rules are inconsistent, they reflect the inconsistency with which we view children who commit crimes. On the one hand, concern for the child's welfare, a belief that youth are malleable, and the fact that children generally are not considered fully responsible for their actions, lead us to consider sympathetically all the factors that may lead youth down the wrong path. On the other hand, we are concerned with our own safety and want protection from minors, who are usually strangers and for many people often of an alien or disvalued heritage. The court, therefore, declares the child delinquent and puts him in the hands of "specialists" whose official task is to work the child back into society. Unfortunately, almost all the data we have indicate that if the specialists help, they do not frequently succeed to the extent of transforming their charges. Recidivism rates for delinquents are high. Only the most severe sanction, incarceration, guarantees a clear social benefit—incapacitation. There is no outcome that clearly helps most youth avoid future crime.

The second reason for the pattern of dispute settlement in juvenile court concerns the nature of the legal order. The monopoly of coercive power in the hands of the state and the inequality of power between the parties in a juvenile court case make the compromises that a wide *res gestae* allows unnecessary. The other procedural reforms designed to encourage relationship settlement— the unavailability of defense counsel, the presence in some cases of police rather

---

19. A relationship decision logic need not reflect any inconsistency if the court is sufficiently mission-oriented and that mission is to settle relationships. Thus the Soviet courts described by Solzhenitsyn explored whatever aspects of the lives of those before them was thought relevant in order to decide whether the accused were good citizens or subverters of the Communist cause. Although these courts were more vicious than the juvenile courts, except in rare instances, they appear untroubled by any internal inconsistency. The problem, however, is that these courts were so mission-oriented and so dominated by the Stalinist leadership, that there is considerable question as to whether the Soviet Troikas, as they performed in the political trials, should be considered courts at all. They lacked the autonomy we generally associate with courts and are perhaps better seen as an extension of the polity, which, except in the shallowest, most formal procedural sense, did not apply legal secondary rules at all.

than law-trained prosecutors, and in some areas the appointment of nonlegally trained judges—means that decisions are often not legalistic, but it does not make them less binary or less imposed. This does not mean that compromise is entirely absent from the juvenile court. It occurs, but largely among the state's agents. The arresting officer (who often prosecutes the matter), the probation officer, and the judge might disagree on the appropriate outcome and proceed to compromise their differences. However, once they arrive at a common solution, it is imposed on the child. These results are not surprising. It may be impossible for a modern legal system in a stratified society to establish courts with the panoply of secondary rules that a fair relationship settlement approach requires.

By according procedural rights, including the right to counsel, to youth in juvenile court, the Supreme Court began a slow movement back in the direction of an issue decision model.[20] Since *Gault* the states have altered their juvenile justice statutes to move further in this direction. In many states the term delinquent is now reserved for children who commit an act that would be criminal if committed by an adult. A new term such as "person in need of supervision" (PINS) describes those children who engage in behavior such as truancy that is not criminal. A child who is a PINS cannot be placed in an institution.[21]

This movement makes the system less oppressive and more internally consistent, but by making the system more like that of the criminal courts, it is a partial return to the situation that the child savers wished to avoid. It is, however, a more moderate policy in two respects. First, it diminishes the extent to which the goal of the adjudication is to decide the essential nature of the child. The juvenile court is less involved in what Garfinkel (1956) called "status degradation

---

20. One should not overstate the movement back. Lefstein, Stapleton, and Teitelbaum (1969) and Stapleton and Teitelbaum (1972) note that due process rights are often honored in the breach, and often defense attorneys refuse to adopt an adversarial model in court (Clayton, 1970). Nevertheless, the reintroduction of counsel has made a difference (Lemmert, 1970) as has the reintroduction of prosecuting attorneys, who adopt a more legalistic posture. Supreme Court decisions since *Gault* have accorded further procedural rights, such as the right to trial by jury for serious offenses and the need to prove criminal charges beyond a reasonable doubt.

Recently, however, in *Schall* v. *Martin*, 104 S.Ct. 2403 (1984), the Supreme Court sustained a statute that allowed juveniles to be preventively detained, that is, denied release on bail following arrest, when there is a "serious risk" that if released the juvenile would before the trial date commit an act that would be a crime if committed by an adult. Most youth so detained were ultimately found not delinquent and released to the community. Thus in many cases the detention statute had the appearance of "impos[ing] punishment for unadjudicated criminal acts" (2409). In sustaining the statute, the Supreme Court used language reminiscent of the early justifications for the special status of the juvenile court. Justice Rehnquist, speaking for a six-person majority wrote, "Society has a legitimate interest in protecting a juvenile from the consequences of his criminal activity . . ." (2411) and he noted that the child's interest in avoiding pretrial confinement "must be qualified by the recognition that juveniles, unlike adults, are always in some form of custody" (2410).

21. In most states these newer statutes contain a Catch 22 provision. If a child is declared a PINS; is put on probation; and then does something to violate the probation, he may be found delinquent for the probation violation and put in an institution. There is as yet little data on how frequently this back door to training schools is used.

ceremonies.'' Second, it limits the degree of official intervention. The delinquency finding is in theory restricted to children who are proven criminals.

At the same time, the move to an issue decision system is an admission of a failure that is both social and institutional. The noble human sentiment that children are special and deserving of special consideration in court has had to bow to two realities. The first is the reality of serious juvenile crime; it is just as painful to be mugged or shot by a juvenile as by an adult, and society must protect itself. The second reality is the institutional situation of the juvenile court; a system of relationship settlement where the parties are of immensely unequal power and the court is on the side of the state is difficult if not impossible to implement.

Recently, an approach called *diversion* has become an important aspect of the juvenile justice system. The objective is to divert children from the juvenile court, thus using it to back up other institutions rather than as a first resort (Carter & Klein, 1976). In some jurisdictions, for instance, the courts refuse to become involved with runaways. This does not necessarily mean that problem children are left to their own devices. Instead, the assistance they receive is not associated with the normal legal process. Diversion too is an admission of failure (Rojek & Erickson, 1981–82). It grew out of the belief that sending children to the juvenile court did little good from either the child's or society's point of view and might, because of either the stigma attached or the treatment received, do positive harm.

Diversion, of course, is more likely with youth who are experiencing their first contacts with the law and with less serious crime. At the other end of the scale, when crimes are most serious, there has been another admission of failure. The penalties the juvenile court can order have typically been limited to the period of the youth's minority. Thus a 17-year-old incarcerated in a juvenile institution for a crime such as rape or homicide that might lead to life imprisonment for an adult could generally expect to be released at no later than age 21. This poses a special problem in the case of older teenagers who are often seen as more dangerous and more responsible than their younger counterparts and as deserving longer sentences than the juvenile court can give them. To deal with the tension caused by the juvenile court's limited sentencing capacity and the fact that individual differences in maturity and criminal commitment mean that no fixed age can neatly separate those the juvenile court might help from those it cannot, juvenile courts have long had the authority to waive jurisdiction over older teenagers charged with serious offenses. This means that the juvenile court has discretion either to hear cases involving older teenagers or to send them to adult court where they will be tried and punished as adults. Today the age at which jurisdiction can be waived is coming down as is, in some states, the jurisdictional age of the juvenile court. Thus at one time a juvenile court might have had jurisdiction over all crimes committed by youth under 18, but if it thought that an accused felon of 17 would not benefit from its processes, it could waive jurisdiction and allow the youth to be tried as an adult. A 16-year-old, however, would always have had to be tried in juvenile court however serious his crime. Today in some courts 16- and 17-year-old alleged felons may be ordinarily tried as adults and jurisdiction over children as young as 13 years old can be waived.[22] Had the juvenile court been regarded as a success, these changes would not have occurred.

Delinquency was invented at the beginning of this century with the creation of the juvenile court. In midcentury it reached its peak, and has begun to decline. By the year 2000, perhaps there will be no more delinquents. Of course, there may still be 15-year-old armed robbers who go to special courts for young robbers, and children will still play hookey and run away. But it is possible that the concept of delinquency will have been overtaken by events.

THE LIMITS OF DOUBLE INSTITUTIONALIZATION

The last three chapters have examined various aspects of the reinstitutionalization of social norms in the law. We have concentrated on secondary rules: rules of evidence, procedure, and outcome. We have tried to show that these rules are at least as important for the operation of a legal system as the primary, substantive rules with which most of us are familiar. We have examined different patterns of dispute processing and the way these patterns relate to the social positions of parties in conflict and the stance that adjudicators adopt. Now we shall summarize the conclusions we draw from the preceding discussion.

From Bohannan's perspective the reinstitutionalization of norms into legal rules is primarily a method of controlling conflict that would otherwise threaten the viability of the institutions in which it occurs. To this we might add that the reinstitutionalization gives aggrieved individuals alternatives to self-help when the use of self-help might increase and exacerbate conflict. By channeling conflict, the law can increase domestic tranquility.

In most cases the effects of legal reinstitutionalization are not confined to the outputs of tribunals and the behavior of the police and other state agents. The potential availability of a legal remedy may advantage one party at the expense of another. Settlements with one eye to the law may terminate partially litigated claims, or the law may discourage the invocation of its dispute processing machinery in the first instance. We saw this most clearly when we looked at business contracts.

Where secondary rules discourage litigation the law walks a narrow path. Often we regard it as a virtue when a set of rules leads people to settle their

---

22. This is true in New York, for example. New York's general jurisdictional age for what it calls Family Court has long been 16 years old. If one looks at different state juvenile court laws over time one will see from the outset a variety of jurisdictional ages and waiver provisions, often varying by type of crime. The important point is not that these limits were always 18, for in some states and for some crimes they never were, but rather that when changes have occurred during the past two decades they have worked generally to lower the age at which the protections of the juvenile court can be claimed.

disputes without turning to courts. Businesspeople are presumably better off than they would be if they were compelled to litigate in court every time a contractual dispute arose. But virtue may turn into vice if in discouraging the use of the legal process the system makes the threat of legal action unavailable or differentially available to potential parties. As we saw in Chapter 6, the threat of taking a case to law complements substantive norms in defining the bargaining arena in which parties may find a solution. If a person cannot resort to law because of the costs involved, she lacks access to a valuable resource and may suffer because her relations with others will be less well regulated by substantive legal rules. The small claims court is one response to this particular problem. Subsidized legal aid, which we have not focused on, is another alternative. It can be particularly important when the law is mobilized against people of limited means, for without free legal help such people might not be able to recognize or assert valid legal defenses.

Not surprisingly, neither legal aid nor the small claims court is completely successful in allowing otherwise disadvantaged members of society that access to law that the affluent take for granted. Differences of wealth and power are always with us (Galanter, 1974). Yet to say that such innovations have not been completely successful is far from saying that they have failed. In many instances they substantially change the terms on which conflicting parties interact. Generally speaking, they have increased the ability of less powerful people to hold others accountable to legal norms.

When courts are called on to resolve cases, the reinstitutionalization of norms in legal rules seems most effective when it employs secondary rules that take account of the relationship between the disputants. Litigants tend to feel most comfortable with and find most satisfying those settlement techniques that reflect their mutual dealings. Techniques that do not reflect these relationships may create serious problems of reintegration after the dispute has been treated. Businesspeople avoid litigation in part because they know that although the court could resolve specific disagreements, the process by which it did so might destroy the rewards of an ongoing relationship.

In general, procedures designed to produce issue decisions are likely to impede the reintegration of disputing parties into viable relationships. If maintaining relationships is an important objective, relationship settlement techniques are generally more effective. Fortunately, the condition of enduring, multiplex relationships that makes maintaining relationships a likely goal facilitates relationship settlement procedures.

Legal innovations such as the juvenile court and small claims court are attempts at legal engineering which reflect a desire to use law to reduce conflict and a sensitivity to some of the shortcomings of the formalized system of issue decision making that characterizes most modern courts. They also reflect the assumption that the provision of legal remedies is the preferred way of dealing with interpersonal troubles. It is true that providing a legal remedy can reduce or resolve conflicts between disputants, especially when the law proceeds by secondary rules that attempt to compromise differences. But, as we have shown in the preceding sections, the assumption is not always correct, and there are limits to the law's ability to settle disputes and achieve fair outcomes.

In the United States today these limits are largely attributable to the power and social structure of our adjudicatory institutions. Although conciliatory approaches can be valuable, they are difficult to integrate into the existing system for dispute settlement. If alternatives to the courts are to be viable, they may have to be segregated from the main legal process. Modern judges and lawyers are not well trained in the skills needed to conciliate deeply felt conflicts. Nor do they share the intimate relationships with parties that are useful when employing mediation techniques for relationship settlement.

Equally important is the fact that when relationships are not multiplex and enduring, forcing people to participate in legal processes designed to yield relationship settlements may increase conflict rather than reduce it. O'Gorman's divorce lawyers were disconcerted primarily because the parties they represented too often wished to escalate conflict far beyond what was necessary to dissolve the relationship. The parties apparently wanted what the juvenile court sometimes provides: a relationship decision. Other parties to divorce want a quick and simple dissolution. The change to no fault divorce accommodates the latter group while denying the emotionally vindictive what they seek. Given the limits of the legal forum, the choice between these groups is a wise one. But it also disadvantages those who seek in the divorce process a last chance for reconciliation. Mediation may be helpful in such cases as well as in cases where there is substantial property to be divided between the spouses. Our analysis does not imply that the state should supply mediative services, but it does suggest that if this is attempted, the coercive machinery of the formal legal system should not be involved except insofar as the threat of formal law is an incentive to mediate.

No matter how much judges seek to be mediators or conciliators, they cannot, over the run of cases, discard the judicial role and the inherent coercive powers that go with it. Coercive relationship settlement, as we have pointed out, effectively reduces conflict only when two circumstances exist. The parties must in fact find themselves in multiplex and ongoing relationships, and they must be of fairly equal power. The relationship settlement technique as practiced among the Lozi, the Zapotec, and even the Moscovites, is essentially a procedure whereby the judges attempt to show the parties the common ground they share. Such proceedings are, in part, educative institutions. They work best when they can demonstrate that the conflict of interest between the parties is relatively low and when they suggest compromise solutions that give both parties some or most of what they want. Not every dispute, however, has such commonalities underlying it. Some disputes are symptomatic of larger conflicts of interest. Relationships between the police and boys in certain areas of our cities are like this. In situations of this sort, widening relevance widens potential areas of conflict. Where, in addition, the parties are of significantly unequal power the relationship settlement technique is easily subverted. The relationship decision logic of the juvenile court is a likely result. This style of adjudication is not only unlikely to lessen conflict, it often offends our traditional sense of justice.

This brings us to a final point: the relationship of domestic tranquility and justice. Macaulay's businesspeople typically avoided lawsuits because they did not believe that the courts could adequately settle their disputes. O'Gorman's divorcees had a more fundamental problem; they wanted the court to take the agony of their marriage into account and do justice. Justice motivations also governed the movement toward the juvenile court. To do justice to juveniles, the child savers believed that a new type of court was necessary. They believed that some deeper assessment of personality was necessary to produce the "fair" solution.

In the divorcee's case, getting what one deserved apparently had a negative connotation, the degradation of the spouse. For the child savers, giving the child what was best for all concerned did not have such a meaning. Unfortunately, the practice did not, and for good institutional reasons could not, live up to the ideal. We do not need to denounce the ideas of just desert held by the child savers or the divorcing spouses to observe that sometimes there is a conflict between the goals of settling disputes and of doing justice.

In this chapter we have concentrated on the way in which law may change in response to a changing society. We have discussed the law's ability to conform its dispute settlement processes to social relationships. The failure of the reforms embodied in the juvenile court and the limited success of the small claims court should alert us to the fact that the rule of law as found in our society in some ways detracts from and undermines the normative order of primary institutions. As Stanley Diamond (1971) argues, the rule of law to some extent corrupts these norms by establishing another set of rules to which parties may turn. In a complex society such as ours, where contact between people is often unsystematic and episodic, it may be impossible and undesirable to seek a legal system that reinstitutionalizes the bulk of the norms that are found in primary institutions. But it would be foolish to conclude that due process is a substitute for them. When law tends to destroy primary institutions, one important alternative is to use less law (see Schur, 1973).

Is it possible, however, to have a different type of legal order? Can the law be used to reduce inequalities between people? Can it help create the sense of community that we must envy in the Barotse? In the last part of the book we concentrate on such questions. We turn from narrower questions of legal engineering to larger questions of social engineering.

PART III

Distribution

The majestic equality of the French Law forbids both the rich and the poor from sleeping under the bridges of Paris.

Anatole France

In the first two parts of this book we have examined what might be called "micro" issues in the study of law and society; that is, issues that focus on the relationship of individuals to the legal system. We have looked at responsibility rules and dispute settlement techniques within the context of individual relationships and organizational constraints. We have discussed the possibility of altering legal rules and procedures to better meet individual needs within an existing social order. The final portion of this book is concerned with systemic issues; that is, with the use of law to influence, control, and at times alter the existing social order.

The law does not itself change things. It is a set of rules that actors may be entitled to draw on in order to achieve certain results. It may, as we have noted, be conceived of as a valuable resource (see also Turk, 1976, p. 276).[1] Its value lies largely in its socialist nature. Law is an instrument of the state and as such it is not only purchased collectively, but it also may have a special claim on the allegiance of the collectivity. Whoever can turn the law to his or her own ends benefits from the investments of others and from whatever general tendencies exist to respect the law for its own sake. Courts, for example, are supported largely by taxpayers rather than by litigants, and those who have the law on

---

1. As a resource, law is more like a raw material than a consumable good. It is useful in making other things. Typically, it is a means that can be used to secure some desired end. Occasionally, however, law is an end in itself because it affirms a moral position. Gusfield (1963) argues that the Eighteenth (prohibition) Amendment was such a law. Its main importance was in affirming traditional morality in a time of change. More commonly, laws that are means to ends also convey moral messages which make them to some extent ends in themselves.

279

their side are backed by a multimillion-dollar enforcement system for which they do not have to pay.

Like most valuable resources law is scarce. Law is not available in many situations, and where it is, its specific provisions are not preordained. Not surprisingly, disputes can arise over whether we should attempt by law to regulate certain areas of social life, and, if so, over what form that regulation should take. Since a legal rule will usually advantage some people at the expense of others,[2] struggles over these issues may be intense. Such struggles are usually played out in the legislature or in the appellate court.[3] In both arenas there are struggles over the existence and meaning of legal rules, although issues of existence are conventionally considered more within the province of the legislature and issues of meaning, especially meaning in the context of particular cases, are thought to be the special concern of the courts.

MEANS AND ENDS

When groups fight for or social scientists assess particular laws, two questions must be addressed. First, there is the question of *purpose*. Some end or ends must justify legal intervention, and it is fair to ask of any law what it seeks to achieve. The second question is one of *means*. If there is an end in view, it is fair to ask how can the law best be employed to achieve that objective. The questions of means and ends are complicated by the variety of ends that one may aim at through law and by the numerous ways that one may approach those ends. Some laws have no clear goal since they are the product of a coalition, each element of which seeks a different thing (Casper & Brereton, 1984). Some means may appear particularly ill-suited to stated ends since they are the product of compromises with groups that endorse the ends without being fully committed to them. Some ends are narrow and the means toward them are clear; for example, a developer may seek to change a zoning law to enhance the value of certain property. Other objectives involve the fundamental reorganization of society and the efficacy of particular means may be doubtful; for example, civil rights organizations may seek laws that mandate forms of ''reverse discrimination'' in order ultimately to eliminate racism from social life. Many laws, of course, fall

---

2. There are cases where everyone has a common interest and one rule best expresses that interest. In such instances the difficulties are those of coordination found in fully cooperative games. The rule that all should drive on the right is perhaps such a rule, although people with English-made cars might not like it. Substantive rules that do not differentially allocate values are unusual in the law.

3. Once a law is passed by a legislature or specified by an appellate court, the struggle may continue in less visible arenas such as the police station or trial courts. Here the issue is how the law is to be *in fact* applied. Obviously, what goes on in these arenas may subvert the goals of those who passed the laws in the first instance. However, in this portion of the book we shall not focus on behavior at this level except insofar as those who make law must and do take this behavior into account.

between our two examples with respect to both the magnitude of the changes sought and the likely efficacy of the legal intervention.

Sorting out these issues is rendered more difficult because there is a good deal of "misdirection" in the law. Some laws that are ostensibly aimed at one goal may in fact be aimed partly or entirely at another goal, and some laws that are honestly aimed at one end may in practice contribute to another outcome. Thus a federal law ostensibly designed to protect the American consumer by establishing minimum size and weight requirements for tomatoes sold in interstate commerce may in fact have been pushed by domestic tomato growers who ripen their crops with gas to eliminate competition from slightly smaller but better tasting vine-ripened Mexican tomatoes. And even if the legislators who passed such a law thought they were protecting the interests of tomato lovers, the effect of the law might be to cut imports, raise prices, and, on balance, hurt consumers.

Regardless of the situation, the questions of means and ends should be discussed together, for often the most effective way of using the law will depend on the ends it is designed to achieve. Martin Rein (1971) states this position well. In an article on policy analysis he says:

> My starting point is that it is not only sterile to pursue techniques of analysis divorced from issues of purpose, but it is also misleading because techniques arise to serve purposes and therefore imply value assumptions. But, if it is no good simply pursuing techniques, neither is it good just to debate issues of social values. . . . We must also look at *implementation outcomes*—how purposes and results relate to each other, what dilemmas and consequences arise from trying to implement a conception of social justice. . . . One of the central concerns in social policy is establishing priorities, or reconciling the goals of economic efficiency, freedom of choice, and equality when they conflict. (pp. 297–301)

In the next five chapters we examine both means and ends, techniques, and policy.[4] Our primary concern in this Part and the unifying theme of these chapters is the role of law in achieving social justice. In Chapter 9 we discuss several schemes of social justice: views of the overarching end toward which the law might be directed. We focus particularly on the perspective developed by John Rawls (1971) in his book, *A Theory of Justice*. Whether or not one accepts Rawls's theory, one must acknowledge the importance of this work. Many find Rawls's framework intuitively appealing and—what is more important to us—believe that one can draw from it implications for action in concrete factual situations.

Following Chapter 9 we occasionally draw on Rawls's model as a standard by which to compare alternative social systems. The reader should remain aware, however, that a different conception of social justice would provide a different

---

4. We should note that much of the best recent work in law and social science that has addressed these questions has done so at a less general level than the one at which we conduct most of our discussion; asking, for example, what types of enforcement regimes by regulatory agencies and courts are most likely to achieve the goals of pollution control. (Bardach & Kagan, 1982; Melnick, 1983; Scholz, 1984).

standard, and that applying a general theory of social justice to particular situations is almost always problematic. Ultimately, however, it is not important that we agree about the correctness of Rawls's theory or that his conception is the measure of justice in a particular circumstance. What matters is that we have a vehicle for discussing issues of justice and a standard of ends against which we can examine the means by which law is used to shape society.

Chapters 10 and 11 pursue this latter task by considering specific problems and the ways in which law has been employed to meet them. Chapter 10 looks at corporate groups, especially business corporations and labor unions. Such groups are essential to the achievement of important social objectives, but they have become sufficiently powerful that they may threaten aspects of social justice. Particularly interesting are the situations in which distributional objectives seem to clash with efficiency and formal law.

Chapter 11 reviews the effort to promote racial equality in the United States. It focuses on law as an independent variable and on the role that law can play in extending voting rights, desegregating schools, and promoting equal employment opportunity. It seeks to draw from this investigation some general lessons regarding law and social change.

Chapters 12 and 13 are pitched at a more abstract level. Chapter 12 explores the meaning of legal autonomy and discusses the possibility of autonomy in the law application process. After specifying what is meant by legal autonomy—a form of independence from society's other social, political, and ethical systems—it is argued that the autonomy of law is at best partial and most fully realizable in the law application process. The implications that autonomy in this sphere has for social change are briefly discussed.

Chapter 13 extends the analysis of Chapter 12 to consider the lawmaking process. Types of lawmaking are combined with styles of law application to yield eight ideal typical kinds of legal systems. The implications of each of these systems for the distribution of social power are examined. The chapter concludes by considering the degree to which those elements that Rawls identifies as the core constituents of social justice can, through law, be simultaneously realized. Conflicts that confront those who would use law to achieve an equal society are emphasized.

Chapter 14 concludes this invitation to law and social science by briefly discussing the main themes of this book and noting where the study of law and social science can lead us.

9

The Ends of Social Justice: John Rawls and the Distribution of Welfare

This chapter deals with the problem of social justice. It is, in important ways, unlike the other chapters in this book. Here there are few references to social science data or even to social science literature. Questions concerning what makes for social justice are largely normative and logical, not empirical and inductive. Answers are unlike most of the hypotheses we advance in this book in that they are not, even in principle, subject to empirical validation or disproof. Thus most of the material we cite and rely on is written by moral philosophers.

We turn to moral philosophy for several reasons. First, it brings systematic and critical thought to issues that are often left to intuition and implicit preferences. Thus it encourages us to think about the objectives law should aim for and it can help us to understand more clearly what objectives a set of rules will advance.[1] Second, as this body of knowledge makes clear, many of our most serious disagreements about rules are not disagreements about just versus unjust outcomes, but rather, are disputes over the priority of competing ends of social justice. Third, and most pragmatically, it is the moral philosophers who have given the most thought to issues that we believe any student of the legal system,

---

1. For example, there has been considerable controversy about the sense in which common law rules advance the objective of "efficiency," and whether the efficient allocation of risks was an objective of the common law. The rhetorical techniques of moral philosophy help to clarify such questions. Ronald Dworkin's "Is Wealth a Value" (1980) and the response by Richard Posner (1980) illustrate this point.

even one who approaches it as a social scientist, should consider. Finally, we occasionally wish to comment on the *justice* of some of the institutional arrangements and efforts at legal change in society that we examine in Chapters 10 and 11, and in Chapter 13 we want to be able to discuss the general question of how different types of legal systems relate to justice in society. These concerns require that reader and author share some reasonable, though not necessarily indisputable or mutually acceptable, conception of social justice to which we can refer from time to time. We believe that these diverse interests are best served not by a general canvass of what moral philosophers have said about justice but rather by attention to a single theory. Thus the central focus of this chapter is on John Rawls's *A Theory of Justice*.

JUSTICE AS RULES AND INSTITUTIONS

In his book Rawls (1971) is concerned not with justice in the "due process" sense, which is the justice one asks for when he says "Gimme a fair trial," but with "social" or "distributive" justice, which involves the just distribution of "goods"[2] in society. Distributive justice is what blacks ask for when they demand a "larger piece of the pie." It is what socialists seek when they argue that goods should be distributed equally or according to human needs. It is what the wealthy want when they argue that marginal tax rates above 50 percent are unfair. As these examples make clear there is no general agreement on what makes for a just distribution of goods.

The philosopher's task is to help clarify our thinking on this matter and, if possible, to persuade us that some distributions of goods or modes of distributing goods are morally more defensible than others. We have chosen to focus on Rawls's theory of justice not only because it is one of the most important statements of recent times, but also because the nature of his major arguments leads quite naturally to questions about the role of law in problems of distribution.[3]

---

2. We mean *goods* in the term's most general sense. It includes all distributable resources that can contribute to social welfare. This includes familiar goods such as food and furniture, but it also includes things such as medical care, access to educational opportunities, and even respect for persons.

3. A full discussion of Rawls's theory goes far beyond our present objectives. Much of Rawls's work is an argument for a *contract theory of distributive justice*, that is, a theory of distributive justice based on the concept of some initial agreement, which in Rawls's case is the agreement that he believes would have been reached if certain original conditions were met. Rawls compares his approach to a utilitarian theory of justice, governed by the concept of an omnipotent observer who allocates benefits according to the principle of the "greatest good for the greatest number." In the body of this chapter we will not present Rawls's argument for why the rational individual would choose his particular theory of justice. The interested reader should see the appendix to this chapter and Part One of Rawls's book.

Those who turn to Rawls's book will find that in addition to being profoundly stimulating it is a lengthy, complex and not altogether consistent work (see, e.g., Hart, 1973). When we refer to

Rawls (1971) argues that the principles of justice apply to and are defined by the basic structure of society. For this reason his theory is sometimes called a structural theory:

> This means, as we have seen, that the first distributive problem is the assignment of fundamental rights and duties and the regulation of social and economic inequalities and of the legitimate expectations founded on these. . . . The basic structure is a public system of rules defining a scheme of activities that leads men to act together so as to produce a greater sum of benefits and assigns to each certain recognized claims to a share in the proceeds. . . . In fact, the cumulative effect of social and economic legislation is to specify the basic structure. (pp. 84, 259)

Thus whatever else rules do, they also combine to produce a system on which social justice depends.

One might judge social institutions like the law by the outcomes they produce. Depending on one's preferences, one might say that a legal system is just if it results in the equal distribution of wealth in society, if it results in a distribution of wealth that reflects efforts expended or if it distributes wealth according to social rank. In each case one can in principle link individuals with the goods they possess and determine whether the pattern is just in the sense described. If it is just, then one may infer that the structure that produced the distribution is just.

Rawls takes a different tack. He argues that the starting point in the quest for a just social order is with the rules and procedures that shape the institutional order of a society and not with the pattern of outcomes that the institutional order produces. Rawls captures this idea in the concept of *pure procedural justice*. If the rules and institutions outline a just scheme for allocating welfare, the resulting pattern of outcomes is in this (procedural) sense just.

Rawls uses outcomes in games of chance to indicate the nature of pure procedural justice. If several people engage in a game of chance where there are a series of fair bets,[4] the distribution of cash after the last bet is fair as long as the procedure followed the rules of the game (e.g., no cheating, bets are voluntary, etc.). The fairness arises from the procedure itself. Thus, in this procedural sense, unequal distributions (we get lucky and win all of your money) may be fair.

Fairness is, of course, a slippery concept. It is hard to ignore substantive outcomes in deciding whether a distributive scheme is fair. If we lose all our money in Rawls's game of chance, we may characterize the outcome as unfair

---

"Rawlsian" ideas of justice later in this book we are referring to Rawls's essential ideas as we present them and not necessarily to refinements that a more detailed reading of his text might suggest. For our purpose, which is not to summarize Rawls's work for its own sake but to think about certain issues of justice both here and in subsequent chapters, treating Rawls in this way is sufficient. For further reflections by Rawls on his theory, which for our purposes we need not consider, see Rawls (1982).

4. A bet that will return N dollars for every dollar wagered is fair if the chance of winning N dollars is $1/N$.

even though we cannot specify a fairer way of proceeding.[5] Or we may change our attitude toward the game and conclude that its rules are in fact unfair. For example, we might agree with Piaget's children that something is wrong when one player gets all the marbles. What is wrong is not that someone cheated, but that the rules of the game permit one person to acquire everything. It is this latter sense of unfairness that is central to a structural theory of social justice. Outcomes may be justified on the basis of procedures, but the procedures must themselves be structured so that they allow only a tolerable range of outcomes.

Suppose, for example, that people are forced to gamble everything they have. Even if the bets are "fair," we may feel that forcing people into a game where they may lose everything is unfair. Or if people are allowed to play a lottery in which the winner is the one whose ticket is first drawn, we would probably find it unfair if one person was given ten tickets with which to enter while another person was given one hundred.

If we regard people's efforts to succeed in life as, in a sense, a contest, we may, for example, wish to establish institutions that do not allow winner-take-all outcomes and/or that equalize the initial positions of the players. Such institutions and their accompanying rules are, according to Rawls, the bases of social justice. If we can agree upon them, he argues, we can treat the outcomes they produce as just since the rules will themselves incorporate the basic criteria of justice. Thus our first task is to describe the basic criteria that the rules and institutions of social interchange should embody or take into account. Some such criteria directly limit the outcomes that are permitted, for we believe that certain outcomes, however arrived at, are unjust, and others establish basic rules for playing life's game. The latter admit of various outcomes, all of which we will regard as legitimate, or even desirable, if the basic rules have been complied with.

Individual liberty, the fair distribution of social welfare, and efficient transformations of the status quo[6] all have a claim to some place in a system of social

---

5. We must not, however, be misled into thinking that when we leave philosophy for the real world judgments of procedural or outcome fairness depend necessarily or entirely on the outcome one has received. The human ability to distinguish the two is most evident in trivial matters like games. Thus one who has been bankrupted in *Monopoly* is unlikely to think that either the game's rules or his defeat are unfair. This is true even if he has played the game, as occasionally happens, with real money. In an area of more interest to us, Tyler (1984) has shown that judgments of procedural fairness and outcome fairness by defendants in a traffic and misdemeanor court are not, for the most part, determined by the absolute level of the outcome they received, the actual outcome as it relates to the outcome they expected, or the actual outcome as it relates to the outcome that they thought others generally received for the same offense. Furthermore, the two procedural fairness judgments (considered as a bloc) are more closely related than the three measures of outcome level (considered as a bloc) to the defendant's expressed outcome satisfaction and to the defendant's evaluation of the judge and the court (p. 65).

6. Efficient transformations of the status quo are "Pareto optimal" in the same sense we used the term in Chapter 6: They make at least one person better off without making anyone worse off than she was prior to the change. When we are talking about Pareto efficient transformations in the context of social justice there is a difficulty in identifying efficient transformations that is generally

justice. Just rules and institutions should attend to each of them. The difficult problem is to determine what place each deserves. Should we sacrifice equal distributions of income for greater efficiency in the production of social and economic goods? Should we trade in some individual liberty for greater equality? Should we allow inequalities in individual liberty if they make for greater efficiency? Answers to such questions define particular schemes of social justice and to answer them is not just an abstract exercise, for they are the kinds of questions we answer all the time in our political life. For example, we answer the first question in the affirmative when we opt for tax cuts that disproportionately benefit corporations and the wealthy in order to stimulate the economy and generate lesser "trickle down" benefits that should aid the less well off. We arguably answer the second question in the affirmative when we establish preference systems that give education and job priorities to people who are identified with groups that in the past have been victimized by discrimination. And many thought we were answering the third question in the negative when we moved to abolish slavery.

Equal Liberty

The trade-offs that may exist between basic values pose a problem for those who would advance schemes of social justice since all seem to be important ingredients. Rawls's solution to this problem is what he calls a *lexical ordering* of the ingredients of justice. This means that one value is more important than another. In a contest between the two, the more important always prevails even if the choice is between a lot of the second and only a little of the first. A good example of lexical ordering in our society is the way we order the goods "freedom from torture" and "crime control." It is conceivable that a little torture of suspected underworld figures—perhaps some electric shock applied to sensitive areas or a few fingers hacked off—would yield substantial dividends in the war against crime, yet we do not allow the trade-off. The goods are lexically ordered and freedom from torture is ranked higher. We will not trade a little bit of torture for a lot of crime control.

---

ignored in welfare economics, the field from which the concept is taken. This is that increased social distance may itself be painful to those on the bottom or give rise to feelings of injustice. Thus, taking account of all social values, a change that advances the lot of the wealthy while leaving the poor no worse off or even slightly better off may not be Pareto efficient since despite the materially stable or even slightly improved situation of those on the bottom, the transformation may lead to a social situation in which they feel—and in this sense are—worse off.

Rawls in his book recognizes the possibility that transfers that are not Pareto efficient can enhance justice, for, as we shall see, those on the bottom in Rawls just society can make different claims from those on the top. Moreover, Rawls largely assumes away the problem we have just described, because except when material differences harm the self-respect of those on the bottom, he considers a preference for more equality rather than more goods to be a kind of "envy" that a theory of justice need not respect.

The first principle, or the most essential good according to Rawls, is liberty:

> Each person is to have an equal right to the most extensive total system of equal basic liberties compatible with a similar system of liberty for all. (1971, p. 302)

The first principle requires equality of liberty and the lexical ordering requires that basic liberty interests should not be sacrificed for other goods.[7] For example, Rawls's scheme does not allow slavery even if the transformation to a slave society would make everyone, including the slaves, materially better off.

The priority of liberty rests on the belief that in a just society liberty would be related intimately to self-respect and valued for its own sake. Although there may be societies where material conditions are so poor that one would trade liberty for food, as societies become better off and basic material needs are met, liberty becomes a relatively more important good. Rawls supports his argument with the claim that if one were describing the society in which he would wish to live without knowing what his position in that society would be, he would not allow institutions premised on the denial of liberty, such as slavery or apartheid, for fear that he would end up in the deprived class.

Liberty has many aspects. In general, Rawls argues, it can be explained by three referents: the agent who is free, the restrictions or limitations from which he is free, and what it is he is free to do or not do. Liberty also imposes on people the duty not to interfere with each other's exercise of liberty.

Basic liberties, Rawls argues, include freedom of conscience and the recognition of individual self-worth. Also fundamental is political liberty, which exists only in the context of institutional structures and public rules defining rights and duties. Central to political liberty is the right to help shape these institutions and rules. In more concrete terms, political liberty involves rights to vote, assemble, and speak.[8]

Equal liberty requires the equal right to participate effectively in the political process. These rights are guaranteed by formal rules, such as one person-one vote, and by rules that make formal equality meaningful. The latter are necessary because a fair distribution of political rights may be eroded by disparities in the distribution of property, wealth, or political power. Universal suffrage by itself is unlikely to ensure political equality. The president of General Motors and an assembly-line worker may both be allowed to vote only once in a given election, but the former is likely to have considerably more political power than the latter. Thus further steps, such as the public financing of political parties, may be appropriate in societies where there are great disparities in wealth.

---

7. Rawls's (1971) theory would, under certain circumstances, tolerate unequal liberty if these inequalities were to the advantage of those with less liberty or necessary for the eventual attainment of a society in which equal liberties can be fully enjoyed. But the advantage would, presumably, have to be in terms of liberty itself, not economic welfare (p. 250) except insofar as a minimal level of welfare is necessary to make liberty worthwhile (p. 225).

8. At one point where Rawls (1971) is more specific he includes as important liberty interests such goods as freedom of thought, freedom of the person, the right to hold (personal) property, and freedom from arbitrary arrest and seizure as defined by the concept of the rule of law (p. 61).

The arrangements needed to ensure political equality extend beyond the legal process narrowly defined. They involve constitutional processes and the ways that societies balance the interests of different groups. We shall discuss in subsequent chapters some of the issues that these concerns raise. Here we concentrate on two narrower issues that more directly relate to specific legal rules. First, there is the fact that each individual element of liberty must be considered within the context of a total system of liberty.[9] This is so because one person's actions often have consequences for others, and the freedom of one party to act may effectively restrict what another can do. This may be true as a sociological matter, or it may be written into law. If hunters frequent a local wood, bird watchers will feel less free to walk there. If the government sells a portion of a national park to a developer, the developer may be free to construct an amusement park, but backpackers will have lost some of their freedom to enjoy nature.

It is not surprising, then, that a person's freedom to act is generally contingent on what her actions imply for the similar rights of others. Law is fundamental here because it is through law that we attempt to reconcile the potentially conflicting liberty claims of individuals. Law not only specifies the bounds between one person's right to act and another's right not to be disturbed, but it also provides a sanctioning system that guarantees, though imperfectly, that these bounds will be respected.

Thus the basic freedom to go where one wishes is limited by the property rights of others and may be forfeited entirely by commission of a crime. The freedom to engage in certain potentially dangerous activities, like driving a car, may through the tort law be conditioned on the obligation to pay for any harm one causes. One can even condition his own future freedom of action by entering into a contract. If promises made therein are not performed, the law will either require their performance or grant the party whose expectations have been breached compensation for his damages.

These laws are all two-sided in their implications for our freedom. Property law prevents us from trespassing on the property of others, but it also allows us to keep uninvited others from using our property. Criminal law and tort law each make it costly to engage in certain behavior and so limit our propensity to do so, but each enhances our freedom by reducing the probability that others will invade our rights. Contract law, while allowing us to restrict our future behavior,

---

9. The discussion that follows is we think in the spirit of Rawls (1971) and reflects our reading of his argument. He writes, "The various liberties specify things that we may choose to do if we wish and in regard to which, when the nature of the liberty makes it appropriate, others have a duty not to interfere" (p. 239). Yet it is only *basic liberties* that are inviolate and must be distributed equally. The liberties that we discuss next may all be derivatives of such basic liberties as freedom of person and freedom of association, but it appears Rawls would allow extensive regulation when these liberties to do things clash with similar liberties of others. Indeed, he would allow restrictions on basic liberties when this is necessary for their enjoyment. Thus rules of order may restrict speech because in doing so they give value to the right to speak. What Rawls is unwilling to tolerate at this level is legal arbitrariness or vagueness that prevents people from knowing what they are free to do and so restricts their actions (p. 239).

also enhances our freedom by creating opportunities, the purchase of a house on a land contract, for example, that might not be available if we could not to some extent make ourselves unfree. Contract law also specifies certain kinds of contracts that are unenforceable and so limits our freedom to make ourselves unfree. In the United States, for instance, an agreement to sell oneself into slavery is not legally binding. Does the inability to enter into such contracts make us as a people freer or less free?

The law is full of trade-offs between actors who know or are presumed to know that certain behavior may be costly and amorphous groups whose liberty is presumably enhanced by rules that impose contingent costs on others. Yet we tend to see the liberty interest lying largely with those whose actions are constrained by government. These negative, Lockean rights to be left free from government regulation are certainly important, but within Rawls's theory they are not the full measure of popular freedom. Rawls's perspective also emphasizes the liberty interest of those whose actions would be constrained but for governmental limitations on the actions of others. Thus gun control is a restraint on the personal liberty of those who would carry guns. As such, it might not be justified if the only arguments for it were that it would reduce police expenditures and so free capital for more worthwhile investments. Welfare or efficiency interests cannot in Rawls's lexically ordered scheme "trump" liberty interests. However, if gun control worked, some people would feel freer to walk alone at night or work in liquor stores. Thus one can find liberty interests on both sides.

Rawls's first principle of justice speaks to the total system of liberties. We must view liberty systemically because, as our example indicates, the value of one liberty depends on the specification of other liberties. The freedom to walk where one wants will be affected by the freedom to hunt, and the freedom of speech may be worthless in a legislative chamber that lacks rules of order. One use of legal rules is to work out the interrelationship of specific liberties.

The second narrow issue that we wish to address here concerns the general function of law in establishing the fair and impartial administration of the rules that govern society. Rawls (1971) calls this "justice as regularity" (p. 235). Justice as regularity requires that there be no offense except those specified by law, that similar cases be treated similarly, that ought implies can (i.e., the law does not require people to do the impossible), and that some rational procedure (system of secondary rules) be followed to establish the truth (cf. Fuller 1964). A legal system that fails in these regards restricts liberty precisely because it fails to inform us as to what our rights and duties are.

> But if the precept of no crime without a law is violated, say by statutes being vague and imprecise, what we are at liberty to do is likewise vague and imprecise. The boundaries of our liberty are uncertain. And to the extent that this is so, liberty is restricted by a reasonable fear of its exercise. The same sort of consequences follow if similar cases are not treated similarly, if the judicial process lacks its essential integrity, if the law does not recognize impossibility of performance as a defense, and so on. (Rawls, 1971, p. 239)

This discussion highlights the importance of procedural rules and formal law generally. Liberty, and hence the just society as Rawls uses the term, requires rules that make legal obligations known and the legal implications of our actions predictable. Even though it might ultimately be determined that a vague but threatening law does not impinge on our liberty, it may have a "chilling effect." For example, people may be reluctant to engage in a protected activity, like giving speeches denouncing the government, for fear that they will overstep their rights and be punished. These principles are so important that they are often expressed in constitutional restrictions and requirements, but they also underlie ordinary statutes and the informal norms of our legal system. Thus the prohibition on *ex post facto* laws (laws that punish people for actions that were not crimes when they were done) is part of our Constitution. Rules of discovery that seek to enhance the rationality of the trial process by allowing litigants to know in advance the essence of their opponent's case, are statutory enactments of relatively recent vintage. The obligation that lower courts follow precedent, which is essential if similar cases are to be decided similarly, is nowhere written into the law, but it is a basic norm of the judicial role and can be enforced by higher courts on appeal from lower court decisions.

Social and Economic Goods

The society that successfully institutionalizes liberty as a first principle has taken an important step, but does not, in Rawls's scheme, thereby ensure justice. It must still confront problems posed by the distribution of social and economic goods.

In modern capitalist societies like the United States, goods tend to be allocated within the context of markets. The main advantage of using markets to determine allocations is their presumed efficiency.[10] Under certain ideal conditions a system of competitive markets ensures that the choices made by producers of goods and the distribution of the goods produced will be in a certain sense optimal. Specifically, there will be no possible rearrangement of the economic configuration that makes one household better off without making some other household worse off. Transfers that tend to bring this state about—which improve the lot of one household without making any other worse off—are said to be "Pareto optimal" or, in the language of welfare economics, "Pareto efficient."[11] Free markets are, as an ideal type, efficient because they tend

10. Rawls argues that there is no essential tie between the use of competitive markets and the private ownership of the instruments of production. This is true at least in the sense that socialist societies could use markets to allocate economic goods (see Bergson, 1967).
11. Some economists adopt a different criterion for efficiency, the Kaldor-Hicks or wealth maximization principle (Posner, 1983, pp. 91–94). A transaction is Kaldor-Hicks efficient if after a transaction the beneficiaries could compensate the losers for all their losses and still come out ahead. But compensation need not be paid to satisfy the Kaldor-Hicks criterion. It need only be hypothetically possible. When we use the word "efficiency" in this chapter, we use it in the sense of Pareto optimality.

toward this state of affairs. As Rawls (1971) notes, "Perfect competition is a perfect procedure with respect to efficiency" (p. 272).

If efficiency were the only criterion of distributive justice, marketplace transactions would yield pure procedural justice. Whatever the final distribution of goods after the market had played itself out, it would be fair in the sense that it would be the result of a series of exchanges, freely entered into, which advantaged one or more parties and left no party worse off than he was before the exchange. But, as with all ideal types, actual markets fall short of what they represent in important ways. First, marketplace competition is never perfect. Problems of monopoly power, high entrance barriers, inequality of information, and the like keep markets from being perfectly efficient allocators of goods.[12] Indeed, with regard to certain types of goods, commonly known as public goods, markets are not efficient at all.[13] Thus even with respect to efficiency, societies require institutions, like antitrust laws or pollution control laws, to make markets more efficient and to deal with situations where they are not efficient.

The second problem with allowing market outcomes to define social justice is even more fundamental. Efficiency is not for Rawls the sole criterion for justice in the allocation of economic and social goods, but the market does not attend to other criteria such as claims that might be made by those with special needs or the claim to some minimal standard of living that, in principle, might be made by anyone. The procedural justice response to such claims, "you made your choice; you were treated fairly; now live with the results," may not be acceptable when people's starting points are unequal. If one person enters the market with less wealth or less skill or less intelligence than another individual and we regard this as unjust, the resulting distributions will not be fair, even if the market is perfectly efficient. Efficiency, in short, is a criterion that does not

---

12. Perfect competition and hence the perfectly efficient market will not exist unless each seller and each buyer have no special control over price. In technical terms each must face a horizontal demand curve. Carson (1973, p. 493) lists the following additional conditions that are important to the existence of perfect competition: (1) Market prices must remain in the neighborhood of equilibrium values that balance supply and demand or price signals will not reflect either scarcity or demand. (2) Efficiency in consumption must prevail. Relative market prices must reflect relative marginal utilities or "consumption prices" for each consumer. Households must behave rationally; they should be neither fooled nor ignorant about either employment opportunities or the menu of consumer goods and saving outlets available. (3) Problems of external effects must be solved. That is, social and private costs and benefits must coincide or else decision makers will be guided by private rather than social indicators. (4) Labor and other factors of production must be fully utilized. If, for example, people are out of work who could easily add to the economy's income, the system is inefficient. (5) Problems connected with economies of scale and mass production must be dealt with effectively. Obviously, any actual market is inefficient to some degree.

13. A public or collective good is a good like street lighting which once produced is open to the enjoyment of all who wish to share in it whether or not they pay for it. We discuss collective goods in detail in Chapter 10. There we give a more precise definition and explain why when collective goods are involved markets are not efficient.

take account of initial starting points, and even if it did, we might be unwilling to accept certain outcomes as just.

What this means is that unless we are willing to take starting points as given (perhaps because we are unwilling to interfere with them on libertarian grounds) and accept any final distribution of economic goods (so long as it is an efficient and fair transformation of an initial distribution) as just, we need nonmarket institutions and rules affecting allocations.[14] Rawls's (1971) second principle of justice involves two such rules. The second principle is:

> Social and economic inequalities are to be arranged so that they are both: (a) To the greatest benefit of the least advantaged, . . .[15] and (b) Attached to offices and positions open to all under conditions of fair equality of opportunity. (p. 302)

Part (a) presents what Rawls calls the "difference principle." Inequalities to be justified must benefit the least well-off members of society. The difference principle is designed to restrict the full implications of the principle of efficiency while at the same time recognizing that everyone may benefit from arrangements that do not result in equally distributed rewards. For example, everyone benefits from having some people trained as doctors, even though society may be forced to invest more in training doctors than in the education of other individuals, and people may have to be paid more to work as doctors than to work at other occupations.[16] At some point, however, the situation will change and giving further advantages to doctors will not benefit the least well-off members of society and so will be unjust. An interesting implication of the medical example is that high salaries for doctors may be justified only if they are needed to secure medical treatment for the poor. Thus whatever other arguments one might make against

---

14. It is here that structural theories such as Rawls's contract theory and most utilitarian theories part company with libertarian theories, at least with respect to economic goods. In the most important recent statement of the libertarian position, Robert Nozick (1974) argues that social justice must take a historical rather than a structural view. If a social distribution is the result of a history of fair voluntary exchanges between individuals, then the outcome that is the product of these trades is itself just regardless of the final distribution of goods.

15. We have replaced Rawls's qualification, that the arrangements also be "consistent with the just savings principle" with ellipses because a discussion of the issue of just savings is unnecessary for our purposes. One area where the principle matters is in dealing with the very difficult problem of justice between generations (see Rawls, 1971, pp. 284–293; Smart, 1978). For example, as this is being written the federal government is running a deficit of one-half billion dollars a day. Whatever else might be said about this debt, it has significant implications for individuals who cannot presently participate in the political process, including, presumably, many who are not yet born.

16. The necessity of economic incentives to allocate abilities efficiently and encourage diligence is disputed in some quarters. Two notable recent attempts to substitute moral incentives and altruism for material incentives and self-interest have occurred in Cuba and China (Richman, 1971; Mesa-Lago, 1972). If altruism ruled and moral incentives sufficed, the difference principle would presumably argue for the equal allocation of goods. The difference principle also argues for the equal allocation of goods where the supply of social goods is constant and cannot be expanded by the special efforts of some.

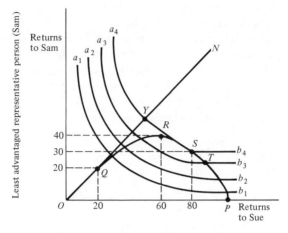

Figure 9.1 Welfare distributions in hypothetical societies.
(Adapted from Rawls, 1971, p. 77.)

medicare and medicaid, these programs are not objectionable because they tend to increase doctor's earnings relative to other members of the society.[17]

For those who find diagrams helpful, Figure 9.1 shows in graph form the nature of the restrictions placed on distributions by the difference principle. In Figure 9.1 the two axes represent the least advantaged and most advantaged representative persons whom we shall call Sam and Sue, respectively. The a—b lines concave to the origin (point O) are societal indifference curves, representing the aggregate welfare provided by particular distributions of goods in society. They indicate the total welfare of all the members of the society. The curves further from the axis represent greater total welfare. The numbers represent units of goods.

The ON line is at 45° to the axis, and represents an equal distribution of welfare expectation between Sam and Sue. In a society that is at this point, the best-off and worst-off person will fare the same, or, in other words, have the same amount of goods. They will, of course, prefer point Y to any other point on line ON, for at this point their society has the most goods to distribute and they are each better off than if they are on an interior curve.

---

17. This illustrates how a philosophical position may have implications for a practical problem. Of course, if one does not accept the difference principle as capturing something essential about justice, nothing follows. The medical example could also be pursued to raise questions about the difference principle. Suppose there is a disease—let us call it gout—that afflicts only the better off members of society. It is difficult to see why gout sufferers should not be allowed to make a transaction—trading wealth for health—even if this will increase the gap between the medical services received by the best off and those received by the worst off, who do not suffer gout. Rawls attempts to sidestep the difficulty of such examples by arguing that the difference principle is intended to apply to the general structure of the whole society but not to each individual situation.

Suppose, however, that the distribution of goods in Sam and Sue's society is unequal and that their well-being is in some way linked. This situation is portrayed by line *OP* which specifies the goods that Sam will receive when Sue is enjoying various levels of benefits. We see from this line that Sam can benefit by Sue's becoming better off, just as Sam, who is sure to get sick, might be better off if Sue had been promised higher wages than he in order to induce her to become a doctor.

Consider three points we have identified along the *OP* line, points *Q*, *R*, and *S*. Point *Q* is the highest point before inequalities arise. The parties could not be better off and still receive identical returns. There are 40 units of welfare to be distributed in this society and Sam and Sue each get 20. A society that made equal welfare its only principle would presumably stop here. But it is very likely that everyone could do better if some inequalities in wealth and power were allowed.

Point *S* describes the point of greatest social welfare. Here the society as a whole is as well off as it can be. The *OP* line is tangent to the highest welfare curve. This is the point that classical utilitarianism would choose—the greatest good for the greatest number.[18] There are 110 units of welfare to be distributed in this society. Sam gets 30 and Sue gets 80.

Point *R* is the point chosen by the difference principle. Here the welfare of the least-advantaged representative person is at its highest point. Although there are only 100 units of welfare to be distributed, Sam gets 40. Further benefits to Sue, even those that do not harm Sam and increase the total societal welfare, are not allowed because inequality itself is undesirable and should be minimized except where minimization will hurt those who are least well off.

The contrast with the Pareto optimal criterion is striking. Transactions that are Pareto efficient in the sense that they help some people and hurt no one are not allowed if they do not help the least-advantaged members of society. Conversely, transactions that are not Pareto efficient because they hurt some people and decrease total social welfare are allowed if they aid the lot of those who are worst off. Many people find the case for preferring the difference principle to the Pareto optimal criterion far from compelling, and for this reason among others the difference principle is perhaps the single most controversial part of Rawls's theory.[19] It has been objected to by libertarians (Nozick, 1974), utili-

---

18. The utilitarian would not wish to move further out on the *OP* curve, for it would reduce total welfare. The gains to the most advantaged would be more than offset by losses to the less advantaged. A libertarian position would presumably allow such a move if it were the result of a set of voluntary exchanges, but most libertarians would properly argue that at least in an economic sense a movement from *S* to *T* is not a likely outcome of voluntary exchanges.

19. The difference principle also allows almost unlimited inequality. A huge gain for the best off is tolerable so long as there is a small gain for the worst off. The only formal limitations on the disparity that Rawls (1971) posits are that (1) the worst off are entitled to the minimal subsistence level needed to make the equal liberties they enjoy worthwhile and (2) disparities cannot grow beyond the point where those on the bottom may reasonably claim that their basic human dignity is being eroded. One may, however, plausibly argue that despite the great room for inequality that

TABLE 9.1
Interpretations of Rawl's Second Principle

Nature of equal opportunity	*Measure of "everyone's advantage"*	
	Principle of efficiency	*Difference principle*
Equality as careers open to talents	Natural liberty	Natural aristocracy
Equality as equality of fair opportunity	Liberal equality	Democratic equality

Source: Adapted from Rawls (1971, p. 65).

tarians (Harsanyi, 1975), and socialists (Nielsen, 1978). In the appendix to this chapter we discuss Rawls's justification for the difference principle and some objections to it.

The second part of the second principle of justice defines the conditions under which individuals should be allowed to compete for advantaged positions in the society. To help answer the basic question of how positions are to be allocated where there is a substantial division of labor, Rawls presents a table (Table 9.1).

We have already dealt with the column headings that distinguish the difference principle from the principle of efficiency. Now we shall consider two possible meanings of equal opportunity. One is that careers are open to talents, which means that socially desirable positions will be awarded to those who can best fill them, and everyone has a right to be considered. It is this kind of equality that Cinderella's stepsisters sought to thwart when they prevented Cinderella from going to Prince Charming's ball even though the Prince's invitation had been addressed to all maidens living in the kingdom.

To require that careers be open to all and be filled on the basis of talent does not, however, correct for differential access to those abilities that a society recognizes as job relevant. Thus where equality is defined in terms of careers open to talents, social and biological factors, such as family wealth and high intelligence, as well as the effects of accident and good fortune, are allowed full play. This can make the promise of equal access to desirable positions a mere chimera for some. One would, for example, have to believe in fairy tales to think that the Prince would have asked Cinderella to dance had she come to the ball in an oxcart and been wearing a threadbare gown.

The equality of careers open to talents is not, however, meaningless. Many talented members of disadvantaged groups have suffered from its absence. Until the last decade, for example, women law students who graduated near the top of their class could not hope to get the kind of law firm positions that lower-

---

the difference principle in theory allows, societies that follow the difference principle would over time tend to relatively low levels of inequality. This is in part because the difference principle argues for the abolition of inequalities that do not aid the worst off and requires the abolition of inequalities that hurt the worst off (p. 79). Thus if lowering the salaries of the best off would make goods more cheaply available to the worst off, in the just society this should occur.

ranked males would routinely acquire. Now that legal jobs are more or less open to people on the basis of their talents, many of the most prestigious judicial clerkships and most sought-after law firm associateships are going to women.

The equal right to compete for positions combined with the principle of efficiency describes for Rawls a system of natural liberty. Everybody gets to race and the winner is the one who runs to the lead. But the contestants start at different points, with some receiving special boosts along the way. This is permissible so long as the advantages are not given by the race officials; that is, by those who determine the rules of the game, or to leave the realm of metaphor, the state. Natural liberty prevails where social institutions are such that those who are most gifted, or perhaps most fortunate, achieve the most rewarded positions. But the successful often owe their achievement in part to initial advantages in talent, family status, wealth, or other unachieved attributes. One never asks in a system where equality is defined in terms of the openness of careers to talent whether initial advantages are deserved. Nor is there any concern for the talents the less successful might have developed had they started with the advantages of their more fortunate counterparts.

The liberal interpretation of "equally open" is essentially an attempt to handicap the race. Positions should be open not only in the formal sense that all have a legal right to compete, but also in a real sense that each should have a *fair opportunity* to attain them. When combined with the principle of efficiency this describes what Rawls calls "liberal equality." When combined with the difference principle it defines what he calls "democratic equality."

We cannot understand either of these concepts unless we know what constitutes a fair opportunity to obtain a particular position. This is not a simple issue. It appears, however, that at a minimum fair opportunity requires the mitigation of disparities attributable to initial differences in social class. Thus Rawls (1971) argues:

> Chances to acquire cultural knowledge and skills should not depend upon one's class position, and so the school system, whether public or private, should be designed to even out class barriers. (p. 73)

In other words, Cinderella's fairy godmother, although the classic tale does not report this, properly included a few dance lessons and some information about royal chitchat when she waived her magic wand. But how much more should fair opportunity require? Should it attempt to even out ability and aspiration, or, as seems more in tune with Rawls's thinking, should it use these natural distributions to achieve maximum efficiency within the constraints of equal liberty and the difference principle?[20] It is also unclear what the mitigation

---

20. Rawls notes that when combined with the difference principle, the idea of careers open to talents describes a natural aristocracy governed by the idea of *noblesse oblige*. Rawls cites George Santayana for this view of the justice of an aristocracy. In *Reason and Society* Santayana says: "an aristocratic regimen can only be justified by radiating benefit and by proving that were less given to those above, less would be obtained by those beneath them" (Rawls, 1971, p. 874, n. 12) Since we are not concerned with this possibility, we do not discuss it in the text.

of class differences requires. If a society does not succeed in the first 12 years of education to obliterate the connections between social class and cultural knowledge, should it attend to social class when admitting people to college in order to eliminate one consequence of its failure to equalize initial advantages? We are not sure what Rawls's argument implies. As we noted at the outset of this chapter, it is difficult to move from a general, formal theory to specific applications.

THE NATURE OF APPROPRIATE INSTITUTIONS

At the level of formal theory the difference principle and the idea of equality of fair opportunity together define basic concepts on which social institutions and rules should be premised if we are to obtain what Rawls would see as a just society. The only essential constraint on our efforts in this direction is that they be consistent with the lexically prior requirement of liberty.[21] A set of institutions and rules that couples the difference principle with fair opportunity will arguably produce the circumstances for a just allocation of social goods. Indeed, one may argue that the outcomes produced by the workings of such rules and institutions are, more or less, the embodiment of justice.

In Part II of his book Rawls discusses the nature of the appropriate background institutions. The following passage captures what Rawls (1971) sees as essential:

> First of all, I assume that the basic structure is regulated by a just constitution that secures the liberties of equal citizenship. . . . Liberty of conscience and freedom of thought are taken for granted, and the fair value of political liberty is maintained. The political process is conducted, as far as circumstances permit, as a just procedure for choosing between governments and for enacting just legislation. I assume also that there is fair (as opposed to formal) equality of opportunity. This means that in addition to maintaining the usual kinds of social overhead capital, the government tries to insure equal chances of education and culture for persons similarly endowed and motivated either by subsidizing private schools or by establishing a public school system. It also enforces and underwrites equality of opportunity in economic activities and in the free choice of occupation. This is achieved by policing the conduct of firms and private associations and by preventing the establishment of monopolistic restrictions and barriers to the more desirable positions. Finally, the government guarantees a social minimum either by family allowances and special payments for

---

21. Fair equality of opportunity is itself lexically prior to the difference principle. Any inequality of opportunity must enhance the opportunities of those with lesser opportunities. Thus one group of citizens cannot deny a worse off group fair access to jobs by arguing that if the society is not forced to invest in fair opportunity there will be a surplus to distribute to the disadvantaged which will make them better off economically than they would have been had fair opportunity been guaranteed. One may argue for this lexical ordering from a long run perspective on the situation of the disadvantaged and from the close relationship between fair opportunity and the good of self-respect.

sickness and employment, or more systematically by such devices as a graded income supplement (a so-called negative income tax). (p. 275)

One could write an entire book as a footnote to this paragraph. We do not propose to do that, but we shall address three issues Rawls's perspective raises as we examine two distributional problems in the following chapters.

The first, and perhaps the central jurisprudential issue that concerns us, is the relationship of laws and the institutions they create to the principles of justice. This requires some analysis of the circumstances giving rise to particular laws and an appreciation of what the laws are intended to accomplish. The second involves the effectiveness of legal rules in achieving their objectives. Rules that promote the ends of social justice must be more than statements of good intentions. We shall examine situations in which laws have offered little more than unfulfilled promises and situations where they have had an obvious impact. The third issue relates to the problems that arise when we must choose between competing precepts of justice. One of our main arguments in the remaining chapters is that the compromises that must be made when we attempt to redistribute goods through law are often compromises between values that are themselves elements of social justice. Thus we look at situations where there are legitimate competing claims of justice and discuss how rules can compromise such claims.

We address these issues first, not in the abstract but within the context of two specific problems: the problem of corporate organizations and the problem of racial inequality. Chapter 10 treats the former problem and Chapter 11 the latter. Both are important problems in our society, and both are areas where the law can significantly affect the distribution of liberty and of social and economic goods. In Chapters 12 and 13 we return to a more abstract level of analysis to address the general questions of the relationship between the legal and the social orders and the ability of law to act as an effective instrument of social justice.

Appendix: The Contract Theory Perspective and the Decision Rule in Uncertainty

This appendix is for those who wish to know more about how Rawls justifies the positions he takes.

John Rawls's theory is basically a "contractarian" theory of justice, with its intellectual roots in Kant and Rousseau. This type of theory is to be distinguished from other theories of just distribution, especially the various utilitarian theories. Indeed, Rawls's work is in part a reaction to what he perceives to be the predominance of utilitarian thinking in informing our ideas of justice. In turn, Rawls's theory has been criticized by philosophers who take a libertarian position. This appendix will briefly discuss these three approaches to defining a just distribution in society.

Rawls (1971) has called his theory "justice as fairness" not because he equates justice with fairness, but to convey the idea that the principles of justice are to be worked out a priori by a group of people in a situation that is fair (pp. 12–13). Now demanding that justice be fair in this way—that is, that it conform to what rational persons would agree to in an initially fair situation—is only a starting place. By itself it gives no content to the concept of justice. It does, however, suggest a procedure for exploring the idea. It is this procedure or point of view that as much as anything distinguishes contractual theories from most utilitarian and libertarian ones.

Classical utilitarianism does not use the contracting party or the idea of an initially fair position as a frame of reference to develop a concept of justice. The utilitarian position, according to Rawls, takes the point of view of the impartial sympathetic observer, a creature who is outside of and above the society (Secs. 3, 4, 5, 30).

Rawls (1971) is particularly concerned with working out the implications of utilitarian and contractarian points of view. He makes two central points. The first is that the impartial sympathetic spectator of classical utilitarianism applies the principle of rational individual choice as a principle of social choice as well (p. 187). The second is that the contractarian view is to be developed from an initial position where the parties are situated behind a "veil of ignorance":

> They do not know how the various alternatives [possible in an actual society] will affect their own particular case and they are obliged to evaluate principles solely on the basis of general considerations. (pp. 136–137)

This latter point distinguishes contract theory from forms of utilitarianism (average utilitarianism) that are not contingent on an initial position of the impartial spectator (pp. 161ff). We shall briefly address these two points.

Rawls argues that a serious shortcoming of classical utilitarianism is that it takes the principle of rational choice as it applies to individual decision making and bases on it a measurement of social (distributive) justice. "Utilitarianism does not take seriously the distinction between persons" (p. 27). A crude example serves to make the point. Suppose that a two-armed person falls in love with someone from a planet of one-armed people. Two-arms may reasonably weigh the costs and benefits of his dilemma. He cannot woo his beloved as long as he suffers from the deformity of two arms, yet to him the arm has value. Is the benefit of the arm worth the cost of unrequited love? Perhaps not. In that case he should give his right arm for her! A rational, utilitarian decision. He has measured the utility of different outcomes and chosen.

Now suppose he decides love is not worth an arm. What should he do if he knows that this decision will cause his intended, who but for his second arm would love him intensely, to suffer more pain than he will suffer by cutting off an arm? He, of course, may wish to take this into account. He may decide to be altruistic and on the basis of her desires give up his arm. We would generally argue, however, that this is his choice, not hers. If he chooses to keep his arm, he is not acting unjustly. And it is not her right to say, "Give up your arm so that I may be happy."

Yet, Rawls argues, this may be the position of the impartial, sympathetic spectator who determines what is just in accordance with classical utilitarian theory. The observer sums costs and benefits across both persons. If, given the honest feelings of both parties, joint happiness would be greatest if the man cuts off his arm, the demand that the man sever his arm is justified by this utilitarian test. Thus principles of individual rational choice become principles of social justice. The assumption is that society is an entity that can and should disregard the suffering of one part of the body politic if the value to the whole is increased.

In his critique of this version of utilitarianism Rawls would be joined by libertarians, but they would add that he also is too willing to allow the rights of one person to be sacrificed for the well-being of another person. If utilitarianism is typically a system created from the position of the sympathetic spectator and Rawlsian contract theory is a system created by the agreement of a group of actors who do not know what their social roles will be, modern libertarian theory, as exemplified by the work of Robert Nozick (1974), is best described as a system that begins by imagining how individuals would want to live in a Hobbes-like state of nature before the emergence of society. People in such a situation, it is argued, have certain rights that act as "side constraints" on the action of others, including the state. Especially, they are entitled to the wealth that they gain by work or voluntary exchanges, and they cannot legitimately be taxed solely to redistribute economic goods as might be required by the difference principle. Thus libertarians would, with Rawls, object to the limitation of our hero's *liberty* that would occur if he were required to forfeit an arm, and they would go further and object to any taking of his property for the purpose of increasing someone else's well-being (Nozick, 1974).[1]

As the preceding comments should make clear, debates concerning what acts or laws are just often flounder because of fundamental differences about how to select principles of justice. One paradigm will generate principles that are very different from those generated by another paradigm, and there is likely

---

1. See *City of Dallas* v. *Mitchell*, 245 S.W. 944 (1922) where Judge Sergeant struck down a zoning law with the following language:

> The rights of the individual are not derived from governmental agencies, either municipal, state or federal, or even from the Constitution. They exist inherently in every man, by endowment of the Creator, and are merely reaffirmed in the Constitution, and restricted only to the extent that they have been voluntarily surrendered by the citizenship to the agencies of government. . . . The Constitution but states again these rights already existing, and when legislative encroachment by the nation, state or municipality invade these original and permanent rights, it is the duty of the courts to so declare, and to afford the necessary relief. [245 S.W. 944, 945–946 (1922)]

to be no generally accepted way to choose between them. A strength of Rawls's theory is its detailed concern with the procedure for the selection of principles and its recognition of the importance of a point of view in this process.

Some people will part company with Rawls at the start, preferring to begin their quest to determine what is socially just from some starting position other than a hypothetical contract between egoists which is where Rawls commences. Those who do not reject this position must confront the problem of specifying the circumstances under which the contracting parties will bargain. If, for example, the parties know what positions they will occupy in the society whose rules they are constructing, this knowledge will certainly influence what they will agree to. A person who knows that he will be a wealthy slaveholder if the society he enters allows slavery is more likely to agree to allow the institution (of slavery) than an individual expecting to be a slave. Similarly, someone who knows he is going to be a murderer would, no doubt, oppose the institution of capital punishment even if it had a deterrent effect.

Thus the kind of agreement that would be generated by egoists who know or think they know their likely place in society would be an accommodation of mutually conflicting interests that reflected relative bargaining strength which we would have no special reason to believe just. Rawls deals with this difficulty by specifying that the basic social rules must be agreed to from behind a *veil of ignorance*. This means that one must choose the arrangements for his ideal society without knowing the position he will occupy in that society or what his own personal preferences or "taste for risk" will be. Rawls (1971) argues that in this situation no one would contract for a society whose social arrangements are such that some positions in it are unacceptable (pp. 26–30). To pursue our earlier suggestion, one might agree to a society that contained wealthy masters and impoverished slaves if he knew he was going to be a master but, Rawls would argue, one would not agree to allow slavery if he did not know whether he would be a master or a slave.

The situation behind the veil of ignorance leads to a key distinction between Rawls's theory and most ethical theories in the utilitarian tradition. In the latter the central ethical choice is that of the rational, risk neutral individual who seeks to maximize average or overall welfare (p. 189). Rawls argues that for one choosing from behind the veil of ignorance the rational strategy is not to maximize the average level of welfare in society. Instead, it is a *maximum minimorum* or *maximin* strategy. The individual should choose so as to maximize his minimum payoff. This, reasons Rawls, is a plausible decision rule when: (1) a person has no idea of his chances of acquiring a particular position in the society he will be entering or even what the distribution of positions in the society will look like; (2) the individual cares little for what he might gain above the minimum level of satisfactions that is guaranteed by the maximin strategy; and (3) other societies with greater possible advantage that the individual might agree to enter carry the risk that he may find himself in an intolerable position. It is out of the maximin strategy that the difference principle is born.

TABLE 9.2
Anticipated Payoffs in Different Societies

Chosen Society	Circumstance		
	C_1	C_2	C_3
S_1	-7	8	23
S_2	-6	7	14
S_3	5	6	8
S_4	3	3	3

Rawls (1971) produces a payoff matrix like that in Table 9.2 to illustrate the application of the maximin rule (p. 153). (We have slightly altered the payoffs he presents and added the S_4 decision.)

The individual behind the veil of ignorance may choose society S_1, S_2, S_3, or S_4. She does not know what her circumstances will be in that society. It could be C_1 or C_2 or C_3. The maximin rule leads the individual to select S_3 where the worst that might occur is a payoff of 5. The argument for the difference principle emerges from the maximin decision rule. If an individual follows this rule, she would always choose the society in which the worst off do the best relative to the other available societies and would seek rules that would allow people to improve their lot only if the least well off were thereby advantaged. This is because once the veil is lifted the person who has agreed to live in the chosen society may find that she has been assigned the position of the least well off. Thus, according to Rawls's analysis, a person behind the veil should prefer a relatively poorer society with no abysmally poor people to a much richer society with a few abysmally poor people. This guarantees that she will avoid a life of abysmal poverty. Rawls thinks that people would prefer to forego the chance of a better life in order to avoid the risk of an intolerably poor position.

The argument for this maximin decision rule is seen by many as a fundamental weakness in Rawls's theory of justice (see, e.g., Arrow, 1973; Barry, 1973; Musgrave, 1974). The critics argue that people behind the veil of ignorance would not necessarily choose such a rule. Harsanyi (1975), for example, has argued for maximizing expected utility as the most appropriate choice in this circumstance. Certainly there is nothing logically irrational about the willingness to risk almost everything for the possibility of a very good life.

From another point of view, since the least-advantaged apparently include those individuals who are worse off because they are lazy and prefer not to work (Rawls, 1971, pp. 310–312), some have criticized the difference principle for failing to consider individual desert in the allocation of goods in the society. Why, they ask, should the lazy be entitled to the substantial standard of living implied by the difference principle, and, perhaps more tellingly from Rawls's perspective, why would people behind a veil of ignorance agree to a basic structure that is so generous to the nonproductive? Lessnoff (1978) proposes an addendum to the difference principle, allowing economic inequalities "either when to the advantage of the less well off; or when it is deserved (where advantage is due to harder work, for example)" (pp. 147–148).

Rawls's argument for the maximin rule appears to be based on a general assumption that people are risk adverse and on a theory of social envy, which suggests that great inequality can produce strains that are difficult for a stable society to endure.[2]

Arguments for other possible decision rules that might be adopted from behind the veil imply different theories of human preferences and social well-being. First, there is a straightforward optimistic rule. This might be adopted if, rather than maximizing the worst one might do (maximin), people generally try to maximize the best they can do (maximax). Such a decision rule would lead to choice S_1 in Table 9.2. If a person should find herself in circumstance C_3, her payoff would be substantially greater than it could be under any other arrangement.

Alternatively, one might choose the situation that produced the minimum variation in outcome (minirange). This leads to choice S_4. Those who believe strongly in equality might make this choice. Some would argue that to select strict equality is necessarily to prefer a poor society where everyone is "in the same boat" to a wealthier society where no one is as badly off but some are much better off than others. The payoff matrix in Table 9.2 reflects such an assumption. Others, however, would argue that the assumption is wrong and that most people would be better off in a strictly equal society than in one where inequalities abound. It is also possible for people to qualify their choice such that they prefer equality provided that everyone obtains a certain minimum standard of living, but they will choose inequality if that is the only way to guarantee that no one falls below the minimum level. The problem may be a real one in deciding between socialist and capitalist economies.

Next, a person might choose a minimum regret decision rule. Regret comes from observing that if one had only known how things would turn out she could have chosen better. For instance, if a person selects S_1 and the world turns out to have placed her in circumstance C_1, she might say, "had I only known I would have chosen S_3" (and got a payoff of 5). (The difference between -7 and 5 is 12.) If she finds herself in circumstance C_2, the person has made the best possible choice in receiving a payoff of 8, and so has no regret. The situation is similar if circumstance C_3 prevails. Thus the maximum regret the person could suffer from choosing S_1 is 12. Likewise, maximum regret from choice S_2 is 11,

---

2. At the beginning of this chapter we noted that questions of social justice are largely normative and logical—not empirical; largely, but not entirely. The question of envy and its role in disrupting the social order is an ancient one. Plato speaks of the "noble lie" designed to keep the people quiet so that they would not feel envy of privilege. Yet the discussion of the role of envy remains largely a matter of speculation and intuition. Social science research on this point would assist the philosophical debate about just distribution. This, however, is not the place for a discussion of social envy or the merits of the maximin rule (see Cook & Hegtvedt, 1983).

from S_3 is 15, and from S_4 is 20. Therefore, the minimum regret rule argues for decision S_2. If social envy contributed to social instability, and if it were a function not of how distant one was from the best off in society but of how distant one was from where she would have been in a subjectively better society, this apparently implausible choice might make some sense.

Finally, there is the expected utility model. Knowing nothing about where one will end up, a person may wish to treat the alternatives as equally likely and choose the society which has on the average the highest expected utility. Average expected utility is determined by summing the payoffs in each possible circumstance for each society and dividing the total by the number of possible circumstances. Choosing the society with the highest average score leads to the selection of S_1. With welfare distributed as it is in S_1, the average return to a member is 8 units. This compares to an average return of 5 units to one who chooses S_2 in order to minimize her maximum regret, an average of 6.3 units to one who selects S_3 to minimize the worst that can happen, and an average of 3 units to one whose taste for equality is so strong as to lead her to choose S_4.

A decision for S_2 seems like a rather odd choice since the decision maker must assume that once the veil is lifted, she will engage in "might have beens" that can do her no good. The other rules, however, pose value conflicts that have no obvious solutions. The choice between S_1 and S_3 depends on whether one is willing to risk the possibility of a very unpleasant outcome for the chance of a very attractive existence, and the choice between either of these rules and S_4 depends on whether one prefers a purely distributive value—equality—to a more attractive material existence. But if the choice is indeterminate and hence difficult, it is also consequential. If the maximin decision rule is not selected, the derived principles of justice may vary substantially from those proposed by Rawls and explicated by us in the text of Chapter 9 (cf. Lave & March, 1975).

10

Corporate Actors and Social Justice: Business Corporations, Labor Unions, and the Problems of Collective Action

One feature that John Rawls's theory shares with utilitarian and libertarian theories of social justice is that value resides in the individual. It is with the happiness, welfare, and freedom of individuals that we are ultimately concerned. People are not, however, the only actors on the social scene. Organizations also act and, indeed, for some purposes are treated by the law as persons. Although they cannot vote, they can own property; they pay taxes, and they may be entitled to broadcast their political views. This chapter focuses on the difficulties and advantages of collective action and on two of the most important and powerful organizational actors in modern society: business corporations and labor unions. We seek through an understanding of collective action to understand these organizational forms, the reasons they were established, and what their activities imply for the welfare and liberty of individuals. We also discuss the role that law has played in facilitating these organizational forms and controlling their behavior.

Our discussion begins by briefly noting the ubiquity and importance of organizations. We then consider problems of collective action. We shall see that organization on a large scale is often difficult to achieve. It is particularly problematic when the rewards an organization offers cannot be easily distributed according to member involvement. To explain why this is so, we examine two barriers to collective action. The first consists of the transaction costs that efforts to organize for collective action entail. The second concerns the *free rider problem* that exists when *collective goods*, that is, goods that must be made available to every member of a group if they are made available to any, are sought. We discuss the free rider problem and the nature of collective goods in detail because one must understand these matters to understand the trade union movement and to appreciate the threat that organizations may pose to individual liberty and other unorganized interests. The discussion is also important because law itself is ordinarily a collective good. Thus in explaining collective goods, we are incidentally illuminating a significant aspect of law and the law-making process.

Next, we examine the rise of big business enterprises and modern trade unions. Growth in each sector meant that various barriers to collective action had to be faced and surmounted. The law in each case was fundamental since the barriers stemmed in part from preexisting legal rules and growth was stimulated by new legal rules that dissolved both legal and nonlegal barriers to collective action. For business, the key development was the invention of the modern corporation, which together with share markets allowed vast stocks of capital to be accumulated as the ownership of businesses was divided into many parts and separated from day-to-day managerial responsibility. For trade unions, what was crucial was legislation that constrained the ways businesses resisted unionization and assured workers that if a majority of them supported the union every worker would have to contribute to the cause.

Finally, we explore the implications of organizational power for various ends of social justice. We argue that both business corporations and trade unions threaten values at the core of the scheme of social justice that we sketched in Chapter 9.[1] They may, however, also be part of the solution to the problems they pose. Competition among businesses is, for example, the best way to prevent production decisions that are not only inefficient but also transfer welfare from consumers to corporate interests. A labor union may enhance its members' liberty interests and promote workplace equality.

Ultimately, however, both unions and business corporations pose threats to justice that only the government seems well situated to control. There is, however, a serious difficulty: Organizations are themselves political actors. Organized interests have always been politically potent, and recent legal changes have

---

1. Recall that we are employing Rawls's scheme as the measure of social justice. Corporate actors might behave so as to be entirely consistent with some schemes of justice (e.g., might makes right) and might pose different problems for defensible non-Rawlsian schemes (e.g., libertarianism). Under Rawls's scheme threats to justice are posed by actions that tend to diminish liberty, especially basic liberties, and to increase the relative distance between the best and the worst off by denying fair equality of opportunity or by advancing the situation of the more advantaged without helping those who are less advantaged.

enhanced the ability of organizations, especially businesses, to directly influence the political process. For individuals to reassert rights that are diluted or negated by corporate power, formidable barriers to collective action must be surmounted, and that preeminent collective good, law, must be employed. In the political arena as in so many others, problems posed by collectivities require collective solutions.

ORGANIZATIONS

Most of us spend much of our lives involved with other people. We constantly interact with each other at home, at work, at school, in church, at play. In these situations and others we engage in what may loosely be called *collective action*; we act with others to achieve common objectives. Collective action usually occurs within the structure of some organization. Social life is organized around institutions such as the family, the workplace, the school or university, the church or synagogue, and even the tennis club. When we think of such institutions we tend to think in personal terms—my family, our church, *the* club. We seldom reflect on the fact that each of these institutions is likely to be recognized to some extent by law, and many have distinct legal identities.

Some organizations, such as the family, have a limited legal existence that is easily altered and does not extend far beyond the current living members. The nuclear family is changed fundamentally in the eyes of the law when a divorce occurs and, perhaps less obviously, when children reach the age of maturity. Other organizations have a legal life that is distinct from their current membership. They exist apart from any individuals. We can think of such organizations as "corporate actors." By corporate actors we mean legally recognized entities that have some of the capacities of "persons" in the eyes of the law. This means, for example, that they can enter into contracts, own property, sue, be sued, and the like. Such persons include the business corporation, the labor union, professional associations, and other bodies. Some, like certain professional associations and private charities, begin as voluntary associations formed by the agreement of a group of people. Others, like trade unions and corporations, fit initially into forms provided by the state.[2]

Organizations are necessary to coordinate cooperative action.[3] The benefits they have brought us are almost coextensive with the benefits of modern life, but the problems they produce are, as we have suggested, equally wide ranging. In particular, organizations tend to take on lives that are distinct from those of

---

2. Professional associations, private charities, and similar groups may at some point become corporations in the legal sense of the word. Today most such organizations are incorporated.

3. The most important nonorganizational device for coordinating social action is the market. Oliver Williamson (1975) in an interesting and important volume has shown that for many purposes market and organizational solutions to the coordination problem may be seen as competing alternatives. His book goes on to specify situations in which one mode or the other is likely to be preferred.

their individual members and to be specially effective when pursuing organizational interests in the face of diffuse individual opposition.

At various times in human history different organizations have enjoyed special influence. Throughout the Middle Ages until recent times the church was the most influential corporate actor in Western society. The church's influence has declined in the last few centuries, partly as a consequence of legal and constitutional transformations in many nations that severed close ties between the church and the state. But if corporate power has declined in the religious sphere, it has increased in the secular sphere, particularly with respect to economic activity.

During the last 150 years there has been a fundamental redistribution of *economic* power in our society. Individuals and families have become relatively less powerful, and corporate actors, especially business corporations and labor unions,[4] have become much more so. To understand why this has occurred and the role that law has played in this development, we must turn first to the general problem of collective action.

THE PROBLEM OF COLLECTIVE ACTION

The Costs of Organizing

There is an old joke about a lecturer on Oriental cultures who would begin her lectures in a darkened auditorium. She would ask the people in the audience to raise their hands and when they did the lights would suddenly be turned on, illustrating, she would say, the old Oriental proverb, "Many hands make light work." As a joke, the story is not particularly funny in the telling, but the central point is sound—people working together can by coordinating their activities accomplish much more than similarly sized groups of noncooperators. The benefits of cooperation are so obvious, and we see so much cooperative activity around us, that cooperation might appear as a normal or even a spontaneous outcome of human interaction. In fact, even when cooperation is in the mutual best interests of potential cooperators, it may, particularly if large numbers of people are involved, be difficult to achieve. It is precisely because of this difficulty that special organizational forms like the business corporation and trade union were invented. These forms often require governmental as well as private support if they are to flourish, and the former often entails legal coercion.[5]

One source of difficulty in mobilizing groups of people to achieve some goal is that when large numbers of people are involved coordinating behavior

---

4. Of at least equal importance, but not a focus of this chapter, is the government.

5. The organization and power of government is itself a solution to the problem of securing cooperation among large numbers of people. It is not surprising that a coercive system of taxation is essential to everything that government does, even acts that are generally seen as advancing the common welfare.

can be expensive. These expenses may be called "transaction costs" and may be contrasted with "production costs" such as the costs of raw materials, which are directly incurred in producing a good.[6] Even if the benefits the producers derive from a good are greater than the direct costs of producing it, they may not be greater than the production costs plus the transaction costs of securing the cooperation that is a prerequisite for production. If this is so, it will not pay to produce the good. Moreover, even when the benefits from producing a good are shared widely and more or less equally, the prospects of a total return that exceeds total costs may not be sufficient to motivate production because the initial coordination costs must often be met, "up front," by a relatively small group of people. Should their efforts fail, they may be out a substantial sum even though they personally will gain little should their efforts succeed. In these circumstances the "lumpiness" of transaction costs is likely to mean that goods that are in a group's best interest, in the sense that each member values his share of the goods more than his proportionate share of the costs, will not be produced.

Suppose, for example, that an eccentric billionaire promises to mail $50 to each and every person named Smith who sends him a birthday card, provided that at least a million Smiths send him cards on his birthday. Several Smiths explore the feasibility of notifying enough Smiths so as to ensure a million birthday greetings. If the average cost of notification and persuasion is $49.50 per Smith and the average cost of birthday cards and postage is $1, it would be senseless to try to take advantage of the offer. But the decision might be the same if the average cost of notification was $10. The coordinators might have to invest hundreds of thousands of dollars for their $50 presents, and they could not be sure that all the benefited Smiths would express their gratitude by paying their fair share of the transaction costs. Furthermore, even if they could be certain that those they benefited would pay, the good might still not be produced because there is a risk that their efforts would not generate one million cards, in which case the organizers would have no way to recoup their organizational investment. Thus even if the risk of failure were slight, no small group of Smiths is likely to underwrite the costs of organization when their personal returns from a successful effort would be only a tiny fraction of the amount they had at risk.

Note how the situation would differ if the world's Smiths happened to be already organized for some other purpose. If they were all members of a club designed to promote the collective interests of Smiths, it would be a relatively simple and inexpensive matter to inform every Smith of the chance for some easy money and what they collectively had to do. Thus, where coordination

---

6. "Good" as it is used here and in the remainder of this chapter is more or less interchangeable with "goal" as it is used in the first sentence of this paragraph. Although we typically think of goods as concrete objects such as dry goods or canned goods, we mean to include in the term all beneficial outcomes that people can get together to accomplish—including intangible goals such as world peace.

requires the participation of large numbers of individuals, it is more likely to be provided if a substantial number of the necessary participants have been previously organized for some purpose other than the provision of that good.

The Free Rider Problem

In the previous example the difficulties and costs of coordination are the primary barriers to collective action. In many situations, however, a second barrier exists, the problem of the *free rider*. Free riders may pose problems whenever collective goods are produced. Collective goods are goods that must be made available to every group member if they are to be made available to anyone (Olson, 1971, p. 14). A strong national defense is a classic example. If aggression against the United States is deterred, there is no way of excluding any resident of the United States, including those who pay no taxes and make no other contribution to the national defense, from the benefits of being neither invaded nor at war. Those who do not contribute enjoy *spillover* effects. Benefits spill over on people who do not contribute to the production of the collective good because of the difficulty of excluding them. This "infeasibility of exclusion" creates the *free rider* problem because it means that actions that are economically rational for a group as a whole may not be rational from the perspective of any one member. That is, each member can perceive both that he will benefit from the good whether or not he contributes to its production, and that the availability of the good is unlikely to depend on whether he in fact makes a contribution.

To illustrate the group member's perspective, let us return to our eccentric billionaire, changing the example slightly, so that it involves a true collective good. We do this by stipulating that the gift rather than being confined to those who send cards (which means that nonparticipants do not benefit) will be sent to everyone named Smith provided that at least one million Smiths send cards. You are a Smith and you learn of the offer. Why should you spend a dollar to mail the billionaire a birthday card? It is most unlikely that your card will affect the outcome. If you send a card and 999,999 others are not received you will be out the dollar you paid to buy and mail the card. If you send a card and one million or more others are received, you will also be out a dollar because your net profit will be $49 rather than the $50 you would have cleared had you sent nothing. It is only in the unlikely event that precisely 999,999 other cards are sent that your action in retrospect would appear wise. Given this, would you mail a card? If you believe you would because you think it would be unfair to take a free ride on the generosity of your fellow Smiths, consider what you would have done if the deal were that if a million checks for $1,000 were received from people named Smith, all Smiths would receive checks for $5,000. Would you risk $1,000 on the chance that 999,999 other Smiths would do the same? Would you send $1,000 if you knew that some Smiths would prefer to risk nothing for a $5,000 profit than to risk $1,000 for a slightly enhanced chance of a \$4,000 profit? In these circumstances it is quite likely that no Smith would benefit from the billionaire's offer, even though all Smiths would have gained substantially if they could have coordinated their actions.[7]

Inclusive and Exclusive Goods

In the preceding example the collective good of the \$50 reward is what Olson (1971, p. 38), calls an inclusive collective good. Not only is exclusion infeasible (the billionaire will pay all Smiths, not only those who send cards), but there is also "jointness of supply" (the fact that one Smith enjoys the collective good does not diminish the enjoyment of another who will also receive \$50). Many collective goods are for most practical purposes of this sort.[8] A frequently used example is streetlighting. If there is a streetlight, one cannot exclude passersby from enjoying the "good" of a brighter night, whether or not they helped pay for the light. Moreover, streetlighting exhibits a jointness of supply. Consumption by one individual does not diminish the amount available to others. My enjoyment of the streetlighting in my neighborhood is not diminished by the fact that you and everyone else on the street also enjoy the light.

Not all collective goods are inclusive. Sometimes the supply of a good is fixed and what is consumed by one member of the group diminishes what remains for the others. We may call such goods exclusive (Olson, 1971, p. 8). Here the infeasibility of exclusion provides a substantial incentive to keep the group that has access to the collective good small. Indeed, if too many people have access to an exclusive good, they may destroy it.[9] When collective goods are exclusive,

---

7. Hardin (1982) in a particularly thoughtful elaboration on Olson's thesis points to one situation in which cooperation might be likely. If there were a contract-like convention among the Smiths mandating cooperation for the common good, there might be sufficient trust to generate coordinated action. The existence and efficacy of such a convention would depend in part on past interaction among the Smiths, their ability to sanction and hence to trust each other, and the likelihood of future interaction. The fact that most Smiths have no past history or future expectation of interacting and a substantial amount at risk makes it almost inconceivable that an efficacious convention would exist when the cooperation of a million Smiths is required. But had the offer involved only the hundred or so Smiths who lived in Smithville (let us say 90 cards were required), preexisting conventions of cooperation and trust might have led to coordinated action even if the Smiths could not consult beforehand. If they were able to contract specifically to cooperate, the likelihood that they would meet the billionaire's demands would be higher still.

8. For practical purposes we can ask whether goods are inclusive for the group that is reasonably situated to take advantage of them. In theory, goods that meet this test might be subject to crowding that would destroy their value. Thus in the example that immediately follows if people were lured from miles around to take advantage of the streetlighting not only would the benefit of a pleasant place to be at night be lost, but people might shade each other so that some might in fact be in the dark.

9. Olson (1971, pp. 36–43) gives the example of an oligopolistic or above market price. If one firm sells more at this price, the price can only be maintained if some other firm sells less. If too many firms enter the market attracted by a supracompetitive price, the price will soon sink to competitive levels.

cooperation among those who enjoy the good is often essential. Not only is a noncooperator often able to skim off most of the benefits of the good for himself, but without cooperation the benefit may be exhausted without substantially helping anyone,[10] even if the number of people enjoying the benefits is small.[11]

A familiar example of an exclusive collective good is the commons, that is, a common grazing land used by cattle belonging to different owners. The land can support a certain number of cattle, and if more than that number is put on the land the cattle will destroy it by overgrazing. Thus if the commons is to retain its value, the number of users must be kept small and those who use it must exercise some restraint. Yet if there are no restrictions on the number of cattle a person can graze, the temptation for any individual to put out a few extra cattle is considerable. For he alone will gain the advantage of the extra income from the cattle, while others must share the costs of overgrazing. Moreover, his extra cattle may have little marginal impact on the commons. It is only if others also push their limits that the commons will be destroyed. But if others are going to graze extra cattle why should not the cattle owner on whom we are focusing do likewise and get at least some of the precious grass while it remains? The problem is, in effect, the mirror image of the problem the Smiths faced in generating birthday cards. What is optimal for the group is not in the immediate self-interest of any one member.

A moment's reflection allows us to see the source of this difficulty. Benefits to individuals do not necessarily reflect expenditures made by the individual or, in the case of the commons, the costs incurred. Therefore, an "incorrect" amount

---

10. In an article in *Scientific American* Douglas Hofstadter (1983, p. 28) provides a particularly ingenious example of how the overuse of a collective good—here the right to enter a lottery—can destroy what is valuable about it. The lottery was called the *Luring Lottery*. The prize it offered could be as much as one million dollars. Hofstadter describes the rules of the game as follows:

> The prize of the lottery is $1,000,000/N$ where N is the number of entries submitted. Just think, if you are the only entrant (and if you submit only one entry), a cool million is yours! Perhaps, though, you doubt this will come about. It does seem a trifle iffy. If you would like to increase your chances of winning, you are encouraged to send in multiple entries without limit. Just send in one postcard per entry. If you send in 100 entries, you will have 100 times the chance of some poor soul who sends in only one entry. Come to think of it, why should you have to send in multiple entries separately? Just send *one* postcard with your name and address and a positive integer (telling how many entries you are making). . . . You will have the same chance of winning as if you had sent in that number of postcards. Illegible, incoherent, ill-specified or incomprehensible entries will be disqualified. Only entries received by 5:00 P.M. on June 30, 1983, will be considered. Good luck to you (but certainly not to any other reader of this column)!

That the offer could be made, even in jest, indicates the point that Hofstadter was trying to make. Problems of coordination can be overwhelming and the overuse of an exclusive collective good can destroy its value for everyone.

11. Thus in the case of Olson's (1971) oligopolists, if one of a small number of oligopolists lowers prices slightly and expands production greatly, he will be able to capture almost all the benefit of the collusive price. If all of the small number of oligopolists cease cooperating, the benefit of the supracompetitive price will disappear entirely, for competition will have been restored.

of the collective good is produced (or consumed). The production of the "right" amount of collective goods is a fundamental problem of social action.

Problems of Adequate Supply

When we talk about the *right* amount of goods being produced, we are not thinking of some specific quantity. Rather, we are thinking, as the economist would, of the amount that would be produced if, after taking into account all the costs and benefits of production, the amount spent to purchase the last unit of the good is equal to the benefits derived from that purchase.[12] When the production of goods that have a collective aspect is left to firms and individuals, the goods tend to be underproduced if they are produced at all. This is because private production stops when the benefits to the producer from the last unit produced equal its costs. If all those who enjoyed the good paid what it was worth to them, there would be more money to finance production and thus more of the good would be available.

For example, if I put a streetlight in front of my house, I will install a light with relatively low wattage near my walk or door. Some light will inescapably fall on the public sidewalk and light the way for passing pedestrians. But the light there will be much dimmer than it would have been had each passerby contributed the few pennies that a brighter street was worth to him and the aggregate amount invested in better lighting. Yet if I had left a box in front of my house with the words "lighting fund" on it and explained where the money would go, I would, for reasons we have already discussed, have been unlikely to collect very much. Indeed, even the government might not produce the optimal amount of lighting, for lighting has relatively localized benefits. Unless there were a city-wide plan that had to be approved in its entirety or not at all, a majority of taxpayers would stand to pay more than they would gain from any particular lighting improvement.

The situation changes if there is an actor who so benefits from the production of a collective good that he has a personal incentive to produce a socially sufficient amount regardless of the others' contributions. If Honest Tom the used car dealer moves into the 600 block of Main Street, pedestrians will enjoy sufficient lighting when they pass his lot even though they are, as taxpayers, unwilling to pay for streetlighting there. Or, to give an actual example, when Howard Hughes, who enjoyed watching westerns and aviation movies on late night television, was frustrated following his move to Las Vegas because the local television station went off the air at 11:00 P.M., he bought the station and created the collective good of late night westerns for everyone in the Las Vegas viewing area (Hardin,

---

12. On units before the last unit we should show a "profit"; that is, the cost of purchasing the good should be less than the value derived from it. It is only when we proceed to the point where costs and benefits are equal that we can be sure that we have milked all possible profits from the production of the good.

1982, p. 42). Had the change of programming required contributions from all insomniacs in the viewing area who enjoyed television movies, it no doubt would never have occurred.

Collective goods are also likely to be supplied in adequate amounts when the group in a position to benefit from the goods is composed of a small number of familiars who expect future interaction.[13] This is because the potential beneficiaries can communicate easily, and they are likely to perceive that an adequate supply of the good cannot be produced unless they all cooperate. Even where total cooperation is not necessary, small groups of potential beneficiaries can apportion responsibility according to likely benefits and can put recalcitrants under substantial normative pressure to do their fair share. Moreover, if the group is small enough the contribution of each member may be essential to overall success. For example, a nation's steel producers are likely to develop a coordinated program to lobby for high tariffs and other subsidies. These subsidies are within the group of steel producers, a collective good in that once they are obtained no domestic manufacturers can be barred from their enjoyment. Yet the steelmakers may correctly perceive that the lobbying effect will not go forward without 100 percent participation and that participation by all is necessary to persuade the Congress.[14] Similarly, if five farmers hold 98 percent of the land in a parched valley, they are likely to be able to agree on hiring a rainmaker to relieve their common suffering, even though once the rain falls those valley farmers who did not help pay for the rainmaking cannot be denied its benefits. If, however, there were 100 ranchers in the valley, and each owned only 1 percent of the land, it is unlikely that any individual or small group would make an adequate rain-making investment.[15]

Olson (1971) states the problem:

> This tendency toward suboptimality is due to the fact that a collective good is, by definition, such that other individuals in the group cannot be kept from consuming it once any individual in the group has provided it for himself. Since an individual member thus gets only part of the benefit of any expenditure he makes to obtain more of the collective good, he will discontinue his purchase of the collective good before the optimal amount for the group as a whole has been obtained. In addition,

---

13. The situation is similar even when the beneficiary group is large if, as Hardin (1982) points out, any small subgroup of this sort is in a position of the single actor, for example, Honest Tom or Howard Hughes in the preceding paragraph.

14. Steelmakers will have a private incentive to join the lobbying effort to the extent that their products are not fungible and a carefully drawn tariff may fail to protect some products they produce. Thus to be sure their steel products are protected from foreign competition, manufacturers of specialized products would want to be part of the lobbying effort.

15. As these examples make clear, the fact that people cannot be excluded from the benefits of a collective good does not mean that everyone will or can enjoy it, for collective goods are like other goods in that one must be in a position to enjoy them. The group that is so positioned is often quite limited. Thus a high tariff on steel is a collective good, but only for domestic manufacturers of steel. The water that falls as a result of rainmaking is a collective good, but only for those whose land lies beneath the seeded clouds.

the amounts of the collective good that a member of the group receives free from other members will further reduce his incentive to provide more of the good at his own expense. Accordingly, *the larger the group, the farther it will fall short of providing an optimal amount of a collective good.*[16] (1971, p. 35)

The spillover benefits that characterize public goods are one kind of *externality* (Carson, 1973, p. 478). Usually, however, when we speak of externalities, we are thinking of spillover costs—costs that are borne not by the beneficiary of an activity, but by some third party or by society as a whole. If a firm or household is able to place some of the costs of producing a good on society, it will not consider these costs in its production decisions and so will produce "too much." This is the situation of the farmer who grazes cattle on the commons since much of the cost of overgrazing is borne by others who use the commons.[17] Likewise, if a chemical company can dump its untreated waste in a river, thus placing some of the costs of its activities on those downstream, the price of its product will not reflect the full costs of production. Consumers will demand more of the product than they would at a higher price that reflected its full costs, and in this sense too much will be produced.

The externalization of costs not only leads to overproduction, it also forces others to consume, in a sense, things they do not want, such as dirty air or water. The externalization of benefits allows others to consume things they value without paying for them. One way to redress these imbalances is to force those who gain from an externality to treat it as a private cost or to pay for it as a private benefit, that is, *to make the costs and benefits coextensive.* Sometimes a rearrangement of property or liability rules is sufficient to achieve this result. In the case of the commons, one solution is to divide the property among the users so that each grazes his cattle only on his land. There are certain types of externalities, however, that are not amenable to this solution. When they are not, the coordinating power of the state, regulatory law, is often invoked.

We shall not, however, probe this aspect of the matter. We are concerned more with the problematics of collective behavior since we are interested in organizational solutions to the problem of collective action and the role law has played in their realization. We shall see how the role of law reflects and at times has exacerbated problems of collective action, and we shall discuss the implications of collective organization in the political arena.[18]

---

16. For some important qualifications, which are not, however, essential to this exposition, see Hardin (1982, pp. 42–49).

17. The commons example is, however, somewhat special since the other users of the commons can impose like costs on the first overgrazer. Furthermore the overgrazer may be motivated not just by the fact that he does not initially bear the full costs of his activities but also by the fear that others will exploit the common ownership if he does not and by the perception that the marginal degradation he is causing is of no consequence, given what others are doing.

18. Law generally, as in our tariff example, is itself a collective good. Thus the problem of securing desirable legislation partakes of the problems involved in securing collective goods. Specifically, we can expect legislation to be most likely when a single actor or small group of actors (rather than

CORPORATIONS AND UNIONS AS RESPONSES
TO THE PROBLEMS OF COLLECTIVE ACTION

The advantages of cooperation are nowhere more obvious than in large-scale business enterprises and trade unions. In businesses capital and labor combine to produce goods and services far beyond the abilities of individuals acting alone. In unions relatively powerless workers band together to effectively challenge business management and to change the way they are treated. To be viable, each of these organizational types had to overcome the barriers to collective action we described. In each case the law was at first relatively uninvolved, but later came to play an important role.

Problems with Partnerships

A crucial problem for a business enterprise is the accumulation of enough capital to begin or expand production. When a business is individually owned, the owner's savings and ability to secure credit will generate capital that the owner will invest in the business if he thinks the likely return will make it worthwhile. But one owner may not have enough resources to launch a business, and although businesses can grow by reinvesting profits or borrowing on assets, growth will be faster if others can be persuaded to invest in the enterprise.[19] The task is to get them to invest. An old solution, which is still with us today, is the ordinary partnership. It gives those who supply capital, credit, or crucial labor some say over how the business is run by making them co-owners.

However, the traditional partnership carries special risks because of long-standing legal rules that make an owner personally responsible for business debts. Under these rules, if a person buys a business for $20,000 and it goes bankrupt with debts of $50,000, he will have to sell personal assets to pay the business debt. Partners, as co-owners, have a similar responsibility for making good on any business debts that cannot be satisfied out of their firm's assets. In particular, if one partner cannot meet this burden, the others must take up the slack. If, for example, your partnership goes bankrupt owing $50,000 due to your partner's mismanagement, and if your partner has no assets, you may be forced to pay

---

a large unorganized group) stands to gain more than the cost of the lobbying effort that appears sufficient to produce the law. H. Ross Perot, for example, through the judicious expenditure of $27,000 in campaign contributions and an unknown sum for lawyers and lobbying, almost secured a change in the tax laws that would have benefited him to the tune of $15 million and would have refunded $150 million to others who individually had much less at stake (Hardin, 1982, pp. 78–79). Also, law may multiply the effects of contributions that people make to secure collective goods and so may enhance the value of collective efforts and stimulate contributions. Hardin estimates that each dollar that environmentalists contribute to political action may buy as much as $2,000 in pollution abatement (p. 135).

19. Once a corporation is well established, borrowing and reinvesting earnings tend to be more important sources of capital than further sale of stock (Conard et al., 1982, pp. 671–678).

the entire amount of the debt even if you must sell some of your personal assets to do it.

This potential liability may be tolerable when one can participate in the day-to-day management of a company, for one can decide at what point the enterprise should be terminated rather than risk further losses. However, if one's ownership interest is merely as an investor and the firm has grown to the point where most owners cannot oversee how the firm is managed, the risks of business failure are more threatening. It is one thing for a person to invest $20,000 in an enterprise and find that he has lost it. It is another thing for a person to find that he has not only lost the $20,000, but also his life savings. Thus once an enterprise reaches a size where all investors cannot participate in the work of the firm, people are unlikely to want to participate as owners unless they trust those who manage to use their money wisely, or, as a substitute for trust, have some way of withdrawing easily from the enterprise if they think it is going poorly.

Although ease of withdrawal is not one of the strengths of traditional partnerships, if there are only a few owners, the problem is manageable. Agreements about what happens when an owner wishes to or must withdraw from the enterprise can be negotiated when the joint venture begins or when the occasion arises. If necessary, the firm may be dissolved and then reconstituted by the owners who wish to remain involved.[20] The need to evaluate the firm's assets, often an expensive proposition, will not occur often since the need to reconstitute ownership in this way is unlikely to be frequent. The situation is different if a firm's ownership has been spread among hundreds or thousands of people in order to raise necessary capital. If succession and withdrawal problems required an evaluation of the firm's assets and the reconstitution of the firm by the remaining owners, the difficulties might prove intolerable.[21]

Business Corporations

These hurdles to mass investment were overcome by the development of the modern business corporation, a legal invention as important to modern life as the invention of the light bulb. Those who become titular owners of business corporations, the shareholders, risk only what they invest. Their liability is by

---

20. Being able to reconstitute the enterprise formally may not deal with the entire crisis that can arise when a partner withdraws from an enterprise. To the extent that the success of the enterprise depended on his skills, reputation, or credit rating, the loss of a partner may have a devastating effect on the ongoing business. However, this problem is attributable to the size of the enterprise and not to the partnership form of organization.

21. In recent years large partnerships such as major law and accounting firms have found ways of dealing with such problems. Modes of dealing with such contingencies are specified as part of the partnership agreement. It is not clear, however, that such devices would have been viable at the time large industrial companies were growing or that they would be feasible for attracting capital from thousands of owners in situations where, unlike the large law firm, returns to ownership are not immediate and substantial.

law limited. The creditors of corporations know this, and so base their decisions to extend credit on the financial health of the corporation rather than on the wealth of the individual owners.[22] Because the ownership of corporations can, again by law, be broken up into literally millions of parts, corporations can attract money from people in very different financial circumstances. Not only are small ownership shares affordable, but people may diversify their investments so that a substantial portion of their wealth does not rest on the success of any one enterprise. Furthermore, the separation of ownership from management which characterizes the large corporation means that the success of the enterprise does not depend on the business acumen of the investors. Since neither the management nor the resources of the corporation depend on the identity of the owners, withdrawals from ownership do not by themselves change the corporate identity or threaten the continued viability of the corporation.[23] Finally, if the corporation is large enough and its ownership widely dispersed, there will be a public market for its shares. The market greatly facilitates the widespread investment by providing a central place where information about a variety of companies can be shared. The market also gives the investor-owner the ability to cut losses or take profits at the first signs of adversity. Thus if a person buys 1,000 shares of corporate stock at $20 per share, he does not have to wait until his $20,000 investment has disappeared before he can pull out of a bad deal. It is true that stock markets move in a somewhat lumpy fashion, but moves are almost always gradual and the unhappy investor will usually have a chance to salvage his investment with a loss that is only a small fraction of the amount he chose to put at risk.

It is, however, true that stock markets can be manipulated, and that investors may be wary of investing in distant companies if they cannot trust the information they receive. A federal agency, the Securities and Exchange Commission, exists primarily for the purpose of guaranteeing the integrity of stock markets. It requires publicly traded companies to furnish potential investors with considerable information, and it polices stock dealers and company officials to ensure that they do not mislead investors or take special advantage of inside information.[24]

The corporation and the stock markets it gave rise to together go a long way toward overcoming three impediments to collective action: coordination problems, incentive problems, and transaction costs. The separation of ownership from control allows investments to be easily coordinated. Owners who are dis-

---

22. Knowing this, creditors of small corporate enterprises often demand that the principal owners sign personal notes insuring debts with their private assets.

23. In small, "closely held" corporations the principal owners are likely to play important roles in the management of the corporation. If one of them dies or resigns his management role at the same time he disposes of his stock, the implications for the corporation can be substantial. The textual analysis is primarily concerned with large, publicly held business corporations.

24. Some economists, in a debate we do not wish to enter, argue that insider trading has important virtues (Manne, 1966; Carlton & Fischel, 1983), and others have suggested that if the S.E.C. had never been established, market forces would lead companies to provide what is essential to investors in the information the law now demands (Stigler, 1964; Benston, 1973).

satisfied with the decisions made can withdraw from the corporation, but unless they withdraw en masse, they will not disrupt it. The change in the liability rule and the existence of active regulated stock markets increase incentives to invest. The former does so by diminishing the risk. The latter disseminates information, reduces the costs of buying and selling shares, and allows shareowners to turn their investments almost instantaneously into cash.

One problem that the corporation does not have to overcome in amassing investors is the free rider problem that is associated with collective goods. The primary incentive for corporate investment is, of course, the desire to make money through the receipt of dividends or by selling one's shares at a profit. This desire motivates investments in small businesses as well as in large ones. The ability to sell one's ownership right is a private good whether a company is large or small as is, in most cases, the ability to share in company profits. In a publicly owned corporation this ability is ordinarily in proportion to the number of shares owned. In an unincorporated company the rights of owners to draw profits may be specified in an agreement that takes into account the relative contributions of each, or those owners that contribute most may receive salaries that exhaust most of what would otherwise be profits.[25] Thus within a business, whether it be a partnership or a corporation, increased wealth is not generally a collective good, because the share each person receives is in theory in proportion to his contribution to the collective well-being.[26] In this sense motivating people to invest or otherwise participate in businesses is not problematic. Those who do not invest do not get free rides on those who do. Those who participate are motivated by the prospect of rewards that are commensurate with their participation. When we look at trade unions, especially industrial unions, we see a different situation.

---

25. Where there are no such agreements or with agreements of some types, the company's profits and other assets may be exclusive public goods. All owners may at law have an equal right to them and the share one owner takes is not available to another. This situation can only work if the partners can trust each other to take only fair shares. This is why arrangements in which more than one party has general operating authority tend to involve only a few such people. The corporate form solves this problem by allocating each owner's share of the company's wealth in accordance with the number and kind of shares held (which presumably reflects individual investments), and by preventing any individual shareholder from distributing or disposing of any portion of the company's income or assets, including the stockholder's proportionate share. The disgruntled shareholder's options are to join with others to elect a board of directors that will distribute the corporation's assets as he wishes or to sell his stock on the open market.

26. A rise in the value of stock on the open market or the distribution of a corporate dividend has collective aspects because if one shareholder in a class benefits, all must benefit, but presumably the contribution of each shareholder is proportionate to the number of shares owned as is the benefit distributed. Thus the benefits distributed as private goods are in proportion to the contribution that was made to obtain the good. Note that in a corporation the contribution is the amount originally paid into the corporation to obtain the shares and not the amount paid for the shares on the resale market. Notice also that a corporation may sell its shares at different prices depending on market conditions. It is only by assumption that the contributions to the corporation that are represented by each share are equal.

Trade Unions

The goods that labor unions work to produce—higher wages and better working conditions—are collective goods in that these benefits of unionization almost inevitably extend to all employees in a workplace whether or not they have joined the union. Labor and management are today often prevented by law from agreeing that union workers will be treated better than nonunion workers in similar positions, but it has almost always been the case that management would give its nonunionized employees in a unionized plant benefits comparable to those that its unionized employees in similar positions had won.[27] Unless such benefits were given, the nonunionized sector would be likely to join the union, creating a yet more formidable adversary for the next round of negotiations.

Since they are in the business of producing collective goods, unions have always faced the free rider problem. A worker realizing that he alone cannot make a union or break a strike might refuse to pay union dues or agree to work during a strike even though he knows that if enough other workers do the same, his own interests will, in the long run, suffer.[28] For a union whose capacity to deliver the goods is inextricably linked with its control over the work force, any defection is threatening. Because the union cannot privatize the most important goods it produces, it must find other ways to induce potential beneficiaries to cooperate in the production effort.[29]

Besides privatization there are at least three methods of dealing with the free rider problem. They are propaganda, normative appeals, and coercion. Although none of these methods may completely eliminate free riders, they can induce enough cooperation to produce a substantial supply of the collective good.

Propaganda involves the effort to persuade people that their individual contributions really do matter and that what is a collective good has important private aspects. Charities, for example, often tell contributors what their individual contributions can buy. Thus a charity whose mission is to fight cancer may tell

---

27. The situation of the unionized trades is somewhat different from the situation of the industrial unions. There contractors and private employers can often hire nonunionized labor and do so because they can pay them less than union rates. Nevertheless, the nonunionized sector still benefits from the activities of the unions, for every time the union secures a wage increase, the nonunionized sector can raise its rates and still compete successfully.

28. The situation is like that of the prisoner's dilemma described in Chapter 6. Regardless of what others do, noncooperation is always in the worker's self-interest (assuming that he will not be punished for this behavior). Yet the worker will be much better off if everyone cooperates than if no one does (cf. Hardin, 1982, pp. 16–37).

29. Again, the argument applies most directly to industrial unions. Craft unions can, despite spillovers, largely privatize their benefits because only those with union cards can command union wages. The major task encountered by craft unions is that of persuading management to hire union labor. One solution, which is to organize all potential craft workers, is not attractive because the high craft union wage is an exclusive collective good. If too many people were unionized it would either drive the union wage down or limit the demand for unionized craftspeople so that the earnings of one worker would come at the expense of another. Thus craft unions strive to limit both their membership and the ability of management to employ nonunion labor.

prospective contributors that $10 will provide the test tubes and beakers that one laboratory technician uses in one month, that $20 will pay for Pap smear tests for ten women, and that $50 will cover the publication and distribution costs of 1,000 leaflets on how to avoid known carcinogens.

However, the fact is that unless the charity receives millions of dollars from other donors, small individual efforts will have no more than a negligible impact in the fight against cancer, and if the charity does receive additional millions, one donation of $10 or $20 will not be missed. Thus propaganda of this sort is misleading in that it suggests that there is a specific return for each gift and that any one small contribution matters, but it is not misleading in the sense that many small contributions may be vital to overall success.

Normative appeals suggest that there is some reason people ought to contribute to the collective good without regard to immediate advantage. Thus the charity might candidly admit, "We won't lick cancer in your lifetime," but then exhort, "Give for your children's sake." Or they might say, "If any of your friends or relations have contracted cancer, they have lived longer and with less pain because of what others gave. Repay that debt. Contribute today."

Finally, there is coercion. So long as efficient mechanisms of coercion are in place, as they are when the state is exercising coercive power through law, this is the most effective way of producing collective goods. Indeed, a good part of the case for the modern state rests on the essential nature of certain collective goods (e.g., internal security, national defense, free markets) and the fact that the state is the organizational form that is most likely to guarantee their production in adequate amounts. In the example we are pursuing, the state collects money through the coercive apparatus of its tax system and with a stroke of the budgetary pen allocates more money to cancer research than all private charities combined.

It is not surprising that labor unions have used each of these methods to attract and hold membership. They have made the individual's contribution seem important by making the immediate goal of unionization not the benefits the union strives to achieve but *solidarity*. This is a brilliant transformation of the issues, as brilliant as any that Madison Avenue has achieved on behalf of business. One defector will not affect the union's ability to achieve its ends, but one defector will destroy solidarity. Every person counts. And, indeed, in a real sense each person does count. Viewing solidarity not as an all or nothing proposition but as a state that can be more or less achieved, unless a substantial degree of solidarity exists, the union will fail in its goals.

Unions have also tried to generate normative claims to the loyalty of unorganized workers. Entire ideologies have been constructed to justify these claims. The union movement's success in this respect is evident in the general opprobrium that attaches to terms that union members coined or appropriated to describe fellow employees and other members of the working class who chose to side with management when it came to a strike. "Goons," "scabs," and "finks" are among the most familiar.

Even the technique of privatizing benefits has been used, and it was important in the early days of some unions. Unions often functioned as social groups as well as the voice of labor. Thus the benefits of good fellowship and a congenial gathering place (the union hall) were an inducement to join unions. Some unions went further and offered financial incentives. Low cost burial insurance was an important early attraction.[30]

And, of course, there is coercion. It is no accident that violence characterized the early days of the industrial labor movement nor that much of it was directed toward other workers rather than toward the company. If workers were not willing to contribute to the common good by refraining from working during strikes, the costs of working in terms of risk to life and limb could be made high enough that many would remain off the job for that reason. Also, it is no accident that labor violence largely ended with the passage of the Wagner Act in 1935 and the institutionalization of the National Labor Relations Board (NLRB). The reason is that the coercive resources of the trade unions, which in large measure could be countered by the resources available to management, were made redundant by the coercive capacity that the state was willing to put at the disposal of whichever party prevailed in organizational elections.

The main legal reform of the 1930s labor laws, indeed, the central change brought about by the Wagner and Norris-LaGuardia acts, was to legitimize coercion. It created the legal elements that both institutionalized and pacified union coercion. These included the representational election, agency shops (all workers must pay union fees even if they do not join the union), dues checkoffs (dues deducted directly from pay), and the concept of the union as an exclusive bargaining agent (only one bargaining agent per unit) charged with representing all workers of a particular type. The acts also protected the right to strike, and, as we saw in the appendix to Chapter 6, imposed on management a duty to bargain in good faith with union officials. In doing so, the state recognized that unions produce inclusive public goods for all workers in organized plants. By lending its monopoly of force to this effort, the state not only recognized the social value of such goods as higher wages and better working conditions, but it also facilitated their production in greater amounts by allowing unions to compel coordination and to overcome the free rider problem.

This analysis indicates why so-called "right to work" laws, that is, laws which prevent unions from requiring that all workers in organized plants join the union, are seen as threatening by organized labor. The fear is not that workers who are opposed in principle to unionization—that is, those whom the laws are ostensibly designed to protect—will refuse to join. Rather, it is that many who

---

30. Such tactics have been used more successfully by craft unions than by industrial unions. The reason is that craft unions, as smaller and more localized groups, do not, as we noted earlier, face the same difficulty in organizing for collective action. In addition, the craft unions, thanks to their guild heritage, achieved considerable success in limiting work of the type they specialize in to union members. This effectively privatized the benefits of collective action and provided a powerful incentive for workers who were interested in a craft to join the relevant union. The pattern of organizing industrial unions through "locals" may be seen as an attempt to achieve the advantages that small groups have in agreeing on collective actions. However, many industries are structured on such a scale that plant-wide locals are not small groups.

enjoy the benefits of unionization will, for reasons of self-interest, opt out. If enough workers take the self-interested route, the union will, if it is not actually destroyed, be unable to act as an effective counterforce to management. Businesses quite understandably often support these laws.

CORPORATIONS, UNIONS, AND THE COMPETING ENDS OF SOCIAL JUSTICE

In the preceding section we have described the central barriers to collective action: the problem of coordination and, in the case of collective goods, the problem of the free rider. We then indicated how laws governing business corporations and labor unions deal with these issues. From this perspective corporations and unions are legal responses to the problem of collective action.[31] Once the difficulties of collective action are resolved for some purposes, however, the high initial transaction costs that might inhibit organizing for other purposes no longer exist. Effectively organized collectivities are potentially powerful social actors. One consequence, as we shall see, is that both organized labor and management can engage in activities that threaten other ends of social justice as defined in Chapter 9. In the next two sections we discuss the ways in which law has been used to facilitate or impede the growing influence of corporate actors and the implications of this influence for a scheme of social justice that values gains to the least well off and equal political rights.

THE BUSINESS CORPORATION

The seeds of corporate organization go back to the Middle Ages and the special status of guilds and towns. Not until the nineteenth century, however, did the corporation become the primary institution around which economic affairs were organized. Before then the dominant view was that corporate entities were to be employed only for great enterprises and for building the resources of the state. The British East India Company was the ideal type. Slowly, however, a different view emerged. It saw the corporation as a convenient instrument for the normal mobilization of capital. Corporate status was granted not only for the great endeavors of the times, but also for everyday business enterprises. By the end of the nineteenth century the advantages of capital mobilization, professional management, abstract personality, and limited liability that the corporate form

---

31. From another perspective the corporate form may be seen as an economic response to the problems of organizing the large firm. For example, an economist might argue that even without the law people would, in principle, bargain for conditions such as limited liability that the law provides. From this perspective the law's virtue is primarily in lowering the transaction costs of what would otherwise be numerous bargained-for agreements (Jenson & Meckling, 1976; Fama & Jenson, 1983; cf. Coase, 1937).

offered were available to all who asked. James Willard Hurst (1956) notes that with this new orientation the corporation became "the most potent single instrument which the law put at the disposal of private decision makers" (p. 15).

The Growth of Corporate Power

From the middle to the end of the nineteenth century, corporations grew with remarkable speed, both in numbers and in power. As they expanded so did the American economy. Although correlations have no necessary implications for causality, clearly, the invention of the corporation in its modern form facilitated the growth of American wealth. This growth was accompanied by a number of other changes: The nation began to change from an agricultural to an industrial society; manufacturing moved from small local plants to factories of mass production; and capital became increasingly concentrated in a relatively few giant concerns.

It is this latter tendency, the concentration of power and wealth in the corporate form, that most concerns us. By the turn of the century the growth of the larger corporations was staggering. Between 1883 and 1906 the Standard Oil combination's assets went from $72 million to $395 million. Between 1890 and 1900 Carnegie and his associates increased steel production from three thousand to three million tons and annual profits from $5 million to $40 million. Somewhat later, between 1903 and 1913, the Ford Motor Company grew from a cash investment of $28 thousand to a value of $22 million. The growth in the company's plant was financed entirely out of retained earnings, while over the same time span $15 million in dividends was paid to stockholders (Hurst, 1956, p. 81).

Recalling Rawls's terms, the last half of the nineteenth century was dominated by a natural liberty conception of social justice. Careers were open to talents in the "rough and tumble" of business, and nothing resembling a difference principle stood in the way of capital concentration or the amassing of great fortunes.[32] In the decades after the Civil War the law either ignored the phenomena of capital growth and concentration or it encouraged them:

> The law provided an open field (assured broad markets), legal instruments (the corporation and manifold tools of contract, especially the devices of corporate finance), legal subsidies (grants of land and public credit, and currency inflation and deflation), and then substantially stood aside. . . . Perhaps the most important contribution which the law's omission made to the concentration of capital was the narrow use of the tax power. After the Civil War income tax ended in 1872, except for the abortive income tax of 1894, tax law not only laid no hand upon capital concentration, but practically promoted it; there were no general income, gift or

---

32. For example, Hurst notes that between 1885 and 1896 John D. Rockefeller received dividends of between $15 and $17 million a year from Standard Oil. C. Wright Mills (1956) provides a more detailed discussion of the nature of some of these great fortunes.

inheritance taxes; the closest analogy to a corporation income tax was state levies on the receipts of railroads and other utilities, which, like the tariff and other excises and the real estate property tax, fell mainly on ultimate consumers or small businessmen and farmers. Thus industry and finance could operate within a framework of social order paid for by other people. (Hurst, 1956, p. 82)

The federal judiciary, using the contract clause and later the due process clause of the Fourteenth Amendment provided corporations with additional protection from the countervailing power of the state. Although early interpretations of the Fourteenth Amendment did not treat it as a substantive safeguard for property and business activity [*Slaughterhouse Cases*, 16 Wall 36 (1873)], this view changed near the end of the century. In 1886 the Supreme Court held, without discussion, that corporations were "persons" within the meaning of the Fourteenth Amendment [*Santa Clara County* v. *Southern Pacific R.R.*, 118 U.S. 394 (1886)]. A year later, in *Mugler* v. *Kansas*, 123 U.S. 623 (1887), the Court announced that it was prepared to examine state legislation for its substantive reasonableness. Armed with these two decisions, the courts over the next half-century struck down a number of laws restricting corporate activity. The most vulnerable were laws regulating wages, prices, and working conditions. [See, e.g., *Lochner* v. *New York*, 198 U.S. 45 (1905) and *Coppage* v. *Kansas*, 236 U.S. 1 (1915)]. Thus taking advantage of the law where it helped and largely unrestrained by the law where it might have hindered,[33] corporations by the end of the nineteenth century had become the primary locus of organized economic power.

Industrial Corporations

By 1900 two-thirds of the nation's manufacturing output was produced by corporations, and a series of mergers were further concentrating resources in the larger corporations.[34] This concentration gave some corporations monopoly power, meaning that certain sectors of the market were no longer, even in principle, efficient allocators of goods.

An early and well-known attempt to monopolize an industry was made by John D. Rockefeller and his associates who began the Standard Oil Trust in

---

33. The rare exceptions included the fledgling Interstate Commerce Commission and some state regulatory activity sustained by a few Supreme Court decisions such as *Munn* v. *Illinois*, 94 U.S. 113 (1877), permitting Illinois to regulate maximum charges of grain warehousemen because their businesses were "affected with public interest." The Sherman Antitrust Act (1890), passed before the turn of the century, had almost no impact until 1904 and the *Northern Securities Case*, 193 U.S. 197 (1904).

34. We lack reliable data on the extent of concentration at the turn of the century. The first solid data on corporate economic concentration is for 1929. In that year the 200 largest corporations controlled 46 percent of the assets of all nonfinancial corporations. If we look only at manufacturing corporations, the 100 largest controlled 40 percent of total assets and 44 percent of net capital assets in 1929. Means (1970, p. 8) estimated that in 1969, 52 percent of total assets and 62 percent of net capital assets were in the legal control of the 100 largest manufacturing corporations (see also Zeitlin, 1970).

1882. Witness the Senate testimony of one C. B. Mathews, head of the Buffalo Lubricating Oil Refinery Works, a company in competition with Standard Oil. He had the misfortune of constructing his refinery in 1881 next to another independent company, the Atlas Refining Company. The Atlas was laying a pipeline from Buffalo to Rock City, a town 70 miles south in the Bradford Oil Field. As Mathews told the Senate:

> They [Atlas] assured me that we should get crude oil at our works for 10 cents a barrel pipeage, and that they would have their line completed in a few days. Meantime the Standard Oil Company hurriedly laid a line to Buffalo, along the line of the Buffalo, and Southwestern and Erie Road [the Erie Railroad], and began pumping oil there, although they had no refineries. The Rock City Pipe Line was prevented from completing their line by the Erie Road refusing to give them a crossing, and the Standard were buying up parties in interest along the line of the right of way, and serving injunctions on the Rock City Pipe Line people, so that they had fifteen or sixteen injunctions at a time, and as soon as the Atlas would raise one injunction they would put on another, so that some months were occupied in getting this independent line through, and it cost them over $100,000—the restrictions and the stoppage which was occasioned by the Standard and Erie Road in trying to prevent them from laying this line. They continued to use this line for a few months, but their business was afterwards destroyed and they sold to the Standard and the Standard took up this line which they had laid along the Erie Road and are now operating the Rock City Line. When they assumed control of the Rock City Line, in 1882, the rates of pipeage went up from 10 cents to 25 cents per barrel.
>
> Q: State whether at that time the railroads also advanced their rates?
> A: The railroads advanced their rates from 15 to 25 cents per barrel.
> Q: That is, about the same time?
> A: Yes sir; from the same points at the same time. (Summers & Howard, 1965, pp. 356–357)

Thus, Standard Oil was not only able to squeeze out a competing pipeline, it also had sufficient power to induce the railroads to raise their shipping charges to the point where they no longer competed effectively. There were fortunes in this way of doing business; Rockefeller and many like him made them.

The managers of the new industrial giants often had substantial proprietary interests in their corporations, but even where they did not, they, rather than their firm's shareholders, often controlled corporate behavior. This remained the case as the twentieth century proceeded and the ownership of corporations—in the form of shareholding—became more widely dispersed. The very rules that protected the investor from the risks of mismanagement also weakened the investor's control over the enterprise. Fifty years ago Berle and Means (1932) in a famous book, *The Modern Corporation and Private Property*, pointed out that corporate ownership was becoming increasingly separated from control. The trend has continued to this day.[35] One corollary has been that corporate managers

---

35. In 1967 Robert Sheehan found that only 150 companies in the Fortune 500 were managed by those who controlled the corporation, and in most of these 150 companies the manager-proprietors owned less than half of the outstanding stock.

seldom attend to the specific concerns of individual shareholders in their day-to-day operation of the business.[36] The typical shareholder despite his titular rights of ownership has no effective control over the policies of the corporations in which he invests.[37]

The basic reasons for this are rooted in the problems of collective action. Managerial authority in a corporation resides ultimately with a board of directors that can hire and fire corporate officers. Members of the board are elected by the shareholders, usually on the basis of one share one vote. These boards are almost always dominated by management and people friendly to it. When the terms of some board members expire, the board of directors typically offers a slate to replace them which can be supplemented by nominations from shareholders. But the nomination and election of nonboard candidates requires either the ownership of a substantial block of shares or coordinated activity.

Individual shareholders are dispersed, and it is difficult for them to coordinate their activities. The costs of keeping sufficiently up-to-date on corporate activities so as to be able to offer managerial advice are, in relation to most investments, prohibitive. The benefits of asserting an owner's ultimate right of control are, unless one can secure a corporate position, the speculative ones of replacing one set of managers with another set. Furthermore, there is the easy option of exit. If one is dissatisfied with what management is doing, he can always sell his stock. Thus in any widely held corporation, however unsuccessful, there is no such thing as a spontaneous revolt from below. The revolts that do happen involve small groups of disgruntled or opportunistic shareholders who try to oust the previous management and take control with their own team. This is explicable because such revolutionaries are seeking not just the collective good of better management but also the private goods that accompany control.[38]

Attempts to take over large publicly held corporations that are not coupled

---

36. Some economists would dispute the implication of nonresponsiveness. They would argue that although business managers do not ordinarily respond to individuals as individuals, they respond to the aggregate of individual concerns through the discipline of various markets (e.g., capital markets, product markets and managerial talent markets) (Jensen & Meckling, 1976; Fama, 1980; Fama & Jensen, 1983). However, these theories are not only unproven, but they hypothesize responsiveness to only the economic interests of the individual shareholders and not to their broader sociopolitical concerns.

37. We are thinking here primarily of individual shareholders, but organizations like insurance companies and pension funds are coming more and more to hold relatively large blocks of shares in the corporations in which they invest (Eisenberg, 1969). However, it appears that these institutional investors ordinarily are not actively involved in the management of companies in which they have substantial interests, and these investors are themselves companies that aggregate the interests of individuals who ordinarily have little control over what they do.

38. Sometimes those who seek control in fact have another goal. They are engaging in what has come to be called "greenmail." What they seek is a corporate decision to buy back at a substantial profit shares they have purchased in their attempt to gain control. Vast profits have been made almost overnight in this way. That the corporate directors to preserve their own power may expend hundreds of millions of the corporation's money to buy back shares from greenmailers is some testimony to how far the ownership of the ordinary shareholder has been separated from the control of important corporate decisions.

with substantial purchases of the company's stock are seen as unlikely to succeed and hence are quite rare. The laws under which corporations are chartered usually give managers substantial advantages of agenda setting, communications, and access to corporate funds when they battle with dissident shareholders. If dissident shareholders are able to obtain a substantial minority of the outstanding stock, the situation changes. Then the dissidents can without significant transaction costs vote their shares as a block, thus putting them well on their way to mobilizing a shareholder majority. Indeed, management in these circumstances often capitulates and allows the minority faction membership on the board of directors and ultimately may relinquish control. For similar reasons, when a substantial minority shareholder already dominates management, he is almost impossible to dislodge. Thus a single individual or family that owns 15 or 20 percent of a corporation's outstanding shares and dominates the board of directors is considered, for all practical purposes, to control the corporation.

Power and Politics

During the ninteenth century and the early part of the twentieth century the large industrial corporations were, for the most part, able to dominate their relationships with their work force. By the use of tactics such as those discussed in the appendix to Chapter 6—yellow dog contracts, dismissal for joining or organizing a union, blacklisting, the use of judicial injunctions, and similar devices—employers were able to deal with employees as isolated individuals. Consider this tale of one worker:

> John Martin came to work in the bitumunous coal fields of West Virginia around the beginning of the twentieth century. He worked underground about fifty-two hours per week. His pay was based on a per-ton rate, but the checking of this tonnage was done by company personnel who often counted 2600 to 3000 pounds per ton. His pay averaged 20 cents an hour. The mine was not unionized, and Martin knew from the talk of other miners that union men would be quickly discharged by the company. One night Martin was visited at home by a United Mine Workers representative who said he was trying to organize the mines so that the West Virginia miners could have the same pay and working conditions as in the mines in Ohio and Illinois. Martin agreed to join the union, but on condition that this be kept quiet. Later his superintendent asked if he had joined and he said, "No," for fear of discharge. "Any union man will be fired on the spot," the superintendent told him.
>
> In 1906, the miners struck for recognition of their union. Martin struck with them. The strike included bloody battles between the miners and private police employed by the mine operators. An injunction was finally issued against the strike and it collapsed. Martin was not allowed to return to work. A mine superintendent told him, "No damned union man is going to work here again." Martin could not find employment in any of the other mines in the area. For ten years, he did odd jobs in the West Virginia coal towns. (Williams, 1965, p. 3)

The economic wealth that corporations amassed also allowed them and those they made rich to gain disproportionate influence in the political process, at least as measured by the Rawlsian ideal which vests liberty interests only in individuals and suggests that equal political liberty, which includes the potential for equal influence in the political process, is the first priority in the just state. In what Arthur Okun (1975) calls the "transgression of dollars on rights," the wealthy are able to enjoy substantial political influence through lobbying, campaign contributions, and occasional outright bribery. Okun (1975) reports from recent times:

> I heard the directors of financing in a campaign organization urge a liberal Democrat to stay away from loophole-closing tax reform as a campaign issue because it would antagonize wealthy potential contributors. Another example was provided by super-rich Howard Hughes, who bought blue chips in the form of a diversified portfolio of campaign contributions to candidates of both parties in an apparent effort to influence particular regional and industrial policies. (p. 24)

Nor is the development new. Similar tales could be told a hundred years earlier (cf. Mills, 1956, p. 166). The power of the large corporations has long excited popular distrust, and corporations for just as long have been involved in politics to forestall efforts to regulate or tax them and to limit the effects of legislation that they have been unable to prevent. Since the first decades of the nineteenth century, periods in which the popular demand for corporate regulation were overwhelming alternated with periods in which corporations have been relatively successful in fending off efforts for greater restraints and in limiting the implications of existing ones.

Corporations have long been free to lobby legislators with respect to matters directly affecting their business interests, but, they have in various ways been restricted by law in their ability to influence electoral processes and to publicize corporate positions on political issues. Generally speaking, the political views of corporations, particularly about which candidates should be elected, and corporate support were for much of this century in large measure mediated through the political contributions and influence of those persons the corporations made rich. This not only ensured that there was some diversity among the voices that were amplified by corporate wealth, but due to the problems of collective action, contributions from the corporate sector were less than they might have been. Even millionaires do not like to invest large sums of their own money in causes to which others with similar interests are not contributing.

Corporate Free Speech. Two developments in the 1970s threaten to change this situation and allow the corporate voices to be more directly heard. First, the Supreme Court has ruled that certain kinds of corporate speech are protected under the First Amendment. For example, in *First National Bank of Boston* v. *Bellotti*, 435 U.S. 765 (1978), the Supreme Court held by a 5–4 majority that Massachusetts could not bar corporations from spending money to influence referenda that did not materially affect their business, property or assets. The law in question had been passed by the Massachusetts legislature after several attempts to secure voter approval of a graduated state personal income tax had failed. In each instance the failure of the proposal followed campaigns against the tax financed largely by the state's banks and corporations.[39] The Supreme Court also held that a state's interest in energy conservation did not allow it to preclude a regulated utility from engaging in advertising that promoted the use of electricity; *Central Hudson Gas & Electric Corp.* v. *Public Service Commission of New York*, 447 U.S. 557 (1980), nor could it bar a utility from including with its bills literature advocating increased reliance on atomic energy; *Consolidated Edison Company of New York* v. *Public Service Commission of New York*, 447 U.S. 530 (1980).

It is conceivable even if it is not likely that a majority of the First National Bank's shareholders supported the Massachusetts personal income tax proposal and that most of Central Hudson's shareholders believed that the national interest in conservation should take precedence over the company's narrow interest in encouraging energy use. The shareholders were certainly not polled on the matter. Moreover, in *Bellotti* one might argue that the principle of majority governance does not justify forcing minority shareholders to share in the cost of personally distasteful political messages unrelated to the bank's business.[40]

The power that the "corporate free speech" cases give certain elements in the political process is enhanced because large corporations have to some extent solved the problem of collective action. Corporate contributions aggregate the wealth of many owners without any new transaction costs, and a contribution from a corporation that is small in proportion to the corporation's total wealth may nonetheless be sufficient to have a noticeable impact on the political process. The latter fact is an incentive that is absent when most individuals consider contributions. *Consolidated Edison* extends to corporations an additional advantage that individuals do not enjoy. The costs of printing the pronuclear power message that the corporation disseminated are small in comparison to the costs of acquiring a broad-based mailing list and mailing out political material. By including the mailing with the bill, the utility uses a list that has been generated for other purposes and can charge off most of the cost of the mailing as a business

---

39. One might reasonably argue that the passage of a graduated state income tax would have affected the property and business of the bank that was the plaintiff in *Bellotti*. However, the Supreme Court decided for the bank without confronting this question, thus accepting for the purpose of the opinion the contention that the expenditures were unrelated. It appears that the question of whether such a tax on individuals would have affected the bank's business interests is a difficult one on which economists differ.

40. The Supreme Court reached this conclusion in a trade union case when it held that a union had to refund to dissenting members that portion of the union dues that was spent on political activities with which they disagreed [*Abood* v. *Detroit Board of Education*, 431 U.S. 209 (1977)]. The dissenting union members in *Abood* differ, however, in an important way from shareholders who may not have agreed with the First National Bank's political stance. They were required to pay union dues to maintain their jobs, while dissenting shareholders can sell their stock and find more or less equivalent investments. It was on these grounds that the majority in *Bellotti* specifically rejected the analogy to *Abood* (435 U.S. 765; 794 at Note 34). Dissenting shareholders might have an action for corporate waste, but realistically the cost would not justify bringing suit.

expense.[41] Only the marginal cost of printing the pronuclear power literature must be borne by the company and its shareholders.[42] Whether a regulatory commission can apportion more than the marginal cost of a political message included in a bill to the shareholders is a question the *Consolidated Edison* court left open.

Decisions like those in *Bellotti, Consolidated Edison*, and *Central Hudson Gas* have been defended, using the imagery of the marketplace of ideas. It is true that these decisions allow certain ideas to be advanced with a louder voice, but it is unlikely that they will lead to genuinely new ideas since corporate executives were always free to advance their own ideas with their own funds. What may happen, though, is that the corporate presence will create as serious imbalances in this market as they have in many economic markets that were once dominated by private individuals. But there will not be the compensating gains in efficiency that arguably justify the tendency of larger companies to drive out smaller ones. There are no economies of scale in the marketplace of ideas. What underlies the metaphor is the belief that we cannot in a democratic society determine by governmental fiat that some ideas are better than others. The public must have access to all of them, for it is only by evaluating competing ideas that the people can determine which are best. Intelligent evaluation requires sufficient balance within the market to expose individuals to a variety of ideas and give them access to enough information so that they can *reasonably* decide which ideas advance their self-interest and value preferences. When one position is more frequently articulated than another, there are two dangers to the ideal of rational decision making by an informed electorate. The first is that the electorate will hear a more complete case for one side than for the other. The second is that it will be the relative frequency of the messages which persuades rather than the relative merits of the competing arguments. When informing an electorate is costly, these dangers increase with disparities in the resources available to the two sides. Thus the Supreme Court, in extending rights of free speech to corporations, may upset a balance that, because of great inequalities in the way wealth is distributed in society and the correlation between wealth and political views, many see as precarious (cf. Rawls, 1982).

---

41. The importance of this advantage was openly acknowledged by Consolidated Edison. Robert Lehman, Con Ed's Vice-President for Public Affairs wrote in an affidavit that was filed as part of Consolidated Edison's brief:

> A separate mailing would be prohibitively expensive. We have a monthly basic bill run of 2.8 million. Postage alone, at first class mail rates, would cost in excess of $350,000. Even at bulk mail rates, postage would cost $210,000. . . . Television is not an adequate or effective medium for communicating lengthy messages on complicated subjects to a mass audience. . . . Newspaper advertising is more expensive in reaching as wide an audience among our customers as bill inserts. (Appendix to Brief for Appellant at 15 as cited in Nicholson, 1980, p. 966)

Consider how much more effective the antinuclear energy movement might be if it could realize similar economies in reaching energy consumers.

42. Presumably the regulatory commission will not include the cost of political messages as a business expense in setting the utility's rates. But billing is an ordinary business expense, so the utilities customers bear most of the costs of the political messages included with their bills.

PACs. The other major development that promises to magnify the direct corporate influence on political life is the invention of the political action committee, or PAC, and the extension of the right to organize PACs to business corporations.

PACs are organizations that solicit money from individuals and either channel the contributions they aggregate directly to candidates or spend the money "independently" on behalf of candidates or causes.[43] PACs may be organized by corporations, trade associations, unions, cooperatives, and individuals, including political leaders. Even the American Nazi party has its PAC.

Contributions to PACs are, in theory, voluntary, but in the case of corporate and labor PACs one suspects that there may be a considerable gap between theory and practice. The National Education Association PAC, for example, until stopped by court order, added PAC contributions to the union dues that were deducted from teachers' salaries. Those who did not wish to contribute had to ask for their money back (*Federal Election Commission* v. *National Education Association*, 457 F. Supp. 1102, D.C. District Court, 1978). On the corporate side, it would be surprising if executive, professional, and supervisory personnel did not feel informal pressures to contribute.[44] Corporate and labor PACs are also special in that corporations and unions may use ordinary funds to establish, administer, and solicit contributions to their PACs. This ability to meet start-up and transaction costs from ordinary funds helps overcome important obstacles to collective behavior.[45]

---

43. The major incentive for independent spending is that there are limits on how much one PAC can contribute to one candidate, but there are no limits on how much money may be spent for a candidate if the PAC is acting independently of the candidate's campaign. The word "independently" is in quotation marks because informal contacts and collusion between PACs running "independent" campaigns and the candidates they support is apparently common. For a concerned perspective on these and other issues relating to PACs and the general issue of money in politics, see Elizabeth Drew's two-part article that appeared in *The New Yorker* magazine (Drew, 1982a; b) and was later published in book form (Drew, 1983). For a response to Drew, see Samuelson (1983). The most a PAC can contribute to a candidate is $5,000. This compares with an individual contribution limit of $1,000. However, in the case of PACs the limit is somewhat misleading since a number of PACs may represent similar interests and contribute to the same candidates. For example, in the 1980 elections four Republican challengers of Democratic incumbents received more than $100,000 each from oil industry PACs (Conway, 1983, p. 137).

44. The law regulating PACs provides that corporations cannot directly solicit ordinary employees and their families except twice a year by mail. Responses to such mail solicitations must be "laundered" so that a PAC cannot distinguish those who do not contribute from those who contribute $50 or less.

45. In 1980 labor PACs received $25.6 million and contributed $13.2 million to candidates; corporate PACs received $33.9 million and contributed $19.2 million; but nonconnected PACs received $40.1 million and contributed only $4.9 million (Conway, 1983, p. 132). The difference in the proportion of receipts contributed by the first two groups and the proportion contributed by the last reflects in part the fact that nonconnected PACs must meet all organizational costs out of funds received. Because potential contributors to nonconnected PACs are not well organized into membership or employee groups, the solicitation costs of such PACs are exceptionally high per dollar received. Trade Membership and Health Associations were more like unions and corporations in their contribution to receipts ratio, although they did not do quite so well ($33.9 million collected, $15.8 million contributed), probably because of greater transaction costs attributed to the more diffuse and looser organization of potential contributors (Conway, 1983, p. 132).

The number of corporate PACs grew from 89 in December 1974 to 1,496 by June 1982. This growth was triggered by an amendment to the federal election law in 1974 which removed a provision that barred organizations with government contracts from maintaining PACs.[46] Since that time PACs have become increasingly important actors on the political scene, and, with the spectacular rise in the number of corporate PACs (labor PACs grew only by about 90 percent from 201 to 389 between 1974 and 1982), the availability of money in politics is becoming an increasing advantage of the Republican party (Drew, 1982a).[47]

PACs seek the election of candidates who are generally sympathetic to their political agendas. Their support obviously matters although the exact difference that PACs and other sources of money make is not clear.[48] But corporate PACs

---

46. This law, as well as some other laws that have worked largely to the advantage of Republicans, was passed by a Congress controlled by the Democrats. These laws not only reflect political short-sightedness by both the Democrats in Congress and their backers in organized labor, but also, if we may say so, a lack of social science sophistication about the relationship between social power and a material base. The 1974 amendments, for example, were supported by organized labor because some unions were beginning to contract with the federal government to train disadvantaged workers. To preserve these union PACs, the Democrats opened the floodgates to corporate PACs that tend to favor Republican candidates.

Perhaps even more telling were the 1979 amendments to the law that allow unions and corporations to spend noncontributed funds and allow unreported individual contributions beyond the federal limits for so-called party building activities like voter registration drives, getting out the vote in presidential elections, and volunteer expenses. The unions, especially the politically powerful United Auto Workers Union, had traditionally focused on such activities and wanted to avoid having them controlled as part of the general controls on expenditures in federal elections. Thus the law was pushed by the Democrats, although what happened almost immediately thereafter should have been entirely predictable: The Republicans far outstripped the Democrats in funds mobilized for these purposes (Drew, 1982b). This source of virtually unlimited funds is particularly threatening to the current party balance because the low voter turnout in U.S. elections means that the party that can organize a truly effective "get out the vote" campaign has potentially an overwhelming advantage even though the distribution of preferences in the voting age population may be decidedly against it.

Finally, congressional Democrats were probably unafraid of increasing the potential role of PACs because PACs in their desire to maximize political influence often support incumbents. However, it turns out that the preference for incumbents is strong only when an incumbent does not seem vulnerable to an opponent whose overall policies are closer to the contributor's preferences. The result has been that over the years corporate PACs have become increasingly likely to fund Republicans challenging Democratic incumbents.

47. On June 30, 1982, the last date of Senate and House political committee filings for the off year elections, the Democratic Party Committees had together raised $24 million from all sources while the Republican Committees had raised $161 million. Most of this money did not come from PACs, but if we pursued the sources of this money, we would see that the success of the Republicans is attributable not only to the greater average wealth of their party's adherents, but also to the greater skill of the Republicans in solving problems of collective behavior. The threat to the political balance would be the same or even greater if it were Democrats rather than Republicans who had a substantial fund-raising advantage, because the Democrats usually receive substantial in-kind services from organized labor.

48. Lee Atwater, deputy assistant to President Reagan for political affairs, gave the following estimate of the role money would play in the 1982 congressional elections:

> I've got to think that the money and all the other resources combined will be worth about two percentage points for about thirty candidates. I think the story of this off-year election is that

are not primarily interested in who is elected; they are more concerned with how the interests they represent will fare in the legislature whoever is there. Thus the bulk of corporate PAC money goes to incumbents (although the share given to challengers, especially Republicans challenging Democrats, is increasing). Large contributions are often given to congressional leaders who face only token or even no opposition, and occasionally PACs will contribute to both the challenger and incumbent in a particular race.

What corporate PACs seek is influence. Not surprisingly, those enterprises that are most entangled with the government are the ones that most value the access that PAC contributions give them. Bernadette Budde, the Business-Industry Political Action Committee's (BIPAC) director of political education commented:

> A clear pattern emerges when reviewing who does and who does not have a PAC—the more regulated an industry and the more obvious an industry is as a Congressional target, the more likely it is to have a political action committee within the associations or within the companies that make up that industry. (Drew, 1982a, pp. 71–72)

And the PACs get influence. In the 1984 elections all PACs together spent, according to Congress Watch, an organization founded by Ralph Nader, more than $28 million. Even candidates opposed in principle to PAC funding often find they cannot afford to reject PAC money because to do so would give their less-scrupled opponents too great an advantage. When money cannot be rejected, it soon must be courted, and this often requires attention to interests that are not important in the congressperson's own state or district. Thus the interests of the local electorate become less significant relative to the interests of national organizations with money to spend. Budde of BIPAC put it this way:

> [A] congressman who was out of touch with his community now hears voices he didn't hear before. If he had never heard from the doctors before, or had never heard from the car dealers before he might have made different decisions because he was operating in a vacuum. (Drew, 1982a, p. 72)

What Budde did not say is that when the voices of the handful of car dealers or doctors in a congressional district are amplified by money from car dealers and doctors throughout the nation their interests may come to count more than those of ordinary citizens who form the bulk of the congressperson's constituency. For example, in 1982 the House and Senate voted to overturn a regulation of the Federal Trade Commission requiring used car dealers to list the known defects in autos they sell, a regulation that one would assume is in the interest of most citizens. But the automobile dealers had spent $675 thousand in the 1980 elections (up from $14,600 6 years before). Of the 268 House members

---

we've marshalled our resources and bought one or two Senate seats and fifteen to twenty House seats, and that's really good. (Drew, 1982a, p. 68)

The 1982 elections resulted, of course, in widespread losses for the Republicans, but Atwater may nonetheless have been close to the mark. The Republican defeat might have been much worse had they not enjoyed a substantial spending advantage.

who voted to overturn the regulations, 242 had received auto dealer money. "Of course it was the money," said one House member. "Why else would they vote for used-car dealers?" (Drew, 1982a, p. 131).

This brings us to the crux of the problem. It is not that PACs and other organized ways of channeling money into politics have upset the political balance. Although this is a cause for serious concern, some balance remains. Labor unions have their PACs, environmentalists have their PACs, and even social scientists have a lobbying group. But the way that balance is achieved is itself a problem. Organization and identification with specific causes, whether defined in left–right terms or as matters of pure self-interest, are becoming increasingly important for political influence. The independent judgments that we expect of our political representatives across a wide range of issues where constituent feelings are not high and expertise is important are growing less independent because the increasing importance of PACs and other nationally based funding sources means that interests that are of little moment to a congressperson's constituents may nonetheless bear on his prospects for reelection. Moreover, when average citizens have their preferences, such as the preference to know about the defects in a used car, organized pressure groups may outweigh their unorganized interests.

In sum, the growth of corporate power threatens the viability of various institutional arrangements and movements that may contribute to social justice. These include: (1) the efficiency of markets, (2) the participation rights of owners, (3) the association rights of workers, (4) the equal political liberty of unorganized members of society, (5) the equal distribution of welfare, and (6) the reallocation of welfare in accordance with the difference principle.[49]

Controlling Corporate Power

Attempts to control by law the threats that corporations pose have met with varying degrees of success. Much of the effort has been directed toward the end of maintaining competitive markets. Here efficiency rather than some other distributional principle such as the difference principle has defined the legal goal.

The effort has probably been most successful with respect to shareholder interests. The creation of capital markets in the form of stock exchanges and the regulation of these markets by the Securities and Exchange Commission (SEC) means that owners dissatisfied with corporate performance can easily exit by selling their shares at a market price. The SEC's task, as we noted earlier, is to ensure as much as possible that transactions in this market are fair, meaning that buyers and sellers are similarly situated in their ability to evaluate corporate stock. The most important element in fairness here is equality of information. Thus the SEC regulates the information in stock prospectuses and corporate

---

49. Note that although Rawls's perspective from which we are defining social justice is not empirically testable, given that perspective these judgments are testable.

reports and attempts to prevent insiders, such as corporate executives, from taking advantage of their special knowledge.

Antitrust laws, beginning with the Sherman Act in 1890, seek to restrict monopoly practices and thus ensure competitive markets. The success of the antitrust laws in achieving this objective has been in dispute since their inception. In many industries, including the automobile industry, aluminum, and more recently mainframe computers, the situation is far from the economist's model of perfect competition. Moreover, even in less concentrated industries, trade associations and other industry-wide organizations provide mechanisms for restricting price competition.

Baran and Sweezy (1966, p. 58, n. 4) relate the comments of one overly candid businessman to the Federal Trade Commission. Speaking of a trade association of chain manufacturers, he said:

> Maybe somebody will say to you, 'You so-and-so Son of a B, what did you do at Bill Jones?' And then somebody calls somebody a liar and so forth, and then maybe he would say, 'Well I have got the evidence that you did, and you are a liar,' and then you would get into a fight with this fellow, and first thing you know somebody else would come up and listen to the conversation, and then there would be six of them there, and they would be picking on you—I don't mean picking on me, but picking on these price cutters, you understand. . . . I have a marvelous vocabulary, I can assure you, when it comes to calling names, and it has been tested by every member of the Institute, and when I call a guy a dirty, low kind of so-and-so price cutter, he knows he has been called a price cutter. I will be frank, and if you want to crucify me, I will add this: I would tell him that if he didn't stop these damned price cuttings, I would show him how to cut prices, and many times I did cut them, and when I cut a price, and if it was your price I was cutting, take it from me, brother, you knew your price had been cut. I could go on and on and on—but I want to say that when any two businessmen get together, whether it is a Chain Institute meeting or a Bible class meeting, if they happen to belong to the same industry, just as soon as the prayers have been said, they start talking about the conditions in the industry, and it is bound definitely to gravitate, that talk, to the price structure of the industry. What else is there to talk about?

Yet such stories do not necessarily mean the laws have failed, for there is no way of knowing how concentrated industries might be or what monopoly profits might be extracted if the antitrust laws did not exist.

Where there is but one source for a good and entry into a market is difficult, the single source can choose to restrict production, raise prices, and extract a monopoly profit.[50] Where there is more than one source that can meet a demand,

---

50. A monopoly profit is the difference between the total profits made when supply and demand are in equilibrium in a fully competitive market and the profit made when production is restricted so that the price of the good times the amount produced yields the highest possible total profit. If only one firm is in a market, a monopoly price may be expected. The situation is different when more than one firm is in the market. If production can be easily expanded, maintaining a supracompetitive price requires an agreement among producers. Without an agreement, one producer can cut his price slightly, expand production, and if the other producers do not meet his price, capture the market.

explicit or tacit collusion must exist to extract monopoly profits, because un-bridled competition will lower the price to the point where the minimal profits needed to maintain the business are made. The antitrust laws seek to ban price fixing and other tactics that thwart competition.

Even without the antitrust laws, price fixing would in some circumstances be difficult because it takes only one substantial noncooperator to upset a price-fixing agreement. Although all businesspeople might like industry-wide price agreements that maximize total profits, many, like the chain manufacturers, find that not infrequently formal or tacit agreements break down as one firm tries to expand its sales at the expense of its competitors. More concentrated industries are, however, a different story. Here the antitrust laws are more important to the maintenance of competitive markets and less successful. This is because small groups, especially those with dominant members, are more likely than large groups to produce collective goods (in this instance a supracompetitive price; Olson, 1971, pp. 22–36). Indeed, in some industries overt communication is not necessary for price fixing. Usually, it will be clear to all that when one of a few dominant firms raises prices, others are to follow. The ability to cooperate without consultation is important, for the antitrust laws are directed against *agreements* in restraint of trade.

This is not the place for a technical discourse on the implications of monopoly practices. It is important, however, to note some consequences of monopoli-zation. First, it produces a deadweight loss because monopolists do not produce as much as would be produced in a competitive market. This means that some of those who would purchase a good at a competitive price will not do so when the price is raised. Second, monopoly prices transfer wealth from the consumer to the monopolist. Consumers pay more for the good than they would at com-petitive prices and the monopolist extracts an extra profit even after taking account of the fact that he sells fewer units of the good than he otherwise would. Thus monopolies are not only inefficient, they alter the distribution of welfare as well.

Although traditional analysis has focused on the efficiency losses caused by monopolies, these may be less distorting than the effects monopolies have on the distribution of welfare. Some analyses have estimated that the efficiency losses due to monopolization fall in the range of 0.1 to 0.5 percent of the gross national product (Carson, 1973, pp. 508–511). Although the absolute sum is large, the percentage figures probably give a better estimate of the impact of monopoly prices on the nation's economy. One reason the efficiency losses attributed to monopolies are relatively small is that they are often offset by

---

If the other producers cut their prices to meet the competition and the cycle repeats, a competitive equilibrium, which is not in the best interest of any producer, will be reached. Price structures that depend on a group of competitors agreeing to restrict output so that they can sell their goods at a supracompetitive price are called *oligopolistic*. The antitrust laws allow certain kinds of monopolies to be broken up and penalize both attempts to monopolize and price fixing. In this way the laws work to maintain competitive markets. An agreement to fix prices is implicitly an agreement to restrict output, since as the price increases less goods can be sold, and the maintenance of a supracompetitive price depends upon the demand at that price being no less than the available supply.

economies of scale. A complicating factor, however, is that the concentrated power of firms with monopolist market positions often enables them to externalize some costs of production, and thus hold down prices. For example, the automobile industry has had some success in stalling efforts that would force them to pay the costs of automobile-generated air pollution, and drug companies may cooperate in not publicizing information about the adverse effects of a drug that several of them manufacture. In these types of situations more cars and drugs will be sold than is "economic," and the manufacturers' profits will rise accordingly. As importantly, people will suffer who would not if the externalities were prevented.

In sum, the efficiency costs of economic concentration may not be enormous, and the antitrust laws have been successful in preventing the worst types of predatory practices such as those exhibited by Standard Oil in the last century. However, the threats that concentrations of capital pose to the distribution of welfare are more serious, and as we noted earlier, corporate political activities can pose serious problems for the democratic process.[51] We return to these problems later. First, however, we deal with threats to efficiency in the labor market. Here we focus on our other type of corporate actor: labor unions.

LABOR UNIONS

Trade unionism has two roots. The first is in medieval guilds, which were essentially cartels designed to control entry to the various trades and to raise the wages that master craftsmen could command. Craft unions, such as those of the plumbers, carpenters, and electricians, are in this tradition. Often they bargain with relatively small localized businesses or associations of businesses like building contractors' groups. The other tradition and the one with which we are primarily concerned is industrial unionism. Industrial unions, as their name implies, organize workers not on the basis of their skills or trade, but on the basis of the industry or even the factory that employs them. Unionization of this sort was seen as necessary to overcome the inordinate bargaining strength that employers, especially large corporate employers, were thought to possess. Industrial unions much more than craft unions historically pitted workers as a class against management and the capitalist interests they represented as a class.

Unionization as a device for promoting the efficiency of labor markets is qualitatively different from the promotion of efficiency through capital markets or the use of antitrust laws. It is a device that follows John C. Calhoun's precept that "Power [can] only be resisted by power and tendency by tendency" (Hurst, 1956, p. 85). The union is, after all, another corporate actor.

---

51. Our focus, by way of example, on recent developments in the areas of corporate free speech and campaign financing is not intended to suggest that these problems are new or that business corporations have only recently become important political actors. Railroads, coal companies, and large industrial corporations have for the past century in some areas at some times dominated local political life.

As a corporate actor, a union can do more than merely counteract the power of a business in the labor market. It can attempt to: (1) create the collective good (for union members) of a monopoly price for labor; (2) exclude people from employment opportunities through artificial barriers to employment; (3) coerce union members in ways that impinge on their rights and opportunities (e.g., allocate seniority on a racially discriminatory basis); (4) cooperate with management in shifting certain business costs to third parties, and (5) use its economic and political power to gain special influence in the political arena.

Unions, unlike corporations, grew initially in spite of the law rather than as a creation of it. The resistance to unions was usually a result of management's perception of its self-interest, but it was often justified on the basis of one or more of the aforementioned possibilities. A little history will be helpful in indicating how management used the law to resist unionization and how unions, like other corporate actors, came to pose problems for the social order.

The Cordwainers

In the United States some of the earliest judicial attempts to deal with unionization involved journeymen cordwainers (shoemakers). *Journeymen* were individuals who were past the stage of learning a skill (apprentices), but were not master craftsmen. Early unions among cordwainers and other crafts consisted of journeymen. They banded together to form collective bargaining groups that dealt with employers as a unit.

Employers attempted to thwart such activity by asking the courts to find that these groups were criminal conspiracies. The courts almost never held that the mere organization by a group of workers to bargain for themselves constituted a criminal conspiracy.[52] In several cases, however, the judiciary's view of the law was clearly hostile to organization. Judge Roberts's instruction to the jury in the *Pittsburgh Cordwainers Case* (1815) (*Commonwealth* v. *Murrow*, see Commons and Gilmore, 1910) is typical:

> It has been truly said that every man has a right to affix what price he pleases on his labour. It is not for demanding high prices that these men are endicted, but for employing unlawful means to extort these prices. For using means prejudicial to the community. Confederacies of this kind have a most pernicious effect, as respects the community at large. They restrain trade; they tend to banish many artisans, and to oppress others. It is the interest of the public, and it so is the right of every individual, that those who are skilled in any profession, art or mystery, should be

---

52. An important exception was the *Philadelphia Cordwainers Case* in 1806 (Commons & Gilmore, 1910). The sealed verdict in this case read, "We find the defendants guilty of a combination to raise their wages." It is not clear that the jurors intended this to be translated into a verdict of guilty, but the court that had charged the jurors that the law condemned a combination of workers to raise their wages whether it was intended to benefit themselves or to injure those not in their society did so (Nelles, 1931, p. 192).

unrestrained in the exercise of it. . . . A conspiracy to compel men to work, at certain prices, is doubtless endictable. It is a restraint of that freedom, which every citizen ought to enjoy, of affixing what prices he pleases on his own labour.

The activity that the judge was proclaiming illegal was a strike brought against employers because they tried to hire journeymen at a price below that agreed upon by the union. On these instructions, the jury found the cordwainers guilty. The court fined them a dollar apiece.

But whose freedom is the judge referring to in the preceding comments? There are three parties: the manufacturers, the laborers, and the rest of the citizenry. Successful unionization means that an employer cannot (is no longer free to) buy labor at a price unaffected by collective organization or bargaining. The worker is restricted from selling his labor at any price he chooses. As for the rest of us, we are no longer free to buy goods in markets that are unaffected by monopolies or restraints of trade. All three "freedoms" are intertwined in the Pittsburgh case. The closing paragraph of the instructions goes from one to the other with more emotion than clarity:

> They [the union] did not indeed drive, by personal violence, from the town, any stranger who happened to come into it: but they adopted means which must eventually drive a journeyman from the town, or immerse him in a jail. It would be mere mockery to say that a journeyman shoemaker (without becoming a member of the society) might exercise his trade freely in Pittsburgh. Was it to be expected that any master workman would employ such a stranger, when the consequences must be the ruin of his own business? No! The stranger must become a wretched wanderer, destitute of employment, and of the means of subsistence. Can anything be imagined more prejudicial to the trade and prosperity of the town? It is the interest of the borough to promote the settlement of mechanics and manufacturers amongst them; and to prevent monopolies. Would it not be monstrous if a confederacy of individuals could exclude those whom it is so much the interest of the community to cherish? Shall they establish a monopoly necessarily prejudicial to the public?[53]

It is important to disentangle the different freedoms threatened by the collective action of the cordwainers if we are to make much headway in understanding the trade-offs posed by trade unions. In doing so, we should recall the three levels of collective action discussed at the outset of the chapter: (1) the simple coordination of individual efforts with the goal of increasing efficiency and productivity; (2) coordination and mutual agreement with the goal of producing inclusive collective goods; and (3) coordination and mutual agreement with the goal of producing exclusive collective goods. The latter two types of collective action require some method of controlling free riders. This is especially important with exclusive collective goods since to the extent free riders consume the good, less is available for those who supply it.[54]

---

53. Recall that this is an instruction to a jury. The passive, neutral referee style of judging has not always been the ideal in American law.

54. With exclusive collective goods, there is also the problem of assuring that someone who was not a free rider to begin with does not become one by consuming more than his share of the good.

The Rights of Employers

First, there is the right of employers to be able to bargain with each individual worker concerning the conditions of employment. This right, if it can be called one at all, is likely to yield just and efficient outcomes only if buyers and sellers of labor meet in competitive markets with relatively equal bargaining power. A common justification for unions rests on the belief that these conditions do not exist in many situations. Where employers are relatively strong unions are instruments of *countervailing power* (Galbraith, 1967) which is needed to offset the bargaining power of employers. Because competitive labor markets often do not exist, employers, according to this view, are able to underpay workers and so create both inefficiencies and inequalities. Countervailing power is to some extent a substitute for competition.

Of course, in certain circumstances unions themselves can gain a position of market dominance and use their monopoly power to raise wages beyond what a competitive market would establish. This also produces inefficiencies and distributional distortions. In many cases, however, where the result of labor–management negotiations is to maximize the combined profit of management and labor, the game that unions and firms play is relatively efficient in that the wage rate and the quantity of goods produced approximate that which would be expected if neither labor nor management had monopoly power (Carson, 1973).

It seems, therefore, that the employer's right to an individualized labor market is a tenuous right indeed. In any situation where the employer would otherwise enjoy some monopoly power on the labor market, the existence of unions will tend to restore the competitive market equilibrium which is the basic justification of the right in the first place. But then the courts never thought much of this right, and we can turn to more difficult cases.

The Rights of Employees

In the nineteenth century the most important legal argument for restricting unions centered on the right of workers not to be coerced by unions. Refusals to work with "scabs" and demands for the discharge of those who worked for less than union wages brought the wrath of the courts down upon unions.

In the first half of the nineteenth century only one case, *Commonwealth* v. *Hunt*, 45 Mass., 1 Met. 111 (1842), permitted the coercion of other workers. The *Hunt* court found no legal violation when a group of journeymen boatmakers pressed an employer to discharge a journeyman who when fined by the union for working for less than scale wages refused to pay the fine. The case, however, did not mark a trend. Over the next half century a pattern emerged whereby unions could lawfully strike for higher wages, shorter hours, or other economic terms, but they could not strike or use economic force to interfere with individual labor contracts or to compel employers to bargain exclusively with the union. Strikes directed to the latter ends were met with injunctions, specific orders that, if violated, would allow a judge, typically the one who issued the injunction, to impose without a jury trial a substantial fine or jail sentence.

The Massachusetts Supreme Court, home of *Commonwealth* v. *Hunt*, as recently as 1921 wrote an opinion in which it said:

> Whatever may be the advantages of "collective bargaining," it is not bargaining at all, in any just sense, unless it is voluntary on both sides. The same liberty which enables men to form unions, and through the union to enter into agreements with employers willing to agree, entitles other men to remain independent of the union and other employers to agree with them to employ no man who owes any allegiance or obligation to the union. [*United Shoe Machinery Co.* v. *Fitsgerald*, 237 Mass. 537, 543–544 (1921) quoting *Hitchman Coal & Coke Co.* v. *Mitchell*, 235 U.S. 229 (1917)]

Note the inconsistency in this position. Although the unions could not legally coerce men to join unions, employers could, as we noted in earlier chapters, use various forms of coercion, such as the blackball, to deter employees from joining a union. If this inconsistency is to be explained by more than a bias in favor of employers, it must be understood as a commitment to one view of individualism. A person should be at liberty to act as an individual, which includes both the freedom to enter into whatever contract he alone can secure and the freedom not to be forced to associate with others in an effort to achieve a common good. These are the basic freedoms that courts were guaranteeing workers. What the courts objected to was not union organization, but union efforts to control free riders by means of coercion. Some might say the freedom being recognized was the freedom to hang separately by not hanging together.

In the industrial context, in particular, the purported freedom of the individual often undermines the individual's ability to join a collectivity that will help him better his lot. The value of the latter ability, which is itself a kind of freedom, is attested to by the hundreds of thousands of people who risked their jobs and sometimes their lives in fighting for it.

Despite substantial judicial resistance, including criminal conspiracy trials and the frequent use of the labor injunction, unions never relented in arguing for the right to coerce their potential members. As we have already noted, the logic of collective action compelled the unions in this course. Yet the judicial concern for worker freedom should not be dismissed out of hand.

Complexities arise because unions often pursue both *inclusive* and *exclusive* public goods. First, unions are interested in the inclusive collective good that comes from the ability to neutralize, through countervailing power, the unequal situation of individual workers confronting large businesses. The union members benefit as a group from their increased power vis à vis management. In pursuing the goal of countervailing power, the union seeks to organize as great a proportion of the work force as it can. The larger the union, the greater their countervailing power, and the more people there are to share relatively fixed organizational costs. Free riders are the undeserved beneficiaries of what the union accomplishes, and their presence in sufficient numbers can undermine the union's ability to accomplish anything. As we pointed out earlier in this chapter, a common response of unions to the free rider problem was to coerce recalcitrants to join their ranks. The Depression era labor laws legitimized some union coercion and made illegal some employer devices that were designed to undermine organizing efforts and to appeal to the self-interest of potential free riders. These laws were designed to assist the creation of unions.

Unions may, however, pursue exclusive collective goods, that is, goods that are limited in supply. Some individuals may be unable to work because a union has sufficient power to insist on especially high wages for those it admits to membership. Craft unions, for example, have a history of attempting to control not only wage rates and working conditions, but also access to jobs and the introduction of new technologies. By restricting entry, the union is able to secure higher wages for its members than those that would prevail if the supply of labor expanded to meet the demand. However, these high wages induce people to develop craft skills even if they are denied entry to the union, and they give employers a substantial incentive to hire nonunion craftspeople who will work for less than union scale. The unions cannot hope to allocate all the work in their specialties to their members, but through tactics such as strikes and boycotts, they try to ensure that the area's principal employers use only union labor.

The attempt to control the introduction of new technologies is similarly motivated. Craft unions have traditional domains of work. If technological change means that traditional work need not be done or can be done by those with less or different skills, there will be less work for union members and their incomes will fall. For example, carpenters have traditionally hung doors in frames on the site of building projects. However, industry can now produce prehung doors, using machines and less-skilled labor. Because such doors are cheaper to install, contractors and consumers have a substantial incentive to insist on them. The carpenter's union has an equally strong incentive to resist this innovation, for the switch to prehung doors effectively transfers money from their pockets to those of consumers and less-skilled factory labor. Strikes develop over such issues, and the law has developed to regulate the conditions under which such strikes will be permitted.

Strikes on work retention issues have a special quality. Although nominally against employers because they seek to extract a promise that the innovation will not be used, the opposing interests are largely those of workers who would benefit if the innovation were used. In the door-hanging example, those who will lose if the carpenters succeed are faceless workers at distant industrial plants.

Union efforts to establish a minimum wage arguably have a similar effect. Minimum wage laws create a collective good for workers with jobs that is similar to a monopoly price for firms. Here, however, the collective action that makes it possible is imposed by the state in the form of a statute making it illegal to pay workers less than a certain amount. A minimum wage law is a two-edged sword. Any minimum wage that is effective—that in fact establishes a wage floor higher than that which would otherwise be paid the most poorly paid worker—puts some people out of work. Not only does it advantage those with jobs at the expense of those who are priced out of the labor market, but it also carries with it some social cost since less is produced than would otherwise be the case.[55] Like monopoly prices, minimum wage laws have both efficiency and wealth distribution consequences. The presence of substantial unemployment means that production is less efficient than it might be, and some of the income that would otherwise go to those whose work is valuable but not worth the minimum wage is paid to those who are employed.[56]

The fact that unions pursue exclusive collective goods lends some credence to the concerns of early courts about the nature of union power, for it is more difficult to justify the exclusive good of labor monopoly than the inclusive good of countervailing power.

The fact that unions pursue both inclusive and exclusive goods also produces tensions within organized labor. These tensions explain the seemingly contradictory behavior of the union movement. On the one hand, the movement as a whole seeks the general expansion of trade unionism, and particular unions want to limit work in their craft or industry to union members.[57] When inclusive goods are pursued, this makes sense. Objectives such as the closed or union

---

55. If the minimum wage is inefficient and has certain undesirable distributional consequences, why do such laws exist? Partly this may be due to an historic failure to understand the economic consequences of such statutes, but it is likely that such laws are due in larger part to the desire to achieve another end of social justice—a more equal distribution of welfare. In particular, minimum wage laws are fueled by the conception that it is unjust to employ someone full time for wages that will not buy the requisites of a decent minimal standard of living. To the extent that the state through "welfare" payments brings the unemployed up to the level that they would achieve by working in a society that lacked minimum wage laws, a case can be made for the laws from a social justice perspective. No one is being hurt socially, except in the marginal sense that everyone's tax expenses are slightly higher, and a substantial portion of the "next to worst off" are being helped.

56. Effects are similar and more substantial, although numerically probably less consequential, when exclusion is more direct, as it is when unions restrict union membership in sectors where employers agree to hire only union labor.

57. The desire to limit work to union members does not have the same meaning for craft and industrial unions. Hence there are different motivations for similar desires. On the craft side the union through its apprenticeship system determines who can be members. If only union members can be hired for a job, the ability to control membership will allow the craft union to achieve the exclusive collective good of a supracompetitive wage rate. On the industrial side, management determines who is hired and the union's demand is that those who are hired join their ranks. This is because once an industrial wage rate has been negotiated, it is an inclusive collective good for all who work in the covered jobs. No one in a covered position may be excluded from the union wage, and if the company hires additional workers who share in the good, returns to other members will not diminish. Thus the incentives to compulsory unionism in the industrial sphere are the desire to spread the production cost of the inclusive good across all who benefit and the fact that if more people share the costs of producing the good, more should be produced. The latter proposition may hold in only a limited sense. A company's ability to weather a strike by all its production workers may not vary much with the numerical size of the striking union (assuming that the strategic nature of the union's position and the ability to replace unionized labor with nonunionized labor is held constant). However, if a substantial proportion of a company's work force is not unionized and does not strike, the company should suffer less than it would if its entire work force was on strike, with the result that the union would be likely to settle for less than it could extract if the entire work force were unionized. Thus it appears that what is most crucial to a union is not the total number of unionized workers in a plant, but the proportion of workers who are in fact union members. Unions behave as if this were the case.

shop and automatic dues checkoffs originate in the desire to eliminate free riders. The deep-seated union opposition to right-to-work laws has similar roots.

On the other hand, unions have at times used their power to limit the work force. Some of the early judicial opposition to unions may charitably be interpreted as reflecting a fear that unions would be able to upset the market price of labor by excluding workers. Whether unions in general have done so is an open question, but to some degree this has been possible. Within restricted areas, unions have created the collective good of a supracompetitive wage that requires the exclusion from the labor market of some who would otherwise be employed. Restrictions of this sort create distributional problems. Not only do they lead to inefficiencies of the kind we have described, but, by creating artificial barriers to entry, they violate Rawls's principle of open offices.[58] The injustice caused by this violation is exacerbated when it is combined with the systematic under-representation of specific groups based on work-irrelevant characteristics such as ethnicity, gender, or the restriction of apprenticeships to relatives of union members.

Nor is the issue of employee rights limited to those who cannot join or are forced to join unions. As with the participatory rights of corporate shareholders, questions arise concerning the individual rights of union members, especially their political right to participate in the affairs of the organization. In many unions, as in most large corporations, the leadership is to some extent beyond member control.

Despite the ethos of democratic trade unionism, this is not surprising. Any group that, like a union, strives to produce a collective good has an interest in coercing members into a single position and subordinating members to the rule of the organization. There operates what Robert Michels (1949) called the *iron law of oligarchy*: "It is organization which gives birth to the dominion of the elected over the electors, of the mandataries over the mandators, of the delegates over the delegators. Who says organization, says oligarchy" (p. 401).

James Coleman (1974) discusses some of the ways in which unions have taken power from their members (pp. 47–50). First, there is the development of a "cult of unity." Unless unity prevails, the organization cannot survive. To promote the cult, some unions have constitutional clauses banning suborganizations that seek to influence the union's course. Thus they "atomize" those who might wish to challenge the leadership in much the same way that management once sought to atomize labor. Second, election procedures can be changed to undermine potential opposition. To nip dissent in the bud, locals may be expelled or brought under the direct rule of the national organization. Third, the funds at the disposal of the union and its control over working conditions give its leaders substantial resources with which to fight organized opposition. Overall, the advantages of incumbency are so great that grassroots

---

58. This latter point applies to professional associations as well as to some trade unions. The American Medical Association, for example, has frequently been accused of using its certification powers and its influence with universities to restrict the supply of physicians.

campaigns to replace union leadership are seldom mounted and rarely successful. In recent years involuntary changes in the leadership of large unions in the United States have usually occurred only when the old leadership or some part of it has been convicted of criminal activity.

The independence enjoyed by union leaders is similar to the independence that managers enjoy in the corporate sphere. In large, publicly held corporations, as we have seen, the owners (shareholders) have little or no control over the operation of the business. Their only real power is the power to sell their stock and thereby abandon the organization. In this regard stockholders have an advantage over union members. They can, when unhappy, easily sever their ties with the organization. The exit option is not available to many workers who face union or agency shops. An alternative mode of protest, voicing complaints, is also not fully satisfactory in the union setting.

In his brilliant book, *Exit, Voice and Loyalty*, Albert Hirschman (1971) suggests that in both cases there is a fundamental inadequacy in the typical response of members. Corporations are not much influenced by the exit behavior of stockholders, and although businesses might be influenced if enough voices are raised together, stockholders for reasons we have already discussed are unlikely to respond in this way. Trade unions, on the other hand, have made exit nearly impossible, although they would be greatly affected by it (p. 122). But voice, the only active response available to dissenting union members, is seriously stifled by organizational needs for solidarity and the rules that some unions pass using solidarity as a justification.

So the solution of one difficulty presents another. In the very process of creating a legal structure that allows workers to organize against corporate power, the law has created a situation in which unions can coerce their members in ways that are not directly related to the procurement of the collective good. Coleman (1974) concisely states the dilemma:

> by giving the corporate body power to act, each member largely loses his power over the direction its actions will take; but by withholding this power through a more restrictive decision rule, the potential benefits brought by the corporate actor vanish. (pp. 40–41)

The Rights of Citizens

The third concern of the judges in the early trade union cases was for the rights of the public at large. This interest was largely directed toward the threat of monopoly power. To the degree that unions act as organizations of countervailing power against employers, the threat seems less serious than the judges made it out to be.[59]

---

59. This statement should be qualified by the possibility that labor and management may collude to promote their joint interest in higher wages and higher prices. To the extent that higher prices are made possible by the monopoly power of one or both, wealth is transferred from consumers to corporations and those who work for them.

A more important consideration in assessing the effect of unions on the public is the ability that unions share with other powerful corporate groups to use their economic power to influence the political process. Union support for the minimum wage is a case in point. Although the minimum wage may protect union members and in some situations improve the union's bargaining position vis-à-vis employers, it works, as we have noted, against the interests of less-skilled people seeking to enter the labor market.

In general, unions and other corporate organizations are able to influence greatly and sometimes dominate those social and economic decisions that affect us all. Philippe Nonet provides a particularly nice example of this in his book *Administrative Justice* (1969). Organized labor cooperated with corporate and insurance interests to transform the California Industrial Accident Commission from a paternalistic, proactive, worker-oriented body in which a worker might recover on his own initiative, to a passive, neutral judicial agency in which a lawyer's aid was important. Those who through their unions had access to experienced lawyers at reasonable rates probably benefited from the transformation because they knew when they were entitled to compensation and, by pushing their legal rights to the fullest, they often were able to secure better outcomes than the paternalistic IAC would have given them. The unorganized sector was clearly less well served by the change than union members and may have been made absolutely worse off. It is the difference principle in reverse. The better off gain at the expense of the less fortunate.

Ultimately, we are dealing with matters that are even more fundamental than the difference principle to the conception of social justice we have borrowed from Rawls. To quote James Coleman (1974):

> among the variety of interests that men have, those interests that have been successfully collected to create corporate actors are the interests that dominate the society . . . decisions about the employment of resources are more and more removed from the multiplicity of dampening and modifying interests of which a real person is composed—more and more the resultant of a balance of narrow intense interests of which corporate actors are composed. Thus to simplify an example, the highway taxes on trucking will be the outcome of the balance of interests among the trucking industry and the Teamsters Union on the one hand, and the railway industry and the railway unions on the other. Interests of natural persons who are not incorporated, not part of the conflicts and bargains among corporate actors, will not enter. (pp. 49–50)

This is the most serious threat, for it allows economic and social inequalities to invade the realm of rights and to undermine the first principle of justice: that each *individual* should enjoy equal liberty.

Our critique is, of course, not aimed only or even primarily at labor unions. The problem is highlighted in the case of unions because in the process of pursuing certain ends of social justice, that is, an efficient labor market and a more equal distribution of resources between labor and management, there is the danger that other precepts of social justice will be violated. But business corporations certainly do as much if not more than unions to undermine equal liberties and subordinate them to issues of economic and social distribution. The problem is not with particular corporate actors, but with corporate actors in general. These actors have altered society in fundamental ways.

Arthur Stinchcombe (1968) provides us with a calculus for this fundamental change. He notes that in a simple society without great concentrations of power, the influence of a given value on that society will ordinarily be largely determined by the average commitment of the society's members to that value. In modern societies, however, the influence of a given value or interest should be understood as an *interaction effect*, in which variations in the degree of commitment to a value have different implications depending on the relative amount of power held by deeply and shallowly committed individuals. Corporate organizations have substantial power. They can accumulate wealth that is not scattered or redirected as death changes generations. They are able to coerce members to participate in the pursuit of given values. And they approach social issues with the transaction costs of collective action prepaid for other purposes. Thus the values and interests of corporate actors are disproportionately influential given the human interests they represent. In particular, there is the danger that shallowly held corporate values will come to dominate deeply held human ones (Stinchcombe, 1968, pp. 182–183). For example, the timber industry's preference for extending roads deep into the national forest to log marginal timber areas may be a weak one, while the human preference (which we shall assume most people share) for leaving the nether reaches of these forests pristine may be a strong one, but the power of the lumber companies and the difficulties of mobilizing diffuse opposition may mean that when the political battle over logging remote areas is fought the interests of the lumber companies prevail.

Yet we cannot return to the *status quo ante*. The problem is how to cope. One solution that has worked tolerably well is that of countervailing power. If corporate actors of relatively equal power advance opposing interests, different voices will be heard and ordinary people, as voters, may choose between them. But as we saw in our discussion of labor and management, even natural antagonists may agree on certain matters. Although such agreement may signify that the accepted solution is generally in the public interest, this is not necessarily the case. Almost always there will be some unorganized sector whose interests are slighted. Indeed, as we noted in Chapter 6, a great facilitator of agreement between antagonists is the ability to transfer costs to third parties. Furthermore, the solution of countervailing power is a delicate one. There is always the danger that things will get out of balance. Recent extensions of corporate rights to free speech and the invention of the corporate PAC, when added to the preexisting ability of the wealthy to fund political action, threaten to create such an imbalance. Ultimately, the only viable solution may depend on law, that is, on the resources of our most powerful and universal corporate actor, the state. But as the political power of private corporate interests increases, legal solutions to the problems posed by such power become less likely, and the possibility that the law will side with corporate interests and slight those of the unorganized citizenry increases as well.[60]

SUMMARY

The growth of corporate power threatens a number of the principles that we identified with social justice in the preceding chapter. Corporate organizations create inefficiencies, produce inequalities that go far beyond the limits established by the difference principle,[61] and threaten equal political liberty. By and large the legal response has been limited to attempts at reestablishing efficiency through the control of monopolistic practices. In most areas of corporate power a natural liberty conception of social justice still dominates.

There have been few attempts to use law to limit the implications of corporate power for equal political liberty. The most important attempts have probably been the laws that limit corporate expenditures to advance political views, but as we have seen, some of these laws are now of doubtful constitutionality and the rise of PACs has opened a new mode of corporate political influence. Other efforts to confine corporate influence include disclosure laws regarding lobbying and the public financing of presidential elections, but the latter has been undercut by loopholes in recent years (Drew, 1982).

Efforts to achieve economic distributions that are compatible with the difference principle have also been limited. One important effort occurred in the 1930s when legal support was given to the trade union movement. Although the Depression era labor laws were passed in part to achieve industrial peace and to limit the ability of businesses to impose wages and working conditions, they can also be viewed as having a modest redistributive goal, transferring money from investors to workers. Later labor law legislation, however, legalized state right-to-work laws. Moreover, for a variety of complex social and economic reasons, among which right-to-work laws play at most a small role, the percentage of workers represented by organized labor in the last 20 years has been in decline.

A second movement in the direction of the difference principle has been the redistributive welfare legislation that began in the Roosevelt years and reached a zenith in President Johnson's Great Society. The first Reagan Administration, though, targeted many of these programs for reduction and, as we write, the

---

60. We do not have the space to pursue the issue, but one way to mobilize the unorganized is through emotion-rousing demagogic appeals. It may be that the apparent rise of such appeals in modern society reflects the dominance of corporate over individual interests in more highly structured political arenas.

61. A decade ago the richest 1 percent of American families held about one-third of the country's wealth and earned about 6 percent of after-tax income. The bottom 50 percent of all families held only 5 percent of the total wealth and received about 25 percent of all income (Okun, 1975, p. 66). News reports indicate that the disparity, in after-tax earnings at least, has been increased by the 1981 "Reagan tax cuts."

second Reagan Administration threatens to reduce many of them still further or to eliminate them entirely.[62]

As this more recent history suggests, many people in our society believe a movement toward greater economic redistribution compatible with the difference principle is an undesirable goal. And any serious movement toward a conception of justice based on the difference principle would involve a substantial alteration of our understanding of the rule of law. We return to this issue in Chapters 12 and 13.

First, however, we examine another endeavor: the use of law to establish formal political equality and to advance social and economic equality by providing equal opportunity rather than by simply opening careers to talents. The effort, to use Rawls's terms, is to move away from a natural liberty conception of social justice and toward a liberal equality conception. Our society has shown some commitment to this definition of social justice for a long time, at least since the establishment of universal public education. In Chapter 11 we focus on a more recent manifestation, the attempt to deal with racial inequality in the United States. We try to explain why the law has had varying degrees of success in enhancing racial equality. In doing so, we hope to gain a better understanding of the relationship between the legal order and the social order under different conceptions of social justice.

---

62. Some might argue that the so-called safety net principle has meant that Rawls's "least well off" group has not been harmed and that the difference principle has been honored in the movement to cut back on the "Great Society" programs. To some extent this depends on what proportion of those at bottom the "least well off" segment encompasses. The justice of the recent cutbacks in a Rawlsian sense would also vary from program to program. One might also consider the justice of programs that enhance the lot of the best off while harming the interests of the less well off but not harming or even improving the lot of those on the bottom. Rawls does not explicitly consider the former circumstance, although it appears that if the lot of the worst off was not improved, the change would not be permitted. Where the lot of the worst off was improved, it appears that the change would be permitted if it were the only way to bring about these consequences.

11

Pursuing Equality: Law as a Force for Social Change

John Rawls's theory of justice with which we began Part III of this book views social or distributive justice as a matter of rules and institutions. Social justice is to be achieved by establishing a set of rules and institutions that, through their normal operations, produce outcomes that accord with the principles of justice. But if rules and institutions can produce just social arrangements by Rawls's or some other standards, they may produce unjust arrangements as well. They can, in the language of Chapter 9, violate the first principle of justice by producing unequal liberty, or the second principle by producing a system that denies fair equality of opportunity, thus destroying efficient markets and barring talented people from some careers. In the United States, throughout most of its history, some rules and institutions have been arranged so as to affect black citizens in these ways.

Racial inequality is older than the Republic. Until the Civil War it was a central part of the social order. After the Civil War, in order to achieve greater equality for blacks, three amendments to the Constitution were, in effect, imposed by the Union States on the states of the Confederacy, and Congress passed several civil rights acts. The latter went largely unenforced, and in 1883 the Supreme Court declared the 1875 Civil Rights Act unconstitutional. This act had provided that all persons in the United States "shall be entitled to the full and equal enjoyment of the accommodations, advantages, facilities, and privileges of inns, public conveyances on land or water, theatres, and other places of public amusement. . . ." *Civil Rights Cases*, 109 U.S. 3, 9 (1883). The decision in the Civil Rights Cases together with the decision in *Plessy* v. *Ferguson*, 163 U.S. 537 (1896), which allowed states to require "separate but equal" facilities, opened the door to "Jim Crow" laws. Soon legislation mandating racial segregation in various social settings was common throughout the southern and border states. Despite the Civil War these states again had in place a set of rules and institutions designed to create fundamental inequalities between blacks and whites.

Over the next 50 years the Supreme Court slowly retreated from its positions in the *Civil Rights Cases* and *Plessy* until in 1954 in *Brown* v. *Board of Education*, 347 U.S. 483, the Court explicitly held that separate schools were inherently unequal. Subsequent decisions extended this principle to all governmentally mandated segregation, and the courts for the next decade were generally far in front of other governmental agencies in trying to use the law to promote racial equality. Finally, in the 1960s Congress once again passed civil rights legislation designed to promote racial equality in the United States.

When the Supreme Court struck down the 1875 Civil Rights Act one approving Arkansas editorial, reflecting the sociology of the day, noted: "Society is a law unto itself, which in matters social in their nature overrides the statutes. Against its decrees the written law is powerless" (Franklin, 1965, p. 5). The editor's view suggests that the prominent role that Rawls (and this book) give to legal rules is misplaced. As written, the editorial is wrong: law and legal institutions do have effects. But its reminder that there are limits to our ability to use law to maintain and, especially, to alter existing distributions should be taken seriously.

Because the question of how law can affect entrenched patterns of social behavior is problematic and intriguing, the civil rights movement has provided an abundance of grist for the social scientist's mill. It has given us the raw material with which to examine the effectiveness of law as an instrument of social justice. Moreover, the topic is not some interesting but rare grain. It deals with an American staple—racial inequality; and it has the additional advantage for our purposes that the settings in which social change has been attempted and the legal actions that have been taken to enhance racial equality are sufficiently diverse so as to illustrate numerous contingencies that affect the implications of law for behavior.

In this chapter we discuss efforts to deal with three types of inequality. First we examine the federal government's role in extending voting rights to blacks in the South. Next we examine attempts to desegregate schools. Third we discuss efforts to create greater equality in employment. After presenting an overview of legal developments in these areas during the last three decades, we seek to generalize from these examples and to identify factors that affect the ability of law to alter the allocation of liberty and welfare in society. These factors fall into five topical areas: (1) The qualities of the rule or regulation. (2) The qualities of the regulator (courts, administrative agencies, etc.). (3) The qualities of the regulated groups. (4) The qualities of the beneficiaries of the rules. (5) The nature of the inequality. Aspects of these topics are by now familiar to you. Thus one of the qualities of the rule or regulation that may influence its effectiveness is whether it is a strict liability rule, and one of the similarly important qualities of both the groups regulated by and the beneficiaries of legal norms is their ability to overcome barriers to collective action. We shall also point to factors we have not heretofore mentioned such as the elasticity and contingency of an inequality. In every case our goal is to arrive at a better understanding of the circumstances under which law is more or less effective in influencing the distribution of political, social, and economic welfare in society.

In looking at efforts to use the law to guarantee voting rights, to desegregate schools, and to end job discrimination we shall see that the effectiveness of legal intervention is in part contingent on the social justice goal to be achieved. Inequalities in the spheres we examine cut across Rawls's two principles of social justice. Voting relates fundamentally to the first principle requirement of equal liberty. School desegregation and employment opportunity relate more closely to a second principle desiderata—the just distribution of economic and social goods (the opportunity to acquire an education is a good in this sense). Using rules to equalize the distribution of such goods may prove more difficult than using rules to promote equal liberty, both because rules that seek to alter the distribution of goods may impinge upon lexically prior (for Rawls at least) first principle values and because there is more ambiguity and conflict—in the society and in the rules themselves—concerning the just distribution of goods than there is when the goal is equal political liberty (see Reynolds, 1984; Marshall, 1984). For example, with respect to both school desegregation and equal employment opportunity, the civil rights laws appear to equivocate between the *Careers Open to Talents* and the *Equality of Fair Opportunity* concepts of equal opportunity. We touch upon this point briefly at the end of the chapter when we discuss the tension between equal opportunity and equal outcome goals. A more complete discussion of this topic is postponed to Chapters 12 and 13 where we discuss legal autonomy and the use of law to achieve various visions of social justice.

EQUAL LIBERTY—THE RIGHT TO VOTE

We begin our discussion with what Rawls would describe as the most important element of social justice, equal liberty: in this case equal participation in the primary political liberty, the right to vote.

Techniques of Disenfranchisement

Beginning shortly after the end of Reconstruction in 1877, and throughout the next 20 years, southern state governments disfranchised black voters. By the turn of the century only a handful of black citizens were voting in the South. The disenfranchisement effort was, in the words of Frederick Wirt (1970) "a testament to the ingenuity of Americans when working out their traditional impulse not to let the Constitution stand in the way of a good thing'' (p. 57). Much of the first half of the twentieth century involved a running battle between the U.S. Supreme Court and southern legislatures concerning the constitutionality of various devices designed to maintain the disenfranchisement of southern blacks.

The earliest and for a long time the most popular of these devices was the white primary. In the then solidly Democratic South, winning the primary was, as they say, tantamount to winning the election. But in 1924 the Supreme Court, in a case originating in Texas, held that statutes limiting state-run primary elections to whites were unconstitutional [*Nixon* v. *Herndon*, 273 U.S. 536, (1924)]. The next 20 years saw numerous attempts to evade the implications of this decision. First, Texas authorized a presumptively private organization, the state Democrat Party, to set up their own standards for determining membership and the right to vote in the party's primary. The Court overturned this, finding that the state was using the party as its agent of discrimination [*Nixon* v. *Condon*, 286 U.S. 73 (1932)]. The state then did nothing, leaving it up to the party to discriminate on its own. This ploy was more successful; the Court's initial view was that the ensuing discrimination was that of a private voluntary association and hence beyond the reach of the Fifteenth Amendment [*Grovey* v. *Townsend*, 295 U.S. 45 (1935)]. In the early 1940s, however, the Supreme Court, taking a more functional approach, held that political parties were not to be treated as private associations when they performed essential governmental activities [*Smith* v. *Alwright*, 321 U.S. 649 (1944)]. The southern states did not immediately give up. South Carolina voided every law pertaining to parties and elections. All to no avail. The Court repeatedly found efforts to preserve white primaries to be unconstitutional evasions.

The battle did not end with the primary, however. The states had other devices in their repertoire, including the poll tax, which often had to be paid on a specific day well in advance of the election; the grandfather clause, which automatically registered voters whose parents or grandparents had been voting prior to 1865; and, either alone or in combination with the grandfather clause, the literacy test. Stories, true and apocryphal, about questions on literacy tests, became famous. One Mississippi registrar allegedly asked a black applicant "How many soap bubbles are there in a bar of soap?" (Wirt, 1970, p. 78).

These various devices allowed the southern states to keep blacks disenfranchised. Literacy tests because of their apparent relationship to informed voting became increasingly prominent. The test usually required the would-be registrant to interpret or explain some section of the state constitution. In comparison to some of the questions asked of would-be black voters, determining the number of bubbles in a bar of soap appears almost easy. For example, some Mississippi registrars asked for a clear interpretation of the section of the state constitution dealing with alluvial land and the conditions under which accretions would produce a change in the ownership of adjacent property. Most people would have to go to law school even to know what this is all about.

With these devices and others, such as lengthy residency requirements, restrictions against those convicted of crimes, and, of course, simple intimidation, the southern states were able to keep blacks disenfranchised. In the early 1950s fewer than 15 percent of the black citizens in the deep southern states of Alabama, Georgia, South Carolina, and Mississippi were registered to vote. In Alabama the figure was under 10 percent, and in Mississippi it was less than 5 percent. Presumably only a fraction of these registered voters exercised the franchise.

In Panola County, Mississippi, the site of an important study by Frederick Wirt, there were in 1960 7,639 whites and 7,250 blacks of voting age. At least 5,343 whites were registered. Only one black was registered. He was H. R. Hightower, a 92-year-old minister who had registered in 1892 [see Wirt, 1970, p. 44; *United States* v. *Duke*, 332 F. 2d 759 (5th Cir. 1964)].

The 1957 Voting Rights Act

Before 1957 the federal government had no legislative authority to sue to enforce a black's right to vote in the South. Legislation is the art of the possible, and from the late nineteenth century until the 1950s it was impossible to pass any new laws on voting over southern opposition.[1] In 1957 the first Voting Rights Act in nearly 90 years was passed. This act authorized suits to be initiated by the Attorney General to redress discrimination against named Negro plaintiffs who sought to vote and created the Commission on Civil Rights to study the extent of discrimination in the South. Of the two, the creation of the commission was the more important. Through its investigations and publications, it publicized the degree of discrimination in the South. The provision for litigation was a total failure.

After 2 years only three suits had been filed, and no black person had achieved the franchise through use of the statute. Part of the problem was that voting registrars in the South were able to avoid giving the government the records needed to prove discrimination by destroying them or by the simple expedient of resigning from office. The courts held that when registrars resigned they were no longer the official custodians of county voting records and had no authority to respond to government subpoenas. Furthermore, the government's suit could change matters only for the named plaintiffs, and it required courage for any black to stand up and claim voting discrimination,[2] a necessary precondition for federal action.

---

1. There had been a group of post-Civil War statutes designed to ensure that the franchise would be extended to all in the South, but most of these laws were repealed in 1894, and the few that survived were rarely used to attack discrimination (see Christopher, 1965, p.1).

2. In 1962 the state of Mississippi changed registration laws so that all applicants' names would be published for two weeks. The applicant then had to return to the registrar after two weeks to determine his acceptance. Failure to return meant nonacceptance and the publication of the applicants' names created a period when they could be pressured not to return (Wirt, 1970, p. 97).

To generalize, the problems with the 1957 Act were of two types. First, it conceived of discrimination against the black electorate as an aggregation of personal troubles rather than as a systematic social problem. Thus the prescribed solution was to redress acts of discrimination one at a time. This did not mean that a group of plaintiffs could not be joined in a single suit, but it did mean that discrimination had to be shown against each member of the group and that the remedy (court-ordered registration) was limited to them. Had a serious effort to register southern blacks proceeded in this way, the court clogging attributable to automobile accident litigation would have paled in comparison.

The second problem with the statute was that it was formalistic. Not only were the plaintiffs individuated, but so were the defendants. Thus suits proceeded as if the defendant registrars rather than the state were being sued. If a registrar resigned his position, he had no further authority over voting records and so could not be compelled to produce them. He similarly lacked authority to accord the desired remedy, that is, the registration of the named plaintiff(s), and so had to be dropped from the suit. A new suit had to be brought against the registrar's successor, who, if the going got hot, could also resign. Given these conditions, proceeding by lawsuit was a waste of time. Perhaps this explains how the statute came to be passed at a time when southern opponents of integration still formed the most powerful regional bloc in the Congress.

The 1960 Voting Rights Act

Within 2 years it was clear that the 1957 Act had had little effect, and in 1960 a new law was passed. This statute required registrars to keep records for 2 years; allowed the Justice Department to make the state a party defendant in a suit, thus continuing the case even if the registrar resigned; and, most importantly, allowed the Justice Department to institute suits against local registrars without pointing to named plaintiffs. If the Justice Department could show a "pattern and practice" of racial discrimination, a referee could be appointed to register any applicant who could show that he was qualified to vote under state election laws and had been denied the opportunity by the registrar or his agent after the court ruling.

The statute was a clear improvement over the 1957 law. It allowed the Justice Department to litigate for a whole county instead of for given plaintiffs, and it guaranteed the Justice Department access to records. But it still left the government with hundreds of separate jurisdictions that it had to take on one at a time, in a piecemeal fashion. And it required that the government show a pattern and practice of discrimination, not an easy matter.

For the government to prove a pattern and practice, it was not sufficient to show that few blacks but many whites were registered. This imbalance might reflect black apathy or the failure to meet permitted standards such as a fair literacy test. What had to be shown was that blacks who had sought to register were rejected by officials while comparable whites were not. This required the review of thousands of documents and countless interviews, a staggering volume of information. Wirt (1970) notes that in the suit against Montgomery County and the State of Alabama the Justice Department's Civil Rights Division (CRD) called 87 witnesses and introduced 69 exhibits, including five filing cabinets of 10,000 documents. The brief of the CRD consisted of a 293-page statement of facts (p. 79).

John Doar (of later Watergate fame) who headed the CRD at the time the 1960 act began to be enforced sent out teams of attorneys to quietly interview blacks about alleged discrimination. If the evidence seemed strong, and if black witnesses could be found, cases would be filed. The CRD's original strategy was to focus on indisputably literate blacks such as college teachers who had been refused registration, but even with college professors it was not difficult for a registrar to point to some misinterpretation of the state constitution in the literacy test. In response, the division shifted to the strategy of presenting as witnesses illiterates of both races. A registrar could not easily explain how an illiterate white could have passed an evenhanded literacy test.

Not only did this strategy have the benefit of making it difficult for a registrar to argue the merits of particular applications, but it also had the further benefit that if a pattern and practice were found, the registrar might be instructed to reregister all voters using the same literacy test, or to allow blacks to register if they met the qualifications of whites, that is, without literacy standards at all.

Nevertheless, the 1960 act was in many ways cumbersome, and in the face of determined opposition its effectiveness was limited. By 1964 only 7 percent of adult blacks were registered in Mississippi. In Alabama the figure was 23 percent (up from 14 percent in 1960). In Louisiana, black registration went from 29 to 32 percent between 1960 and 1964. In other southern states the results were more dramatic—Virginia went from 23 to 46 percent and South Carolina from 16 to 39 percent. But nowhere in the deep South except Florida did black registration reach 50 percent of the voter eligible population.

The 1960 act was more effective than the 1957 act partly because it was actively enforced (The CRD did not sit back and wait for complaints, but instead searched out suits) and partly because it permitted remedies for whole counties where a pattern and practice of discrimination could be proven. But the law still required litigation wherever a county discriminated, with all the due process and delay that litigation entails.[3]

The 1965 Voting Rights Act

Then came the 1965 Voting Rights Act, a radical departure from earlier attempts to enfranchise blacks. The 1960 law, like its predecessor, was explicitly designed to restrain actions that were for the "purpose of" interfering with registration

---

3. The 1964 Civil Rights law had a few provisions relating to elections, but by and large it was directed at other aspects of segregation such as job discrimination.

and voting. Its concern with purpose meant that the state of mind of the interferer had to be shown. Not surprisingly, when officials were asked about their intent they never acknowledged that their purpose was to keep blacks from voting. Wirt (1970) notes, "In one case, a sheriff beat a black rights worker in the registrar's office; [Federal District Court] Judge Cox accepted the sheriff's word he did it only because the black was blocking the corridor and interfering with registration" (p. 88).

Since state officials would not admit their discriminatory intent and since states of mind cannot be known directly, the forbidden purpose had to be proven in the way that evil motives are often proven, by examining the history and surrounding circumstances of the act. In part this became a matter of showing a pattern and practice of registering voters that could bear but one interpretation— that the registrar was attempting to disenfranchise blacks.

The 1965 act swept all of this aside. It ignored motives and focused solely on the results of behavior. It established an arbitrary test of whether discrimination existed. The only evidence needed to show presumptive discrimination was the demographic data on registration. If fewer than half the eligible voters were registered on November 1, 1964, *or* voted in the 1964 presidential election, and if the attorney general determined that the jurisdiction on November 1, 1964, maintained as a prerequisite for voting or registration for voting requirements of literacy, education, or good moral character, the provisions of the act took effect (42 U.S.C. 1973b (b)). The voting percentage was to be determined by the Director of the Census.[4]

Where presumptive discrimination existed, as was the case in the six deep southern states and portions of several others, the Attorney General was empowered to appoint federal examiners to take over the task of registering voters. The statute effectively eliminated literacy tests as a force for disenfranchisement. Literacy tests could not be applied unless they were applied to all prospective registrants, and, where they were applied, education through the sixth grade established a conclusive presumption of literacy.

Nor was this all. The poll tax was declared illegal (later the Twenty-fourth Amendment constitutionalized the ban), and any attempt by covered jurisdictions to legislate on prerequisites to voting had to be cleared with the Attorney General. If the Attorney General objected within 60 days after a change was submitted, the change could not go into effect, and the only remedy available to the jurisdiction was to request a declaratory judgment from the district court for the District of Columbia. To decide for the state, this court had to find that the proposed change would not have the purpose or *effect* of denying or abridging the right to vote because of race or color. The District of Columbia court, perhaps the most liberal in the nation at the time, was not one to cast a sympathetic eye on southern legislation that might adversely affect black voting.

---

4. The original act ran for 5 years and has been renewed three times. It is now in effect, not only in the South, but in a few northern jurisdictions that do not achieve the statute's minimal levels of participation.

The preclearance provision became a major barrier against efforts to frustrate black voting. Even minor changes, such as the designation of different polling places, were held to require prior approval. And the statute was broadly interpreted to include related matters as well. Thus in *Allen* v. *State Board of Elections*, 393 U.S. 544 (1969) the Supreme Court held that the following changes fell within the purview of the act: permitting members of county boards of supervisor to be elected at large rather than by district; requiring that county superintendents of education be appointed; and empowering election judges to provide illiterate voters with assistance in marking their ballots. In *Gaston County* v. *United States*, 395 U.S. 285 (1969) the Supreme Court upheld a trial court's refusal to permit the county to reinstate its literacy test for voter registration because the historical effect of a segregated dual system had been to "deprive black residents of equal education opportunities, which in turn deprived them of an equal chance to pass the literacy test" (395 U.S. at 297). Thus even impartially administered literacy tests could be voided for tending to perpetuate inequalities.[5]

The results of the 1965 Act were dramatic, especially in those states that had most successfully resisted the earlier attempts to end voting discrimination. Between 1964 and 1967 the percentage of potential black voters registered in Alabama went from 23 to 52 percent. By 1969 it was up to 61 percent. Most striking of all was Mississippi. In 1964 7 percent of blacks in Mississippi were registered. In 1967 60 percent were. By 1969 the percentage had climbed to 67. Overall in the South black registration increased by nearly one million voters between the 1964 and 1968 presidential elections. Three-fourths of the increase came in the six states that were fully covered by the act (Alabama, Georgia, Louisiana, Mississippi, North Carolina, and South Carolina). This effectively doubled the number of registered blacks in these areas (Logan & Winston, 1971, p. 27).

The 1965 Act, however, did not mark the end of southern resistance. New attempts were made to dilute the black vote. These included switching from elections by district to elections at large and racially motivated redistricting and reapportionment statutes.[6] And, of course, various forms of harassment and intimidation, including arrests and economic reprisals, were still used. As of early 1969 nearly 38 percent of voting age blacks in the South remained unregistered, and in the six fully covered states, 43 percent of the eligible blacks were not registered compared to 21 percent of eligible whites.

Nevertheless, the 1965 law through its impact on black registration and voting had significant consequences for black political power. In 1965 there were

---

5. The 1970 amendment to the Voting Rights Act abolished literacy tests throughout the country.
6. We touched briefly on these efforts in a different context in Chapter 4. Switching from single member districts to at large elections meant, for example, that if blacks constituted 40 percent of the population in a county with five Commissioners they were unlikely to be able to elect any black commissioners. If elections in the county had been by district, residential patterns would almost certainly have guaranteed a black majority in one or two districts.

approximately 70 elected black officials in the southern states. By 1969 this had risen to around 400, and in 1981 there were approximately 2,500 elected black officials in the 11 states of the old Confederacy, including a black mayor in Atlanta (Scher & Button, 1984, p. 45).

Why was the 1965 Act relatively more successful than its predecessors in gaining voting rights for blacks? The elements that seem most important are the switch from a judicial to an administrative mechanism of control and the adoption of a strict liability rule logic to determine actionable discrimination. In addition, the agency responsible for enforcing the law and the courts that ultimately interpreted it were committed to an expansive vision of equal justice.

Putting the responsibility for assessing discrimination in the hands of a committed agency eliminated much of the delay and the piecemeal nature of the solutions that were associated with the earlier laws. The movement to a strict liability rule stripped away almost all excuses states could use to explain unequal registration. The judicial attitude made appeals fruitless. To generalize from this one case, it appears that the use of an active, powerful, and committed agency increases legal impact, as does both the use of a liability standard that looks to results rather than to intention or due care (criminal or negligence rule logics) and an appellate system that shares the commitment of the enforcement agency.

It is unwise, however, to place too much faith in generalizations based on one case. Several caveats are in order. First, the 1965 Act combined a strict liability rule with an enforcement system that vested primary responsibility in an executive agency. The relative effectiveness of agencies and courts may be quite different in situations where the rule logic is not one of strict liability.

Second, the comparison between courts and agencies is a *ceteris paribus* statement. It assumes other things are equal such as the effective political power of the regulated group and beneficiaries. This assumption may not always be justified. Moving from judicial to administrative enforcement may alter the relative power of the parties by providing the regulated groups an opportunity to ''capture'' the agency and turn it to their own ends.

Third, in this instance the agency that had enforcement authority was deeply committed to the ends of the act, and except in one region of the country popular support for the act was substantial. In other instances where the law aims at major social reform, these supporting conditions may not exist. If an agency responsible for enforcing a statute is less committed to the statute's goals than are the courts, the courts may be more effective enforcement agents. Also, courts being further removed from the political process may be more effective than administrative agencies in enforcing laws that are the source of deep divisions in society or that have fallen into popular disfavor. However, any relative advantage that courts enjoy over agencies in the latter circumstances does not necessarily translate into greatly effective enforcement.

Finally, giving one person the vote does not take the vote from anyone else. In this sense the vote is what Wirt (1970) calls a perfectly elastic good. It is similar to an inclusive collective good in that one person may enjoy the right to vote without *noticeably* diminishing the similar enjoyment of others. This is not true of all inequalities. Where one person's increased equality means that others must do without a salient advantage, the problems of law enforcement might be quite different. Thus before we generalize any further we should look at inequalities in other areas. One of the most prominent in recent years has involved education.

EDUCATION—DESEGREGATING PUBLIC SCHOOLS

The watershed of renewed interest in the use of law to alter race relations in America was, of course, the Supreme Court opinion in *Brown* v. *Board of Education*, 347 U.S. 483 (1954). The *Brown* Court held that separate schools for blacks and whites denied black students the equal protection of the law as guaranteed by the Fourteenth Amendment. In a separate opinion a year later the court held that school districts must eliminate dual school systems "with all deliberate speed" *Brown* v. *Board of Education* (No. 2) 349 U.S. 294 (1955). Although the Court implied in the second opinion that any delay was to be justified only to accommodate necessary administrative changes, school transportation, and personnel shifts, the phrase "deliberate speed" came in the deep South to stand for interminable procrastination.

In the border states which were not part of the old confederacy but which had at least some dual school systems before *Brown*, there is considerable evidence of compliance. By 1959, the first year for which complete data is available, 45 percent of all black students attending public school in these states were doing so with white students. Even in Kentucky, perhaps the most "southern" of the border states, 39 percent of all black students were attending schools that included white students (Bullock and Lamb, 1984, p. 65). To some extent these changes mirrored other socioeconomic changes that were occurring in the region, but it also appears that judicial pronouncements had an important catalytic effect.

In the eleven states of the old Confederacy the situation was different. Change was nearly too small to measure. Ten years after *Brown*, at the time of the passage of the 1964 Civil Rights Act, fewer than one-fifth of southern school districts had even begun the desegregation process. It has been estimated that only 1 percent of the black children attending public schools in these states were going to desegregated schools (U.S. Commission on Civil Rights, 1964). Wirt notes that in Mississippi in 1964, ten years after *Brown*, no school district was yet desegregated (Wirt, 1970, p. 183).

Part of the reason for this lack of progress is to be found in what we have called the qualities of the regulated group, in this case opponents of change were well organized around governmental institutions. A strategy of southern resistance was signaled early on with the so-called Southern Manifesto, issued in the spring of 1956 and signed by 101 senators and representatives from the eleven states of the old Confederacy. According to the Manifesto the *Brown* decision was a "clear abuse of judicial power." The signers pledged "to use all lawful means to bring about a reversal of this decision which is contrary to the constitution.'' But it was not only the organized resistance of southern leaders which led to the disregard of *Brown*. Congress did not come to the aid of the Court with any civil rights legislation. In an important symbolic statement, the Eisenhower administration did mobilize the executive branch to support the federal courts when Governor Orval Faubus defied judicial desegregation orders in Little Rock in 1957. However, when federal authority was not challenged directly, the administration appeared at best neutral toward school desegregation. President Eisenhower refused to endorse the *Brown* opinion with the statement that, ''I think it makes no difference whether or not I endorse it'' (Kluger, 1976, p. 753).

With minimum support from the executive and no tangible support from the legislature, progress was difficult. As Burke Marshall wrote in 1964, ''It is as if no taxpayer sent in a return until he personally was sued by the federal government'' (Marshall, 1964, p. 7–8). Some writers doubted whether desegregation would ever occur (see Surrant, 1966).

The Civil Rights Act of 1964

It was not until the political events of the early 1960s, including the Civil Rights movement in the South, the march on Washington, the cattle prods and police dogs of Sheriff ''Bull'' Connor on Good Friday in Birmingham, and the assassination of President Kennedy that the executive and the legislature finally acted. The consequence was the Civil Rights Act of 1964. One important provision with respect to school desegregation was Title VI.

Title VI provided that:

> No person in the United States shall, on the ground of race, color, or national origin be excluded from participation in, be denied the benefits of, or be subjected to discrimination under any program or activity receiving Federal financial assistance. (42 U.S.C. 2000d)

The act further provided that agencies providing federal financial assistance were empowered to issue rules, regulations, and orders that, when approved by the President, must be complied with if federal financial assistance were to continue. Provisions were made for a hearing within the appropriate governmental agency [ordinarily HEW (Department of Health, Education and Welfare)], and ultimately for judicial review of the agency's actions. Thus judicial delays were possible, but the ''shoe would be on the other foot.'' If funds were cut off, the delays involved in the judicial process worked against those who wished to continue segregation.

The provisions of Title VI took on added significance with the passage in 1965 of the Elementary and Secondary Education Act. This law made the nations' school districts eligible for billions of dollars in federal aid.

The second important provision of the 1964 Act, Title IV took a different tack. It increased the powers of the Justice Department by permitting the Attorney

General to initiate desegregation actions against school districts if he received meritorious complaints from children or their parents in that district.

Armed with these two new weapons, the Justice Department and the Office of Civil Rights of HEW acted. Although resistance to Title VI never abated, for the next 5 years the Justice Department and HEW together radically altered the nature of school attendance patterns in the South (Orfield, 1969; 1978).

Tied to these changes were changes in judicial standards. Originally freedom-of-choice plans were treated by some courts as an appropriate way to desegregate schools. Under such plans all children in a school district had, in theory, a choice as to which school they would attend. In *Green* v. *County School Board of New Kent County*, 391 U.S. 430 (1968) the Court held that such a plan did not comply with the law. The case involved a rural school district in eastern Virginia with 740 blacks and 550 white students, and little or no residential segregation. After 3 years of freedom of choice no white and only 115 black children had changed schools. The Court stated that: "The burden on a school board today is to come forward with a plan that promises realistically to work, and promises realistically to work *now*" (391 U.S. 430, 439).

Green in its demand for action that would effectively dismantle dual school systems (rather than merely end discriminatory practices), supported the HEW guidelines, which required such a standard. By 1968 both HEW and the Justice Department were making significant gains in the desegregation of schools, especially in the South. With the coming of the Nixon Administration, however, the enforcement situation began to change.

A Retreat on Enforcement

In July of 1969 the Secretary of HEW and the Attorney General made a joint statement that affirmed a commitment to ending racial discrimination in the schools, but they argued that too much emphasis had been placed on deadlines, coercion, and punishment. At that point 121 school districts had lost federal funds for failing to comply with Title VI. The statement also said that henceforth litigation by the Justice Department would be de-emphasized. It rather quickly became clear that de-emphasis was an understatement. HEW had initiated approximately one hundred enforcement proceedings in both 1968 and 1969. Between March 1970 and February 1971 no proceeding was initiated, and only a token number were started thereafter. Not only did this slow desegregation in the South, it nipped in the bud a movement by HEW to investigate northern and western school districts.

In 1968 HEW had begun reviewing 28 cases involving school districts outside the South to determine if its guidelines were being met. In 1969 the number dropped to 16. Table 11.1 shows the pattern in the subsequent years.

This pattern led to resistance within HEW. The director of HEW's Office for Civil Rights, Leon Panetta, was fired in the spring of 1970, purportedly for his efforts to continue administrative enforcement of Title VI (Bell, 1973,

TABLE 11.1
Title VI Enforcement Reviews

Year	No. of Reviews Initiated
1970	15
1971	11
1972	9
1973	1
1974	0

p. 468). Justice Department personnel also protested. During the first 6 months of 1969, 19 attorneys resigned and others sought jobs elsewhere. The immediate cause of concern at the Justice Department was a motion filed by the Department of Justice (supplemented by a recommendation from the Secretary of HEW) seeking to delay the implementation of desegregation plans in several Mississippi school districts. A few months before the Justice Department had supported these plans. Now the federal government which in the years since *Brown* had never opposed counsel for black plaintiffs sided with defendant school boards. The Fifth Circuit agreed, postponing the date by which 33 Mississippi school districts had to submit desegregation plans, but the case was appealed to the Supreme Court. In *Alexander* v. *Holmes County Board of Education*, 396 U.S. 19 (1969) the Supreme Court, headed by Chief Justice Burger, rejected arguments that there was not enough time to accomplish a complete and orderly desegregation plan by the coming school year. The Court's *per curiam* decision stated:

> The question presented is one of paramount importance, involving as it does the denial of fundamental rights to many thousands of school children, who are presently attending Mississippi schools under segregated conditions contrary to the applicable decisions of this Court. Against this background the Court of Appeals should have denied all motions for additional time because continued operation of segregated schools under a standard of allowing ''all deliberate speed'' for desegregation is no longer constitutionally permissible. Under explicit holding of this Court the obligation of every school district is to terminate dual school systems at once and to operate now and hereafter only unitary schools. (396 U.S. 19, at 20)

Even with the *Alexander* case in hand, however, the Justice Department, which following the *Green* opinion had filed 68 motions to further facilitate desegregation failed to initiate contempt actions in districts where there were apparent violations of orders. Nor did HEW act. Not only did they reduce the number of reviews, they effectively stopped the practice of cutting off funds to noncomplying school boards after the summer of 1970.[7]

---

7. In 1973 a Federal Appeals court in Washington, D.C., said that while HEW has some discretion in this area, it is not unlimited. After a substantial period of time has elapsed and no voluntary compliance is forthcoming, HEW must proceed with enforcement proceedings as provided under Title VI [*Adams* v. *Richardson*, 480 F. 2d 1159 (D.C. Cir. 1973)].

However, this change in policy with respect to the most visible goods of school desegregation came too late to "save" most southern schools from desegregation. In fact, the most startling fact about the school desegregation movement from 1964 to 1972 is the substantial desegregation that occurred in the South.

The March of Desegregation

Before the 1964 Act took effect there was little or no school desegregation. But once the Justice Department and the Office of Civil Rights began using Titles IV and VI in 1967 and 1968, change was rapid. Although funds had been cut off in only 122 districts by the end of 1967, the effect of the new laws was widespread. Of 4,588 school districts in 17 southern and border states, 3,013

TABLE 11.2

Percentage of Black Students in Schools With Fewer Than 50 Percent Blacks and in Schools With 90–100 Percent Blacks, by Region, 1968–1980

	Year				Percent Change 1968–1980
Area	*1968*	*1972*	*1976*	*1980*	
Percentage in 0–49 Percent Minority Schools					
South	19.1	44.7	45.1	42.9	+23.8
Border	28.4	32.8	39.9	40.8	+12.4
Northeast	33.2	30.1	27.5	20.1	−13.1
Midwest	22.7	24.7	29.7	30.5	+7.8
West	27.8	31.9	32.6	33.2	+5.4
United States Average	23.4	36.4	37.8	37.1	+13.7
Percentage in 90–100 Percent Minority Schools					
South	77.8	24.7	22.4	23.0	−54.8
Border	60.2	54.7	42.5	37.0	−23.2
Northeast	42.7	46.9	51.4	48.7	+6.0
Midwest	58.0	57.4	51.1	43.6	−14.4
West	50.8	42.7	36.3	33.7	−17.1
United States Average	64.3	38.7	35.9	33.2	−31.1

Note: States in each region are as follows
South: AL, AR, GA, FL, LA, MS, NC, SC, TN, TX, VA
Border: DE, DC, KY, MD, MO, OK, WV
Northeast: CT, ME, MA, NH, NJ, NY, PA, RI, VT
Midwest: IL, IN, IA, KS, MI, MN, NE, ND, OH, SD, WI
West: AZ, CA, CO, ID, MT, NV, NM, OR, UT, WA, WY

Source: Orfield, 1983, p. 4.

reported they would be under compliance, 1,225 were already under voluntary compliance, and 350 were under court orders (Wirt, 1970, p. 185).

As enforcement increased so did desegregation. In the 1963–1964 school year only 1 percent of all school children in the 11 Confederate states were in integrated schools (Wirt, 1970, p. 185). In the school year 1965–1966, the first full year of Title VI, the figure reached 6 percent. In 1966–1967 there was a jump to 17 percent, and in 1967–1968 it rose to over 20 percent. The combined pressure of HEW, the Justice Department, and the federal courts finally succeeded in dismantling the dual school system. Table 11.2 indicates the precipitous change since 1968. As the table indicates, most of the change in racial composition occurred between 1968 and 1972. Table 11.3 brings this change into even sharper focus.

The third column, "Within District Segregation," is the most revealing. The segregation index reported in that column is a standardized measure of the amount of segregation between two groups in a school district. The measure has a value of 0 if there is no segregation between the two groups, and a value of 1.0 if the segregation is complete. In 1968 the Southeast led the nation with a segregation score of .75. But in 1972 the segregation score in the Southeast was only .19, the lowest in the nation. The old Confederacy was substantially desegregated. By comparison northern and western schools were still substantially segregated. Table 11.3 graphically illustrates the size of the change. If people still wish to use the South as a "whipping-boy" on the issue of integration, they will have to choose an area other than schools.

There is one puzzle in these data. Most southern school desegregation occurred between 1968 and 1972, the years of the first Nixon administration, when rigorous enforcement was relaxed. The most likely explanation for this apparent

TABLE 11.3
Black–White School Segregation in 1968 by Region

	Proportion				*Black–White Segregation*	
	1 *White*		*2* *Black*		*3* *Within District*	
	1968	*1972*	*1968*	*1972*	*1968*	*1972*
United States	.79	.77	.15	.16	.63	.37
New England	.93	.92	.05	.06	.34	.33
Middle Atlantic	.81	.78	.14	.16	.43	.43
Border	.79	.79	.21	.21	.48	.44
Southeast	.69	.68	.29	.30	.75	.19
West South Central	.78	.76	.16	.17	.69	.48
East North Central	.87	.86	.12	.13	.58	.57
West North Central	.90	.89	.09	.09	.61	.56
Mountain	.81	.80	.03	.03	.49	.25
Pacific	.78	.75	.07	.08	.56	.42

Source: Coleman et al., 1975, p. 15.

anomoly is that desegregation during this period reflects earlier efforts to secure compliance. By the end of 1967, as we have noted, most southern school districts were not in compliance with the law but had reported their intentions to comply. As they followed through on these commitments, desegregation increased dramatically. It is also important that while the Nixon Justice Department was willing to tolerate further delay and HEW was reluctant to act to cut off funds, neither agency invited wholesale backsliding in commitments already made. Indeed, the visible changes in the rigor with which the desegregation laws were enforced may obscure more routine work by HEW and Justice Department bureaucrats to promote desegregation. Ultimately, the clear change in enforcement policy may be less responsible for the drop in enforcement actions during the first Nixon administration than the fact that forces previously set in motion meant that fewer formal enforcement actions were necessary. While, no doubt, some actions were not brought that would have been brought a few years earlier, the effects of the diminution were muted because the courts continued to be vigorous where they played an enforcement role.

Understanding What Occurred

How are we to understand what occurred? There are two related questions: (1) Why after 15 years of almost no desegregation did the southern schools make so much progress in less than 5 years? (2) Why has so little progress been made in northern and western school districts?

The answer to the first question is fairly straightforward. In 1964 the three branches of the federal government began to play an active role in school desegregation, thus greatly increasing enforcement powers. Congress provided administrative remedies, and it gave the Justice Department power to bring suit in its own right. Moreover, the Supreme Court finally stripped away many of the excuses school districts had used to delay or subvert desegregation.

Green and *Alexander* were followed by the key case of *Swann* v. *Charlotte-Mecklenberg*, 402 U.S. 1 (1971). *Swann* brought *Green* to the city and ordered pupil transportation to achieve "root and branch" desegregation. Following *Swann* the objective in desegregation cases was the creation of an attendance pattern in which the racial mix in each school was not substantially different from the school district average.

Results more than intentions mattered and thus freedom-of-choice plans were rejected as were excuses based on administrative and personnel considerations. Consequently, there again appears to be a relationship between legal effectiveness and the adoption of administrative enforcement techniques and between effectiveness and stricter rule logics.

However, caveats are once more also in order. First, HEW's power rested as much or more on the 1965 Primary and Secondary Education Act as it did on the 1964 Civil Rights Act. The 1964 Act provided the rules, but the 1965 Act in providing funds to be taken away gave bite to the sanctions. It does no good to cut off funds if there are few funds to cut off. In general, administrative agencies can be effective only insofar as they have viable sanctions at their disposal. The 1965 Act allowed HEW to be effective.

Second, the HEW experience in the Nixon years carries an important lesson. Agencies do not have the independent status of the judiciary. They are less autonomous, which means they are more responsive to shifts in the political wind. After 1970 HEW's formal enforcement effort came nearly to a standstill while judicial enforcement proceeded.

Finally, in the South, once the citadel of dual school systems was breached and school districts began to run unitary systems, little stood in the way of desegregation. The residential patterns in much of the South were such that assigning children to schools by attendance zones rather than by race effectively desegregated many districts. Thus once intentional segregation was arrested, the consequence was within district integration. This leads us to the second question, Why has so little progress been made in northern and western school districts?

Outside the South

Certainly an important factor in the higher levels of segregation in northern schools is the relative lack of enforcement of the 1964 Act in the North and the West. HEW fund cutoffs ended at the very time when the department began to focus on the North. The Justice Department did not pursue northern cases with the vigor it once pursued southern cases under Title IV, leaving most litigation to private plaintiffs. Even school boards that intentionally segregated, for instance, by drawing school boundaries and constructing new schools so as to maximize racial homogeneity, have been seldom challenged by the federal government.

The change from a Democratic to a Republican administration at about the time the desegregation movement looked North may have played a role, for Republicans now draw less of their political support from blacks than do the Democrats, but the return to a Democratic administration under President Carter did not lead the Justice Department to mount an all out assault on school segregation in the North and West—as they had done earlier in the South. Other aspects of the political situation precluded this and made possible costs of integration efforts more salient.

Pure politics was important. The spread of desegregation efforts to the North and West expanded the anti-desegregation constituency. Elected representatives who once could support desegregation at little political cost, found such support to be a political liability as desegregation moved North. In Congress northerners and southerners joined forces to block certain federal expenditures in aid of court ordered desegregation.

Moreover, new and more respectable arguments against desegregation emerged. One could support integration, but oppose busing. One could be against segregation, but for community control and neighborhood schools (Mazmanian &

Sabatier, 1983). One did not get educated on a bus, nor, although this often went unspoken, did one get as well educated in school facilities that had been allowed to run down, in settings where interracial hostility was palpable, or in classes that were dominated by children from educationally disadvantaged backgrounds.[8]

The loss of popular support for desegregation in the North is only partly explained by the fact that the process affected northern children. The early southern cases reflected the sense that Jim Crow laws created segregated schools which injured the self-image of black students and hampered their learning, and that these harms could be remedied by forbidding intentional segregation. This perspective provides both a simple model of the cause of unequal educational opportunity (state mandated segregation) and an equally simple model of the cure (prohibition of color conscious rules in the assignment of children to schools). However, later cases in both the North and the South reveal this perspective to be inadequate with respect to both the cause of inequality (segregation is only in part a matter of state action) and the cure (integration requires color conscious racial balancing of schools) (Loh, 1984, pp. 156–157).

The retreat from the imperative of integration manifested itself not only among politicians and the public, but also within the Supreme Court. The unanimity of Supreme Court opinions which had been a hallmark of school desegregation cases since *Brown* slowly eroded. The change is only in part attributable to the more conservative makeup of the Burger Court, for in the area of race relations the Supreme Court under Burger's leadership acted initially very much in the Warren Court tradition. What is more important is that as desegregation moved north the old jurisprudence broke down. Constitutional violations are not obvious where assigning pupils to schools on the basis of race neutral criteria such as neighborhood can yield schools that are largely of one race and where neither state nor local history is replete with efforts to discriminate legally against blacks. Has a constitutional violation been shown when a school board's reasonably compact and contiguous zones yield segregated schools which would have been less segregated had other equally compact and contiguous zones been chosen? In such circumstances the existence of a constitutional violation may turn on whether the school board's motivations matter, and if the intent to segregate rather than just the fact of segregation matters, the ability to prove a constitutional violation is likely to turn on how forbidden intention may be shown.

The relationship between the violation and the remedy, when school boards were found to have impermissibly fostered racial segregation, likewise became more tenuous. Should the remedy be limited to restoring the system to the state it would have been in had the school board chosen the most racially balanced neighborhood plan, or should the remedy strive to produce similar proportions of black and white students in every school in the school district? The Justices

---

8. The reality of these fears does not concern us here. The educational implications of desegregation programs vary by school district and plan. Research into the effects of desegregation on learning reveals mixed results (see, for example, Rist, 1979; Crain & Mahard, 1983).

on the Supreme Court could and did disagree. [See *Dayton Board of Education* v. *Brinkman* I, 433 U.S. 406 (1977) and *Dayton Board of Education* v. *Brinkman* II, 443 U.S. 526 (1979).] The Justices' disagreement both symbolizes and reflects the increased complexity and ambiguity that confronted the courts as they wrestled with the question of to what extent institutional arrangements, like neighborhood schools, should be altered to combat segregation.[9]

An important source of the ambiguity and complexity that led to the breakdown of judicial consensus is manifested most clearly in large, central city school districts. Table 11.4 indicates that throughout the country, but especially in the North, large school districts are much more segregated than small ones. (The values in the table are again segregation index scores, with 0 reflecting complete integration in the sense that every school in a district has the same proportion of black and white students and 1 reflecting complete separation.)

Thomas Pettigrew has argued that there are four major causes of public school segregation in urban areas. They are (1) long-term trends in racial demography, (2) the anti-metropolitan nature of school district organization, (3) the effects of private schools, and (4) intentional segregation within districts (Pettigrew, 1975, p. 226). The first two factors pose the most substantial problems. Overcoming segregation in urban areas, especially in the North, requires that pupils be moved to counteract the effects of residential racial segregation. Yet considerable movement of children within school districts will leave many metropolitan areas segregated with largely black central city schools and largely white suburban ones. For example, approximately 76 percent of the students in public elementary and secondary schools in 1978 were non-Hispanic whites, but in Washington, D.C., only 5 percent were white, in Atlanta 10 percent and in Detroit 14 percent. (Farley, 1984, p. 32) Any desegregation plan involving just the central city's schools can only distribute students within the confines of these percentages. Plans that encompass surburban as well as urban schools are needed for greater integration.

In *Milliken* v. *Bradley*, 418 U.S. 717 (1974) the Supreme Court confronted this problem in the context of the Detroit desegregation suit. The Court reversed a District Court desegregation plan that required Detroit and its suburbs through "cross-district busing" to exchange students. The Court held that multidistrict

---

9. The history of early attempts to generate legal theories that would cause the courts to order desegregation of northern cities is long and tortured. Finally, in *Keys* v. *School District #1*, 413 U.S. 189 (1973) the Court imposed a *Swann*-like remedy on Denver, Colorado. Although this made possible numerous lawsuits and numerous plaintiff victories in northern cities from Boston to San Francisco, the law has remained somewhat precarious. As Table 11.3 indicates, northern desegregation levels never reached the levels of those in the South. The legal uncertainty in post-*Keys* decisions is discussed from two different perspectives in Graglia (1980) and in Yudof (1980). Matters came to a head in 1979 when it appeared that the Supreme Court might make a substantial retreat by limiting desegregation remedies to the undoing of specific intentional segregative acts of school boards, rather than the "root and branch" desegregation remedies ordered in *Swann* and *Keys*. A divided court maintained the *Keys* standard [*Columbus Board of Education* v. *Penick*, 443 U.S. 449 (1979); *Dayton Board of Education* v. *Brinkman*, 443 U.S. 526 (1979)]. Since the two Ohio opinions there has been a general reduction in the amount of litigation.

TABLE 11.4
Average Within District Segregation in 1972 by Region According to District Size

District Size (000)	U.S.	New England	Middle Atlantic	Border	Southeast	West South Central	East North Central	West North Central	Mountain	Pacific
100	.65	—	.55	.55	.44	.76	.79	.84	—	.78
25–100	.39	.56	.53	.43	.20	.47	.60	.59	.25	.25
10–25	.22	.20	.22	.17	.16	.31	.38	.20	.29	.16
5–10	.14	.08	.12	.06	.13	.17	.17	.19	.28	.05
2.5–5	.09	.02	.05	.03	.09	.14	.07	.11	.09	.16
2.5	.03	0	.03	.02	.04	.02	.02	.01	.03	.05

Source: Coleman, 1975, p. 33.

remedies cannot be ordered without proof that school district lines have been drawn in a racially discriminatory manner or that other discriminatory acts of state officials or school boards have caused substantial inter-district segregation. To the degree that such inter-district segregation is *de facto*, that is, results from the consequences of individual residential decisions and not from the acts of the school officials, it is according to *Milliken* beyond the reach of the Fourteenth Amendment. Yet without area-wide desegregation plans "white flight" from systems under court order may substantially defeat desegregation efforts (Rossell & Hawley, 1981; Armor, 1980; Farley, 1984). Unable to control the school situation, parents use residential location to control their children's educational experience.[10]

Thus the fact that school segregation is in some places contingent on residential segregation makes it difficult to remedy through law, because it leads to disputes about what the law should require and raises the costs of an adequate remedy (Orfield, 1981). These problems are not limited to the area of school desegregation. Inequalities contingent on other inequalities are generally more resistant than noncontingent inequalities to remediation through the law. As we shall see, this and other problems exist in employment discrimination as well.

EMPLOYMENT DISCRIMINATION—THE KEY ISSUE

The workplace is a fundamental battleground in the struggle for racial equality. Jobs are the capstone of equal opportunity because they are the cornerstone of economic equality. The law has attempted to reduce job discrimination just as it has attempted to desegregate schools and extend the right to vote. In several respects, however, this effect has been less successful than efforts in the other two areas, at least if success is measured by the degree to which blacks have come to enjoy the same job opportunities and incomes as whites.[11]

---

10. In perhaps the most significant recent development along these lines the parties to a desegregation suit in St. Louis reached an out-of-court settlement calling for a metropolitan plan. Several other cities, including Benton Harbor, Indianapolis, Little Rock, and Wilmington have been proceeding with various types of cross-district plans while efforts to achieve such remedies in cities like Atlanta and Houston have failed. Indeed, some of the current legal activity has been by districts such as Mobile, Baton Rouge, and Houston, attempting to have themselves declared "unitary." If the district is declared unitary it is no longer under the continued jurisdiction of the federal district court and, presumably, resegregation that reflects demographic patterns rather than the school board's intent will not be remediable. For a general review of events through 1984 see Smylie (1984).

11. There is a serious measurement problem here. It may be that job discrimination if measured by employment decisions that close opportunities to blacks simply because they are black have largely disappeared in recent years and that the law has played an important role in this disappearance, or it may be that such direct racial discrimination is still a frequent occurrence. Generally speaking, all we can measure is the distribution of blacks and whites by jobs and income level. Disparities exist, but they may be attributable to education, job performance, job experience, and the like as well as to pure responses to race. We shall treat the long-term goal of job discrimination legislation as reducing the disparities between both the opportunities available to black and white workers and the incomes that blacks and whites earn. Pure discrimination is just one factor that contributes to job inequality, and it is the latter which is ultimately our concern.

The 1964 Civil Rights Act is the statute that placed the federal government in the forefront of the fight against employment discrimination. Title VII established the Equal Employment Opportunities Commission (EEOC), a new regulatory agency. The EEOC was not, however, the first regulatory agency operating in this area. The 1964 Act had a number of state and local precursors. We look at these state efforts before turning to the federal law.

State Fair Employment Commissions

State fair employment laws usually created a regulatory agency to implement their guarantees of equal opportunity. Collectively known as Fair Employment Practice Commissions (FEPCs) these groups had limited success at best. According to Alfred Blumrosen, former Chief of Conciliations of the EEOC:

> the history of [FEPCs] is one of timidity in investigation, vacillation in decision making, and soft settlements that failed to aid the victim of discrimination and did not remedy the broader social problem. . . . A quarter century of administrative effort has failed to produce a body of law which defines discrimination. . . . The pure administrative process has proved incapable of coping with employment discrimination. (Blumrosen, 1971, quoted in Hill, 1972, p. 246)[12]

The failure of the FEPCs may be attributed to several factors. First, many of the statutes that created these agencies had no enforcement provisions. The commissions could only conciliate; they could not coerce. Even in states where the commission had enforcement powers there was little progress. The best study of a single commission is that of Leon Mayhew (1968) who looked at the Massachusetts Commission Against Discrimination (MCAD) in the early 1960s. The commission had significant enforcement powers, but for political reasons it rarely used them.

The Massachusetts Commission Against Discrimination

Early Orientation. The law establishing the MCAD had been passed in 1947, backed by a coalition of religious, labor, and civil rights organizations. Although most businesspeople opposed the law, they found it politically unwise to speak up against it. They had no trepidations, however, about working behind the scenes, and were able to influence the wording of the law so that it emphasized the educational and conciliatory functions of the commission and explicitly allowed the application of "bona fide standards" in employment decisions. The business community's hopes that the commission would be "moderate" were fulfilled when the commission adopted a policy of education, persuasion, and moderation (Mayhew, 1968, p. 120).

---

12. There is a large body of literature dealing with various FEPCs around the nation (see Hill, 1972, n. 11). For a general history of the FEPCs see Sovern, 1966.

The commissioners did not see their choice of a conciliatory approach as a prescription for failure. Indeed, one reason they opted for this strategy was their concern for the survival of the commission. When the Massachusetts commission was formed, the demise of the Federal Committee on Fair Employment Practices was fresh in the minds of its members. Although the federal committee had never been very aggressive, it had only a brief existence (from 1941–1946) before it was destroyed by the concerted assault of business interests and southern politicians (Maslow, 1946; Ruchames, 1953).

Mayhew notes that perhaps the most important lesson the Massachusetts commissioners learned from the federal committee experience was the danger of being shown to have no effective power. At one point in its stormy career the federal committee issued a formal order on employment practices to the railroad industry. The industry refused in writing to follow the order and despite committee appeals to President Roosevelt, the order was not enforced. Thus the federal committee was shown to have no effective power when confronted with determined opposition. The MCAD did not want to suffer a similar fate (Mayhew, 1968, p. 123). One way to avoid this was to avoid clear confrontations; that is, they would try to conciliate and persuade.

But it was not only the fear of an early demise that led to the conciliatory posture of the commission. The commissioners believed in this approach. This is not surprising, for the governor of Massachusetts at the time the statute was enacted promised business that he would appoint some "good people" to the commission. Good people apparently were those who believed in the general good will and reasonableness of businesspeople and regarded the needs of business as a value to be weighed against the objectives of minority groups. The commissioners were chosen, and at least once dismissed, with an eye to their acceptability in the business community. Advisory committees established by the commission were similarly staffed.

One of the tasks of the commission was to create a set of community councils to use in its programs of research and education. The most important council, that of the Greater Boston Area, had as its first four chairmen the vice-president of Filene's Department store, the president of the Bay State Milling Company, the vice-president of the Liberty Mutual Life Insurance Company, and the chairman of the board of the Gillette Company (Mayhew, 1968, p. 127). Throughout its first 25 years, the Boston Area Council was overwhelmingly made up of business and labor leaders. Given this membership, it is not surprising that affirmative action initiatives were not pursued.

Cooptation. It is not unfair to say that the MCAD was *coopted* by the business interests of Massachusetts. *Cooptation* occurs when an organization in order to forestall actual or potential threats to its well-being selects people to fill organizational roles on the basis of the roles they play in the organization's environment (Lempert & Ikeda, 1970). The organization acquires "friends" who will support it in the milieu in which it acts. The friends acquire influence within the organization which makes it likely that it will adopt policies they can support.

At the extremes we can say that cooptation comes in two varieties, each of which involves selling out. Either an organization, fearful for its existence, sacrifices core principles by giving power to those who do not share its core commitments in order to avert their hostility, or people withdraw their opposition to organizational activity in exchange for the trappings of office unaccompanied by real power.

With these as the poles, one can appreciate the space for maneuver. Organizations obviously seek to give up as little actual power as is necessary to secure outside support or neutralize opposition. Outsiders, on the other hand, seek the greatest possible gains from their participation. These gains, however, need not be in influence. Some people can be coopted by prestige or money. In the case of the MCAD the business interests that the commission needed to woo could not be bought with the latter currencies. Influence was the "coin" of the realm.

As Philip Selznick (1966), who introduced the concept of cooptation to sociology, notes:

> The significance of coöptation for organizational analysis is not simply that there is a change in or a broadening of leadership, and that this is an adaptive response, but also *that this change is consequential for the character and role of the organization or governing body.* Coöptation results in some constriction of the field of choice available to the organization or leadership in question. The character of the coöpted elements will necessarily shape the modes of action available to the group which has won adaptation at the price of commitment to outside elements. (pp. 15–16)[13]

Selznick also tells us that cooptation typically:

> reflects a state of tension between formal authority and social power. . . . Where the formal authority or leadership reflects real social power, its stability is assured. On the other hand, when it becomes divorced from the sources of social power its continued existence is threatened. (p. 15)

The latter characterization describes the situation of the MCAD in its early years. The coalition of religious and civil rights groups that mobilized to pass the statute creating the MCAD turned to other endeavors after the act's passage. The businesses whom the commission was to control remained on the scene.

The theory of cooptation suggests a naturalness to the process by which regulatory agencies can be captured by the regulated. Mayhew (1968) does not argue that the Massachusetts commission entered into a conspiracy with Boston businesspeople to circumvent the statute. Rather, he writes:

> In choosing cooptation as a technique of administration the Commission cut itself off from other possible techniques. It could not make use of the findings of the council-sponsored research projects in any way that would compromise continuing cooperation. Industry-dominated community councils were not interested in initiating

---

13. Selznick's study concerned the Tennessee Valley Authority (TVA) and the development of cooptative relationships between the TVA and business and agricultural elements in the Tennessee River Valley.

and sponsoring programs designed to facilitate systematic use of the Commission's broad enforcement powers. Accordingly, the mode of the council organization chosen by the Commission supported a policy that tied the enforcement process to proceedings initiated by private complaints. (p. 132)

To the degree that the commission measured its success in terms of its acceptability to business, which, we should not forget, implies some acceptance by business of the commission's goals, the MCAD was successful. A 1952 survey of businesses showed favorable responses to the commission outnumbered unfavorable ones by 6 to 1. Among employers who actually had dealings with the commission, the ratio was 10 to 1. This is not surprising since as of that time no employment case had ever gone to court, and only 3 of 1,600 complaints of employment discrimination had received a formal hearing[14] (Mayhew, 1968, pp. 132–33). Clearly, in comparing the likely effectiveness of administrative and judicial modes of enforcing statutes, one must consider the possibility of cooptation.

The Locus of Complaints. Before leaving the MCAD, one other finding of Mayhew's deserves mention. Mayhew (1968) reports that most of the alleged employment discrimination brought to the commission's attention involved companies with work forces that were substantially more integrated than those of the average Massachusetts employer. Although this finding seems at first blush surprising, the reason for it is not hard to discern. Employment discrimination requires some contact between employers and blacks who are either seeking work, fighting dismissal, or hoping to advance in jobs they already have. The latter two require a preexisting employment relationship, and the more blacks a business employs, the greater is the number of potential grievants. The first requires blacks seeking employment. Since black workers are disproportionately likely to know of and pursue opportunities at firms that are known to hire blacks, firms with integrated work forces are likely to turn down substantially more black applicants, some of whom will attribute the decision to discrimination, than companies that have few or no black job applicants because few or no blacks work for them. To some degree this pattern might have been changed and more actual discrimination might have been discovered if the MCAD had adopted a *proactive* enforcement strategy. Sending out pairs of equally qualified white and black workers to firms that had no black employees, for example, might have uncovered clear cases of racially based hiring, but the commission refused to do this. Instead, it waited *reactively* for complaints.

The fact that a company has a substantial black work force does not, of course, mean that the company does not discriminate against blacks. It might, for example, establish pay rates for job categories dominated by blacks that are

---

14. The extent to which the MCAD avoided even the appearance of adjudication is striking. Mayhew interviewed 27 former respondents in employment discrimination cases and not one of them thought he had "lost" his case. This was true even where the commission had formally found that there was probable cause to believe that discrimination had occurred (p. 246).

lower than the rates for similarly skilled white-dominated positions. It might dismiss black workers for behavior that would earn a white worker only a reprimand. And it might refuse to promote its black workers beyond a certain level. Yet for all of this, it is difficult to make out a case of discrimination against a business that is known to have one of the better records for employing blacks in the area. Thus reactive enforcement generated a pattern of cases that the black complainants found particularly hard to prove. Their difficulties were exacerbated, because in evaluating complaints the MCAD adopted a reasonable basis test. If a black were fired because he reported to work drunk, his case was dismissed because it is reasonable to fire someone who was drunk on the job. If an employer could show that the black he had refused to hire had a criminal record, the complaint was dismissed because it is reasonable to refuse to employ someone with a criminal record. The MCAD never sought out, and, indeed, was not receptive to, evidence bearing on the crucial question: namely, whether the firm in our examples fired whites who reported to work drunk and refused to hire whites with criminal records. We have here yet another example of case logics determining the implications of rules.

Title VII of the 1964 Civil Rights Act

The Equal Employment Opportunity Commission. In light of the fate of most state FEPCs, consider Title VII of the 1964 Civil Rights Act and the Equal Employment Opportunity Commission that it created. In many ways the 1964 Act was weak. Most importantly, the EEOC as it was established in 1964 was a paper tiger. It could receive complaints of discrimination from individuals, file complaints for individuals, investigate complaints, and upon finding reasonable cause to believe discrimination had occurred, it could attempt to conciliate the complaint by *voluntary* means. From the statute, the impression one gets of the EEOC is that it was to be the federal counterpart to the early Massachusetts Commission Against Discrimination. It was to wait for complaints rather than to investigate discrimination on its own. It was to conciliate rather than to adjudicate. It was to cajole rather than to coerce. It was to be passive, persuasive, and ultimately powerless.

Moreover, the few processes at the EEOC's disposal were fraught with delay. If a state or municipality had a fair employment practice forum, this could not be bypassed by complainants desiring federal relief. Yet many of these forums also had no enforcement powers, and their processes could be quite time-consuming (Norgren, 1967; Hill, 1972).

The one coercive device in the EEOC's repertoire was its right to refer cases to the Attorney General for litigation if the parties could not reach a voluntary settlement.[15] Given the EEOC's passive posture and an overworked Justice

---

15. The Justice Department, if it so chose, could bring suit on its own where the Attorney General found a pattern of practice of discrimination. And individual complainants themselves could sue after at least 60 days following their EEOC filing—210 days in jurisdictions that had local forums for settling grievances.

Department, this stick was rarely employed (Bullock, 1975, p. 83). Not surprisingly, the early EEOC did not appear to be an effective agency. In its first 32 months, the EEOC's conciliation efforts involved only 754 complaints, of which only 358 were even partially settled. These actions affected at most 20,000 workers (Nathan, 1966).[16]

The one important thing that the EEOC did do during this period was to establish a set of guidelines that constituted its interpretation of Title VII's provisions. Although the EEOC could not enforce these guidelines, they had a significant impact on later judicial interpretations.

Statutory Provisions. In 1972 Title VII was amended in several ways. The most important amendment gave the EEOC the power to bring suits in the federal courts in its own right upon a finding of reasonable cause and a failure of conciliation. This meant that a committed agency now had substantial power to enforce the law.

There remained, however, the question of statutory interpretation. The remedies that Title VII makes available to a federal court when there is a finding of discrimination are extensive.[17] However, the substantive provisions of the statute do not clearly specify whether an intent to discriminate must be found for a Title VII violation, and the statute contains exceptions and limitations that under some plausible interpretations would severely limit the law's effectiveness.

The operative provisions of Title VII are in section 703. For employers it is an unlawful employment practice:

(1) to fail or refuse to hire or to discharge any individual, or otherwise discriminate against any individual with respect to his compensation, terms, conditions, or privileges of employment, *because* of such individual's race, color, religion, sex or national origin; or (2) to limit, segregate, or classify his employees or applicants for employment in any way which would deprive or tend to deprive any individual of employment opportunities or otherwise adversely affect his status as an employee, *because* of such individual's race, color, religion, sex or national origin. (emphasis added) [42 U.S.C. Sec. 2000e-2(a)]

Labor unions have similar duties, and it is also unlawful for a union to cause or attempt to cause an employer to discriminate. In addition, the statute laid out

---

16. In addition to Title VII, there have been two other federal efforts to reduce job discrimination. First, there have been a series of executive orders since the Roosevelt Administration that have prohibited discrimination by federal contractors. These orders have had a spotty career at best, the most noteworthy success being the so-called Philadelphia plan establishing quota-like employment rules in the construction industry [see *Contractors Association of Eastern Pennsylvania* v. *Secretary of Labor*, 422 F. 2d. 159 (3d Cir. 1971) cert. denied, 404 U.S. 854 (1972), and Nash (1971)].

Second, there have been many federal programs designed to create jobs that presumably would improve the employment situation of minorities. Although a discussion of such programs is beyond the scope of this chapter, it is fair to say that they have met with relatively little success in view of their expense.

17. They include: injunctions against unlawful practices and "such affirmative action as may be appropriate, which may include, but is not limited to, reinstatement or hiring of employees, with or without back pay . . . or any other equitable relief as the court deems appropriate" [42 U.S.C. Sec. 2000e-5(g)].

two important exceptions to these provisions: It specifically permitted (1) different standards of compensation or other conditions of employment if they were "pursuant to a bona fide seniority or merit system, provided the system was not the result of an intention to discriminate," and (2) the giving of and acting on the results of "any professionally developed ability test provided that such test, its administration or action upon the results is not designed, intended or used to discriminate" [42 U.S.C. Sec. 2000e–2(h)].

Thus the statute contained many potential loopholes through which the discriminating employer or union might slip. Apparently, many employers and unions believed they could slip through these loopholes, for they frequently refused conciliation. In doing so, they provided a body of factually potent cases for the federal courts, which, it soon became apparent, welcomed the strong enforcement postures suggested by the otherwise weak EEOC.

As one might suspect, the passage of Title VII led to the end of overt refusals to hire or promote for racial reasons. Justification for employment practices that resulted in the disproportionate exclusion of minorities centered around special educational qualifications, training, experience, seniority, test scores, family connections, arrest records, and wage garnishments. Many of these appear neutral on their face, and therefore are not compelling indicia of intent to discriminate. Judicial interpretation, however, maximized the statute's impact.

Employment Tests. Among the most important issues litigated under Title VII in the early 1970s were the use of educational requirements and the impact of seniority systems. In *Griggs* v. *Duke Power Company*, 401 U.S. 424 (1971) and *Albermarle Paper Co.* v. *Moody*, 422 U.S. 405 (1975) the Supreme Court cast a skeptical eye on job qualification tests. These cases involved tests of a type that commonly were given as prerequisites for certain jobs or promotions. The lower courts in these cases had held that the use of such tests did not violate Title VII unless they were given for some discriminatory purpose, but the Supreme Court adopted a more restrictive standard.

The Court recognized that the tests used had to be taken by everyone and thus on their face were neutral instruments, but it held that this alone was not enough to justify them. In *Griggs*, Chief Justice Berger wrote, "Under the Act, practices, procedures, or tests neutral on their face, and even neutral in terms of intent, cannot be maintained if they operate to 'freeze' the status quo of prior discriminatory employment practices" (401 U.S. 424, 430).

The company that was sued in *Griggs* gave an aptitude test to those without high school diplomas. (In 1960 only 12 percent of the black male population had a diploma.) For one set of jobs 58 percent of the whites passed the test used by the company as compared to only 6 percent of the blacks. The Court responded by holding that the act, "proscribes not only overt discrimination but also practices that are fair in form, but discriminatory in operation. The touchstone is business necessity. If an employment practice which operates to exclude Negroes cannot be shown to be related to job performance, the practice is prohibited" (401 U.S. 424, 431). The Court went on to find that there was no demonstration that either having a high school diploma or passing the test was related to successful performance on the job. Indeed, there was evidence to the contrary. White employees who had neither taken the test nor completed high school performed as well and were promoted as frequently as those who had. Thus so long as there was discrimination in fact, a showing of no intent to discriminate would not save the tests. "Congress directed the thrust of the Act to the *consequences* of employment practices, not simply the motivation" (401 U.S. 424, 432).

Albemarle was just going to trial when the Court rendered the *Griggs* opinion. The defendant, Albemarle Paper Company, attempted to save its testing program from a similar fate. It gave tests like those it gave at the time of hiring to 105 employees in ten job groupings, all of the groupings being high in the plant's skilled lines of progression. The test scores of actual employees were compared with supervisor evaluations of competence. Scores on the IQ test that was part of their battery correlated significantly with supervisors' judgments in three job groups. One form of a verbal aptitude test was significantly related to evaluations in seven of the ten groups. The trial court found this to be an adequate demonstration of job relatedness, and refused to enjoin Albemarle's testing program. The Fourth Circuit reversed the trial court in a divided decision. The Supreme Court affirmed the appellate decision. It reiterated its position that once the plaintiff shows that a test disproportionately eliminates minority group members from employment, the employer must bear the burden of proving the test is job-related. Albemarle, the Court found, did not meet this burden. The court implied that this could not be done merely by showing that a test had "construct validity," that is, it was fairly designed with specific job skills in mind. Instead, the Court, following EEOC guidelines, suggested that performance validation studies should be conducted where feasible. This requires controlled statistical analysis relating test scores to subsequent job performance.

The Court also held in *Albemarle* that even if a defendant is able to prove that a test is job-related, the plaintiff may still prevail by showing that an alternative selection device exists that would have the same business utility but less of an adverse impact (422 U.S. 405, 425).

Several questions were left open by these two opinions, such as: What should be the standard of adverse impact?[18] and, What do "job-relatedness" and "business necessity" mean in practice? We need not, however, probe the law in detail for current purposes nor need we canvass the burgeoning case law and literature

---

18. In 1978 the EEOC and other federal agencies jointly adopted a set of Uniform Guidelines on Employee Selection Procedures. Among other things the guidelines adopted a "rule of thumb" standard of 80 percent for determining adverse impact. Thus a test or other employment criterion is considered to have an adverse impact if it has a "selection rate for any race, sex, or ethnic group which is less than four-fifths (⅘) (or eighty percent) of the rate for the group with the highest rate . . ." In addition, adverse impact is to be measured by a "bottom line" standard. If the total selection process used by an employer does not adversely affect a protected group, the components do not have to be evaluated or validated separately. The bottom line standard was challenged successfully, however [*Connecticut* v. *Teal*, 457 U.S. 440 (1982)].

involving sex-based rather than race-based discrimination. We simply note that in the years since *Griggs* and *Albemarle* the courts have dealt with these and other questions while holding to the basic rule enunciated in the two early cases (see Schlei & Grossman, 1983).

Seniority Systems. The other major body of case law involving race discrimination under Title VII concerns seniority systems. Here the usual issue is not whether current seniority systems are "legal," but rather, what must be done to remedy the effects of a past seniority system that discriminated between the races or of a current one that, without discriminating, will perpetuate past discrimination. A typical situation is one in which certain job categories involving the worst and lowest paying jobs in the plant are disproportionately filled with minority workers and seniority instead of being plant-wide accrues only within job categories. Thus in switching to a different line of progression through the firm, seniority is lost. Yet promotions to better positions are significantly, if not totally determined, by the seniority of the applicants.

Title VII contains language that is amplified by statements in the Civil Rights Act's legislative history, indicating that it is not the purpose nor should it be the effect of the law to allow "reverse discrimination." Until recently, however, the courts have systematically refused to let bygones be bygones. They have held that workers disadvantaged by discriminatory seniority systems are entitled to more than the forward-looking remedy of holding that such systems will be henceforth illegal. As one judge put it:

> The history [of the legislation] leads the court to conclude that Congress did not intend to require "reverse discrimination"; that is, the act does not require that Negroes be preferred over white employees who possess employment seniority. It is also apparent that Congress did not intend to freeze an entire generation of Negro employees into discriminatory patterns that existed before the act." [*Quarles* v. *Philip Morris Inc.*, 279 F. Supp. 505, 516 (E.D. Va. 1968)]

The Fifth Circuit, in *Local 189* v. *United States*, 416 F. 2d 980 (1969), outlines three strategies for dealing with the effects of past discrimination. The first, called "freedom now" would eliminate all "but for" effects of past discrimination. It would require that blacks displace whites with lesser plant seniority who hold jobs that, but for the discrimination, the blacks would have had. At the other extreme is a "status quo" strategy. It finds the Act satisfied if the illegal system is terminated and treats the disadvantaged position of longtime black employees as the unfortunate but irremediable consequence of past actions.

Between these poles there lies what the Fifth Circuit called a "rightful place" theory. It neither extinguishes all the but for effects of past discrimination nor does it accept the status quo. Rather, it prohibits future job assignments on the basis of a seniority system that "locks in" prior racial classification. It does not, however, bump whites from their present jobs. The rightful place approach is the one that is most generally accepted by the courts.

The rightful place approach probably reached its zenith in 1979 in the case of *United Steelworkers* v. *Weber*, 443 U.S. 193 (1979). That case involved a Louisiana company that had long drawn its craft work force from men trained by the local craft unions which were known to have had a long history of racial discrimination. To counteract the discriminatory effects of past hiring practices, the company and union agreed to an in-plant craft training program into which workers would be fed, alternately, from two seniority lists, one for white workers and one for black ones, until the proportion of black craft workers in the plant equaled their proportion in the company's work force. Brian Weber, a white worker who sought to enter the program but was displaced by black workers with lesser seniority sued to have the program declared illegal under Title VII.

It is clear that if a dual seniority system like that in *Weber* had disadvantaged black workers, it would have been invalidated immediately. But the Supreme Court, on a 5–4 vote, rejected Weber's claim. Particularly important to the Court were the facts that the program had been privately agreed to by the company and the union and that the program was designed to overcome the effects of past discrimination, albeit not in the first instance by the company, that had effectively excluded blacks from craft positions.[19]

Weber involved voluntary remediation. This, it turned out, marks a limit on the use of the rightful place approach. The Supreme Court in *International Brotherhood of Teamsters* v. *United States*, 431 U.S. 324 (1977) held as a matter of statutory interpretation that a bona fide seniority system (i.e., one not created for purposes of discrimination) was lawful even though it perpetuated pre-Title VII discrimination. In 1982 the *Teamsters* holding was extended to cover seniority systems created after the passage of Title VII, a more dubious judgment given the language of the act. In *Patterson* v. *American Tobacco Co.*, 456 U.S. 63 (1982) the Supreme Court held that such systems do not violate Title VII unless they are the result of "discriminatory intent" even if they perpetuate past discrimination. *Teamsters* and *American Tobacco* do not, however, eliminate rightful place relief entirely, because they apply only to bona fide systems and do not bar a rightful place remedy for post-1964 (i.e., post act) discrimination.[20]

---

19. Frequently employers argue that "business necessity" makes a rightful place remedy infeasible. Their position is that because blacks have been excluded from certain lines of progression, they have not received the "on-the-job" training needed to advance into new lines on a par with whites whose time with the company has been spent entirely within the desirable lines of progression. Employers have also argued against disrupting the seniority system because of its adverse effect on the morale of (white) workers. In *United States* v. *Bethlehem Steel*, 446 F. 2d 652 (2d Cir. 1971) the Court responded that the business necessity doctrine "must mean more than that the transfer and seniority policies serve legitimate management functions. . . . Necessity connotes an irresistible demand" (446 F. 2d 652, 662). More generally, the courts have been unwilling to recognize the defense of business necessity except in very clear cases where the employee is not qualified. Any other policy would severely limit a court's ability to remedy past discrimination or prevent future bias.

20. Much of the post *Teamsters* litigation has concerned the issue of *bona fides*. Some of the criteria to be used in making this judgment are: (1) Whether the seniority system operates to discourage all employees equally from transferring between seniority units; (2) Whether the seniority units are in the same or separate bargaining units (if the latter, whether that structure is rational and in conformance with industry practice); (3) Whether the seniority system had its genesis in racial discrimination; and (4) Whether the system was negotiated and has been maintained free from any illegal purpose [*James* v. *Stockton Valves and Fittings Co.*, 559 F. 2d 310, 352 (5th Cir 1977), *cert denied*, 434 U.S. 1034 (1978)].

Backpay. The other important remedy that Title VII makes available is the award of backpay to persons adjudged to have been discriminated against. Specifically, the courts have rejected a good faith defense to backpay liability. The Supreme Court in *Albemarle* noted that the primary thrust of Title VII is twofold: elimination of employment discrimination and compensation for the victims. The second objective implies backpay as a matter of course, although this remains within the discretion of the court. Thus, for instance, if awarding backpay would bankrupt an employer, causing all employees to lose their jobs, the remedy may be denied. Nevertheless, the Court declared that there should be a "reasonably certain" prospect of a backpay award when the statute is violated as an inducement for employers to eliminate discrimination without judicial intervention. The Supreme Court noted that "If employers faced only the prospect of an injunctive order, they would have little incentive to shun practices of dubious legality" [422 U.S. 405, 417 (1975)].

In summary, the cases in the 1970s established a strong body of law designed to promote equality in the workplace.[21] Among the more important rules are: statistics showing racial disparity constitute at least a prima facie case of discrimination; proof of discrimination does not ordinarily require proving discriminatory intent; qualifications that are neutral on their face but that are not demonstrably related to job performance are unlawful if they create an avoidable racial imbalance or perpetuate past discrimination; and relief to compensate for past discrimination and pay attorney's fees can be obtained.

Administrative Action. The effectiveness of a law, however, cannot be judged solely by the quality of the case law that develops. Focusing on the law as it has been applied since 1972 when the EEOC gained enforcement power reveals problems. The first is delay. For a number of years the EEOC suffered a serious backlog problem. In 1972 there was a 50,000-case backlog. This rose to over 100,000 in 1974 and was at 70,000 in 1979. More recently a reorganization of intake and case disposition procedures has substantially reduced this backlog. Processing time has fallen from a high of over 2 years in the mid-seventies to closer to one-half year in 1982 (Bullock, 1975, p. 83; Schlei & Grossman, 1983, p. 938). However, the Reagan EEOC appears substantially less zealous in pursuing cases on behalf of black complainants than its predecessor.

Another limitation on the EEOC is that by and large it has been a reactive agency, waiting for complaints to be brought to it.[22] Indeed, the heavy caseload means that the greater proportion of the agency's staff must devote its time to handling complaints.

---

21. Some decisions by the Supreme Court in the 1980s limit rather than extend trends that the earlier case law appeared to sanction. See, for example, *Firefighters Local 1784* v. *Stotts*, 104 S. Ct. 2576 (1984).

22. A potentially important exception is the EEOC's Office of Systemic Programs. This is an internal group with the mission of finding and processing cases against employers and unions responsible for systemic employment discrimination (Schlei & Grossman, 1983, p. 951). However, it appears that this office has chosen to rely on patterns of complaints to trigger its investigations.

Reactivity, as we have already noted, poses problems that extend beyond forcing plaintiffs to bear the initial burden of filing complaints. It may limit the impact of the resources at the agency's disposal. Mayhew (1968) in his study of the MCAD distinguishes strategic from nonstrategic complaints. By his definition:

> We shall call a complaint strategic when, if it were successful, it would produce a more even distribution of Negroes in the community. We are simply asking whether the targets of complaints are firms and neighborhoods that already include an average number of Negroes, or whether they are pioneering, strategic complaints against underrepresented firms or neighborhoods. (p. 169)

As we saw in the case of the MCAD, reactivity means that strategic complaints are likely to be only a small proportion of the agency caseload. They may be lost in the mass of valid but nonstrategic complaints and so command neither special attention nor extra resources. A more proactive EEOC would search out industries or firms where blacks are not hired and bring actions against these employers. In those relatively few instances where the EEOC has been proactive, it has had some important successes.[23]

Although one can point to specific employment policy changes and backpay awards attributable to Title VII, the question remains whether the law has had any appreciable tendency to promote racial equality in the job market. The answer is not clear. Unlike voting and even school desegregation, it is much more difficult to know whether any reduction in job inequality should be attributed to the law or whether the reduction would have occurred in any event because of nonlegal factors.

Job Market Equality

Some data suggest a general improvement in the situation of black employees during the last quarter century. Monthly labor force reports from the Bureau of Labor Statistics place persons into 11 major categories, each of which has been assigned a prestige score using a system developed by Duncan (1961). At one end laborers are assigned a score of 7 and at the other professionals are assigned a score of 75. Using these scales we can calculate an index of dissimilarity in occupational prestige. The index runs from 0 to 100, with a lower score indicating less of a difference in the occupational status of blacks and whites as groups. In 1940 the dissimilarity index for males was 43. By 1950 it had fallen to 37 and it was still at this level in 1960, indicating that blacks had drawn no closer

---

23. Industry-wide conciliation efforts have been undertaken in airlines, shipping, trucking, steel, and other industries, and the EEOC has been effective in intervening in the policymaking of other regulatory commissions. Most noteworthy perhaps was the EEOC appearance before the Federal Communications Commission which led to a delay in a rate increase requested by AT&T, until the company agreed to change certain personnel policies. Ultimately AT&T paid $15 million in back wages and gave $23 million in raises to women and minority men against whom it had allegedly discriminated.

to whites in average occupational prestige during the decade of the fifties. The index began again to drop in 1962 reaching 30 in 1970 and 26 in 1975. Since then there has been little change. In 1982 the index stood at 23. The decline in the disparity in occupational prestige scores for black and white women has been greater. The index fell from the mid-forties in 1960; greater than it was for men, to 17 in 1982. But the trend began before the passage of the 1964 act and it had substantially accelerated by the time of the 1972 amendments. These facts coupled with changing attitudes toward race in other spheres, preclude the easy conclusion that post-1964 improvements in the occupational prestige of blacks relative to whites are attributable to Title VII. When we examine other indicators of black employment gains, we see that other apparently favorable signs are equally ambiguous.

Table 11.5 indicates how the ratio of minority workers to white workers in eight major nonfarm occupational categories has shifted between 1950 and 1980. Since 1965 there has been a significant increase in the ratio of minority to white employees in the top six categories, while there has been a decrease in the two lowest categories. Most of this improvement has occurred since 1965.

Table 11.6 compares the actual 1980 occupational distribution of *black* workers with a hypothetical 1980 distribution based on 1965 percentages from EEO reports. The table indicates that there are more black workers in the higher occupational categories and fewer black workers in the lower occupational categories than one would have predicted using the 1965 occupational distribution data.

These data suggest that blacks have made considerable progress toward job equality in recent years. But the data tell only part of the story. First, we should not lose sight of the fact that there remains a significant gap between whites and

TABLE 11.5
Ratio of Minority Worker Employment to White Worker employment

Occupation	1950	1955	1960	1965	1970	1975	1980
Officials & managers	21.5	20.7	21.5	23.4	30.7	39.2	43.3
Professional & technical	37.5	35.7	36.7	52.3	61.5	73.5	77.0
Sales	17.3	18.8	22.2	26.7	31.3	39.1	42.6
Clerical	25.3	34.5	46.2	50.3	73.3	86.7	98.9
Craftspersons (skilled)	35.0	36.8	43.0	49.6	60.0	65.7	72.2
Operatives (semiskilled)	90.2	103.4	113.5	117.0	139.4	136.9	143.7
Laborers (unskilled)	282.0	336.2	306.0	282.0	251.2	193.3	160.5
Services (excluding household)	233.3	233.3	213.4	218.3	194.6	184.9	176.1

Note: Ratio = $\dfrac{\text{percentage of minority workers in occupation}}{\text{percentage of white workers in occupation}} \times 100$

Source: Blumrosen, 1984, p. 335.

TABLE 11.6
Comparison of Actual 1980 Occupational Distribution of Black Workers With Hypothetical 1980 Distribution Based on 1965 Percentages From EEO Reports

Occupation	Column 1: Number of Black Workers in Actual Distribution	Column 2: Number of Black Workers in Hypothetical Distribution	Column 3: Difference in Number of Black Workers (Column 1 − Column 2)
Officials & managers	148,765	35,490	113,275
Professionals	139,972	43,377	96,595
Technical	161,229	86,753	74,476
Sales	216,335	78,867	137,468
Office & clerical	603,404	283,920	319,484
Craftspersons (skilled)	356,467	244,486	111,981
Operatives (semiskilled)	1,115,255	1,324,959	−209,704
Laborers (unskilled)	516,947	989,776	−472,829
Services	684,995	851,759	−166,764

Sources: EEOC. Equal Employment Opportunity Report No. 1, Job Patterns for Minorities and Women in Private Industry, 1966 (1968): EEOC. Job Patterns for Minorities and Women in Private Industry, 1980 (1982); Blumrosen, 1984, p. 341.

blacks in employment. As Farley (1977) notes, the average prestige score for nonwhite workers in 1975 was lower than that for white workers in 1940 despite employment shifts, which meant that the average prestige score for all workers, white and black, increased substantially.

Moreover, the gains blacks have made, relative to whites, in job status must be examined in light of several other factors. First, black unemployment is higher than white unemployment, especially among younger persons. For example, in 1980, when white unemployment was 12 percent for youth between 16 and 24 years old, black unemployment was 26 percent in this age bracket (Mare & Winship, 1984, p. 39). And unemployment rates themselves do not capture people who have dropped out of the labor market entirely. In 1982, among white men in the prime working ages of 25 to 54, 89 percent were employed, 6 percent were unemployed (looking for work), and 5 percent were out of the labor market either because of ill health, school attendance, or other reasons. For black men, 77 percent were employed, 11 percent were unemployed, and 12 percent were out of the labor force. Whatever the reasons for the higher rate of black men out of the labor force (see, e.g., Farley, 1984, pp. 52–55), when labor force "dropouts" are included in our analysis apparent gains in black employment and earnings since 1964 are diminished (Brown, 1984).

Second, even if we consider only employed workers, nonwhite men with occupational prestige scores equal to white men earn less. A gain of one point on the prestige scale is worth about one-half as much to a nonwhite as to a white (Farley, 1977, p. 203). This is in part due to the fact that black employment is generally lower in larger firms that pay more (Bullock, 1975, p. 94).

Third, even if Title VII were perfectly enforced, racial inequalities in employment would probably persist for a considerable period of time. Studies of the disparity between the job success of white and black males suggest that it is in large measure attributable not directly to race but to such things as educational attainment, occupation, father's occupation, residential location, region of the country, and number of hours worked per year (Duncan, 1969; Kain, 1968; Lieberson & Fugitt, 1967; Mooney, 1969; Smith & Welch, 1977; Featherman & Hauser, 1978; Farley, 1984).[24]

Finally, employment gains have not been reflected in gains in family income. Indeed, the gap between black and white family income is as great now as it was in 1966. In that year black median family income was 58 percent of white median income (black income = $4,507; white income = $7,792). In 1983

---

24. The opposite side of this coin is that differences which remain after such factors are taken into account are often thought to be measures of "the cost of being a Negro" (Seigel, 1965) or the cost of racial discrimination in the labor market. Thus, for example, the results of an analysis by Farley (1984) indicate that in 1979 the hypothetical earning of a black male with success-relevant characteristics identical to those of the typical white male worker and working the same number of hours would be 88 percent of what the white worker earns. A similar analysis for 1959 produces a 19 percent difference (1984, p. 75). But, as Farley notes, considerable caution is needed in interpreting these data as measures of discrimination. See Conway and Roberts (1983) for a discussion of various techniques of producing these estimates.

black median income was 57 percent of white median income (black income = $14,506; white income = $25,757) (Rodgers, 1984, p. 105; U.S. Bureau of the Census, 1984). Part of this continuing gap is due to the fact that single parent, female-headed households constitute a larger percentage of all black families than of all white families, but a substantial gap remains when intact families are examined (Reimers, 1984).

Limits on Title VII

Since occupational inequality is tied to other types of inequality, as long as blacks are less well educated, live in areas of higher unemployment, and are residentially segregated in areas with inferior job opportunities, racial inequality in the work force will persist even in the absence of discrimination as defined by Title VII. Equal employment opportunity if it means only that race will play no role in determining who will be hired from among a pool of equally qualified job applicants does not mean that jobs or incomes will come eventually to be distributed equally across races. As we emphasize in Chapter 13, equal opportunity in an unequal society does not lead to equal results.

Thus there appear to be inherent limits on what the laws that have been passed to deal with employment discrimination can do. Within these limits, there remains substantial room for legally induced change, but whether the law has induced important changes is not easy to ascertain. As we noted earlier, the gains that blacks have made since 1964 are not necessarily attributable to civil rights legislation. Market forces are particularly powerful in the employment area, and the status and income of employed black workers would have risen in the prosperous sixties regardless of the 1964 Act.[25] Also, other laws and more general normative changes have made overt discrimination less acceptable over the years. This change in attitude, no doubt, has affected employment decisions. Rising black political power in parts of the South and in some northern industrial cities may have had a similar effect.

Finally, changes in the aspirations of black youth and desegregation or affirmative action in other sectors of society could have been expected to produce some increase in the status of black workers even if fair employment laws did not exist. For example, it was not until the early 1970s that the higher status white universities were producing more than a trickle of black graduates who were qualified to enter the worlds of law, business, and medicine. Today thousands of black students receive degrees in these areas each year.

---

25. There may also be an interaction between market forces and the law. In the case of women, who are also protected from discrimination by Title VII, we think such an interaction occurred. Title VII helped to overcome entrenched habits of discrimination, but once this happened, the market, together with a large pool of qualified women, was probably primarily responsible for the substantial advances that women made in many previously closed job areas. If this is the case, repealing Title VII should have little effect on future patterns of female employment, although, had it never been enacted, the pattern of jobs available to women might be very different.

For all these reasons, we, as social scientists, must withhold judgment on the question of whether Title VII of the 1964 Civil Rights Act and the 1972 Amendments had a substantial effect on patterns of black employment. Viewing the lower average status of black workers as a social problem, improvements since World War II are obvious, but differences between black and white employment are still substantial, and it is unlikely that they will be greatly diminished in the near future. It is also not clear what the future contributions of Title VII and the EEOC are likely to be. But this analysis reflects the social scientist's bias toward viewing troubles in the aggregate. There are thousands of black workers who have money in their pockets, better jobs, and more promising futures because of the existence of Title VII and the efforts of the EEOC. On occasion and in dealing with personal troubles, the law has had its intended effect. Some people are happier and enjoy greater equality because of the law. Some employers who have made backpay awards or revised their employment policies will also attest that Title VII has mattered.

VOTING, SCHOOLS, AND JOBS: THE LAW AND INEQUALITY

What conclusions might we draw from the various attempts to use law to desegregate our society and to reduce racial inequality? Our thoughts on this matter are greatly influenced by Frederick Wirt's (1970) discussion in his study of Panola County, Mississippi. Not only is the organization of this chapter similar to the organization of his book, but we arrrive at many of the same conclusions.

The question is, under what circumstances is law a more or less effective instrument in reducing inequality? Put more concretely, what differences in effectiveness can we find among the various laws we have examined, and to what should we attribute their relative success? Following Wirt, we suggest that five basic factors are important to the effectiveness of legal interventions in promoting racial equality. These are: (1) qualities of the regulation, (2) qualities of the regulator, (3) qualities of the regulated, (4) qualities of the beneficiary class, and (5) other factors, of which the most important are the elasticity, availability, and contingency of the resource being sought.

Qualities of the Regulation

Perhaps the single most important observation emerging from our discussion of these three laws is that regulations are more effective when they use a strict liability standard and are less effective when they use a criminal liability standard. In other words, the need to show intentionality gets in the way of enforcement. For example, significant strides were made in voting registration once the intentions of registrars were no longer an issue.

To adopt a regulation that uses a strict liability standard is to assess actions by their results, rather than by their purposes. Regulations that do this focus not on individual actions but on aggregate patterns of behavior. Focusing on aggregate patterns tends to make regulation more effective by (1) providing a clear standard of what constitutes a violation, (2) reducing the amount of time and effort involved in fact-finding, and (3) allowing situational rather than case-focused remedies. Together these factors maximize aggregate impact while holding down processing costs. All three factors not only allow enforcement to proceed more efficiently, but they also give the regulated a better idea of what is expected and an incentive to comply before becoming enforcement targets.

Maximizing aggregate impact is to some extent achieved only at the cost of what many think of as justice in individual cases. These costs may be paid by third parties or by the beneficiaries of the regulation as well as by the regulated parties. Brian Weber, who did nothing to discriminate against blacks, must step aside so that a black worker with less seniority may receive the training he covets (443 U.S. 193, 1979). Or a black who because of his special skills was substantially disadvantaged by his employers' racially biased employment policies receives substantially less as part of an aggregate settlement than he would if his case had been decided alone. The justification for such outcomes is the feeling that aggregating responses to past discrimination enhances justice in some social sense.

Although the school desegregation and job discrimination laws differ from the Voting Rights Act in that neither of the former has employed a strict liability rule logic, enforcement efforts have been greatly enhanced by the willingness of the courts to accept aggregate statistical evidence and to shift burdens of proof. These steps, like the adoption of a strict liability rule logic, undercut the defendant's ability to advance motivational excuses against charges of discrimination.[26] A shallow case logic, in effect, creates a regime that approximates one of strict liability.

Also important in assessing the likely success of a regulation are the sanctions it allows. A popular view is that the criminal sanction and the punishment it entails is the most effective way of channeling behavior. The threat of imprisonment seems more likely than milder sanctions to deter resisting defendants and encourage others to obey the law. From this perspective it may seem surprising that none of the laws we have dealt with employs criminal sanctions as its primary deterrent weapon.

Criminal sanctions, however, are not the most promising legal tool when the goal is to promote equality. First, criminal sanctions are usually applied against individuals, but if we are concerned with eliminating inequality, altering individual actions will rarely be sufficient. Instead, we must change institution-

---

26. For example, statistics on the relative proportions of black and white job applicants passing a test may be sufficient to establish a normal meaning of discrimination. The defendant then may bear the burden of proving that a different interpretation is true, and the law, by limiting the relevance of intentionality, may make this task particularly difficult.

alized patterns of behavior and the organizations that embody them. Organizations can usually insulate themselves from the legal problems of their individual agents. If we seek to penalize organizations criminally, our choice is limited to either fining or destroying the institution. In the situations we have dealt with neither of these remedies is likely to be of much help. Those whom we seek to benefit will suffer if the organizations that might help them are weakened or destroyed for the dubious possibility that similarly situated organizations will be deterred.

Criminal sanctions are also of limited usefulness because they are tied to criminal responsibilty. We are reluctant to use harsh criminal penalties unless illegal intentions have been shown and the state has met a substantial burden of proof. Yet, as we have suggested, the usefulness of law in promoting equality has depended in large measure on the construction of a jurisprudence that avoids these requirements.

Given the deficiencies of the criminal sanction, the law must rely on other threats. One remedy that combines civil and criminal elements is the injunction. It allows a court to order people to act in a specific way and threatens those so ordered with fines or imprisonment for contempt of court should they refuse to comply. Injunctions were used extensively in school desegregation litigation and have occasionally been important in the other areas we have examined. However, it may take years of litigation and appeals before complex injunctive orders finally take effect. Moreover, injunctions and the threats they imply affect only those who have been brought to court. What is needed for widespread social change are sanctions or procedures that avoid the need for litigating every instance of the behavior to be changed.

In the job cases there is the obvious sanction of a backpay order as a deterrent to discriminatory practices. When the issue is voting rights or school segregation, there is no obvious natural sanction. In the case of voting, the ultimate solution was not the discovery of a way to threaten registrars; rather, it was the elimination of their function. Attempts to enforce the law by the use of sanctions, for instance, by threatening to jail registrars for contempt if they did not obey court orders produced at best only the limited, specific deterrence of the threatened registrar. There was no general deterrent impact against other registrars, nor was there reason to expect any. The situation was similar with respect to injunctions aimed at school boards.

In the case of schools the federal government was able to devise a sanction by creating something school boards needed, federal grants, which could then be taken away. Although the sanction was used for only a short period of time, it appears to have been quite persuasive. In the employment area federal contractors have proved particularly vulnerable for the same reason. Uncorrected discrimination could cost them money (Wirt, 1970). To generalize from these instances, enforcement is likely to be most effective if the enforcer can ignore individual actors in restructuring a situation and has something of value that it can routinely give to or withhold from the regulated party.

Qualities of the Regulator

One important distinction we have made in this chapter is between enforcement by the courts and enforcement by an administrative agency. This clearly affects how a regulatory regime is implemented and what it achieves, but the relationship depends on many factors. Enforcement by administrative agencies is not always superior to judicial enforcement, nor is the reverse true.

In comparing judicial and administrative modes of regulation, we need to distinguish between the creation of rules and their enforcement. School desegregation was originally required by the Supreme Court. For 10 years there was no statutory support for the Court's mandate. Equality of employment, on the other hand, was first made a right by the 1964 Civil Rights Act. When the judiciary creates regulations, the development of rules will tend to be more particularistic and incremental: There will be a case-by-case determination of the circumstances in which the rule does or does not apply. What appears to be the rule in one case may be substantially modified in the next.[27] Regulations created by legislatures ordinarily have a more general flavor; they are designed to deal with classes of situations. Close attention to context, if it occurs at all, is at the level of administrative elaboration and enforcement.

Arthur Stinchcombe (1968) has suggested that the effectiveness of any regulatory agency in enforcing rights depends in part on its ability to rely on other sources of power to support its decisions. According to Stinchcombe, "A legitimate right or authority is backed by a *nesting of reverse sources of power* set up in such a fashion that the power can always overcome opposition" (p. 160). This reserve has normative as well as legal dimensions, for "*A power is legitimate to the degree that, by virtue of the doctrines and norms by which it is justified, the power-holder can [in case of need] call upon sufficient other centers of power . . . to make his power effective*" (p. 162).

From this perspective the most important quality of the regulator is its ability to depend on other powerful actors to help it in times of conflict. In the first 10 years of the school desegregation effort, the Supreme Court had no backup institutions to aid it in conflicts with school boards. The executive and legislature did little to assist in enforcement. With the commitment of the legislature and the HEW in the early 1960s, desegregation increased significantly. This does not mean, however, that the Supreme Court's efforts did not matter. The Court

---

27. The often piecemeal nature of judicial action and the difficulty courts may have in getting an overall picture when they hear cases one at a time are among the reasons that have led some to suggest that courts should be wary of reaching decisions that dramatically alter existing social policies and, in particular, that courts should avoid judgments that attempt to structure in detail complex situations or require close, ongoing judicial involvement in the business of some other institution (Glazer, 1975; Horowitz, 1977). Others have argued that the courts should tackle broad issues of social and institutional structure and that they have developed considerable technical competence in dealing with the problems such cases pose (Cavanagh & Sarat, 1980; Fiss, 1984).

contributed crucially to the establishment of norms that helped later to generate other institutional support. Moreover, in the border states *Brown* itself stimulated desegregation. Backup aid was less important because resistance was weaker to begin with.

A similar situation existed with voting rights and jobs. In both cases the pace of change increased when different agencies began to work toward the same end. In the case of voting rights the law created a group of federal registrars backed up by the federal court in Washington, D.C. In the employment area enforcement was shared by the federal courts, the Office of Contract Compliance, and the EEOC.

Stinchcombe's perspective helps clarify the apparently contradictory evidence concerning the relative ineffectiveness of state fair employment commissions such as the Massachusetts Commission Against Discrimination. Their failure was in large part due to their inability to turn to other sources of power to assist in their enforcement efforts. The regulated groups, on the other hand, had access to other power sources, such as the governor's office, in attempting to gain support for their interpretation of the statute and their favored modes of enforcement. Morevoer, the example of the MCAD suggests that when an agency is isolated, opportunities for cooptation and "capture" are greatly increased, and to that degree its ability to enforce a statute is diminished. Judicial enforcement also suffers from isolation effects. However, the core problem is not cooptation. Rather, it is the limited and incremental nature of purely judicial remedies.

Qualities of the Regulated Groups

The most important factor here, as it is for the regulators, is the ability to garner support. The legitimacy and ultimately the success of those who wish to resist regulation depends on their ability to mobilize powerful individuals and institutions that are willing to support resistance with time, money, and ideological commitments. In the area of school desegregation, for instance, the Southern Manifesto provided resisting school boards with a general promise of support in the Congress of the United States and an official affirmation that their views were not aberrant. For 20 years thereafter one could see faded remnants of this support in teetering signs on back roads calling for the impeachment of Chief Justice Earl Warren. Further normative support was found in some popular and academic publications (Wirt, 1970, p. 304, n. 23), and the absence of firm presidential commitment to speedy desegregation must have been of some comfort. Resistance was, however, ultimately doomed, in part because the broader support for the resisting school boards was largely confined to one region and so from a national standpoint was isolated.

In order to take advantage of third-party support, regulated groups must be organized. If coordination is expensive or difficult, perhaps for reasons we noted in Chapter 10, regulated groups will have trouble mobilizing others to help them resist when the occasion arises. Consider, for example, the strong and continuous resistance to school desegregation in Boston and the way it contrasts with the lesser resistance of some apparently similar towns. This may be because Boston is noted for its relatively tight-knit ethnic communities which provide a natural core of organization. More generally, we should find that resistance to court-ordered integration in the North is greatest where (1) the local communities involved already have organized power, such as we might find in certain ethnic neighborhoods and (2) support exists for resistance outside the community, particularly at other levels of government (see Bullock & Rodgers, 1976; Dentler & Scott, 1981).

In the employment area employers and unions have ongoing organizational structures and ties to government and other powerful actors that can be mobilized to resist regulation. This aided them in what were initially largely successful efforts to neutralize the potential power of state FEPCs. The greater effectiveness of the federal law may be attributed in part to the relatively greater power of federal agencies vis-à-vis any one employer and union. For the states the problem is in part one of collective action. Although it might be in the interest of the states as a group to act against employment discrimination, each state individually is confronted with the prospect that its behavior will drive business elsewhere. The federal government does not confront this problem.

Nevertheless, it is perhaps surprising that federal fair employment legislation has not met more resistance. One possible explanation is that corporate interests are not strictly opposed to such legislation. It may be that to the degree that such legislation coerces all employers, it injures none of them. The risk of hiring black salespeople, for instance, is that a customer will take his business elsewhere. But if there is nowhere else to go because the competition must also hire black salespeople, an apparent cost of employing blacks disappears. Furthermore, expanding the pool of potential employees by removing artificial restrictions on who may hold what jobs should work to keep labor costs down.

Unions are a different matter. There actual jobs are at stake. To the degree that unions control hiring practices, and to the degree they are segregated, we might expect sterner opposition. This appears to have been the case with some craft unions. Construction jobs, in particular, seem to have been difficult to integrate. The opposition of the large industrial unions to integration has been to some extent foreclosed by their ideology of worker equality. In addition, for reasons we discussed in Chapter 10, industrial unions have a strong interest in organizing all workers, including minority group members, hired at plants they wish to control.

Finally, part of the ability of groups to resist regulation depends on their ability to sanction those who are willing to comply with or assist in the regulatory process. Friedman (1975, p. 106) argues that in some cases subcultures may be able to neutralize regulatory efforts completely through countersanctions. These countersanctions may run from fear of "what the neighbors will think," to the murder of those assisting in the enforcement effort, as occurred in Neshoba County, Mississippi, during the summer of 1964.[28]

Qualities of the Beneficiary

It is said that "God helps those who help themselves." Likewise with the law. Most laws are not self-starting. They require an angry or aggrieved citizenry to set them in motion. If no citizen is so aggrieved or if those aggrieved have compelling reasons not to engage the legal process, nothing will happen. For example, the law does not search out breached contracts. Someone must come to court and demand action because she has been hurt by another's breach. If the individual does not feel that she is harmed by the breach or feels that the legal remedy is too costly or time-consuming or is intimidated from pursuing a legal remedy, nothing will occur.

Early civil rights laws, such as the 1957 Voting Rights Act, were reactive in much the same way as contract law. The individual who felt harmed had to take action. When the class of potential plaintiffs is well organized such reactive remedies may be sufficient to allow effective enforcement of the regulation. Where, as was the case with southern blacks in 1957, the potential plaintiffs are not only unorganized but vulnerable to intimidation, a reactive law may have no impact at all.

But more than intimidation may deter people from seeking legal benefits to which they are entitled. The delay and cost inherent in using a legal remedy may make the remedy useless for the individual, unorganized plaintiff. The problems of collective action—difficulties of coordination and the temptations to free riders—may lead unorganized individuals to avoid legal solutions for fear that they will bear substantial costs while the benefits of their efforts spill over onto others. What is the personal good of suing to desegregate a school system if an integrated system will be realized only after all one's children have graduated?

But the law can, within limits, encourage collective action by a set of potential plaintiffs. First, barriers to getting together can be removed. For example, the Supreme Court in a series of decisions held that a state could not prohibit lawyers from taking referrals channeled through membership organizations like unions (*Brotherhood of Railway Trainmen* v. *Virginia*, 377 U.S. 1, 1964), that organizations could fund lawsuits on behalf of individuals (*NAACP* v. *Button,* 371 U.S. 415, 1963), and that the membership lists of civil rights organizations were protected from state scrutiny (*NAACP* v. *Alabama*, 357 U.S.

---

28. One of the most revealing studies in this regard is that of Gregory Massell (1968, p. 179; 1974) on the failure of the Soviet government's legal effort to change personal and family relationships in Islamic Soviet Central Asia during the 1920s. Moslem men were able to use sabotage, retribution against those who cooperated with the regime, and ultimately assaults on representatives of the regime in their resistance effort. Much of this effort was the work of local citizens employed by the central government who were in a good position to delay, avoid, and sabotage Soviet efforts.

349, 1958). Second, litigation to promote collective interests may be subsidized or mandated. Thus the 1960 Civil Rights Act permitted the Attorney General to sue on behalf of a whole class of plaintiffs where there was a pattern and practice of discrimination. Here the law actually produces organization. The individual(s) for whom the suit is brought may not be organized, but the new plaintiff, the Civil Rights Division of the Justice Department, is. Less extreme are provisions like those in the Civil Rights Attorney's Fees Award Act of 1976 that allow plaintiffs to recover attorney fees when they sue successfully to redress discrimination. This promotes the financial integrity of those organizations, like the NAACP (National Association for the Advancement of Colored People) or ACLU (American Civil Liberties Union), that commonly sponsor such suits and so invites more litigation than would otherwise take place.

Where suit is brought by the government or by a group of well-organized plaintiffs (e.g., the NAACP Legal Defense Fund), it is likely to be more expertly litigated and better funded than if it is privately instigated. But this is only one of the advantages of organizational litigation. Organizations tend to produce more suits that are "strategic" in the sense that they attack the areas of greatest or most consequential inequality. Mayhew (1968) found this to be the case when he examined the MCAD's efforts to prevent housing discrimination (pp. 168–177). Civil rights groups would target areas to be opened up and develop cases for the commission. And although the Justice Department brought relatively few suits during the early years of Title VII, those that were filed promised to have an area-wide or industry-wide impact (Bullock, 1975, p. 87).

In addition, government agencies or private organizations suing on behalf of groups of people may find it easier to prove discrimination than individuals suing in their own right. Demographic and statistical proofs are more readily available to organized complainants. A person suing under the 1957 Voting Rights Act, for example, would find it difficult to prove discrimination if he had failed a literacy test. However, in a Justice Department suit on behalf of all blacks in a county, evidence of a pattern excluding illiterate blacks while allowing illiterate whites to register to vote is likely to be persuasive.

Even when litigation is not contemplated, there are good reasons for the beneficiaries of rules to organize. The ability of a regulated group to capture or coopt an agency is greatly reduced if there is an organization of beneficiaries who continue to pressure the agency to adopt their views as to the agency's role. Beneficiaries fail to pressure agencies at their peril.

The Nature of the Inequality

Finally, there are three factors that we have lumped together under the heading "the nature of the inequality."

The first, raised by Wirt (1970, p. 310), is what he calls the *elasticity* of the right sought. A right is elastic when giving it to some does not take the good it protects from others. As Wirt notes, giving black citizens the right to vote does not take the vote from whites (although, of course, it dilutes the vote of whites as a group). Here at least on an individual level, the right is elastic. But the job market in Panola County at the time Wirt was writing his book was stagnant. Enforcing Title VII meant in many cases that if a black applicant were hired it was at the expense of a white applicant. Jobs are relatively inelastic. One would expect regulatory resistance to grow with the inelasticity of the right provided.

Consistent with this expectation is the serious backlash that certain "affirmative action" programs have engendered. When a white is denied admission to medical school and a black with inferior credentials is admitted, the inelasticity of the situation is obvious [cf. *Bakke* v. *Regents of the University of California*, 438 U.S. 265 (1978)]. Furthermore, the implications of the inelasticity are likely to be exaggerated. Several hundred whites can attribute their failure to obtain a coveted slot to the fact that ten places were given to blacks. Even where those applying for jobs or other positions are all basically qualified, so long as some appear to be more qualified than others, the use of quotas, that is, the use of ascribed statuses to assign positions, may increase group conflict.

The second factor that relates to the nature of the inequality is the *availability* of resources. If there are no jobs, Title VII will not create them. If a school district's students are 80 percent black, integration as it is usually understood cannot be achieved.[29] In cases where producing equality is unlikely unless new resources can be created, laws that serve only to guarantee equality provide a limited remedy. Enforcing Title VII will not lead industry in a recession year to hire more blacks.

The third factor we call the *contingency* of the inequality. The equal right to vote, once poll taxes and literacy tests are removed, is contingent on no other inequalities. It is an equality that can be produced directly. Integrated schools and equality in the workplace are, however, contingent in part on equality in other areas. The racial composition of schools is associated with residential patterns. Thus an end to housing discrimination may be essential if effective school desegregation is to occur in the North. Even this may not be enough, for ethnic group concentration may reflect both "tastes" for neighbors as well as the ability to pay certain rents. The former may be countered only by interfering with an aspect of liberty, while the latter is inextricably bound up with job discrimination. Equal employment opportunity is still more contingent. It depends in some measure on both educational equality and on residential equality. It is one thing to abolish most educational requirements for semiskilled jobs in textile plants. It is another thing to do this for more responsible, well-paying white-collar jobs. And if minority group members cannot easily travel to certain jobs, the fact that they are filled without regard to race will be of little benefit.

---

29. In such a situation it is not altogether misleading to view white students as resources. In cities like Detroit, not only are there few such resources, they are rapidly being depleted as whites leave the city for the suburbs. Attempts to cross school district boundaries, as in the Detroit case, are attempts to collect sufficient resources to make desegregation possible.

Inequalities that are contingent on other inequalities are relatively less amenable to change through the creation of equal opportunity. Moving beyond equal opportunity is a topic addressed in Chapter 13.

EQUAL OPPORTUNITY AND EQUAL RESULTS

Looking back on the civil rights legislation of the 1960s, we see that the movements toward school desegregation and equal job opportunity have had, as at least part of their justification, the goal of a more equal distribution of goods between races.[30] One result of segregated schools and segregated jobs, like the consequence of political suppression, is to relegate minority citizens to an inferior standard of living. Where aspects of political, economic, and social life are reserved for a dominant majority, the minority will end up with less. From this perspective equal opportunity is valued in large measure because it promises to contribute to equal outcomes. But as we saw in our discussion of job discrimination, equal opportunity is difficult to achieve in a society riddled with inequalities. Indeed, it is not even clear what equal opportunity means, for we must agree on the bases of differentiation that are permissible before we can say whether opportunities are or are not equal.

Focusing on race relations, as we have in this chapter, invites one to overlook a substantial proportion of the inequality in society. Inequality between racial and ethnic groups is great, but not so great as inequality between individuals:

> It seems quite shocking, for example, that white workers earn 50 percent more than black workers. But we are even more disturbed by the fact that the best-paid fifth of all white workers earn 600 percent more than the worst-paid fifth. From this viewpoint, racial inequality looks almost insignificant. (Jencks, 1972, p. 14)

Equalizing opportunity is apparently not the key to eliminating such substantial income differences. Neither family background nor occupational status explains much of the variation in men's incomes. When we compare men who are identical in these respects, we find only 12 to 15 percent less inequality than we find among randomly paired individuals (Jencks, 1972). Thus we can expect that altering opportunity structures will to only a limited extent equalize income.

Of course, there are direct ways to influence income inequality. The most obvious is to use the tax system to redistribute wealth. A steeply progressive income tax combined with a negative income tax or income maintenance program for the poor would decrease the amount of income inequality in society. A policy establishing minimum and maximum wages would, within the group of employed workers, have a similar effect. Civil service government jobs, in fact, follow

---

30. This is not to deny the existence of other goals, such as the reduction of racial conflict that some think separatism nourishes or the affirmation of the individual's right to advance to the limit of his or her ability.

such a model, but the possibility has never been entertained seriously for the private sector.

Our failure to exploit such methods is not due to our inability to see how they would alter inequality, but to other considerations. Many think we should not use law to directly alter outcomes. They would limit law to the role of establishing efficient markets open to talents, or, in Rawls's terms, to establishing a regime of Natural Liberty. Civil rights law is interesting because the goal of much of it goes beyond a Natural Liberty conception of social justice toward a regime of Liberal or even Democratic Equality where there is some attempt to alter starting points. But, as we have seen, there are limits to the willingness of courts and legislatures to alter institutional arrangements even to produce an equality of Fair Opportunity. The political boundaries of existing school districts and bona fide seniority systems are two such institutional arrangements. They serve other goals that many are not prepared to lightly cast aside.

We have in this chapter, as we shall see in the next two, discussed the very stuff of justice. We have been concerned with the allocation of rights that relate fundamentally to both liberty and the difference principle. Whether one equates justice with moves toward greater equality between the races depends both on the character of racial inequalities and on one's theory of justice. We have tried to describe some aspects of racial inequality as it has and continues to exist in the United States. Theories of justice, however, to the extent their premises are logically coherent and beyond empirical validation, allow controversies that we cannot, even in principle, resolve.

But justice has not been our only or indeed a primary concern in this chapter. Our focus has been on how law may be used to affect institutionalized patterns of behavior. The issues that most concerned us are essentially empirical. If we have done nothing else in this chapter, we hope we have laid to rest the old saw, commonly associated with William Graham Sumner, that ''stateways [law] cannot change folkways [culturally entrenched patterns of behaving].'' The proposition is simply wrong (cf. Ball et al., 1962). Although there is no guarantee that a particular law will alter behavior, the question is not whether law can do this. It is instead, under what conditions and to what extent will such changes occur?

12

Law Application and the Possibility of Autonomy

In the last two chapters we have studied examples of how the law has been used in the United States in an attempt to close the gap between ideals of social justice and injustices that are perceived to exist in society. How successful have these attempts been? Opinions differ.

From Chapter 10 it would appear that "social engineering" through law has been able to ameliorate certain threats posed by corporate power, but that most efforts have not gone beyond attempts to control threats to market efficiency and establish labor as a countervailing force to industrial management. From Chapter 11 we may conclude that legal reforms have to some extent increased equality of opportunity in the political and economic spheres, but that substantial inequalities between groups remain.

Thus the empirical data provide support for both those who conclude that law can work to reduce power and status differences in society and those who argue that reforms such as the ones we have discussed are essentially cosmetic because law is ultimately but the instrument of powerful groups. In this chapter and the next we wish to examine at a more abstract level than we have heretofore taken the arguments that support these conflicting positions. The key variables in our discussion are *legal autonomy* and *legislative endowments*. The concept of legal autonomy, which is a difficult one, we discuss in some detail. First, we describe what we mean by legal autonomy in the ideal case. We shall see that it involves the ability of a legal system to act independently of other sources of power and authority in social life. Next, we consider the possibility of its existence, arguing that legal autonomy is at most partially achieved, and that it is in fact partially achieved in the modern, Western democracies. Finally, we ask what legal autonomy entails in the law application process. Here we focus on administrative and judicial courts, although other agencies like the police and prosecutor play an important role and much of our discussion could be extended to include them if space allowed. We suggest that as an ideal, legal autonomy has three components: formality, equal competence, and normative neutrality. We discuss each of these components as ideal types and examine the degree to which the ideal breaks down in the real world and what this implies for issues of social justice. The subject of legislative endowments and the conclusion of our discussion is reserved for Chapter 13.

LEGAL AUTONOMY

An autonomous legal system is one that is independent of other sources of power and authority in social life. Legal action, be it a decision to prosecute, an award of damages, or the reapportionment of a state legislature, is in an autonomous system influenced only by the preestablished rules of the legal system. These rules determine not only the consequences of social action, but also—for all legal purposes—its meaning, and it is from the assigned meaning that legal consequences follow (cf. Teubner 1983; 1984).

Where a legal system is genuinely independent of other social systems, differences in meaning can be substantial. For example, consider the case of 79-year-old Hans Florian whose wife, Johanna, was in a nursing home suffering from advanced Alzheimer's disease. She lived in her bed, she would not talk, and she spent much of her time screaming. On a visit to the nursing home, Mr. Florian pushed his wife's wheelchair down the nursing home hall and into a stairwell where he shot and killed her. He was found holding a smoking pistol and weeping (Malcolm, 1984). To Mr. Florian his act, no doubt, was intended to bring an end to his wife's suffering and to allow her to die with dignity. To the public that read of the incident in the newspapers the death was a "mercy killing." But to one assistant district attorney, it was "a classic first-degree murder case." And so it was, for first-degree murder is the meaning that the law gives to the unauthorized, planned, intentional taking of another's life.

If the law is to be autonomous in the sense of defining events in its own terms and detailing the consequences that follow, it must in the ideal case be fully independent of society's other mechanisms of social control. Although law is itself part of the governing apparatus of the state, to be autonomous it must be independent of the political branches of government, that is, free from the influence of those branches that respond to and embody power relations in society. Although law, as Bohannan told us, abstracts cases from and returns solutions to the larger society, if autonomy is to be maintained law must not be influenced by the power and status differences that permeate social life. And although law is itself a normative system, autonomous law remains impervious to the ethical codes of the surrounding society.

A good example of this first aspect of autonomy—political autonomy—is the Abscam investigation that resulted in the conviction of several congressmen and one Senator for bribe taking. If U.S. district attorneys were not largely insulated from the political power of individual congressmen, an investigation with Congress as its target would have been unlikely. The second aspect of autonomy, social autonomy, is a major theme in the "access to justice" literature (Cappelletti & Garth, 1978). The movement, for example, to provide free legal services to the poor reflects in large measure the belief that personal wealth should not determine how one fares in the legal system. The story of the 79-year-old mercy killer, mentioned above, nicely illustrates the third aspect of autonomy, ethical autonomy. Clearly, the prosecutor's ethical system—at least when he was acting in his official capacity—was no slave to the larger society's view of right and wrong. In this case, however, Mr. Florian was never prosecuted because the grand jury refused to issue the indictment the prosecutor sought. Thus the legal system as a whole did not maintain its ethical autonomy from the larger society (cf. Sanders, 1969).

If autonomy in these senses is to be realized, the legal system should be autonomous in one further sense. It must be *self-legitimating*, for to depend upon political, social, or ethical forces for authority is to be vulnerable to the encroachment of such forces on decision making. A legal system is self-legitimating when its rules and rulings are accepted because they are legal. If we keep in mind the distinction between primary and secondary rules that we have used several times in this volume, this proposition is less circular than it may sound. In terms of this distinction, a legal system is self-legitimating when its primary rules and statements of them are accepted as binding because they are enacted in accordance with the system's secondary rules. Thus in a self-legitimating legal system a law will be recognized if it is *duly* enacted and the legal system itself determines what is meant by "duly." Similarly, a court ruling will be regarded as binding because it specifies the implications of a primary rule (i.e., a substantive law, like the law of theft) for the parties in accordance with appropriate secondary rule procedures (i.e., procedural rules, like the rules of evidence and the rules of procedural due process).

It should be obvious from the foregoing discussion that the autonomy of a legal system is, at best, a relative matter. The legal system exists as part of the social system, and legal activity involves a constant interplay with other sectors of society. Empirically, it would be surprising if any legal system could fully resist the influences of popular ethics or political or social power. It would be similarly surprising if a legal system could maintain its legitimacy if its primary rules, however properly enacted, continually clashed with generally accepted ethical precepts or with the interests of those who enjoy political and social power.

But the problem is more than empirical. Complete legal autonomy is, even in theory, unattainable. Law is a normative system and its norms must, at least in the first instance, come from somewhere.[1] Furthermore, most legal systems have secondary rules describing procedures by which new laws can be made. These procedures usually allow for the orderly incorporation of extra legal values into the legal system. In the process the legal system is necessarily penetrated by interests that are external to it.

Not surprisingly, groups seek to advance their interest by infusing their preferred values into law. We have discussed many such attempts in earlier chapters. Recall, for example, the history of the struggle for workers' compensation or our brief description of the origins of the juvenile court. Two aspects of the way law incorporates values are especially important. First, the values infused into law may be more or less specific. Thus the law may seek to set the price of corn at the desired level of so many dollars per bushel, or it may try to establish the conditions for a free market in corn on the theory that any price reached in a free market exchange is desirable. Second, except in periods of revolution or other massive social change, new laws—that is, new instances of value infusion—are embedded in an encompassing legal culture. In the process laws may be transformed so that their ultimate behavioral implications are not precisely what their original sponsors intended. The more autonomous the legal system is, the greater the transformation is likely to be. In the extreme case, apparent law making, for example, an attempt to mandate a daily prayer to Jesus Christ in the public schools, will have no legal effect because the legal culture will contain higher norms that nullify the attempt at value infusion.

In this chapter we explore the implications of the relative autonomy of law for social justice. We begin by looking at claims that have been made about the possibility of legal autonomy. We then ask what it means for the law to be autonomous, not as a matter of definition, which is how we have approached this question thus far, but in terms of the institutional requisites of an autonomous legal order. We suggest that two factors are crucial: (1) a sociopolitical structure such that no group can enlist the law in the service of a particular private agenda and (2) formalism, which distances the law from ethical systems that hold particular ends in view. Having established the importance of these factors, we treat them as variables and develop typologies of legislation and adjudication that embody the implications of their different states for justice between classes and within society.

We do not summarize our views on law and social justice until the end of Chapter 13, but many of the examples with which we illustrate our discussion

---

1. Weber (1968) in describing rational legal authority, which is self-legitimating in the way we describe, postulated a legal code that was gapless in the sense that one could derive logically from the code legal implications for any possible case that might arise under it. In this sense the legal system is fully self-contained. However, that code must have its roots in some external institution(s) and in this sense at least the legal system will be penetrated by the norms and power relations of the larger society.

in this chapter relate to issues of liberty or the distribution of welfare among classes. Recall that for Rawls (1971), whose concept of justice we have used as a standard in the last two chapters, liberty and the fair distribution of welfare are the crucial components of the just society, and, of these, liberty is primary. We shall see, as we proceed through this chapter and the next one, that a legal order that seeks to achieve maximal justice by one of Rawls's criteria may perpetuate or increase injustice by the other. There are many possible responses to this fact. They include, but are by no means limited to, accepting Rawls's preference for liberty, rejecting Rawls's approach entirely, redefining what is meant by liberty or a fair distribution of welfare, and attempting to institutionalize some mix of liberty and a fair distribution of welfare as a base from which further advances can be made. We have our preferences, but we cannot choose for others.

LAW AS AN AUTONOMOUS FORCE IN SOCIETY

To say that law is autonomous in the partial sense is to say that law is to some extent a product of itself and implies that legal power alone may influence social life. The claim of autonomy does not deny the possibility that law, insofar as it purports to regulate social life, may do nothing more than reinstitutionalize the norms and values of some other authority system (Bohannan, 1965). But it does mean that once reinstitutionalization has occurred, legal norms and values and the actions these entail are no longer fully reducible to the actions, norms, and values of that other system and so may have an independent influence on social life.

A Reductionist View

Some would deny that autonomy in this sense is ever possible. They would argue that the law is reducible to the norms of some other authority system or that the law cannot by itself affect social life or that both these propositions are true at once. The classic proponent of the latter position, at least by one interpretation of his writing, is Karl Marx. Marx in the preface to *A Contribution to the Critique of Political Economy* wrote:

> In the social production of their life, men enter into definite relations that are indispensable and independent of their will; these relations of production correspond to a definite stage of development of their material forces of production. The sum total of these relations of production constitutes the economic structure of society— the real foundation, on which rises a legal and political superstructure and to which correspond definite forms of social consciousness. [Kamenka (Ed.), 1983, pp. 159–160]

In the *Communist Manifesto* Marx and Engels sound the same theme. They say to the bourgeoisie:

[Y]our jurisprudence is but the will of your class made into a law for all, a will whose essential character and direction are determined by the economical conditions of existence of your class. [Kamenka (Ed.), 1983, p. 222]

These passages reflect Marx's belief that the rules for allocating political power like all other social arrangements reflect an economic base. Dominant groups achieve their eminence not because they control the state but because they dominate the means of production. From this economic dominance comes control over the state which carries with it the ability to make law. Law is made as a way of wielding power, that is, as an *instrument* of the will of the economically dominant class. It has no life of its own, for its norms and procedures follow from and are reducible to the agenda of the dominant class. Law may well bring with it momentary terror for the dominated, but fundamentally it is powerless. For law neither establishes nor changes the economic base, and law must change as the inexorable dialectic alters the relations of production.

Although most modern Marxists still believe that law must be understood in relation to the economic base, the idea that law is simply a tool to maximize the immediate interests of those in power is now dismissed as "crude instrumentalism," and the view that law helps shape rather that merely reflects the structure of society is widely accepted. Crude instrumentalism should, perhaps, have been rejected from the beginning by anyone who looked carefully at society. Certainly, there is now too much evidence against the "simple tool" theory for this crudely instrumentalist perspective to be maintained. Through studies by scholars like Balbus (1973) and Thompson (1975) we have learned that attempts at domination through law differ in their consequences from attempts at domination through other "superstructural" institutions such as the brute force of the state or the mystification of religion. This means that the rules in one sphere cannot be reduced to those in another, nor can they be reduced to a common core. Furthermore, proceeding through law may yield particular outcomes that favor the dominated in society and run counter to what one might assume would be the will of the dominant class (Hay, 1975).

Consider, for example, the situation in a capitalist society that has just invented the "checking account." Here is a new and important instrument to facilitate the transfer of wealth, but the institution cannot work if checks are routinely forged. Clearly, the society must find some way to discourage forgery. If the decision is to proceed through law rather than, for example, by brute force (boil in oil everyone suspected of forging checks), those who desire the new law must confront the fact that they are not writing on a blank slate. If the populace is to identify the capitalists' rule as law, certain characteristics must exist. In our society, for instance, to proceed through law means that violators must be identified and sanctioned through some judicial procedure and that the rule must be stated in more or less general terms.

With these constraints, the outcomes in particular cases may not obviously favor capitalist interest or reflect the class will that led to the law in the first place. Let us suppose a law that states "Forging checks is punishable by death." A court may acquit a suspected forger because the state's burden of proving forgery has not been met, even though deterrence would be maximized if everyone suspected of forging checks were summarily shot. Or a member of the dominant class might find that he is sentenced to be shot when all he did was forge the checks of several workers for the admirable capitalist purpose of acquiring money to expand his woolen mill.

Given the possibility of these inconvenient outcomes, one might wonder why capitalists or any other dominant class would elect to govern through law. This is a fundamental question that we examine in Chapter 13.

A Formalist Vision

At the opposite extreme from a crudely instrumental Marxist conception of law there is the vision of law as a purely autonomous system which we sketch and reject in our introduction to this chapter. We may think of this vision as the *formalist vision*. It is formalist in two senses. First, it is the casting of rules in the "legal form" (i.e., as "laws") that makes for autonomous application (i.e., without regard to the subject's political, social, or ethical status).[2] Second, and more importantly, it is the law's attention to form that maintains the system's autonomy. "All," it is said, "are naked before the law." That is, those who seek to invoke the law have in theory no extralegal identity, such as large corporation, poor widow, campaign contributor, congressperson, and the like. How can the law deal with such anonymous entities? The answer is by fitting them into forms the law possesses. Common legal forms include citizen, person, plaintiff, and defendant. The list could go on in greater detail (contract defendant, tort defendant, personal injury defendant, etc.), but the bloodless nature of these legal actors is clear. The situation is similar with the stories these actors tell (cf. Noonan, 1976).

The law, in the formalist ideal, strips the stories it hears of any extralegal ethical content. The moral meaning of action is to be determined not by ordinary morality but by how the facts that describe the action fit preexisting legal concepts such as negligence, murder, and breach of contract. If the law could succeed in abstracting both the identity of actors and their stories from everything that gives them social meaning, and if it had a stock of forms and concepts sufficiently wide to encompass either directly or by logical derivation all those actors and actions that might come to its attention, the law might, by confining itself to

---

2. There remains the question of why the legal form is status blind. We address this question as well as the consequences this entails in Chapter 13. We shall see that other visions of law do not require status blindness.

this stock, act without regard to other power and authority systems. Such independence is obviously unachievable and even if it could be achieved the law would only be maintaining a degree of autonomy. As we pointed out earlier, there would still be the question of where the stock of norms came from.

Thus the situation of the law, as we know it in Western society, is one of partial autonomy.[3] Law is influenced by the political, ethical or social order, but this does not mean that the law must be in essence a tool of the dominant class's immediate self-interest, the plaything of those in high office, or the obedient servant of some moral majority. If it is important to recognize that law is only partially autonomous, it is also important to realize that partial autonomy can allow for considerable independence.

Relative Autonomy

We may think of relative autonomy as *the degree to which the legal system looks to itself rather than to the standards of some external social, political, or ethical system for guidance in making or applying law*. We have already seen how this depends on the stock of legal forms and the law's ability to fit actors and actions to them. But we have also noted a problem: A particular group may capture the law-making process and embed its own standards or interests in the legal form. Given this possibility, we must confront the task of distinguishing legal systems that are more or less dominated by the interests and standards of external groups.

Distinctions may be made along two dimensions. The first involves the extent to which a standard once embedded in law acquires meaning through the law's own canons of construction rather than by reference to the interests that gave it birth. Where the law's canons of construction dominate, the law will be more autonomous of the external system than where they do not. For example, consider our earlier discussion of the law forbidding check forgery. Clearly, this law is designed to facilitate capitalist economic transactions and to this extent the law is penetrated by capitalist interests. But the law also appears to reflect

---

3. We suspect that no legal system can ever maintain complete autonomy. But a complete lack of autonomy or something close to it is quite possible. Our discussion does not suggest this because our implicit focus on Western capitalist democracies, and, in particular, on the United States has led us to concentrate our empirical attention on the law's autonomy from sources of private power and status in response to the Marxist challenge. It may well be that as an empirical matter, Marx— or at least one reading of Marx—is always wrong, and the law is always to some degree autonomous of the economically dominant group. But the same is not necessarily true of the two other prime threats to legal autonomy that we have identified: political power and extralegal ethical systems. Although neither of these destroys the law's autonomy in the countries that most concern us, arguably the polity has dictated all important legal activity in some totalitarian states at some times and the extralegal norms of religion have apparently had a similar influence in Calvin's Geneva and Khomeni's Iran to name just two instances.

a generally accepted ethical proposition about how people should and should not acquire property. Suppose Sam, a clever criminal, drains Jane's bank account not by forging her check but by fraudulently inducing her to write a genuine check in exchange for a promise to deliver goods that Sam neither owns nor intends to deliver. Sam is then charged with forgery under the statute. If the legal system looks either to the capitalist interests that secured the forgery statute or to the popular ethical code, it might convict because fraud of this sort both threatens the free exchange of checks and offends popular morality. But by certain legal canons of construction, forgery is not the same as fraud, and no one should be punished unless his behavior has been previously and specifically declared criminal. Since the legislature seeking to protect the security of checks overlooked the need to protect against fraud, if the law's canons of constructions control, Sam will escape on a "technicality": The legislature neglected to define his crime. Legal systems that look to their own canons of construction to determine the meaning of law rather than to external morality or the interests that support the law are more autonomous than those that take the opposite approach.[4]

The second dimension that allows us to distinguish more autonomous legal systems from less autonomous ones is the degree to which laws are generally applicable. The more general the applicability of legal language, the less close will be the tie between the legal norm and the interests of a particular status group. Thus a system that forbids anyone from forging a check is more autonomous than one that protects only capitalists from forgery.[5] Put another way, a legal system characterized by generally applicable rules is likely to be more autonomous than one riddled with particularistic enactments.

The first of these dimensions, the degree to which external interests influence legal construction, is more important in assessing the degree of autonomy that characterizes the law application process, while the second, the degree to which the law is generally applicable, relates more closely to lawmaking. One important point they have in common is that the more autonomous law is along both of these dimensions, the more legal concepts can be manipulated without apparent reference to the particular substantive concerns that led to the legal norm in the first instance. Laws, in other words, are distanced from narrow, externally grounded, substantive concerns both through the generality of their commands and by internally defined rules of interpretation.

---

4. We do not mean to suggest by this example that the law's canons of construction are rigid or that a foreordained logic inexorably controls. Llewellyn (1950) has shown that the common law's stock of canons is sufficiently diverse that it would allow considerable flexibility of interpretation even if there were a rule, which there is not, that in interpreting a statute a court must always cite some relevant canon.

5. This might be done not only in so many words, but also by protecting business checks from forgery but not the checks of individuals. If the possibility that such an undisguised class-based distinction will enter the law appears remote, consider the numerous societies that had laws broadly protecting masters from violence at the hands of their slaves but only narrowly or not at all protecting slaves from violence at the hands of their masters.

Judicial Formalism

The ideal of legal autonomy can be more closely achieved in the law application or judicial process[6] than in the law creation or legislative process. The legislature sits at the intersection of the political and legal spheres. It may be captured by interests and organizations that have substantial social power, and it often responds to the entreaties of those who support private ethical systems. This does not mean that the concept of autonomy has no place in a discussion of legislation. We discuss the possibility of legislative autonomy in Chapter 13. For the moment, however, we shall focus on the way laws are applied by courts.

Autonomy in the law application process is characterized by and to a large extent is attributable to what we call *judicial formalism* (cf. Nonet & Selznick, 1978, pp. 60–65). Judicial formalism is in turn characterized by three concerns: a concern for procedure, a concern for rules, and a concern for legal categories.

A Concern for Procedure. The elevation of procedural concerns above more immediately substantive ones is perhaps the distinguishing feature—and to some the most jarring feature—of a formal legal system. For example, in *Dobbert* v. *Wainwright* several courts, including the U.S. Supreme Court, refused to consider Dobbert's claim that he was about to be executed for behavior that under Florida law did not constitute a capital offense. Review was refused because 10 years earlier in 1974 the accused's counsel had not objected at trial to a jury instruction that may have erroneously defined the accused's behavior as capital, and the matter was not raised on a first federal appeal.[7] At the other extreme, likely murderers may go free because the rules of evidence preclude the admission of the most probative evidence against them. In between the extremes there are more prosaic cases that arise every day in which outcomes are partly or entirely determined by a litigant's inability or failure to comply with one of the law's procedural rules.

To say that in these cases the law elevates procedure above substance is accurate when one considers only the substantive merits of a claim, but from the perspective of the legal system it is somewhat misleading. There are usually good substantive reasons that justify the law's procedural rules and the influence they have.

Although it may seem unfair or even intolerable to execute Dobbert because his counsel failed to object to a jury instruction, even this outcome can be defended. The rule that objections must ordinarily be made at trial if they are

---

6. Law application, as we have already noted, also involves nonjudicial agencies such as the police and prosecutors. The analysis of judicial autonomy might be extended to consider action in these spheres, but for simplicity's sake we confine our textual attention to courts and administrative tribunals.

7. *Dobbert* v. *Wainwright*, cert. denied, 105 S. Ct. 34, 43 (1984), opinion of Marshall, J. dissenting. The case was also one in which the jury that convicted the defendant recommended mercy by a 10–2 vote, but the judge, as is permitted under Florida law, ignored the recommendation and imposed a death sentence.

to be made at all prevents counsel from intentionally withholding objections until appeal and promotes justice and efficiency in important ways. For example, had Dobbert made his objection at trial, the matter might have been corrected and either no appeal would have been necessary because no capital conviction would have been returned or Dobbert might have been found deserving of death under a correct view of the law. Furthermore, Dobbert may be wrong in his claim of error, and to allow a new appeal 10 years after the trial might delay the law's mandated penalty for another year or two. Worse still, crucial evidence can erode or disappear over time.[8] Thus if the appeal were meritorious and a new trial was ordered, an accused who had committed a serious crime might be subsequently acquitted for lack of evidence.[9]

Thus the fact that the law may insist on honoring its procedural rules when injustice apparently results should not be condemned as an elevation of form over substance for its own sake. There are often good systemic reasons why procedural forms should be followed. Nevertheless, there is a problem here. Where judicial formalism prevails, the law's preference schedule appears to many as unduly *self-regarding*. The values that underlie legal procedures tend to "trump" the apparent demands of substantive justice without regard to the relative merits of the competing claims.[10] In *Dobbert*, for example, we might think that preventing the execution of a man for behavior that the state never made punishable by death, is worth any slight, long-run erosion in the rule requiring that objections be made at trial. Or consider the argument of Yale Kamisar, the leading academic defender of the rule excluding illegally seized evidence. He maintains that the primary justification for the exclusionary rule is not that it deters police malfeasance, but that the integrity of a court is compromised when it officially considers evidence seized in violation of the Fourth Amendment (Kamisar, 1978). This may be true, for it is easy to see how a constitutional court's integrity may be diminished when it considers evidence seized in violation of the Constitution from which it draws its authority. But ordinary citizens might be happy to trade a bit of judicial integrity for a better record in convicting criminals caught with the goods.

It is only the court's privileged position with respect to the law that allows it to impose system-regarding legal values in settings where ethical or political

---

8. In the *Dobbert* case, for example, the key witness against the accused, his son, claimed after his father's execution date had been set that as a 13-year-old boy he had lied about crucial matters at trial. Justice Brennan saw this recantation, which on its face was credible, as a further reason to delay the execution and hold a full hearing *Dobbert* v. *Wainwright*, 105 S. Ct. 34, 34–41 (1984).
9. In *Dobbert* the accused had certainly committed serious child abuse and may have been guilty of manslaughter or murder.
10. Note that although the examples with which we illustrate the concern for procedure have been drawn from the present-day United States we are nonetheless portraying an ideal-typical system. Looking only at appellate cases, one can find numerous instances in which immediate substantive considerations are arguably crucial to decisions that override apparently settled rules of procedure [see, e.g., *Henry* v. *Mississippi*, 379 U.S. 443 (1965); Sandalow (1965)]. When courts are deciding some issues, such as whether to reverse criminal convictions because of evidentiary errors, attention to substance may be quite common (Davies, 1982).

considerations call strongly for different action. It is this ability to hew to distinctively legal values and the propensity of courts to do so that makes the law's procedural orientation an important component of autonomous justice. We have seen from our examples that this procedural allegiance can have important consequences when the law is applied. In particular, attempts to use the law to achieve specific ends may be hampered by legal rules of procedure. The exclusionary rule, for example, has implications for how the war against narcotic drugs is fought. Advertisements found to be misleading by the Federal Trade Commission may be broadcast for years while the advertisers exhaust their appeals. The right to jury trial has at one time or another helped injury victims secure adequate compensation from the giants of industry, restrained governmental efforts to censor or oppress those who disagreed with official policies, hampered efforts to enforce game laws in rural areas, and allowed people who have violently resisted desegregation efforts to escape punishment. As this potpourri of examples illustrates, procedural formalism may inhibit the law's ability to achieve a variety of political and legislative ends, for there is no necessary consistency in how the law's allegiance to procedures will cut.[11] At the same time, the formal requirement that those who proceed through law conform to preexisting legal procedures has important implications for how such values are realized.

A Concern for Rules. The second aspect of judicial formalism is a concern for what legal rules require. A formalist judge treats the law as given. He does not in deciding cases try to promote some extralegal value system, even one congruent with the law, but looks internally to the law for the source of all values. What the law requires must be done, and what the law does not forbid is allowed. Thus a hungry child may be sentenced to death for picking pockets in search of the wherewithal to live, and one who steals money entrusted to him for investment may escape without any punishment if the law of theft at the time forbids only forcible or stealthy takings.

Being guided by exclusively legal norms does not mean that the formal judge looks only to the legislature for guidance. Depending on the system, legal norms may be drawn from such sources as constitutions, the rulings of administrative agencies, treaties, proclamations by high officials, and prior court decisions. Nor does the internal orientation mean that a court cannot declare a law invalid. Courts recognize hierarchies of law, and constitutional provisions can override legislation just as legislation can reverse nonconstitutional judicial precedent. What distinguishes the formalist system with respect to both the sources of legal norms and the ways conflicts are resolved among them is the fact that the legal system's rules determine what is permissible. Thus a formalist judge

---

11. Note the special nature of the right to jury trial. It is a procedural device that permits an input of localized, popular morality. Allegiance to this procedure may undercut the values that have been embodied in the substantive law and thus the aim of government, but it does so by allowing extralegal values to penetrate the law and in this respect makes the legal system less autonomous.

does not enforce administrative restrictions on pollution because he thinks they are desirable. Rather, the rules are enforced because the legislature has delegated to an agency the authority to regulate by rule and the legislature has the legal (in this case constitutional) authority to do so. Similarly, a formalist judge will strike down legislation he thinks desirable if it conflicts with the Constitution. Thus a feminist judge may strike down laws seeking to prevent the degradation of women through pornography because the laws conflict with the First Amendment's strictures on the regulation of speech.

Perhaps, most surprisingly, treating preexisting law as the source of all legal norms does not prevent the formalist judge from making law, if by making law we mean the elaboration of doctrine to fit specific behavior. The important point is that in making law the formalist judge does not look to some external ethical system or political interest, but instead looks inward to the law to ascertain what, if anything, the body of law fairly and logically implies for the behavior that has come before the court. This determination involves a close inspection of the language of the law and an effort to interpret that language in the light of the lawgiver's meaning.

Consider, for example, a statute that defines theft as "the intentional taking of another's property without permission." A formal court faced with someone who had accessed another person's computer and used CPU time would probably have little trouble in creating the new crime of "hacking" by defining the activity as theft. CPU time is valuable; one may have a property interest in it, and for someone else to use it may be reasonably characterized as a form of taking. Although the long since deceased drafters of the theft statute were unfamiliar with computers, from their language it is fair to assume that they intended to forbid the unauthorized use of anyone else's property.

On the other hand, had the statute defined theft as "the intentional carrying away of another's property without permission" a formalist court would be unlikely to define hacking as a crime. Hacking would be recognized as equally immoral regardless of the language of the law, but it is hard to see in the unauthorized use of CPU time a "carrying away" of anything. CPU time is used on the spot. The intention behind the law suggests that the drafters would have considered hacking a form of theft had they thought of it. However, they did not, and the formalist judge is confined to logical implications of the language used as illuminated by other authoritative aids to interpretation like precedent and legislative history.

Taking rules as given enhances autonomy in the judicial process because it relegates all political and ethical considerations to another sphere—that of the lawmaker (Nonet & Selznick, 1978, pp. 57–58). The concerns that motivate the lawmakers are taken into account only as an aid in interpreting language whose logical implications are not clear; so what may appear from one perspective as making new law is from another perspective only the determination and logical application of what was meant by the old law.

Attention to rules, like attention to procedure, may lead to substantive injustice and, for better or worse, interfere with attempts at regulation. A formalist court will not ask what is fair or what the ruler wants or what the good of society demands, but will instead ask what the rules provide. If in the context of a specific case the rules do not yield a just result, they nevertheless will be followed. But the converse is also true. In particular cases the formalist interpretation of oppressive legislation will not always yield oppressive results. For example, a statute might prohibit the publication of newspapers without clearance by a censor. The editor of a monthly journal that is highly critical of the government may escape punishment even though the journal is full of the kind of material the government sought to suppress because the statute does not apply to magazines. The formalist judge may know the government wishes to suppress all criticism in the press and may share this desire, but for him neither the governmental interest nor his own preferences are a valid source of norms.

A Concern for Legal Categories. The third element of formalism is the tendency to fit actions, actors, and, in particular, statutory language into legal forms. Once this is done, applying law involves only the proper categorization of acts and actions and the logical manipulation of concepts internal to the legal system.

We have already noted the way in which people and actions in an autonomous legal system are abstracted from their social settings and treated as members of predefined legal categories. Thus a mercy killing is as premeditated and as much murder as the assassination of a president. In much the same way, Citizen Kane, who owns a newspaper empire and is worth millions is in court no different from citizens Lempert and Sanders who will be lucky if they sell a few books. As plaintiffs, defendants, or witnesses each will have the same status and the same rights. What we wish to add here is that the statutory language, from which the formalist court draws its norms, is similarly transformed into categories that the law routinely manipulates, but instead of plaintiffs and defendants we have rights and duties.

A formalist judge interprets a statute in terms of the rights and duties it creates and then applies the statute by logically analyzing the implications of these rights and duties for the parties before the court. The specification of the statutorily created rights may consider the purposes of the statute, but once the rights have been specified, the original purpose fades from view. The system is autonomous in that it no longer attends to the political and ethical concerns that spurred the legislation but operates only with legal concepts. If the legislature did not specify rights that are sufficient to achieve the goals it had in mind, a formalist jurisprudence will mean that the goal will not be achieved. This contrasts with a more substantively oriented jurisprudence that interprets rights on a case-by-case basis with an eye in each instance to the achievement of a politically given or ethical end.

As with the other aspects of formalism, the tendency to freeze statutory intent in concepts of right and duty has important implications for how a law is enforced. Philippe Nonet's (1969) fine study of the California Industrial Accident Commission (IAC) again is particularly revealing because the effects of a rights-oriented formalism are contrasted with those of a more substantively oriented tribunal.

Recall that the California legislature created the IAC to help rehabilitate injured workers and to relieve the poverty that industrial accidents too often entailed. Nonet (1969) follows the agency's slow but steady change from an administrative organization committed to these goals to an adjudicative organization that was increasingly formalistic:

> In the early IAC, compensation was taken as a means of reducing poverty, of rehabilitating the disabled; benefits could always be withdrawn if they were not shown to contribute to that end. Being responsible for results, the administrator insists on preserving the freedom to respond to concrete problems on their own terms; he cannot afford to let policies become binding upon him and sources of entitlement to the constituents. But those are precisely the issues with which adjudication is concerned—to what extent does a policy carry binding authority and establish rights? To what extent should it be restricted in view of other binding standards and vested rights? The adjudicator emphasizes the *normative* aspect of standards. . . . It is typical, however, of adjudication that the decider is not free to manipulate applicable standards in view of the outcome he desires in particular cases. He is expected to "let the chips fall where they may," in accordance with binding norms; he is not free to extend or restrict a policy for the sole reason his decision will produce some "good" or "bad" result. (pp. 235–236)

To simplify only slightly, in the early days of the IAC an injured worker received compensation if, and only for so long as, he needed it. The IAC felt considerable responsibility to facilitate claims, and in deciding whether compensation was due, it was always conscious of the needs of the injured worker. What perhaps best symbolized the early IAC's approach was the agency's general reluctance to allow the parties to convert the long-term payments due the most severely injured into one time, lump sum judgments. The fear was that the injured worker would soon squander the money he received and poverty would have been only temporarily forestalled rather than prevented.

These attitudes were gradually transformed. Compensation became not a means to a goal, but a right of injured workers and a duty placed on management. [12] Workers were expected to prosecute their claims with minimal aid from

---

12. The law of compensation was from the start one of rights and duties, even if the early IAC took a purposive stance. Payments to injured workers came directly or indirectly out of their employer's pockets, so the employer and its employees had genuinely conflicting interests. The hearing procedures in giving each party a voice were, to the discomfort of the early IAC, adversarial in form. The form in turn allowed the parties to highlight their opposing rights and interests, and by so doing forced the IAC to attend to them. Gradually the agency came to define its primary responsibility as one of protecting or conciliating these interests. Thus the procedural form of adversariness helped bring about the jurisprudential stance we call formalism.

Political controversy also caused a drift toward formalistic interpretations. Nonet (1969) tells us why:

> In the setting of organized group conflict that characterizes workmen's compensation, political consensus is hard to create and remains always precarious. Policy-making is a controversial enterprise, in which the legitimacy of authority is exposed to continuing assault. That is what the IAC sought to avoid when it retreated from administration to the determination of claims. To the agency, the focus on individual claims was a way of depoliticizing the compensation controversy. . . . In the eyes of the commission, a judicial posture would offer a refuge from the responsibilities and hazards of policy-making. (p. 237)

the IAC. The availability and amount of compensation became matters of entitlement. Judgments were not even to be colored by the needs of the injured worker. The only questions for the agency, whose hearings by this time had many of the trappings of a trial, were whether the injury was of a kind that the legislature had made compensible, and, if so, what was the appropriate recovery?

Long-term payment obligations were routinely converted into lump sums even though the danger of squandering remained, and the agency knew that a substantial fraction of the lump would probably go to a lawyer as a contingent fee. Indeed, one reason to allow the conversion was the need to pay lawyers. Compensation law had become so complex and the agency's approach to cases so formalistic that it was the foolish worker who proceeded without one.

The retreat to formalism did not mean that the IAC's hearing examiners (later called "judges") lost all discretion. Rather, it confined their discretion within bounds set by the rights of individual litigants and the need to conform to general rules and authoritative standards. Nor did the retreat to formalism mean that workers, as a class, were worse off vis-à-vis management. Instead, it seems to have redistributed advantages among workers. Injured workers who belonged to unions that alerted them to their rights, directed them to experienced compensation attorneys, and helped pay their attorneys if necessary were probably better off under the formalistic system than they were under the purposive but paternalistic system that preceded it. The unorganized sector of the work force that lacked the advantages of information and access to attorneys was probably worse off. Thus, even within the working class we see that formalism can mean the rich get richer.

The tendency of courts to fit actors into legal categories that obscure social differences and to treat substantive legislation not entirely in its own purposive terms but in terms of the rights and obligations that can be abstracted out of the legislation poses problems for those who attempt to use the law as an instrument of social justice. Statutes as reinterpreted by courts often do both more and less than is intended. They do less because the purposes of the statute may be blunted or its scope narrowed when the focus is on the rights or obligations the statute clearly entails. Furthermore, when the differential opportunities that people have to invoke the law are not acknowledged many potential litigants may be denied that access to the legal process which is necessary if the substantive goals of the statute are to be obtained. Thus the California IAC by treating unionized and nonunionized workers as equally competent to invoke its procedures developed a set of procedures that hurt the latter.

Formalism allows legislation to do more than intended when the tendency to focus on formalistic abstractions leads to a reading of the law that covers situations that were not within the intended scope of the act or extends benefits to classes of litigants who were not intended beneficiaries of the law's protections. Thus a law that provides that medical school applicants may not be discriminated against because of sex may have been intended to eliminate discrimination in medical school admissions in order to open up to women a profession that was once largely closed to them. However, if a court focuses on the sex-neutral term "applicant" and ignores the substantive end in view, the law might be used to strike down, at the instance of a male applicant, an affirmative action program that promises to increase substantially the proportion of physicians who are female. In such circumstances a court, by extending rights in ways not contemplated by the legislature, may undermine the very goals a law was intended to serve.

Pseudo-formalism

The three aspects of formalism just described all serve to distance the law as it is applied from the interests of external ethical and political systems, even to some degree when those interests have captured the legislative process and embedded their preferences into law. For this reason judicial formalism goes a long way to ensuring legal autonomy. There is, however, another kind of judicial behavior that goes by the name "formalism" which often has the opposite effect.

Courts sometimes look at the actions they must deal with in formalistic terms. Adopting a shallow logic, they assume that appearances are reality and render decisions that are blind to the actual reality not because legal categories abstract actors and actions from their social context, but because the courts eschew any indepth investigation of reality to determine what legal categories are appropriately applied. The motivating force behind such formalism is not the self-regarding attitude that underlies those aspects of formalism that contribute to autonomy. Rather, it is a sense that the autonomous manipulation of legal concepts will yield results that are inconsistent with some external political or ethical standard unless reality is distorted. The judge who is a formalist in this sense—we call him a "pseudo-formalist"—is both blind to reality and conscious of it, for it is the judge's awareness of reality and attention to external interests that leads to apparent blindness.

The contrast between this externally oriented psuedo-formalism and the kind of internally oriented formalism that is a crucial constituent of legal autonomy is nicely illustrated by the case of *Plessy* v. *Ferguson*, 163 U.S. 537 (1896). This case arose out of the arrest of a man, by ancestry one-eighth Negro, who insisted on riding in a railroad car reserved for white passengers. In it the Supreme Court enunciated the "separate but equal" doctrine.

The task the Court faced was to decide whether a Louisiana statute requiring "'equal but separate' accommodations for white and black railway passengers," was constitutional. The crucial issue was whether this statute conflicted with the Fourteenth Amendment to the Constitution, which provides in pertinent part:

> No State shall make or enforce any law which shall abridge the privileges or immunities of citizens of the United States; nor shall any state deprive any person of life, liberty, or property, without due process of law; nor deny to any person within its jurisdiction the equal protection of the laws.

Justice Brown, writing for himself and six other justices, held that the Louisiana statute did not run afoul of these proscriptions:

> The object of the (Fourteenth) amendment was undoubtedly to enforce the absolute equality of the two races before the law, but in the nature of things it could not have

been intended to abolish distinctions based upon color, or to enforce social, as distinguished from political equality, . . . *Laws permitting, and even requiring, their separation in places where they are liable to be brought into contact do not necessarily imply the inferiority of either race to the other*, and have been generally, if not universally, recognized as within the competency of the state legislatures in the exercise of their police power. (163 U.S. 537, 544; emphasis added)

This language suggests that the Louisiana statute would have been overturned as stigmatizing or unequal had it stated that its purpose was to preserve the superior status of the white race or had it provided that white passengers shall have reserved for them the better of the available cars. But the statute on its face does *not necessarily imply* black inferiority. Whether it did in fact stigmatize blacks and whether it inevitably led to unequal treatment did not concern the *Plessy* majority.[13] On this theme Justice Brown wrote:

We consider the underlying fallacy of the plaintiff's argument to consist in the assumption that the enforced separation of the two races stamps the colored race with a badge of inferiority. If this be so, it is not by reason of anything found in the act, but solely because the colored race chooses to put that construction upon it. (163 U.S. 537, 551)

Brown is in one sense right, for the language of the statute is neutral with respect to the issue of which race is superior. But the neutrality vanishes if one considers, as Brown did not, the society in which the law was to be enforced.

The first Mr. Justice Harlan, in dissent, pierces the form of the statute.

The thing to accomplish was, under the guise of giving equal accommodation for whites and blacks, to compel the latter to keep to themselves while travelling in railroad passenger coaches. No one would be so wanting in candor as to assert the contrary. The fundamental objection, therefore, to the statute is that it interferes with the personal freedom of citizens. . . . (557)

But this is only half the story. Justice Brown's ultimate justification for *Plessy* is very much concerned with the real world as he perceives it, "If one race be inferior to the other socially, the Constitution of the United States cannot put them upon the same plane" (552).

And Justice Harlan eloquently asserts the formalist ideal:

The white race deems itself to be the dominant race in this country. And so it is, in prestige, in achievements, in education, in wealth and in power. So, I doubt not, it will continue to be for all time, if it remains true to its great heritage and holds fast to the principles of constitutional liberty. But in view of the Constitution, in the eye of the law, there is in this country no superior, dominant, ruling class of citizens. There is no caste here. Our Constitution is color-blind, and neither knows

---

13. Later Courts, accepting *Plessy*'s gloss on the Fourteenth Amendment as received law, were concerned with the reality and possibility of actual equality. Thus the *Plessy* standard, before it was superseded by a rereading of the Fourteenth Amendment, eventually became a viable tool for challenging segregation. See, e.g., *Sweat* v. *Painter*, 339 U.S. 629 (1950). But before *Plessy* could be used in this way the Court had to look beyond the language of statutes, not to the legislature's motives, but to the reality they created.

nor tolerates classes among citizens. In respect of civil rights, all citizens are equal before the law. The humblest is the peer of the most powerful. The law regards man as man, and takes no account of his surroundings or of his color when his civil rights as guaranteed by the supreme law of the land are involved. (559)

Harlan is the true formalist in the sense that he is concerned with applying the law's standards, regardless of their upshot, to the reality of social action. Brown reasons formalistically, but he does so to obscure his attention to substantive considerations. It is crucial to Brown's conclusion that blacks are an inferior race. If they were not, the law mandating segregation would be unconstitutionally irrational.[14] Thus Brown is forced almost immediately to rely on socially rather than legally defined statuses to support his analysis. Harlan does not obviously differ from Brown in his evaluation of the relative virtues of the white and black races, but for Harlan the socially defined categories of white and black are not recognized in the Constitution. For him the Constitution acknowledged only the larger class, *citizen*, and the Fourteenth Amendment does not allow some citizens to be denied rights that others have on the basis of race. Harlan, in short, finds that Plessy fits the legal category (form) "citizen" and treats the Court's task as determining the rights associated with that category.[15] Although social characteristics had to be attended to in order to determine whether Plessy was someone defined legally as a citizen, once that was determined the legal category rather than the social category carried forward the analysis.

OTHER ASPECTS OF AUTONOMY

Although legal formalism is a central constituent of legal autonomy, it is not the only one, for the autonomy of law, as we have defined that term, is not solely a matter of the stance judges take toward it. If access to the law or the

---

14. Brown recognizes this in acknowledging that a "separate but equal" law dividing persons by, for example, hair color would be vulnerable to challenge as unreasonable and not enacted in good faith for the common good.

15. This does not mean that Harlan did not differ from Brown and from the other members of the majority about where the common good lay. It may have been such a difference that led him to a true formalist position. We are constructing an ideal type. In the real world judges may be true formalists, pseudo-formalists, or not at all formalist, depending on their view of where the common good lies. There are, however, tendencies in many Western societies toward true formalism, and this can and often does lead to decisions that run counter to the value preferences of judges as individuals. We see this every day when lower court judges apply higher court precedent with which they are known to disagree. The norms of the legal system demand a certain result and the judge complies. Ironically, the greatest testimony to the strength of the pull toward formalism is the presence of pseudo-formalism. Judges often find it easier to ignore or distort reality so that the formalist manipulation of legal language yields desired results than to eschew the appearance of legal formalism and opt openly for what they think is substantively sound. An important way in which social science tends to delegitimize the law is that it makes reality obvious to all, exposing the substantive orientation that underlies pseudo-formalist reasoning and challenging received formalist doctrine where it it based on the misinterpretation of how the social world fits into legal categories.

ability to use it effectively varies with political power or social status, social disparities will affect how the law is applied even if the court takes no official account of extralegal status. Thus if filing fees and attorneys costs are such that low-income debtors cannot afford to defend themselves when sued, the judicial output will disproportionately reflect the interests of wealthy litigants. Legal rights belonging to the less well off will not be recognized because they will not be effectively asserted. Also, if those legal norms the formalist court treats as given take extralegal status into account, the judicial output will reflect this. Although formal application of a law designed to promote the ethics or interests of one group over another may, for reasons we have noted, leaven the substantive orientation of the law, the rights and duties that are abstracted from the law and enforced will consistently favor one set of interests over another.

This second consideration draws our attention from the law application to the law creation process. We will address the issues that this raises shortly. For the moment, we focus on the issue of effectiveness in court, a matter we call *legal competence* (cf. Galanter, 1974; 1976). If those who use or are subject to the law are of unequal legal competence, the judicial output over the run of cases will reflect this inequality. For legal competence to be equal, parties to a dispute must have equal access to legal remedies and must be equally capable of influencing judicial outcomes. If such equality exists, the court's decision should be determined entirely by the law as it applies to the facts of the case. Except insofar as the law takes into account the parties' extralegal status, extra-legal sources of authority will have no effect on the decision.

Legal Competence

Courts are by and large reactive bodies. They wait for parties to bring cases to them; they evaluate the evidence presented by each side with the help of the parties' briefs[16] and arguments; and after considering the evidence in light of the law, they determine which party should prevail. In principle, people are equally able to initiate legal action and have equal influence in courts. Anyone with a cause of action may institute a lawsuit and the party sued must respond or a judgment will be entered "by default" against him. Once in court, the parties are, as we have seen, stripped of their extra-legal identities and the case proceeds as plaintiff (or prosecution) against defendant. The parties are presumed to have equal access to information pertaining to the lawsuit,[17] and subject to rules of evidence, each party may offer any information that favors his case.

---

16. A *brief* is a document prepared by a party that sets forth the facts of a case, discusses the applicable law, and argues that, given the facts of the case and the applicable law, the party's position should prevail.

17. In civil cases rules of "discovery" allow each party to inquire extensively before trial about information possessed by the other. In criminal cases there is considerable variation among the states, but the permissible range of discovery is less extensive than it is in civil cases.

Equal legal competence is the second crucial ingredient of legal autonomy. Formalism guarantees that the law will be applied by reference to legal norms and procedures. But without equal legal competence formal adjudication will yield outcomes that disproportionately favor the more powerful and better off and to this extent reinforce social disparities that the law does not recognize. The better off are advantaged both because they are better able to bring or avoid litigation and because once in court they are better able to muster the facts and legal arguments that aid courts in determining how the law should be applied. To the extent that the ideal of equal competence breaks down, the legal system will be less autonomous, for although the court may be blind to extralegal power and status differences, its output will reflect such disparities.

The ideal of equal competence is just that, an ideal. Despite the formal equality that pertains in court, some litigants, like the pigs in George Orwell's *Animal Farm*, are "more equal" than others. Those who are better off generally, are usually better off when they go to law.

In litigation, perhaps the most ubiquitous inequality is between what Marc Galanter (1975) calls "one shotters" (OS) and "repeat players" (RP). One shotters are those who have only occasional recourse to the courts. They tend to be people of average or less than average means. Repeat players are those who, over time, engage in many similar lawsuits. They are typically government agencies or business organizations. Galanter (1975) argues that the RPs have a significant advantage in gaining favorable outcomes in courts and other legal settings:

> Briefly, these advantages include: ability to structure the transaction; expertise, economies of scale, low start-up costs; informal relations with institutional incumbents; bargaining credibility; ability to adopt optimal strategies; ability to play for rules in both political forums and in litigation itself by litigation strategy and settlement policy; and ability to invest to secure penetration of favorable rules. (p. 347)

Thus in small claims courts, RPs, often business creditors, sue OSs, typically individual debtors, more often than they themselves are sued and enjoy great success in the lawsuits they bring (Yngvesson & Hennesey, 1975).[18] In criminal court, prosecutors do better than defendants. In the auto franchise area RPs parlay their advantages beyond specific cases to fundamental issues of legal interpretation. Here the large auto manufacturers have been able to choose cases to be litigated and appealed through the simple expedient of extending generous settlement offers in cases they did not want the courts to pass on. Thus the courts first interpreted the Dealer's Day in Court Act in factual contexts that suggested the reasonableness of the manufacturers' positions. This helped generate a body of precedent that ameliorated some of what the manufacturers saw as the worst

---

18. Vidmar (1984) points out that the success that business plaintiffs enjoy in small claims court is largely due to the large number of business suits that end in default judgments. In many of these cases in which individual defendants do not appear the default judgment is worthless, for either the individual cannot be found or he has no assets with which to pay the judgment.

features of a law they had opposed in the first instance (Macaulay, 1966). Of course, terminated franchisees who as OSs could not match the automakers litigation strategy probably evaluated these precedents quite differently.

Experience alone does not, however, guarantee a substantial advantage in the litigation process. Some drunks and prostitutes have been in court more times than they can count, with no better and often times worse results on each successive occasion. In addition to their experiential advantage over OSs, RPs are usually the wealthier and more powerful party. Business corporations, insurance companies, and state prosecutors are familiar RPs. Aggrieved consumers, injured individuals, and criminal defendants are typical OSs.

When one uses or contemplates using the law, wealth is important for many reasons. Litigation is expensive. Attorneys' fees mount rapidly and other court costs can easily run into thousands of dollars. Uncovering facts and securing expert testimony cost even more. The delay that is built into the legal process may lead an impoverished party with a meritorious case to settle quickly because he needs some money immediately.

Moreover, the stratification of the American Bar draws much of the best legal talent (as measured by success in law school and prestige in the profession) into the service of large corporations and wealthy individuals, leaving the criminal law, tort law, and divorce law to the rest of the profession (Carlin, 1962; Smigel, 1964; Heinz & Laumann, 1982). Public defenders and legal aid attorneys who serve an exclusively poor clientele are notoriously overworked and prone to give bureaucratic rather than client-centered services (Sudnow, 1965; Bellow, 1977). People who are not impoverished may, ironically, be even worse off, for without subsidies legal assistance may be entirely out of reach.

Clearly, success at law is linked to success in social life. Those who are legally competent have usually succeeded in other areas as well. Yet even in an unequal society partial autonomy may endure. Law as it is applied in the United States tends to ameliorate rather than simply reproduce power discrepancies. Institutions like the contingent fee and legal rules like the right to appointed counsel in criminal cases, together with legal formality, tend to equalize the situation of parties who go to law. Nor are these efforts empty. Judges at and before trial routinely make rulings that disadvantage the more powerful litigant. Juries regularly acquit defendants who have been prosecuted with all the financial and symbolic power the state can muster. Appointed counsel often work diligently for their clients, and some of the most important victories that poor people have won as a class have been engineered by lawyers on the state's payroll.

But whether partial autonomy as it exists in this country is a glass that is half full or half empty depends on one's attitude and where one looks. The death penalty for rape in the South was, for example, largely reserved for black men who raped white women (Wolfgang & Reidel, 1976). The lack of effective legal counsel no doubt contributed to this.[19]

In most situations, however, it is difficult to show that the legal system

---

19. See, for example, the transcript in the case of *State* v. *Brooks* in Lempert and Saltzburg (2d. ed., 1982, pp. 1115–1180).

responds with substantial bias to indicators of differential social advantage such as race. The process by which "the poor pay more" is more subtle. In bail setting (Nagel, 1983) and sentencing (Hagan, 1974; Hagan & Bumiller, 1983), for example, racial and income effects are hard to find after one controls for variables such as offense seriousness and past record. In other words, standards internal to the law rather than race or poverty explain the fact that the poor and the black as groups are sentenced more harshly than the wealthy or the white. But it is also the case that the poor and the black tend to be arrested for more serious crimes and to have more extensive records than the wealthy and the white. It is likely that poverty and perhaps race contribute to this. Similarly, in deciding whether to set bail or release an accused without bond, "community ties," as evidenced by such things as an intact family and a steady job are thought to be and probably are a factor increasing the likelihood that the accused will show up at trial. Since this likelihood is the principle legal criterion for the bail decision, community ties are appropriately considered by a court in setting bond. But since poverty and discrimination are associated with difficulties in securing employment and with family instability, impoverished victims of discrimination are for permissible legal reasons disproportionately unlikely to be released on their own recognizance.

Status Neutral Law

Returning to the plane of the ideal, we note that we have identified two of the conditions that must be met if the legal system is to be autonomous and thereby resist the penetration of the social, political, and ethical systems that surround it. First, the law must be applied in a formal, self-regarding way, which means that legal disputes are decided by reference to legal norms and categories in accordance with preexisting legal procedures. Second, actors must be equally competent in their use of law. Without such equality the socially better off will disproportionately benefit from a formal law application process.

Both formality and equal competence are at best only partially achieved in modern Western societies. If they could be fully achieved, the law would be autonomously applied. But even if they were fully achieved, the law as applied would not necessarily be autonomous of other social systems, for built into the very texture of the law are norms that redistribute values from one political or social group to another. This brings us to the last component of pure legal autonomy: The law itself must be blind to all differences in social status.

Some law, including much of the common law, fits this description. It gives actors rights apart from their social or political status. Thus anyone may own property and those who do are generally free to use it or transfer it as they see fit. Anyone injured through the fault of another may recover in tort. And within broad limits any two people may agree to enter into a contract that will be enforced in court. If all laws were "status neutral" in this way, if people were equally well situated to take advantage of such status neutral entitlements, and if the other requisites of legal autonomy were met, the ideal of pure legal autonomy would be achieved. The legal system would proceed in a purely self-regarding way. The law application process would in accordance with its own procedures manipulate distinctively legal concepts in the light of legal norms. A party's extralegal status would have no implications for either his rights— since these would be equally accessible to all—or his treatment in court. Similar social action would everywhere have the same legal implications. Thus in the ideal case legal autonomy and personal autonomy coincide. Freedom is at a maximum.

Obviously, this ideal of legal autonomy is nowhere achieved. We have already noted the distance between formalism and equal competence as ideals and as phenomena that exist in the real world, and we have examined some of the causes and implications of these discrepancies. What remains is to consider the third component of legal autonomy, a component we may label *normative neutrality* and discuss how the real world falls short of the ideal.

Status neutral law, that is, law that on its surface attaches no special benefits to social, political, or ethical status, is essential if normative neutrality is to be achieved. Thus one way normative neutrality can fail is that law may be overtly oriented to external political, ethical, or social considerations. Laws are not status neutral when, for example, they tax the rich at higher rates than the poor; they force blacks to use separate railway carriages or drinking fountains, they give those with incomes under $12,000 a year food stamps; or they give special depletion allowances to oil producers that enable them to escape most tax obligations. In Chapter 13 we are concerned with the substantive orientation of such laws. Here we are interested in another reason for the failure of neutrality: the fact that laws that are status neutral on their face are applied in a world where considerable inequality exists. In an unequal world, the implications of such laws are contingent on aspects of social status.

Status neutral law eschews the task of setting social directions and recognizes only the values of individualism. If a court applies such norms formalistically, the resulting outcomes will have an appearance of neutrality, for extralegal distinctions will not have been imported into the law and will have no place in the legal analysis. Yet in an unequal society the formal analysis will tend to enforce power relationships that exist outside the law. Those who have substantial social power will be able to use the law to reaffirm the advantages they have over others in their day-to-day affairs. This is best illustrated by the contract law jurisprudence of the nineteenth century:

> At the heart of contract, as one English judge put it: . . . there is one thing more than any other which public policy requires, it is that men of full age and competent understanding shall have the utmost liberty of contracting, and that contracts, when entered into freely and voluntarily, shall be held good and shall be enforced by courts of justice. (Hurst, 1956, p. 12)

Such a standard provides a body of interpretive rules that do not concern themselves with the "fairness" of the bargain one party seeks to enforce. If, for example, a black tenant farmer in 1870 had willingly agreed with his former master to exchange 60 percent of his next fall's cotton crop for some seed and the loan of a mule for plowing, a formalist court would enforce the agreement even if the expected value of the promised cotton was many times the value of the goods given. After all, what justifies a court in substituting its idea of relative value for that of the parties? Some might argue that the fact that the parties were so disparate in wealth, education, and the like provides sufficient justification, but the formal analysis of nineteenth-century contract law (which in large measure is still with us today) did not attend to such considerations. The parties appeared before the law as formally equal and all that mattered was that they had willingly agreed to exchange items of value.

Note, however, that even in the extremely formalistic system of nineteenth-century contract law substantive values were not entirely absent. In defining what was an enforceable contract, the law adopted some of the values and meanings of the larger social system. Thus the courts would not enforce agreements that one party was induced to enter by fraud or threats, that were entirely one-sided in the sense that one party gave the other nothing of value, or that were only apparent in the sense that the parties mistook each other's meanings and never really agreed about the terms of the exchange. Moreover, even when the circumstances of the parties were as disparate as in the case we hypothesized, formalism gave some protection to the weaker party. Had the former master, seeing an abundant crop, taken 70 percent of the harvest, a formalist court would have enforced the ex-slave's demand for the value of 10 percent of the harvest. Thirty years before a master who had promised a slave 40 percent of the value of what he grew as an incentive for hard work could at harvest time have left him with 30 percent, and the courts would have done nothing to interfere. Slave and master were not formally equal before the law, and lawsuits did not proceed as if they were.

In an unequal society, even where inequality is not as extreme as in this example, the formal application of laws that do not take into account initial disparities of wealth and power will produce injustice not only in the Rawlsian sense discussed in Chapter 9, but also in the minds of many people. Even those who opposed the abolition of slavery might have thought it unjust to enforce an agreement by an illiterate ex-slave to exchange a cotton crop expected to be worth $200 for seed and some help in plowing that was, for example, worth $3. Why one might ask, did legislatures not often intervene? One answer is that legislatures were not (and are not) perfectly democratic institutions. Powerful elements in society have more influence with legislatures than do ordinary individuals, and it is not surprising that the legislation of a particular era disproportionately reflects their interests.[20] But there is more to the story than this, for to say that legislative democracy is imperfect is not to deny its existence, and

---

20. One can, of course, point to instances where legislatures did recognize status differences in legislation and come to the aid of parties who, individually, had little economic power. Much rate-setting legislation, at least initially, had this quality. In an extreme and celebrated example, the Kansas legislature barred several insurance companies from doing business in the state because they refused to pay a woman money allegedly due under her husband's life insurance policies, contending, with some substantial evidence to back them up, that the husband was not dead but that his alleged corpse was that of someone the husband had killed in order to give his wife an apparent claim to the insurance (Maguire, 1925).

even in the nineteenth century, that golden age of industrialization, legislatures often turned down requests by the powerful for special privileges.

The power of the well-to-do was apparently complemented by the appeal that a formalist jurisprudence based on the assumption of equality among individuals had for many people. Willard Hurst (1956) nicely captures the prevailing spirit. The emphasis was on "human nature," that aspect of personhood that is common to all, and the openness of opportunity:

> The base lines of nineteenth-century public policy . . . are three: (I) Human nature is creative, and its meaning lies largely in the expression of its creative capacity; hence it is socially desirable that there be broad opportunity for the release of creative human energy. (II) Corollary to the creative competence which characterizes human nature, the meaning of life for men rests also in their possessing liberty, which means basically possessing a wide practical range of options or choices as to what they do and how they are affected by circumstances. (III) These propositions have special significance for the future of mankind as they apply in the place and time of the adventure of the United States; here unclaimed natural abundance together with the promise of new technical command of nature dictate that men should realize their creative energy and exercise their liberty peculiarly in the realm of the economy to the enhancement of other human values. (pp. 5–6)

Although there was some status regarding legislation in the nineteenth century,[21] and even more in the early twentieth century, it was not until the Great Depression shattered the myth of the efficacy and fairness of the free market that the jurisprudence of individualism and legal neutrality began to collapse. With the coming of the New Deal, legislatures unashamedly took status regarding interventionist positions, and distributively oriented norms began to infuse a steadily increasing portion of everyday legal life.[22] This movement corresponds in general to the rise of the welfare state (Unger, 1976, pp. 192–200).

In the law-making process there is now considerable attention given to the particular status characteristics of groups and individuals and in this sense a retreat from formalism. Legislation is increasingly designed to enhance values that are not necessarily "legal" but are embedded in some other normative system. But this diminution in one of the aspects of pure autonomy does not necessarily mean that autonomy in the law application process is diminishing.

---

21. Status regarding legislation can, of course, further enhance the well-being of the better off. We are concerned here primarily with legislation aimed at advancing the interests of the worse off. We are describing jurisprudential themes of different epochs. One can in the nineteenth century find status regarding legislation looking both ways, and one can find in the post-depression twentieth century legislation that creates new status neutral norms and legislation that takes account of status to advance the material interests of the already better off.

22. Antitrust law, labor law, civil rights law, and welfare law are, for example, all designed to redistribute welfare between groups or classes. Antitrust law is designed to restrict the economic power of certain groups. Labor law has as its objective increasing the economic and legal power of unions vis à vis management and of workers in general. Civil rights law is aimed at arming minorities with legal powers because of their minority status. And welfare law is law in its most purely redistributive role, taking general tax revenues and channeling them to the less well off.

By increasing legal competence and general access to status neutral legal rights, we may expand the sphere of autonomous legal action.

CONCLUSION

In this chapter we have introduced the idea of legal autonomy and have discussed the possibility of its achievement in the law application process. We have suggested that in Western societies partial autonomy prevails. Law is not fully reducible to the norms of some other authority system, but the application process is constantly penetrated by extralegal social, political, and ethical interests. However, even when the penetration is great, there are distinctions between the rule of law and a reign that rests on some other basis of social power.

Autonomy in the application process depends, we have argued, on three factors: judicial formalism, equal legal competence, and normative neutrality. Only if they are simultaneously realized in an already equal society will the ideal of pure autonomy exist. Judicial formalism is in turn a composite of three factors: a concern for procedure, a concern for rules, and a concern for legal categories. Each of these concerns, we have seen, can temper the goal-oriented impetus of substantive laws and limit the law's ability to achieve the lawmaker's ends. The tempering applies whether a law subverts or promotes liberty, equality, or any other good thing.

In the next chapter we combine these components in different ways. We consider specifically the substantive content of laws, the distribution of power in society, and the stance that courts take in applying legislation. With these dimensions in mind, different implications for the preservation of liberty and the distribution of welfare in society can be identified. We look at each type of law and ask what it portends for the goal of a just society.

13

Styles of Law and the Attainment of Social Justice

In the last chapter we focused on the meaning of legal autonomy and on the constituent elements of the ideal type. We noted two requisites for the autonomous application of law: judicial formalism and equal competence. But we also argued that the autonomous application of law does not guarantee that the law as applied will not perpetuate or advance socioeconomic differences. For applied law to be autonomous in this further sense, legal norms, in addition, must be status neutral, and the distribution of welfare in society must be such that the neutral norms do not disproportionately benefit some people. These latter requisites mean, in practice, that there must be substantial equality in the political, social, and economic structures external to the legal system. If there is not, the advantaged are likely to be able to use law to maintain or better their positions. The norms of property law, for example, will perpetuate existing class distinctions, and through contract law disparities associated with unequal bargaining power will penetrate the legal system.

The discussion of legal norms with which we concluded the previous chapter is a good bridge to this one. Here we are first concerned with the law creation process, the source of legal norms. In discussing law creation, our focus will be on the legislature rather than on the courts or the executive branch, although these latter actors can also make legal norms. We discuss at the outset the possibility of legislative autonomy and suggest that at one level a legislature can be partially autonomous but at another legislatures are inescapably oriented to the demands of nonlegal political, ethical, or social schemes. We next specify four types of law that vary with social equality and overt attention to status. Once we have specified the types of law, we consider how the law application process interacts with the legislative types to define styles of law that characterize legal relations in society. The basic concepts are developed at the level of ideal types, but approximations to the types can be found in the real world. Throughout this chapter issues of social justice are addressed, and in our conclusion we discuss the implication of this chapter and the preceding one for the realization of liberty and equality, the core components of justice from the Rawlsian perspective.

THE POSSIBILITY OF LEGISLATIVE AUTONOMY

The legislature sits at the intersection of the political and legal spheres. As we saw in Chapter 10, it is open to the influence of wealth as well as to other sources of social and political power and to the vociferous entreaties of those who support private ethical systems. At the same time, the legislature is a crucial legal actor, for it pours norms into the judicial and regulatory systems. It is fair to ask whether a legislature can ever share the partial autonomy we have identified with law. If not, the autonomy of law is likely to be of little import, for the stock of legal forms and concepts that regulate and sanction behavior will soon reflect the interests of powerful extralegal status groups. To note this is to suggest our answer, for we have consistently and intentionally implied that the partial autonomy we see in the legal systems of the capitalist democracies reflects meaningful independence from extralegal sources of authority.

There are several reasons why some degree of legislative autonomy is possible. First, the structure of the legislature contributes to its ability to act autonomously. Interest groups can capture legisla*tors,* but it is difficult to generate a coalition to capture the legisla*ture.* Thus the ready translation of the interests of social, political, or ethical groups in ways that substantially threaten, rather than simply fail to promote, the interests of others is difficult to achieve. In the United States this difficulty is enhanced by constitutional requirements for super majorities when fundamental liberty interests or the independence of the courts is directly threatened, and by the veto power given to the president.

Second, there are distinctively legal norms about the form, content, and procedure of legislation that legislatures routinely honor. Some norms such as the prohibition in the United States of *ex post facto* laws and bills of attainder are written into a constitution. Others such as the need to respect the separate jurisdictions of the judiciary and executive are implied by one. Still others such as the preference for legislation that fits in as far as possible with the body of existing law and the idea that legislation should be open to public comment are part of the legislative culture. Adherence to such cultural rules not only promotes autonomy in legislation, but is itself an important expression of autonomy.

Third, in the United States by long-standing precedent and in other countries, to differing degrees, the judiciary, the branch of government best insulated from the pressures that threaten autonomy, has authority to void specific legislative enactments.

Three further propositions are also important. First, although particular laws may reflect the influence of identifiable status groups, the body of laws may mix such a variety of concerns that the legal system can be identified with no particular external interests, except possibly at the highest level of generality, such as whites in a segregated society or the propertied in a class-stratified society. Second, not all instances of externally oriented legislative behavior reflect the influence of some *special* interest group. Recall Bohannan (1965). Some norms—like much of the criminal law—are so generally accepted in society that the legislative reinstitutionalization of these norms is not problematic. Third, it is not necessarily the case that an autonomous legislature is likely to promote social justice or that a legislature more accessible to special interests and extralegal ethical systems is likely to decrease it. Often it is just the opposite.

LAW CREATION

But the fact that legislation is insulated to some extent from the pressures of particular extralegal interests and is shaped to some extent by distinctively legal concerns does not mean that legislatures are autonomous in the way courts are. Even at the level of the ideal, there are fundamental differences. The formalist court, as we saw in Chapter 12, takes legal norms as given and in this sense can be entirely *self-regarding*[1] in disposing of cases. But a legislature must ordinarily look beyond existing sources of law in deciding what new legal norms will be. In doing so, it is almost always acting with a substantive end—as valued in some extralegal social, political, or ethical order—in sight. This is true even if that end is, for example, a regime of contract law that does not take into account values other than the desirability of enforcing private agreements. The creation of a status netural legal order can itself be a substantive goal.

LEGISLATIVE ENDOWMENTS

Laws specify the conditions under which the power of the state will be addressed to certain ends.[2] These ends will, in practice, always be in some person's or

---

1. In the term "self-regarding" as we use it in this chapter, the legal system is the "self." Here by self-regarding we mean that only the requirements of the law are attended to in deciding how a dispute should be resolved. The implications of extralegal power and normative orders are not considered.

2. These ends may specify specific goals directly as in laws designed to limit pollution, or they may be more general as in much of tort law which has as its goal protecting people from the economic aspects of harm caused by others, or as in much of contract law, the end of law may be to guarantee arrangements specified by private parties.

group's interest. Thus legislation, or lawmaking, increases the probability that certain ends will be achieved because if they are not realized either the state will enforce the law proactively, or the beneficiary of the legislation may call on the courts, on the police, or on some other administrative agency to enforce the law. In this sense law is said to "guarantee" behavior, and for this reason we may think of a law as a kind of *endowment*. It endows actors with a power to achieve their goals that they otherwise would not have.[3]

Legislative endowments, that is, laws, vary in the extent to which they acknowledge social differences and have a distributive end openly in view. Some laws are on their face status neutral in that they create categories extracted from all social context (e.g., the categories of citizen, defendant, property owner) and give the same rights and duties to all who fit the category created. Other laws take explicit account of social or economic positions and seek to allocate values accordingly. Laws that are status neutral do not specify a particular distributive goal to be achieved; that is, they do not on their face mandate actions that will impose special costs on a preexisting class of organizations or individuals or give special benefits to another such class. The distributive consequences of status neutral laws are instead determined by the actions of individuals and organizations and the ways these parties choose to invoke the law. Thus status neutral laws often have the appearance of distributive neutrality and seem to be motivated by an abstract evaluation of the kinds of rights and duties that will allow communal life to flourish rather than by some conception of a desired end state; or if there is a desired end state, the end, such as deterring homicide or keeping traffic within a speed limit, will not be tied to or directed against the interests of some discrete social group. Status neutral legal language is well suited to judicial formalism and is apparently removed from redistributive concerns. We must, however, be cautious in taking the appearance for reality. Status neutral laws are nonetheless purposive. Legislatures pass them to achieve certain ends. The end may be the promotion of individual achievement or the enhancement of communal life in a status neutral fashion. Or it may be to create legal rules that will allow one group or class to advance itself at the expense of another group or class. In Chapter 12 we saw how the application of status neutral laws in an unequal society could have this effect. A legislature enacting laws for such a society presumably knows what neutral norms imply for the distribution of

---

3. The endowment may be less than what is promised or it may never have to be invoked. Legislative endowments may be less than what is apparently promised because the administration or enforcement of a law may be only partial, generally lax, or even subversive of the legislative intent. They may never have to be invoked because the legislation may command behavior that would occur anyway or the existence of the law may, without more, be sufficient to bring about the behavior ordered. Yet except in the extreme cases where a law is clearly a dead letter or where no one would think of doing otherwise, legislative endowments are real and consequential even if they do not fully determine how the behavior they purport to deal with is ordered. In particular, we saw in Chapter 6 on negotiation that law may be vitally important to the resolution of disputes even if cases do not officially enter the legal system (cf. Mnookin & Kornhauser, 1979).

welfare. Nevertheless, in examining legislation, it is helpful to treat status neutral law as a distinct type.

The opposite type consists of laws that take social status specifically into account and subordinate the ideals of legal neutrality and individual rights to the attainment of particular ends. Laws of this type aim at specific end states that usually involve some redistribution of welfare in society. Thus we shall call such laws *distributively oriented*. Courts act consistently with the legislature's goals if they interpret such laws with a close eye to the distributive goals the legislature hoped to achieve. This requires a judiciary that is sensitive to the extralegal values and interests that stimulated the legislation.

We can also distinguish two ways in which laws come to be enacted. At the extremes powerful status groups may have effective control over the legislative process or those affected by the laws may be relatively equal in their influence on what is enacted. In the former instance, legislation can be expected to systematically advantage the most influential groups. In the latter, legislation should ideally reflect some general consensus, but in practice, it is likely to reflect shifting coalitions that temporarily gain control over the legislative process to advance positions that they value. The process of building a coalition, however, often tempers the gains of those who seek a particular law and cushions the impact on those who will be disadvantaged by it. Thus where relatively equal influence prevails there is frequently a distinction between what the groups that most strongly support a law desire and what they get.

Keeping the concept of the legislative endowment in mind and cross-classifying the types of law by equality of influence, we obtain the following fourfold table (Table 13.1):

TABLE 13.1
Law Creation and Legislative Endowments

	Type of Law	
The Law-Making Process	*Status Neutral*	*Distributively Oriented*
(More or less) equal influence	Equally accessible general endowments (3)	Welfare-oriented endowments (4)
(Greatly) unequal influence	Differentially accessible general endowments (2)	Class-oriented endowments (1)

Distributively Oriented Endowments

Where dominant groups have inordinate control over the rule-making process, and where the legislature is not bound in any way by a commitment to neutral rules, we have the situation specified in cell 1. The organized power of the state is at the service of a particular class. Laws of this type are "instrumental" in that they are instruments or tools used by socially dominant groups to achieve their ends. Logical consistency if it is part of the legal culture is required only with reference to self-defined interests, not with regard to some internal logic of rules. Much of the law of slavery falls in this cell, as do those English laws that facilitated the private exploitation of what had been publicly available pastures and American legislation that hampered the activities of trade unions. In each case the dominant class bent the state to its will and so could proceed legally to pursue its narrow class interests. Laws in this cell take explicit account of the status differences of the affected parties and allocate values accordingly.

The dividing line between cell 1 and cell 4 is not discoverable by looking at the law itself, for welfare-oriented endowments like class-oriented endowments are purposive statutes that openly seek to advance specific subsets of social interests. However, law in cell 1 is a powerful force for the preservation or extension of existing inequalities, since it reinstitutionalizes the power of the dominant class in the legal arena, while law in cell 4 seeks to advance the common welfare[4] and is potentially a means to increased social justice.

These differences reflect differences in political power; that is, in power to influence the law-making process. In cell 1 in the ideal case a class or status group clearly dominates, and it can make law without attending to the interests of any other social group. The only restraints on how such powerful interests use the legal system are the benevolent restraints of *noblesse oblige* and the calculated restraints of self-interest. In cell 4 no one group can control the legal process, so legislation will reflect either widely shared interests or the give-and-take needed to form winning coalitions. In the latter instance, laws will either compromise the interests of various groups or be part of a package deal in which interest groups support each other so that they will be supported in turn.

Instances of these three different processes are common. For example, laws regulating pollution are in the perceived interest of so many people that the vested interests in opposition have been unable to resist effectively much of what has been attempted. Laws establishing determinate sentencing programs were originally a compromise between liberals and conservatives who each had their own reasons for wanting to discard a penal system oriented toward rehabilitation and the system of indeterminate sentencing that went with it. The result in many jurisdictions was a new, less flexible sentencing structure with average prison terms that were longer than the liberals thought appropriate but shorter than the conservatives wanted. Finally, the logrolling process that has congressman A

---

4. What we call welfare law, like the AFDC program, fits this cell, but the term *welfare* is used more generally to refer to all kinds of redistributive legislation aimed at some vision of the common good. Again, the line between cell 1 and cell 4 is blurred because a dominant minority can claim that laws that further enhance their status are in the common good. However, at the extremes we think the distinctions between cell 1 and cell 4 are clearly recognizable. They are also recognizable if we focus on the process since in cell 1 unlike cell 4 a particular group or class consistently dominates the legislative process and the law consistently reflects their domination.

voting to support a shipyard in congressman B's district on the condition that B vote to construct a dam for A's constituents is a familiar political phenomenon.

If perfectly equal influence, the situation that *ideally* characterizes cell 4 (and cell 3), in fact existed, social justice would not be problematic because equal influence in the legislative process will not exist unless there is an equal division of wealth, power, and privilege in the larger society. Law in such a society would be in the common interest, for if it ceased to be, the condition of equal influence that defines the pure type would disappear. In the real world, or at least in the portion of the real world we call Western democracies, the influence that different identifiable interests have on the legislative process is not equal, but it is not so unequal that one group or class consistently dominates. To capture this and to better relate our analysis to actual legal systems, we have relaxed the defining condition for laws in cells 3 and 4 and have posited a society in which individual welfare and influence on the law-making process are only "more or less" rather than absolutely equal. Given that some inequality persists in such a society, it is not obvious why the interests of weaker groups occasionally prevail, with justice, in the Rawlsian sense, being advanced by something like the difference principle. Why, for example, do we have a large body of welfare law that transfers money from the wealthier to the less well off? Why do not the more powerful elements of society consistently form coalitions to advance themselves at the expense of the least well off?

We do not propose to deal with these questions at length, but a word is in order. There are several reasons why legislation may give special advantages to groups that have little social power. First, the interests of stronger groups are often antagonistic. If their power is closely balanced, weaker groups may be in a position to strike a balance between them and, in exchange for their support, they may be able to demand substantial benefits. The institutional requirements for coalition building are crucial in determining the power that relatively weak groups possess. Thus, in Israel, where the parliamentary system allows small parties to flourish, extremely orthodox religious parties, whose support has been needed to form a government, have been able to insist that some religious practices they favor be imposed throughout the state. In the United States the single member district system is death to third parties, but because large numbers of otherwise powerless people participate in elections the dominant parties cannot afford to ignore their interests entirely. Indeed, the Democratic party is, to a large extent, organized around the expectation that they will get the vote of the less well off, and legislation that the party passes when in office often responds to the interests of this core constituency.

Other reasons welfare-oriented legislation often benefits the less well off include the altruistic instincts of the powerful, self-interested judgments about the cheapest way to keep the dominated under control and the fact that distinctions between the weak and powerful are by no means clear-cut.

Altruism is a particularly powerful instinct when restated in an ideology that demands certain actions. Thus the idea that humans were equal in the eyes of God helped create the climate for a war that was in part about freeing slaves, and the idea, a century later, that humans were equal before the law led, as we saw in Chapter 11, to a series of legal skirmishes that enhanced the social and political power of those slaves' descendants. Pure self-interest may also lead dominant coalitions to share benefits with less powerful groups. Sharing benefits may be a cheap way to secure popular cooperation with laws that disproportionately aid those on top. Some would argue that the modern welfare state was invented to prevent repetitions of the Russian revolution, and colonial regimes typically reward some elements of the native population to keep other elements under control. Sharing benefits is, of course, a strategy that may inform cell 1 type laws as well.

Finally, there may be important ties between members of more influential and less influential groups that lead the former to support legislation in the latter's interest. For example, future accident victims by virtue of being both unknown and unorganized have little direct influence on the legislative process. Yet their interests are well-represented when industries or insurance companies seek to make tort recoveries less lucrative or more difficult to attain. This is because personal injury lawyers, a quite influential group, realize that their financial interests are inextricably linked with the rights accorded future victims. Perhaps more to the point, even if the elderly were not a potentially powerful political force, it would be difficult to cut back on the Social Security retirement program because many of the more active and influential younger citizens who are children of the elderly would feel obligated to support their parents if the state subsidy were not available.

This litany of reasons why the interests of the relatively less influential are likely to be advanced by welfare-oriented endowments when political influence is divided more or less equally across individuals and groups should not mislead one into thinking that in such a society it is better to have less influence than more. The more powerful are likely to benefit disproportionately from the legislative process even if they cannot effectively bend the law into the specific instrument of class domination that it is in cell 1. Special benefits to the more powerful are endemic in modern capitalist democracies. Yet an important qualification must be added. The very features that cause a group to stand out as influential can make its interests a natural target when other, individually less influential groups, coalesce. Indeed, it may be the disproportionate influence of a powerful group that stimulates the formation of more powerful counter coalitions. At the extreme the result will be a social revolution that strips the previously most powerful single element of its power base. Less extreme but more common is the mobilization of a coalition to pass a particular law when an especially powerful element appears to be overreaching. Thus the railroads, the most powerful of the nineteenth century industries, could not forestall the popular movement for regulated freight rates that led to the Interstate Commerce Commission, and the large trusts could not derail the perceived need for laws attacking the monopolies that they spawned. However, in each instance the fate of the enacted regulatory schemes reminds us of the tenacity of powerful organizations and the transience of many coalitions.

A more or less equal distribution of legislative influence among actors and social groups is also consistent with endowments that trample on the interests of some weaker parties. Coalitions are formed that increase social injustice. For much of this century a coalition of well-to-do and poor southern whites enforced a system of segregation that disadvantaged the black population. American Indians and aliens in many countries have had to confront legislation that sought to give portions of their wealth to more dominant groups. At some points in our history there has been an overwhelming consensus supporting laws designed to stifle political dissent. And even where legislative majorities have not oppressed minorities, the interests of some groups, such as the interest that short people have in avoiding discrimination, are almost entirely ignored. This then is the dark side of cell 4. Although welfare-oriented legislation has the potential to enhance justice by endowing weaker parties with state-supported entitlements, it may also do the opposite. In particular, there is the danger that has been called the "tyranny of the majority," a situation in which the dominant coalition dismisses the interests and rides roughshod over the rights of those who are collectively less powerful. The tyranny of the majority is particularly likely where the same stable coalition dominates on many issues.

In any given society that is sufficiently egalitarian so that welfare-oriented endowments are possible, the quality of the legislation that is enacted will turn on the interests of identifiable groups, on their potential influence in the legislative process, and on institutional arrangements that allow groups to link up or channel the exercise of power. In short, it will turn on politics, for in cell 4 as in cell 1 the way that law orders behavior is the realization of a political process; not autonomous from it.

Status Neutral Endowments

The situation is somewhat different when we look at cells 2 and 3. Laws that fit these cells are characterized by the appearance of status neutrality. They create entitlements that are, in theory, open to all; impose duties that are, in theory, binding on all; or establish conditions under which any private party can invoke the power of the state in pursuit of personal ends. Some examples include the rights that people have to use their private property as they see fit, the restraints imposed on all by the criminal law, and the ability that contract law gives people to hold others to their promises.

Status neutral laws attribute meaning to behavior based on the legal categories into which the behavior fits and not on the meaning it may have in the larger society. Thus the destruction of draft board records to protest the arms race is in law like throwing a rock through a school window for the hell of it. Both are the malicious destruction of public property. The protestor who believes he should be treated differently from the vandal will be told in a status neutral system that the law perceives no essential difference in the two behaviors. Similarly, a poor woman who agrees to sell her wedding ring for a quarter of its known value because she desperately needs money to feed her children will, if she later tries to renege on the deal, be treated no differently from a wealthy woman who agreed to sell a ring cheaply because she wanted to rid herself of a reminder of her former husband and was indifferent to what she was paid. The relevant legal categories do not attend to the social status of the contracting parties or to the immediate motivations of specific agreements. Only certain aspects of agreements are regarded by the law as important, and if these aspects have the proper form, the law will proceed to enforce the agreement as if that were all that mattered.

The problem with status neutral law from a social justice standpoint is, as we saw in Chapter 12, that it treats people from all walks of life as if they are equally well situated to comply with the law or to benefit from it. By not attending to differences of power and status, it cannot correct for them. And by distributing rights or responsibilities as if social status had nothing to do with their enjoyment or burden, status neutral law in a substantially unequal society differentially endows people with legal power or differentially exposes them to state regulation.

In a generally egalitarian society, status neutral law is more likely to enhance mutual well-being and advance social justice. The law establishes conditions under which individual action will be protected without specifying in detail the direction those actions should take. Ordinarily this is liberty enhancing. People know, for example, that their agreements will be enforced, but they are free to agree on whatever suits them. Guarantees against overreaching derive not from the law, but from the fact that power and status are equal to begin with. Rights and obligations with respect to property cannot further entrench the power of one group vis-à-vis another when preexisting disparities are absent.

Thus we see that the implications of formally neutral law for social justice depend crucially on the distribution of power in nonlegal spheres. But this is not the whole story. Law also affects that distribution. Where power is initially distributed more or less equally but not perfectly so, status neutral law inhibits planned social change that might wipe out vestiges of inequality. There are two reasons for this. The first is that if the law does not recognize the way that individuals are unequally situated it can neither compensate for inequalities nor develop programs to obliterate them. The second is that status neutral law tends to democratize the state's power, that is, to endow all the state's citizens more or less equally with legal entitlements. This interferes with planned change both by dispersing power rather than focusing it and by investing people with rights that allow them to resist concerted efforts to reach egalitarian goals. Indeed, the point is more general. In a more or less equal society people may have rights protected by status neutral law that allow them to resist laws that the majority of the moment thinks are in the common interest.

Where the distribution of power is markedly unequal to begin with, status neutral law acts as a restraint on the dominant class. It must be general and tends to be consistent across a wide body of law. Thus it is not a finely tuned instrument designed to meet the specific, immediate needs of a powerful group. The advantage of status neutral law for the better off is that its entitlements are more accessible to the wealthy than to the poor, and the duties it imposes on the wealthy are less onerous. However, it can cut against the interest of specific members of the dominant class even if its tendency as a whole is to better their positions. Rich murderers, for example, are occasionally hanged for their crimes, and an ordinary homeowner who is sentimentally attached to his property may thwart the plans of a wealthy developer.

REASONS FOR STATUS NEUTRALITY

Law that is not overtly purposive, *is nonetheless passed with a purpose*. We can always ask of a law, in whose interest is it? If status neutral law imposes limits on efforts to advance both the common good and the good of groups with overwhelming political power, why do such laws ever get passed and why is the common law, which is by and large a body of status neutral case law, not overturned by legislation? Why, in other words, does not the majority of the moment in a more or less equal society or the dominant group in a decidedly unequal society limit their lawmaking to legislation that is aimed overtly at the distributive ends they seek to achieve?

One reason has to do with culture and tradition; some values are taken for granted even if they are not in an actor's immediate interest. It is probably important that the common law is largely status neutral. Not only is the common law at the core of Anglo-American legal education and thus important in shaping the expectations that young lawyers have about law, but it also provides a context into which new legislation must fit.[5]

Here, however, we want to focus on another part of the explanation, for status neutral law can be in the perceived interest of those who dominate the political process. In a more or less equal society there will be no one group that dominates. Instead, policy will be the product of temporary majorities and shifting coalitions. All groups are likely to be satisfied with the way some issues are resolved and dissatisfied with the resolution of others. Influential groups may, however, fear that the coalition structure will change to exclude their interests. In particular, groups that do not dominate but have relatively more power and influence at a particular moment may feel that their privileged status might lead others to coalesce against them, and if so, they will be hopelessly outnumbered. Status neutral law is a protection against the "tyranny of the majority" that

---

5. In the next section we discuss issues of judge made law. The common law is judge made. Some of its norms seem to be judicial distillations of what was once popular or specialized (e.g., among merchants) morality. An exploration of the origins of the common law is beyond the scope of this book. Its general status neutrality may reflect ideals or requisites of judicial neutrality. Judges should not legislate, and one way to avoid the appearance of legislating while making law is to suggest that natural law, precedent or statutory law, mandates the particular decision and to present that decision in language that is addressed to the general well-being of society rather than to the particular ends of some status group. Also, it may be that the specialized and popular moral codes that have been assimilated over the years into the common law are themselves status neutral.

might otherwise result. Thus in a more or less equal society the coalition favoring neutral solutions will often be dominant, and there will be a tendency to build such solutions into constitutions, schemes of representation, and other institutions that cannot be changed at the will of a temporarily dominant majority.

Status neutral law may also reflect the difficulties of planning for desired ends. Extending rights to all in a more or less equal society means that the effects of the law will reflect individual judgments and desires as mediated by some approximation to a market. Not only might such an approach appear more efficient than an attempt at detailed regulation, but it is also a way of compromising differences among groups that generally agree about how social life should be regulated but disagree on the details.

In decidedly unequal societies there is another reason for status neutral law. It tends to mask the exercise of power and obscure the degree to which law is the servant of one class. This is important because the fact that one class clearly dominates does not mean that control is not problematic. Maintaining control is often difficult, expensive, and precarious. If the legal system is seen as a naked tool by which one group rules others, it will be opposed by those hostile to the group in power. If, however, the law is seen as rising above class differences, it may be accorded respect and its commands may be taken for granted as right (Hay, 1975).

We call this attitude toward law "legitimacy." The fact that a legal order is regarded as legitimate does not necessarily mean that there will be compliance when self-interest suggests that lawbreaking holds greater promise of reward. But it does increase the probability of compliance and, more importantly, increases the probability that those whose self-interest is not obviously affected by the law will cooperate with the lawmaker rather than with the lawbreaker. As a result, legitimacy reduces the frequency with which legal commands must be backed up with force.

It appears that laws which endow everyone with entitlements that only the best off are likely to be in a position to enjoy and restrict everyone with prohibitions that are disproportionately likely to pinch the worst off are more likely to be regarded as legitimate than laws that more openly enhance the position of the best off or diminish the position of the worst.[6] Contrast, for example, your reaction to a law that says "Jews and blacks may not join the Elite Country Club" and a law that says "Private clubs are free to choose their own members." The two laws may be equally effective in keeping Jews and blacks from joining the Elite, but reactions to them, particularly on the part of "good thinking" white Christians, will probably differ.

If you were intent on keeping the Elite a WASP organization, which law

---

6. This may well be contingent on the prevailing ideology. In a society where the ideals of freedom and equality are regarded as important the textural argument is most likely to hold. In a highly stratified society where the stratification is accepted as in the order of things, laws that openly distance the dominant strata from the lower orders may be accepted by both the upper and lower strata as legitimate.

would you prefer? The choice is not completely clear, for you might find some day that a less-bigoted clique had come to dominate the club. But formally neutral law is likely to be less expensive to enforce since the Elite is less likely to be attacked for bigotry, and it is likely to be more enduring since everyone, including Jews and blacks, may see some advantage in laws that allow private clubs to choose their own members. To generalize, the prospect of enhanced legitimacy is, in many situations, likely to be sufficiently attractive to those who dominate a legal order that status neutral law will be preferred to more openly distributive enactments. Although the former is not so neatly tailored to the end in view as the latter and some slippage may be inevitable, proceeding by neutral rather than by clearly distributive rules may appear to offer greater prospects for promoting class interests in the long run.

LAW APPLICATION

Now that we have considered four basic types of law and some reasons for these approaches, we must consider how these types interact with the ways that law may be applied. Thus we return to a topic that we discussed in detail in Chapter 12, but we examine it from a different perspective. First, we discuss senses in which courts make law while applying it. Next, we contrast the substantively oriented court with the formalist court we considered in Chapter 12. Finally, we see what these judicial stances imply when courts apply laws of the types specified in Table 13.1.

Judicial Lawmaking

In moving from lawmaking to law application, we shift our attention from legislation to adjudication and from legislatures to courts. In doing so, we must first address the fact that there are some senses in which courts make law. Courts are directly responsible for the law of the case, which is the law as it applies specifically to the litigating parties. When John Jones came to court charged with burglary the law was that anyone who breaks into the dwelling of another at night is guilty of burglary and may be punished by a prison term of from 1 to 10 years. When John Jones left court, a convicted felon, the law insofar as it applied to John, was that he had broken into the dwelling of another at night and as a consequence had to serve 3 years in prison. The situation is similar for Susie Smith who was stopped at a red light when an Ajax moving van ploughed into her. When Susie sued Ajax the law was that if Ajax's driver had not exercised the care that might have been expected of a reasonable person and in consequence had injured someone, Ajax would have to pay the injured person's damages. When the lawsuit was concluded, the law, insofar as it concerned Susie and Ajax, was that Ajax's driver had not, in fact, been exercising reasonable care when his van struck Susie, and Ajax was obliged to pay her $126,000.

Now this kind of lawmaking is inherent in any adjudicative process. Courts cannot help but engage in it. Indeed, one of the features that distinguishes adjudication from mediation is the adjudicator's ability to determine the law of the case without seeking the parties' consent (McEwen & Maiman, 1984). Thus if courts did not make law in this sense, they would not be adjudicating.

At the extreme, all that courts are doing when they make law in this way is finding facts. John Jones either did or did not break into the dwelling of another at night. If he did, he is guilty of burglary; if not, he is innocent. Once the facts are determined, the implications of the law are self-evident. But almost invariably, applying the law to cases involves some interpretation. What, after all, does it mean for a truck driver to exercise the care of a reasonable person? Is it reasonable to look back at one's load after hearing a loud crash and so risk not seeing a light turn red up ahead? Interpretive tasks like these are routine occurrences at trials (Stone, 1966).

Often, however, questions of interpretation rise that are easily extracted from the facts of the case. If the court interpreting the law has the power to pronounce rules that will guide other courts in similar cases, law in a more extended sense may be created. Not only is the rule pronounced binding on the parties to the case, but it is also binding on similarly situated parties in future cases. It is a new rule to guide behavior. For example, suppose that John Jones had just moved into a new subdivision in which all houses look alike. Coming home late one night he turned into the wrong cul-de-sac and walked to the wrong house. Frustrated at finding that his key did not work, he broke a window pane and entered the house. He is charged with burglary.

To decide whether John is guilty of burglary is to decide whether the law that criminalizes breaking into the dwelling of another person at night applies when one reasonably believes he is breaking into his own house. However the highest court in a jurisdiction resolves this issue, there will be a new rule of general applicability. Either a good faith mistake will be a defense to the crime of burglary or one breaks into a home he thinks is his own at his peril.

A court in this instance is clearly making law, and the type of rule it enunciates is not very different from the kinds of rules that legislatures enact. For example, had the legislature contemplated the case we describe, it might have specifically provided that the burglary statute did not apply where the proscribed actions were the result of a good faith mistake. Yet the practice by which the court made law is sufficiently distinct from the legislative approach to lawmaking that it makes sense to call it adjudication. The Court was not deciding on the best policy to apply in *State* v. *Jones*. Instead, it was trying in good faith to determine how the legislature wanted its rules to be interpreted. The judges were not trying to impose their values on the case, but were instead trying to determine what the values of the legislature—the accepted lawmaker— had been.

Now, in practice, when legislative language is open to interpretation in a case of first impression it is almost impossible for a judge to determine what the legislature would have intended without being in some degree influenced by his or her own values.[7] To vary our burglary example somewhat, consider the case of Sally Smith who was lost in the woods for ten days surviving on insects and berries. One night, shortly after sundown, she stumbled into a clearing and saw a hunting cabin. When no one answered her knock, she broke a window, entered the cabin, found food, and prepared a decent meal. This case involves two issues of legal interpretation. The first is whether a hunting cabin that is ordinarily vacant qualifies as a "dwelling" within the meaning of the statute. The second is whether the statute contains an implicit exception for starving people who break into dwellings in search of food.

The legislation is ambiguous on both points. Indeed, had the problem been posed, different legislators might have had different views. Yet the court is supposed to determine legislative intent. A judge who believes firmly in the sanctity of private property is more likely than a judge with socialist leanings to find that the statute covers any property in which people sometimes dwell and is likely to hold that although the particular motivations for breaking into another's dwelling might justify a lenient sentence or a gubernatorial pardon, they do not change the fact that the behavior is proscribed by the law. A judge who places a high value on human life and a lesser value on private property might hold that the legislature did not intend its proscription to apply in emergency situations, or if the judge felt constrained by the legislative language on this point, he might interpret "dwelling" to mean a "regularly inhabited building."[8]

Here the court is clearly close to lawmaking in a legislative sense. The judges are applying their own values to determine not what the legislature would have intended had they contemplated the situation that arose, but rather, what the legislature *should* have intended. Nevertheless, we would still call this adjudication provided two conditions are met: (1) that the interpretation be interstitial in nature; that is, the court is filling in gaps in what is, generally speaking, a legislatively ordered scheme of things; (2) that the court interpret in good faith the cues that exist concerning legislative intent. These include committee reports and other legislative history as well as the statutory language. Good faith interpretation requires an awareness of one's own values and the ability to perceive and respect conflicting values that are embodied in legislation.

Finally, we come to the other extreme in which legislative texts give no guidance or, fairly read, suggest a different interpretation from that which the court endorses. Here judges are, in effect, stating what they think is the best policy to govern a situation. This is pure judicial lawmaking. Perhaps the best example of judicial lawmaking in recent years is the abortion case, *Roe* v. *Wade*,

---

7. On some occasions there are clear guides such as statements in floor debates, committee reports, or other legislative history that contemplate the situation that has arisen and state how it would be resolved under the law. Judges will also consult for guidance related laws and precedents in their own and other jurisdictions.

8. Note that both judges might find they had to refine their interpretations further in future cases. The first judge might think a different rule justified when the entrance was to save those in a dwelling from a fire, and the second judge might come to interpret "regularly inhabited" differently when confronted with cases in which vacation homes had been entered by vandals or thieves.

410 U.S. 113 (1973) and, in particular, the detailed lines the Court draws. Nothing in the Constitution (or readily derived therefrom) suggests that states cannot regulate abortions during the first trimester of pregnancy, can engage in limited regulation during the second trimester, and can regulate extensively during the final three months. Yet this is what a majority of the Supreme Court held.

We do not mean to imply by this analysis that the decision in *Roe* was wrong. We express no opinion on that matter. We are saying that the Supreme Court in this case, as in other cases, crossed the fuzzy line that usefully, if somewhat unclearly, separates adjudication from legislation. The majority in *Roe*, almost completely unconstrained by the language of the Constitution or the received body of law, enunciated what they thought was the wisest policy given the conflicting values involved.

In defense of the Court one might argue that it was forced to act as it did. For the Constitution as it had been interpreted to that point did not clearly imply that there was not a right to abortion or that states were free to restrict abortions as they chose (Regan, 1979), and the body of precedent involving privacy rights on the one hand and the states' police power on the other cut in two directions. This is often the situation when courts make law in this sense. They are called on to resolve a conflict, and the received law either fails to give substantial guidance or, especially in the case of precedent, is too dated to merit respect. Judges are, in effect, forced to make legislative judgments. But even in these circumstances there is an important sense—perhaps the most important sense— in which the decision making remains adjudicative. When courts make law, norms of judicial behavior are salient, and courts follow judicial procedures. Adjudicative processes differ from legislative ones, and the differences can have important implications for the law that results.[9] Moreover, courts generally see their task not as deciding on the best possible rule to govern a situation but as choosing from among a more limited set of rules that it is plausible for a court to enunciate given the case posed by the parties. Thus in *Brown v. Board of Education* the Supreme Court could make law by declaring legally segregated schools unconstitutional. It could not in *Brown* have ordered the Congress to allocate special funds to southern school boards that dismantled dual school systems. While the Court's decision in *Brown* was arguably legislative in nature,

---

9. One difference is that adjudication centers around a particular case while legislation usually focuses on a particular problem. A second difference is that legislators can reach out to inform themselves through constituent polls and legislative hearings, and may count on hearing from those interested in the legislation in any event. Only the parties to a case have a right to inform a court no matter how widespread the implications of a prospective ruling, but courts knowing they shall make law often allow a few interested parties to state their concerns in what are called "amicus" or "friend of the court" briefs. Finally, and perhaps most saliently, legislators are expected to represent constituents and must regularly stand before them in genuinely contested elections. High court judges are usually appointed for life or for long terms punctuated by elections that are either seldom seriously contested because incumbency is such a substantial advantage (Dubois, 1984) or turn more on a judge's party affiliations than on the decisions he or she has reached.

it was appropriate for a court although other kinds of legislative commands would not have been.

Finally, to make law judges must write opinions, for it is the opinion that identifies the legal rule. While in a particular case a ruling broadly favoring either party might be appropriate, not all justifications for possible rulings are permissible. This need to justify decisions constrains the kinds of legal rules that courts make. *Roe*, arguably, would have appeared much less exceptional had a different justification been advanced (Regan, 1979).

Styles of Judging

When we look at judicial decision making, we can distinguish two approaches. Following Weber (1968) we call these stances *formal rationality* and *substantive rationality*. These terms describe styles of thought—ways that courts position themselves vis-à-vis the *corpus juris* they must apply and interpret. Formal rationality is the mode of thought associated with judicial formalism as we describe it in Chapter 12. As we have noted, it abstracts persons and actions out of the real world, fits them into legal categories, proceeds to manipulate those categories as the law specifies, and decides cases accordingly.[10] A formally rational court might reason as follows in the case of our suburbanite, John Jones, who turned down the wrong cul de sac:

> The statute proscribes breaking and entering the dwelling of another at night. When Jones smashed a window pane and then lifted the window and walked through it, he was certainly breaking and entering. The dwelling was owned by another person and the act occurred after sundown and before sunrise. Therefore Jones is guilty of burglary.

The formally rational jurist might find the result that his analysis leads to dissatisfying, but that does not concern him *as judge*. What concerns him is that the result follow logically from the facts as he understands them and from the law as it is written.

Perhaps the best example of a judge who was able and felt compelled to make such a separation was Felix Frankfurter. In one case *(Louisiana ex rel Francis v. Resweber,* 329 U.S. 459 (1947) the Court confronted the situation of a young man who was condemned to die in the electric chair. For some reason the chair was faulty, and although electric current apparently shot through the man, he survived. The issue was whether a second electrocution could proceed or whether it was barred by the constitutional proscription of cruel and unusual

---

10. For those familiar with Plato's allegory of the cave, we can offer a nice analogy to formal rationality. Real people and real actions are, in all their complexity, like the live people walking before the mouth of the cave. The law is the sun that casts images on the wall of the cave. Legal categories are the two-dimensional shadows that only partly capture the nature of the real people and objects that they represent. Formally rational jurists are people who have been in the cave for such a long time that they take the shadows for the real thing and proceed to act accordingly.

punishment, double jeopardy and other violations of due process. Frankfurter, finding that the chair's deficiency was entirely accidental, concurred in the decision of the majority of the Supreme Court that nothing in the Constitution prevented the state from proceeding with a second execution, but he also implied that the situation was one in which a governor might be expected to intercede with executive clemency. Not content with this, Frankfurter, after the opinion was filed, wrote a personal letter to the governor urging the extension of mercy. Thus the man who could have prevented the execution as a judge (the case was decided by a 5–4 vote) felt that in this capacity the law required him to let the execution proceed, but as a private person he directed his immense prestige toward the end of sparing the life of a young black man he did not know. Power, however, lay in the role and not the person, for the governor allowed the execution.

The substantively rational judge proceeds, by contrast, with an end in view. The end must to some extent be derived from some normative system that is external to the legal system, for if the end were fully specified by law, substantive and formal rationality would collapse into the same set of prescriptions for legal affairs. To draw on the "Case of the Confusing Cul-de-Sac" for one last time, a substantively rational judge might have acquitted Jones by looking not at the language of the law,[11] but at the ends that the legislature that passed the breaking and entering statute might have had in mind. He might argue that the legislature was concerned with breaking and entering because this was a common prelude to evils such as vandalism or theft and that they wished to be able to punish those who were interrupted before they had completed the crimes for which they entered. Finding that John Jones did not enter with the intent to engage in any criminal act, this substantively rational judge might acquit. Another substantively rational judge might decide that the legislature's goal was to deter breaking and entering the dwellings of others for any reason. Finding that John Jones could not have been deterred even had he known of the statute because he did not know that the house he was entering was not his own, this substantively rational judge might also acquit.

In each of the preceding cases the judge in interpreting the statute purports to be deciding what end the legislature that enacted that law had in view and is refusing to apply the statute when it does not serve the legislative end. However, by hypothesis neither the statute nor its legislative history suggest any end except the punishment of those who break into the homes of others at night. John Jones clearly did this. In deciding that he should not be punished, our first substantively rational judge is relying on the Judeo-Christian normative ethic as it relates to the moral implications of intent, and the second substantively rational judge is guided by the ethic of utilitarianism. Thus concepts from extralegal ethical systems get infused into the law since they are a reference point for determining what the legislature was about. If the goal is to interpret faithfully the legislative

---

11. Recognized guides to statutory interpretation such as statements in legislative debates explaining the meaning of legislative language might be consulted by the formally rational jurist as part of an internally focused analysis of legislative meaning.

intent, this is not necessarily improper. The legislature probably never contemplated poor John Jones lost in a too familiar cul-de-sac, but if they had, they might well have rewritten the statute to exempt good faith mistakes. Nor is this surprising; the values of judges and legislators are often likely to be rooted in the same extralegal ethical systems.

There are two circumstances in which the substantively rational judge may look to different sources of norms and values from those that influenced the legislature. One is when the cultural milieu in which the legislature acted has been so transformed over time that to be true to what were perhaps the specific understandings of the legislature is to be untrue to the concerns that motivated the legislation. In this situation a substantively rational court may try to discern the concerns of the legislature that enacted the law and interpret the statute so as to best realize those concerns in the context of contemporary culture. For example, the Congress that proposed the Thirteenth, Fourteenth, and Fifteenth Amendments to the Constitution was trying to guarantee political equality for black people and by so doing wipe out the "badge of slavery." They probably did not think that the Fourteenth Amendment would someday entail the destruction of segregated school systems. Indeed, schools in Washington, D.C., whose practices the Congress could have controlled, were segregated at the time the Civil War amendments were passed. Yet by 1954 the effort to guarantee political equality and to stamp out the vestiges of slavery required the destruction of legally segregated school systems. In this context, to be guided by what the lawmakers thought the Fourteenth Amendment entailed for segregated schooling would be to undercut the grander purposes they hoped to accomplish. If the Amendment was to remain an effective vehicle for the abolition of vestiges of slavery, it would have to be interpreted in the light of contemporary culture and not by reference to the normative understandings of a century before.

The second circumstance in which a substantively rational court looks to extralegal norms and values different from those that motivated the legislature is when the court subscribes to a different ethic and is trying to achieve a different substantive goal. Thus in *Lochner* v. *New York,* 198 U.S. 45 (1905) the Supreme Court struck down a state law establishing a 10-hour maximum workday and a 6 day workweek for bakers, holding that because baking was not an especially unhealthful profession, the legislature could not interfere with people's rights to sell their labor. The state legislature was seeking to enact a set of norms grounded in their perception of the nature of professional baking and what the welfare of the workers required. The Court was advancing its conception of freedom of contract, a conception that was closely linked to entrepreneurial values in a capitalist society. Judges, however, are not supposed to substitute their normative views for those of legislatures; therefore, in cases like *Lochner* the process has to be disguised.

Perhaps the simplest solution is to ignore issues or dismiss them without serious consideration when good faith attention to what the law implies might mandate a result inconsistent with substantive goals. Appellate decisions in routine criminal cases suggest that this technique is frequently applied (Davies, 1982). Courts often dismiss in a sentence or two a defendant's possibly substantial objections to the way his case has been processed when it is clear that the defendant has committed the crime charged. Alternatively, evidentiary or procedural errors at trial are acknowledged, but they are dismissed as "harmless," even though to one reading the opinion—and sometimes to dissenting judges— it appears that the error might well have affected the verdict. The other side of this, and equally revealing of a substantive orientation, is that when an appellate court believes that an injustice has been done at trial, it will if necessary seize on relatively trivial errors that are unlikely to have affected the verdict and reverse the case on these grounds.

A second technique is to misinterpret the legislature's intent and claim to be upholding it while in fact embellishing or even subverting it. This was the technique of the *Lochner* majority who found in the language of the Fourteenth Amendment an intent to preclude certain kinds of state interference with the ability of people to set the terms on which they sold their services. Yet there is no reason to believe that drafters of the Fourteenth Amendment had any intention to preclude racially neutral labor regulations like those in *Lochner*, nor is such an intention fairly deducible from the language or history of the amendment.[12]

A third method is to retreat to pseudo-formalism. A court interpreting ambiguous language may pretend it is constrained by the language used when the legislative language could be fairly construed to mean something very different and the legislature obviously meant to attach the different meaning. Or a court may distort reality in order to reach a desired result. In *Lochner*, for example, the legal rule the Court purported to be following was that legislation setting maximum hours of work was an unconstitutional interference with freedom of contract unless there was a valid health-related reason that justified the limitation. Since the majority of the Court found that baking was not an especially unhealthy occupation, it followed that the rule had to be struck down. However, the dissent made it clear that there was substantial evidence that baking was a particularly difficult and unhealthy profession. The majority simply ignored this evidence so that their conclusion appears required by a logical, formal analysis. It is only when we read the dissent that it appears that the decision is controlled not by a true commitment to formalism, but by a desire to achieve substantive ends that are inconsistent with the concerns that motivated the legislature.

In separating formalistic from substantive stances in judging, we do not mean to imply that one style necessarily yields better results or, indeed, is more

---

12. Earlier Supreme Court decisions had extended the scope of the Fourteenth Amendment in this direction, so the *Lochner* majority was building on precedent. To the extent that judges in the *Lochner* majority were actually responding to the fair implications of precedent that they felt constrained by rather than to some extralegal perspective of where the good of society lay, the Court was looking to a recognized source of legal authority in a common law system and there is a formalist element to *Lochner*.

appropriate for a court than the other (cf. Kennedy, 1976; pp. 1710–1711). As we shall see in the discussion that follows, depending on the context in which a law is applied, one or the other style may be more likely to enhance justice or aspects of justice in the sense we have been using that term.

It is also important to note that the separation in styles that we can make at the level of ideal types is far neater than what one finds when the behavior of actual judges is examined. Formalist judges must work with language that is not defined by the legislature but is comprehensible because judges and lawmakers share a community of meaning. Behind this community of meaning are shared extralegal norms including rules of grammar and ethical norms that help a judge understand what a legislature means by the language it uses. Moreover, cases continually arise which are hard because the implications of legal language are not clear, and the formalist judge must do more than reason logically from distinctively legal sources of authority. Even with respect to procedural issues, that special province of formalism, results that appear substantively absurd properly shape the interpretation of legal language, for it is usually reasonable to assume that a legislature did not intend absurd results to follow from procedures it specified. Thus, a judge often cannot understand what a legislature means by certain language unless he shares an extralegal standard that allows certain interpretations to be ruled out because their implications would be silly or intolerable.

A substantively oriented judge on the other hand is still working within the confines of law and legal procedures. As we earlier noted, even if a variety of decisions may be reached on the facts of a case, many decisions that might be possible for a legislature (or a dictator, for that matter) are unavailable to a judge. Similarly, not all plausible justifications for a permissible decision may be advanced by judges. Usually a judge motivated by substantive concerns must at least be able to dress up an opinion—if the case requires one—in formalistic language, and if such dressing up is difficult it may be that the decision is changed. Also substantively oriented judges are likely to proceed formalistically in much of what they do. The role of judge contains a commitment to formalism at its core. Where the implications of legal language and procedures are clear, the substantively oriented judge is likely to accept them even though this results in an outcome that is by reference to some nonlegal standard undesirable. If a judge only drew on nonlegal sources as guides to decisions, he would, in a modern Western society, not be acting like a judge.

Despite the necessary commingling of formalist and substantive tendencies in actual judging, it is helpful to separate the two styles as ideal types. As we shall see next, strong tendencies in these directions when combined with different types of laws can yield legal systems with distinct implications for relations between classes and the quality of justice in society. These systems too are ideal types, but we shall show by way of example that laws in the spirit of such systems do exist, and that actual legal systems are mixtures of laws that tend in several of the directions we identify.

THE QUALITY OF APPLIED LAW

In looking at legislation, we noted that at the extremes it is either status neutral or distributively oriented in character. Building on Chapter 12 and on the foregoing discussion, we can characterize a court's approach as either formalistic or substantive when it is called on to apply legislation. A formalist court is one that approaches law in the way that we describe in Chapter 12 as judicial formalism. Judicial formalism is characterized by a formally rational approach to the interpretive problems arising when courts apply law. This entails two elements that we discussed separately in Chapter 12. The first is close attention to legislative meaning. The law is taken by a formalist court as given and is interpreted in accordance with the logical implications of the statutory language, supplemented where the language is ambiguous, by legislative history, precedent, and other recognized sources of legal meaning. The second is the attempt to reduce legislative meaning to a set of distinctly legal categories that are used to classify behavior and determine its legal implications. In addition, judicial formalism also includes a commitment to procedural regularity regardless of what is in dispute.

It is important to note that these factors taken together do not necessarily guarantee a specific outcome in a particular case. The law is often sufficiently open textured that formalist reasoning does not yield a unique answer to the questions a case poses. What is important is the stance the judge takes toward the law. A formalist judge not only proceeds as described in the preceding paragraph, but is also not influenced in his reasoning by the outcome the interpretive process yields except to the extent that the law or other sources of legal authority specify that the particular outcome is to be taken into account.

A substantive approach, on the other hand, looks, as we have seen, to sources outside the law in determining the legal implications of action. The extralegal sources of authority may be of a social, ethical, or political sort. A court may, as some nineteenth-century courts apparently did (Horwitz, 1977), ask what kinds of rules would best promote industrialization and decide accordingly. It might, in deciding on the constitutionality of Sunday closing law be influenced by its view that Sunday is the Lord's day. And it might in deciding the constitutionality of rules that, in effect, imprison citizens who have committed no crime [*Korematsu* v. *United States,* 323 U.S. 214 (1944)] or in trying alleged subversives (Solzhenitsyn, 1973), be responding to what the political exigencies of the day seem to require.

The extralegal sources of normative authority that a substantively oriented court looks to in applying the law may or may not be the same sources that influenced the legislature in its law-making activity. If the source is not the same, the court may hamper or even forestall a legislative effort to achieve certain goals. At certain points in U.S. history, most notably before the Civil War and in the early New Deal period, crises developed because the Supreme Court in interpreting the Constitution was influenced by a set of extralegal social and ethical values that were antithetical to those that were motivating the legislature. At other points the receptiveness of courts to values other than those that motivated the legislature has been celebrated for its contribution to freedom. Indeed, one institution, the jury trial, is largely predicated on the value of building into the legal system a decision maker that may freely import values from extralegal spheres.

Although cases in which a substantively oriented court seeks to subvert the legislative intention are striking, it is no doubt more common for a court to share the values that motivated the legislature. After all, judges and legislators are both politically sensitive elite decision makers and typically share a common culture. Where a substantively oriented court shares legislative values, decisions are typically outcome-driven. The court strives to achieve the ends that motivated the legislature even when the legislative language, higher law (e.g., the Constitution), or its own procedural requirements do not countenance the desired result. This situation is particularly evident in appellate decisions in criminal cases where courts routinely overlook procedural and constitutional flaws when they think the defendant is in fact guilty (Davies, 1982; Lempert & Saltzburg, 1982, p. 2).

In the discussion that follows we identify different ideal types of applied law and examine their implications for social justice. To do this without writing another book, we must make a number of simplifying assumptions. First, we assume that a substantively oriented court shares the legislature's extralegal values, and that these shared values include a concern for equality where legislative influence is more or less equal and a concern for the dominant class's interests where great inequalities of influence exist. The substantively oriented court differs from a formalistic court in that in seeking to achieve these and other shared values, it is relatively unconstrained by the features that define judicial formalism, although in writing opinions it may appear to bow to them. Because the substantive courts we consider aim at ends the legislature seeks to achieve, ordinarily these courts will decide cases in the same way as formalistic courts which are, at the level of the ideal, oriented solely to legal norms. We shall ignore such cases and focus on situations in which the judicial stance makes a difference.

We assume also that in a society in which people have more or less equal influence, the parties also have more or less equal competence in making claims on the legal system, and that in societies where political influence is very unequal, legal competence similarly varies.[13] Thus where political and social equality prevails people will be generally familiar with their legal rights, will know how to pursue claims on their own, will know when to turn to lawyers, and will be able to retain legal counsel where necessary. In highly unequal societies access to law will be closely associated with other indices of social power.

---

13. This assumption collapses one requisite of legal autonomy with one of the dimensions that distinguishes the four types of legal endowments that we specified earlier in this chapter. This congruence is not necessary, but we expect that as an empirical matter a correlation between the two is likely.

Finally, we are concerned here only with what the legal system—by which we mean the law and the way it is applied—implies for individual rights and for the distribution of power and welfare across classes or other identifiable social groups. This concern means that we are at least as interested in the run-of-the-mill adjudication that occurs in ordinary trial courts as we are in the less frequent but more visible decisions that emerge on appeal. Also we do not concern ourselves with aspects of the law as applied that have no systematic distributive consequences.

If we cross-classify the four types of endowments that legislatures can create (Table 13.2) with the different stances that courts can take when applying them, we get the following possibilities:

TABLE 13.2
The Quality of Applied Law

Type of Legislative Endowment	Judicial Stance Toward Legislation	
	Substantive	*Formalistic*
Class-oriented endowments	Unrestrained class domination (1)	Bounded class domination (2)
Differentially accessible general endowments	Illusory rights (3)	Formal autonomy (4)
Equally accessible general endowments	Egalitarian justice (5)	Pure autonomy (6)
Welfare-oriented endowments	Substantive justice (7)	Formal justice (8)

At the outset it is important to note one distinction that pervades this table. Recall from Chapter 12 that formalism is a core component of legal autonomy in the law application process. The other two components, equal competence and neutral norms, are in this table aspects of the four types of legal endowments we identified earlier. *Formalism by itself is sufficient for partial autonomy.* A legal system characterized by judicial formalism is, other things being equal, more autonomous than one in which substantive adjudication is common. Note also that legal autonomy may sound like a good thing, but its full implications should be considered before making value judgments.

Unrestrained Class Domination

Cell 1 of Table 13.2 describes the situation that exists when one class openly dominates both the legislative and judicial processes.[14] In such a system laws are passed to promote the interests of the dominant class, and they are interpreted by courts with the same end in view. If it should happen that a law designed to

---

14. We speak throughout of a dominant class, but it may be that groups with somewhat different class interests share dominance.

advance the interests of the dominant class threatens to run counter to those interests, the law will be interpreted to avoid these untoward results.

For example, a powerful immigrant group may choose to move less powerful natives from rich farmlands to barren territory. The move may be formalized in a treaty by which the chiefs of the native groups agree to trade their fertile land for the new territory. If the legal system is of our first type, a suit by a native seeking title to his ancestral homeland on the ground that he did not consent to the treaty and that the consent of his chief was coerced will be rejected by the courts even if all other land transfers in the society require the consent of the landowner and are void when consent is coerced. On the other hand, should valuable minerals be discovered on the land given to the natives, they will be again moved, and should they seek to resist the move in court, the treaty guarantees will be found in some way deficient. For example, a court might argue that the presence of substantial mineral wealth meant that the guarantees were void because of mutual mistake. The appropriate remedy will, however, not be the return of the native's original property as would have happened had a contract between two members of the dominant group been voided for mutual mistake. Instead, the remedy will be to find land as valueless as the original land was thought to have been, and to move the natives to it. Of course, had it been the rich farmlands that yielded even more valuable minerals, the native's claim that the treaty should be voided for mutual mistake would be dismissed out of hand. This is because a court in this cell does not look first to what the facts and the law imply for the outcome, but instead decides what outcome is most in the interest of the dominant class and finds facts or interprets the law so as to yield that outcome.

A system in which law is both enacted and applied in such a purely instrumental fashion is one of *unrestrained class domination*. The legal system in such a society is insofar as it applies to transactions between classes a sham. It is a convenient form of governance, designed to give the appearance of legality to a use of state power that is *entirely* predictable from the relative class positions of the parties to the dispute. In its pure form, the legal system defined by cell 1 is the legal system of a tyranny which, in fact, rules by force.

Bounded Class Domination

Cell 2, which we call *bounded class domination*, is more interesting. As in cell 1, legislation is openly designed to advance the interests of the dominant class. Unlike cell 1, though, the decision to proceed through rules is respected in the judicial process, and rules, even those enacted to advance one class's interests, have a certain generality to them. In particular, even as applied they only order behavior with reference to categories and in ways that the legislature has specified in advance, and they can only be applied through legal procedures. The fair application of these rules will not always leave those of higher status in a dominant position and will limit the ways in which the wishes of the powerful can be realized. E. P. Thompson (1975) makes the point convincingly in his study of the Black Act, an English law that made capital a variety of offenses that were common in forested areas, such as stalking deer in disguise at night, poaching hares or fish while armed and disguised, and cutting down planted trees. Although the acts were bloody, enforcement was far more restrained than many landed gentry would have liked. At a minimum it was necessary to prove guilt in a court of law. Knowing that someone is guilty does not necessarily mean that the offense can be proven. Tactics that might have been more effective in preventing poaching such as the abduction and slaying of suspected poachers were precluded once the decision was made to proceed through law.

Even slave law that validates the dominance of the master class may as part of the scheme of domination accord rights to slaves that are respected in court. Marc Tushnett (1975) in an erudite article on the antebellum South shows how the ultimately unsuccessful attempt to define slaves simultaneously as chattel, personal property, and, in some respects, human beings, resulted in a set of rules that restrained the general power of whites over blacks and, in some measure, the power of masters over their own property. Eugene Genovese (1972, p. 36) describes the particularly poignant story of a slave named Will, who had attempted to run away from an overseer who was trying to whip him. The overseer got a gun and tried to shoot Will. Will killed the overseer instead and pleaded innocent by reason of self-defense. The Supreme Court of North Carolina sustained Will's plea, but fearing extralegal retaliation Will's master sold him and his wife to a slave owner in Mississippi. A few years later the wife arranged to have herself sold back to her former master, but Will was not with her. He had killed a fellow slave in Mississippi, and he had been tried for murder, convicted, and executed. As his wife recalled, "Will sho'ly had hard luck. He killed a white man in North Carolina and got off, and then was hung for killing a nigger in Mississippi." Formal justice triumphed in both instances.

Systems of bounded class domination are found in societies in which marked stratification is so entrenched that substantial inequalities are taken for granted. There is no need for the dominant class to act as if its supremacy was not preordained or to eschew using the legal system to institutionalize the dominant order. At the same time, there are pressures on the dominant class to rule through law. This may in part be because a measure of legitimacy attaches to the rule of law even when the legal order perpetuates inequality. It may also, and in larger measure, be because law has become the accepted way of regulating relationships within the dominant classes, and it is natural to use the same device to regulate relations between classes. In regulating behavior within classes, the legal system is largely autonomous of class interests because social class does not substantially differentiate the parties. This autonomy and, in particular, the formalistic approach to law application that is its hallmark, carries over to some degree when intraclass differences are in issue.

Illusory Rights

Cell 3 defines a system in which differentially accessible general endowments are interpreted and applied by a substantively oriented court. We call such a system a system of *illusory rights*. Where such a system exists the decision of the dominant class to proceed by creating differentially accessible endowments rather than class oriented endowments is a kind of mystification. Rights are apparently open to all, but, in fact, they are largely accessible only by those in the dominant class, and so the enforcement of those rights serves to perpetuate the existing system of domination. Rights to private property in a markedly unequal society have something of this character as does the right to sue in court when this is, in practice, conditioned on the ability to pay substantial lawyer and filing fees.

From the point of view of the dominant element the problem with differentially accessible general endowments is that the *in principle* openness of rights means that on occasion those from the dominated groups will be in a position to assert rights against those who are ordinarily on top. This flaw may be "corrected" by a substantively oriented judiciary, that is, a judiciary that values the same ends as the dominant class and will sacrifice formalism to obtain them.

In these circumstances rights prove illusory. When the less-advantaged attempt to assert them they disappear, for they were not meant to be asserted by the less advantaged in the first instance. For example, a society may purport to value freedom of speech, and cloaked with this freedom, those who control the media establishment may disseminate whatever message they choose. But when less powerful groups through their own media try to organize unions, promote pacifism, or suggest revolution the right to free speech may be reinterpreted so that it does not apply where there is a clear and present danger to the national security and the likelihood of imminent harm may be found even though a fair reading of the facts does not justify the conclusion. Thus, the desirability of the outcome from an extralegal political perspective determines how the facts and law are manipulated to yield a decision.

Pseudo-formalism of this sort is likely because the decision to proceed through status neutral law in the first instance probably reflects the belief that there are advantages to be gained from the appearance of neutrality. Pseudo-formalism helps preserve this appearance. The illusion of neutral rights can, of course, be heightened if the rights of the less advantaged are genuinely respected in situations where this carries no implications for the relative power of contending classes.

To some extent laws creating differentially accessible general endowments are found in contemporary capitalist and socialist states. However, in the case of the Western democracies at least, the pure type is too extreme to capture what is going on. Class structures are not so extreme; and it is not clear that most rights were established largely to advantage superior classes. Moreover, only some courts some of the time interpret rights differently depending on the status of the claimant, so rights in the system are not fully or generally illusory.

Formal Autonomy

Cell 4 describes a type of law we call *formal autonomy*. Such systems are like systems of illusory rights in that legal endowments are created with full knowledge that they are differentially accessible. They differ in that once legal endowments are created, all those in a position to assert a right can enjoy its benefits regardless of whether they are members of the initially privileged classes. Systems of formal autonomy tend to reproduce the existing class structure, but it is a permeable structure that is reproduced. By acquiring wealth and power despite a legal system skewed in favor of those who are already well off, the initially disadvantaged can move into the advantaged strata. Those of higher status can similarly slip if they fail to take advantage of the benefits that are specially accessible to them. Such transpositions of places have few if any implications for the distribution of power between classes, for the class system is more or less indifferent to the specific people who occupy the dominant or subordinate positions in society or the backgrounds from which they come (Balbus, 1977, Pashukanis, 1980).

Formal autonomy is often associated with law under capitalism. Positions are open to talent and there is considerable movement of people across positions, but it unquestionably helps to start life as a well-off member of society. Furthermore, the system of rights is structured so that those who have power can use the legal system to reinforce and legitimate the power they choose to exercise. The legal system of the United States in the late nineteenth century most resembled a system of formal autonomy, and residues of that system are still very much with us.

Egalitarian Justice

Cell 5, which we call *egalitarian justice*, describes a system in which legal endowments created by status neutral laws are in theory and to a large extent, in practice, equally accessible to all. Where egalitarian justice exists there can be no gross inequalities that deny large numbers of people access to rights that are in principle theirs or the ability to invoke the law effectively. In an absolutely egalitarian society, cell 5 would collapse with cell 6 because everyone would have the same access to rights and a formalist jurisprudence would treat everyone asserting a particular legal right or duty the same. Absolute equality is, of course, achieved nowhere, a fact we recognized when we constructed our endowment types.

In the less than ideal world the difference between the social conditions of a society that can expect the egalitarian justice of cell 5 and one that is likely to be characterized by the illusory rights of cell 3 is one of degree. In cell 3 disparities in social status and legal competence are so extreme that some groups are largely precluded from enjoying rights apparently extended by the legal system. In cell 5 differences in social status are small and if neutral endowments are not in fact equally accessible, they are more or less so. Indeed, in such a society we may expect welfare-oriented legislation, like laws providing free legal services to the poor, that provides nothing of value except access to the legal process.

The most striking difference between law in cell 5 and that in cell 3 is not, however, in the quality of rights available nor is it even in the ability of people to take advantage of the law. Rather, it is in the attitude courts take when hearing cases that involve parties of unequal status. Where rights are illusory it is because substantively oriented courts deny claims that would be honored if the social status of the litigants was reversed. Where egalitarian justice prevails, a sub-stantively oriented court, equally aware of differences in social status, but re-sponding to a different set of extralegal normative imperatives acts in almost the opposite fashion. It seeks to ameliorate some of the advantages that the better off enjoy because of their social status. This follows from our assumption that courts (and legislatures) value equality in societies where equality of influence is more or less achieved. Cases consistent with this assumption are in fact encountered.

Everyone, for example, has a right to enter into contracts, but more powerful parties generally enjoy important advantages in contracting with those who are weaker. These include better access to information, access to many alternative contracting partners, familiarity with legal negotiations, and the ability to wait for a better deal because immediate needs are not pressing. These and similar advantages can, however, be offset if a court is willing to take the contracting situation into account in deciding if or in what ways contractual agreements are binding. Where egalitarian justice prevails, courts do this by considering the bargaining situation that would have existed had the parties negotiated as equals. Thus contracts may be voided because one party with special access to infor-mation did not share it with another, and in the extreme cases bargains that are on their face too one-sided will be struck down as unconscionable. Recall the judge in Chapter 8 who refused to compensate the garage mechanic for the repairs he had made to the car he sold a Mexican-American. From one perspective the judge ignored the law governing the rights of parties to contracts, but from another perspective he was enforcing the contract the parties might have reached had they been in a more or less equal bargaining position.

In the area of contracts, courts have been most active in constructing "as if" equalities in their interpretation of "contracts of adhesion." *Contracts of adhesion* are contracts between parties who are so unequally situated that one party to a bargain has little choice but to accept a deal on the terms the other offers. We are all familiar with contracts of adhesion, for we are parties to many of them every year. Look at the print on the back of the next ticket you buy for a train, plane, or boat, or check on the back of your motel door for the details of the management's liability should a thief break into your room and steal your valuables. Do you really consent to the limitations on liability that these forms state? Do you have any ability to bargain over the terms? If you were chartering a plane or filling a hotel for a convention, you might, but not if you are a lone customer. Persist in objecting to the imposed terms and you will walk to the next town and have no place to sleep.

Some courts, responding to the obvious inequalities of bargaining power that underlie such contracts, have declared particularly onerous clauses void as against public policy and have held that ambiguous language should be interpreted against the interest of the party who dictated the terms. Judge Clark, a distinguished federal judge, nicely summed up for one subset of such cases a result that might be frequent in a regime of egalitarian justice. "An insurance contract," Judge Clark said, "is interpreted just like any other contract, except the insurance company always loses."[15] Similar substantively rational decision making may occur on the criminal side when the poor are not punished as seriously as the wealthy would be for similar acts because their initial disadvantage makes their criminal behavior more understandable. Thus decisions that embody egalitarian justice occur, although they do not predominate, in the courts of the modern welfare state.

Pure Autonomy

Cell 6 defines a system whose prerequisites we laid out in Chapter 12. We call it *pure autonomy*. In the ideal case where absolute equality prevails in society the outcomes of a purely autonomous system are pure procedural justice. We discuss this possibility in the final section of this chapter. In its real-world approximations pure autonomy occurs in societies that are more or less equal when courts accept the inequality that exists and enforce rights and obligations accordingly. The important difference between the pure autonomy of cell 6 and the egalitarian justice of cell 5 is that in the former unlike the latter courts do not try to "correct" in deciding cases for the status disparities that persist in a more or less equal society.

There are two important differences between law in this cell and the formally autonomous law of cell 4. They both have to do with what it means for legal endowments to be differentially accessible. First, differential accessibility is a function of the rights that are extended. Thus the protections accorded private property are available only to those who own property in the first instance. This type of difference is tolerable in systems of both pure and formal autonomy. But in systems where autonomy is only formal, the degree of inequality is by

---

15. Reported by Professor Charles Alan Wright, a former clerk to Judge Clark, to a first year class in civil procedure at the Harvard Law School in the academic year 1964–1965. The quotation may be inexact and the precise date is forgotten. The rule was called by Professor Wright "Judge Clark's law." The occasion for the pronouncement was to avoid breaking up a dinner party when two law review students who were present proposed to retire to prepare for their insurance law exam. One can only imagine what the professor grading the exam must have thought when two of his students cited such a rule and attributed it to one of the country's leading judicial authorities on insurance law.

definition much greater than in systems of pure autonomy. Thus the enjoyment of rights and the burdens of duties are substantially more skewed by class in the formally autonomous system.

Second, differential accessibility is a function of one's ability to make a claim in court. Thus a property owner whose property is wrongfully repossessed to satisfy an alleged debt has no effective property right if he cannot hire a lawyer to object to the repossession and bring suit. State or private programs may, however, equalize people's access to court by establishing centers for informal justice or by paying for attorney's fees, court costs, and the like. Such subsidies do not improve the general position of a less well-off party, for they do not improve his social position or expand his stock of rights.[16] But the subsidies make it possible for less well-off parties to claim in practice whatever legal rights are theirs in theory. Subsidized access to law is, we would argue, necessary to pure autonomy and antithetical to formal autonomy. In both types of systems inequalities may affect the arrangements that parties enter into, but where pure autonomy prevails there is a guarantee that the privately made arrangements will be enforced as such. In other words, social differences in a purely autonomous system affect the arrangements parties make between them and may systematically advantage the more powerful, but the advantage will stem from social power generally and not from superior access to the legal system.

This is why the funding of legal services to the poor is often such a hot political issue. Easy access to legal services threatens to transform a system of formal autonomy into one of pure autonomy or even egalitarian justice. This is no small redistribution of power. Pure autonomy like formal autonomy and egalitarian justice is part of the mix of law found in the modern welfare state. It is perhaps most prevalent in such common law fields as tort, property, contract law, and criminal law.

Substantive Justice

Cell 7 describes the law that arises when a legislature enacts laws directed toward particular goals, and the judiciary, responding to the same values that motivated the legislature, takes a substantively oriented stance toward the statutes. Although legislation can further almost any end a legislative majority approves of, we will focus on laws designed to reallocate benefits from the better off to the less well off and thus increase justice according to Rawls's difference principle. Where a court interprets such statutes with the legislature's redistributive ends in view, the scheme is what we call *substantive justice*.

For example, suppose a legislature enacts a public housing program designed to provide decent subsidized housing to poor people. Such programs commonly

---

16. Except, of course, by adding a right to legal services, but the value of this right depends entirely on the range of other rights that exist.

provide for a local housing authority that oversees the construction of housing projects and then rents apartments to low-income tenants. The housing authority might, as most authorities do, rent its units with a month-to-month lease that, in accordance with local landlord–tenant law, allows either party to terminate the lease on 30 days notice for any reason whatsoever. Suppose a tenant whose lease has been so terminated alleges that she is being discharged for her efforts to organize tenants into a union that can pressure the authority to act less like a bureaucratic landlord and more in the tenants' interests. Tenants' unions appear consistent with the goal of the statute, which is to improve the position of the poor in respect to housing; so if the woman is being evicted for attempting to found a tenants' union, the goals of the statute are being subverted. A substantively oriented court will read the Public Housing Act or more general principles of constitutional law as prohibiting the local authority from evicting the woman or acting in other ways that are inconsistent with the overriding goal of the statute even though neither source of law specifically addresses the issue and the Housing Act contemplates housing authorities that rely on local law to manage evictions [cf. *Thorpe* v. *Housing Authority of the City of Durham*, 393 U.S. 268 (1969)].

When legislatures attempt to reallocate wealth to the needy and courts subscribing to the same ethic cooperate by reading reallocative statutes so as to maximally advance the interest of the intended beneficiaries, we have a system oriented to substantive justice. Of course, reallocations may flow in the opposite direction, for welfare-oriented endowments are not necessarily designed to enhance the welfare of the worst off. If they are not, and a judiciary that shares the legislature's values interprets the legislation in the light of those values, marked injustice as measured by Rawls's difference principle can result. The law as applied will tend to worsen rather than correct for existing inequalities.

In the extreme, there is the danger of going full circle and returning to cell 1. This will occur if the group that enjoys legislative ascendency is during its period of triumph able to redistribute wealth sufficiently so that the condition of more or less equal influence that supports welfare-oriented endowments no longer pertains. What is more likely, however, is not the transformation of society that would occur if the legal system became overtly class-oriented, but the consistent exclusion of certain interests from legislative majorities, with the result that these minority interests are sacrificed to the majority's self-interested vision of the common good. For example, legislation might criminalize membership in the Communist party or make membership in the Communist party a basis for denying passports. When a court that shares the majority's values takes a substantive stance toward such legislation, we have what we may call unrestrained majority domination, or the tyranny of the majority. The dominated and dominating groups may or may not be identifiable social classes. If they are, domination is likely to be across many areas of social life. If they are not, domination may be along one dimension. In either case the possibility of majoritarian tyranny should alert us to the fact that even in a more or less equal society in which distributive justice is valued, the ideological argument for a substantively oriented judiciary is fraught with danger. If the political climate changes, the jurisprudential habits that are engendered by such a regime give courts a license to promote injustice.

Formal Justice

Just as cell 2 dampens the substantive tendencies that make law in cell 1 a force for tyranny, so can the formalism of cell 8 limit the justice enhancing effects of legislation that in cell 7 is a potent force for change. For example, in the case of the tenants' union leader we have just described, a formalistic court would not look to the political and ethical values that it shares with the legislature that enacted the public housing laws. Instead, the judge would look at the means or form by which the legislature sought to accomplish its end. The primary means was by creating local housing authorities to stand in the place of private landlords in renting apartments to poor people. Since the authorities take the form (legal category) of private landlords, a formalistic court might hold that they have the private landlord's right to evict anyone, tenants' union leader or inveterate troublemaker, so long as the statutory notice is given.[17] Such a court would not attempt to look behind the law of *tenancies at will* to see whether, when applied to public housing tenants, it furthered the values that underlie public housing or the purposes of the public housing statute.[18]

---

17. Complexities arise if the legislative history or some other recognized guide to statutory interpretation spells out the social, political, or ethical values the law is designed to promote. If a court relies on such an aid—like a preamble that says the purpose of a statute is to provide better housing for poor people—to reach a conclusion regarding permissible grounds for eviction is it reasoning formalistically or substantively? The answer turns on the extent to which it is permissible to rely on such guides given the clarity of the legislative language and on whether the court is motivated by its interpretation of the language of the preamble and about its views of the weight such language should bear or whether it is motivated by some extralegal sense of where justice or wise policy lies. In other words, the court is reasoning substantively if it would reach the opposite decision if its values were different. We can, however, seldom know whether this is the case, so we are often unable to determine empirically, at least in individual cases, whether a decision is controlled by substantive or formal considerations. Often, however, when we look at a series of cases, consistencies or the lack thereof in the ethical content of decisions and the use made of statutory language or guides to interpretation allow us to identify some judges as being oriented more to formal justice and others as moved more often by substantive concerns. In addition, the formalistic judge will in the ideal case seek to reduce the implications of legislation to manipulable rights, duties, and other legal categories in the way we describe in Chapter 12.

The fact that we may not always be able to neatly label decisions as formal or substantive does not threaten the basic analysis advanced. The formalistic judge is still subjectively more constrained by legal language and categories with the restraints this implies than is the substantive judge. The fact that there is genuine debate about the weight that is appropriately given to various guides to statutory construction when statutory language is of varying clarity is one reason why a commitment to legal formality will not necessarily yield a unique decision. What will result, however, is a decision that reflects judgments about the weight to be accorded statutory language and various guides to interpretation rather than judgments about the most desirable outcome given some extralegal normative perspective.

18. It would, however, also consider constitutional requirements. A formalistic interpretation of the law and precedent might lead a court to conclude that the authority's actions were unconstitutional.

This does not mean that law in cell 8 cannot enhance justice in the sense we are using this term. It can to the extent that the legislature clearly mandates justice-enhancing redistributions. In the example we have been pursuing, hundreds of thousands of poor tenants who refrained from rocking the boat and did not ask of the authority more than it was willing to give would benefit from subsidized housing. However, the justice-enhancing aspect of the legislation would be limited by the forms the legislature chose to follow and the specific endowments that were given. For this reason we think of the law that results from the intersection of a formalistic stance toward law and welfare-oriented endowments as "formal justice."

MIXED JUSTICE

We have often noted that the types we create in this book through cross-classification are ideal and may not be found in any actual system. In the instant case we think the different types of law may be identified—sometimes in their pure forms—in actual legal systems. However, no legal system is purely of one type. Instead, different stances toward law may be found within the bounds of a single legal system. Thus in Nazi Germany the law relating to the affairs of Jews may in its application have fit nicely into cell 1, but the law relating to contracts between Germans may have fit into cell 4 and in some instances into cell 5 or 6. In the United States one may argue that laws representing all the types we have defined exist now or at one time could have been found.

The Anglo-American legal system is, however, special in one respect. The institution of the jury guarantees that in wide areas of law tendencies toward judicial formalism will to some extent be counterbalanced by substantive tendencies. These tendencies need not, of course, reflect the substantive values that motivated the legislature. Consider, for example, the role that juries played in worker injury cases or the role that they continue to play in auto accident cases as discussed in Chapter 5. In these examples jury justice apparently advances the interests of the less advantaged parties. This is not necessarily the case. Recall that extralegal substantive concerns motivated southern juries in the 1950s and 1960s to acquit whites in the face of overwhelming evidence that they had beaten or killed black people.

The situation can be similar when judges interpret law. To simplify our discussion, we have thus far assumed that substantively oriented judges share the values that underlie legislative policies. This need not be the case, and institutional arrangements like lifetime judicial tenure work to ensure that a segment of the judiciary will not at any given point in time share the legislature's values. Where values are not shared, a substantively oriented court may pronounce rules that are inconsistent with or even opposed to those of the legislative majority.

Yet there are limits on what a judiciary that does not share the legislature's values can do to thwart the will of the majority, limits so substantial that one of the leading students of the Supreme Court, Alexander Bickel (1962), was led to call the judiciary the "Least Dangerous Branch." Perhaps the most substantial limit is that courts ultimately do not command armies; they depend on the cooperation of the other branches for enforcing their orders. But this naked limit on the judiciary's power is seldom apparent, for courts almost never escalate conflicts with the other branches to the point that raw power is an issue. The judicial role ultimately demands deference to insistent political forces. This is because judges always purport to be applying laws that may be changed by nonjudicial processes. If the laws are sufficiently clear, a judge will almost always comply. Thus a substantively oriented court with values different from the legislature's may gut a statute by interpreting it to mean almost the opposite of what the legislature intended. Yet if the legislature reenacts the law to make its purposes inescapably clear, the court will usually enforce the revised law as written. Judges acknowledge the legislature's right to have the last word, and our respect for courts depends to some extent on this acknowledgment.

Within these limits, however, courts have substantial leeway to promote their own substantive agendas. A legislature may be deeply divided on an issue, and it may be impossible to get a majority to pass any new law. In these circumstances the judicial interpretation of a statute will stand whether or not it accords with the values of the majority that originally drafted and passed the law. Furthermore, judicial decisions, particularly when they appear to be a fair reading of the law and evidence, are accepted by many as legitimate and help shape the popular conception of where justice lies. Thus courts motivated by different values from those of the legislative majority may limit a statutory scheme by a formalist interpretation. Judicial formalism does not obviously advance the court's own values and, perhaps for this reason, seems to mute opposition that might exist if the court acted with specific reference to an antimajoritarian substantive agenda. Moreover, some judicial action may not be overturned by simple legislative majorities. This is most often the case when courts are interpreting constitutions that can be amended only by some supramajoritarian process. When the difficulties of overturning a court decision are coupled with an authoritative text so open textured that its various provisions can mean almost anything, a substantively oriented judiciary has the opportunity to pronounce binding rules that advance values quite different from those to which the majority of the moment subscribes. Such rules may be justice enhancing in the Rawlsian sense, or they may be just the opposite.

The issues that arise when courts, either through judicial lawmaking or under the guise of fact finding, respond to substantive concerns that differ from those of the legislature are fascinating, but we do not have the space to pursue them further here. The purpose of our brief introduction of these issues, together with our more extended general discussion of the qualities of different types of law, is to stress how important it is, in viewing any legal system, to study systematically the ways in which institutional arrangements affect how courts apply law and the social implications of law as applied.

THE PROSPECTS FOR CHANGE: RISKS AND GAINS

The American legal order, as we have just pointed out, is not a pure type. Yet some species of law are more predominant than others. In particular, over the past half century, especially with regard to the distribution of social and economic goods, the dominant tendency has been toward redistributive welfare-oriented laws. The new laws do not, however, all tend in the same direction. Some seem likely to increase existing inequalities, many seem designed to reduce inequality, and some seem aimed at improving the general interest with little attention to how welfare is distributed among groups or classes. Thus we have the Reagan "tax reform" of 1981 which left the wealthy better off relative to the poor than they had been previously. We have numerous transfer programs that like the food stamp program or public housing enhance the relative status of the poor. And we have programs like those regulating toxic dumps that appear to be in almost everyone's interest.

The allocative aspect of legal rules has gained new prominence not only in areas like civil rights law, but in more mundane areas such as automobile accidents and worker's compensation. It is a movement that from a Rawlsian perspective has mixed implications for social justice. It involves not only potential gains, but potential losses as well. In the final section of this chapter, we discuss some of the prospects and risks facing those who would use law as an instrument of social justice.

LEGAL ARRANGEMENTS: LAW AND THE ENDS OF JUSTICE

We saw in Chapter 9 that in John Rawls's theory social justice is treated as a product of the arrangement of rules and institutions. What we have just been discussing is a set of such arrangements at the societal level. We call it the "legal system" and our ideal types have been designed to illustrate the themes that may predominate in particular societies at particular points in time.

Liberty Interests

To focus on the situation we know best, the American legal order as it is presently constituted comes fairly close to achieving the first principle of justice as defined by John Rawls. It secures a good deal of the basic individual liberties for citizens, both liberty of conscience and political liberty; and its legal institutions guard against the possible encroachments of a police state. The movement to enfranchise blacks which we examined in Chapter 11 removed what had been until recently the most glaring imperfection. But despite these virtues, the system is by no means perfect. One great danger to the equal distribution of basic liberties is, as Chapter 10 points out, the potential for economic inequality to encroach on rights. A related danger is that the level of welfare in some segments of society is below the minimum needed for self-respect and meaningful political rights. Finally, there are still identifiable social groups, such as immigrant aliens, whose members lack full political rights.

The Trend Toward Equality

When we turn from liberty interests to equality interests and Rawls's second principle of justice, imperfections mount. The lack of a fair opportunity structure and large inequalities of welfare that are not justified by the difference principle are serious problems with which the legal order is just beginning to deal.

When a society is unequal to begin with, the move toward equality through law is problematic because, as we saw in Table 13.1, relative equality (as opposed to gross inequality) is necessary for both equally accessible general endowments and welfare-oriented endowments. The former tend to preserve a more or less equal status quo in which people rise and fall according to their ability rather than because of some ascribed status. The latter can take status into account, with the goal of eliminating status differences.

It might seem that the only way to achieve equality is through revolution rather than by law, yet the rise of modern welfare democracies tends to belie this. We shall not at this point attempt even a brief history of how this could happen, but a few speculations are in order.

To begin, the absolute wealth and power of those in the lower social ranks has increased substantially over the years and their aggregate power relative to the higher classes has almost certainly increased as well. Consider, for example, the implications of some well-known developments. The advance of capitalism created competition for labor, thereby increasing its value. Changes in the way warfare was conducted made the ability to conscript masses of men and hold their allegiance essential to military success. The development of specialized labor forces and a monetary economy opened up numerous opportunities for small businesses which could become independent bases of power. The possibility of migration to or within underdeveloped countries further increased the value of labor and allowed those who migrated to set themselves up as land-owning farmers or in businesses that served the growing farming class. Education, spurred by the value of an educated work force and literate consumers, added to the knowledge of the lower classes and made possible the widespread dissemination of ideas that threatened to mobilize them for concerted action. In short, the technological and social developments associated with the rise of capitalism not only destroyed the old system of feudal privileges, but it also dispersed power in society, creating a powerful bourgeoisie and a potentially powerful working class.

The increase in the aggregate power of the lower ranks and the demise of traditional dependency relationships made government more problematic. One option that took hold because it seemed to work was the attempt to establish legitimacy. In the political arena this involved first giving leading citizens and then giving almost all citizens a role in government as electors. In the legal arena this involved regulation through apparently status neutral laws and judicial formalism, the result being a regime of formal autonomy. This as we have seen tends from a systemic point of view to preserve existing disparities, but it also allows both upward and downward mobility, and it permits those of lesser rank to stake out positions vis-à-vis the higher classes that are legally protected.

From this point the trend toward greater equality has been an iterative process. With increased power comes the ability to use force and the threat of force. In the United States labor no doubt benefited both from the costs they could inflict on industry and third parties through strikes and from the specter of European revolutions. The spread of the franchise without regard to wealth and the consequent competition for the voting allegiance of the less well off has also contributed. Promises have been made and kept to those on the lowest rungs of society. This in turn increases their power and gives force to demands for further improvements. The rise of modern Communist and Socialist states has kept the issue of class inequality at the forefront of the political process. Ideology has also been important. Although the mechanisms by which ideologies rise and flourish are poorly understood, the idea of equality has undoubtedly been a driving force in modern social life.[19]

This capsule description of some trends over several centuries may read as if we mean to suggest that we are in the midst of a inexorable movement toward increased equality in social life. This is not our conclusion. We should not be deceived by our ability to make sense of history. It is only in retrospect that trends appear inevitable. There is no guarantee that the patterns we describe will continue into the future.[20]

---

19. Note that even if we have accurately described a general trend, it may still be the case that some groups have been left out, and that the general increase in social wealth has made them *relatively* less powerful and relatively poorer with respect to average levels of power and well-being in society than their counterparts were several centuries ago.

20. In particular, it is possible that material circumstances are less conducive to equality (including equal liberty) than they were a century ago. Modern weaponry makes the allegiance of the masses less important militarily than it was when fire power had a closer relation to the number of troops that could be mustered. They also make a military coup more of a threat and a popular revolt less of a threat to those who control power in modern states. Techniques of social organization and communication that give those who govern direct access to masses of people, as well as the government's ability to target threats to people, may make the need to maintain the general legitimacy of government less important than it once was. These techniques also allow governmental power to be further removed physically (the movement of power from local to state to federal government) and psychologically (the development of bureaucracy) from the people and in these senses may also tend to limit the power of the masses. If these speculations are sound, the structure of institutions, like democratic procedures for choosing those in power, and ideologies, like the ideal of equality, are increasingly important for maintaining the freedom we enjoy and for the future enhancement of social equality. To the extent that ideologies change or the workings of democratic processes allow tyrannical majorities to control the government, liberty and the advance of equality are accordingly threatened.

Law as an Instrument for Equality

Consider the situation of the United States. Considerable inequality exists and with it disparities of political and social power. Those on top have both the potential for disparate influence and incentives to resist changes that make them absolutely, and maybe even relatively, worse off. Indeed, they not only stand to gain from changes that do not give anything to the disadvantaged, but they may gain by exploiting the few goods the disadvantaged possess.[21] How in such a society may law be used to open up opportunities for the worst off and otherwise increase their enjoyment of valued goods, actions that following Rawls, will be justice-enhancing so long as basic liberties are not sacrificed in the process.

Three conditions must be met if law is to be an effective force for increased equality in social life. First, the legal system must in large measure be insulated from the special pleadings of those who are better off. Second, legal norms must aim at reducing status differences and at transferring wealth and power from the better to the worse off.[22] Third, such norms must be able to penetrate the existing socioeconomic structure and bring about the changes they aim at.

---

21. Other things being equal, in a society where one person has 10 units of absolute pleasure and another 5, one would expect the person on top to approve of a change that gives each person 11 units of pleasure. Consistent with this, it appears that movements toward increased equality fare best when the "pie" is increasing for all. However, at some point satisfactions may attach to differences in relative positions and the difficulty of judging absolute well-being may lead those on top to believe that increased equality is absolutely harmful. For example, in one affirmative action suit a white worker sought to overturn a plan that admitted black workers with less seniority to an in-plant craft training program ahead of him [*United Steelworkers* v. *Weber*, 443 U.S. 193 (1979)]. He probably felt that this effort to enhance interracial equality hurt him. Yet the in-plant program had been established because the local craft unions from which the company had previously recruited its craft workers had historically barred blacks thus precluding them from high-paying skilled positions. The white plaintiff was seeking to enhance his salary and position by getting into a program that would not have existed but for a history of discrimination against blacks. Clearly, he had not been made worse off by this development. Indeed, while blacks with low seniority were admitted to the in-plant program ahead of whites with greater seniority, whites were admitted separately according to their seniority. In the long run, the plaintiff would be made better off by the movement for enhanced equality because he would eventually have an opportunity that otherwise would not have existed. Nevertheless, the case he brought suggests he felt victimized by what had occurred.
22. An exception exists according to Rawls when these differences improve the lot of the better off. *Thus when we discuss the movement toward equality as justice-enhancing, we intend to implicitly include the limitation on movement toward equality implied by the difference principle.* It is our view that although some inequalities of wealth and status enhance the lot of the worst off, given our current starting point considerable movement toward equality may be accomplished without any necessary detriment to those on the bottom. The set of equality enhancing changes that the law must specially aim at and the ones we are most concerned with are those that narrow the gap between the rich and poor by simultaneously diminishing the advantages of the rich and increasing the well-being of the poor (cf. Rawls, 1971, p. 79). Particularly important are changes that diminish the access of the advantaged to positions of wealth and power by creating conditions of fair equality of opportunity that allow the disadvantaged to compete successfully for higher status positions.

Formal Autonomy. The first of these, the insulation of the legal system from the special pleadings of the better off is largely accomplished by a legal regime of formal autonomy. Formal autonomy, as we have seen, is characterized by differentially accessible general endowments coupled with a formalistic application process.

The move to formal autonomy from the more status-oriented legal systems of earlier years appears in retrospect to be a natural development for emerging capitalist societies. The switch from class-oriented endowments to general ones eliminated ancient privileges that stood in the way of economic development. The development of a formalist jurisprudence made the legal consequences of investments and trades predictable. The status neutral character of both general endowments and formalist jurisprudence lent legitimacy to the class system, for it made legal outcomes turn on the actions of organizations and individuals rather than on their social status.

In addition to these virtues, there are important ways in which formal autonomy promotes liberty. The hallmark of formally autonomous law is a system of basic rights, which are in principle enjoyed by all. So long as these rights are exercised in ways that respect the rights of others, the law does not constrain action. Nor is liberty constrained by uncertainty about what the law implies. The allocation of wealth and status is mediated not by governmental intervention but by market-like mechanisms that depend on individual choices rather than on collective decisions. This means that the legal system does not seek to reallocate welfare over individual objections. Quite to the contrary, some rights it creates, like the right to own private property, stake out areas of individual sovereignty, and other rights, like right to enter into contracts, open up areas for action by allowing people to plan more confidently for the future. To the extent that these rights involve basic liberties, formal autonomy preserves the core component of justice. Formally autonomous law cannot, however, reshape the status quo in the direction of increased equality. It makes only the "negative" contribution of limiting the extent to which law can be used to forestall tendencies toward equality rooted in other spheres.[23]

Formally autonomous law extends rights equally to all individuals, but, as we pointed out when we first discussed formal autonomy, rights are useful only to the extent that one can take advantage of them. The right to own property is, for example, not worth much to a person who lacks the ability to acquire any. Indeed, it limits certain kinds of redistributions that might make people more equal since a corollary of the right is that the unconsented taking of property is theft. The example may be generalized. One aspect of being better off is being

---

23. Formally autonomous law is, in other words, more conducive to equality than a system of class-oriented endowments or one of illusory rights. Unlike class-oriented endowments, the differentially accessible general endowments associated with formal autonomy do not muster the state's power with the specific goal of maintaining or extending the advantages of the better off. And unlike systems of illusory rights, formally autonomous systems respect the legal entitlements the worse off are able to obtain even if this threatens the interests of persons of higher status.

better able to take advantage of the rights that formal autonomy extends to all.[24] Thus in an unequal society formal autonomy tends to reproduce the status quo or even to increase existing inequality.

The Transfer of Welfare. If law is to be an independent force for equality, it must recognize social differences and seek to eliminate them. This is the second of the three requisites we identified: Legal norms must aim at reducing status differences and at transferring wealth and power from the better to the worse off.[25] They must be redistributive welfare-oriented endowments. How is this state of affairs to come about? If we have an unequal society, why should the better off, who presumably have disproportionate influence in the law-making process, consent to laws that transfer welfare to those beneath them? These questions are, of course, not rhetorical, for thousands of laws that effect such transfers exist. Nor are the answers simple. Here we can only sketch some possibilities.

First, because it is most obvious, there are ideological elements. The Judeo-Christian ethic has an important egalitarian aspect, in that human differences pale before God, as well as an important charitable component. Helping the less well off is a Judeo-Christian virtue. In the United States this ideology energized redistributive efforts ranging from the localized poor relief programs that have existed in this country from colonial days onward to the movement to free the slaves which became a central cause of reform Protestantism during the first half of the nineteenth century. Complementing this ethic and, no doubt, related to it is a political culture, in which, as evidenced by the Declaration of Independence and portions of the Constitution, egalitarian themes have long been deeply embedded.

Also important is the ideology of formal law. Formal law is legitimating because it suggests that legal rights are equally available and that when people come to law, status differences do not matter. The more obviously false these propositions are, the less likely the law is to be accepted for its own sake, and the more likely it is that believers in the ideology will support corrective action.

The deficiencies in the formally autonomous model are especially glaring when the impoverished are unable to call on courts to enforce their rights or are unable to exercise their rights when called into court by others. The appeal of the formal autonomy is best revealed in the reception accorded steps taken to rectify these situations. On the criminal side, the Supreme Court decisions requiring the state to appoint counsel in felony [*Gideon* v. *Wainwright*, 372 U.S.

---

24. The better off are also ordinarily more able to avoid the duties that a regime of formal autonomy imposes on all.

25. At the point where transfers from the well off diminish the amount of goods available to the worst off, transfers, according to Rawls, should stop. This might happen, for example, if taxes were so high that skilled people had no incentive to do more than a minimal amount of work and everyone's standard of living dropped accordingly.

335 (1963)] and many misdemeanor [*Argersinger* v. *Hamlin,* 407 U.S. 25 (1972)] cases have caused virtually no controversy. Yet in comparison to the highly controversial exclusionary rule, the right to appointed counsel has, no doubt, cost the state considerably more money, and it has probably allowed more factually guilty people to escape conviction for the behavior with which they were charged. On the civil side, the federal government is currently spending more than a quarter of a billion dollars a year on legal aid to the poor. Most revealing was the outcome of the battle early in the Reagan Administration, which may be repeated in Reagan's second term, to eliminate the federal legal service program entirely. The administration appeared motivated by both a principled commitment to minimize redistributions[26] and the sense that empowering the poor to assert their legal rights hurt the interests of valued constituents and interfered with their agenda for government. That the administration's plan was thwarted largely due to the defection of conservative congressmen who would ordinarily support the administration testifies to the ability of an ideology to motivate action and to the general fit between the ideology of formal autonomy and conservative views of government.[27]

A second reason why redistributive legislation gets passed which is less obvious than ideology but probably more important has to do with the nature of inequality in the United States and the character of political life. Inequality is not constant across all areas of social life, nor are the interests of the more advantaged uniformly antagonistic to those of the less well off. Equality is itself a relative matter.

For example, each black person's vote counts the same as each white person's vote. It is true that money counts in politics as it does elsewhere, but if the average black does not have much influence beyond his vote, neither does the average white. Thus blacks are probably more equal to whites in the political arena than they are in economic matters. Moreover, in systems of territorial representation the ability to aggregate votes within defined boundaries is crucial to a political voice. Blacks together with other relatively impoverished minority groups now dominate the political machines in many of the country's largest urban areas. With local domination there comes not only representation at higher

---

26. The widespread state funding of counsel in both criminal and civil cases is a relatively recent phenomena, yet the ideology of formal rationality and the realization that not everyone in fact had access to the courts or could perform effectively once in court has been around for a long time. This suggests that even if we are right about the importance of the ideology of formal autonomy in this area, the disparity between ideology and actuality was not sufficient to motivate change. What was missing until recent decades was the idea that the government had an affirmative responsibility for the well-being of individual citizens (cf. Sandalow, 1981).

27. The lobbying efforts of the organized bar were also important and perhaps essential in the struggle to save legal services. However, while the self-interest of the bar is obvious, the elites who supported the lobbying had little at stake personally. They were probably motivated by their professional commitment to formal autonomy. In arguing to the Congress, the theme of equal access to justice was one to which they constantly returned.

levels of government but also the obvious potential to swing state or even national elections. The end result is that relatively greater equality in the political sphere can lead to transfers that increase equality in economic and social life.

Also the monolithic nature of those on top can easily be overemphasized while the implications of conditions that cut across class lines are ignored. In the United States, for example, both major political parties are multiclass coalitions. Although the Democrats do much better with those at the very bottom of the socioeconomic scale and the Republicans are the predominant choice of those at the top, the Republican coalition now extends well into the ranks of the working class, and Jay Rockefeller, to argue by way of example, is a Democrat. In order to maintain coalitions like these, the parties must offer rewards to those on the bottom. The rewards may be largely symbolic, such as the support for school prayer which in recent presidential elections has helped tie fundamentalist Christians to the Republican coalition, but symbols will often not do. Instead, concrete rewards that can only be realized by transfers from the better to the worse off are necessary.

In this connection it is important to note that government transfers are not confined to the downward direction. Not all welfare-oriented endowments are aimed at enhancing the welfare of the worst off, nor do they all draw from the well-to-do. Minimum wage laws, as we pointed out in Chapter 10, transfer wealth from the least skilled workers whose labor is not worth the minimum wage to those slightly more skilled who receive more than a market wage because of the laws. The tax deduction for home mortgages, coupled with the failure to tax imputed rent, tends to transfer wealth from renters to homeowners, although the class of homeowners are clearly better off than the class of renters. What we call welfare payments, like AFDC, transfer money collected largely from the middle class to those closer to the bottom. Thus one reason laws that aim at increasing equality exist is that welfare-oriented endowments aim at all sorts of transfers. Given that the poor play a role in the political process, it is not surprising that they gain some benefits. Whether as a purely economic matter the most advantaged have a larger share of the country's wealth than they would have in a system without massive government transfers (assuming such a system were possible) is an empirical question that has not yet been satisfactorily answered.[28]

Equality is, of course, more than economic. Perhaps the most important legal contributions to equality have aimed at equalizing political and social rather than economic well-being. The laws we focused on in Chapter 11 when we discussed the role of law in promoting racial equality are an obvious example. Other recent examples include laws designed to prevent discrimination against women, laws mandating that new construction accommodate the handicapped,

---

28. Indeed, it may be impossible to answer since there is no obviously correct way to allocate the benefits of certain governmental expenditures, like those for national defense, across classes. Does everyone benefit the same? Do the poor benefit the most because they are most likely to be cannon fodder? Or do the wealthy benefit disproportionately because they have the most to lose from a destructive war or invasion?

laws relating to the "mainstreaming" of handicapped children, and laws limiting compulsory retirement. The groups benefited by these laws illustrate our point that being disadvantaged in one area (e.g., age) does not mean that one is disadvantaged along some other dimension (e.g., wealth). The justice-enhancing character of such laws is obvious for they aim to increase liberty and self-respect.

Another part of the explanation for laws that redistribute wealth downward is that the classes that dominate society are often beset by cleavages, and some elements of the dominant classes may be natural allies or even champions of those who are worst off. For example, in the effort to increase racial equality regional cleavages between elites played an important role. Indeed, the Civil War is often attributed more to the socioeconomic conflicts that divided the North and South than to a northern passion to abolish slavery. The two flurries of civil rights legislations, one following the Civil War and the other in the 1960s involved statutes supported by northern elites who did not foresee that any of the interests they represented might be threatened by such laws. When northern interests were threatened, however, as in school busing cases, the quality of some laws changed dramatically. For example, instead of laws mandating greater efforts toward equality, legislation sought to limit court-ordered busing. The point is, of course, general. Some laws that redistribute welfare to the worse off can be explained by the fact that they do not run counter to or are in the interest of the more elite segments of society. We offer as a general hypothesis the proposition that people are not reluctant to distribute welfare downward when it is someone else's welfare they are distributing.

Consideration of elite interests brings us to our last point. Generally speaking, wealth and status in society is distributed much like a pyramid with the base being considerably broader than the apex. Although those on the bottom individually lack power, their numbers may mean that in the aggregate they can mount a genuine threat to those above them. Welfare endowments that enhance equality may reflect neither ideological considerations nor cleavages in the upper ranks. Instead, they may reflect calculations rooted in self-interest. Thus the labor laws we discuss in the appendix to Chapter 6 might never have been passed had not bloody and sometimes successful strikes suggested that industrial peace was in the national interest. And, somewhat more speculatively, the money and attention given to urban ghettos following the riots of the mid-1960s probably stemmed in part from a desire "to keep the lid on."[29]

---

29. To the extent that sheer numbers count in the exercise of both raw power and electoral politics, it may be that the forces leading to laws that enhance equality are self-limiting. As more people move out of the lower ranks into a broad middle class, the power of those on the bottom and the momentum for further egalitarian redistributions are likely to diminish. In this connection it is interesting to speculate on the effects of the inflation of the 1970s. Without increasing people's real wealth, it raised the dollar incomes of many people substantially and often placed them in higher tax brackets. By increasing the dollar disparity among those in the lower third of the country's income distribution and increasing the burden that transfers to the very poor placed on those at the upper end of this "low budget" range, it may have broken up a broad coalition of interests and substantially reduced the political power of those at the very bottom.

This brief survey of reasons why law-making processes dominated by elites may yield a substantial body of redistributive legislation does not pretend to depth or completeness. It does, however, begin to explain why, in capitalist democracies, laws that aim toward increased equality are neither rare nor surprising events.

Problems of Implementation. This brings us to our third requisite for using law to enhance justice. The enactment of a law is not the same as its implementation. If norms that seek to redistribute welfare are actually to contribute to increased equality, they must be able to penetrate the existing socioeconomic structures and bring about their intended reforms. In the case of some laws this is not problematic. With direct transfers of the money, like the AFDC or food stamp programs, for example, an efficient mechanism, the tax system, is already in place for taking welfare from those who have it, and self-interest leads most people who qualify for aid to seek it.

When increased social, political, or certain types of economic equality are the goals, the problems of penetrating the socioeconomic structure are much greater. The Voting Rights Act, for example, was only the first step toward giving southern blacks real political power. The consistent, sympathetic attention of federal administrators and courts was needed to make legal provisions for federal registrars, federal poll watchers, and the preclusion of structural changes (from single member to multimember districts, for example) that might dilute black votes effective. The law, in other words, is not self-executing, but in the case of the Voting Rights Act it apparently worked as intended.

Efforts to integrate schools by legal fiat have had a different history, and success in many areas has been limited. In many northern cities integration meant the destruction of a few mostly white schools, large-scale busing, and a resulting system in which every school was predominantly black. When white parents responded by moving to the suburbs or sending their children to private schools, the legal system was unable to cope.

This is not to say that coping was in theory impossible. It is conceivable that a substantively oriented court might have enjoined the opening or expansion of private schools where this would tend to hinder integration, and cross-district busing that consolidated largely black inner-city school districts with white suburban ones at one time seemed to be the wave of the future. But ultimately formalism prevailed. The private school option was never constrained except in the limited sense that some private schools that discriminated against blacks were denied the right to a tax exemption. Cross-district busing was severely restricted by a formalistic view of district boundary lines and because an association was required between the locus of the wrong and the remedy. Anything other than formalism might, however, have provoked a clash between the courts, on the one hand, and the president and Congress, on the other, that the courts could never have won.

We offer these brief summaries of matters discussed earlier by way of example. Our intention here is not to develop a theory of legal impact. Instead, we are concerned with the possibility that law may be used to enhance social justice. Note how far we have come. We have seen that removing society from law, as in systems of formal autonomy, is not a promising option unless society is equal to begin with, in which case formal autonomy melts into pure autonomy and we reach the Nirvana of maximal freedom, given the available goods, and pure procedural justice. We have also seen that laws that aim at increased equality can be enacted in an unequal society and enforced despite social resistance. The possibility for an iterative progression toward complete equality exists. If the groups on the bottom grow relatively more powerful, they should be able to demand more in the way of further equality. They will seek laws that give them more and a judicial system that acknowledges their interests.[30]

Liberty and Equality

If the goal is social justice, however, a contradiction may arise. As you will recall from Chapter 9, liberty is given priority over equality in Rawls's (1971) scheme of justice. Equality-enhancing changes are not permitted if they infringe on basic rights. Yet when law gets into the business of redistributing welfare it necessarily curtails the freedom of some. Endowments are status-oriented rather than neutral, and if the redistributive effort is to be maximally effective courts must eschew formalism and consider the ends to be achieved by the norms they are enforcing. A regime of substantive justice that aims for social equality is required.

But such a regime conflicts with liberty interests. Rights in property are diminished, for people are not free to spend their wealth as they wish. Instead, resources are taken from some and given to others. In addition, freedom of association might be limited. To promote fair equality of opportunity, male-only clubs might be ordered open to women and private schools might be forced to integrate along with public ones. Liberties enhanced by the good faith interpretation of written law are also diminished as courts respond to extra legal status considerations.

Now these consequences might strike many as tolerable if equality would in fact be enhanced. Indeed, Rawls's scheme would allow some of them, because not all liberty interests are "trump" but only certain basic ones are. And one might argue that enhancing economic equality enhances the total system of liberty as well. But if true equality were the goal, law would have to do still more. Free speech might have to be suppressed, at least to the extent of banning any language that degrades any status group. People might have to be assigned to jobs, for discrimination in the workplace can be subtle indeed. Procedural formalism would disappear from the legal process because it could interfere with

---

30. Repression, however, is another possibility as those on the top seek to stop the gradual erosion of their advantages before it is too late.

doing justice. And even the ballot might have to go, for a majority might not vote for a regime that sought to impose equality through state action. Ultimately, the picture one gets is not one of pursuing equality through law, but of pursuing equality despite it. The rule of law, in other words, entails constraints on the state. The pursuit of total equality at some point requires their elimination.

Of course, the last scenario is farfetched. The pursuit of equality is unlikely ever to extend so far as to encompass our parade of "horribles." But this is only because of the extreme way in which we have stated these possibilities. In less extreme form all of them have occurred. To prevent the degradation of women, statutes barring pornography have been passed, even though some of the material the statutes seek to suppress has heretofore been considered protected free speech. Quotas have led to choices between job candidates on the basis of race. Courts have ignored or overridden established procedural rules to reach decisions based on litigant status. And the ballot was certainly rendered meaningless for many southerners who sought policies that would forestall integration. Some or even all of these actions may be justified, but the threats they pose to basic liberty interests must be acknowledged.

Here we come to the inescapable dilemma. Liberty and equality, which we take to be the two fundamental desiderata of justice, cannot be maximized simultaneously.[31]

Not only do statutes that attempt to make people more socially and economically equal threaten liberty interests, but the pursuit of more equal liberty in the long run may also seem to call for the destruction of liberties that are currently enjoyed. The tension between the demands of liberty and the ideal of equality is clearly visible when we examine alternative legal systems. Formal autonomy, which protects basic liberty, does so for much of the population only in theory or only in part. The right to vote is not worth much if the lack of bus fare keeps one from the polls. The right to enter into contracts is of little value

---

31. Rawls (1971), of course, recognizes this, for much of a *Theory of Justice* is devoted to the relationship between these two goods. When equality is equality of liberty it is required, but Rawls never adequately confronts the fact that achieving equal liberty may require that seemingly basic liberty interests be overridden. Rawls would probably allow such overriding because he would allow the sacrifice of some liberty for a greater, more equal liberty in the long run (pp. 247–248). However, Rawls's discussion is ambiguous because infringing on some liberties, like liberty of conscience, seems not to be allowed. Moreover, since one could always argue that a liberty interest was being infringed in the interest of greater long-run liberty, unless Rawls meant his concession to apply only where liberty interests were in immediate conflict or in a few limited circumstances, the right to destroy liberty in the interests of long-run liberty would in actuality be a way of circumventing liberty's priority.

When equality concerns the more material aspects of well-being, the priority of liberty is clear, but the situation is complicated by the ways in which equality in material goods contributes to more equal liberty. Rawls also touches on this issue in a way that is not completely satisfactory. He suggests that some minimal level of material well-being may be necessary to enjoy basic liberties, but the level seems truly minimal and the implications for equal liberty of the difference between those above the minimum and those far above it are not adequately addressed. See, however, Rawls (1982).

if a lack of bargaining power means that one must always accept the terms another has set. All the rights in the world may seem meaningless if one's child has perished from a disease that adequate medical care could have prevented. In an unequal society, formal autonomy by treating everyone as equal will place the state's power behind arrangements that keep some people in second-class status.

Substantive justice, on the other hand, need not be directed at increased equality, and when it is, liberty interests are almost certain to be infringed. To some extent such infringements will be offset by the greater ability of those who have been aided to enjoy the liberties they have. However, as the pursuit of equality continues, the balance is likely to shift.

The difficulty confronting those who wish to use law as an instrument of social justice is to do so in a way that retains those aspects of formal autonomy that guarantee valued freedoms of individual action. The task is to achieve fair equality of opportunity, open offices, and a distribution of welfare in which the only inequalities are those allowed by the difference principle. This requires redistributive welfare-oriented endowments and is more likely when such laws are interpreted by sympathetic substantively oriented courts. Yet the goal must be accomplished without sacrificing political and moral liberty. These are protected by the legal autonomy associated with general endowments and formalism.

Ultimately, we must turn from Rawls to ourselves in order to decide on the type of legal system we prefer. Rawls's judgment of how to value liberty and equality is just one of many possible balances that may be struck (Hart, 1973). We must think philosophically, for we must weigh competing values. And we must develop law and social science, because we need more detailed knowledge about how law relates to valued outcomes.

The Seamless Web: The Legal Order and Modern Society

One of the many aphorisms with which the new law student is confronted is the statement that *the law is a seamless web*. The phrase recalls that orientation toward law that Max Weber called "formal rationality" and the idea of a "gapless system." We, however, like the metaphor for a different reason. The visual image invites us to search for the many strands of the web and the ways they interweave to form the tapestry of the legal order. This book is a response to that invitation. We have not traced all the threads to be sure, but we hope that we have shown you some intriguing patterns.

Our central concern in this book has been to understand the nature of the legal system and its relationship to the structure of society. In each part we have developed ideal types, describing in turn the attribution of responsibility, dispute settlement techniques, and the law's ability to alter distributions. Generally speaking, within each typology one cell more than others defines a type of legal order that in Western society is held up as a social ideal.

When the attribution of responsibility is in issue the ideal involves the logical analysis of what conduct means. This entails a concern for intention and ability and the use of what we call a deep case logic. In dealing with disputes, the ideal procedure narrows the arena of conflict and yields binary decisions. As a distributive system the ideal involves the interaction of status neutral legislative endowments with judicial formalism in the application process.

These types are ideal in that for many Westerners they define the best possible type of legal order. They are also ideal in that from Weber on many observers have seen in them what is, or until recently, what is thought to have been, the essence of Western law. A major theme of this book is that in both these senses the ideal is being challenged. We have sought to explore the situations in which these ideals are most likely to be realized and to contrast them with situations in which other types are more likely to emerge. We also have sought to examine some of the ends that people seek to achieve through law and to discuss the relationship between types of law and the likelihood that given ends will be achieved.

THE ASCRIPTION OF RESPONSIBILITY

In Part I our primary concern was to discuss the ascription of responsibility as a normative and social process. We saw that the choice of responsibility rules (rule logics) and the process by which responsibility is determined (case logics) are influenced by the bureaucratization of the adjudication process. Bureaucratized decision making is a relatively cheap and efficient way of disposing of large numbers of cases. It may also aid in preventing criminal or tortious behavior. But these goals are achieved at what some see as a substantial cost. Bureaucratic adjudication tends toward shallow case logics that ignore much of what it is to be a human actor in a complex situation. Thus the law as administered challenges the ideal that is implicit in those laws that demand the logical analysis of the meaning of action. Nor is the challenge confined to a disjunction between the law as administered and the law as it appears on the books. We saw in Chapter 5 that when caseloads mount and shallow case logics become routine, rule logics may change so that the law attends less fully to the dimensions of human action. Negligence liability in particular has come increasingly to appear as a legalistic roadblock to the efficient operation of the legal system.

The movement away from negligence liability cannot, however, be understood solely as an outcome of bureaucratic decision making. Bureaucratic adjudication is also common in criminal cases. Yet here the formal rule logic has remained relatively stable. The switch from negligence to no fault or strict liability also reflects the perception that a system that attempts an individualistic understanding of certain common types of accidents does so at the cost of coping adequately with the allocative problems they entail. Thus many people have come to believe that the individualistic orientation of negligence liability cannot deal with such collective community problems as workplace injuries and automobile accidents. Instead, the law must understand accidents not as the personal problems or delicts of individuals, but as a public problem rooted in the social structure (Mills, 1959). When such understandings arise we are likely to turn to less individualistic solutions.

DISPUTE SETTLEMENT

Part II focused on the secondary rule systems used to deal with disputes[1] that have been removed for resolution from the settings of ordinary life to some special legal institution. These systems reflect both the typical relationship of disputing parties and the larger sociopolitical structure. In the United States these factors contribute to a system of secondary rules that narrow the scope of the dispute to a small set of legally relevant issues, the resolution of which will allow one side or the other to be declared a winner. This combination of narrow *res gestae* and binary decisions yields what we call *issue decisions*. Issue decision systems define disputes in legal terms and resolve them as matters of right and duty. This means that the law in practice may attend to only a portion of what the parties are quarreling over.

Although the issue decision style of dispute processing appears well suited to some types of disputes, especially relatively impersonal conflicts between strangers, it has been criticized for failing to deal with the conflicts that often underlie disputes between close acquaintances and for ignoring communal perspectives on what a dispute is all about. The juvenile court, mediation in small claims court, and the wide variety of alternative dispute resolution forums that have emerged in the last decade are all attempts to move away from the issue decision style of dispute settlement toward a style that treats disputes less legalistically.

Many of the reform efforts seek a dispute settlement process that considers all the issues implicated by the dispute and strives for a flexible, integrative outcome. The issue decision style fails to achieve these objectives insofar as it tends to treat individuals as legal entities that exist separate and apart from actual substantive relationships in ongoing communities. Reformers are looking for settlement techniques that can express and capture the personal relations that the parties, and sometimes their judges, share and the communal interest in the outcome of the process.

The obvious attractions of modes of dispute processing that eschew legal formalism should not blind us to the costs that may attend efforts to implement such systems in modern society. If participation in a forum that allows a wide *res gestae* is coerced, a person may find that he has to answer for behavior that appeared permissible because it was not illegal. And if decisions are flexible rather than binary, a person may find that rights he has counted on are not fully enforced. In either case expectations will be frustrated and planning will be hampered.

In some situations and societies secondary rules of this sort pose no problems. Problems arise when the secondary rule structure seeks to impose community where it does not exist. There is a difference between accommodating those who

---

1. We use the term *dispute* broadly to encompass cases in which any two actors, including groups, states, and organizations as well as individuals, disagree as parties about the quality or consequences of an actor's behavior.

feel that an issue decision technique does not reflect the multiplex and enduring relationships they share with their opponents and compelling people to treat their disputes as if they were in fact with such opponents. Nevertheless, dispute settlement forums tend to adopt a single style and seek to shape the disputes brought to them in accordance with it. We saw this in examining the New York courts as they once dealt with matrimonial cases and in looking at how the Lozi kuta sought to resolve the case of the Jehovah's Witnesses.

When parties are not in enduring multiplex relationships or when communal ties do not bind the adjudicator and the adjudicated, there is a risk that settlement techniques that ostensibly aim at flexible, integrative outcomes may be corrupted. The pressures toward shallow case logics emerging from bureaucratic typification, the high levels of relative conflict of interest that are common between disputing strangers, and the lack of clear rules of relevance when the *res gestae* is wide, may, as in the juvenile court, produce a relationship decision system. In the words of the U.S. Supreme Court:

> There is evidence, in fact, that there may be grounds for concern that the child receives the worst of both worlds: that he gets neither the protections accorded to adults nor the solicitous care and regenerative treatment postulated for children. [*Kent* v. *United States*, 383 U.S. 541, 556 (1966)]

DISTRIBUTION

In Part III we examined the relationship between the legal order and the distribution of power and welfare in society. Here the ideal combines judicial formalism with status neutral legal norms. This combination ignores both social status and starting points. The commitment is to formalistic rules that treat individuals as juridic equals regardless of their actual conditions. It is most nearly described by what in Chapter 13 we called *formal autonomy*. Others would add an additional component to the ideal. They would argue that the virtues of formal adjudication and status neutral norms are not realized unless people have relatively equal access to the law creation and law application processes. This version of the ideal is closest to the system that we call *pure autonomy* in Chapter 13.

Chapter 10 looked at problems of collective behavior and the corporate form. Corporate actors because they aggregate wealth and power are in a position to benefit disproportionately from a system committed to formal autonomy. For similar reasons these creatures of the law are able to influence it profoundly. Not only are corporate actors likely to be a force for formal autonomy rather than for pure autonomy, but the particularistic endowments they seek and their potentially disproportionate influence on the political process may threaten even the former.

In Chapter 11 our general concern was with the use of law to alter the distribution of social and economic welfare in society. We concentrated on legal efforts to promote racial equality in voting, jobs, and education. These efforts have as their objectives the promotion of equal liberty and real equality of opportunity. These are compatible with, and, indeed, help to create a society dominated by the ideal of liberal equality as John Rawls uses the term. As we read Rawls, this social justice ideal finds its legal counterpart in systems of pure autonomy.

But this type of legal order is challenged by those who argue that attempts to institutionalize pure autonomy are doomed to yield outcomes that are insufficiently egalitarian unless society is truly equal to begin with. Without absolute initial equality, even purely autonomous legal orders[2] will tend to reproduce and exaggerate existing inequalities. Indeed, the conjunction of a purely autonomous legal system and a less than egalitarian society is in the long run unstable, and a retreat toward formal autonomy is a likely result. Thus if the law is to be effective in counteracting the social and economic inequalities that persist, even in the face of equal individual opportunity, the law must move beyond not only formal autonomy but also pure autonomy. To repeat Max Weber's (1968) observation of nearly a century ago:

> Formal justice guarantees the maximum freedom for the interested parties to represent their formal legal interests. But because of the unequal distribution of economic power, which the system of formal justice legalizes, this very freedom must time and again produce consequences which are contrary to the substantive postulates of religious ethics or of political expediency. (p. 812)

Or as Karl Klare (1978) more recently wrote, at the conclusion of an article critical of early Supreme Court interpretations of the Wagner Act:

> Until lawmaking becomes a quest for justice in each concrete historical setting, until the "rule of law" ideal (the separation of law and ethics) is abolished and ethics brought directly into daily life as a continuous, participatory practice of mediation and redefinition of relations among people . . . there can be no hope of the emancipation of labor. (p. 338)

Klare's criticism of judicial interpretations of the Wagner Act is in part that the courts tended to address labor law problems as if they were dealing with disputes between disengaged private individuals. Thus the courts proceeded from a private law perspective. Klare argues for a public law perspective that recognizes the way labor law problems are rooted in the communal social structure.

Important values are, however, at risk when a legal system strives to bring "ethics . . . directly into daily life." Klare recognizes that his program calls for the "politicization of law" but abjures any desire to abolish the public–private distinction where it affirms individual integrity. However, Klare does not tell us how this distinction is to be eliminated in some areas of legal regulation while maintained at full strength in others. The politicization of law, which in the extreme case involves a continuous input of status-oriented endowments and

---

2. That is legal orders that more nearly resemble pure autonomy than any other type. As the typology was constructed, pure autonomy in its purest form *requires* social and political equality.

little or no autonomy in the law application process, can lead to a tyranny of the majority even when there is equal access to the rule making and rule application processes. Where such access is unequal the politicizing of law supports systems of unrestrained class domination.

TWO CHALLENGES

Extrinsic Formality

This brief review of some of the themes developed in this book suggests two challenges that confront the modern legal order. The first presupposes that we value, at least in some circumstances, the deep-principled analysis of human action. The danger is that the legal order will bend under the pressures of bureaucratization and interest group influence and will increasingly tend toward that type of shallow formalism that Max Weber (1967) described as the ''absolute formalism of classification according to 'sense data characteristics''' (p. 64) and Rheinstein (1954), an important translator of Weber, called ''extrinsically formal law'' (p. xlii). Extrinsically formal law equates the legal concepts it manipulates with outward signs that are not necessarily associated with the ideas they represent. Thus for Ross's insurance adjusters hitting someone from behind was negligence no matter how careful one had in fact been.

When judgments of responsibility must be made, extrinsic formality is found in shallow case logics which disregard much of what it is to be a human actor. In dispute settlement processes the forces that lead toward extrinsic formality are likely to be associated with adjudicative systems that are removed from the life of the community. Such systems are either unable to avoid an issue decision style even when the parties are in enduring, multiplex relationships or, if they allow for relationship settlement processes, they either permit substantial inequalities in bargaining strength or provide for only a shallow analysis of the matters in dispute. When distributional issues are confronted, tendencies toward extrinsic formality are closely associated with what we have called *pseudo-formalism*. We see extrinsic formality, for example, in a system that accepts the outward symbols of equal rights (separate but equal schools) and equal procedure (right to counsel) as necessary and sufficient indicia of equality before the law.

Formal law, by which we mean the formalistic application of status neutral norms, even when it purports to require a deep analysis of meaning, often tends toward extrinsic formality. Since formal law does not itself recognize social differences, easy to grasp, generalized indicia of status and behavior become crucial to the determination of legal consequences. In so attending to surface forms, law disguises the real relationships between people and between human actors and their acts. To resist tendencies in this direction, the modern state must erect organizations and structures that minimize the bureaucratization of the legal order and the extrinsic rationality that follows. This is the first challenge to which we referred. Yet the analysis in this book suggests that in many places just the opposite is occurring. Whether this is an inevitable correlate of the social changes of the last half-century is an open question.

Values of Justice

The second challenge facing the legal system is the challenge of providing institutions that protect individual liberty, while at the same time working to achieve other ends of social justice such as the more equal distribution of welfare. Problems arise because, as we have seen at several points in this book, the maximization of liberty is not fully compatible with the maximization of equality or of other values that we might incorporate along with liberty and equality in a definition of social justice. Our most urgent problems tend to be collective ones requiring communal solutions. But communal solutions almost inevitably slight rights that some individuals thought they possessed. Indeed, when faced with a collective problem, the tendency is to ignore individual claims and to seek substantive outcomes that aggregate to an acceptable pattern at the group or societal level.

The Ascription of Responsibility. When responsibility is to be ascribed, this tendency reflects itself in rule systems that deal superficially, if at all, with the questions of meaning that arise if the law seeks a genuine understanding of human action. Surface indicia of responsibility suffice because they promise to resolve masses of cases in an efficient and generally fair fashion. At first, there may be a tendency to judge the new system by the standards of the older one. Errors are perceived in the sense that certain judgments seem unfair, but they are accepted as a cost of the new more workable system and perhaps are rationalized by the perception that the errors cancel out in the aggregate. Eventually, however, new systems may be accepted in their own right and older conceptions of error may disappear. Justice for individuals is no longer individuated. Thus, to speak hypothetically since we have not done the research, in the early days of a worker's compensation scheme it may seem unfortunate that workers can recover for injuries caused by disobeying orders or by their own clear negligence. Later the failure to sanction workers who are clearly responsible for their own injuries may be accepted as in the order of things.[3]

Dispute Processing. When dispute processing is in issue, the collective problem is changed and the tendency to slight individual rights manifests itself in a different fashion. The problem is rooted in the nature of dispute resolution

---

3. A good example is provided by the Federal Employers' Liability Act, a tort compensation scheme for employees of interstate railroads. Cases arising under the act tended to transform it from a negligence scheme (which it remained at law) to a compensation scheme. See, for example, *Gibson* v. *Thompson*, 355 U.S. 18 (1957); *Ringhiser* v. *Chesapeake & Ohio Railway Co.*, 354 U.S. 901 (1957).

systems. A rights-oriented judicial system is expensive, in that experts on legal rights, that is, lawyers, are typically needed for the effective resolution of cases. It is also less than fully satisfactory, because in many cases a rights orientation does not encompass all the issues that the parties seek to raise. The solution is to move to informal modes of dispute processing that, as we saw in Chapters 7 and 8, exist in various degrees and come in many guises. Informalism does not necessarily lead to shallow adjudications, for, as we saw among the Lozi, subjective meaning and human relationships may be probed deeply. However, informalism diminishes the importance of legal rights. People, like youngsters in juvenile court, may not be in a good position to assert their rights or, as happens in negotiations and some mediations, they may be pressured to relinquish valid claims or, as can happen in various informal forums, the inquiry may expand so that claims of legal right are balanced against a variety of extralegal normative considerations.

Rights and Distributions. This last theme is picked up when we look at distributional issues. Here values rooted in extralegal ethical systems are incorporated into the legal system. This has many aspects. The one that concerns us here is that as the law reinstitutionalizes norms that value particular distributive outcomes, the practice of vesting rights in individuals and accepting the outcomes of their lawful dealings as just tends to be replaced by a system that defines a particular distribution of welfare as just and seeks through law to achieve that distribution. Thus claims of individual right come to be subordinated by law to group claims for distributively just outcomes. When courts and legislatures cooperate to shape the law toward the same distributive goal, we have what we call in Chapter 13 a regime of substantive justice or, in a society that seeks to perpetuate marked inequality, unrestrained class domination.

A THREAT TO LEGITIMACY

The tendencies toward extrinsically formal law and a jurisprudence oriented toward the solving of collective problems have different implications for society and the role that law can play. The tendency toward extrinsically formal law poses threats to the relevance and legitimacy of the law itself. Law is, to be sure, guaranteed by force, but it is validated by its norms and processes. If its norms attend to symbols that are obviously removed from popular concerns and if its processes—like plea bargaining—undercut public confidence in the legal enterprise, the likely result—although we cannot prove it—will be a sense that law, except when one is brutally confronted with it, has little to do with ordinary life and only a feeble claim to generalized allegiance. The long-run effects of the tendency toward extrinsic formality will be to divorce the legal process from the relationships people have with each other and with the deeds they perform. Following this course the law, as Weber noted, must finally exhaust itself in casuistry.

DILEMMAS OF JUSTICE

The tendency toward a problem-oriented jurisprudence that aims for substantive justice raises yet more interesting questions. As we have suggested, there is a tension between law's capacity to seek aggregate justice and its role in protecting individual rights. Underlying the latter role is a sense of the uniqueness and autonomy of individuals, complemented by the view that people deserve to benefit from or be accountable for what they can and actually do. Law promotes these values by providing people with, among other things, liberty, security, the possibility of dominion over property, and responsibility rules that take full account of unique human natures. This vision is most clearly realized in legal regimes that approximate the ideal of pure autonomy. But an important aspect of what it is to be human is not recognized in such regimes: To be human is not only to be unique and autonomous, it is also—at least in any situation where there is law and hence a state—to be involved in a community.

An alternative vision of the legal order sees law's basic contributions in communal terms. Law reflects and regulates the interdependence and mutual responsibility that exists wherever people live in groups and is heightened when people care not only for their own well-being but also for the well-being of each other. A legal order that aims for substantive justice recognizes this sense of community and common fate. Legal orders in modern states, perhaps because lesser communities have broken down, have tended in this direction. But the outcome of an orientation toward substantive justice is often not a larger sense of community but rather a kind of official caring. Indeed, groups may compete to secure the benefits or avoid the burdens of the state's largess. However, despite these arguable costs, if equality is valued, and if we want a legal system that does more than loosely reproduce the status quo, some orientation to outcomes is necessary.

Nor is this the only dilemma that those who value rights yet espouse more distributively oriented legal orders must confront. An outcome-oriented jurisprudence often replaces deep analyses of meaning with shallower ones. As we noted in Chapter 4, this move promises greater efficiency in the attainment of particular ends. Yet we have just decried the tendency of formal law to degenerate into an extrinsically formal rationality, which is the kind of movement from a deeper to a shallower logic that an outcome-oriented jurisprudence often entails.[4] At one level this is a cost to be acknowledged. However, the choice our legal system faces may not be between a legal order that is more fully cognizant of what it is to be human and one that is less aware. The quality of formalism in modern society appears to be moving for many reasons from the formalistic manipulation of concepts that require a deep understanding of human behavior to an extrinsic formality that works only with surface symbols. The lesson to

---

4. Freiberg and O'Malley (1984), for example, note how in administrative regulations the deeper logic of the criminal law is being replaced by the "civil offense" which necessitates less of an inquiry into the action meaning of untoward behavior.

be learned from the discussion of automobile accidents and industrial injuries in Chapter 5 is that in many areas the idea that the legal significance of an actor's conduct should be determined by a deep case logic is not only no longer an ideal; it is no longer among the choices available. Instead, the choice appears to be between a purposive rule, like strict liability for workers' injuries, which considers typical party relationships and goals to be achieved, and a bureaucratized, extrinsic formalism, like the rules of thumb that adjusters and lawyers use to settle most auto accident cases.

The final dilemma is the most basic. If formal rights remain strong and the law treats the redistribution of welfare as a secondary goal, a capitalist democracy such as ours can at best aspire to the condition Rawls calls liberal equality. Liberal equality has substantial virtues. There are many who think that conditions in the present-day United States approximate liberal equality and see no reason to attempt anything more. This position may be a defensible choice both philosophically and empirically, but it implies a general acceptance of the substantial inequalities that exist in contemporary social life. As we have seen in Chapters 12 and 13, the formally autonomous legal order that best guarantees liberal equality tends to reproduce the social and political disparities of the status quo. To go beyond liberal equality and to ameliorate such disparities requires a purposive, outcome-oriented jurisprudence.

Yet if along with Rawls we value basic freedoms above other primary goods, to run heedlessly toward something we vaguely call substantive justice without giving due consideration to the values served by legal rights and judicial autonomy is to risk a good deal. E. P. Thompson (1975) put it nicely at the conclusion of his book on the Black Act:

> I am told that, just beyond the horizon, new forms of working class power are about to arise which, being founded upon egalitarian productive relations, will require no inhibition and can dispense with the negative restrictions of bourgeois legalism. A historian is unqualified to pronounce on such utopian projections. All that he knows is that he can bring in support of them no historical evidence whatsoever. His advice might be: watch this new power for a century or two before you cut your hedges down. (p. 266)

The task is to use law to achieve social and economic justice without in the name of justice destroying the substantial benefits of legal autonomy and formal rules. The challenge is to have a legal order that supports a sense of community while maintaining individual liberty as a first virtue (see Unger, 1976; p. 266). Until the equality necessary for a stable system of pure autonomy exists, our preference is to create and move cautiously from what in Chapter 13 we called a regime of formal justice.

Thus the challenge posed by the trend toward extrinsic formalism is a challenge to avoid a degenerate legal system that responds to short-term bureaucratic exigencies rather than to the law's inner ideals or some systematic program for a more just society. The challenge posed by the trend toward a more purposive jurisprudence is a challenge to use law to strive for the best possible society. It is, however, easier to give the ideal a name than to describe the concrete set of institutional arrangements and legal decision rules that promises to most nearly achieve this outcome. For the student of law and social science the task is to understand the ways in which responsibility rules, settlement techniques, and the content and application of rules may interact to promote both individual liberty and a sharing community. In short, we must not only be able to understand, but we must also be able to unravel and reconstruct the seamless web.

EPILOGUE: AN INVITATION TO LAW AND SOCIAL SCIENCE

Thus we come to the end of our invitation to law and social science. We hope we have given you an appreciation of the enterprise. It is to explore with the aid of social science techniques and learning all aspects of law and the legal system. Our goal is an empirically based understanding of law and the role it plays in social life. This requires a multitude of specific, careful studies from a variety of social science perspectives. Examples are scattered throughout this book. But specific studies are not enough. They must be combined in a coherent theoretical framework. We have tried to move in this direction with the typologies we developed and the ways we built on them.

In the first 11 chapters of this book we assimilated a substantial amount of empirical data in analyzing the problems we addressed. In the concluding two chapters we dealt with global themes that are only rarely the subject of careful empirical treatment. Here the data are more impressionistic than systematic, and the theoretical exercise is largely conceptual. In Part III, which is concerned with the law's role as a distributive agency, we began by looking beyond social science and toward philosophical positions on justice. We closely examined the position of one philosopher, John Rawls, because to put the social science and conceptual research that followed in context, we first had to consider what justice might entail. Indeed, for some of our discussion we had to assume, if only by fiat, that you, the reader, and we, the authors, shared values.

In this concluding chapter we have occasionally gone further, and at places it is difficult, even in principle, to separate our social science observations from certain value preferences. We have intentionally left positivist science behind because the empirically based understanding of how law and the legal system operate is not for us an end in itself. The larger concern is justice and how to construct a better society. It is to such questions that the invitation which we accepted many years ago, ultimately leads. The discipline of law and social science matters because it seeks to answer some of the most fundamental questions that can confront a society. If this is your first exposure to law and social science, we invite you to join in the enterprise.

Bibliography

Abel, Richard L. (Ed.). (1982a). *The politics of informal justice* (Vol. 1: *The American experience*). New York: Academic Press.

Abel, Richard L. (Ed.). (1982b). Contradictions of informal justice. In Richard Abel (Ed.), *The politics of informal justice: Vol. 1 (pp. 267–320).* New York: Academic Press.

Allen, Frances. (1964). *The borderland of criminal justice: Essays in law and criminology.* Chicago: University of Chicago Press.

Alschuler, Albert. (1975). The defense attorney's role in plea bargaining. *Yale Law Journal, 84*, 1179–1314.

Ares, Charles, Rankin, Anne, & Sturtz, Herbert. (1963). The Manhattan Bail Project: An interim report on the use of pre-trial parole. *New York University Law Review, 38*, 67–95.

Aristotle. (1951). *The Nicomachean ethics* (Bk. III, ch. 1). Oxford: Clarendon Press.

Armor, David. (1980). White flight demographic transition and the future of school desegregation. In Walter Stephan and Joel Feagin (Eds.), *School desegregation: Past, present and future* (pp. 187–226). New York: Plenum Press.

Arrow, Kenneth. (1973). Some ordinalist-utilitarian notes on Rawls's theory of justice. *Journal of Philosophy, 70*, 245–263.

Auerbach, Jerold. (1983). *Justice without law?* New York: Oxford University Press.

Austin, J. L. (1956–57). A plea for excuses. *Aristotelian Society Proceedings, 57*, 1–30.

Austin, John. (1832) (1955). *The province of jurisprudence determined.* London: Wiedenfeld & Nicholson.

Axelrod, Robert. (1970). *Conflict of interest.* Chicago: Markham Press.

Axelrod, Robert. (1984). *The evolution of cooperation.* New York: Basic Books.

Baier, Kurt. (1970). Responsibility and action. In Myles Brand (Ed.), *The nature of human action* (pp. 100–116). Glenview: Scott, Foresman & Co.

Baker, Harvey. (1961). Procedure of the Boston juvenile court. *Survey, 23.* Cited in Anthony Platt, *The child savers: The invention of delinquency* (Note 17, p. 142). Chicago: The University of Chicago Press.

Balbus, Isaac. (1973). *The dialectics of legal repression: Black rebels before American criminal courts.* New York: Russell Sage Foundation.

Balbus, Isaac. (1977). Commodity form and legal form: An essay on the 'relative autonomy' of the law. *Law and Society Review, 11,* 571–588.

Baldwin, John, & McConville, Michael. (1977). *Negotiated justice: pressures to plead guilty.* London: Martin Robertson.

Ball, Harry, Simpson, George, & Ikeda, Kiyoshi. (1962). A re-examination of William Graham Sumner on law and social change. *Journal of Legal Education, 14,* 299–316.

Baran, Paul, & Sweezy, Paul. (1966). *Monopoly capital.* New York: Modern Review Press.

Bardach, Eugene, & Kagan, Robert. (1982). *Going by the book: The problem of regulatory unreasonableness.* Philadelphia: Temple University Press.

Barry, Brian M. (1973). *The liberal theory of justice: A critical examination of the principal doctrines in a theory of justice by John Rawls.* London: Oxford University Press.

Bartosic, F., & Hartley, R. C. (1972). The employer's duty to supply information to the union—A study of the interplay of administrative and judicial rationalization. *Cornell Law Review, 58,* 23–50.

Becker, Howard S. (1963). *The outsiders: Studies in the sociology of deviance.* Glencoe, IL: Free Press.

Bell, Derrick. (1973). *Race, racism and American law.* Boston: Little, Brown & Co.

Bellow, G. (1977). Turning solutions into problems: The legal aid experience. *NLADA Briefcase, 34,* 106.

Bennett, W. Lance, & Feldman, Martha S. (1981). *Reconstructing reality in the courtroom: Justice and judgment in American culture.* New Brunswick, NJ: Rutgers University Press.

Bentson, George. (1973). Required disclosure and the stockmarket: An evaluation of the Securities Exchange Act of 1934. *American Economic Review, 63,* 132–155.

Bergson, Abram. (1967). Market socialism revisited. *Journal of Political Economy, 75,* 655–673.

Berle, Adolf Agustus, & Means, Gardiner C. (1932). *The modern corporation and private property.* New York: Macmillan & Co.

Berlin, Isiah. (1959). *Historical inevitability.* London: Oxford University Press.

Bickel, Alexander. (1962). *The least dangerous branch: The Supreme Court at the bar of politics.* Indianapolis: Bobbs-Merrill.

Bittner, Egon. (1969). The police on skid row: A study of peace keeping. In William Chambliss (Ed.), *Crime and the legal process* (pp. 135–155). New York: McGraw-Hill.

Black, Donald. (1976). *The behavior of law.* New York: Academic Press.

Black, Donald. (1980). *The manners and customs of the police.* New York: Academic Press.

Blum, Alan, & McHugh, Peter. (1971). Social ascription of motives. *American Sociological Review, 36,* 98–109.

Blumberg, Abraham. (1967). The practice of law as a confidence game: Organizational cooptation of a profession. *Law and Society Review, 1,* 15–39.

Blumrosen, Alfred. (1984). The law transmission system and the southern jurisprudence of employment discrimination. *Industrial Relations Law Journal, 6,* 313–352.

Bohannan, Paul. (1957). *Justice and judgment among the Tiv.* London: Oxford University Press.

Bohannan, Paul. (1965). The differing realms of the law. *American Anthropologist,* Special Publication, *The Ethnography of Law,* Laura Nader (ed.), Vol. 67, No. 6, Pt. 2, 33–42.

Bordua, David J. (Ed.). (1967). *The police: Six sociological essays.* New York: John Wiley & Sons.

Brand, Myles. (Ed.). (1970). *The nature of human action.* Glenview, IL: Scott, Foresman & Co.

Brereton, David, & Casper, Johnathan. (1981–82). Does it pay to plead guilty? Differential sentencing and the functioning of criminal courts. *Law and Society Review, 16,* 45–70.

Brown, Charles. (1984). Black–white earnings ratios since the Civil Rights Act of 1964: The importance of labor market dropouts. *Quarterly Journal of Economics, 99,* 33–44.

Bullock, Charles S. III, & Lamb, Charles M. (Eds.). (1984). *Implementation of civil rights policy.* Monterey, CA: Brooks/Cole Publishing.

Bullock, Charles. (1975). Expanding black economic rights. In Harrell Rodgers (Ed.), *Racism and inequality: The policy alternatives.* San Francisco: W. H. Freeman & Co.

Bullock, Charles, & Rodgers, Harrell. (1975). *Racial equality in America.* Pacific Palisades, CA: Goodyear Publishing Co.

Bullock, Charles, & Rodgers, Harrell. (1976). Coercion to compliance: Southern school districts and school desegregation guidelines. *Journal of Politics, 38,* 987–1011.

Calabresi, Guido. (1970). *The cost of accidents: A legal and economic analysis.* New Haven: Yale University Press.

Cappeletti, Mauro & Garth, Bryant. (1978). *Access to justice: A world survey.* Milan: Sijthoff Giaffre.

Carlin, Jerome. (1962). *Lawyers on their own: A study of individual practitioners in Chicago.* New Brunswick, NJ: Rutgers University Press.

Carlin, Jerome. (1966). *Lawyers' ethics: A survey of the New York City bar.* New York: Russell Sage Foundation.

Carlton, Dennis, & Fischel, Daniel R. (1983). The regulation of insider trading. *Stanford Law Review, 35,* 857–895.

Carson, Richard L. (1973). *Comparative economic systems.* New York: Macmillan.

Carter, Robert, & Klein, Malcolm. (Eds.). (1976). *Back on the streets: The diversion of juvenile offenders.* Englewood Cliffs, NJ: Prentice-Hall.

Casper, Jonathan, & Brereton, David. (1984). Evaluating criminal justice reforms. *Law and Society Review, 18,* 121–144.

Cavanagh, Ralph, & Sarat, Austin. (1980). Thinking about courts: Toward and beyond a jurisprudence of judicial competence. *Law and Society Review, 14,* 371–420.

Chambliss, William, & Seidman, Robert. (1971). *Law, order and power.* Reading, MA: Addison-Wesley.

Chayes, Abram. (1976). The role of the judge in public law litigation. *Harvard Law Review, 89,* 1281–1316.

Chevigny, Paul. (1969). *Police power.* New York: Vintage Books.

Chisholm, Roderick. (1967). He could have done otherwise. *Journal of Philosophy, 64,* 409–417.

Christopher, Warren. (1965). The constitutionality of the Voting Rights Act of 1965. *Stanford Law Review, 18*, 1–26.

Church, Thomas Jr. (1976). Plea bargains, concessions and courts: Analysis of a quasi-experiment. *Law and Society Review, 10*, 377–401.

Clayton, Charles. (1970). The relationship of the probation officer and defense attorney after *Gault*. *Federal Probation, 34*, 9–13.

Coase, Ronald. (1937). The nature of the firm. *Economica* (new series), *4*, 386–405.

Coffee, John. (1978). The repressed issues of sentencing: Accountability, predictability and equality in the era of the sentencing commission. *Georgetown Law Journal, 66*, 975–1107.

Colasanto, Diane, & Sanders, Joseph. (1976). *Methodological issues in simulated jury research*. Unpublished manuscript.

Coleman, James. (1974). *Power and the structure of society*. New York: W. W. Norton.

Coleman, James, Kelly, Sarah, & Moore, John. (1975). *Trends in school desegregation, 1968–1975*. Washington, DC: Urban Institute.

Columbia University. (1932). *Report by the Committee to Study Compensation for Automobile Accidents*. Philadelphia: International Printing Co.

Commons, John R., Phillips, Ulrich B., Gilmore, Eugene A., Sumner, Helen L., & Andrews, John B. (Eds.). (1910). *A documentary history of American industrial society: Vols. III & VI. Labor Conspiracy Cases*. Cleveland, OH: Arthur H. Clark Company.

Conard, Alfred F., Knauss, Robert L., & Siegel, Stanley. (1982). *Enterprise organization* (3rd ed.). Mineola, NY: Foundation Press.

Conard, Alfred F., Morgan, James N., Pratt, Robert W. Jr., Voltz, Charles E., & Bombaugh, Robert L. (1965). *Automobile accident costs and payments: Studies in the economics of injury reparation*. Ann Arbor: University of Michigan Press.

Conway, Delores A., & Roberts, Harry V. (1983). Reverse regression fairness and employment discrimination. *Journal of Business and Economic Statistics, 1*, 75–78.

Cook, Karen S., & Hegtvedt, Karen A. (1983). Distributive justice, equity, and equality. In Ralph H. Turner & James F. Short, Jr. (Eds.), *Annual Review of Sociology* (pp. 217–241). Palo Alto: Annual Reviews, Inc.

Cooper, Richard C. (1966). Boulwarism and the duty to bargain in good faith. *Rutgers Law Review, 20*, 653–695.

Cox, Archibald. (1958). The duty to bargain in good faith. *Harvard Law Review, 71*, 1401–1442.

Crain, Robert, & Mahard, Rita. (1983). The effect of research methodology on desegregation-achievement studies: A meta-analysis. *American Journal of Sociology, 88*, 839–854.

Currie, Elliott P. (1968). Crimes without criminals: Witchcraft and its control in Renaissance Europe. *Law and Society Review, 3*, 7–32.

Cyert, Richard, & March, James. (1963). *A behavioral theory of the firm*. Englewood Cliffs, NJ: Prentice-Hall.

Damaska, Mirjan. (1975). Presentation of evidence and factfinding precision. *University of Pennsylvania Law Review, 123*, 1083–1106.

Dannefer, Dale. (1984). Who signs the complaint? Relational distance and the juvenile justice process. *Law and Society Review, 18*, 249–271.

Danto, Arthur. (1965). Basic actions. *American Philosophical Quarterly, 11*, 141–148.

Danzig, Richard. (1973). Toward the creation of a complementary decentralized system of criminal justice. *Stanford Law Review, 26*, 1–54.

Danzig, Richard, & Lowy, Michael. (1975). Everyday disputes and mediation in the United States: A reply to Professor Felstiner. *Law and Society Review, 9,* 675–694.

Davidson, Donald. (1963). Actions, reasons and causes. *Journal of Philosophy, 60,* 685–700.

Davies, Thomas. (1982). Affirmed: A study of criminal appeals and decision-making norms in a California Court of Appeal. *American Bar Foundation Research Journal,* 543–648.

Dentler, Robert, & Scott, Marvin B. (1981). *Schools on trial: An inside account of the Boston desegregation case.* Cambridge, MA: Harvard University Press.

Department of Transportation. (1971). *Motor vehicle crash losses and their compensation in the United States.* Washington, DC: U.S. Government Printing Office.

Diamond, Stanley. (1971). The rule of law versus the order of custom. *Social Research, 38,* 42–72.

Drew, Elizabeth. (1982a). A reporter at large: Politics and money: 1. *The New Yorker, LVIII:* 42, 54–149.

Drew, Elizabeth. (1982b). A reporter at large: Politics and money: 2. *The New Yorker, LVIII:* 43, 57–111.

Drew, Elizabeth. (1983). *Politics and money: The new road to corruption.* New York: Macmillan.

Dubois, Philip. (1984). Voting cues in nonpartisan trial court elections: A multivariate assessment. *Law and Society Review, 18,* 395–436.

Dubois, Philip (Ed.). (1982). *The analysis of judicial reform.* Lexington, MA: Lexington Press.

Duncan, Otis D. (1961). Properties and characteristics of the socioeconomic index. In Albert J. Reiss (ed.), *Occupations and Social Status.* New York: Free Press.

Duncan, Otis Dudley. (1968). Patterns of occupational mobility among negro men. *Demography, 5,* 11–22.

Duncan, Otis Dudley. (1969). Inheritance of poverty or inheritance of race. In Daniel Moynihan (Ed.), *On understanding poverty* (pp. 85–110). New York: Basic Books.

Duvin, Robert. (1964). The duty to bargain: Law in search of policy. *Columbia Law Review, 64,* 248–292.

Dworkin, Ronald. (1980). Is wealth a value? *Journal of Legal Studies, 9,* 191–226.

Eckhoff, Torstein. (1966). The mediator, the judge and the administrator in conflict-resolution. *Acta Sociologica, 10,* 148–172.

Eisenberg, Melvin. (1969). The legal role of shareholders and management in modern corporate decisionmaking. *California Law Review, 57,* 1–181.

Eisenberg, Melvin. (1976). Private ordering through negotiation: Dispute-settlement and rulemaking. *Harvard Law Review, 89,* 637–681.

Eisenstein, James, & Jacob, Herbert. (1977). *Felony justice: An organizational analysis of criminal courts.* Boston: Little, Brown & Co.

Ellsberg, Daniel. (1975). The theory and practice of blackmail. In Oran Young (Ed.), *Bargaining: Formal theories of negotiation* (pp. 343–364). Urbana: University of Illinois Press.

Emerson, Robert. (1969). *Judging delinquents.* Chicago: Aldine Publishing Co.

Emerson, Robert. (1983). Holistic effects in social control decision making. *Law and Society Review, 17,* 425–456.

Erikson, Kai T. (1966). *Wayward puritans: A study in the sociology of deviance.* New York: John Wiley & Sons.

Erlich, Eugene. (1936). *Fundamental principles of the sociology of law*. Cambridge, MA: Harvard University Press.

Fallers, Lloyd. (1969). *Law without precedent: Legal ideas in action in the courts of Colonial Bugosa*. Chicago: University of Chicago Press.

Fama, Eugene. (1980). Agency problems and the theory of the firm. *Journal of Political Economy, 88*, 288–307.

Fama, Eugene, & Jenson, Michael. (1983). Separation of ownership and control. *Journal of Law and Economics, 26*, 301–325.

Farley, Reynolds. (1984). *Blacks and whites: Narrowing the gap*. Cambridge, MA: Harvard University Press.

Farley, Reynolds. (1977). Trends in racial inequalities: Have the gains of the 1960's disappeared in the 1970's? *American Sociological Review, 42*, 189–207.

Featherman, David L., & Hauser, Robert M. (1978). *Opportunity and change*. New York: Academic Press.

Feeley, Malcolm. (1979a). Pleading guilty in lower courts. *Law and Society Review, 13*, 461–467.

Feeley, Malcolm. (1979b). *The process is the punishment: Handling cases in a lower criminal court*. New York: Russell Sage.

Feiffer, George. (1964). *Justice in Moscow*. New York: Simon & Schuster.

Felstiner, William. (1974). Influences of social organization on dispute processing. *Law and Society Review, 9*, 63–94.

Felstiner, William. (1975). Avoidance as dispute processing: An elaboration. *Law and Society Review, 9*, 695–706.

Finkelstein, Michael. (1975). A statistical analysis of guilty plea practices in the federal courts. *Harvard Law Review, 89*, 293–315.

Finnis, John. (1980). *Natural law and natural rights*. New York: Oxford University Press.

Fiss, Owen. (1984). Against settlement. *Yale Law Journal, 93*, 1073–1092.

Fletcher, George. (1972). Fairness and utility in tort theory. *Harvard Law Review, 85*, 537–573.

Frank, Jerome. (1949). *Courts on trial*. Princeton, NJ: Princeton University Press.

Franklin, John Hope. (1956). History of racial segregation in the United States. *Annals of the American Academy of Political & Social Science, 304*, 1–9.

Freiberg, Arie, & O'Malley, Pat. (1984). State intervention and the civil offense. *Law and Society Review, 18*, 373–394.

Freund, Julian. (1969). *The sociology of Max Weber*. New York: Vintage Books.

Friedman, Lawrence. (1966). On legalistic reasoning—A footnote to Weber. *Wisconsin Law Review*, 148–190.

Friedman, Lawrence. (1975). *The legal system: A social science perspective*. New York: Russell Sage.

Friedman, Lawrence, & Ladinsky, Jack. (1967). Social change and the law of industrial accidents. *Columbia Law Review, 67*, 50–82.

Fuller, Lon. (1964). *The morality of law*. New Haven: Yale University Press.

Fuller, Lon. (1971). The adversary system. In H. Berman (Ed.), *Talks on American law*. New York: Vintage Books.

Galanter, Marc. (1974). Why the "haves" come out ahead: Speculations on the limits of legal change. *Law and Society Review, 9*, 95–160.

Galanter, Marc. (1975). Afterword: Explaining litigation. *Law and Society Review, 9*, 347–368.

Galanter, Marc. (1976). Delivering legality: Some proposals for the direction of research. *Law and Society Review, 11*, 225–246.

Galanter, Marc. (1983). Reading the landscape of disputes: What we know and don't know (and think we know) about our allegedly contentious and litigious society. *UCLA Law Review, 31*, 4–71.

Galbraith, John Kenneth. (1967). *The new industrial state.* Boston: Houghton Mifflin.

Garfinkel, Harold. (1956). Conditions of successful degradation ceremonies. *American Journal of Sociology, 61*, 420–424.

Genovese, Eugene. (1972). *Roll, Jordan, roll: The world the slaves made.* New York: Vintage Books.

Gilmore, Grant. (1974). *The death of contract.* Columbus: Ohio State University Press.

Glaser, William. (1968). *Pretrial discovery in the adversarial system.* New York: Russell Sage.

Glazer, Nathan. (1975). Toward an imperial judiciary. *The Public Interest, 41*, 104–123.

Gluckman, Max. (1967). *The judicial process among the Barotse of Northern Rhodesia.* Manchester: Manchester University Press.

Goffman, Erving. (1970). Private communication reprinted in H. Lawrence Ross, *Settled out of court* (p. 162). Chicago: Aldine.

Goffman, Erving. (1971). *Relations in public. Microstudies of the public order.* New York: Basic Books.

Goffman, Erving. (1974). *Frame analysis.* New York: Colophon Books.

Gold, Martin. (1970). *Delinquent behavior in an American city.* Belmont, CA: Brooks/Cole Publishing Co.

Goldstein, Joseph. (1960). Police discretion not to invoke the criminal process: Low visibility decisions in the administration of justice. *Yale Law Journal, 69*, 543–589.

Gottfredson, D., Wilkins, L., & Hoffman, P. (1978). *Parole and sentencing guidelines.* Lexington, MA: Lexington Books.

Gould, David. III. (1972, April 12). *Staff report on the small claims court.* Submitted to the National Institute for Consumer Justice. Staff Studies.

Graglia, Lino. (1980). From prohibiting segregation to requiring integration. In Walter Stephan & Joe Feagin (Eds.), *School desegregation: Past, present and future.* New York: Plenum Press.

Green, Leon. (1930). *Judge and jury.* Kansas City: Vernon Law Book Co.

Green, Leon. (1958). *Traffic victims—Tort law and insurance.* Evanston, IL: Northwestern University Press.

Green, Thomas A. (1976). The jury and the English law of homicide, 1200–1600. *Michigan Law Review, 74*, 413–499.

Green, Thomas A. (1985). *Verdict according to conscience: Perspectives on the English criminal trial jury, 1200–1800.* Chicago: University of Chicago Press.

Griffiths, John. (1970). Ideology in criminal procedure, or a third 'model' of the criminal process. *Yale Law Journal, 79*, 359–417.

Gulliver, P. M. (1963). *Social control in an African society: A study of the Arusha.* London: Routledge & Kegan Paul.

Gusfield, Joseph. (1963). *Symbolic crusade: Status politics and the American temperance movement.* Urbana: University of Illinois Press.

Hagan, John. (1974). Extra-legal attributes and criminal sentencing: An assessment of a sociological viewpoint. *Law and Society Review, 8*, 357–383.

Hagan, John, & Bumiller, Kristin. (1983). Making sense of sentencing: A review and critique of sentencing research. In A. Blumstein, J. Cohen, S. Martin, & M. Tonry

(Eds.), *Research on sentencing: The search for reform*, vol. II, pp. 1–54. Washington, DC: National Academy Press.

Hagan, John, Nagel, Ilene, & Albonetti, Celesta. (1980). The differential sentencing of white collar offenders in ten federal district courts. *American Sociological Review*, *45*, 802–820.

Hardin, Russell. (1982). *Collective action*. Baltimore: Johns Hopkins University Press.

Harsanyi, John. (1975). Can the maximin principle serve as a basis for morality?: A critique of John Rawls's theory. *American Political Science Review*, *69*, 594–606.

Hart, H. L. A. (1949). Ascription of responsibility and rights. *Proceedings of the Aristotelian Society, New Series*, *49*, 171.

Hart, H. L. A. (1961). *The concept of law*. Oxford: Clarendon Press.

Hart, H. L. A. (1968). *Punishment and responsibility: Essays in the philosophy of law*. New York: Oxford University Press.

Hart, H. L. A. (1973). Rawls on liberty and its priority. *University of Chicago Law Review*, *40*, 486–534.

Hart, H. L. A., & Honore, H. M. (1959). *Causation and the law*. Oxford: Clarendon Press.

Hay, Douglas. (1975). Property, authority and the criminal law. In Douglas Hay, Peter Linebaugh, John Rule, E. P. Thompson, & Carl Winslow (Eds.), *Albion's fatal tree: Crime and society in eighteenth century England* (pp. 17–63). New York: Pantheon Books.

Heinz, John, & Laumann, Edward. (1982). *Chicago lawyers: The social structure of the bar*. New York: Russell Sage.

Henry, Stuart. (1985). Community justice, social structures and the dialectics of decentralized, collective socialist legality. *Law and Society Review*, *19*, 303–327.

Heumann, Milton. (1975). A note on plea bargaining and case pressure. *Law and Society Review*, *9*, 515–525.

Heumann, Milton. (1977). *Plea bargaining: The experiences of prosecutors, judges and defense attorneys*. Chicago: University of Chicago Press.

Hill, Herbert. (1972). The new judicial perception of employment discrimination—Litigation under Title VII of the Civil Rights Act of 1964. *Colorado Law Review*, *43*, 243–268.

Hirschman, Albert. (1971). *Exit, voice and loyalty: Response to decline in firms*. Cambridge, MA: Harvard University Press.

Hoebel, Adamson. (1969). *Keresan Pueblo law*. In Laura Nader, *Law in Culture and Society* (pp. 92–116). Chicago: Aldine Publishing Co.

Hofstadter, Douglas. (1983, June). Metamagical themas: The calculus of cooperation is tested through a lottery. *Scientific American*, *248*(6), 14–28.

Holmes, Oliver Wendell Jr. (1881). *The common law*. Boston: Little, Brown & Sons.

Holmes, Oliver Wendell Jr. (1897). The path of the law. *Harvard Law Review*, *10*, 457–478.

Horowitz, Donald L. (1977). *The courts and social policy*. Washington, DC: The Brookings Institution.

Horwitz, Morton J. (1977). *The transformation of American law: 1780–1860*. Cambridge, MA.: Harvard University Press.

Howard, Charles, & Summers, Robert. (1965). *Law: Its nature, functions and limits*. Englewood Cliffs, NJ: Prentice-Hall.

Hurst, James Willard. (1956). *Law and the conditions of freedom*. Madison: University of Wisconsin Press.

James, Flemming, & Law, Stuart. (1952). Compensation for auto accident victims: A story of too little too late. *Connecticut Bar Journal, 26,* 70–81.

Jencks, Christopher, Smith, Marshall, Acland, Henry, Bane, Mary Jo, Cohen, David, Gintis, Herbert, Heyns, Barbara, & Michelson, Stephan. (1972). *Inequality: A reassessment of the effect of family and schooling in America.* New York: Harper/Colophon Books.

Jensen, Michael, & Meckling, William H. (1976). Theory of the firm: managerial behavior, agency costs and ownership of structure. *Journal of Financial Economics, 3,* 305–360.

Johnson, Earl. (1980–81). Lawyer's choice: A theoretical appraisal of litigation investment decisions. *Law and Society Review, 15,* 567–610.

Jones, Edward, & Nisbett, Richard. (1972). Actor and observer: Divergent perceptions of the cause of behavior. In Edward Jones, David E. Kanose, Harold H. Kelley, Richard E. Nisbett, Stuart Valins, & Bernard Weiner, *Attribution: Perceiving the causes of behavior* (pp. 79–95). Morristown, NJ: General Learning Press.

Kain, John F. (1968). Distribution and movement of jobs and industry. In James Q. Wilson (Ed.), *Metropolitan enigma: Inquiries into the nature and dimensions of America's urban crisis* (pp. 1–23). Cambridge, MA: Harvard University Press.

Kalven, Harry, & Zeisel, Hans. (1966). *The American jury.* Boston: Little, Brown & Co.

Kamashima, Takeyoshi. (1963). Dispute resolution in contemporary Japan. In Arthur T. von Mehren (Ed.), *Law in Japan: The legal order of a changing society* (pp. 41–52). Cambridge, MA: Harvard University Press.

Kamisar, Yale. (1978). Is the exclusionary rule an 'illogical' or 'unnatural' interpretation of the Fourth Amendment? *Judicature, 62,* 66–84.

Kaplan, Abraham. (1964). *The conduct of inquiry.* San Francisco: Chandler Publishing Co.

Keeton, Robert, & O'Connell, Jeffery. (1965). *Basic protection for the traffic victim.* Boston: Little, Brown & Co.

Kelley, Harold. (1967). Attribution theory in social psychology. In David Levine (Ed.), *Nebraska Symposium on Motivation.* Lincoln: University of Nebraska Press.

Kelley, Harold. (1971). Attribution in social interaction. In Edward E. Jones, David E. Kanose, Harold H. Kelley, Richard E. Nisbett, Stuart Valins, & Bernard Weiner. (Eds.), *Attribution: Perceiving the causes of behavior* (pp. 1–27). Morristown, NJ: General Learning Press.

Kelsen, Hans. (1967). *The pure theory of law* (M. Knight, Trans.). Berkeley: University of California Press.

Kennedy, Duncan. (1976). Form and substance in private law adjudication. *Harvard Law Review, 89,* 1685–1778.

Klare, Karl E. (1978). Judicial deradicalization of the Wagner Act and the origins of modern legal consciousness, 1937–1941. *Minnesota Law Review, 62,* 265–339.

Klein, John. (1976). *Lets make a deal: Negotiating justice.* Lexington, MA: Lexington Books.

Kluger, Richard. (1976). *Simple justice.* New York: Alfred Knopf.

Kohlberg, Lawrence. (1969). *Stage and sequence: The cognitive development approach to socialization.* Chicago: Rand McNally.

Kritzer, Herbert M., Felstiner, William L., Sarat, Austin, & Trubek, David M. (1985). The impact of fee arrangement on lawyer effort. *Law and Society Review, 19,* 251–278.

Kronman, Anthony. (1983). *Max Weber.* Stanford, CA: Stanford University Press.

Larson, Arthur. (1952). The law of workmen's compensation. New York: Mathew Bender & Co.

Lave, Charles, & March, James. (1975). *An introduction to models in the social sciences.* New York: Harper & Row.

Lefstein, Norman, Stapleton, Vaughn, & Teitlebaum, Lee. (1969). In search of juvenile justice: *Gault* and its implementation. *Law and Society Review, 3,* 491–562.

Lemmert, Edwin. (1970). *Social action and legal change: Revolution within the juvenile court.* Chicago: Aldine Publishing Co.

Lempert, Richard, & Ikeda, Kiyoshi. (1970). Evictions from public housing: Effects of independent review. *American Sociological Review, 35,* 852–860.

Lempert, Richard. (1972). Norm-making in social exchange: A contract law model. *Law and Society Review, 7,* 1–32.

Lempert, Richard. (1978). More tales of two courts: Exploring changes in the ''dispute settlement function'' of trial courts. *Law and Society Review, 13,* 90–138.

Lempert, Richard. (1981). Organizing for deterrence: Lessons from a study of child support. *Law and Society Review, 16,* 513–568.

Lempert, Richard. (1982). From the editor. *Law and Society Review, 17,* 3–6.

Lempert, Richard, & Saltzburg, Steven. (1982). A modern approach to evidence (2nd ed.). St. Paul: West Publishing Co.

Lessnoff, M. H. (1978). Capitalism, socialism and justice. In John Arthur & William Shaw (Eds.), *Justice and economic distribution* (pp. 139–149). Englewood Cliffs, NJ: Prentice-Hall.

Licht, Walter. (1983). *Working for the railroad: The organization of work in the nineteenth century.* Princeton, NJ: Princeton University Press.

Lieberson, S., & Fugitt, G. (1967). Negro–white occupational differences in the absence of discrimination. *American Journal of Sociology, 73,* 188–200.

Llewellyn, Karl. (1930). A realistic jurisprudence—the next step. *Columbia Law Review, 30,* 431–465.

Llewellyn, Karl. (1950). Remarks on the theory of appellate decision and the rules of canons about how statutes are to be construed. *Vanderbilt Law Review, 3,* 395–406.

Llewellyn, Karl. (1960). *The common law tradition: Deciding appeals.* Boston: Little, Brown & Co.

Llewellyn, Karl, & Hoebel, Adamson. (1941). *The Cheyenne way: Conflict and case law in primitive society.* Norman: University of Oklahoma Press.

Loftin, Colin, Heumann, Milton, & McDowall, David. (1983). Mandatory sentencing and firearms violence: Evaluating an alternative to gun control. *Law and Society Review, 17,* 287–318.

Logan, Rayford W., & Winston, Michael. (1971). The Negro in the United States (Vol. 2: The ordeal of democracy). Princeton, NJ: Van Nostrand Reinhold.

Loh, Wallace. (1984). *Social research in the judicial process: Cases, readings, and text.* New York: Russell Sage Foundation.

Luce, R. Duncan, & Raffia, Howard. (1957). *Games and decisions.* New York: John Wiley & Sons.

Macaulay, Stewart. (1963). Non-contractual relations in business: A preliminary study. *American Sociological Review, 28,* 55–67.

Macaulay, Stewart. (1966). *Law and the balance of power: The automobile manufacturers and their dealers.* New York: Russell Sage.

Macaulay, Stewart. (1984). An empirical view of contract. Working Paper no. 8, Madison, WI: Disputes Processing Research Program.

Maguire, John M. (1925). The Hillmon case—Thirty-three years after. *Harvard Law Review*, *38*, 709–732.

Maine, Henry. (1963) (1861). *Ancient law: Its connection with the early history of society and its relation to modern ideas*. Boston: Beacon Press.

Maitland, F. W. (1936). *The forms of action at common law*. Cambridge, England: The University Press.

Malcolm, Andrew H. (1984, October 3). As euthanasia rises, society seeks rules. *International Herald Tribune*.

Malone, Wex. (1970). Ruminations on the role of fault in the history of torts. In Department of Transportation, Automobile Compensation & Insurance Study Series, *The origin and development of the negligence action* (pp. 1–33). Washington, DC: U.S. Government Printing Office.

Manne, Henry. (1966). In defense of insider trading. *Harvard Business Review*, *44*, 113–122.

March, James, & Simon, Herbert. (1958). *Organizations*. New York: John Wiley & Sons.

Mare, Robert, & Winship, Christopher. (1984). The paradox of lessening racial inequality and joblessness among black youth: Enrollment, enlistment, and employment, 1964–1981. *American Sociological Review*, *49*, 39–55.

Marshall, Burke. (1964). *Federalism and civil rights*. New York: Columbia University Press.

Marshall, Burke. (1984). A comment on the nondiscrimination principle in a "Nation of Minorities." *Yale Law Journal*, *93*, 1006–1012.

Marx, Karl. (1983). *The portable Karl Marx* (Eugene Kamenka, Ed.). New York: Viking Press.

Maslow, Will. (1946). FEPC—A case history in parliamentary maneuver. *University of Chicago Law Review*, *13*, 407–444.

Massell, Gregory. (1968). Law as an instrument of revolutionary change in a traditional milieu: The case of Soviet Central Asia. *Law and Society Review*, *2*, 179–228.

Massell, Gregory. (1974). *The surrogate proletariat: Moslem women and revolutionary strategies in Central Asia*. Princeton, NJ: Princeton University Press.

Mather, Lynn. (1974). Some determinants of the method of case disposition: Decision-making by public defenders in Los Angeles. *Law and Society Review*, *8*, 187–216.

Mather, Lynn. (1979). *Plea bargaining or trial? The process of criminal case disposition*. Lexington, MA: Lexington Books.

Matthews, Douglas. (1973). *Sue the b*st*rds*. New York: Arbor House.

Matza, David. (1964). *Delinquency and drift*. New York: John Wiley & Sons.

Mayhew, Leon. (1968). *Law and equal opportunity*. Cambridge, MA: Harvard University Press.

Mayhew, Leon. (1975). Institutions of representation: Civil justice and the public. *Law and Society Review*, *9*, 401–429.

Maynard, Douglas M. (1984). The structure of discourse in misdemeanor plea bargaining. *Law and Society Review*, *18*, 75–104.

Mazmanian, Daniel, & Sabatier, Paul. (1983). *Implementation and public policy*. Glenview, IL: Scott, Foresman & Co.

McBarnet, Doreen. (1981). *Conviction: Law, the state and the construction of justice*. Atlantic Highlands, NJ: Humanities Press.

McEwen, Craig, & Maiman, Richard. (1981). Small claims mediation in Maine: An empirical assessment. *Maine Law Review*, *33*, 237–268.

McEwen, Craig, & Maiman, Richard. (1984). Mediation in small claims court: Achieving compliance through consent. *Law and Society Review, 18,* 11–50.

McFadgen, Terrence. (1972). Dispute resolution in the small claims context: Adjudication, arbitration or conciliation? LLM Thesis, Harvard University.

McIver, Robert. (1964). *Social causation.* New York: Harper & Row.

Means, Gardiner C. (1970). Conglomerates and concentration. *University of Miami Law Review, 25,* 1–40.

Meier, Paul, Sacks, Jerome, & Zabell, Sandy L. (1984). What happened in Hazelwood: Statistics, employment discrimination and the 80% rule. *American Bar Foundation Research Journal,* 139–186.

Melden, Arthur I. (1961). *Free Action.* New York: Humanities Press.

Melnick, R. Shep. (1983). *Regulation and the courts: The Case of the Clean Air Act.* Washington, DC: Brookings Institution.

Menkel-Meadow, Carrie. (1983). Legal negotiation: A study of strategies in search of a theory. *American Bar Foundation Research Journal,* 905–937.

Menkel-Meadow, Carrie. (1984). Toward another view of legal negotiation: The structure of problem solving. *UCLA Law Review, 31,* 754–842.

Merry, Sally. (1982). The social organization of mediation in non-industrial societies: Implications for informal community justice in America. In Richard Abel (Ed.), *The politics of informal justice, 2* (pp. 17–45). New York: Academic Press.

Mesa-Lago, Carmelo. (1972). Ideological, political and economic factors in the Cuban controversy on material vs. moral incentives. *Journal of Interamerican Studies and World Affairs, 14,* 49–110.

Michels, Robert. (1949). *Political parties: A sociological study of the oligarchical tendencies of modern democracy.* New York: Free Press.

Mileski, Maureen. (1971). Courtroom encounters: An observation study of a lower criminal court. *Law and Society Review, 5,* 473–538.

Miller, Herbert S., McDonald, William F., & Cramer, James A. (1978). *Plea bargaining in the United States.* Washington, DC: National Institute of Law Enforcement and Criminal Justice.

Miller, Richard U. (1965). The enigma of Section 8(5) of the Wagner Act. *Industrial and Labor Relations Review, 18,* 166–185.

Mills, C. Wright. (1940). Situated actions and vocabularies of motive. *American Sociological Review, 5,* 904–913.

Mills, C. Wright. (1956). *The power elite.* New York: Oxford University Press.

Mills, C. Wright. (1959). *The sociological imagination.* London: Oxford University Press.

Mnookin, Robert, & Kornhauser, Lewis. (1979). Bargaining in the shadow of law: The case of divorce. *Yale Law Journal, 88,* 950–997.

Mooney, Joseph. (1969). Housing segregation, Negro employment and metropolitan decentralization: Alternative perspectives. *Quarterly Journal of Economics, 83,* 299–311.

Moynihan, Cornelius. (1962). *Introduction to the law of real property.* St. Paul: West Publishing Co.

Murray, Charles, & Cox, Louis. (1979). *Beyond probation.* Beverly Hills, CA: Sage Publications.

Musgrave, R. A. (1974). Maximin, uncertainty and the leisure tradeoff. *Quarterly Journal of Economics, 88,* 625–632.

Nader, Laura. (1969). Styles of court procedure: To make the balance. In Laura Nader (Ed.), *Law in culture and society* (pp. 69–92). Chicago: Aldine Publishing Co.

Nagel, Ernest. (1961). *The structure of science*. New York: Harcourt, Brace & World.

Nagel, Ilene. (1983). The legal/extra-legal controversy: Judicial decisions in pretrial release. *Law and Society Review, 17*, 481–515.

Nash, John. (1950). The bargaining problem. *Econometrica, XXI*, 155–162.

Nash, Peter. (1971). Affirmative action under executive order 11,246. *New York University Law Review, 46*, 225–261.

Nathan, Richard. (1969). *Jobs and civil rights*. Washington, DC: U.S. Government Printing Office.

National Safety Council. (1969). *Accident facts*. Chicago, IL: National Safety Council.

Nelles, Walter. (1931). The first American labor case. *Yale Law Journal, 41*, 165–200.

Newman, Donald. (1956). Pleading guilty for considerations: A study of bargain justice. *Journal of Criminal Law, Criminology and Police Science, 46*, 780–790.

Newman, Donald J. (1966). *Conviction: The determination of guilt or innocence without trial*. Boston: Little, Brown & Co.

Nicholson, Marlene Arnold. (1980). The constitutionality of the federal restrictions on corporate and union campaign contributions and expenditures. *Cornell Law Review, 65*, 945–1010.

Nielsen, Kai. (1978). Class and justice. In John Arthur & William Shaw (Eds.), *Justice and economic distribution* (pp. 225–245). Englewood Cliffs, NJ: Prentice-Hall.

Nonet, Philippe. (1969). *Administrative justice: Advocacy and change in a government agency*. New York: Russell Sage.

Nonet, Philippe, & Selznick, Philip. (1978). *Law and society in transition: Toward responsive law*. New York: Harper & Row.

Noonan, John T. (1976). *Persons and masks of the law: Cardozo, Holmes, Jefferson and Wythe as makers of the masks*. New York: Farrar, Straus & Giroux.

Norgren, Paul H. (1967). Fair employment practice laws—Experience, effects, prospects. In Arthur Ross & Herbert Hill (Eds.), *Employment, race and poverty* (pp. 541–570). New York: Harcourt, Brace & World.

Note. (1957). Employers' duty to supply economic data for collective bargaining. *Columbia Law Review, 57*, 112–123.

Nozick, Robert. (1974). *Anarchy, state and utopia*. New York: Basic Books.

O'Gorman, Hubert J. (1963). *Lawyers and matrimonial cases*. New York: Free Press.

Ofstad, Harold. (1961). *An inquiry into the freedom of decision*. Oslo: Norwegian Universities Press.

Okun, Arthur. (1975). *Equality and efficiency, the big tradeoff*. Washington, DC: Brookings Institution.

Olson, Mancur. (1971). *The logic of collective action: Public goods and the theory of groups*. New York: Schocken Books.

Orfield, Gary. (1969). *The reconstruction of southern education: Schools and the 1964 Civil Rights Act*. New York: John Wiley & Sons.

Orfield, Gary. (1978). *Must we bus?: Segregated schools and national policy*. Washington, DC: Brookings Institution.

Orfield, Gary. (1981). Housing patterns and desegregation policy. In Willis Hawley (Ed.), *Effective school desegregation: Equity, quality and feasibility* (pp. 185–221). Beverly Hills, CA: Sage Publications.

Orfield, Gary. (1983). *Public school desegregation in the United States 1968–1980*. Washington, DC: Joint Center for Political Studies.

Owen, David. (1982). Problems in assessing punitive damages against manufacturers of defective products. *University of Chicago Law Review, 49*, 1–60.

Packer, Herbert. (1964). Two models of the criminal process. *University of Pennsylvania Law Review, 1134,* 1–68.

Packer, Herbert. (1968). *The limits of the criminal sanction.* Palo Alto, CA: Stanford University Press.

Paige, Jeffery. (1975). *Agrarian revolution: Social movements and export agriculture in the underdeveloped world.* New York: Free Press.

Palay, Thomas. (1984). Comparative institutional economics: The governance of rail freight contracting. *Journal of Legal Studies, 13,* 265–287.

Parrinder, E. G. (1965). *Witchcraft: European and African.* London: Faber & Faber.

Pashukanis, Ergenii B. (1980), [1924]. The general theory of law and Marxism (Peter Maggs, Trans.). In Piers Beirne & Robert Sharlet (Eds.), *Pashukanis: Selected writings on Marxism and law* (pp. 40–131). London: Academic Press.

Peters, R. S. (1958). *The concept of motivation.* London: Routledge & Kegan Paul.

Pettigrew, Thomas. (1975). The racial integration of the schools. In Thomas Pettigrew (Ed.), *Racial discrimination in the United States* (pp. 224–239). New York: Harper & Row.

Piaget, Jean. (1965). *Moral judgment of the child.* New York: Free Press.

Plato. (1937). *Euthyphro.* New York: Random House.

Platt, Anthony. (1969). *The child savers: The invention of delinquency.* Chicago: University of Chicago Press.

Posner, Richard. (1983). *The economics of justice* (2nd ed.). Cambridge, MA: Harvard University Press.

Posner, Richard. (1977). *Economic analysis of law* (2nd ed.). Boston: Little, Brown & Co.

Posner, Richard. (1980). The value of wealth: A comment on Dworkin and Kronman. *Journal of Legal Studies, 9,* 243–252.

Pound, Roscoe. (1906). The causes of popular dissatisfaction with the administration of justice. *American Law Review, 40,* 729–749.

Pound, Roscoe. (1922) (1956). *An introduction to the philosophy of law.* New Haven: Yale University Press.

Prosser, William L. (1953). Comparative negligence. *Michigan Law Review, 51,* 465–508.

Prosser, William L. (1971). *Law of torts* (4th ed.). St. Paul: West Publishing Co.

Raab, Francis. (1968). History, freedom and responsibility. In May Brodbeck (Ed.), *Readings in the philosophy of the social sciences* (pp. 694–704). New York: Macmillan.

Rabin, Robert (Ed.). (1983). *Perspectives on tort law* (2nd ed.). Boston: Little, Brown & Co.

Raffia, Howard. (1982). The Art and Science of Negotiation. Cambridge, MA: Harvard University Press.

Rains, Prue. (1984). Juvenile justice and the boys' farm: Surviving a court-created population crisis, 1909–1948. *Social Problems, 31,* 500–513.

Rawls, John. (1971). *A theory of justice.* Cambridge, MA: Harvard University Press.

Rawls, John. (1982). The basic liberties and their priority. In Sterling M. McMurrin (Ed.), *The Tanner lectures on human values* (pp. 1–87). Salt Lake City, UT: University of Utah Press.

Regan, Donald. (1979). Rewriting *Roe* v. *Wade. Michigan Law Review, 77,* 1569–1646.

Reimers, Cordelia. (1984). Sources of the family income differentials among Hispanics, blacks and white non-Hispanics. *American Journal of Sociology, 89,* 889–903.

Rein, Martin. (1971). Social policy analysis as the interpretation of belief. In Lee Rainwater (Ed.), *Social problems and public policy: Inequality and justice* (pp. 62–67). Chicago: Aldine Publishing Co.

Reiss, Albert J. (1971). *The police and the public.* New Haven: Yale University Press.

Rescher, Nicholas. (1970). On the characterization of actions. In Myles Brand (Ed.), *The nature of human action.* Glenview, IL: Scott, Foresman & Co.

Reynolds, William B. (1984). Individual vs. group rights: The legacy of *Brown. Yale Law Journal, 93,* 995–1005.

Rheinstein, Max (Ed.). (1954). *Max Weber on law in economy and society.* Cambridge, MA: Harvard University Press.

Rhodes, William. (1978). *Plea bargaining: Who gains? Who loses?* (PROMIS Research Project No. 14, Final Draft). Washington DC: Institute for Law and Social Research.

Richman, Barry. (1971). Ideology and management: The Chinese oscillate. *Columbia Journal of World Business, 6,* 23–35.

Rist, Ray (Ed.). (1979). *Desegregated schools: Appraisals of an American experiment.* New York: Academic Press.

Rodgers, Harrell. (1984). Fair employment laws for minorities: An evaluation of federal implementation. In Charles Bullock & Charles Lamb (Eds.), *Implementation of civil rights policy* (pp. 93–117). Monterey, CA: Brooks/Cole Publishing.

Rojek, Dean, & Erickson, Maynard. (1981–82). Reforming the juvenile justice system: The diversion of status offenders. *Law and Society Review, 16,* 241–264.

Rosenberg, Maurice, & Sovern, Michael. (1959). Delay and the dynamics of personal injury litigation. *Columbia Law Review, 59,* 1115–1170.

Rosenthal, Douglas. (1974). *Lawyer and client: Who's in charge?* New York: Russell Sage.

Ross, H. Lawrence. (1970). *Settled out of court: The social process of insurance claims adjustment.* Chicago: Aldine Publishing Co.

Ross, Lee. (1977). The intuitive psychologist and his shortcomings. In L. Berkowitz (Ed.), *Advances in experimental social psychology* (Vol. 10, pp. 174–220). New York: Academic Press.

Ross, Philip. (1965). *The government as a source of union power: The role of public policy in collective bargaining.* Providence, RI: Brown University Press.

Rossell, Christine, & Hawley, Willis. (1981). Understanding white flight and doing something about it. In Willis Hawley (Ed.), *Effective school desegregation: Equity, quality and feasibility* (pp. 157–184). Beverly Hills, CA: Sage Publications.

Rubinstein, Michael, & White, Teresa. (1979). Alaska's ban on plea bargaining. *Law and Society Review, 13,* 367–383.

Ruchames, Louis. (1953). *Race, jobs and politics: The story of the FEPC.* New York: Columbia University Press, (1953).

Ryan, William. (1971). *Blaming the victim.* New York: Vintage Books.

Samuelson, Robert J. (5 Sept. 1983). The campaign reform failure. *The New Republic, 189*:10, 28–36.

Sandalow, Terrance. (1965). Henry vs. Mississippi and the adequate state ground: Proposals for a revised doctrine. *Supreme Court Review, 1965,* 187–239.

Sandalow, Terrance. (1981). Constitutional interpretation. *Michigan Law Review, 79,* 1033–1072.

Sanders, Joseph. (1969). Euthanasia: None dare call it murder. *Journal of Criminal Law, Criminology & Police Science, 60,* 351–359.

Sartre, Jean Paul. (1977). *Existentialism and humanism* (Philip Mairet, Trans.). Brooklyn, NY: Haskell House.

Scher, R., & Button, J. (1984). Voting Rights Act: Implementation and impact. In Charles

Bullock & Charles Lamb (Eds.), *Implementation of civil rights policy* (pp. 20–54). Monterey, CA: Brooks/Cole Publishing Co.

Schleffler, Israel. (1963). *The anatomy of inquiry.* New York: Alfred A. Knopf.

Schlei, Barbara, & Grossman, Paul. (1983). *Employment discrimination law* (2nd ed.). Chicago: American Bar Association.

Schmitt, David. (1964). The invocation of moral obligation. *Sociometry, 27,* 108–117.

Scholz, John. (1984). Cooperation, deterrrence, and the ecology of regulatory enforcement. *Law and Society Review, 18,* 179–224.

Schrag, Philip G. (1969). Bleak house 1968: A report on consumer test litigation. *New York University Law Review, 44,* 115–158.

Schulhofer, Stephan J. (1984). Is plea bargaining inevitable? *Harvard Law Review, 97,* 1037–1107.

Schur, Edwin. (1973). *Radical non-intervention: Rethinking the delinquency problem.* Englewood Cliffs, NJ: Prentice-Hall.

Schutz, Alfred. (1970). *On phenomenology and social relations* (Helmut Wagner, Ed.). Chicago: University of Chicago Press.

Schwartz, Richard, & Skolnick, Jerome. (1962). Two studies of legal stigma. *Social Problems, 10,* 133–142.

Scott, Austin. (1923). Small causes and poor litigants. *American Bar Association Journal, 9,* 457–459.

Scott, Marvin, & Lyman, Stanford. (1968). Accounts. *American Sociological Review, 33,* 46–62.

Seidman, Robert. (1965). Witch murder and *mens rea*: A problem of society under radical social change. *Modern Law Review, 28,* 46–61.

Selznick, Philip. (1966). *The T.V.A. and the grass roots.* New York: Harper Torchbook.

Severence, Laurence, & Loftus, Elizabeth. (1982). Improving the ability of jurors to comprehend and apply criminal jury instructions. *Law and Society Review, 17,* 154–197.

Shavell, Steven. (1980). Strict liability versus negligence. *Journal of Legal Studies, 9,* 1–25.

Shedlin, Leslie. (1980). Regulation of disclosure of economic and financial data and the impact on the American system of labor-management relations. *Ohio State Law Journal, 41,* 441–473.

Sheehan, Robert. (15 June 1967). Proprietors in the world of big business. *Fortune,* 179–183. Reprinted in Maurice Zeitlin (Ed.), *American Society, Inc.* Chicago, IL: Markham (1970).

Sheppard, Blair, & Vidmar, Neil. (1980). Adversary pretrial procedures and testimonial evidence: Effects of lawyer's role and Machiavellianism. *Journal of Personality and Social Psychology, 39,* 320–332.

Shubik, Martin. (1982). *Game theory in the social sciences.* Cambridge, MA: MIT Press.

Siegel, Paul M. (1965). On the cost of being a negro. *Sociological Inquiry, 35,* 41–57.

Simmel, Georg. (1955). *Conflict and the web of group affiliation.* New York: Free Press.

Simmons, Robert. (1974). *Winning before trial: How to prepare cases for the best settlement or trial result.* Englewood Cliffs, NJ: Executive Reports Corp. 2 vols.

Simon, Rita. (1967). *The jury and the defense of insanity.* Boston: Little, Brown.

Simpson, Laurence. (1965). Contracts (2nd ed.). St. Paul: West Publishing Co.

Skinner, B. F. (1971). *Beyond freedom and dignity.* New York: Alfred A. Knopf.

Skolnick, Jerome. (1966). *Justice without trial.* New York: John Wiley & Sons.

Skolnick, Jerome. (1967). Social control and the adversary system. *Journal of Conflict Resolution, 11*, 52–70.

Smart, J. J. C. (1978). Distributive justice. In John Arthur & William Shaw (Eds.), *Justice and economic distribution* (pp. 103–115). Englewood Cliffs, NJ: Prentice-Hall.

Smigel, Edwin O. (1964). *The Wall Street lawyer.* New York: Free Press.

Smith, James P., & Welch, Finis R. (1977). Black/white male earnings and employment: 1960–70. In F. Thomas Juster (Ed.), *The distribution of economic well-being* (pp. 233–295). Cambridge, MA: Ballinger.

Smith, Jeremiah. (1914). Sequel to workmen's compensation acts. *Harvard Law Review, 27*, 235–344.

Smith, Russell. (1941). The evolution of the "duty to bargain" concept in American law. *Michigan Law Review, 39*, 1065–1108.

Smylie, Mark. (1984). *Covering school desegregation: A deskbook for education writers: The educational equity project institute for public policy studies.* Nashville, TN: Vanderbilt University.

Solzhenitsyn, Aleksandr I. (1973). *The gulag archipelago* (Vol. 1). New York: Harper & Row.

Sovern, Michael. (1966). *Legal restraints on racial discrimination in employment.* New York: Twentieth Century Fund.

Stapleton, Vaughn, & Teitlebaum Lee. (1972). *In defense of youth: A study of the role of counsel in American juvenile courts.* New York: Russell Sage.

Starr, June, & Yngvesson, Barbara. (1975). Scarcity and disputing: Zeroing-in on compromise decisions. *American Ethnologist, 2*, 553–566.

Steele, Eric H. (1975). Fraud, dispute and the consumer: Responding to consumer complaints. *University of Pennsylvania Law Review, 123*, 1107–1186.

Stern, Gerald M. (1976). *The Buffalo Creek disaster.* New York: Random House.

Stigler, George. (1964). Public regulation of the securities market. *Journal of Business, 37*, 117.

Stinchcombe, Arthur. (1968). *Constructing social theories.* New York: Harcourt, Brace & World.

Stone, Julius. (1966). *Social dimensions of law and justice.* Stanford, CA: Stanford University Press.

Stone, Roy. (1966). The compleat wrangler. *Minnesota Law Review, 50*, 1001–1025.

Storms, Michael. (1973). Videotape and the attribution process: Reversing actors' and observers' points of view. *Journal of Personality and Social Psychology, 27*, 165–175.

Sudnow, David. (1965). Normal crimes: Sociological features of the penal code in a public defender office. *Social Problems, 12*, 255–276.

Summers, Robert, & Howard, Charles. (1965). *Law, its nature, functions and limits* (2nd ed.). Englewood Cliffs, NJ: Prentice-Hall.

Surrant, Reed. (1966). The ordeal of desegregation. New York: Harper & Row.

Sutton, John. (1983). Social structure, institutions and the legal status of children in the United States. *American Journal of Sociology, 88*, 915–947.

Sutton, John R. (1985). The juvenile court and social welfare: Dynamics of a progressive reform. *Law and Society Review, 19*, 107–145.

Sykes, Gresham, & Matza, David. (1957). Techniques of neutralization: A theory of delinquency. *American Sociological Review, 22*, 664–670.

Taylor, Charles. (1964). *The explanation of behavior*. London: Routledge & Kegan Paul.

Taylor, Richard. (1966). *Action and purpose*. Englewood Cliffs, NJ: Prentice-Hall.

Taylor, Richard. (1969). Thought and purpose. *Inquiry, 12*, 149–169.

Teubner, Gunther. (1983). Substantive and reflexive elements in modern law. *Law and Society Review, 17*, 239–286.

Teubner, Gunther. (1984). Autopoiesis in law and society: A rejoinder to Blankenburg. *Law and Society Review, 18*, 291–301.

Thibaut, John, & Riecken, Henry. (1955). Some determinants and consequences of the perception of social causality. *Journal of Personality, 24*, 113–133.

Thibaut, John, Walker, Laurens, & Lind, Allan. (1972). Adversary presentation and bias in legal decisionmaking. *Harvard Law Review, 86*, 386–407.

Thompson, E. P. (1975). *Whigs and hunters: The origin of the Black Act*. New York: Pantheon Books.

Toulmin, Stephen. (1969). Concepts and the explanation of human behavior. In Theodore Mischel (Ed.), *Human action: Conceptual and empirical issues* (pp. 71–104). New York: Academic Press.

Trubek, David. (1972). Max Weber on law and the rise of capitalism. *Wisconsin Law Review*, 720–753.

Trubek, David. (1977). Complexity and contradication in the legal order: Balbus and the challenge of critical social thought about law. *Law and Society Review, 12*, 529–569.

Trubek, David, Sarat, Austin, Felstiner, William, Kritzer, Herbert, & Grossman, Joel. (1983). The costs of ordinary litigation. *U.C.L.A. Law Review, 31*, 73–129.

Turk, Austin. (1976). Law as a weapon in social conflict. *Social Problems, 23*, 276–291.

Tushnett, Marc. (1975). American law of slavery 1810–1860: A study in the persistence of legal autonomy. *Law and Society Review, 10*, 119–184.

Tyler, Tom. (1984). The role of perceived injustice in defendants' evaluations of their courtroom experience. *Law and Society Review, 18*, 51–74.

Uhlman, Thomas, & Walker, Darlene. (1979). A plea is no bargain: The impact of case disposition on sentencing. *Social Science Quarterly, 60*, 218–234.

Unger, Roberto M. (1976). *Law in modern society: Toward a criticism of social theory*. New York: Free Press.

Uniform Commercial Code. (1972). Philadelphia: American Law Institute.

U.S. Bureau of the Census. (1984). *Money income & poverty status of families and persons in the U.S., 1983* (Current Population Reports, series P-60 No. 145). Washington, DC: U.S. Government Printing Office.

U.S. Commission on Civil Rights. (1964). *Public education*. Washington, DC: U.S. Government Printing Office.

Utz, Pamela J. (1978). *Settling the facts: Discretion and negotiation in criminal court*. Lexington, MA: Lexington Books.

Vidmar, Neil. (1984). The small claims court: A reconceptualization of disputes and an empirical investigation. *Law and Society Review, 18*, 515–550.

Vidmar, Neil, & Laird, Nancy MacDonald. (1983). Adversary social roles: Their effects on witnesses' communication of evidence and the assessments of adjudicators. *Journal of Personality and Social Psychology, 44*, 888–898.

Von Mehren, Arthur T. (Ed.). (1964). *Law in Japan: The legal order of a changing society*. Cambridge, MA: Harvard University Press.

Wahrhaftig, Paul. (1982). An overview of community-oriented citizen dispute resolution programs in the United States. In Richard Abel (Ed.), The politics of informal justice (Vol. 1, pp. 75–98). New York: Academic Press.

Walton, Richard, & McKersie, Robert. (1965). *Negotiations: An analysis of a social interaction system.* New York: McGraw-Hill.

Weber, Max. (1949). *The methodology of the social sciences* (Edward Shils & Henry Fitch, Eds. & Trans.). Glencoe, IL: Free Press.

Weber, Max. (1967). *Max Weber on law in economy and society* (Max Rheinstein, Ed.). New York: Simon & Schuster.

Weber, Max. (1968a). *Economy and society* (Vol. 1). (Guenter Roth & Claus Wittich, Eds.). New York: Bedminster Press.

Weber, Max. (1968b). *Economy and society* (Vol. 2). (Guenter Roth & Claus Wittich, Eds.). New York: Bedminster Press.

Weiner, Bernard, & Kukla, Andy. (1970). An attributional analysis of achievement motivation. *Journal of Personality and Social Psychology, 15,* 1–20.

Werthman, Carl, & Piliavin, Irving. (1967). Gang members and ecological conflict. In David Bordua (Ed.), *The police: Six sociological essays* (pp. 56–98). New York: John Wiley & Sons.

Wheeler, Stanton (Ed.). (1968). *Controlling delinquents.* New York: John Wiley & Sons.

Williams, Gerald. (1983). *Legal negotiation and settlement.* St. Paul: West Publishing Co.

Williams, Jerre. (1965). *Labor relations and the law* (3rd ed.). Boston: Little, Brown & Co.

Williamson, Oliver E. (1975). *Markets & hierarchies.* New York: Free Press.

Wirt, Frederick. (1970). *The politics of Southern equality: Law and social change in a Mississippi county.* Chicago: Aldine Publishing Co.

Wolfgang, Marvin, & Reidel, Marc. (1973). Race, judicial discretion, and the death penalty. *Annals of the American Academy of Political and Social Science, 407,* 119–133.

Wolfgang, Marvin E., & Riedel, Marc. (1976). Rape, racial discrimination and the death penalty. In Hugo A. Bedau & Chester M. Pierce (Eds.), *Capital punishment in the United States* (pp. 99–121). New York: AMS Press.

Yngvesson, Barbara, & Hennessey, Patricia. (1975). Small claims, complex disputes: A review of the small claims literature. *Law and Society Review, 9,* 219–274.

Yudof, Mark. (1980). Nondiscrimination and beyond: The search for principle in Supreme Court desegregation decisions. In Walter Stephan & Joe Feagin (Eds.), *School desegregation: Past, present and future* (pp. 97–116). New York: Plenum Press.

Zeisel, Hans, Kalven, Harry, & Buchholtz, Bernard. (1959). *Delay in court.* Boston: Little, Brown & Co.

Zeitlin, Maurice. (Ed.). (1970). *American society inc.* Chicago: Markham Publishing Co.

Zeitlin, Maurice. (1974). Corporate ownership and control: The large corporation and the capitalist class. *American Journal of Sociology, 79,* 1073–1119.

List of Cases

Abood v. *Detroit Board of Education*, 431 U.S. 209 (1977).
Adair v. *United States*, 208 U.S. 161 (1908).
Adams v. *Nichols*, 19 Pick (Mass.) 275 (1837).
Adams v. *Richardson*, 480 F. 2d 1159 (D.C. Cir. 1973).
Albermarle Paper Co. v. *Moody*, 422 U.S. 405 (1975).
Alexander v. *Holmes County Board of Education*, 396 U.S. 19 (1969).
Allen v. *State Board of Elections*, 393 U.S. 544 (1969).
Aluminum Company of America v. *Essex Group Inc.*, 499 F. Supp. 53 (W.D. Pa. 1980).
Argersinger v. *Hamlin*, 407 U.S. 25 (1972).
The Attorney General for Nyasaland v. *Jackson*, 1957 R. & N. 443 (1957).
Bakke v. *Regents of the University of California*, 438 U.S. 265 (1978).
Brotherhood of Railway Trainmen v. *Virginia*, 377 U.S. 1 (1964).
Brown v. *Board of Education*, 347 U.S. 483 (1954).
Brown v. *Board of Education* (No. 2), 349 U.S. 294 (1955).
Budd Manufacturing Co. v. *N.L.R.B.*, 138 F. 2d 86 (1943).
Butterfield v. *Forrester*, 11 East 60 (K.B. 1809).
Carter v. *Galligher*, 452 F. 2d 315 (8th Cir. 1972).
Central Hudson Gas & Electric Corp. v. *Public Service Commission of New York*, 447 U.S. 557 (1980).
City of Dallas v. *Mitchell*, 245 S.W. 944 (1922).
Civil Rights Cases, 109 U.S. 3 (1883).
Columbus Board of Education v. *Penick*, 443 U.S. 887 (1979).
Commonwealth v. *Hunt*, 45 Mass. (1 Metc.) 111 (1842).
Connecticut v. *Teal*, 457 U.S. 440 (1982).
Consolidated Edison Company of New York v. *Public Service Commission of New York*, 447 U.S. 530 (1980).
Contractors Association of Eastern Pennsylvania v. *Secretary of Labor*, 442 F. 2d 159 (3rd Cir. 1971), *cert. denied*, 404 U.S. 854 (1974).

Coppage v. *Kansas*, 236 U.S. 1 (1915).

Cousins v. *City Council of the City of Chicago*, 466 F. 2d. 830 (7th Cir. 1972).

Crawford v. *Board of Education of the City of Los Angeles*, 458 U.S. 527 (1982).

Davies v. *Mann*, 10 M. & W. 545 (Exchequer, 1842).

Dayton Board of Education v. *Brinkman I*, 433 U.S. 406 (1977).

Dayton Board of Education v. *Brinkman II.*, 443 U.S. 526 (1979).

Dobbert v. *Wainwright*, cert. denied 105 S. Ct. 34 (1984).

Erika Galikuwa (Uganda), 18 E.A.C.A. 175 (1951).

Ermolieff v. *R.K.O. Pictures Incorporated*, 122 P. 2d 3 (1942).

Fabiano (Uganda), 8 E.A.C.A. 96 (1941).

Farwell v. *The Boston and Worcester Railroad Corp.*, 4 Metc. 49 (Mass., 1842).

Federal Election Commission v. *National Education Association*, 457 F. Supp. 1102 (D.C. District Court 1978).

Firefighters Local 1784 v. *Stotts*, 104 S. Ct. 2576 (1984).

First National Bank of Boston v. *Bellotti*, 435 U.S. 765 (1978).

Fortson v. *Dorsey*, 379 U.S. 433 (1965).

Frazier v. *Pokorny*, 359 P. 2d 324 (Wyo. 1960).

Gadam (Nigeria), 14 W.A.C.A. 442 (1954).

Gaston County v. *United States*, 395 U.S. 285 (1969).

General Electric Company, 150 N.L.R.B. 192 (1964).

Gibson v. *Thompson*, 335 U.S. 18 (1957).

Gideon v. *Wainwright*, 372 U.S. 335 (1963).

Gomillion v. *Lightfoot*, 364 U.S. 339 (1960).

Green v. *County School Board of New Kent County*, 391 U.S. 430 (1968).

Greenman v. *Yuba Power Products, Inc.*, 59 Cal. 2d. 57, 377 P. 2d 897 (1963).

Griggs v. *Duke Power Co.*, 401 U.S. 424 (1971).

Grimshaw v. *Ford Motor Co.* No. 19-77-61, Super. Ct. Orange Cty., Cal., Order Dated 3-30-78 (1978); 74 Cal. Rptr. 348 (1981).

Grovey v. *Townsend*, 295 U.S. 45 (1935).

Hennington v. *Bloomfield Motors, Inc.*, 32 N.J. 358, 161 A. 2d 59 (1960).

Henry v. *Mississippi*, 379 U.S. 443 (1965).

Hitchman Coal & Coke v. *Mitchell*, 245 U.S. 229 (1917).

Horton v. *Greyhound Corp.*, 241 S.C. 430, 128 S.E. 2d 776 (1962).

In Re Gault, 387 U.S. 1 (1967).

In Re Winship, 397 U.S. 358 (1970).

Ince v. *Rockefeller*, 290 F. Supp. 878 (S.D.N.Y. 1968).

International Brotherhood of Teamsters v. *United States*, 431 U.S. 324 (1977).

James v. *Stockton Valves and Fittings Co.*, 559 F. 2d 310 (5th Cir. 1977), *cert. denied,* 434 U.S. 1034 (1978).

Johnson v. *Hot Springs Land & Improvement Co.*, 76 Ore. 333, 148 P. 1137 (1915).

Jones v. *Falcey*, 48 N.J. 25, 222 A. 2d 101 (1966).

Kent v. *United States*, 383 U.S. 541 (1966).

Keys v. *School District #1*, 413 U.S. 189 (1973).

Konkomba, 14 W.A.C.A. 236 (1952).

Korematsu v. *United States*, 323 U.S. 214 (1944).

Local 189 v. *United States*, 416 F. 2d 980 (1969).

Lochner v. *New York*, 198 U.S. 45 (1905).

Lockett v. *Ohio*, 438 U.S. 586 (1978).

Logan v. *Zimmerman Brush Co.*, 455 U.S. 422 (1982).

Washington v. *Seattle School District # 1*, 458 U.S. 457 (1982).

Whitcomb v. *Chavis*, 403 U.S. 124 (1971).

White v. *Island Amusement Co.*, Sub. Nom. Brown v. Hayden Island Amusement Company 378 P. 2d 953 (Ore. 1963).

Wright v. *Rockefeller*, 376 U.S. 52 (1964)

Acknowledgments

Table 1.1, "The Typology of Legal Systems Classified by Formality and Rationality of Decisionmaking Processes," from David M. Trubek, "Max Weber on Law and the Rise of Capitalism," *Wisconsin Law Review*, 720–753, table at p.729. Copyright © 1972 by the Wisconsin Law Review Association. Reprinted with permission. From Plato's *Euthyphro* in Benjamin Jowett (ed. and trans.), *The Dialogues of Plato*. New York: Random House, 1937. Reprinted with permission of Oxford University Press, London. From H. L. A. Hart, *Punishment and Responsibility: Essays in the Philosophy of Law*. London and New York: Oxford University Press, 1968. Reprinted with permission of Oxford University Press. From Herbert Packer, *The Limits of Criminal Sanction*. Palo Alto, CA: Stanford University Press, 1968. Reprinted with permission of Stanford University Press. Table 2.3, "Benefits and Costs Related to Fuel Leakage Associated with the Static Rollover Test Portion of FMVSS 208," from David G. Owen, "Problems in Assessing Punitive Damages against Manufactures of Defective Products," *University of Chicago Law Review, 49*, 1–60, table at p. 56. Reprinted with permission of the *University of Chicago Law Review* and the author. From Isiah Berlin, *Historical Inevitability*. London: Oxford University Press, 1959. Reprinted with permission of Oxford University Press. From J. L. Austin, "A Plea for Excuses," *Aristotelian Society Proceedings, 57*, (1956–57), 1–30, quotations at p. 17 and p. 14. From Erving Goffman, *Frame Analysis*. Copyright © 1972 by Colophon Books, Harper & Row, New York. From Edward Jones and Richard Nisbitt, "Actor and Observer: Divergent Perceptions of the Cause of Behavior," in Edward Jones, David E. Kanose, Harold H. Kelley, Richard E. Nisbitt, Stuart Valins, and Bernard Weiner, *Attribution: Perceiving the Causes of Behavior*, pp. 79–95. Morristown, NJ: General Learning Press, 1972. From Aleksandr I. Solzhenitsyn, *The Gulag Archipelago*, Vol. 1. Copyright © 1972 by Aleksandr I. Solzhenitsyn. New York: Harper & Row. From Lon Fuller, "The Adversary System," in H. Berman (ed.), *Talks on American Law*. New York: Vintage Books, 1971. Table 4.2, "The Effect of Procedure on Decision Making: Mean Final Opinions," from John Thibaut, Laurens Walker, and Allan Lind, "Adversary Presentation and Bias in Legal Decision-making," *Harvard Law Review, 86*, 386–407, table at p. 395. Copyright © 1972 by the Harvard Law Review Association. Reprinted with permission. Table 4.3, "Legal Instructions and Jury Decision-making," from Diane Colasanto and Joseph Sanders, *Methodological Issues in Simulated Jury Research*. Unpublished manuscript. Copyright © 1972 by Diane Colasanto and Joseph Sanders. Reprinted with permission of the authors. From David Sudnow, "Normal Crimes: Sociological Features of the Penal Code in a Public Defender Office," *Social Problems, 12*, 255–276, quotations at pp. 259–260 and p. 274. Copyright © 1965 by the Society for the Study of Social Problems. Published with the permission of the Society for the Study of Social Problems. From William L. Prosser, "Comparative Negligence," *Michigan Law Review, 51*, 465–508, quotation at p. 465. Copyright © 1953 by the Michigan Law

Review Association. From Leon Green, *Traffic Victims—Tort and Law Insurance*. Copyright © 1958 by the Northwestern University Traffic Institute. Reprinted with permission. From H. Lawrence Ross, *Settled Out of Court: The Social Process of Insurance Claims Adjustment*. Hawthorne, NY: Aldine Publishing Co., 1970. From William L. Prosser, *Law of Torts*, 4th Edition. © 1971 West Publishing Co., St. Paul. Reprinted with permission. From Philippe Nonet, *Administrative Justice: Advocacy and Change in a Government Agency*. Copyright © 1969 by the Russell Sage Foundation. Reprinted with permission of the Russell Sage Foundation, New York. From Jean Piaget, *The Moral Judgment of the Child*, translated by Marjorie Gabain. London: Routledge and Kegan Paul, plc.; first Free Press paperback edition, New York, 1965. Reprinted with permission of Routledge and Kegan Paul, plc., and Free Press, Macmillan. From David Trubek, Austin Sarat, William Felstiner, Herbert Kritzer, and Joel Grossman, "The Cost of Ordinary Litigation," *U.C.L.A. Law Review, 31* (1983), 73–129, formula at p. 114. From Gerald Williams, *Legal Negotiation and Settlement*. © 1983 West Publishing Co., St. Paul. Reprinted with permission; from Robert Simmons in *Winning Before Trial: How to Prepare Cases for the Best Settlement or Trial Result*, 2 vols. Englewood Cliffs, NJ: Executive Reports Corp., 1974. Table 7.2, "Power, Culture, and Types of Law," and quotations from Paul Bohannan, "The Differing Realms of the Law," *American Anthropologist* Special Publication, *The Ethnography of Law*, Laura Nader (ed.), Vol. 67 (1965), No. 6, Part 2, 33–42. Reproduced with permission of the American Anthropological Association from the *American Anthropologist*. Not for further reproduction. From Max Gluckman, *The Judicial Process among the Barotse of Northern Rhodesia*. Copyright © 1967 by Manchester University Press. Reprinted with permission. From Laura Nader, "Styles of Court Procedure: To Make the Balance," in Laura Nader (ed.), *Law in Culture and Society*, pp. 69–92. Hawthorne, NY: Aldine Publishing Co., 1969. Figure 7.2, "The Case of the Headman's Stepson," and quotations from Lloyd Fallers, *Law Without Precedent: Legal Ideas in Action in the Courts of Colonial Bugosa*. Copyright © 1969 the University of Chicago Press. Reprinted with permission. From Egon Bittner, "The Police on Skid Row: A Study of Peace Keeping," in William Chambliss (ed.), *Crime and the Legal Process*, pp. 135–155. Copyright © 1965 by McGraw-Hill, New York. Reprinted with permission of Macmillan Publishing Company, from *Justice Without Trial: Law Enforcement in a Democratic Society* by Jerome Skolnick. New York: Macmillan, 1966, p. 221. From Stewart Macaulay, "Non-contractual Relations in Business: A Preliminary Study," *American Sociological Review, 28*, 55–67. Copyright © 1963 by the American Sociological Association. Reprinted by permission of the American Sociological Association. From George Feiffer, *Justice in Moscow*. New York: Simon & Schuster, 1964. Reprinted by permission of the author. From Douglas Matthews, *Sue the B*st*rds*. New York: Arbor House, 1973. From Martin Rein, "Social Policy Analysis as the Interpretation of Belief," in Lee Rainwater (ed.), *Social Problems and Public Policy: Inequality and Justice*, pp. 62–67. Hawthorne, NY: Aldine Publishing Co., 1971. Table 9.1, "Interpretations of Rawls's Second Principle," adapted and quotations reprinted by permission of the publishers from *A Theory of Justice* by John Rawls, Cambridge, MA: Harvard University Press and London: Oxford University Press. From Douglas Hofstadter, "Metamagical Themes: The Calculus of Cooperation Is Tested Through a Lottery," *Scientific American*, 248(6), June 1983, 14–28, quotation at p. 28. From James Willard Hurst, *Law and the Conditions of Freedom*. Copyright © 1956 by Northwestern University Press. Reprinted with permission of the University of Wisconsin Press. From *Monopoly Capital* by Paul A. Baran and Paul M. Sweezy. Copyright © 1966 by Paul M. Sweezy. Reprinted by permission of the Monthly Review Foundation, New York. From *Power and the Structure of Society* by James S. Coleman. Copyright © 1974 by the Fells Center of Government, University of Pennsylvania. Reprinted by permission of W.W. Norton & Company, Inc. Table 11.2, "Percentage of Black Students in Schools with Fewer than 50 Percent Blacks and Schools with 90-100 Percent Blacks, By Region, 1968–1980," from Gary Orfield, *Public School Desegregation in the United States 1968–1980*. Copyright © 1983 by the Joint Center for Political Studies, Inc. Reprinted with permission. From Philip Selznick, *The T.V.A. and the Grassroots*. Copyright © 1966 by Harper & Row. Reprinted with permission. Table 11.5, "Ratio of Minority Worker Employment to White Worker Employment," and Table 11.6, "Comparison of Actual 1980 Occupational Distribution of Black Workers with Hypothetical 1980 Distribution Based on 1965 Percentages from EEC Reports," from Alfred Blumrosen, "The Law Transmission System and the Southern Jurisprudence of Employment Discrimination," *Industrial Relations Law Journal, 6* (1984), 313–352, tables at p. 335 and p. 341. Reprinted with permission of the author. From *The Portable Karl Marx* edited by Eugene Kamenka. Copyright © 1983 by Viking Penguin Inc. Reprinted by permission of Viking Penguin Inc.

Index